Professional Digital Compositing

Essential Tools and Techniques

Professional Digital Compositing

Essential Tools and Techniques

Lee Lanier

Wiley Publishing, Inc.

Acquisitions Editor: Mariann Barsolo
Development Editor: Gary Schwartz
Technical Editor: Tim Turner
Production Editor: Rachel McConlogue
Copy Editor: Judy Flynn
Editorial Manager: Pete Gaughan
Production Manager: Tim Tate
Vice President and Executive Group Publisher: Richard Swadley
Vice President and Publisher: Neil Edde
Media Associate Project Manager: Jenny Swisher
Media Associate Producer: Josh Frank
Media Quality Assurance: Doug Kuhn
Book Designer: Mark Ong, Side By Side Studios
Compositor: Chris Gillespie, Happenstance Type-O-Rama
Proofreader: Rebecca Rider
Indexer: Ted Laux
Project Coordinator, Cover: Lynsey Stanford
Cover Designer: Ryan Sneed
Cover Image: Lee Lanier

Library of Congress Cataloging-in-Publication Data

Lanier, Lee, 1966–
  Professional digital compositing : essential tools and techniques / Lee Lanier.
    p. cm.
  ISBN 978-0-470-45261-5 (paper/dvd)
  1. Cinematography—Special effects—Data processing. 2. Computer animation. 3. Image processing—Digital techniques. 4. Adobe After Effects. I. Title.
  TR897.7.L375 2010
  778.5'345—dc22
                                        2009035139

Dear Reader,

Thank you for choosing *Professional Digital Compositing: Essential Tools and Techniques*. This book is part of a family of premium-quality Sybex books, all of which are written by outstanding authors who combine practical experience with a gift for teaching.

Sybex was founded in 1976. More than 30 years later, we're still committed to producing consistently exceptional books. With each of our titles, we're working hard to set a new standard for the industry. From the paper we print on to the authors we work with, our goal is to bring you the best books available.

I hope you see all that reflected in these pages. I'd be very interested to hear your comments and get your feedback on how we're doing. Feel free to let me know what you think about this or any other Sybex book by sending me an email at nedde@wiley.com. If you think you've found a technical error in this book, please visit `http://sybex.custhelp.com`. Customer feedback is critical to our efforts at Sybex.

Best regards,

Neil Edde
Vice President and Publisher
Sybex, an Imprint of Wiley

Acknowledgments

My thanks to the excellent editorial, design, and production staff at Sybex and John Wiley & Sons, including the acquisitions editor, Mariann Barsolo; development editor, Gary Schwartz; production editor, Rachel McConlogue; technical editor, Tim Turner; copyeditor, Judy Flynn; and proofreader, Rebecca Rider.

Special thanks to the compositing supervisors, lead compositors, and compositing experts who provided invaluable information through sit-down and long-distance interviews. Special thanks to Elena, the Las Vegas-based professional model who appears in many of the figures and video tutorials in this book. Also, special thanks to my friends and family who supported my wild ambitions. And my biggest thanks to my beautiful wife, Anita, who encouraged me all the way.

About the Author

Lee Lanier is a 3D animator, digital compositor, and director. His films have played in more than 200 museums, galleries, and film festivals worldwide. Before directing the shorts "Millennium Bug," "Mirror," "Day Off the Dead," "Weapons of Mass Destruction," and "13 Ways to Die at Home," Lee served as a senior animator in the lighting and modeling departments at PDI/DreamWorks on *Antz* and *Shrek*. He got his start at Buena Vista Visual Effects at Walt Disney Studios, where he created digital visual effects for such films as *Mortal Kombat*. Lee currently splits his time between Los Angeles and Boulder City, Nevada (just outside of Las Vegas). He creates his animation work through BeezleBug Bit, LLC (www.BeezleBugBit.com), serves as executive director of the Dam Short Film Festival (www.DamShortFilm.org), and teaches lighting at the Gnomon School of Visual Effects.

Contents

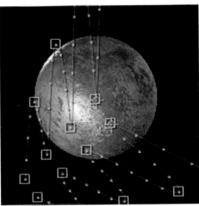

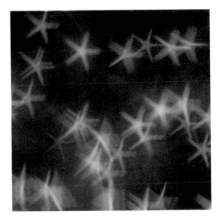

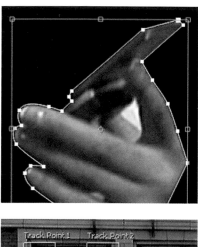

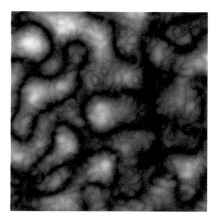

Figure I.2 *The optical printer used to create the visual effects on* Star Wars. *The machine currently resides at the Industrial Light & Magic facility in San Francisco. (Photo courtesy of Industrial Light & Magic)*

Who Should Buy This Book

This book is written for beginning- to immediate-level animators and compositors who would like to expand their knowledge of compositing theory and improve their professional technique. If you've never composited before, this book supplies you with all the fundamental information you need to know to start creating successful shots. If you already have experience as a compositor, it provides advanced information and late-breaking industry approaches to compositing.

After Effects and Nuke

The examples in this book were created with Adobe After Effects CS3 and The Foundry Nuke 5.1v1. Newer versions of the software packages are available. However, CS3 and 5.1v1 were chosen to ensure backward compatibility and stability. Since the differences between these versions and the latest releases are minor, it will not affect your learning experience. A large number of After Effects project files and Nuke scripts are included on the companion DVD.

   If you do not own After Effects and Nuke, free trials are available through the softwares' developers. Adobe offers a 30-day, fully functional trial of After Effects at www.adobe.com, while The Foundry offers a Personal Learning Edition (PLE) of Nuke at www.thefoundry.co.uk. (Note that the PLE version of Nuke places a dotted watermark on any render and does not support the Primatte keyer, which is discussed in this book.)

The Companion DVD

The companion DVD is a critical part of *Professional Digital Compositing*. It includes over a gigabyte of After Effects project files, Nuke scripts, video footage, CG renders, texture bitmaps, digital stills, and interview transcripts. The files are located in the following directory structure:

ProjectFiles\Chapter1\Tutorials\	After Effects project files (.aep) and Nuke scripts (.nk)
ProjectFiles\Chapter1\Footage\	Video footage, CG renders, texture bitmaps, and digital stills
Interviews\	Full transcriptions of the book's interviews

The After Effects projects and Nuke scripts assume that the source files are located on a C: drive. Hence, I suggest that you copy the DVD contents onto your own C: drive. If space is not available, you can reload the necessary files once you are in the program. Methods for reloading the files are discussed in Chapter 1.

Naming Conventions

The tutorials and step-by-step guides in *Professional Digital Compositing* use common conventions for mouse operation. Here are few examples:

LMB	Left mouse button
MMB	Middle mouse button
RMB	Right mouse button
LMB+drag	Click and hold button while dragging mouse
RMB+click	Click button and release
Double-click	Rapidly click LMB twice
Ctrl+LMB+drag	Click and hold mouse button while pressing Ctrl key and dragging mouse

When referring to different areas and functions of After Effects and Nuke, I have used the terminology employed by the software's own help files. Whenever there is a deviation in terminology (usually for the sake of clarity), a note is included to explain the change. As such, Figure I.3 denotes the main areas of the After Effects interface.

Figure I.4 and Figure I.5 denote the main areas of the Nuke interface.

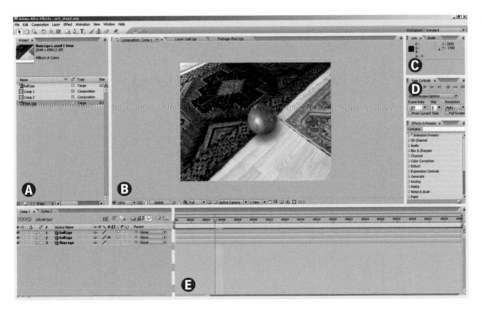

Figure I.3 The After Effects CS3 interface. The Project panel (visible) and Effect Controls panel (hidden) share area A. Composition panel (visible), Layer panel (hidden), and Footage panel (hidden) share area B; each panel carries its own viewer. The Info panel is found at C. The Time Controls panel is found at D. The Timeline panel (E) is broken into two portions—the left side features the layer outline and the right side features the timeline. Each composition receives its own tab in the Timeline panel and thus has a unique layer outline and timeline.

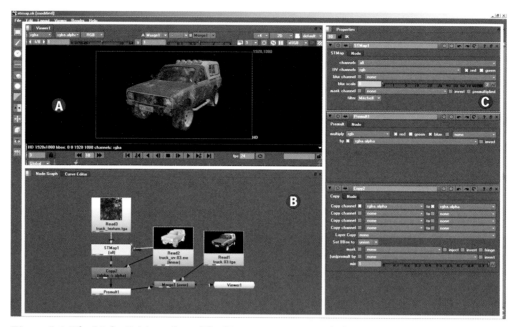

Figure I.4 *The Nuke 5.1 interface. The Viewer pane (A) includes all viewers, as well as the timeline and time controls. The Node Graph pane (visible) and the Curve Editor pane (hidden) share area B. The Properties pane (C) displays one or more properties panels for selected nodes.*

Menu bar

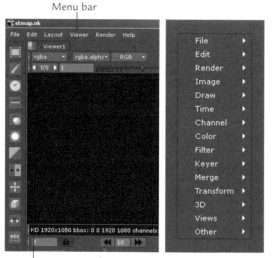

Toolbar with content menu buttons

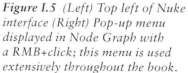

Figure I.5 *(Left) Top left of Nuke interface (Right) Pop-up menu displayed in Node Graph with a RMB+click; this menu is used extensively throughout the book.*

How to Contact the Author

Feel free to contact me at comp@BeezleBugBit.com. If you're a fan of short films, visit
www.DamShortFilm.org.

CHAPTER **one**

Setting Up a Composite

"Education is important—I think people need to make sure that they're learning to be artists and not just learning tools."

—GIANNI ALIOTTI, lead lighter, DreamWorks Animation

Before beginning a composite, *it's important to understand the fundamental differences between layer- and node-based compositing systems. A strong knowledge of common image resolutions and frame rates will allow you to make correct decisions. Once the fundamentals are grasped, setting up a compositing project or script becomes fairly easy. Since this book uses both After Effects and Nuke, you will be required to learn two different workflows. However, if you master both, you will be well suited for work in the feature animation, visual effects, and commercial production industries. To add perspective to the lessons, professional compositing examples are included. In addition, the first 3 of 19 interviews with professional compositing supervisors, lead compositors, and compositing experts are added at the end of this chapter. Two tutorials are also provided to get you started in After Effects and Nuke.*

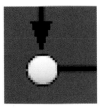

Compositing Challenge

Digital compositing is the process of digitally assembling multiple images or image sequences into a single piece of motion picture or digital video footage. The goal of a successful digital composite is to make the source material appear as if it has always existed in the same location or scene. Digital compositing is closely related to photomontage and compositing (without the word *digital*). *Photomontage* is the process of cutting apart, reassembling, and rephotographing photographic prints. *Compositing*, as it's used for professional photography, is the digital assembly of still images; compositing, when used this way, is often referred to as *Photoshopping*. The compositing and composites mentioned in this book refer to digital compositing. Professional digital compositors are simply known as *compositors*.

While this book focuses on the theoretical and technical aspects of digital compositing, it dedicates a limited amount of space to the aesthetic component. Ultimately, the success of a composite does not rely solely on specific effects or nodes. Instead, a successful composite makes a particular shot *look real* or *appear attractive*. If the composite is a visual effect, then the goal is to make all the elements (background plate, computer graphics [CG] renders, matte paintings, and so on) look like they exist in a real-world location. If the composite is for feature animation and the sets and characters are fantastic, the goal is to make the elements visually interesting yet, at the same time, plausible for the world fabricated by the story. If the composite uses abstracted motion graphics and text for a commercial, the goal is to make the elements fascinating, exciting, or just plain worth watching.

Whatever the destination of the composite, it always pays to study related fields. In particular, photography, cinematography, stage and film lighting, and classic painting will help you develop an eye for what works. Composition, color balance, light quality, and shadow quality are important aspects of these fields and are equally applicable to compositing. As you follow the step-by-step guides and tutorials in this book, ask yourself how each composite can be improved. Not only are there many different approaches to each compositing task, there also are numerous ways to fine-tune any given shot.

Compositing Examples

If you are fairly new to compositing, it may be difficult to imagine what types of footage, rendered elements, or layers are regularly combined. As such, several examples are included in this chapter. All the listed techniques are demonstrated in the various chapters of this book.

Freestyle Collective for Cartoon Network

Figure 1.1 shows eight steps of an After Effects composite created by Entae Kim at Freestyle Collective, a collaborative design and production studio in New York City. (To read an interview with Entae Kim, see Chapter 7, "Masking, Rotoscoping, and Motion Tracking.") The composite is one shot of an extended network ID (identification) that features popular Cartoon Network characters battling each other. The breakdown is as follows:

1. A gradient is used to create a sky. Stock images of clouds are added with transparency.
2. A CG render of a city block is imported as a layer.
3. A CG robot is imported as a layer. Although the render has self-shadowing, there is limited specularity.
4. A specular render pass and decal render pass of the robot are blended with the original robot layer. The result is color graded to create greater contrast. In addition, a new CG ground plane with debris is placed on top.

5. The ground plane layer is color graded to make it lighter. In addition, a CG female warrior is brought in as a layer. At this point, it's difficult to see the warrior over the background.

6. The warrior layer is color graded. A smoke render is sandwiched between the foreground and the robot. A glow render is added to the end of the warrior's weapon.

7. A smoke render is added to the foreground as a top layer. CG lasers and starbursts are imported.

8. Environmental fog is added to the background to make the foreground characters easier to see. The CG buildings are also blurred. All the layers are color graded toward a sepia tone and are given artificial film grain and dirt.

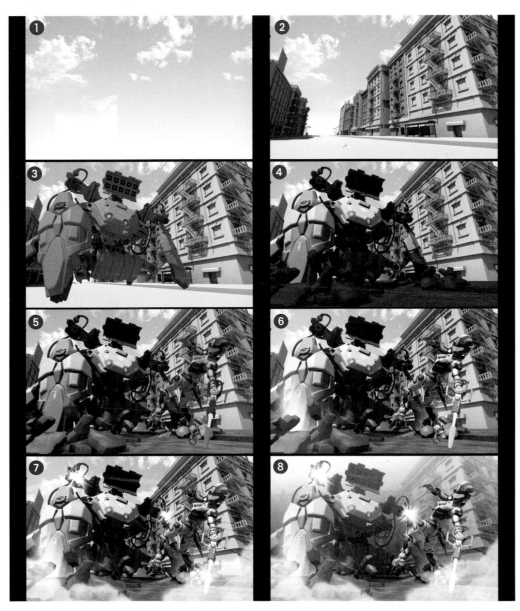

Figure 1.1 *Eight compositing steps used by Freestyle Collective to create a network ID for Cartoon Network (Images courtesy of Freestyle Collective)*

Click 3X for Sharp

Figure 1.2 shows five steps of a Flame composite created by Aaron Vasquez at Click 3X, a motion graphics and visual effects studio in New York City. (To read an interview with Aaron Vasquez, see Chapter 11, "Working with 2.5D and 3D.") The composite is one shot of a commercial for Sharp featuring the Aquos television. The breakdown is as follows:

1. A peacock is filmed against greenscreen. The bird slowly rotates on a turntable.
2. The peacock footage is motion tracked. The tracking information is brought into Flame and applied to a 3D camera. Simple geometry is added to the background in the composite. (Flame provides geometry primitives and is able to import geometry files.) After greenscreen removal, the peacock footage is placed over the background. Since the 3D camera uses tracking information from the footage, it dollies at an appropriate speed and perspective to fit the background to the peacock. Hence, the 3D background doesn't slide under the peacock's feet. A shadow is created by offsetting, transforming, and darkening the peacock footage. The body of the bird is removed and replaced by a CG body, thus creating different color feathers. The motion tracking data ensures that the CG fits tightly to the bird.
3. A prop tail, shot against greenscreen, is brought into the composite and layered to create new tail feathers for the peacock.

4. The layered feathers are fit to the body through spline warp tools and motion tracking. The deformation of the feathers is animated over time to create the illusion of rustling. A separate iteration of the feathers is used to create an appropriately shaped shadow on the background.
5. New wing and neck feathers are fit to the body by spline warping and motion tracking CG renders. The resulting composite is merged with a CG render of a television and background. The final result is color graded.

Figure 1.2 *Five compositing steps used by Click 3X to create a commercial for Sharp (Images courtesy of Click 3X)*

AILV for Spec Commercial

Figure 1.3 shows six steps of an After Effects composite created by the author and students at the Art Institute of Las Vegas (AILV). The composite is one shot of a spec commercial advertising a futuristic copier. (A *spec* is a demo used to show filmmaking or animation skills.) The breakdown is as follows:

1. An actress is shot against bluescreen.
2. Stock footage of a city is defocused (that is, blurred in an optically accurate way).
3. The bluescreen is removed from the footage of the actress. A scaled and transformed copy is given reduced opacity and a blur to emulate a window reflection. A texture bitmap is added with low opacity to create the illusion of dirt on the same window.
4. A CG render of a pillar is imported.
5. A single frame of the bluescreen footage is isolated. The frame is taken into Photoshop, color graded, and touched up to remove the wrinkles and seams on the tablecloth. The frame is imported back into the composite and placed on top of all the other layers.
6. The final composite combines the defocused city, the CG pillar, the fake window reflection, the actress, and the touched-up table. All the elements are color graded so that they work as a whole. A glow is added to create light wrap along the edges of objects in front of the window.

Tonya Smay for Westchester Medical Center

Figure 1.4 shows two shots composited by Tonya Smay in After Effects for the Westchester Medical Center. Tonya works as a freelance compositor in the New York area. (To read an interview with Tonya Smay, see Chapter 12, "Advanced Techniques.") The breakdown is as follows:

1. A CG render of a medical center grounds, created in Maya, is brought into the composite as separate render passes. The camera is moving during the shot. The renders remain somewhat bare and are missing the sky.
2. A camera is exported out of Maya and imported into After Effects. In addition, several nulls, indicating specific locations within the model, are imported. The composite is converted to a 3D environment. Several 3D cards are set up with trees, bushes, water spray, and a sky. Because the composite uses a camera exported from the 3D program, the cards' motion follows the 3D render perfectly. To prevent occlusion

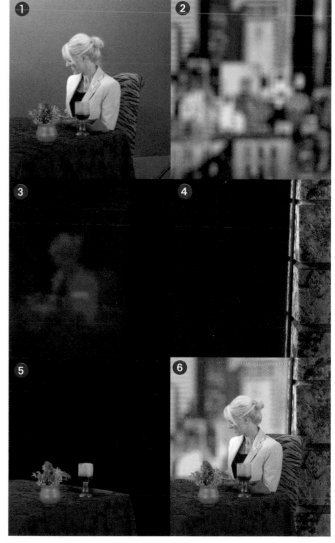

Figure 1.3 *Six compositing steps used by AILV to create a spec commercial*

issues, RGB ID render passes of the model are imported and are converted to holdout mattes. ID passes offer a means to separate 3D objects. In this case, foreground, mid-ground, and background objects are separated. The final composite is color graded. Depth of field is applied to the composite to soften the immediate foreground and background. Artificial glare is also added to make the daylight lighting appear more intense.

3. A CG render, featuring a medical lab, is imported into the composite. Although convincing, it lacks people.

4. Two actors are shot against greenscreen. After greenscreen removal and additional rotoscoping, they are imported into the composite. To allow the central actor to appear as if he's walking across the floor, the composite is converted to a 3D environment. The footage of the central actor is converted into a 3D card and is animated moving across the z-axis. To help sell the effect, reflections for each leg are applied to separate cards and are animated individually. To create the reflections, copies of the actor footage layer are vertically inverted and masked.

Figure 1.4 *Before and after images of two shots composited by Tonya Smay for a medical center commercial (Images courtesy of Tonya Smay)*

Layers vs. Nodes

After Effects and Nuke exemplify the two major approaches to compositing: layer based and node based. Layer-based programs represent each imported and utilized digital still or image sequence as a layer along a timeline. Each layer possesses its own set of transformations and special-effect filters. The layers are stacked and processed in order from bottom to top (see Figure 1.5). If there are three layers, the bottom layer and middle layer are blended and then the result is blended with the top layer.

Node-based programs, on the other hand, represent each imported and utilized digital still or image sequence as a node. The output of a node is connected to the inputs of other nodes, which may be special-effect filters, input/output controls, and viewers (see Figure 1.6). Any given node accepts a limited number of inputs. However, the output of a node may be connected to an almost unlimited number of nodes through their inputs. *Node*, as a term, refers to a discrete unit used to build linked data structures. The data structure in Nuke and similar node-based programs is referred to as a *tree graph*, *node tree*, or *node network*. More specifically, the structure is a Directed Acyclic Graph (DAG), wherein data flows in one direction along the node connections. The direction is usually indicated by arrows.

1	engine_fog.tga
2	engine_spec.tga
3	engine_fan_rim.tga
4	engine_rim.tga
5	engine_rcf_holdout.tga
6	engine_reflect.tga
7	engine_ao.tga
8	engine_self_shadow.tga
9	engine_diffuse.tga
10	engine_shadow.tga
11	engine_background.tga

Figure 1.5 *The layer outline in the Timeline panel of After Effects. The 11 layers are processed in order from bottom to top.*

There are several advantages to layer-based programs:

- Layers are intuitive to use. It's fairly easy to imagine the result of dropping one layer on top of another, particularly when the majority of digital artists are familiar with the Photoshop layer workflow.
- You can quickly set up a simple composite utilizing a limited number of layers. The same simple composite in a node-based program can require additional steps. For example, Nuke may require the addition of a Bezier node whereas After Effects automatically provides the Pen tool.
- When layers are stacked, they are merged automatically. A node-based program requires some type of merge node to supply the blending mathematics.

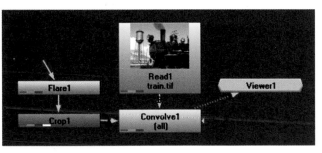

Figure 1.6 *A Nuke node network with five nodes. The arrows of the connection lines (pipes) indicate the direction information is flowing.*

There are several advantages to node-based programs:

- You can use the output of one node as the input to numerous other nodes. Although you can nest composites in a layer-based program, it becomes difficult to manage on complex projects.
- Once you are familiar with a node-based workflow, complex node networks are easy to interpret. Inputs and outputs in a node network are clearly indicated by node connection lines. With a complex layer-based composite, it becomes difficult to trace inputs and outputs because the main graphic representation only indicates position within a layer outline of a particular composite.
- Generally, node-based systems do not require precomposites, or *precomps*. Precomps are necessary with layer-based systems because it is difficult to send outputs of particular layers or filters to the inputs of other layers.
- High-end feature animation and visual effects work is generally created on node-based systems. Flame, Inferno, Shake, Fusion, Toxik, and Combustion are node based.

Industry Perspective: Compositing Software Overview

In preparation for this book, 19 expert compositors from feature animation studios, visual effects houses, and commercial production facilities in Los Angeles, New York, and San Francisco (as well as New Zealand and the United Kingdom) were interviewed. As such, a survey of popular compositing software was taken. The two most consistently named programs were Flame (or its sister, Inferno) and After Effects. These were followed by Shake and Nuke. Fusion, Toxik, and Combustion were used more sporadically. A few studios, including Sony Pictures Imageworks and DreamWorks Animation, continue to use proprietary compositing software.

Flame and Inferno are distributed by Autodesk and are prized for their real-time, high-resolution workflow. They are strongly favored in commercial production where clients prefer to sit in on color grading and other final adjustments. Seats of Flame and Inferno are extremely expensive and can run several hundred thousand dollars. Because of the expense and difficult maintenance of the Flame and Inferno systems, artists have traditionally learned them by apprenticing under an experienced compositor on site. Between the two programs, Inferno is considered the more advanced due to resolution independence and advances in hardware design.

After Effects is distributed by Adobe and is now bundled with its production set of software. It was developed in the early 1990s and was purchased by Adobe in 1994. Since that time, the After Effects interface has stayed fairly consistent, with minor adjustments accompanying every release. Because of its low price and ease of use, it is employed widely in various graphics-related fields by professionals, students, and hobbyists. That said, professional compositors at larger studios tend to employ it as a secondary compositing program. Of all the programs discussed in this section, After Effects is the only one that is layer based.

Shake was developed by a team of compositors at Sony Pictures Imageworks in the mid-1990s. In 2002, Apple purchased the software. Shake has been a preferred compositor in the visual effects industry due to its long-time support of high resolutions such as 2K, 4K, and IMAX. Shake supports 8-, 16-, and 32-bit workflows.

Nuke was developed by Digital Domain in 1993 as an in-house compositor. It was released to the public in 2002. In 2007, The Foundry, a London-based software distributor, took over the development of the program. Nuke has always enjoyed 32-bit floating-point architecture and has been ported to every major operating system. Although Nuke continues to be used by Digital Domain, it tends to be a secondary program at other animation studios. However, many compositors have found it to be a worthy replacement for Shake, which has suffered from lack of development in the last several years. At the time of this writing, several major studios, including Industrial Light & Magic and Weta Digital, have purchased site licenses for Nuke.

Fusion (previously known as Digital Fusion) is distributed by Eyeon Software Inc. and has found its niche in episodic television, feature visual effects, and the video game industry. Toxik is a relative newcomer to the Autodesk suite of programs and is aimed at high-resolution film and video work. In August 2009, Autodesk announced the integration of Toxik with Maya 2010; as such, the use of Toxik (which has been renamed Maya Composite) will likely become more widespread. Combustion, also distributed by Autodesk, has long been an inexpensive desktop rival to After Effects. Combustion is unique in that it is node based but offers a layer outline similar to After Effects. Combustion, due its architecture, is best suited for low-resolution projects.

Resolutions and Frame Rates

Compositors are faced with a wide array of image resolutions and frame rates. However, international broadcast standards and motion picture precedents make the choices logical for specific media.

Common Resolutions and Aspect Ratios

You can break image resolutions into three categories: SDTV, HDTV, and motion picture film. SDTV (Standard-Definition Television) includes broadcast television and video that possesses *fewer* than 720 lines of vertical resolution. SDTV may be analog or digital. HDTV (High-Definition Television) includes broadcast television and video that possesses 720 or more lines of vertical resolution. HDTV, as a newer format, is digital. Motion picture resolutions, on the other hand, are dependent on film scanner and film recorder technologies. Nevertheless, resolutions common to film scans are similar to resolutions captured by the latest generation of HD digital video cameras.

Video and broadcast television resolutions are determined by a number of international standards, including NTSC, PAL, SECAM, ATSC, and DVB. NTSC (National Television System Committee) is the standard for North America, Japan, South Korea, Taiwan, and parts of South America. PAL (Phase Alternating Line) is the standard for Europe, South America, Africa, India, Australia, and parts of the Pacific Rim. SECAM (SEquentiel Couleur Avec Mémoire) is the standard for France, Russia, and parts of Africa. PAL and SECAM use the same SDTV resolution and frame rate. ATSC (Advanced Television Systems Committee) is the digital broadcast successor for NTSC in North America. DVB (Digital Video Broadcasting) is the digital broadcast successor for PAL and SECAM in Europe, Australia, and parts of Africa.

Image aspect ratios are intrinsically linked to resolutions. An aspect ratio is represented as *x:y* or *x*, where *x* is the width and *y* is the height. For example, the SDTV aspect ratio can be written as 1.33:1 or 1.33. That is, SDTV has a width that's 1.33 times greater than its height. HDTV has an aspect ratio of 16:9 or 1.78. Mixing different aspect ratios leads to compositional problems. For example, broadcasting SDTV on a high-definition TV requires the footage to be stretched horizontally or letterboxed with two side bars. Broadcasting HDTV on an SDTV set requires the footage to be cropped at the sides or letterboxed with top and bottom bars. In terms of compositing, mixing footage with different aspect ratios necessitates additional transformations to fit the components together. (See the tutorials at the end of the chapter for more information.)

In addition, each resolution carries a specific Pixel Aspect Ratio (PAR). A PAR is the mathematical ratio between the pixel width and height. A square PAR has an equal width and height and is expressed as 1:1 or 1.0. A non-square PAR has an unequal width and height. Non-square PARs are feasible because television hardware is able to stretch non-square pixels into square pixels at the point of display. For example, NTSC SDTV has a PAR of 10:11, which is rounded off as 0.9. Thus, NTSC SDTV pixels are slightly taller than they are wide. As such, NTSC SDTV composites appear slightly "squished" on a computer monitor (which uses square pixels). However, once the NTSC SDTV composite is transferred to video and broadcast, the image appears normal.

A list of common resolutions follows. If the PAR is not listed, it's assumed to be 1.0.

640×480 The visible broadcast size of NTSC SDTV as well as a variation of ATSC EDTV (Enhanced Digital Television) is 640×480. In addition, 640×480 is a common size for web-based videos (in fact, it's sometimes called PC Video). A half-size version, 320×240, is often used for web-based video that is severely restricted by bandwidth.

NSTC and PAL D1 D1 (or D-1) was the first widely used digital video format. Although D1 is no longer common, its size is conducive to any compositing project destined for SDTV. The NTSC square-pixel version is 720×540. The NTSC non-square version is 720×486 with a PAR of 0.9. The non-square PAL version is 720×576 with a PAR of 1.07. In contrast, D-3, D-5, and D-5 HD are newer digital formats developed by Panasonic. D-5 HD supports common HDTV resolutions and frame rates.

NTSC and PAL DV DV has been the standard for SDTV consumer digital video capture since the mid-1990s. The NSTC version is 720×480 with a PAR of 0.9. PAL DV is identical to PAL D1.

NTSC and PAL 16:9 Widescreen variations of D1 and DV are commonly called 16:9. The resolutions remain the same, but the NTSC PAR becomes 1.21 and the PAL PAR becomes 1.42.

HDTV 1080 and HDTV 720 There are two HDTV resolutions: 1080 and 720. The 1080 format runs 1920×1080, while the 720 format runs 1280×720. The 720 format utilizes progressive frames, as is indicated by the *p* in 720p. The 1080 format supports interlaced and progressive variations, as is indicated by the names 1080i and 1080p. Although the resolutions for ATSC HDTV and DVB HDTV are identical, the frame rates remain different. (See the next two sections for information on frame rates and interlacing.) HDTV formats are often written as *height-fields-frame rate*. For example, 720p24 is 1280×720 with 24 progressive frames-per-second.

1K, 2K, 3K, and 4K If a resolution ends with *K*, it refers to the number of pixels available horizontally. You can multiply the number by 1024 to get the result. For example 2K is 2048 while 4K is 4096. These resolutions are often employed by motion picture film scanners and recorders. As such, the number of vertical lines of resolution is dependent on the aperture used. An *aperture* is an opening in a plate that allows light to strike the film or the digital sensor. In order for a film scanner to capture the full motion picture frame, it must match its aperture to the one used by the film camera. Two common film formats, Academy and Full Aperture (also known as Super 35 or full-ap), use two different apertures, which leads to two different resolutions. Full Aperture uses the full width of the film to expose the frame (no room is left for the optical soundtrack). Full Aperture scans create a 2048×1556 2K image. Academy shrinks the exposure to make room for the optical soundtrack. Thus, the 2K Academy resolution is reduced to 1828×1332. Note that projectors employ apertures that have a slightly smaller opening than camera, scanner, and recorder apertures; thus, the edges of the image are cropped. Also note that HD digital video cameras operate at common *K* resolutions. For example, a 4096×2048 resolution is referred to as 4K 2:1.

Cinemascope and VistaVision Cinemascope is an anamorphic system that uses a special lens to squeeze an image horizontally so that it fits either the Academy or Full Aperture format. The projector uses a matching lens to restretch the image into its correct shape. A common Cinemascope scan size is 1828×1556. In this case, the compositing program must set the PAR to 2.0 to view the image in a nonstretched fashion. VistaVision (also known as 8-perf) rotates the film frame by 90° so that the frame has twice the film stock with which to work. A common VistaVision scan size is 3096×2048.

Common Frame Rates

There are three common frame rates: 24, 25, and 30.

The frame rate of motion picture film is 24. The 1080p and 720p ATSC HDTV formats, in addition to 480p EDTV, support 24 fps variations. Some digital video cameras support 24p, which records progressive frames at 24 fps. Other cameras offer 24p Advanced, which records 24 fps by repeating frames with a 30 fps format.

The frame rate of PAL, SECAM, and DVB video and broadcast television is 25. The ATSC HDTV formats 1080p, 1080i, and 720p, as well as 480p EDTV, support a frame rate of 30. If the video is interlaced, 30 fps is sometimes expressed as 60, or 60 fields-per-second.

Tips & Tricks: NTSC and ATSC Frame Rates

When a frame rate is listed for an NTSC or ATSC SDTV, EDTV, or HDTV format, it is usually rounded off. Thus 30 fps is actually 29.97 fps and 24 fps is actually 23.98 fps. When whole-value frame rates are listed for PAL or DVB formats, the frame rate is accurate. Note that 29.97 is a simplification of the more accurate 30/1.001 and 23.98 is a simplification of 24/1.001.

Tips & Tricks: Frame Rate Conversions

Converting between frame rates has been a problem since the advent of television. Converting from 24 fps to 30 fps requires a *3:2 pulldown,* whereby frames must be duplicated. This leads to hesitation in the motion known as *judder.* Converting from 30 fps to 24 fps requires the removal or averaging of 6 frames per second. Converting between different international video and broadcast standards is equally difficult and often leads to some type of motion artifact. Thankfully, recent improvements in time warping and optical flow techniques allow compositors to change frame rates without unduly affecting the footage. For more information on time warping and optical flow, see Chapter 12, "Advanced Techniques."

Interlaced vs. Progressive

The process of interlacing breaks each frame of video into two fields. One field carries the even line numbers and a second field carries the odd lines numbers (see Figure 1.7). When interlaced footage is broadcast or played as video, the fields are displayed one at a time. Hence, NTSC SDTV displays 60/1.001 fields per second (often rounded to 59.94) and PAL SDTV displays 50 fields per second. Interlacing provides improved picture quality without requiring additional bandwidth. In contrast, progressive frames are not split apart but are displayed intact. CG renders, for example, are generally delivered to a compositor as progressive frames.

Figure 1.7 Close-up of interlaced frame. The footage features a rapid camera zoom in. If the camera movement was slower, the interlacing would be less perceptible.

Tips & Tricks: Progressive-Frame Tutorials

21 out of 22 tutorials included in this book use progressive-frame footage. Any footage that was shot interlaced has been converted to progressive frames. This was done to keep the tutorials relatively compact and to place the emphasis on various techniques, tools, effects, and nodes. In addition, this allows footage to be shared between After Effects and Nuke. At present, Nuke possesses a limited toolset for working with interlaced footage. Nevertheless, the ability of both programs to work with interlacing is discussed later in this chapter.

Setting Up a Composite

After Effects and Nuke each require a unique set of steps for creating a new project, importing footage, previewing composites, and rendering the result.

After Effects Projects

After Effects composites are referred to as *compositions*. Multiple compositions can exist in a single project. To create a new project, choose File → New → New Project. To adjust the project's global properties, choose File → Project Settings. In the Project Settings dialog box, you can choose the timeline measurement by switching between the Display Style radio buttons (Figure 1.8). If you are working exclusively with video footage, the default Timecode Base radio button is suitable. In this case, the timeline uses base 25 or base 30 measurements; that is, the time is counted in units of 25 frames for PAL and 30 frames for NTSC. If you are working with motion picture film or CG, it's generally best to select the Frames radio button, whereby the frames are counted upward from 1. (For the tutorials in this book, the Display Style is set to Frames.) The Project Settings dialog box also carries settings for bit depth and color space, which are discussed in Chapter 2, "Choosing a Color Space."

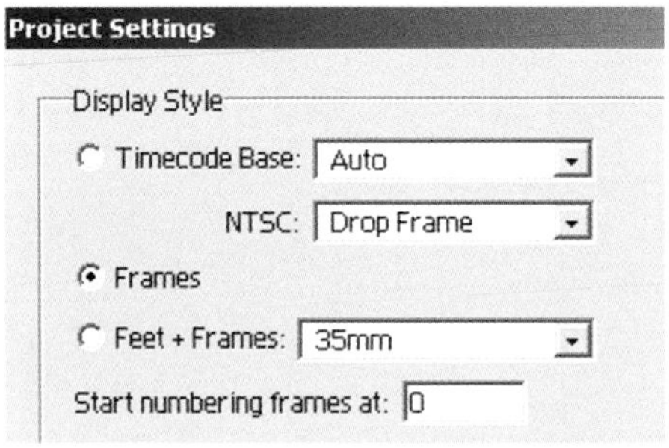

Figure 1.8 The Display Style section of the Project Settings dialog box

To create a new composition, choose Composition → New Composition. The Composition Settings dialog box opens, allowing you to set the composition's critical properties. The Preset menu sets common formats and their appropriate resolution, frame rate, and PAR (see Figure 1.9). You can also manually set the resolution Width and Height cells, plus enter a custom value into the Frame Rate cell. You can manually choose different PARs through the Pixel Aspect Ratio menu. The composition length is set by the Duration cell.

When a new composition is created, it's placed in the Project panel and named Comp *n* (see Figure 1.10). To see the composition as a tab in the Timeline panel, double-click the composition name. If you create more than one composition, each composition receives a separate tab in the Timeline panel. Initially, a composition is empty. However, you can create layers for the composition by importing and adding footage (see the next two sections).

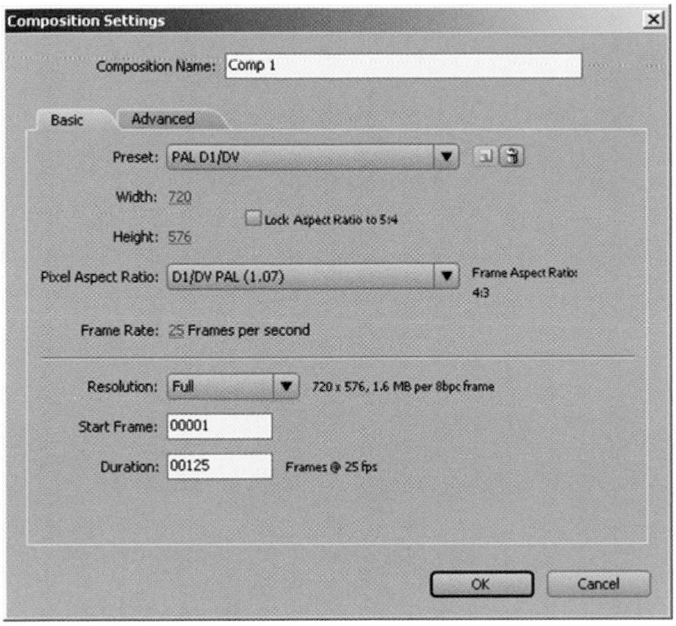

Figure 1.9 The Composition Settings dialog box

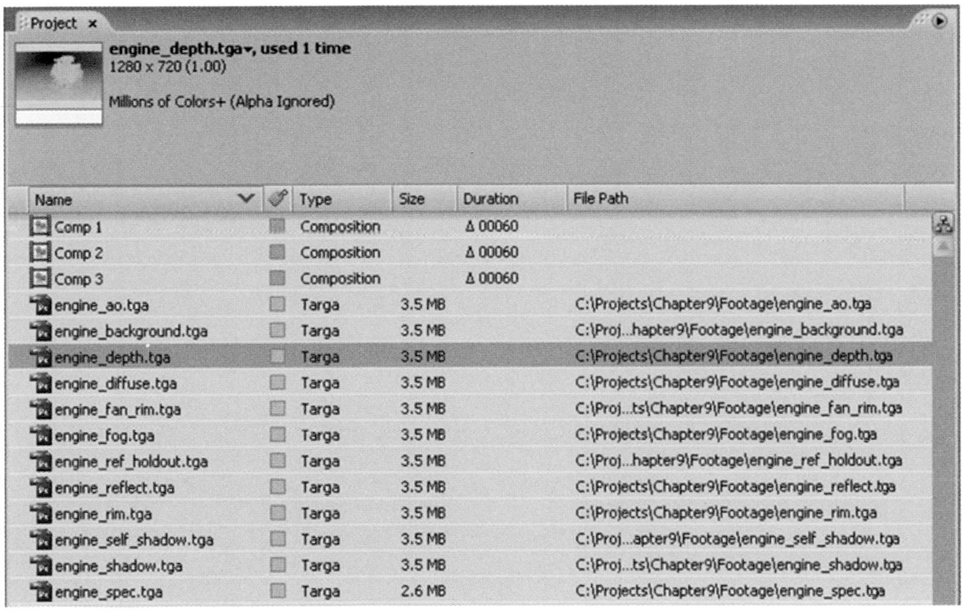

Figure 1.10 The expanded Project panel with 3 compositions and 12 pieces of footage

Importing Footage

To import an image, image sequence, QuickTime movie, or AVI movie into After Effects, choose File → Import → File. If you are importing an image sequence, select the first image of the sequence. By default, the program imports consecutively numbered frames as a single unit. This assumes that the files follow the following naming convention: *name.#.extension. Extension* is the three-letter file format code, such as tga. The program also requires a consistent number of numeric placeholders within the sequence. For example, if a sequence has 200 frames, there must be three placeholders, as with *name.###.ext.* When footage is imported, it's placed in the Project panel.

By default, an imported image sequence or movie is assumed to be a particular frame rate, such as 30 fps. To change the frame rate interpretation, select the footage name in the Project panel, RMB+click, and choose Interpret → Main from the menu. In the Interpret Footage dialog box, change the Assume This Frame Rate value to a number of your choice and click OK.

Tips & Tricks: Missing Files and Assumed Frames Rates

If you open a project file and find that the footage is missing due to an incorrect file path, you can retrieve it by selecting the footage name in the Project panel, RMB+clicking, and choosing Replace Footage → File.

You can change the default frame rate interpretation for all imported footage by choosing Edit → Preferences → Import and changing the Frames Per Second cell.

Using the Layer Outline

To add imported footage to a composition as a layer, LMB+drag the footage name from the Project panel and drop it on top of the layer outline of a composition tab in the Timeline panel. (For a review of the After Effects interface, see the Introduction.)

The layer outline occupies the left side of the Timeline panel. Each composition receives its own tab and its own layer outline (see Figure 1.11). Once a layer exists in a layer outline, it can be selected with the Selection tool. If multiple layers exist in a composition, you can change their order by selecting a layer and LMB+dragging it up or down the layer stack.

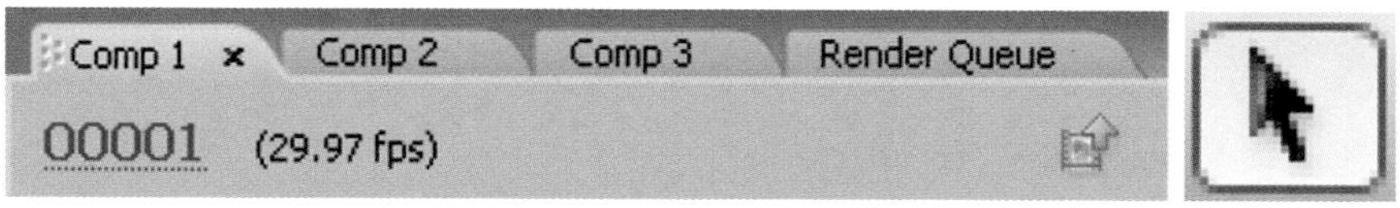

Figure 1.11 (Left) Three compositions, and the Render Queue, receive tabs in the Timeline panel. (Right) The Selection tool

The layer outline functions in a similar fashion to the Layers panel within Photoshop. By default, higher layers occlude lower layers, except where the upper layers are transparent due to alpha channels. The way in which a layer is blended with the layer directly below it is controlled by a blending mode. Blending modes are set by RMB+clicking the upper layer name and choosing Blending Mode → *mode.* You can also set the blending mode by clicking the Toggle Switches/Modes button at the bottom left of the Timeline panel, which reveals Mode menu buttons beside each layer name in the layer outline.

The layer outline carries a number of additional composition switches, layer switches, and menus (see Figure 1.12).

Figure 1.12 *Layer outline of Timeline panel. The composition switches include (A) Open Parent, (B) Live Update, (C) Draft 3D, (D) Hide Shy Layers, (E) Frame Blending, (F) Motion Blur, (G) Brainstorm, and (H) Graph Editor. The layer switches include (I) Video, (J) Audio, (K) Solo, (L) Lock, (M) Shy, (N) Collapse Transformations, (O) Quality, (P) Effect, (Q) Frame Blending, (R) Motion Blur, (S) Adjustment Layer, and (T) 3D Layer.*

Composition switches affect all the layers of a composition while layer switches affect individual layers. Composition switches include the following:

Open Parent, when clicked, displays a menu that lists the nested location of the current composition. For example, if Comp 1 is nested inside Comp 3, the menu reads Comp 3, Layer *n*. If you select a menu item, the Timeline panel will jump to the composition tab where the nesting occurs.

Live Update, when toggled on, updates the composition in the viewer while its layers are transformed or otherwise manipulated. If Live Update is toggled off, manipulated layers are drawn as wireframe boxes.

Draft 3D, when toggled on, disables 3D lights, shadows, and camera depth of field. 3D setups are discussed in Chapter 11, "Working with 2.5D and 3D."

Hide Shy Layers, if toggled on, hides all Shy layers (see the list of layer switches later in this section).

Frame Blending, if toggled on, enables frame blending for all layers. This is necessary for time warping, which is described in Chapter 12, "Advanced Techniques."

Motion Blur, if toggled on, enables motion blur for all layers and is described in Chapter 6, "Convolution Filters."

Brainstorm, if clicked, creates multiple, temporary variations of the composition. To activate the Brainstorm dialog box, you must first select layer properties. The Brainstorm function randomly offsets the values of the selected properties to create the composite variations.

Graph Editor, if toggled on, reveals the Graph Editor in the Timeline panel. For information on the Graph Editor, see Chapter 5, "Transformations and Keyframing."

As for layer switches, the Frame Blend switch is discussed in Chapter 12, the Motion Blur switch is covered in Chapter 6, and the 3D Layer switch is detailed in Chapter 11. Additional layer switches follow:

Video toggles the layer's visibility. The layer remains in the layer outline, but it is not used for the composite.

Audio mutes any audio attached to the layer. (Since this book is concerned with digital compositing, the audio functionality of After Effects is not covered.)

Solo displays the layer for which the switch is activated but disables all other layers.

Lock, when toggle on, prevents alteration of the layer's properties or transformations.

Shy hides the layer if the Hide Shy Layers composition switch is toggled on. If a layer is hidden, it is no longer visible in the layer outline, but it continues to influence the composite.

Collapse Transformations, if toggled on, preserves image integrity for nested compositions. For example, the following may occur:

1. Layer A, which is carried by Comp A, is transformed.
2. Comp A is nested within Comp B.
3. Comp B is transformed.
4. As a result, layer A is essentially transformed two times. This double transformation can destroy pixels unless the transforms are collapsed and a net transformation is calculated at the start. This process is known as *concatenation*, which is discussed further in Chapter 5. (For more information on nesting, see the next section.)

Quality toggles between a draft and best-quality render. A backward slash indicates draft, while a forward slash indicates best quality.

Effect, if toggled off, disables any effects applied to the layer.

Adjustment Layer, when toggled on, converts the layer into an adjustment layer, which automatically applies any effects it carries to all layers below it. The RGB information of the layer itself is hidden.

By default, the layer outline is set to display switches. However, you can toggle to the menu view by clicking the Toggle Switches/Modes button at the bottom left of the Timeline panel. The menu view includes Mode menu buttons, which set each layer's blending mode, and Track Matte menu buttons, which convert the layer to a matte. The Track Matte functionality is discussed in Chapter 3, "Interpreting Alpha and Creating Mattes."

Nesting, Parenting, and Precomping Compositions

You can place one composition inside a second composition. This is called *nesting*. To do so, LMB+drag a composition from the Project panel and drop it on top of the layer outline of a different composition tab in the Timeline panel. When a composition is nested, the entire contents of the composition are represented by a single layer.

You can parent one layer to another by changing a layer's Parent menu (to the right of the layer switches). For example, you can parent an upper layer to a lower layer. When the lower layer is transformed, the upper layer inherits the same transformation. (Transformations are discussed at length in Chapter 5.)

As discussed earlier in this chapter, one disadvantage of the layer-based system is the difficulty with which the output of an adjusted layer or layers is sent to another composition. One workaround is to create a precomposite (also known as a precomp) through precomposing. To precompose one or more layers, follow these steps:

1. Select a layer or layers in a layer outline. Choose Layer → Pre-compose. In the Precompose dialog box, enter a name into the New Composition Name cell (see Figure 1.13). If a single layer is selected, you can select a radio button for Leave All Attributes In Comp or Move All Attributes Into The New Composition. If more than one layer is selected, only the Move All Attributes Into The New Composition radio button is available. Click the OK button.

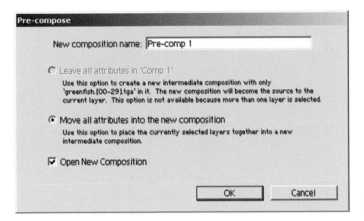

Figure 1.13 The Pre-
compose dialog box

2. If a single layer is selected and Leave All Attributes In Comp is chosen, the selected
layer is left at its original location. However, a duplicate of the layer is placed in a new
composition with a name determined by the New Composition Name cell. If Move
All Attributes Into The New Composition is selected, the selected layer or layers are
moved to the new composition. The new composition is placed at the layers' original
location.

3. You can nest, transform, or apply effects to the newly created layers within the new
composition as you would any other composition.

You can manually create a precomp by rendering a composite through the Render
Queue and importing the resulting footage. To isolate particular layers for a render, toggle
off the Video layer switch for any layer that is unwanted.

Using Composition, Footage, and Layer Panels

There are four types of panels that appear in the central section of the After Effects interface: Composition, Footage, Layer, and Flowchart. To see a particular composition in
the Composition panel, double-click the composition name in the Project panel. To view
imported footage in the Footage panel, double-click the footage name in the Project panel.
To view a layer, by itself, in the Layer panel, double-click the layer name in the layer outline
of the Timeline panel. The Footage and Layer panel differs from the Composition panel
in that they possess their own timelines. If the Composition panel is open and you switch
between composition tabs in the Timeline panel, the active composition is automatically
displayed. The Composition, Footage, and Layer panels each carry their own viewer. The
viewer may show the default 2D view or carry multiple views of a 3D environment. (3D environments are described in Chapter 11; the Flowchart panel is discussed in the next section.)

Aside from carrying viewers, Composition, Footage, and Layer panels include a number of menus and controls (see Figure 1.14).

▣	50%	▼	⊞	▣	00000	▣	♟	◉	Full	▼	▣	▓	Active Camera	▼	1 View	▼	▭	▣	▥	⚓	▚	+0.0
A	B		C	D	E		F	G H		I		J	K		L			M		N O P	Q R	S

Figure 1.14 Composition panel switches and menus: (A) Always Preview This View, (B) Magnification Ratio
Popup, (C) Choose Grid And Guide Options, (D) Toggle Mask And Shape Path Visibility, (E) Current Time,
(F) Take Snapshot, (G) Show Last Snapshot, (H) Show Channel, (I) Resolution/Down Sample Factor Popup,
(J) Region Of Interest, (K) Toggle Transparency Grid, (L) 3D View Popup, (M) Select View Layout, (N)
Toggle Pixel Aspect Ratio Correction, (O) Fast Previews, (P) Timeline, (Q) Comp Flowchart View, (R) Reset
Exposure, (S) Adjust Exposure

While the switches and menus will be described throughout the remaining chapters, a few are worth noting here:

Magnification Ratio Popup menu zooms in or out of the view. To scroll left/right or up/down in a viewer, LMB+drag with the Hand tool (to the right of the Selection tool).

Choose Grid And Guide Options menu allows you to apply Title/Action Safe, Grid, and Ruler overlays to the view.

Tips & Tricks: Title/Action Safe and Overscan

The Title/Action Safe overlay is designed for SDTV. It offers a quick way to make sure critical text and action doesn't get too close to the edge of frame. Due to the design limitations of CRT-based televisions, the frame edge is lost and is not seen by the viewer. This lost region is known as *overscan*. Although digital televisions offer greater control of the broadcast image display, overscan remains a feature. For example, HD televisions generally show the viewer the central 1776×1000 set of pixels out of a possible 1920×1080 pixels. If a project is intended for motion picture film, the Title/Action Safe overlay doesn't apply. Nevertheless, due to projector apertures and masks, a portion of the film frame is lost when shown in theaters. To compensate for this, some compositors import a custom field chart into the compositing program; a *field chart* indicates the area of exposure and projection for a particular camera setup.

Toggle Mask And Shape Path Visibility, if toggled off, hides mask and shape paths. Masks are discussed in Chapter 7, "Masking, Rotoscoping, and Motion Tracking."

Take Snapshot, when clicked, captures the current view and stores it in a cache. You can examine snapshots by clicking the Show Last Snapshot button. Snapshots are useful when comparing different frames or the results of different effect settings.

Resolution/Down Sample Factor Popup menu reduces the resolution of the composition to speed up the viewer update. If this is set to Full, the composite is set to 100% quality. If it's set to Half, half the pixels are discarded and a pixilated view is thus created.

Region Of Interest, if toggled on, allows you to LMB+drag interactively in the viewer to isolate a small area. This improves the update speed of the viewer.

Toggle Transparency Grid, if toggled on, changes the empty black background of the viewer to a white and gray checkerboard. This is useful for identifying subtle holes in a layer.

Toggle Pixel Aspect Ratio Correction, if toggled on, stretches non-square pixels into square pixels. For example, if a composition is set to DV resolution with a 0.9 PAR, Toggle Pixel Aspect Ratio Correction stretches the view horizontally to create a 1.0 PAR. Note that the new PAR only exists in the viewer and does not affect the composite when it's rendered through the Render Queue.

Fast Previews, if clicked, reveals a menu with the different display and graphics card options available on your machine.

The AE Flowchart

After Effects can display compositions and their relationships as a flowchart (node network). To display the flowchart, toggle on the Comp Flowchart View switch in the Composition panel or choose Composition → Comp Flowchart View. The flowchart is opened in a new Flowchart panel. You can display footage, solids, layers, and effects nodes by toggling on the display buttons at the bottom left of the Flowchart panel. Connection lines show the flow of information (see Figure 1.15). You can collapse a composition node and thus hide its inputs by clicking the + sign at the top of the node icon. Note that the flowchart is intended as reference. Connections cannot be changed within the flowchart view.

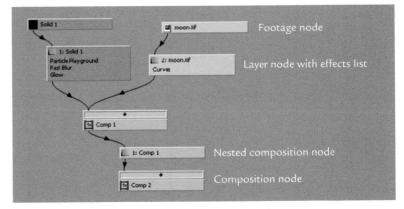

Figure 1.15 *Flowchart view in the Viewer panel*

Tips & Tricks: Composition Navigator

After Effects CS4 adds the Composition Navigator bar to the top of the Composition panel. The bar displays node network information for nested compositions. The bar includes the Composition Mini-Flowchart button. When clicked, the button displays the names of compositions immediately upstream and downstream of the active composition. (Upstream nodes provide information while downstream nodes accept information.)

Previewing a Composition

To play back the timeline, use the playback controls in the Time Controls panel. As the timeline is played, each frame is composited and stored in a cache. Once all the frames have been composited, the timeline is able to achieve real-time playback speeds. The playback speed is indicated by an Fps readout in the Info panel. The target frame rate is determined by the Frame Rate parameter of the Project Settings dialog box. However, you can change the rate through the Frame Rate menu of the Time Controls panel to achieve a different playback rate temporarily.

Rendering a Composition

To render out a composition, select the composition name in the Project panel and choose Composition → Add To Render Queue. A Render Queue tab is added to the Timeline panel (see Figure 1.16). Each queued item in the Render Queue is divided into four sections: Render Settings, Output Modules, Log, and Output To.

Render Settings controls the quality of the render. To adjust the quality, click the words *Best Settings*. In the Render Settings dialog box, you can adjust the Quality property (Best, Draft, or Wireframe), choose a custom frame range, and toggle on or off render features such as Motion Blur or Frame Blending (see Figure 1.17). By default, Quality is set to Best and the full frame range of the timeline is used. However, the Field Render and 3:2 Pulldown options are off by default (see the next section).

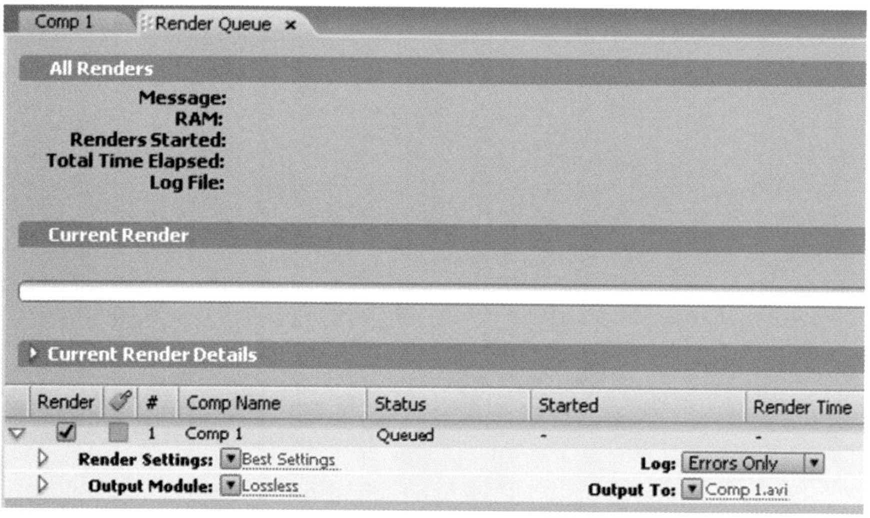

Figure 1.16 The Render Queue tab with Comp 1 queued

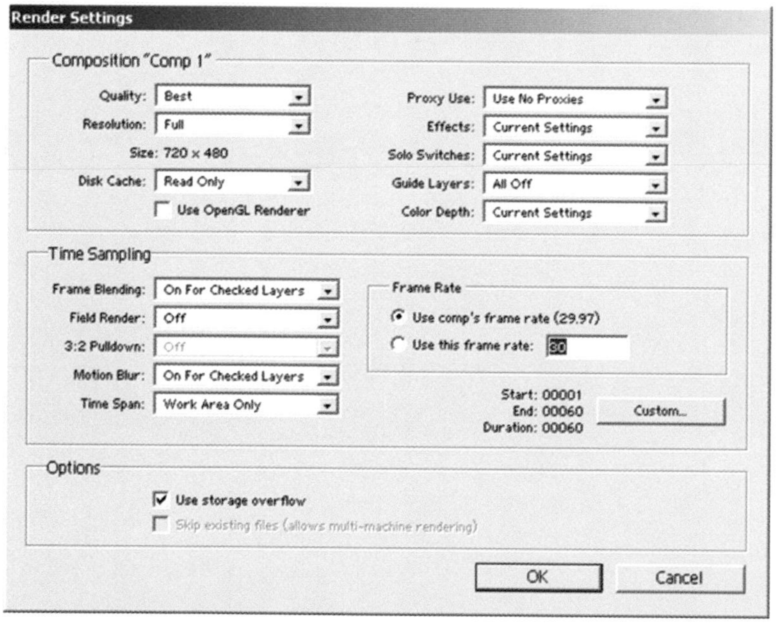

Figure 1.17 The Render Settings dialog box

The Output Module section sets the render format. To choose a different format, click the word *Lossless*. In the Output Module Settings dialog box, the Format menu lists all the formats supported by After Effects that are detected on the local machine (see Figure 1.18). QuickTime, AVI (Video For Windows), and Windows Media formats are suitable for tests, while image formats such as Targa and TIFF are superior for final renders. (For more information on image formats, see Chapter 2.) Once a specific format is selected, you can adjust the format compression and quality settings by clicking the Format Options button. The Channels menu determines which channels are rendered. For example, to render with an alpha channel, change the menu to RGB+Alpha. You can also choose to render straight or premultiplied alpha through the Color menu. (For information on alpha and premultiplication, see Chapter 3). Finally, the Output Module Settings dialog box offers a means to rescale or crop an output through the Stretch and Crop check boxes. Note that the dialog box carries a Color Management tab, which allows you to render a composite to a specific color space. This process is discussed in Chapter 2.

The Log section sets the style of an error log text file that's written to disk. Output To sets the name and location of file(s) to be written. To select a name and location, click the current filename (for example, Comp1.avi). The Output Movie To dialog box opens. Enter the name into the file name cell using the format *name*.[#].*extension* for an image sequence and *name.extension* for QuickTime or AVI movies. For example, test.[##].tga is suitable for a Targa image sequence with 10 to 99 frames because it includes two numeric placeholders.

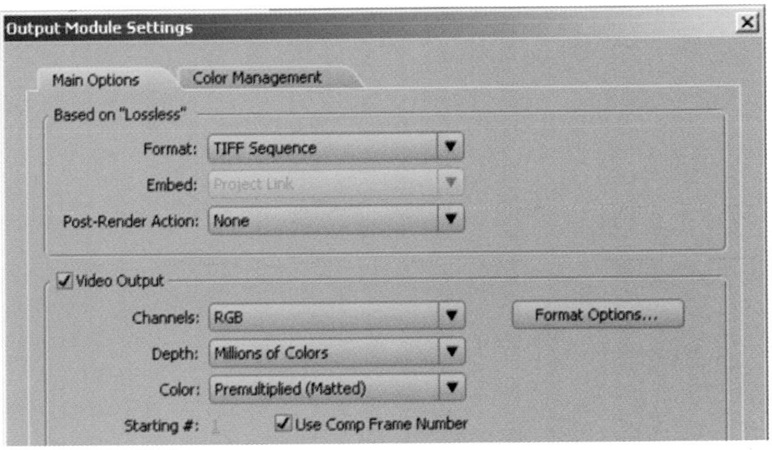

Figure 1.18 The top of the Output Module Settings dialog box

Once the various render settings are selected, you can launch the render by clicking the Render button at the top right of the Render Queue tab. When the render finishes, the queued item remains listed. If you queue an additional composition, it's added to the queue list. You can delete an old queue by selecting the item name in the list and pressing the Delete key.

Interlacing in AE

If you import interlaced video footage, the interlacing is recognized and is indicated by the footage statistics provided at the top of the Project panel. The word *separating* is included with an indication of which field is dominant (upper or lower, see Figure 1.19). An upper field contains the odd lines of a frame, while the lower field contains the even lines of a frame. Different video formats carry different field dominances, which affect the way edits are made and how de-interlacing is carried out. When After Effects identifies interlacing, it separates the fields and converts them to individual frames. In essence, this doubles the frame rate. If you open the footage in the Footage panel, you can examine each separated field by stepping through the Footage panel timeline with the Page Down and Page Up keys. For example, if the footage has lower dominance and the timeline is at frame 1, the lower field of frame 1 is displayed. Pressing the Page Down key once displays the upper field of frame 1. Pressing the Page Down key a second time displays the lower field of frame 2. The frame number is indicated by the Footage panel's Current Time button.

If footage is field-separated and dropped into a composition, only the dominant field of each frame is displayed by the Composition panel as you play the timeline (see Figure 1.20). Both fields continue to exist and are used if the composition is rendered with interlacing. You can force interlacing on the render by changing the Field Render menu in the Render Settings dialog

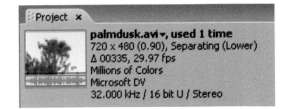

Figure 1.19 Interlaced footage identified by the word Separating *in the Project panel*

box to Upper Field First or Lower Field First (the field dominance should match the intended output format). During the render, the program creates the appropriate interlacing. Note that the interlacing will be successful only if QuickTime Movie, AVI (Video For Windows), or Windows Media is selected as the output format; if you choose to render an image sequence, the fields are combined without averaging or interpolation. On the other hand, if a field-separated composition is not rendered with interlacing, half the information for each frame is discarded and the final image quality may suffer (particularly if you're using low resolution footage for the project). You can mix and match field-separated and progressive-frame footage in a composition with no penalty, although you should take care when you set up a render through the Render Queue (the render will convert field-separated footage into progressive frames or the render will convert progressive frames into interlaced fields).

Figure 1.20 *(Left) Close-up of model lifting a water bottle. The dominant upper field, as seen in the viewer of the Footage panel, is displayed. (Center) Lower field of same frame. Note the significantly higher position of the bottle and index finger. (Right) Upper field of the same frame, as seen in the viewer of the Composition panel.*

If you are working with D1 or DV footage, it's generally best to leave the field dominance interpretation to the program. However, you can choose a different field dominance or select a field dominance for a different video format through the Interpret Footage dialog box. To access this, select the footage name in the Project panel, RMB+click, and choose Interpret → Main from the menu. You can set the Separate Fields menu to Off, Upper Field First, or Lower Field First. If field dominance is chosen incorrectly for a piece of footage, objects will appear to move erratically in the viewer of the Footage panel. If the footage possesses a field dominance but the Field Separation is set to Off, the fields are combined without averaging and heavy artifacts appear around objects in motion.

Various interlacing/de-interlacing plug-ins, such as RE:Vision Effects Twixtor, are available for After Effects and are generally superior to the program's native tools when handling interlacing tasks.

3:2 Pulldown in AE

As mentioned earlier in this chapter, a 3:2 pulldown is required when converting between 24 fps and 29.97 or 30 fps. If you drop 24 fps footage into a 29.97 fps composition, After Effects automatically applies the pulldown by repeating frames of the 24 fps footage. To remove the resulting hesitation in the movement, you can apply time warping and frame blending (which is detailed in Chapter 12). If you drop 30 fps footage into a 24 fps composition, frames are removed from the 30 fps footage. To remove resulting skipping within the movement, you can apply time warping and frame blending.

In addition, After Effects provides a means to remove a 3:2 pulldown that was *previously* applied to footage. For example, if motion picture footage was transferred to video and that interlaced video is imported into After Effects, you can remove the 3:2 pulldown and thus return the motion picture footage to 23.976 fps, which is close to its original 24 fps. This process is commonly referred to as *inverse telecine*. To apply inverse telecine, open the Interpret Footage dialog box, set the Separate Fields menu to the appropriate field dominance, and click the Guess 3:2 Pulldown button (see Figure 1.21). The program identifies the style of pulldown and removes the duplicated frames. (Different pulldown styles repeat the original film frames in different patterns.)

Figure 1.21 *The Fields And Pulldown section of the Interpret Footage dialog box. The WSSWW listed by the Remove Pulldown menu is the identified pulldown style, where W indicates a whole frame and S indicates a split frame. Split frames are composed of two neighboring whole frames.*

Tips & Tricks: 24Pa Pulldown

After Effects includes a Guess 24Pa Pulldown button in the Interpret Footage dialog box. This is designed to remove the pulldown created by 24p Advanced video systems, which record 24 progressive fps within a 30 fps interlaced video format.

Nuke Scripts

Nuke composites are called *scripts*. To create a new script, choose File → New from the main menu bar. (For a review of Nuke panes and menus, see the introduction.) To edit the script's global properties, choose Edit → Project Settings. In the properties panel, the Frame Range parameter determines the duration, the Fps parameter sets the frame rate, and the Full Size Format parameter establishes the composite resolution. (A Nuke parameter is any property with a slider, numeric cell, or check box.)

Importing Files

To import footage into a Nuke script, create a Read node. To do so, RMB+click in the Node Graph and choose Image→ Read from the menu. (Throughout this book, the RMB+click technique is used almost exclusively when creating new nodes.) You can also LMB+click the Image button at the top of the left toolbar and choose Read from the menu. Once the Read1 node exists, its properties panel opens in the Properties pane. If the properties panel is not visible, double-click the Read1 node in the Node Graph. You can browse for the footage by clicking the File browse button (see Figure 1.22). Nuke automatically recognizes image sequences and represents them with the following syntax: *name.padding.extension*. *Padding* indicates the number of numeric placeholders used for the sequence numbering. This is encoded as %01d, %02d, %03d, and so on. %02d, for example, signifies that there are two placeholders, which creates 01, 02, 03, and so forth. *Extension* is the three-letter file format code, such as tga.

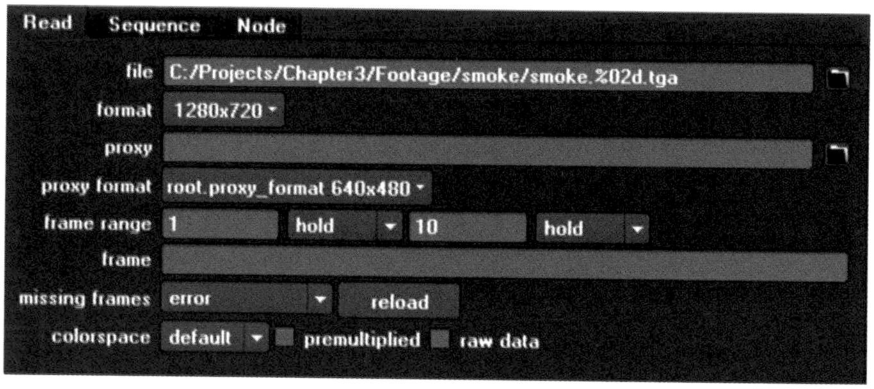

Read
Sequence
Node
file
C:/Projects/Chapter3/Footage/smoke/smoke.%02d.tga
format
1280x720
proxy
proxy format
root.proxy_format 640x480
frame range
1
hold
10
hold
frame
missing frames
error
reload
colorspace
default
premultiplied
raw data

Figure 1.22 A Read node's properties panel

Within the Read node's properties panel, you can set the color space and alpha premultiplication of the imported files. These parameters are discussed in Chapter 2 and Chapter 3.

If the resolution of imported footage does not match the Full Size Format setting in the Project Settings properties panel, the footage will not "fit" the project resolution frame. Thus it may be necessary to connect a Reformat node. For a demonstration of this, see the section "Nuke Tutorial 1: Working with the Reformat Node" at the end of this chapter.

Connecting Nodes

You can connect nodes in an almost endless fashion in the Node Graph. Here are a few approaches to keep in mind:

- To connect two nodes, LMB+drag an unused pipe (connecting line) from one node and drop it on a second node. Each pipe has a specific input or output function. Input pipes are indicated by a line and arrowhead pointing toward the node (see Figure 1.23). Input nodes are generally labeled. The exception to this rule is a Mask input, which takes the form of an inward-pointing arrow stub at the right side of the node. Output pipes are indicated by an outward-pointing arrow stub at the bottom edge of the node.
- If a node is selected and a new node is created, the new node is automatically connected to the selected node's output.

Input A pipe
Input B pipe
A
B
Merge1 (over)
Mask input
arrow stub
Output arrow stub

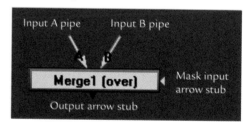

Figure 1.23 Pipes and arrow stubs of a node

- To disconnect a node, LMB+drag the pipe away from the connected node. When you release the mouse button, the pipe is broken. You can also select the node that is downstream (that is, the one that receives the input) and press Ctrl+D.
- To select a node, LMB+click the node icon. To open a node's properties panel, double-click the node icon. To select multiple nodes, Shift+click the node icons.
- To disable a node so that it no longer influences the node network, select the node and press D. To enable the node, press D again.
- To delete a node, select the node icon and press the Delete key.
- To rename a node, open its properties panel and enter a new name into the top cell.

- To duplicate a node with its current setting, select the node and choose Edit →
  Duplicate from the menu bar.
- You can clone a node by selecting the node and choosing Edit → Clone from the menu
  bar. Cloning differs from duplication in that the cloned node maintains an active link
  to the original node (see Figure 1.24). Thus, if the properties of the original node are
  updated, the updated information is passed to the cloned node. You can sever the link
  between the clone and the original by choosing the cloned node and selecting Edit →
  Declone.

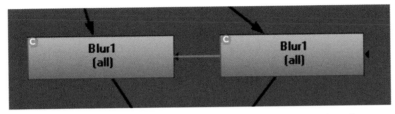

Figure 1.24 *A cloned node (left) is automatically connected to the source node (right), as indicated by the orange pipe and the orange C symbol at the top-left corner of each node icon.*

- To help organize the node network, you can force bends into pipes. To do so, choose
  the node that is upstream (that is, provides the output), RMB+click and choose Other →
  Dot. A dot icon is inserted into the pipe (see Figure 1.25). You can LMB+drag the dot
  and thus force a right angle into the connection. The dot carries no parameters. You can
  also insert a dot by pressing the Ctrl key while
  the mouse is in the Node Graph. A diamond
  appears at the midpoint of every pipe. Continue
  to hold the Ctrl key while LMB+dragging a
  diamond. The diamond is instantly converted
  to a dot.

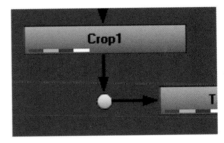

- To zoom in or out of the Node Graph,
  Alt+MMB+drag. To pan, Alt+LMB+drag.
  To frame the node network automatically,
  MMB+click while the mouse pointer is over
  the Node Graph.

Figure 1.25 *A dot creates a bend in a pipe.*

Using the Viewer Pane and Viewers

To view a composite, you must connect a viewer to the node network. By default, a Viewer 1
node is provided. To connect Viewer 1, LMB+drag the 1 pipe and drop it on top of the node
you wish to view. Once a viewer is connected, its output is displayed in the Viewer pane.
You can also connect a viewer by selecting the node you wish to view and pressing the 1
key. You can connect more than one node to a viewer (see Figure 1.26). To do so, select the
nodes one at a time and press the next available viewer number on the keyboard, such as 2,
3, or 4. To have each connection's output appear in the Viewer pane, press the appropriate
number key.

You can create additional viewers and connect each viewer to a different node. To do
so, choose Viewer → Create New Viewer from the menu bar. If more than one viewer exists
in a script, each viewer receives a tab in the Viewer pane.

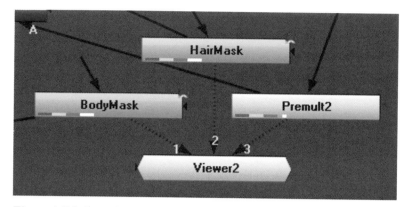

Figure 1.26 *One viewer connected to three nodes*

Aside from displaying the outputs of various viewers, the Viewer pane carries a number of menus and controls (see Figure 1.27). These include the ability to control the timeline; display different channels; adjust the viewer f-stop, gain, and gamma; pick a particular display LUT; and switch between 2D and 3D camera views.

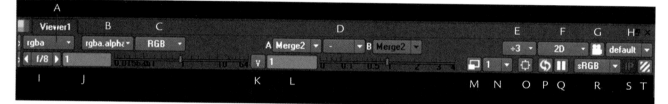

Figure 1.27 *Top of the Viewer pane: (A) Channels, (B) Channel In Alpha, (C) Display Style, (D) Wipe controls, (E) Zoom, (F) View Selection, (G) 3D View Lock, (H) Default Camera/Light, (I) Gain via stops, (J) Gain via slider, (K) Gamma Toggle, (L) Gamma via slider, (M) Toggle Proxy Mode, (N) Downrez, (O) Region-Of-Interest, (P) Update, (Q) Pause, (R) Display_LUT, (S) Input_process, (T) Cliptest*

While most of the Viewer pane menus and controls will be described throughout the remaining chapters, a few are worth noting here:

Channels determines which channels are available for view in the viewer. To cycle through the chosen channels, press the R, G, and B keys while the mouse hovers over the Viewer pane. You can also step through the channels by changing the Display Style menu.

Channel In Alpha allows you to select a different channel to display where the alpha channel would be normally. For example, you can change the menu to Rgb.red and press the A key while the mouse hovers over the Viewer pane to view the red channel. If the menu is set to None, pressing A will display the alpha channel.

Zoom controls its namesake. You can interactively zoom in the Viewer pane by Alt+MMB+dragging. You can scroll in the Viewer pane by Alt+LMB+dragging. Pressing the MMB will maximize the view frame automatically without cropping the edges.

Downrez displays a simplified version of the viewer output. If Downrez is set to 1, the viewer displays the output at 100% quality. If it's set to a value other than 1, pixels are averaged to speed up the viewer update. For example, if the Downrez menu is set to 16, the project's horizontal and vertical resolution is reduced to 1/16th.

Toggle Proxy allows you to switch to a low-resolution version of the composite. For this to work, the Proxy check box in the Project Settings properties panel must be selected. The degree to which the image is reduced is based upon the Proxy Mode menu, which can be set to Format or Scale. If the menu is set to Scale, the proxy works like the Downrez menu, whereby pixels are averaged together. If the Proxy Mode menu is set to Format, the proxy resolution is based on the Proxy Format menu.

Tips & Tricks: Proxy Resolutions

The Read node supports the importation of a full-resolution and a proxy-resolution version of the same piece of footage. The full-resolution version is loaded through the File parameter, while the proxy-resolution version is loaded through the Proxy parameter. If the Toggle Proxy button is toggled on in the Viewer pane, the proxy footage is used.

Wipe displays the output of two nodes simultaneously within the same viewer frame (see Figure 1.28). To activate the wipe, you must connect two nodes to the active viewer. Once the nodes are connected, select each node name from the A and B drop-down menus in the Viewer pane. Change the Combine A And B menu to Wipe. A wipe handle appears in the viewer. You can interactively LMB+drag the handle left or right to change the screen split between the two outputs. You can adjust the opacity of node B by LMB+dragging the handle's diagonal arm.

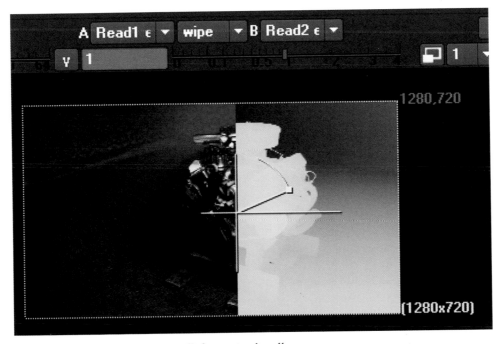

Figure 1.28 Two outputs are split by a wipe handle

Region-Of-Interest, when toggled on, creates a region box in the viewer. Updates occur only within the region box. You can alter the size of the box by LMB+dragging the box edges. To reposition the box, LMB+drag the center crosshair.

Pause, when toggled on, prevents the viewer from updating, even when the node network is updated or parameter values are changed.

Update, when clicked, forces an update, even if the Pause button is toggled on.

Cliptest, when toggled on, applies zebra stripes to any part of the output that exceeds an RGB value of 1, 1, 1.

Playing the Timeline and Creating a Flipbook

There are two ways to test a composite over time within Nuke: play back the timeline or create a Flipbook.

To play back the timeline, use the time controls in the Viewer pane. As the timeline is played, each frame is composited and stored in cache. Once all the frames are composited, the timeline is able to achieve real-time playback speeds. The playback speed is indicated by the Desired Playback Rate cell, which is to the immediate right of the playback controls. The target frame rate is determined by the Fps parameter of the Project Settings properties panel. However, you can change the value in the Desired Playback Rate cell to temporarily achieve a different playback rate.

To create a Flipbook, select the node whose output you wish to see and choose Render → Flipbook Selected from the menu bar. In the Frames To Flipbook dialog box, enter a frame range. Each frame of the composite is written to a disk cache as an RGB file (with an .rgb extension). Once the render is complete, the IRIDAS FrameCycler window opens. FrameCycler is an external program and thus has its own unique interface (see Figure 1.29).

Figure 1.29 FrameCycler window

To center the rendered movie in the FrameCycler viewer, press Ctrl+Home. To scroll within the viewer, Ctrl+MMB+drag. To zoom in or out, set the Zoom menu (directly above the time controls). To see the render at full size, set the Zoom menu to Resample Off. You can interactively scrub the timeline by RMB+dragging left or right in the viewer or LMB+dragging the playhead bar on the timeline. The time controls function as they do in any standard player. The first time you play the timeline, the rendered frames are reloaded into memory. You can save a flipbook movie as an image sequence, QuickTime, or AVI by clicking the Render tab, choosing an output tab in the Render dialog box, and clicking the Render button. You can load previously rendered sequences or movies by pressing the Desktop tab and browsing for files. To add a file to the timeline, press the + sign that appears over the file icon. Multiple movies and image sequences can exist on the timeline simultaneously.

Additional Resources: FrameCycler Documentation

FrameCycler is a robust player that includes support for basic editing, color grading, 3D LUTs, version management, network file sharing, command-line control, and stereoscopic vision. For documentation on the extensive interface and built-in toolsets, see the HTML Documentation Index in the `FrameCyclerWindows/doc/` folder located within the Nuke program directory.

Writing an Image Sequence

To render a composite to disk, create a Write node. To do so, select the node whose output you wish to render, RMB+click in the Node Graph, and choose Image → Write. Browse for a location by clicking the browse button beside the File parameter in the Write node's properties panel (see Figure 1.30). Add the filename to the path cell using the format *name.#.extension*. For example, enter `C:/render/test.###.tga` if you are rendering between 100 and 999 frames. Click the Save button. The program automatically recognizes the filename extension and sets the File Type menu for you. Each File Type setting adds a unique set of quality menus to the bottom of the properties panel. For example, TIFF adds a Data Type (bit depth) and a Compression menu. Once you've set the quality menus, click the Render button. In the Frames To Render dialog box, enter the desired frame range. For instance, if you want to render frame 10, enter 10. If you want to render frames 5 to 20, enter 5,20.

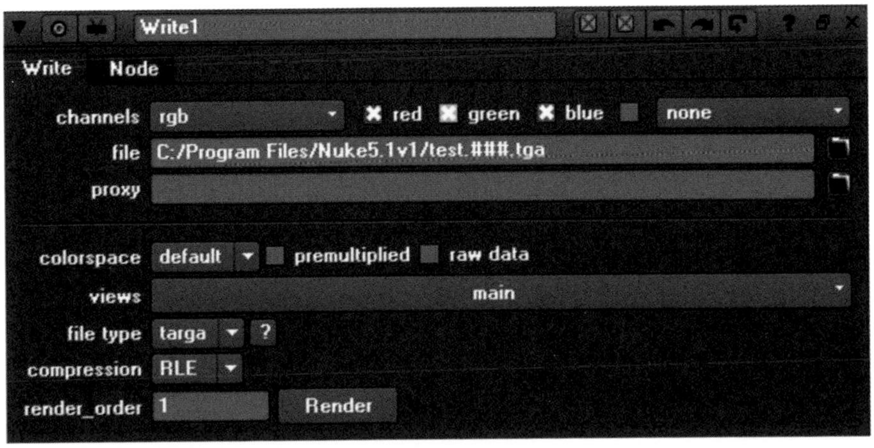

Figure 1.30 Write node properties panel

Interlacing and 3:2 Pulldown in Nuke

Nuke 5.1 carries a hidden DeInterlace node. To access the node, press the X key to bring up the Command Line window. With the Script radio buttons set to TCL, enter **DeInterlace** in the cell and click OK (note the capitalization). A DeInterlace node is added to the Node Graph. Connect the DeInterlace node to the output of a Read node that carries interlaced footage. The interlacing is removed. However, since the DeInterlace node carries no adjustable parameters, the output may be scaled vertically. To correct this, connect Transform and Reformat nodes to scale and fit the output back to the project resolution. For example, in Figure 1.31, interlaced HDTV footage is imported. The DeInterlace node removes the interlacing but stretches the footage vertically by 125%. A Transform node is added with its Scale property set to 1,0.75. A Reformat node is included so that the result of the Transform node is snapped back to the correct 1280×720 bounding box size.

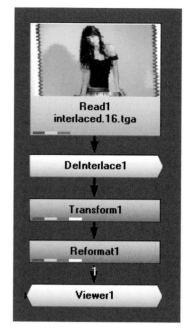

Figure 1.31 A *DeInterlace node removes interlacing with the help of a Transform and Reformat node. A sample Nuke script is included as* deinterlace.nk *in the Tutorials folder on the DVD.*

In addition, Nuke 5.1 includes two gizmo nodes for working with pulldowns: Add 3:2 Pulldown and Remove 3:2 Pulldown. Both are found in the Time menu. Each carries a Phase parameter, which you can use to offset the fields incrementally. Various interlacing/deinterlacing plug-ins and gizmos are available for Nuke. For example, the FieldsKit gizmo is available at www.creativecrash.com.

Tips & Tricks: Nuke Primitives

Nuke provides a number of primitives that are useful for testing networks or seeing the results of particular filters. You can add a primitive to the Node Graph by RMB+clicking and choosing either Image → *node* or Draw → *node*. The Image menu carries the Constant (solid color), Checkerboard, and Colorbars (NTSC test pattern) nodes. The Draw node includes the Radial (solid circle), Ramp (gradient), and Rectangle nodes.

AE and Nuke Tutorials

In this chapter's tutorials, you'll create new projects and scripts. In After Effects, you'll work with interlaced footage and in Nuke you'll work with footage that has different resolutions.

AE Tutorial 1: Working with Interlaced Footage

Working with interlaced video footage presents its own unique set of challenges.

1. Open After Effects. Choose File → New → New Project. Choose File → Project Settings. In the Project Settings dialog box, select the Frames radio button in the Display Style section. This consecutively numbers frames on the timeline. Note that the Project Settings dialog box includes Depth (bit-depth) and Working Space (color

space) menus. It's important to set these menus at the start of each project. Chapter 2 discusses bit depths and color space in great detail. For this tutorial, Depth may be left at 8 Bits Per Channel and Working Space may be left set to None. Click the OK button.

2. Choose Composition → New Composition. In the Composition Settings dialog box, change the Preset menu to HDV/HDTV 720 29.97. This sets the width to 1280, the height to 720, and the frame rate to 29.97. Change the Duration cell to 60, and click the OK button. Comp 1 is added to the Project panel.

3. Choose File → Import → File. In the Import File dialog box, browse for `interlaced.mov` in the Footage folder on the DVD. `interlaced.mov` is added to the Project panel. LMB+drag the QuickTime from the Project panel to the outline layer of the Comp 1 tab in the Timeline panel.

4. Play back the timeline. The motion of the camera zoom appears smooth. In reality, After Effects has incorrectly interpreted the field dominance as upper. This is not visible in the viewer of the Composition panel. This is due to the program displaying only one field per frame when playing back the timeline for the composition. To see all the fields, double-click the footage name. This opens the footage in the Footage panel. To step through the fields one at a time, press the Page Down and Page Up buttons. Page Down moves forward, starting with the dominant field for each frame. Page Up moves backward. Note that the fields appear out of order. Play back the footage using the Footage panel's time controls. The motion appears erratic.

5. To solve the field problem, select the `interlaced.mov` footage in the Project panel, RMB+click, and choose Interpret Footage → Main. In the Interpret Footage dialog box, change Separate Fields to Lower Frame First and click OK. Play the footage using the Footage panel's time controls. The motion is now smooth (that is, the fields are no longer out of order).

6. To convert the field-separated footage into progressive-frame footage, you can render out an image sequence. To do so, select Comp 1 in the Project panel and choose Composition → Add To Render Queue. A Render Queue tab is added to the Timeline panel with Comp 1 listed as the first queue. Click the word *Lossless*. In the Output Module Settings dialog box, change the Format menu to Targa Sequence. Click the OK button. In the Render Queue tab, note the phrase `Comp 1_[##].tga` next to Output To. This is the default name given to the soon-to-be-rendered frames. To change to a different render directory, click the phrase `Comp 1_[##].tga`. In the Output Movie To dialog box, browse for a directory. You can also type in a new render name in the File Name cell. The `[##].` portion of the name is critical for proper frame numbering. Two pound signs indicate two numeric placeholders, which is suitable for a timeline duration that runs between 10 and 99 frames. Click the Save button to close the Output Movie To dialog box. Click the Render button.

7. To examine the rendered footage, import it into the project. Choose File → Import → File. In the Import File dialog box, browse for the rendered footage. Because it's an image sequence, you need only select the first frame of the sequence. The program automatically imports the entire sequence as a single unit. Double-click the new footage's name in the Project panel to open it in the Footage panel. Step through the footage one frame at a time to examine the quality. Since the footage was rendered without interlacing, there are no fields. Note how the footage progresses in coarser steps. Every other field was lost during the render. Nevertheless, the footage is fairly high resolution, so it still creates smooth motion. The tutorial is complete. A sample After Effects project is included as `ae1.aep` in the Tutorials folder on the DVD.

Nuke Tutorial 1: Working with the Reformat Node

Working with source footage that possesses different resolutions can lead to formatting and composition problems unless special steps are taken.

1. Open Nuke. Choose Edit → Project Settings from the menu bar. In the Project Settings property panel, set the Full Size Format menu to 1K_Super_35(full-ap). This creates a project with a resolution of 1024×778. Note that the resolution bears no indication of a PAR. In contrast, the NTSC format displays a size of 720×486 .9, where the .9 is the non-square PAR. If a PAR is not listed, it's assumed to be 1.0.

2. In the Node Graph, RMB+click and choose Image → Read. In the Read1 node's properties panel, browse for symbols.tga in the Footage folder on the DVD. Select the Premultiplied check box to interpret the alpha channel correctly. Connect a viewer to the Read1 node. A graphic with five symbols is shown. The viewer indicates the size of the graphic by adding a 1024,778 notation to the top-right corner of the view frame. In this case, the graphic is the same size as the project resolution (see Figure 1.32). The project resolution is indicated at the lower-right corner of the frame.

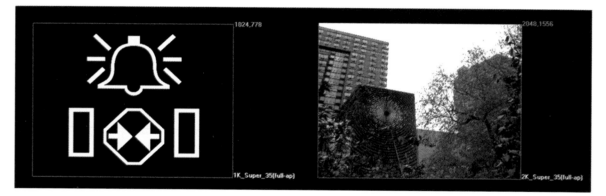

Figure 1.32 *(Left) 1024×778 symbols graphic (Right) 2048×1556 city photo*

3. In the Node Graph, RMB+click and choose Image → Read. In the Read2 node's properties panel, browse for square.tif in the Footage folder on the DVD. Connect the viewer to Read2. A city square is displayed. However, the view adapts to the new, larger resolution of the square.tif image. This is indicated by the 2048,1556 notation at the top-right of the view frame (see Figure 1.32).

4. With no nodes selected, RMB+click and choose Merge → Merge. Connect the viewer to the Merge1 node. Connect input B of the Merge1 node to the output of the Read2 node. Connect input A of Merge1 to the output of Read1. The Merge1 node applies a blending operation to combine the two images. Because symbols.tga carries an alpha channel, it appears on top of the city square. However, since square.tif is larger than symbols.tga and the project resolution, the view frame remains fixed at 2048×1556. In addition, the symbols graphic is forced to the bottom left of the frame (see Figure 1.33). If you were to render the Merge1 node's output, the resolution would remain 2048×1556.

5. To force the Merge1 node to create a project-sized resolution, feed the Read2 node through a Reformat node. To do so, select the Read2 node, RMB+click, and choose Transform → Reformat. A Reformat1 node is inserted after Read2. The composition instantly returns to the proper size of 1024×778, and the symbols take up the entire

frame. The Reformat node forces the Read2 output to conform to the output format established by the project settings. For additional information on the Reformat node, see Chapter 5. The tutorial is complete (see Figure 1.34). A sample Nuke script is included as nuke1.nk in the Tutorials folder on the DVD.

Figure 1.33 The initial composite. The ouput size is forced to 2048×1556.

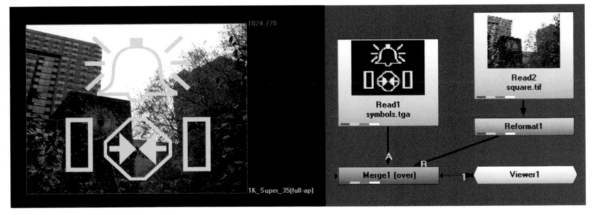

Figure 1.34 (Left) The final composite with the proper size of 1024×778 (Right) The final node network

Tips & Tricks: The Crop Node

The Crop node (in the Transform menu) allows you to reduce the resolution of an output by cropping the image edges. The Box X, Y, R, and T cells define the left crop edge, bottom crop edge, right drop edge, and top crop edge respectively. If the Reformat check box remains unselected, the cropped area is rendered black and the frame edges remain unaffected. If the Reformat check box is selected, the output resolution is forced to the cropped size.

Interview: Dorne Huebler, Industrial Light & Magic, San Francisco

Dorne Huebler graduated from the California Institute of the Arts in 1980. By the time he graduated, he was already creating graphics and visual effects for commercials. In 1995, he served as visual effects supervisor for *James and the Giant Peach.* Since joining ILM

in 1998, he's served as a compositor, sequence supervisor, and compositing supervisor on such features as *Harry Potter and the Chamber of Secrets*, *The Chronicles of Riddick*, *Hulk*, *Pirates of the Caribbean: At World's End*, and *Iron Man.*

Industrial Light & Magic (ILM) was founded 1975 in by George Lucas as a means to create the special effects for *Star Wars.* The studio has since gone on to become a powerhouse in the visual effects industry, garnering multiple Academy Awards and a long list of top-grossing feature films. ILM pioneered many of the computer animation and filmmaking technologies taken for granted today, including 24 fps digital video, morphing, and photo-real 3D characters.

Dorne Huebler at his workstation. Note the CRT monitors, including one made by SGI.

(Left) R2-D2 and a storm trooper stand guard over the lobby. (Right) A statue of Eadweard Muybridge, a pioneer of the photographic study of motion, watches over the ILM facility. ILM moved to the Presidio in 2005, restoring the buildings of an abandoned army hospital. (Photos courtesy of Industrial Light & Magic)

(At the time of this writing, ILM was transitioning from Sabre, a modified version of Flame/Inferno, to Nuke.)

LL: You've been involved with visual effects work for close to 30 years—long before the term *digital compositing* was used. Can you describe the route you took to ILM?

DH: While at school at Cal Arts, I was doing graphics for commercials and titles with visual effects.... I didn't run an optical printer. I was prepping [work] for optical printers and art directing [work] with optical printers. So that was my focus in the early 1980s—art direction and design along with animation and film graphics, really. Initially, I was just freelancing for [small companies] in L.A. [T]he first big studio I worked for was Dream Quest Images in the late 1980s. My first feature film was *Superman IV*. I also worked at a place called Chandler Group on *Pee Wee's Playhouse*. I worked for Universal Studios on feature film trailer titles, which was kind of a niche at that point. In the early 1990s, I joined Buena Vista Visual Effects (the early digital effects division of Walt Disney Studios)—that was the real transition into digital compositing. And I worked there until I came to ILM [11 years ago].

LL: Approximately, how many compositors are at ILM at any given time?

DH: It fluctuates based on [the number of] shows that we're working on at once. We might have three to five big shows at once going through here at any time.... The size of the crew will expand and contract based on that. [W]hen I got here in 1998, there were around 20 staff compositors. At present, I'm guessing that there are around 60 to 70 (including freelancers).

LL: Since you joined ILM, you've served as a compositing supervisor. How many compositors would you work with on one project?

DH: I was compositing supervisor for *Star Wars: Episode II*. At one point, we had close to 35 compositors in my group. [A] smaller show may only need 6 to 10 people.... A lot of the times, there are technical directors who will do their own compositing, so you'll work with them as well.

LL: Do you prefer working with the proprietary compositing software or off-the-shelf compositing software?

DH: What I've found is, with every package I use, [I] always find things that I just love.... [E]very package also has idiosyncrasies—like, this is the one thing that bugs me about it. So I think that it's really about the type of work you're doing, [and whether] one program might be more efficient than another. It really depends on what you're up to....

LL: ILM helped popularize the use of HD digital video for feature film work. What has been your own experience with HD in comparison to film?

DH: I'm actually trying to think about the last time I worked on an HD show. I mean, we'll have elements that are shot in HD and it can be really convenient because you don't have to get a film scan. I think it's been three or four years since I've worked on an all-HD show. When you're working with HD, you're going to deal with different green [channel] structure, for instance. It can present challenges for [greenscreen] extractions. But, overall, it's pretty seamless. At the beginning of a show, you think, "Oh my God—it's HD! It's all going to be different!" And then, once you're working, you realize that it's the same as working in film. It's pretty much invisible....

Additional Resources: The Full Interview

To read the full interview with Dorne Huebler, see the Interviews folder on the DVD.

Interview: Michael Coleman, Adobe, Seattle, Washington

Michael Coleman graduated with a degree in business economics from Seattle University. He went on to work as a graphic designer, visual effects artist, and compositor for such companies as Aldus and Will Vinton Studios. In 1999, he joined Adobe and helped redesign the Adobe Creative Suite. In 2007, he became the product manager of After Effects.

Michael Coleman

Adobe Systems Incorporated was founded in 1982 by John Warnock and Charles Geschke. Although its initial products were PostScript tools and digital fonts, the company has gone on to develop a wide array of desktop publishing, digital imaging, digital editing, and compositing software. As of 2009, Adobe had grown to over 7,000 employees with offices in San Jose, Seattle, Orlando, and San Francisco as well other cities in the United States and abroad.

LL: What are your duties as product manager?

MC: The product manager position has many facets, but my main responsibility is to define the product strategy and to ensure that After Effects meets our customers' needs. I spend a lot of time talking with customers. It's important that I immerse myself in their concerns, from business trends to the gritty details of production workflows. The After Effects team takes its inspiration from an understanding of what our customers need. Staying close to our customers gives us confidence that every version of After Effects will help our customers be more creative and more productive. If we do this one thing and do it well, everybody wins.

LL: Over its 15-year history, what have been the most significant changes to After Effects?

MC: If you go back and use After Effects 1.0, you can animate your content in nested, hierarchical, high-definition compositions, but you might spend some time looking for the timeline panel. That's because it didn't have one. The timeline came in version 2.0 and would certainly be one of the more significant early changes. Since then, I would say that 3D compositing with cameras, lights, and shadows was a huge leap forward. And 32-bit color, painting tools, and the animation engine for text and shapes have also opened up a universe of creative opportunity....

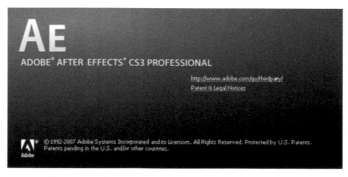

After Effects CS3 logo

LL: There is a great deal of competition when it comes to compositing software. How does After Effects differentiate itself from the pack?

MC: After Effects is surprisingly easy to use and has a great deal of flexibility to handle a broad range of projects. It integrates very well into broader workflows, and it's almost guaranteed that the people you hire already know how to use it.... When it comes to other compositing products, I think you'll find that After Effects is more of a complement than a competitor. If you ask someone who owns another compositing product if they also use After Effects, the answer is probably yes.

LL: After Effects is layer-based. What is the greatest advantage of a layer-based system when compared to a node-based system?

MC: Most people have a mental model of a composite that looks like a stack of layers. The After Effects user interface is organized around a timeline that reflects the stacking order of the layers.... When animation and timing come into play, the advantages of a layered timeline begin to shine. After Effects has the best timeline in the industry, and it's truly a joy to animate with it.... [With After Effects CS4, we] introduced a new feature called the mini-flowchart that visualizes the nesting structure and makes navigating among compositions much faster. It's quite handy and provides some of the advantages of nodes within the layered timeline. Our goal is to have the best of both worlds.

Additional Resources: The Full Interview

To read the full interview with Michael Coleman, see the Interviews folder on the DVD.

Interview: Richard Shackleton, The Foundry, London

Richard Shackleton graduated from the Imperial College of Science, Technology and Medicine in London with a degree in software engineering. He began his career at Nortel Networks and Avid Technology, where he specialized in software development for the visual effects and editing markets. Richard joined The Foundry in 1999 but left to work with Digital Vision. He returned to The Foundry in 2008 and now serves as product manager for Nuke.

The Foundry was founded in 1996 by Bruno Nicoletti and Simon Robinson. The company developed the Tinder plug-in set for Flame and went on to create a wide range of tools for all the major compositing packages. At present, The Foundry is a leading developer of visual effects and image processing technologies for film and video postproduction.

Richard Shackleton

Nuke 5.1 logo

LL: Nuke was developed in-house at Digital Domain. Describe the path it took from Hollywood to The Foundry.

RS: Nuke was [written] as a command-line image-processing program.... [In 1993,] it was used by Digital Domain on the film *True Lies*. The first version, [which] became Nuke 2, was created to read scripts, draw, and show data flow down the tree. It was used for *Titanic* and the *T2* 3D ride along with many other films.... Nuke 4 was the first commercially available version...from the newly-formed D2 Software in 2002.... Selling commercial software is outside Digital Domain's core interests. Both Digital Domain and The Foundry realized that Nuke could have far greater potential if it was developed and marketed by The Foundry. Today, The Foundry owns the Nuke IP (intellectual property).... Digital Domain remains one of The Foundry's most important customers.

LL: Nuke is node based. What is the greatest advantage of a node-based system over a layer-based system? Are there times when a node-based system is a disadvantage?

RS: A node-based system allows you to change earlier operations without having to repeat the later steps manually. It also allows a free flow of operations, whereas a layer-based system will direct an artist's approach to working with a particular application model. Such freedom in constructing the flow of data and operations promotes many advantages, such as intermediate result reuse, the creation of operation templates, more creative and powerful use of scripting and expressions, 3D data flows, and nonimage data use.... A disadvantage is that the program actually does allow such flexibility and may repeat the later steps for you, so this can be slower when you change a step other than the last one. A layer-based system can support a better time-based view, useful when working with multiple shots together in a sequence.

LL: Nuke has always operated in 32-bit floating point. How would you summarize the advantages of floating point over lower, fixed bit depths?

RS: Even in 1993, floating-point calculations were faster than integers on modern processors. Floating point also offers a wider latitude, [which] allows linear data representation rather than having gamma to encode detail in specific areas.... This allows artistic and technical freedom during image processing, [thereby] removing the need to carefully manage clipping in the data. For example, this is useful in color correction (where values are pushed up and down multiple times in succession), with depth or motion data (where great accuracy is needed), and in HDR workflows that need to support a wide range of exposure values.

LL: Nuke is designed for a feature film production environment. Do you consider the core client to be visual effects professionals?

RS: The core client is visual effects professionals, supporting artist and production needs in feature films, commercials, CG animation, and high-value television drama and documentaries.

Additional Resources: The Full Interview

To read the full interview with Richard Shackleton, see the Interviews folder on the DVD.

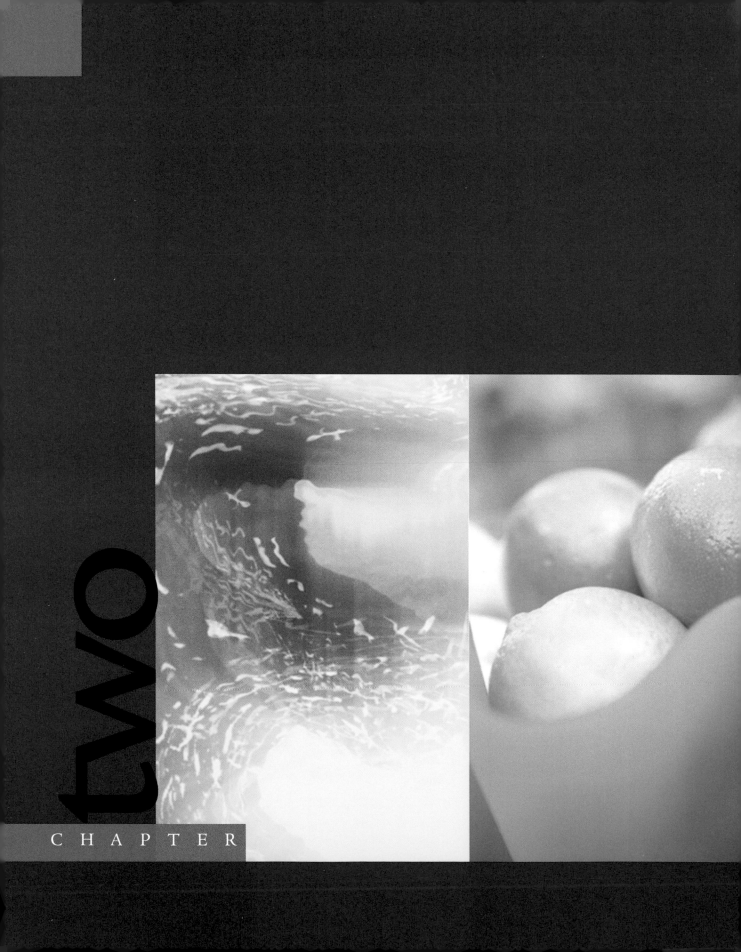

CHAPTER

two

Choosing a Color Space

A firm understanding of color *theory, color space, and color calibration is critical for a successful compositor. Knowledge of color theory will help you choose attractive palettes and shades. An understanding of color space will ensure that your work will not be degraded when output to television or film. A firm grasp of calibration will guarantee that your compositing decisions are based on an accurate display. It's not unusual for professional compositors to be handed pieces of footage that come in various bit depths, color spaces, and image formats. Thus it's necessary to convert the various files. The After Effects and Nuke tutorials at the end of this chapter will present you with just such a scenario.*

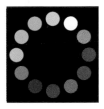

Color Theory Overview

Color is not contained within the materials of objects. Instead, color is the result of particular wavelengths of light reaching the viewer through reflection or transmission. Different materials (wood, stone, metal, and so on) have different atomic compositions and thereby absorb, reflect, and transmit light differently. This natural system is therefore considered a *subtractive* color system. When a wavelength of light is absorbed by a material, it is thus subtracted from white light, which is the net sum of all visible wavelengths. Hence, the red of a red object represents a particular wavelength that is not absorbed but is reflected or transmitted toward the viewer.

RYB and RGB Color Models

When discussing color in the realm of fine arts, *color models* are invoked. Color models establish primary colors, combinations of which form all other visible colors. The red-yellow-blue (RYB) color model, used extensively for nondigital arts, traces its roots back to eighteenth-century color materialism, which assumes that primary colors are based on specific, indivisible material pigments found in minerals or other natural substances. The popularization of specific RYB colors was aided by printmakers of the period who employed the color separation printing process.

The development of computer graphics, however, necessitated a new color model with a new set of primary colors: red, green, and blue, commonly known as RGB. Through an additive process, computer monitors mix red, green, and blue light to produce additional colors. Added in equal proportions, RGB primaries produce white. In contrast, the RYB color model is subtractive in that the absence of red, yellow, and blue produces white (assuming that the blank paper or canvas is white). Modern printing techniques follow the subtractive model by utilizing cyan, magenta, and yellow primary inks, with the addition of black ink (CMYK, where K is black). The RGB color model is based upon mid-nineteenth-century trichromatic color theories, which recognized that color vision is reliant on unique photoreceptor cells that are specifically tuned to particular wavelengths.

Both the RYB and RGB models are often displayed as color wheels (see Figure 2.1). Despite the difference between the RYB and RGB models, artistic methods of utilizing an RYB color wheel are equally applicable to an RGB color wheel.

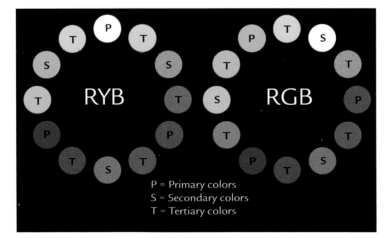

Figure 2.1 *RYB and RGB color wheels. Secondary colors are mixtures of two primary colors. Tertiary colors are mixtures of a primary and a secondary color. An RGB version of this figure is included as* `colorwheel.tif` *in the Footage folder on the DVD.*

Employing Color Harmony

The goal of color selection is *color harmony*, which is the pleasing selection and arrangement of colors within a piece of art. The most common methods of choosing harmonic colors from a color wheel are listed here:

Complimentary Colors A pair of colors at opposite ends of the color wheel. With an RGB color wheel, blue and yellow are complimentary colors (see the left image of Figure 2.2).

Split Compliment One color plus the two colors that flank that color's complimentary color. With an RGB color wheel, green, blue-violet (purple), and red-violet (pink) form split compliments (see the right image of Figure 2.2).

Analogous Colors Colors that are side by side (see the left image of Figure 2.3). With an RGB color wheel, yellow and orange are analogous.

Diad Two colors that have a single color position between them (see the right image of Figure 2.3). With an RGB color wheel, cyan and green form a diad. Along those lines, a triad consists of three colors that are equally spaced on the wheel (such as red, green, and blue).

Figure 2.2 *(Left) Complimentary blue and yellow patterns appear on an angelfish. (Right) Green, blue-violet, and red-violet light in a broadcast graphic create a split compliment. (Images © 2009 by Jupiterimages)*

Color Space and Monitor Calibration

Gamut represents all the colors that a device can produce. *Color space* refers to a gamut that utilizes a particular color model. (For example, sRGB and Rec. 709 are color spaces, while RYB and RGB are color models.) The color space available to various output devices varies greatly. For example, the color space that a high-definition television can output is significantly different from the color space available to a computer monitor or an ink-jet printer. The variations in color space necessitate the calibration of equipment to ensure correct results when it comes to color reproduction. As a compositor, you should know if your own monitor has been calibrated. In addition, it's important to know what type of color grading will be applied to your work. *Color grading* is the process by which the colors of the footage are

Figure 2.3 *(Left) The yellow and orange of an abstract digital painting function as analogous colors. (Right) the green of limes and the cyan of a glass bowl form a diad. (Images © 2009 by Jupiterimages)*

adjusted or enhanced in anticipation of its projection on film, broadcast on television, display on the Internet, or inclusion in a video game. (Prior to digital technology, the motion picture grading process was known *color timing*.)

Working with Gamma

Computer monitors operate in a nonlinear fashion. That is, the transition from darks to lights forms as a delayed curve (see Figure 2.4). With a CRT (Cathode Ray Tube) monitor, this curve results from the nonlinear relationship between the grid voltage (voltage applied to the electron gun) and luminance (the net effect of electrons shot at the screen's phosphors). Mathematically, the curve is shaped by *gamma*, which is the exponent of a power function. That is, the voltage of the gun must be raised by the power of gamma for an equivalent raise in the screen's luminance. When discussing the specific gamma of a particular monitor, the term *native gamma* is used. Liquid Crystal Display (LCD) and plasma screens do not employ electron guns; however, they do apply varying amounts of voltage to liquid crystals or plasma electrodes. As such, LCD and plasma screens exhibit gamma curves similar to CRTs.

If there is no compensation for a monitor's native gamma, the digital image will gain additional contrast through its mid-tones and may lose detail in the shadows or similarly dark areas (see Figure 2.5).

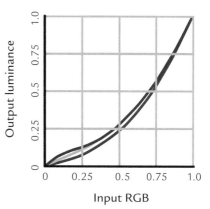

Figure 2.4 *The uncalibrated gamma curve of a mid-priced LCD monitor. Note that the red, green, and blue channels each have a slightly different response. The graph has been normalized to a range of 0 to 1.0.*

Figure 2.5 *(Left) A digital photo with gamma correction applied. (Right) Same photo without gamma correction. The contrast is exaggerated for print. (Photos © 2009 by Jupiterimages)*

Industry Perspective: LCDs vs. CRTs

LCD and plasma screens are rapidly replacing CRTs in the professional world of animation and visual effects. Unfortunately, this has led to additional calibration difficulties. LCD screens have a viewing angle that is narrower than a CRT. Thus, the effect of a display gamma curve is subject to how off-center the viewer is as he or she sits or stands. In addition, LCDs have a poor record when it comes to color accuracy and consistency. "Color critical" LCD monitors have been available to studios for a number of years, but their high price tag has made them impractical when outfitting a large number for seats for animators or compositors. This situation has led some studios to stockpile CRT monitors in anticipation of their disappearance. Fortunately, recent advances in technology have begun to address this issue. For example, the moderately priced Hewlett-Packard DreamColor LCD monitor, codeveloped by DreamWorks Animation, offers a 30-bit color space (10-bits per channel), hardware support for industry-standard color profiles, and an LED backlight that produces a contrast range of 1000:1.

To avoid this, operating systems apply gamma correction. *Gamma correction* is the inverse power function of the monitor's native gamma. That is, gamma correction creates a curve which neutralizes the monitor's native gamma curve, thus making the monitor's response roughly linear. The gamma correction curve is defined by a single number. With Windows operating systems, the default is 2.2. With Macintosh OS-X, the default is 1.8. Ideally, gamma correction would adjust the pixel values so that their displayed luminance corresponds to their original values. However, since native gamma curves generally don't match the gamma correction curves, this becomes difficult. For example, the average CRT monitor carries a native gamma of 2.5. Hence the resulting *system* or *end-to-end gamma* on a Windows system is 1.14, which equates to 2.5 / 2.2. In other words, a pixel with a value of 0.5 ultimately receives an adjusted value of 0.46 (see Figure 2.6). Thus, the gamma correction formula can be written like this:

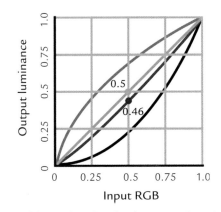

Figure 2.6 Pixel value curve (cyan), native gamma curve (black), gamma correction curve (orange), and final adjusted curve (violet). The green dot indicates the original pixel value of 0.5. The red dot indicates the final adjusted pixel value of 0.46.

$$\text{new pixel value} = \text{pixel value}^{(\text{native gamma} / \text{gamma correction})}$$

Calibrating a Monitor

Monitor calibration ensures that a monitor is using an appropriate gamma correction curve and guarantees that the system's contrast, brightness, and color temperature settings are suitable for the environment in which the workstation is located. Accurate calibration requires two items: color calibration software and a colorimeter. Calibration generally follows these steps:

1. The calibration software outputs color patches of known values to the monitor. The colorimeter reads in the monitor's output values. To reduce the disparity between values, the user is instructed to adjust the monitor's contrast and brightness controls as well as the system's gamma and color temperature. *Color temperature*, which is the

color of light as measured by the kelvin scale, determines the white point of the hardware. A *white point* is a coordinate in color space that defines what is "white." Colorimeters take the form of a physical sensor that is suction-cupped or otherwise positioned over the screen (see Figure 2.7).

2. The software compares the measured values to the known values and creates a monitor profile. A *monitor profile* describes the color response of the tested monitor within a standard file format determined by the International Color Consortium (ICC). The profile includes data for a Look-Up Table (LUT) for each color channel. A LUT is an array used to remap a range of input values. The system graphics card is able to extract gamma correction curves from the LUTs. As part of the calibration process, the user may decide to choose a white point different from the system default.

3. When an image is to be displayed, it is first loaded into a framebuffer (a portion of RAM storage). Each pixel is then remapped through the LUTs before its value is sent to the monitor. When LUTs are used, the original pixel values are temporarily changed and the original image file remains unaffected.

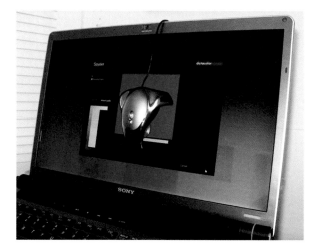

Figure 2.7 A Spyder 3 Elite colorimeter calibrates the LCD of the laptop with which this book was written. The colorimeter is able to read ambient light sources and take them into consideration.

Tips & Tricks: Switching Between White Points

The flexibility of a white point is necessary to match potential output formats. For compositing intended for video, 6500 K (kelvin) matches the white point of SDTV televisions. For composites intended for a movie theater, 5400 K matches the standardized white point of projected motion picture footage. Many HDTV sets offer the option to switch between different white points; 5400 K, 6500 K, and 9300 K options are common.

By default, operating systems supply a default monitor profile so that the computer system can be used before calibration. Although the profile is functional, it is not necessarily accurate. In addition, the system supplies a default gamma correction value and color temperature.

Colorimeters are generally bundled with matching calibration software. Manufactures such as Pantone, MonacoOPTIX, and X-Rite offer models ranging from those suitable for home use to ones designed for professional artists. In any case, it's not necessary to use monitor calibration software to create a display LUT. In fact, many studios write custom LUTs for specific projects by using various programming languages or by employing tools built into compositing packages. For additional information on LUTs and how they are utilized for the digital intermediate (DI) process, see Chapter 8, "DI, Color Grading, Noise, and Grain."

Industry Perspective: Monitor Calibration

When it comes to monitor calibration, there is no universally accepted standard at animation studios, visual effects houses, and commercial production facilities. A few studios skip monitor calibration completely, preferring to send their work to another facility that specializes in color grading. Others undertake a rigid schedule of calibration (as often as every three days) and employ specifically tailored LUTs for each project. In either case, the compositors' monitors still retain a finite color space due to the physical nature of their CRT or LCD screens. To help compensate for this, some studios install a limited number of quality control (QC) stations consisting of broadcast monitors or screening rooms set up with high-end digital projectors. Others retain in-house Autodesk Flame or Inferno bays that are well-suited for real-time color manipulation. More recently, large studios have started purchasing digital intermediate color grading stations, such as those provided by Autodesk Lustre.

Understanding Bit Depth

Standard digital images carry three channels: one for red, one for green, and one for blue. (An optional fourth channel, alpha, is discussed in Chapter 3, "Interpreting Alpha and Creating Mattes.") The bit depth of each channel establishes the number of tonal steps that are available to it. Each tonal step is capable of carrying a unique color value. The term *bit depth* refers to the number of assigned *bits*. A *bit* is a discreet unit that represents data in a digital environment. (A *byte*, in contrast, is a sequence of bits used to represent more complex data, such as a letter of the alphabet.)

When bit depth is expressed as a number, such as *1-bit*, the number signifies an exponent. For example, 1-bit translates to 2^1, equaling two possible tonal steps for a single channel of any given pixel. Other common bit depths are listed in Table 1.1. When discussing bit depth, tonal steps are commonly referred to as *colors*.

Table 1.1: Common bit depths

Bit-Depth	Mathematical Equivalent	Number of Available Colors (One Channel)	Number of Available Colors (Three Channels)
8 bit	2^8	256	16,777,216
10-bit	2^{10}	1,024	1,073,741,824
12-bit	2^{12}	4,096	68,719,476,736
15-bit	2^{15}	32,768	$3.51843721 \times 10^{13}$
16-bit	2^{16}	65,536	$2.81474977 \times 10^{14}$

Bit depth is often expressed as *bpc*, or bits per channel. For example, an RGB image may be labeled 8-bpc, which implies that a total of 24 bits is available when all three channels are utilized. The 2 used as a base in each Table 1.1 calculation is derived from the fact that a single bit has two possible states: 1 or 0 (or true/false or on/off).

When discussing bit depth, specific ranges are invoked. For example, an 8-bit image has a tonal range of 0 to 255, which equates to 256 tonal steps. A 15-bit image has a tonal range of 0 to 32,767, which equates to 32,768 tonal steps. To make the application of bit depth more manageable, however, the ranges are often normalized so that they run from 0 to 1.0. In terms of resulting RGB color values, 0 is black, 1.0 is white, and 0.5 is median gray. Regardless, an 8-bit image with a normalized range continues to carry 256 tonal steps, and a 15-bit image with a normalized range carries 32,768 tonal steps. The tonal steps of an 8-bit image are thus larger than the tonal steps for a 15-bit image. For example, the darkest color available to an 8-bit image, other than 0 black, is 0.004 on a 0 to 1.0 scale. The darkest color available to a 15-bit image is 0.00003 on a 0 to 1.0 scale. (Note that normalized ranges are used throughout this book in order to simplify the accompanying math.)

Tips & Tricks: After Effects 16-bit

What Photoshop and After Effects refer to as "16-bit" is actually a 15-bit color space with one extra step. Hence, After Effects represents 15-bit color space with a scale of 0 to 32,768, which equates to 32,769 tonal steps. Thus, the darkest After Effects "16-bit" color value available above black is 0.00003 on a 0 to 1.0 scale, or 1.0 on a 0 to 32,768 scale. Keep in mind that such small changes in color value will not be visible on a standard monitor, which is limited to 8 bits per channel.

Two bit depth variants that do not possess such limited tonal ranges are 16-bit floating point (half float) and 32-bit floating point (float). Due to their unique architecture, they are discussed in the section "Integer vs. Float" later in this chapter.

Bit Depth Conversions

When it comes to bit depth, there is no universally accepted standard at animation studios, visual effects houses, and commercial production facilities. Although full 32-bit float pipelines have become more common in the last several years, it's not unusual to find professional animators and compositors continuing to work with 8-, 10-, 12-, 15-, or 16-bit formats with linear, log, integer, and float variations. In fact, a single project will often involve multiple formats, as there are specific benefits for using each. Hence, one troublesome aspect of compositing is back-and-forth conversions.

Converting a low-bit-depth image to a high-bit-depth image does not degrade the image. However, such a conversion will create a *combed* histogram (see Figure 2.8). A *histogram* is a graph that displays the number of pixels found at each tonal step of an image. (For more detail on histograms, see Chapter 4.) The combing is a result of a program distributing a limited number of tonal steps in a color space that has a greater number of tonal steps. Visually, this may not affect the image since the gaps in the comb may be as small as one tonal step. However, if successive filters are applied to the converted image, quality may be degraded due to the missing steps. When the gaps grow too large, they result in posterization (color banding).

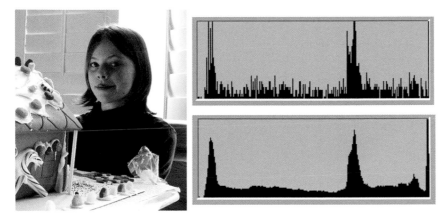

Figure 2.8 *(Left) 8-bit image converted to 16 bits (Top Right) The image's combed blue-channel histogram (Bottom Right) The same histogram after repair*

There's no automatic solution for repairing the combing. However, there are several approaches you can take:

- Apply a specialty plug-in that repairs the histogram and fills in the missing tonal steps. For example, the Power Retouche plug-in is available for Photoshop and After Effects. The GenArts Sapphire Deband plug-in is available for After Effects and Nuke.
- If posterization occurs, blur the affected area and add a finite amount of noise. (You can find a demonstration of this technique in the Chapter 8 tutorials.)
- Avoid the situation by working with higher-bit-depth footage whenever possible.

Tips & Tricks: Histogram Displays

When you convert an 8-bit image to a 16-bit image in Photoshop or import an 8-bit image into a 16-bit project in After Effects, combing occurs. However, due to the 8-bit nature of the programs' histogram, the combing is not displayed (256 vertical lines are used to represent both 8- and 16-bit value ranges). However, if filters are applied that induce additional combing, the new combing is displayed.

In contrast, Nuke displays combing in its histogram for all imported bit depths.

Converting a high-bit-depth image to a low-bit-depth image is equally problematic because information is lost. Either superwhite values (values above the low bit-depth's maximum allowable value) are thrown away through clipping or other value regions are lost through tone mapping. *Tone mapping*, the process of mapping one set of colors to a second set, is demonstrated in Chapter 12, "Advanced Techniques."

Compositing packages, such as After Effects and Nuke, offer built-in solutions that make managing multi-bit-depth projects somewhat easier. These solutions are discussed and demonstrated at the end of this chapter.

Log vs. Linear

As light photons strike undeveloped film stock, the embedded silver halide crystals turn opaque. The greater the number of photons, the more opaque the otherwise transparent stock becomes. The "opaqueness" is measured as *optical density.* The interaction between the photons and the stock is referred to as *exposure*. The relationship between the density and exposure is not linear, however. Instead, the film stock shows little differentiation in its response to low-exposure levels. At the same time, the film stock shows little differentiation in its response to high-exposure levels. This reaction is often represented by film characteristic curve graphs (see Figure 2.9).

The typical characteristic curve for film includes a toe and a shoulder. The *toe* is a flattened section of curve where there is little response to low-exposure levels. The *shoulder* is a semi-flattened section of curve where there is a slowed response to high levels of exposure. Ultimately, the reduced response in these two areas translates to a reduced level of contrast in the film. Hence, cinematographers are careful to expose film so as to take advantage of the characteristic curve's center slope. This exposure range produces the greatest amount of contrast in the recorded image, and it is referred to as the film's *latitude*.

Characteristic curves are logarithmic. With each equal step of a logarithm, the logarithmic value is multiplied by an equal constant. For example, in Figure 2.9 the log is in base 10. Hence, each step is 10 times greater (or less) than the neighboring step. For example, the exposure level, as measured in lux seconds, is mapped to the x-axis. (A *lux* is an international unit for luminous emittance, and it is equivalent to one candela source one meter away; a candela is roughly equivalent to an average candle.)

The values run from –1.0 to 2.0. On the logarithmic scale, –1.0 equates to 10^{-1}, or 0.1; 0 equates to 10^{0}, or 1.0; and 2.0 equates to 10^{2}, or 100. Hence, the x-axis indicates a range in from 1/10 of a second to 100 seconds. At 1/10 of a second, the film is exposed to 1/10 of a lux. At 100 seconds, the film is exposed to 100 lux. The x-axis of characteristic curves can also be assigned to generic relative exposure units or f-stops. The y-axis is assigned to the optical density and is also measured on a logarithmic scale. A value of 3 marks the maximum "opaqueness" achievable by the film stock.

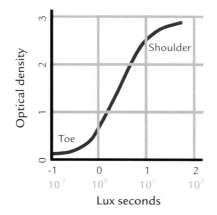

Figure 2.9 A generic film characteristic curve

Log File Formats

To take advantage of film's nonlinear nature, several image formats offer logarithmic (log) encoding. These include DPX and Cineon (which are detailed in the section "Favored Image Formats" later in this chapter). Although the formats can reproduce the film fairly accurately, they are difficult to work with. Most digital imaging, visual effects, and animation pipelines, whether at a studio or through a specific piece of software, operate in linear color spaces. Hence, it is common to convert log files to linear files and vice versa. The difficulty lies in the way in which log and linear files store their data.

Linear files store data in equal increments. That is, each tonal step has equal weight regardless of the exposure range it may be representing. For example, with 8-bit linear color space, doubling the intensity of a pixel requires multiplying a value by 2. You can write out the progression as 1, 2, 4, 8, 16, 32, and so on. As the intensity doubles, so does the number of tonal steps required. Each doubling of intensity is equivalent to an increase in stop. (*Stop* denotes a doubling or halving of intensity, but does not use specific f-stop notation, such as 1.4 or 5.6.) Hence, each stop receives a different number of tonal steps. The disparity between low and high stops becomes significant. For example, the lowest stop has 1 tonal step (2 – 1), while the highest stop has 128 steps (256 – 128). In contrast, 8-bit log color space only requires an incremental increase in its exponent to double the intensity. The logarithmic formula is written as $\log_b(x) = y$, where $_b$ is the base and y is the exponent. For example, the log base 10 of 100 is 2, or $\log_{10}(100) = 2$; this equates to $10^2 = 100$. If log base 10 has an exponent progression that runs 0, 0.5, 1.0, 1.5, 2, the logarithmic values are 1, 3.16, 10, 31.62, 100. In this case, each logarithmic value represents a stop. If the logarithmic values are remapped to the 0 to 256 8-bit range, those same stops earn regularly-spaced values (0, 64, 128, 192, 256). As such, each of the four stops receive 64 tonal steps. If you restrict the linear color space to four stops, the progression becomes 32, 64, 128, 256. When the 4-stop linear color space is placed beside the 4-stop logarithmic color space, the uneven distribution of tonal steps becomes apparent (see Figure 2.10).

White and Black Reference

The incremental nature of the linear steps becomes a problem when representing logarithmic light intensity and, in particular, white reference and black reference. *White reference* (also known as the *white point*) is the optical density of motion picture film at the high end of an acceptable exposure range, whereby a 90 percent reflective white card is exposed properly. *Black reference* (also known as the *black point*) is the low end of an acceptable exposure range, whereby a 1 percent reflective black card is exposed properly. On a 10-bit scale, black reference has an equivalent value of 95 and white reference has an equivalent value of 685. Values above 685 are considered *superwhite*.

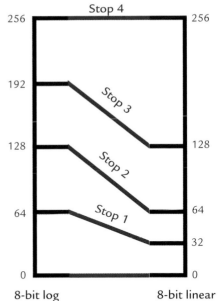

Figure 2.10 *4-stop, 8-bit log and 4-stop, 8-bit linear color ranges. Note how each stop has a dissimilar number of tonal steps. Each stop captures twice the amount of light, or is twice as intense, as the stop below it.*

When a 10-bit log file is imported into a compositing program, it can be interpreted as log or converted to a linear color space. If the log file is interpreted as log, the full 0 to 1023 range is remapped to the project range. For example, if the project is set to After Effects 16-bit (which is actually 15-bit plus one step), 95 becomes 3040 and 685 becomes 21,920. If the log file is converted to linear color space, the 95 to 685 range is remapped to the project range. If the project is set to After Effects 16-bit, 95 becomes 0 and 685 becomes 32,768. Hence, the acceptable exposure range for a linear conversion takes up 100% of the project range, while the acceptable exposure range for the log interpretation takes up roughly 58% of the project range. With the log interpretation, 33% is lost to superwhite values and 9% is lost to superblack values (values below 95 on a 10-bit scale). As a result, the log file appears washed out in an 8-bit viewer. This is due to the acceptable exposure range occurring between 3040 and 21,920. Because the range is closer to the center of the full 0 to 32,768 range, the blacks are raised, the whites are reduced, and the contrast is lowered.

Fortunately, After Effects and Nuke provide effects and nodes that can convert log space to linear space while allowing the use of custom black and white points. These effects and nodes are demonstrated at the end of this chapter.

Integer vs. Float

Common image formats, such as JPEG or Targa, store integer values. Since an integer does not carry any decimal information, accuracy is sacrificed. For example, if you snap a picture with a digital camera and store the picture as a JPEG, a particular pixel may be assigned a value of 98 even though a more accurate value would be 98.6573. Although such accuracy is not critical for a family photo, it can easily affect the quality of a professional composite that employs any type of filter or matte.

Floating-point image formats solve the problem of accuracy by allowing for decimal values. When a value is encoded, the format takes a fractional number (the *mantissa*) and multiplies it by a power of 10 (the *exponent*). For example, a floating-point number may be expressed as 5.987e+8, where e+8 is the same as ×10^8. In other words, 5.987 is multiplied by 10^8, or 100,000,000, to produce 598,700,000. If the exponent has a negative sign, such as e−8, the decimal travels in the opposite direction and produces 0.00000005987 (e−8 is the same as × 10^{-8}). Additionally, floating points can store either positive or negative numbers by flipping a *sign bit* from 0 to 1.

Floating-point formats exist in two flavors: half float and float. Half float (also known as half precision) is based on 16-bit architecture that was specifically developed for the OpenEXR format. Half float file sizes are significantly smaller than 32-bit float files. Nevertheless, OpenEXR half float supports dynamic ranges as large as 30 stops.

Aside from decimal accuracy, float formats offer the following advantages:

- Practically speaking, float formats do not suffer from clipping. For example, if you introduce a value of 80,000 to a 16-bit linear image, 80,000 is clipped and stored as 65,535. At the same time, a value of −100 is stored as 0. In comparison, a 16-bit half float can store 80,000 as 8.0e+4 and −100 as 1.0e+2 with the sign bit set to 1.
- Float formats support real-world dynamic ranges. Whereas a 16-bit linear image is limited to a dynamic range of 65,535:1, a 32-bit float TIFF has a potential dynamic range of well over 2^{100}:1. (For more information on HDR photography, which specializes in capturing such large dynamic ranges, see Chapter 12.)

Despite the capacity for a monstrous dynamic range, float formats remain linear and are thus not as accurate as log formats when film is encoded.

Favored Image Formats

Digital image formats support various bit depths and fall into two major categories: linear and log (logarithmic). Within these two categories, there are two means in which to store the data: integer and float (floating point). If a format is not identified as float, then it operates on an integer basis. Here is a partial list of image formats commonly favored in the world of compositing:

DPX and Cineon (.dpx and .cin)   The DPX (Digital Picture Exchange) format is based on the Cineon file format, which was developed for Kodak's FIDO film scanner. DPX and Cineon files both operate in 10-bit log and are designed to preserve the gamma of the scanned film negative. DPX differs from Cineon, however, in that it supports 8-, 12-, 16-, and 32-bit variations as well linear encoding. Whether a DPX file is linear or log is indicated by its header.

TIFF (.tif, .tiff)   The Tagged Image File Format was developed in the mid-1980s as a means to standardize the desktop publishing industry. It currently supports various compression schemes and offers linear 8-bit, 16-bit, 16-bit half float, and 32-bit float variations.

OpenEXR (.exr)   The OpenEXR format was developed by Industrial Light & Magic and was made available to the public in 2003. OpenEXR offers linear 16-bit half float, 32-bit float, and 32-bit integer variations. In addition, the format supports an arbitrary number of custom channels, including depth, motion vector, surface normal direction, and so on. In recent years, the format has become a standard at animation studios that operate floating-point pipelines.

Targa (.tga) Targa was developed by Truevision in the mid-1980s. Common variants of the format include linear 16-bit, 24-bit (8 bits per channel), and 32-bit (8 bits per channel with alpha).

Radiance (.hdr, .rgbe, .xyze) The Radiance format was pioneered by Greg Ward in the late 1980s and was the first to support linear 32-bit floating-point architecture. Radiance files are most commonly seen with the .hdr filename extension and are used extensively in high dynamic range photography.

Raw Raw image files contain data from the image sensor of a digital camera or film scanner that has been minimally processed. The format is sometimes referred to as a *digital negative* as it contains all the information needed to create a usable image file but requires additional processing before that goal is achieved. The main advantage of the Raw format is that its data has not been degraded by the demosaicing process (reconstruction using a color filter array) that is needed to convert the Raw format to an immediately useful one, such as JPEG or TIFF. The Raw format has numerous variations and filename extensions that are dependent on the camera or scanner manufacturer. One variation of Raw, designated DNG, has been put forth by Adobe in an attempt to standardize the Raw format.

Working with Color Space

After Effects and Nuke support a wide range of bit depths. In addition, they are able to simulate color spaces commonly encountered in the professional world of compositing.

Working in AE

Recent versions of After Effects support 8-bit integer, 16-bit integer, and 32-bit float projects. To select the bit depth, choose File → Project Settings. In the Project Settings dialog box, change the Depth menu to 8 Bits Per Channel, 16 Bits Per Channel, or 32 Bits Per Channel (Float). If lower-bit-depth footage is imported into a higher-bit-depth project, After Effects automatically upconverts the footage. Note that Adobe's 16-bit space is actually a 15-bit color space with one extra step.

Color Management in AE

By default, After Effects does not apply any type of color management. That is, no special color profiles are applied to any input or output. However, if the Working Space menu is switched from None to a specific color profile in the Project Settings dialog box, the following occurs:

1. Each piece of imported footage is converted to the working color space as defined by the Working Space menu. The native color space of the footage is either retrieved from its file as an embedded ICC profile or defined by the user in the Interpret Footage dialog box (see the section "AE Tutorial 2: Working with DPX and Cineon Files" later in this chapter).
2. After Effects performs all its color operations in the working color space.
3. To display the result on the screen, After Effects converts the images to system color space via a LUT generated by the monitor profile (which is carried by the computer's operating system).
4. When rendered through the Render Queue, the images are converted to output color space, which is defined by the Output Profile menu of the Color Management tab in the Output Module Settings dialog box.

Common Color Profiles

After Effects offers a long list of profiles through its Working Space menu, including the following:

sRGB IEC6 1966-2.1 The sRGB IEC6 1966-2.1 profile is an RGB color space developed by Hewlett-Packard and Microsoft. Since its inception in the mid-1990s, it has become an international standard for computer monitors, scanners, printers, digital cameras, and the Internet. The *IEC6 1966-2.1* component refers to an official specification laid down by the International Electrotechnical Commission (IEC).

HDTV (Rec. 709) As its name implies, HDTV (Rec. 709) is the standard color space for high-definition television. The *Rec. 709* component refers to a specific recommendation of the International Telecommunication Union (ITU).

SMPTE-C The SMPTE-C profile is the standard color space for analog television broadcast in the U.S. The space was standardized by the Society of Motion Picture and Television Engineers in 1979.

SDTV NTSC and SDTV PAL The SDTV NTSC and SDTV PAL profiles are the color spaces for standard-definition video cameras. The profiles use the same tonal response curves as HDTV (Rec. 709).

Tips & Tricks: 16-235 Profiles

Several profiles, including SDTV NTSC, SDTV PAL, and HDTV (Rec. 709), have a variant with 16-235 as a suffix. The 16-235 profiles are designed to maintain proper luma levels when you import and export video. When video is captured, the image values are represented by voltages measured as mV (millivolts) or IRE (a unit developed by the Institute of Radio Engineers). When the voltages are converted to Y'CbCr (a video color space with luma, blue chroma, and red chroma components), the voltage values are often fixed to an 8-bit range of 16 to 235. (With NTSC video, values under 16 and over 235 are considered to be "unsafe.") Hence, After Effects offers 16-235 profiles to maintain or compress the luma range. If a 16-235 profile is selected through the Working Space menu of the Project Settings dialog box and the Assign Profile menu of the Interpret Footage dialog box, the 16-235 luma range is maintained. If a 16-235 profile is selected for the Output Profile menu but the Working Space menu is set to a non-16-235 profile, the luma range is compressed at the point of render. For a definition of *luma*, which varies from luminance, see Chapter 4, "Channel Manipulation."

Color Profile Converter

In addition to the Working Space menu, After Effects provides a Color Profile Converter effect (Effect → Utility → Color Profile Converter). With the effect, you can choose an input profile and an output profile for the layer to which it's applied. The style of the conversion is controlled by the Intent menu. The Perception property attempts to maintain the visual consistency of colors between color spaces. The Saturation option preserves high saturation values at the expense of color accuracy. Relative Colorimetric remaps values from one color space to the next. Absolute Colorimetric does not alter values but instead clips any colors that fall outside of the range of the new color space. The Color Profile Converter should not be used in conjunction with color management, however, as errors may occur. If the effect is used, the Working Space menu in the Project Settings dialog box should be set to None.

Linearization

In After Effects, it's possible to switch from a gamma-corrected color space to a non-corrected color space. Within a non-corrected color space, no gamma curve is applied and values are not altered in anticipation of display on a monitor. There are two methods with which to apply the conversion. In the Project Settings dialog box, you can select a profile through the Working Space menu and then select the Linearize Working Space check box. This linearizes the entire project. Otherwise, you can leave Working Space set to None and select the Blend Color Using 1.0 Gamma check box. In certain situations, a linearized space offers greater accuracy when blending layers together.

Color Space Simulation

If you've chosen a profile through the Working Space menu, you can simulate a color space other than sRGB through the viewer. For example, you can simulate an NTSC video output on your computer monitor even though the monitor has a color space inherently different than a television. To select a simulation mode, choose View → Simulate Output → *Simulation Mode*. You can create a custom simulation mode by choosing View → Simulate Output → Custom. The process occurs in four steps in the Custom Simulation Output dialog box (see Figure 2.11):

1. In the first step, the imported image is converted using the Working Space profile. This profile is listed at the top of the dialog box as the Project Working Space.
2. In the second step, the resulting image is converted using the output profile. Although the menu defaults to Working Space, you have a long list of optional profiles. Special profiles provided by Adobe include those that emulate specific 35mm motion picture film stocks and specific makes of HD digital video cameras. Note that this Output Profile option operates independently of the one found in the Color Management tab of the Output Module Settings dialog box.
3. In the third step, the resulting image is converted using the simulation profile. The conversion preserves the color appearance of the image within the color limits of the simulated device, but not the numeric color values. If the Preserve RGB check box is selected, however, the opposite occurs, whereby the color values are maintained at cost to the visual appearance. Preserve RGB may be useful when working exclusively with film stock. In either case, the simulation does not affect the way in which the image is rendered through the Render Queue.
4. As a final step, the resulting image is converted to the monitor profile provided by the computer's operating system so that it can be displayed on the screen.

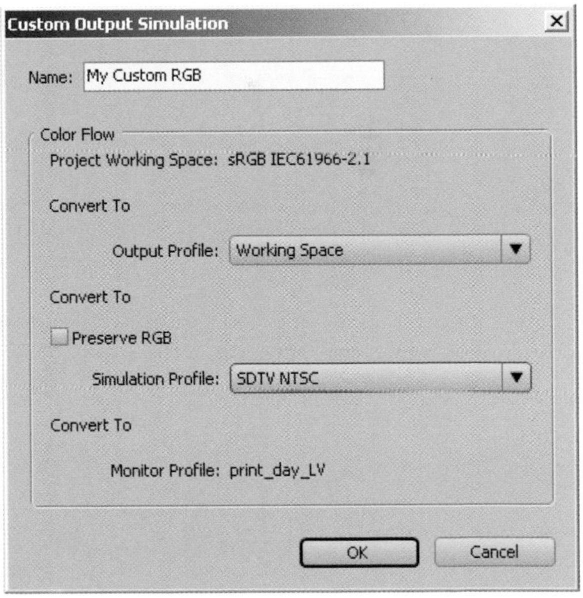

Figure 2.11 Custom Output Simulation dialog box

Log-to-Linear Conversions in AE

After Effects provides a means by which to convert log images to linear through the Project panel. To do so, follow these steps:

1. In the Project panel, RMB+click over the log file name and choose Interpret Footage → Main. In the Interpret Footage dialog box, switch to the Color Management tab and click the Cineon Settings button. The Cineon Settings dialog box opens.

The 10 Bit Black Point cell represents the value within the log file that is converted to the Converted Black Point value. The 10 Bit White Point cell represents the value within the log file that is converted to the Converted White Point value. The Gamma cell establishes the gamma curve applied to the log file to prepare it for viewing. You can enter values into the cells or choose one of the options through the Preset menu. (For information on black and white points, see the section "Log vs. Linear" earlier in this chapter.)

2. When you change Preset to Video, the program undertakes a conversion that is designed for video. With this setting, the Converted Black Point cell is set to 16 and the Converted White Point cell is set to 235. This is equivalent to the broadcast-safe 16 to 235 range for Y'CbCr color space.

3. If you change the Preset menu to Custom, you can enter your own values. This may be necessary when preparing digital sequences for film out (recording to motion picture film) at a lab that requires specific black and white points. Changing the Units menu to 8-bpc or 16-bpc affects the way the various values are displayed in the dialog box; however, the conversion continues to happen in the current bit depth of the project.

4. To retrieve lost highlights, raise the Highlight Rolloff cell. This crushes the upper range so that the highest output values are no longer at the bit-depth limit. For example, a Highlight Rolloff value of 20 prevents any value from surpassing 29,041 in After Effects 16-bit color space.

A second approach to working with log files involves the use of the Cineon Converter effect. To apply the effect, follow these steps:

1. Select the log file or log footage in the layer outline of the Timeline tab. Choose Effect → Utility → Cineon Converter. The Cineon image will instantly gain contrast in the viewer.

2. To adjust the overall contrast within the image, change the Black Point and White Point sliders. The sliders are divided into two groups: 10 Bit and Internal. The 10 Bit sliders function in the same manner as the 10 Bit sliders found in the Cineon Settings dialog box. The Internal sliders function in the same manner as the Converted sliders found in the Cineon Settings dialog box. The Highlight Rolloff and Gamma properties are also identical. Note that Conversion Type is set to Log To Linear.

Tips & Tricks: 10-Bit Log Files

By default, when the Preset menu in the Cineon Settings dialog box is changed to Standard, Video, or Over Range, the 10 Bit Black Point cell is set to 95 and the 10 Bit White Point cell is set to 685. This represents the acceptable motion picture film exposures of 10 percent and 90 percent reflective cards. For more information, see the "Log vs. Linear" section earlier in this chapter.

If you need to render 10-bit log files, you can open the Output Module Settings dialog box through the Render Queue tab. In the dialog box, change the Format menu to Cineon Sequence, switch to the Color Management tab, click the Cineon Settings button, and change the Preset menu to Full Range. Note that the Gamma property is automatically returned to 1.0. You can choose between FIDO/Cineon 4.5 or DPX flavors by selecting one of the File Format radio buttons.

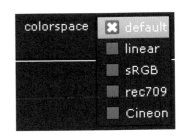

Working in Nuke

Nuke is based on linear 32-bit floating-point architecture. All operations occur in linear 32-bit floating-point space. When lower-bit-depth images are imported into the program, they are upconverted to 32-bpc. Whether or not the incoming data is interpreted as linear or log, however, is determined by the Colorspace menu of the Read node (see Figure 2.12).

Color Space in Nuke

Each color space accessible through a Read node is emulated by a LUT provided by Nuke. The following spaces are available:

Figure 2.12 *The Colorspace menu in the properties panel of a Read node*

> **Linear** has no affect on the input pixels. On a normalized scale, 0 remains 0, 0.5 remains 0.5, and 1 remains 1.

sRGB is the standard sRGB IEC6 1966-2.1 color space.

rec709 is the standard HDTV color space. Both sRGB and rec709 use a gamma curve.

Cineon is a 10-bit log color space. If the Colorspace menu is set to Cineon, the Read node converts the log file to linear space using conversion settings recommended by Kodak, author of the Cineon format. To override the conversion, you can select the Raw Data check box. In this case, the Colorspace parameter is disabled. You are then free to connect a Log2Lin node to the Read node (see the next section).

Default is a color space determined by the script's Project Settings properties panel. Nuke allows the user to select default color space LUTs for various imported/exported file formats and interface components. For example, an sRGB LUT is automatically assigned to the default viewer. Hence, images sent to a viewer are first processed by the sRGB LUT.

You can view the current script's LUT settings by choosing Edit → Project Settings and switching to the LUT tab of the properties panel. The default LUT settings are listed at the bottom. You can change any listed inputs/outputs to a new LUT by selecting a LUT from the corresponding pull-down menu. If you click on a LUT listed at the top left, the LUT curve is displayed in the integrated curve editor (see Figure 2.13).

In the editor, the x-axis represents the input pixel values and the y-axis represents the output pixel values (normalized to run from 0 to 1.0). You can create a new LUT by clicking the small + button at the bottom of the LUT list and entering a name into the New Curve Name dialog box. The new LUT curve is displayed in the curve editor and is linear by default. You can manipulate the shape of the curve by inserting and moving points. To insert a new point, select the curve so that it turns yellow and Ctrl+Alt+click on the curve. To move a point, LMB+drag the point. In addition, you can LMB+drag the resulting tangent handles. To reset the curve to its default linear shape, click the Reset button at the bottom of the LUT list.

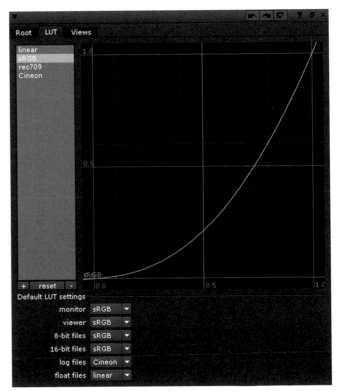

Figure 2.13 *The LUT tab curve editor with the sRGB LUT displayed*

Log-to-Linear Conversions in Nuke

Nuke offers a node with which to convert a log input to a linear output. To apply the node, follow these steps:

1. Select the node you wish to convert from a log space to a linear space. If the node is a Read node, make sure that the Raw Data check box is selected in the Read node's properties panel. In the Node Graph, RMB+click and choose Color → Log2Lin. Open the Log2Lin node's properties panel.

2. The Black parameter establishes the black point (the value within the log file that will be converted to 0 value within the current 32-bit linear color space). The White parameter establishes the white point (the value within the log file that will be converted to a maximum value within the current 32-bit linear color space). The Gamma parameter defines the gamma correction curve that is applied to the output in anticipation of its display on the monitor.

Color Space Tutorials

Discussions of color space, color profiles, and simulation modes can be confusing. Therefore, it's often easier to think of specific scenarios that may be encountered in the professional world.

AE Tutorial 2: Working with DPX and Cineon Files

You may be tasked to composite a shot that involves effects and greenscreen footage. Ideally, the footage would be digitized using a single image format at a consistent bit depth. However, the reality is that multiple formats and bit depths are usually employed. This is due to the varied technical limitations of camera equipment, the distribution of work to different production units or companies who have different working methodologies, and the fact that different formats and bit depths are better suited for specific shooting scenarios. Regardless, you will need to convert all incoming footage to an image format and bit depth that is suitable for the project to which the composite belongs.

More specifically, you may be faced with the following situation. Greenscreen footage is shot on 35mm and is provided to you as 10-bit log Cineon files. Effects footage, shot several years earlier, is culled from the studio's offline shot library; 10-bit log DPX is the only format available. Background plate footage is shot with an HD digital video camera; the 12-bit linear TIFF files are converted to 16-bit before they are handed to you. Your composite is part of a visual effects job for a television commercial. Due to budget considerations, the clients have decided to deliver the project as standard definition (SD). Your shot will be passed on to a Flame bay for color grading. Nevertheless, you will need to have your work approved by your supervisor. You're using a CRT monitor to judge your work. Although the monitor is calibrated, it can only approximate the look of an SDTV system.

In light of such a situation, you can take the following steps in After Effects when setting up a new composite:

1. Create a new project. Choose File → Project Settings. In the Project Settings dialog box, set Depth to 16 Bits Per Channel. 16-bit depth is necessary to take advantage of the 10-bit DPX, 10-bit Cineon, and 16-bit TIFF footage that will be imported. Although the ultimate project output will be 8-bit images for SDTV, it's best to work in a higher bit depth until the final render. Set the Working Space menu to SDTV NTSC. It's also best to work within the color space utilized by the final output. Select the Frames radio button (see Figure 2.14).

2. Choose Composition → New Composition. In the Composition Settings dialog box, set the Preset menu to NTSC D1 Square Pixel, the Frame Rate to 30, and Duration to 30, and click OK. Choose View → Simulate Output → SDTV NTSC. Henceforth, the viewer will simulate SDTV broadcast color space.

3. Choose File → Import → File. Browse for the `bg_plate.tif` file in the Footage folder on the DVD (see Figure 2.15).

4. Choose File → Import → File. Browse for the `greenscreen.cin` file in the Footage folder on the DVD. RMB+click over the `greenscreen.cin` filename in the Project panel and choose Interpret Footage → Main. In the Interpret Footage dialog box, switch to the Color Management tab. Note that the Assign Profile menu is automatically assigned to Working Space - SDTV NTSC. Since the footage was not shot in an SDTV format, check the Preserve RGB check box to avoid color filtering. Despite this setting, the image appears washed out in the simulated SDTV NTSC color space of the viewer (see Figure 2.15).

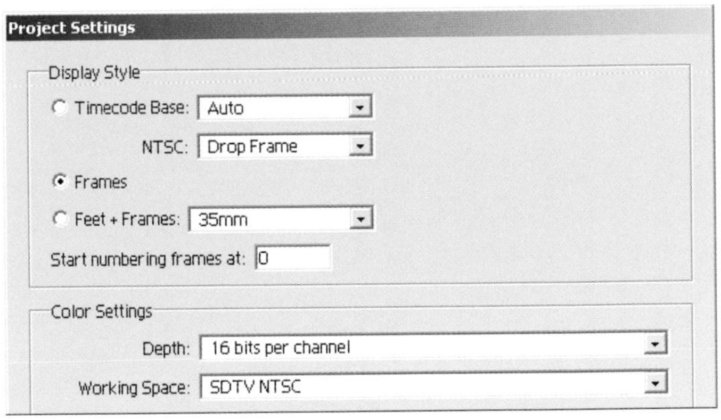

Figure 2.14 *The top of the Project Settings dialog box*

Figure 2.15 *(Left) Background plate (Right) Unaltered greenscreen file. Since the file is a 10-bit log Cineon, it appears washed out in the simulated SDTV NTSC color space of the viewer.*

5. To restore contrast to the greenscreen, click the Cineon Settings button in the Interpret Footage dialog box. In the Cineon Settings dialog box, change the Preset menu to Standard (see Figure 2.16). When you choose Standard, the program undertakes a conversion that expands the log file's 95 to 685 tonal range to a 0 to 32,768 project tonal range. For more information on the conversion process, see the section "Log-to-Linear Conversions in AE" earlier in this chapter.

6. Choose File → Import → File. Browse for the `effect.##.dpx` sequence in the Footage folder on the DVD. Through the Interpret Footage dialog box, select the Preserve RGB check box and match the Cineon settings of the `greenscreen.cin` file.

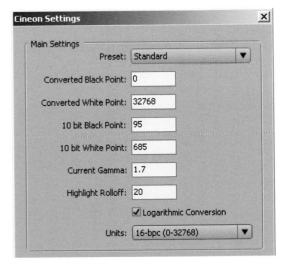

Figure 2.16 *Log-to-linear conversion is carried out by the Standard preset in the Cineon Settings dialog box.*

Tips & Tricks: Film and Video Profiles

The Assign Profile menu of the Interpret Footage dialog box includes a list of specific motion picture film stocks and digital video camera formats. The profiles are designed to match the characteristic curves of the stocks and formats. Providing an exact profile match is desirable when possible.

7. To assemble the composite, LMB+drag `bg_plate.tif` from the Project panel into the layer outline of the Timeline panel. LMB+drag the `effect.##.dpx` footage on top of the new `bg_plate.tif` layer. LMB+drag `greenscreen.cin` on top of the new `effect.##.dpx` layer (see Figure 2.17). Both `bg_plate.tif` and `greenscreen.cin` are 2K in resolution, and `effect.##.dpx` is 1K in resolution. To fit each layer to the smaller composition resolution, select one layer at a time and press Ctrl+Alt+F. The layers are automatically downscaled.

8. To remove the greenscreen quickly, select the `greenscreen.cin` layer and choose Effect → Keying → Keylight. In the Effect Controls panel, click the Screen Color eyedropper and choose a bright portion of the greenscreen in the viewer. The effect will remove the majority of the green, revealing the fire layer beneath. Adjust the Screen Gain and Screen Balance sliders to remove remaining noise. A Screen Gain value of 120 and a Screen Balance value of 75 will make the alpha fairly clean (see Figure 2.18). (Greenscreen tools are discussed in greater depth in Chapter 3.)

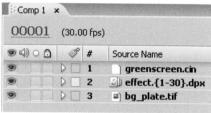

Figure 2.17 The layer outline of the Timeline panel

9. To remove the black surrounding the fire quickly, select the `effect.##.dpx` layer and choose Effect → Keying → Color Key. In the Effect Controls panel, click the Key Color eyedropper and select a dark portion of the background in the viewer. Set the Color Tolerance slider to 75 and the Edge Feather slider to 4 (see Figure 2.18). The black is removed. However, a dark ring remains around the edge of the flame. Select the `effect.##.dpx` layer in the layer outline, RMB+click over the layer name, and choose Blending Mode → Screen. The screen operation maintains the bright areas of the fire while suppressing the black. (Blending modes are discussed in more detail in Chapter 3.)

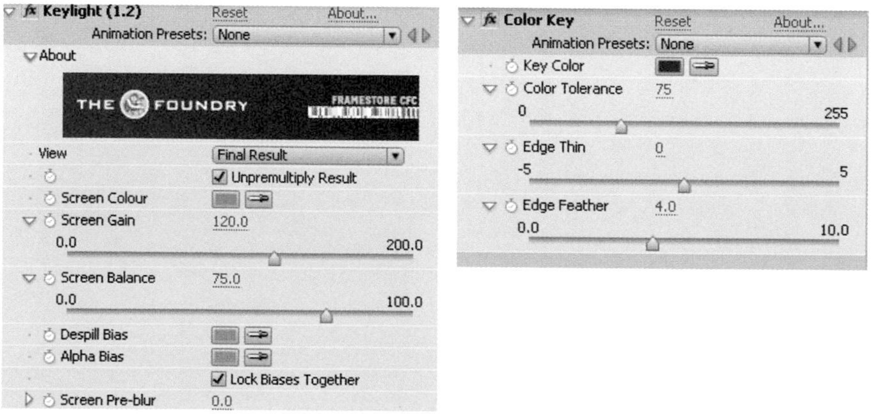

Figure 2.18 (Left) Keylight effect settings (Right) Color Key effect settings

10. At this point, the statue is not sitting on the street. Expand the `greenscreen.cin` layer's Transform section and change Position X and Y to 355, 285. The statue location is improved (see Figure 2.19). However, the statue's brightness, contrast, and color do not match the background. In addition, the edge of the statue is "hard" compared to the surrounding scene. Both of these issues will be addressed in an After Effects follow-up tutorial in Chapter 3. In the meantime, save the file under a new name. A sample After Effects project is saved as `ae2.aep` in the Footage folder on the DVD.

Figure 2.19 *The initial composite. The brightness, contrast, and color of the statue will be adjusted in the Chapter 3 After Effects follow-up tutorial.*

Nuke Tutorial 2: Working with DPX and Cineon Files

You're working on a project with specific image bit depth and image format limitations. Greenscreen footage is shot on 35mm and is provided to you as 10-bit log Cineon files. Effects footage is culled from the studio's offline shot library; 10-bit log DPX is the only format available. Background plate footage is shot with an HD digital video camera. The 12-bit linear TIFF files are converted to 16-bit before they are handed to you. Your composite is part of a visual effects job for a feature film. Therefore, you must deliver 10-bit log Cineon files to the DI house. Nevertheless, you will need to have your work approved by your supervisor. You're using an LCD monitor to judge your work. Although the monitor is calibrated, it can only approximate the log quality of film.

You can take the following steps in Nuke to set up a new composite:

1. Create a new script. Choose Edit → Project Settings. In the properties panel, set Frame Range to 1, 30, set Fps to 30, and change the Full Size Format menu to 2k_Super_35mm (Full-ap). Switch to the LUT tab. Note that the Viewer is set to sRGB, 16-Bit is set to sRGB, and Log Files is set to Cineon.

2. RMB+click over the Node Graph and choose Image → Read. Open the Read1 node's properties panel. Browse for `bg_plate.tif`, which is included in the Footage folder on the DVD. Note that the Colorspace menu is set to Default. Since the16-Bit menu is set to sRGB in the Project Settings properties panel, the TIFF is interpreted through the sRGB LUT. The 16-Bit preset is designed for any integer data greater than 8-bits. The plate features a city street (see Figure 2.20).

Figure 2.20 (Left) Background plate (Right) Unaltered greenscreen file. Since the file is a 10-bit log Cineon, it appears washed out in the sRGB color space of the viewer.

3. RMB+click over the Node Graph and choose Image → Read. Browse for greenscreen .cin, which is included in the Footage folder on the DVD. In the Read2 node's properties panel, select the Raw Data check box. This prevents the Read node from applying a log-to-linear conversion. This causes the statue against greenscreen to appear washed out in the sRGB color space of the viewer (see Figure 2.20).

4. RMB+click over the Node Graph and choose Image → Read. Browse for the effect .##.dpx footage, which is included in the Footage folder on the DVD. Select the Raw Data checkbox. Because the footage is only 1K in resolution, it will not fit the 2K composition properly. To fix this, select the Read3 node, RMB+click, and choose Transform → Reformat. With the default settings, the Reformat1 node resizes the footage to the project output size.

5. Select the Read2 node, RMB+click, and choose Color → Log2Lin. Connect the Viewer1 node to the Log2Lin1 node. (Whenever you need to view the output of a node, reconnect the Viewer1 node or create a new viewer via Viewer → Create New Viewer.) The Log2Lin1 node, with its default settings, restores contrast to the statue (see Figure 2.21). For more information on the Log2Lin node, see "Log-to-Linear Conversions in Nuke" earlier in this chapter.

6. With the Read3 node selected, RMB+ click and choose Color → Log2Lin. The default Log2Lin2 node settings are also suitable for the linear conversion of the fire footage.

7. Select the Log2Lin1 node, RMB+click, and choose Keyer → Keyer. To remove the greenscreen from the statue quickly, open the Keyer1 properties panel and change Operation to Greenscreen. LMB+drag the bottom-left yellow bar in the Range field to the far right (see Figure 2.22). The green remains, although it is darkened. To remove the green completely, choose the Keyer1 node, RMB+click, and choose Merge → Premult. The Premult node multiplies

Figure 2.21 Detail of Cineon greenscreen footage after the application of a Log2Lin node

the input RBG values by the input alpha values (created by the keyer). Since Nuke expects premultiplied input when merging, the output is properly prepared for the viewer. (In this case, the Keyer1 output is merged with the empty black background.) For more information on merge nodes, premultiplication, and keyers, see Chapter 3. To examine the resulting alpha channel, connect a viewer to the Premult1 node, click the Viewer pane, and press the A key. To return to an RGB view, press A again.

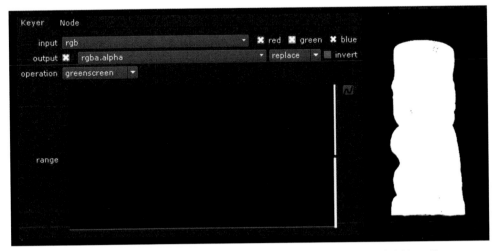

Figure 2.22 (Left) The Keyer1 properties panel with adjusted Range field handle (Right) Detail of resulting alpha channel (black indicates transparency)

8. Select the Log2Lin2 node and apply new Keyer and Premult nodes. Leave Operation set to Luminance Key. There's no need to adjust the Range field bars since there is a high level of contrast in the image of the fire.

9. With no nodes selected, RMB+click in the Node Graph and choose Merge → Merge. Connect input A of the Merge1 node to the Premult2 node (belonging to the fire effect). Connect input B of the Merge1 node to the Read1 node (which holds the city plate). See Figure 2.23 for the completed node network. This places the fire on top of the sky. Open the Merge1 node's properties panel, and change the Operation menu to Screen. This blends the fire more naturally. (The Screen mode is detailed in Chapter 3.)

10. With no nodes selected, RMB+click in the Node Graph and choose Merge → Merge. Connect input A of the Merge2 node to the output of the Premult1 node (belonging to the statue). Connect input B of the Merge2 node to the output of the Merge1 node. This places the statue on top of the fire/city composite. Unfortunately, the statue is floating slightly off the ground. To remedy this, select the Read2 node, RMB+click, and choose Transform → Position. A Position node is inserted between the Read2 and Log2Lin1 nodes. Open the Position node's properties

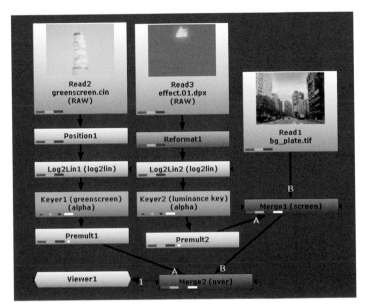

Figure 2.23 The completed node network

panel and change Translate X and Y to −12, −45. The statue moves to a more believable location (see Figure 2.24).

11. At this stage, the statue's brightness and color does not match the background plate. In addition, the edge of the statue is "hard" compared to the surrounding scene. Both of these issues will be addressed in a Nuke follow-up tutorial in Chapter 3. In the meantime, save the file under a new name. A sample script is included as `nuke2.aep` in the Tutorials folder on the DVD.

Figure 2.24 *The initial composite. The brightness, color, and edge quality of the statue will be adjusted in the Chapter 3 Nuke follow-up tutorial.*

Interview: Jason Greenblum, Sony Pictures Imageworks

Jason Greenblum started in the industry as an art department production assistant. He was serving as an art department coordinator at Digital Domain on *Supernova* when he made the transition to compositing. He went on to work at Rhythm & Hues and Weta Digital. In 2004, he joined Sony Pictures Imageworks. Jason's roster of feature film work includes *How the Grinch Stole Christmas*, *Harry Potter and the Sorcerer's Stone*, the second and third *Lord of the Rings* installments, and the second and third *Spiderman* sequels. He has served as a senior and lead compositor on recent projects.

Sony Pictures Imageworks began operation in 1993. The studio creates visual effects and character animation for a wide range of feature film projects and has earned a number of Oscar nominations. Imageworks's sister company, Sony Pictures Animation, opened in 2002 to create feature animation projects such as *Open Season* and *Surf's Up!*

(Compositing falls under the lighting department at Sony Pictures Imageworks.)

Jason Greenblum at his compositing workstation. Note the dual CRT displays.

(Left) The front entrance to the Sony Pictures Imageworks Culver City facility (Right) One of the many art deco style buildings tucked behind rows of trees (Right photo courtesy of Sony Pictures Imageworks)

LL: What is the main compositing software used at Sony Pictures Imageworks?

JG: We have a proprietary package that we use that we've been writing (Katana). We've actually just moved over to it the last six months…. We used to use a tool called Bonzai, which was written to replace Composer. We do have a little bit of Shake. We tend to keep other tools in-house so that we can evaluate them. Everything has its own niche that it can be used for.

LL: Can you describe Katana in more detail?

JG: Because it's a 3D engine, it's got the 3D viewer—it's got all the attribute setting tools that you would need to render through Renderman—there are very clean ways to get from that to the 2D world. [For example], you can put images on planes and [create] environments, or get tracking data from a 3D scene into your comp [so that it] can be applied to roto (rotoscope).

LL: As a compositor, what involvement do you have with color management?

JG: [We had] a really cool process at Weta that made the images less breakable. The idea is to neutralize the plate when it comes to you. So it gets scanned and it goes to color timing where it's neutralized—you essentially try to make your 18 percent gray and then, since everything goes to a digital intermediate (DI) these days, [there's] a temp color timing number that they will give [the compositor] that can be looked at to see if the images are going to track. As long as you're compositing to that neutral plate and you match everything to the neutral plate, [when] they crank everything around in the DI, you're safe. [At Sony Pictures Imageworks], it's a similar process [compared to the one used at Weta]….

LL: What bit depth do you work in at Sony Pictures Imageworks?

JG: In the last two years, it's become fully float. Textures are painted in float, renders are done in float, [and] the composite is done in float. The only thing that isn't float [are the scans of the live-action plates]. They're 10-bit Cineon files.

LL: Is there any special calibration applied to the compositors' monitors?

JG: On the show I'm currently working on (*G-Force*), we have an environment where, while in the composite, we're looking at things in a one-stop-up, color-timed environment. Since it's a linear float, we can back out those color timing numbers into the Raw [files]. [That is], we write out a [un-color-timed] Raw with our images comped into it. We also write out a color-timed [version] that we can show the director. The DI house will get a Raw composite....

LL: Are LUTs used to create the proper viewing environment?

JG: You used to have a [software-based] monitor LUT that would take you from a log space into more of a viewable space. Now, most of that is done in the monitor for the compositing tool. What's nice about our proprietary [system] is that it has stopping-up [and] stopping-down tools within the hardware accelerator itself. So it's really easy to look into your blacks or look at it with different LUTs applied to it.

LL: Are the monitors calibrated?

JG: Our monitors are meant to be calibrated monthly if you're doing color-sensitive work. We'll have two CRTs next to each other because they're still the best calibratable viewers, and you tend to see how fast they drift because you have one next to the other—you'll see one go warm and one go cool....

Additional Resources: The Full Interview

To read the full interview with Jason Greenblum, see the Interviews folder on the DVD. For more information on the DI process, see Chapter 8.

Interview: Rod Basham, Imaginary Forces, Hollywood

Rod Basham started in the industry as a visual effects editor. While at Cinesite, he worked on such features as *Air Force One* and *Sphere*. He joined Imaginary Forces in the same capacity but was soon able to train under an Inferno artist. He shifted his concentration to Inferno compositing and has since worked on visual effects and title sequences for such films as *Minority Report*, *Blade: Trinity*, and *Charlotte's Web* and a host of television commercials and related projects.

Rod Basham in his Inferno bay. He uses a HD CRT among other monitors.

Imaginary Forces is a design studio with offices in Los Angeles and New York. It creates film titles, commercials, broadcast design, experience design, and general branding. The studio's recent work includes title sequences for the feature film *Beverly Hills Chihuahua* and the television show *Mad Men*.

LL: You work on an Autodesk Inferno in a 12-bit environment. Do you output 12-bit footage?

RB: Our broadcast deliverables are always 10-bit when going to DigiBeta or HDCam. Our film drops go out as [10-bit] DPXs or Cineons. So for us to go from 12-bit to 10-bit is a good thing. Most of our conversions or LUTs are set up to go from 10 to 12 or 12 to 10. [The bit depth] is high enough that we don't get any banding.

LL: When you receive live-action footage, what format is it in?

RB: We typically receive 10-bit log DPX files. Everything we generate internally is generated in linear space. Because we're so graphic heavy, it makes more sense to keep everything in a linear pipeline. So, if we receive logarithmic material, we make it linear. [A]t the end, we turn everything back into a log file.

LL: When your work is destined for film, what type of color space issues arise?

RB: [D]igital intermediates are one of the biggest things to have [affected] me over the last few years. We used to have a Celco [film recorder] here, so we would actually deliver negative for our projects. A big part of my learning was figuring out how to get things from Inferno to the Celco and onto film correctly. That, happily, has gone away. Now, when you're delivering work to a DI facility, you have another level of quality control. The biggest challenge we have is that [each] DI facility may [use a different lab and a different] film stock for their film-outs. I can take one frame and make a Cineon [file] and send it to nine different [facilities] with nine different screening rooms and it will look [nine different ways]. (Other factors include the different display systems, 3D LUTs, and projector color spaces.)

The Imaginary Forces facility in the heart of Hollywood (Image courtesy of Imaginary Forces)

In fact, we've started working on a digital handshake where we call the facilities up [and have them] send us a 3D display LUT [from their DI software, whether it is True Light or Lustre]. I'll load that up into Inferno, convert my work to Cineon 10-bit log, and then view it through the 3D display LUT to see how much our work is being damaged from its original linear presentation. It's my job, from this lin[ear]-to-log conversion, to know how to [return] the colors to where they need to be when the work goes to the DI setup....

LL: For commercials, do you do the final color grading in-house?

RB: The final color grading happens here. We do it in the Flame.

LL: Do you calibrate your monitors?

RB: We have a technician who comes in periodically and does our monitors for us. Our biggest challenge these days is the different flavors of monitors. When it was all CRT, it was very straightforward. [Now], we have LCDs, CRTs, and plasma [screens]. We try to keep them all very close; they will never be exact. In fact, we just purchased one of the last remaining HD CRTs in town.

Additional Resources: The Full Interview

To read the full interview with Rod Basham, see the Interviews folder on the DVD.

three

Interpreting Alpha and Creating Mattes

Alpha channels, and their *associated matte information, are cornerstones of compositing. Alpha allows the combination of two or more images, whether the images are part of a layer within After Effects or a node output within Nuke. Although 3D programs generate alpha as part of the rendering process, motion picture and video footage does not contain alpha information. As such, it's necessary to create alpha values. One of the most common techniques for creating alpha is to "key out" blue or green from bluescreen or greenscreen footage. Both After Effects and Nuke offer tools designed specifically for this process. The tutorials at the end of this chapter will give you the opportunity to use these tools by removing a greenscreen from a digital video shoot. In addition, you'll have a chance to revisit the tutorials from Chapter 2 in order to refine alpha edge quality and the overall color balance of the composite.*

Alpha Support and Premultiplication

Alpha is a channel of a digital image that is designed to store matte information. In traditional filmmaking, a matte is a device used to control the exposure of film when two or more elements are optically combined. In the digital realm, the matte establishes pixel transparency and takes the form of a grayscale image stored in the alpha channel. When alpha is examined in a compositing program, a pixel value of 1 (white) represents 100 percent opaqueness and a value of 0 (black) represents 100 percent transparency (see Figure 3.1). (The word *mask* is often used to describe a matte; for more information, see Chapter 7, "Masking, Rotoscoping, and Motion Tracking.")

Various image formats support alpha by making it an integrated fourth channel (written as RGBA). Those formats include Maya IFF, OpenEXR, RLA, SGI, Targa, and TIFF.

Figure 3.1 (Left) CG flower (Right) Corresponding alpha channel. Since the petals have a slight transparency, the alpha values are gray in those areas. The render is included as `flower.tga` *in the Footage folder on the DVD.*

3D programs, such as Autodesk's Maya and 3ds Max, give the user the option of rendering out the alpha channel. It's also possible to create an alpha channel from scratch in digital imaging programs such as Photoshop. Digitized motion picture footage and digital video, however, do not provide an alpha channel; as such, an alpha channel must be generated or otherwise "pulled" in the compositing program through various matte tools.

Premultiplication, on the other hand, is an optional alpha process. When a 3D program, such as Maya or 3ds Max, renders an image with an alpha channel, the RGB channel values are multiplied by the alpha channel values. For example, if the normalized RGB values of a pixel are 1.0, 0.5, 0.7 and the corresponding alpha value is 0.5, then the premultiplied RGB pixel values become 0.5, 0.25, 0.35. Premultiplied pixel values are mathematically more efficient during the compositing process because the alpha values have been preinterpreted. One disadvantage, however, is that the premultiplied color values are less accurate than unpremultiplied values, which can affect the accuracy of color filters, color grading, and greenscreen removal (see Chapter 8, "DI, Color Grading, Noise, and Grain," for more information).

When an image file is imported into a compositing program, it must be interpreted as premultiplied (matted with color) or *straight* (unmatted). The process can be described with this simplified scenario:

1. A 3D program renders a surface with anti-aliasing. An edge pixel is assigned an alpha value of 0.5. The RGB values of the pixel are determined to be 1, 1, 1. However, because premultiplication is applied, the RGB values are multiplied by the alpha value and the final assigned RGB values are 0.5, 0.5, 0.5.

2. The resulting render is brought into a compositing program. The program interprets the render as premultiplied. If the render is composited over the top of a red layer and

a Normal blending mode is used, the overlapping pixel value becomes 1, 0.5, 0.5 (light red), which you would expect when placing semitransparent white over red (see Figure 3.2). (The mathematical formula for the Normal blending mode is described in the next section.)

3. If the alpha is incorrectly interpreted as straight, each color channel is multiplied by the alpha channel at the point that the render is blended with the red background. Therefore, the edge pixel is assigned an incorrect color value of 0.75, 0.25, 0.25. This forms a gray line around the surface that becomes exaggerated when motion blur is present and there are a greater number of semitransparent pixels (see Figure 3.2).

Figure 3.2 (Top Left) A CG surface with motion blur, composited over a red background, has its alpha interpreted as straight. This produces a gray line along the edge. (Top Right) Same surface with its alpha interpreted as premultiplied. (Bottom Left) A CG jar, composited over a white background, has its alpha interpreted as straight. This produces a gray line around the edge. (Center) Same jar with alpha interpreted as premultiplied. The renders are included as blur.tga *and* jar.tga *in the Footage folder on the DVD.*

Fundamental Math Operations

Alpha channels, and their corresponding mattes, are a critical part of compositing. Yet there are many methods by which the matte is used when combining or layering images. These combinations are commonly known as *blending modes.* (Nuke refers to them as *merge operations.*) As a compositor, it's important to understand the various blending modes and have a strong concept of the math that lies behind them.

Keep in mind that alpha channels are optional. It's possible, and quite common, to apply blending modes to two images that do not carry alpha channels. In such a case, the blending happens to the full image, whereas a matte limits the effect to whatever is defined as opaque or semi-opaque.

Common blending modes include Normal (Over), Stencil, Add (Plus), Screen, Multiply, Lighten (Max), and Darken (Min). There are numerous additional variations of blending modes. In fact, After Effects and Nuke each offer over 30.

Normal (Over) and Stencil

The most common blending mode is Normal (Adobe) or Over (Nuke). In a layer-based compositing program, this means that the top layer (A) obscures the lower layer (B), except where the top layer is transparent. In a node-based compositing program, this means that input A obscures input B. In traditional compositing math, the A and B relationship is often laid out as a formula. The small a or b signifies the alpha channel value of A or B. The C represents the resulting pixel value:

A + (B × (1 − a)) = C

This formula assumes that the alpha values have been premultiplied. Otherwise, we can write the formula like this:

(A × a) + ((B × b) × (1 − a)) = C

This formula processes one color channel at a time. For example, the red channel pixel values are dealt with first. With this formula, the alpha channel of A, which is a, is inverted and multiplied by the red channel pixel value of B. Hence, if a has a value of 1.0, the contribution of the corresponding B pixel value becomes 0. On the other hand, if a has a value of 0.5, the A and B red channel pixel values are averaged. For example, if A has a value of 1.0 and B has a value of 0.2, the following occurs:

(1.0 × 0.5) + ((0.2 × 1.0) × (1 − 0.5)) = 0.6

The Normal/Over method can also be represented visually (see Figure 3.3).

Figure 3.3 *(Top Left) Layer A mushroom element over black (Top Center) Layer A alpha channel (Bottom Left) Layer B mountain plate (Bottom Center) Layer B alpha channel (Right) Resulting composite with Normal (Over) blending mode. The images are included as* mushroom.##.tif *and* mountain.tif *in the Footage folder on the DVD.*

In contrast, the Stencil blending mode uses a section of the Normal (Over) formula:

B × (1 − a) = C

For example, if a is 0.75, then B is multiplied by 0.25. If B started with a value of 1.0, its end value is 0.25. Thus, B appears only where a is less than 1.0. In other words, a hole in the shape of a is cut into B (see Figure 3.4).

Whereas Nuke offers a Stencil operation for its Merge node, After Effects provides two variations. The Silhouette Alpha blending mode cuts a hole in the shape of a into B. The Stencil Alpha blending mode does the opposite by cutting B out into the shape of a.

Figure 3.4 *Result of a Stencil blending mode*

Add (Plus) and Screen

Add (Adobe) and Plus (Nuke) offer a simple formula:

A + B = C

This allows the final pixel to exceed the normalized 1.0 threshold and carry super-white values—for example, 0.7 + 0.6 = 1.3. This often results in a washed-out, overexposed composite. To avoid the superwhite values, the Screen blending mode is offered. Screen uses the following math:

(A + B) - (A × B) = C

(0.7 + 0.6) - (0.7 × 0.6) = 0.88

1.3 - 0.42 = 0.88

Screen is useful for blending bright elements against a darker background. Screen does not employ alpha values; as such, A does not have to carry an alpha channel. Screen is suited for blending smoke, fire, or flares into a background plate (see Figure 3.5). For an additional example of the Screen blending mode, see the next section.

Figure 3.5 (Left) Layer A smoke element against black (Center) Layer B smokestack plate (Right) Resulting composite using the Screen blending mode. A sample After Effects project is included as screen.aep *in the Tutorials folder on the DVD.*

Multiply

Multiply fulfills its namesake with the formula AB, or A × B. Multiply uses a conditional that tests for negative numbers and converts them into zeroes. This prevents C from becoming a negative value. Multiply is useful for compositing dark elements against lighter backgrounds without allowing the element to become 100 percent opaque. For example, you can use Multiply to blend a stormy sky into a clear one (see Figure 3.6).

Figure 3.6 (Top Left) Layer A stormy sky (Bottom Left) Layer B desert plate with a bright sky (Right) Result of composite using Multiply blending mode. A sample After Effects project is included as multiply.aep *in the Tutorials folder on the DVD.*

Lighten (Max) and Darken (Min)

Lighten (Adobe) and Max (Nuke) simply use the highest value of two corresponding pixels found in A and B. Darken (Adobe) and Min (Nuke) use the lowest value. The modes can be written as max(A,B)and min(A,B). Lighten is useful for adding bright elements to dark backgrounds. Although Lighten can produce results similar to the Add (Plus) blending mode, it is not subject to clipping. Darken, on the other hand, is useful for blending dark elements into light backgrounds. For instance, in Figure 3.7, the top layer is a CG spaceship render; its blending mode is set to Darken. The middle layer contains a CG render of smoke; its blending mode is set to Screen, allowing the smoke to pick up intensity and the illusion of a glow. The lowest layer holds a background plate of the sky.

When A and B operations are discussed, only two layers, or two inputs, are considered at one time. Hence, the spaceship is multiplied over the net result of the layers below it. Since Nuke is node based, it takes two Merge nodes to create a similar composite. The first Merge node, set to Screen, combines the smoke and the sky. The second Merge node, set to Multiply, combines the spaceship with the output of the first Merge node.

Figure 3.7 (Top Left) CG spaceship render (Center Left) CG smoke render (Bottom Left) Sky plate (Right) Result of composite. A sample After Effects project is included as darken. aep *in the Tutorials folder on the DVD.*

Chroma Key

Chroma keying forms a major portion of compositing work for feature visual effects, episodic television, and commercial production work. Compositing packages attempt to automate the process by supplying built-in tools and support for production-strength plug-ins. The automation is rarely perfect, however. Thus it's important to understand what technical steps the keying requires and different approaches that may be available.

Bluescreen vs. Greenscreen

Aside from referring to a particular color of backdrop, bluescreen and greenscreen are contemporary names for the chroma key process. All three terms trace their roots to traveling mattes. *Traveling mattes* were developed in the 1930s by RKO Pictures and fellow studios as a way to combine, with an optical process, foreground action and background images that were otherwise impossible to shoot together. (The mattes were referred to as "traveling" because each frame of the matte changed along with the foreground action.) Motion picture film stock, due to its physical nature, is more sensitive to blue wavelengths; hence, when shooting the foreground action for a traveling matte, cinematographers placed a blue backdrop behind the actors. Blue is also a complimentary color to (Caucasian) human skin tone, which makes keying (the pulling of mattes) somewhat easier. Over the decades that followed, other key colors were utilized, such as sulfur yellow, red, magenta, and green. Greenscreen increased in popularity in the late 1970s due to the growth of video. With analog YUV or digital Y'CbCr video color space, green is indirectly carried by the Y or Y' channel, which means there is generally more data set aside for it than the blue or red channels. (Green is derived by subtracting the blue and red channel values from the luminance or luma channel.)

Tips & Tricks: Chroma Subsampling

The quality of a digital video is often indicated by three numbers: x:y:z. The numbers represent the subsample ratios between the luma (gamma-adjusted luminance) and chroma (color) channels of Y'CbCr or similar color space. For example, with 4:2:2 video, chroma is sampled at half the horizontal frequency of luma.

Chroma key paints and fabrics, on the other hand, refer to specifically formulated materials that produce blues and greens that are optimal for videography and cinematography. The greenscreens shot for this book, for instance, are derived from foam-backed chroma key fabric.

Common Approaches to Keying

The first step to using a bluescreen or greenscreen plate is to key out the unwanted blue or green using a keyer. *Keying out*, which is also referred to as *keying*, removes the unwanted color so that an alpha matte is created for the desired foreground elements. (A *plate* is a particular piece of footage from a particular camera setup or shot destined for compositing or other visual effects work.) There are several standard approaches to keying that make use of luma, color, and difference mathematics. After the shot is keyed, there are additional techniques that will improve the quality of the matte. These include spill suppression and matte erosion/expansion.

Luma Key One of the simplest approaches to keying a plate is to use the luminance information found in the frames. This is achieved by converting the frames to grayscale and adjusting the values to create a high-contrast (hicon) version that contains mostly 0 blacks and 1.0 whites. The adjustment can be made to all three color channels or to a single color channel where a high degree of contrast between the foreground and background already exists (see Figure 3.8). The RGB values are then

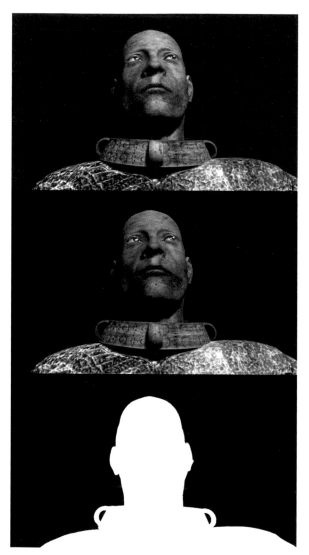

Figure 3.8 *(Top) CG render of man (Center) Unadjusted blue channel (Bottom) Blue channel adjusted to create a hicon matte. The CG render is included as* man.tga *in the Footage folder of the DVD.*

fed to the alpha channel of an unmolested version of the plate. Since luma keys ignore color information, they are prone to failure when you're working with plates with little luminance variation. Nevertheless, luma keys are not dependent on bluescreen or greenscreen and can be created from a wide variety of footage that contains sufficient contrast. In fact, generating a matte in such a manner is often referred to as *pulling a matte*. (Note that the term *luma key* is shorthand for *luminance key* and is not directly related to the luma channel of Y'CbCr video.)

Color Key   The most logical approach to keying a chroma key plate is to take advantage of a key color. To do so, the frames must be converted from RGB to HSV or HSB color space. By dividing the color range into hue, saturation, and value (or brightness), the keyer is able to identify pixels for keying by examining saturation values. One disadvantage of color keyers is their tendency to produce hard matte edges. However, they can target any color and are not limited to green or blue.

Difference Matte   A difference matte necessitates two plates: one with the foreground action against the background (a target plate) and one with only the background (a difference plate). Corresponding pixels of the two plates are compared. Pixels that show significant variation are assigned opaque pixel values in the resulting alpha matte. In anticipation of the difference matte, the camera producing the plates must be locked down; in addition, any significant change in lighting will affect the difference matte's success.

Color Difference Matte   A more sophisticated method of keying uses a color difference matte, which determines the difference in values between the RGB channels within a pixel. For example, if a pixel has a value of 0.2, 0.8, 0.2, then it's recognized to be heavily biased toward green. If the plate includes a greenscreen, then the pixel is targeted for transparency because its green channel is significantly different from the red and blue channels. A foreground pixel, on the other hand, may have a value of 0.7, 0.5, 0.6. Because the difference between the green channel and the red and blue channels is relatively minor, the pixel is targeted for opaqueness. Color difference mattes offer the advantage of soft matte edges, where the transition from transparent to opaque pixels can be fairly gradual.

Despill   Due to the nature of bluescreen and greenscreen shoots, there is often blue and green that "spills" onto the foreground subject (see Figure 3.11). This is particularly evident when the foreground is physically close to the background screen or the lighting on the foreground is not designed to neutralize any blue or green wavelengths that are reflected from the background. Despill operations target pixels that are heavily saturated by the key color and perform an adjustment. The algorithms controlling despill operations vary. One method clips the values of the offending channel, such as green, to the values of another channel, such as red. A second method generates an internal spill map, which records areas of spill that can be used to subtract the spill color from the image.

Matte Erosion and Expansion It's common for a matte created through keying to suffer from a loose fit. That is, the matte extends past the edge of the foreground object to reveal an inappropriate white or colored line. Conversely, the matte may be too "tight" and therefore erode into the object. Hence, a means by which you can expand or contract the alpha matte is often necessary. In general, erosion and expansion tools, often called *chokers*, operate by manipulating the alpha channels color curve. The curves are scaled so that the gray, semitransparent values are pushed toward white for a greater degree of opaqueness or pushed toward black for a greater degree of transparency.

After Effects and Nuke offer a wide range of keying effects and nodes that utilize the techniques discussed in this section. Their functionality is detailed in the section "Working with Alpha" later in this chapter.

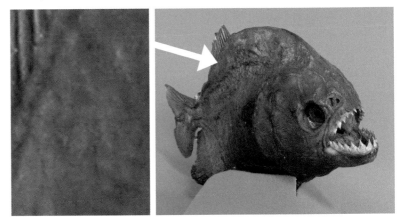

Figure 3.09 Taxidermied fish shot against greenscreen. The close-up on the left shows the high degree of green spill.

Keying Workflow

Here are a few steps to keep in mind when keying:

Multiple Keyers When keying, you are not limited to using a single keyer. Instead, feel free to apply a different keyer with a different setting to various regions of the image. You can define particular regions by drawing masks. You can then combine the alpha channels of the various regions to create a final matte (see Chapter 7, "Masking, Rotoscoping, and Motion Tracking," for examples).

Alpha Color Correction You can apply various color-correction effects and nodes to help improve the quality of a resulting alpha channel. In After Effects, you can use a filter that can target the alpha channel without influencing the RGB channels. The Curves and Levels effects do so by offering a Channel menu. In Nuke, you can change the Channels menu in any node's properties panel to Alpha.

Timeline Test When working with footage, test the keyer settings at different frames. If necessary, animate the keyer settings over time. If the foreground objects are changing too dramatically, consider applying multiple keyers to individual portions of the timeline. For example, apply keyer 1 from frames 1 to 100 and keyer 2 from frames 101 to 150.

Rotoscoping If you're having difficultly keying a piece of footage or the key is producing unclean matte edges, consider rotoscoping. Despite the advances in keyer technology, rotoscoping remains a common practice at animation studios and visual effects houses. In addition, rotoscoping is generally required when there is no green-screen or bluescreen, the screens are not large enough to cover the entire background, or reflective surfaces are involved. (Rotoscoping is discussed in Chapter 7.)

Lab and YUV Color   Consider converting the footage to L*a*b* or YUV color space. L*a*b* (often written as Lab) separates luminance information from chrominance information. The L* channel handles luminance, or "lightness." The a* channel controls the green-red color balance. The b* channel controls the blue-yellow color balance. In the realm of computer graphics, YUV generally refers to digital file formats encoded in Y'CbCr color space. YUV divides the luminance and chrominance information in a similar manner. U (or Cb) encodes the blue chroma component. V (or Cr) encodes the red chroma component. The green chroma component is indirectly carried by the Y channel.

Since the noise found in film and digital video footage is more strongly represented in chrominance channels, it can pay to apply noise suppression techniques (such as subtle blurs) to the a*/U/Cb or b*/V/Cr channels only. Ultimately, the presence of noise interferes with the proper operation of chroma keyer effects and nodes. Conversely, many compositors prefer to sharpen their images in L*a*b* or YUV space. By applying a sharpen filter to the L*/Y channel, you bypass the greater degree of noise inherent in the a*/U/Cb and b*/V/Cr channels. This results in fewer sharpening artifacts, including white edge "halos."

After Effects supports L*a*b* and YUV through the Color Range effect, which is discussed later in this chapter. It supports YUV through the Channel Combiner effect, which is demonstrated in Chapter 4, "Channel Manipulation." Nuke can operate in L*a*b* or Y'CbCr through the Colorspace node, which is detailed in Chapter 4.

Working with Alpha

Alpha channels are an inescapable part of compositing. When alpha is not present, it must be pulled or otherwise generated. As such, After Effects and Nuke offer a wide variety of tools and plug-ins to achieve this goal.

Alpha in AE

After Effects tests each imported file for the presence of an alpha channel. If an unlabeled alpha channel is found, the program pops up the Interpret Footage dialog box, which lets you choose the alpha interpretation (see Figure 3.10).

The program also offers the option to pick a different color to be used in the matting process. For instance, if you import a render from Maya that has a green background color, you can set the Matted With Color cell to green and thus carry out a successful premultiplication interpretation. (If the Matted

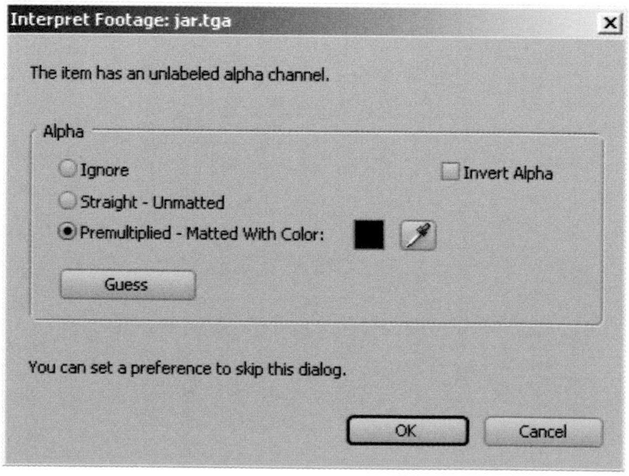

Figure 3.10 The Interpret Footage dialog box

With Color cell doesn't match the background color of the render, the background color will be trapped within a thin line running around the edge of the rendered element.)

In general, any imported 3D render should be interpreted as premultiplied. However, on occasion it becomes useful to ignore the premultiplication. For example, CG glow, fog, and optical effects may retain better edge quality when the Straight radio button is selected. To avoid having After Effects prompt you for alpha interpretation, choose Edit → Preferences → Import, and change Interpret Unlabeled Alpha As to the interpretation of your choice.

After Effects offers the following additional support for alpha:

- When rendering through the Render Queue, you can choose to render an alpha channel by changing the Channels menu in the Output Module Settings dialog box to RGB + Alpha (assuming the selected image format supports alpha). In addition, you can choose to render premultiplied or straight files by changing the Color menu to Straight (Unmatted) or Premultiplied (Matted). Straight files may be required when importing the After Effects output into another program, such as an editing software that doesn't support premultiplication.
- You can view the alpha channel in the viewer of the Composition panel at any time by changing the Show Channel menu to Alpha.
- It's possible to invert the alpha channel by choosing Effect → Channel → Invert and changing the effect's Channel menu to Alpha. What was opaque becomes transparent and vice versa.
- The TrkMat (Track Matte) menus, which are visible when the Toggle Switches/Modes button is clicked, offer a quick way to cut a hole into the alpha of a layer. For example, you can set a layer's TrkMat menu to the name of a hidden layer that is directly above. The named layer's alpha or RGB luminance values are converted to new alpha values for the layer whose TrkMat menu was set.

Blending Modes

Each layer of each composition receives its own blending mode. The blending mode determines how the layer will be blended with the net result of the layers below it. By default, the blending mode is set to Normal. However, there are two ways you can change a layer's mode:

- RMB+click over the layer's name in the layer outline of the Timeline panel. Choose Blending Mode → *blending mode* (see Figure 3.11).
- Click the Toggle Switches/Modes button at the bottom-left of the Timeline panel. This reveals the Mode menus beside each layer (see Figure 3.11). Change each menu to the blending mode of your choice.

Commonly-used blending modes are described in the section "Fundamental Math Operations" earlier in this chapter. For additional documentation on the remaining blending modes, see the "Blending Mode Reference" page in the After Effects help files.

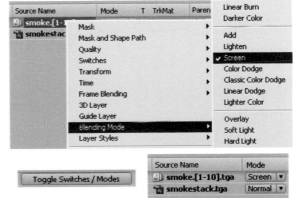

Figure 3.11 *(Top) A small section of the Blending Mode menu (Bottom Left) Toggle Switches/Modes button (Bottom Right) Mode menus for two layers in the layer outline*

AE Keyers and Chokers

Keying effects in After Effects are broken into two categories: keyers (Effect → Keying) and chokers (Effect → Matte). While keyers remove unwanted color from bluescreen or greenscreen plates, chokers refine the resulting alpha matte edges.

Simple Choker and Matte Choker

Simple Choker is designed to erode or expand the edge of a matte. It has a Choke Matte slider, which controls the amount of erosion or expansion.

Matte Choker offers the same erosion or expansion but provides greater control. Two sets of Choke sliders are supplied to erode or expand the matte. For example, you can use Choke 1 to expand the matte and thus fill small holes (see Figure 3.12). At the same time, you can use Choke 2 to erode the matte to improve the outer edges. It's not necessary to use both Choke sliders. If Choke 1 produces acceptable results, Choke 2 can be left at 0. Values above 0 for either Choke slider erode the matte (that is, reduce the number of pixels with 1.0 alpha values). Values below 0 for either Choke slider expand the matte. In addition, each Choke has a Gray Level Softness slider which controls the amount of blur applied to the matte edge. (Gray Level Softness 2 must be above 0 for the blur to appear.) High values will anti-alias the matte edges but tend to round off any sharp corners. In addition, each Choke has a Geometric Softness slider that sets the aggressiveness of the erosion or expansion.

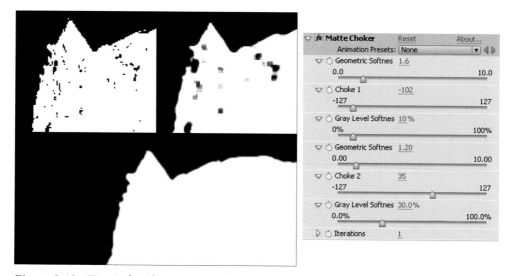

Figure 3.12 *(Top Left) Close-up of alpha matte with hard edges and holes (Top Center) Same matte after Matte Choker is applied with default settings (Bottom Left) Matte Choker adjusted to smooth edge and remove holes (Right) Adjusted matte choker settings. A sample After Effects project is saved as* matte_choker.aep *in the Tutorials folder on the DVD.*

Since keyers are unable to provide clean matte edges in some situations, Simple Choker and Matte Choker can give you an extra level of control. In addition, you can easily remove stranded pixels with either effect. For demonstrations of both effects, see the next section, plus the section "Difference Matte" later in this chapter.

Color Key, Linear Color Key, and Luma Key

The Color Key, Linear Color Key, and Luma Key effects target specific value information within an image. The values may be expressed as color, hue, chroma, or luminance.

The Color Key effect bases its matte creation on a color established by its Key Color swatch. You can choose any color found within the image with the associated eyedropper. The keyer is suited for footage in which the background color does not appear in the foreground object. For example, in Figure 3.13, the proper exposure for a building face has left the sky overexposed. The Color Key keyer, in conjunction with a Matte Choker, is able to remove the sky without affecting the building's windows. With the Color Key effect, you can refine the aggressiveness of the matte by adjusting the Color Tolerance slider. The higher the Color Tolerance value, the wider the color range targeted for keying. You can erode or expand the matte with the Edge Thin slider. You can soften the edge with the Edge Feather slider. The Edge Feather slider can help disguise stair-stepped edges, which the keyer is prone to.

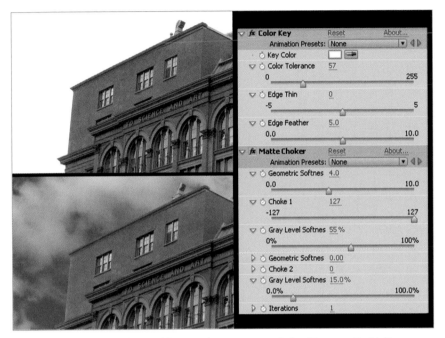

Figure 3.13 (Top Left) Building with overexposed sky (Bottom Left) Footage composited over a new sky after application of Color Key and Matte Choker (Right) Color Key and Matte Choker settings. A sample After Effects project is saved as color_key.aep *in the Footage folder on the DVD.*

Whereas Color Key simply keys out any color that matches the color determined by the Key Color option, Linear Color Key bases pixel transparency on the closeness of the color match. In other words, Linear Color Key is able to apply falloff to the pixel transparency. For example, in Figure 3.14, a Color Key matte is compared to a Linear Color Key matte. When the Color Key has it Edge Feather left at 0, the edge reveals the binary (on/off) nature of the keyer. When Edge Feather is raised, the edge becomes softer, but the softness is equal at all edge points. Linear Color Key, in comparison, tapers the pixel transparency based on

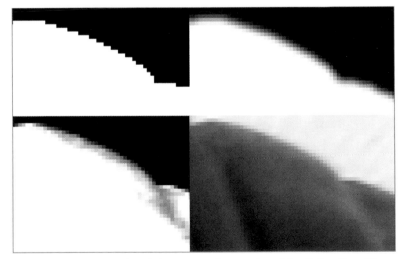

Figure 3.14 (Top Left) Alpha matte edge produced by Color Key (Top Right) Edge produced by Color Key with a high Edge Feather value (Bottom Left) Edge produced by Linear Color Key (Bottom Right) Close-up of plate

pixel color value. To make the taper more gradual, you can increase the Linear Color Key's Matching Softness slider.

The Linear Color Key effect adds the ability to match colors through RGB, Hue, or Chroma color spaces, as set by the Match Colors menu. RGB causes Linear Color Key to operate in the same space as Color Key. Hue, on the other hand, forces the examination of pixel hue while ignoring saturation values. Chroma operates on the color purity of a pixel. Although RGB works for most situations, Hue and Chroma may be desirable when the color to be removed is very saturated or has a narrowly-defined value. The Linear Color Key effect's Matching Tolerance slider operates in a manner similar to the Color Key effect's Color Tolerance slider.

Tips & Tricks: Hue, Colorfulness, Chroma, and Saturation

Hue is the main property of a color. Specific hues correlate to specific wavelengths of light. Colors with primary hues are given names such as *red, green,* and *blue. Colorfulness* is the degree to which a color is different from gray at a given luminance. *Chroma* is the colorfulness of a color in reference to perceived white (which varies with the environment). *Saturation* is the colorfulness of a color relative to its own brightness. In the realm of computer graphics, chroma and saturation are often used interchangeably. This is due to the computer monitor serving as the sole source of light. With a digital image, chroma and saturation can be considered the purity of a color. A pure color is one that has a very specific hue. *Value* is the luminance, or lightness and darkness, of a color. The HSV and HSB color spaces utilize these components. With HSB, value is referred to as *brightness.*

The Luma Key effect bases its matte creation on image luminance. The keyer can affect brighter, darker, similar, or dissimilar pixels through its Key Type menu. The keyer is useful for any image that carries extreme variations in luminance levels. For example, in Figure 3.15, the fire from a burning structure is separated from its background. With the Luma key effect, you determine the targeted luminance value with the Threshold slider. The Tolerance slider sets the width of the luminance range. Edge Thin and Edge Feather control the erosion and softness of the matte.

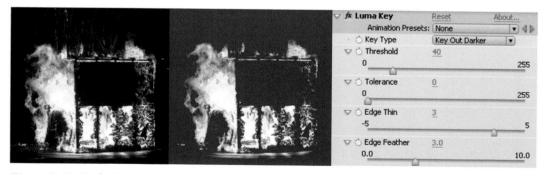

Figure 3.15 (Left) Burning structure (Center) Luma Key applied to footage and result layered over red background (Right) Luma Key settings. A sample After Effects project is saved as luma.aep *in the Footage folder on the DVD.*

Color Difference Key

The Color Difference Key effect divides the image into intermediate mattes and recombines them into a final alpha matte. Although it bases its functionality on common color difference key techniques (see the section "Common Approaches to Keying" earlier in this chapter), its workflow is unique:

1. A color is selected through the Key Color eyedropper.
2. Intermediate mattes *Partial A* and *Partial B* are created automatically. Partial B bases it transparency on the Key Color hue. (The operation occurs in HLS, or Hue/Lightness/Saturation, space.) Partial A bases its transparency on a hue offset on the HLS color wheel.
3. Partial A and Partial B are adjusted through A and B sliders, which include In White, Out White, In Black, Out Black, and Gamma. The sliders have the effect of setting the white and black points for the partial mattes. (For information on white and black points, see Chapter 2.) The points can also be set by clicking the A or B buttons below the small matte preview window and using the White eyedropper or Black eyedropper (see Figure 3.16). In addition, you can preview the mattes in the viewer of the Composition panel by changing the View menu to Matte Partial A Corrected, Matte Partial B Corrected, or Matte Corrected. (Matted Corrected displays the final combined matte.)
4. The final matte is automatically generated by blending Partial A with Partial B in a screen blending operation. No alpha values are allowed to exceed a normalized 1.0. Final adjustments to the alpha matte can be made with the Matte In White, Matte In Black, and Matte Gamma sliders.

Although the Color Difference key is fairly unintuitive, it does offer the advantage of partial mattes. By using two partial mattes, you can maintain fine edge quality without the risk of opening up holes in the main body of the foreground objects. That is, you can adjust one matte to protect the interior of the object and ensure that it appears solid; at the same time, you can adjust the second matte to keep feathered edges. For example, in Figure 3.16, clouds are separated from the sky and composited over a new background.

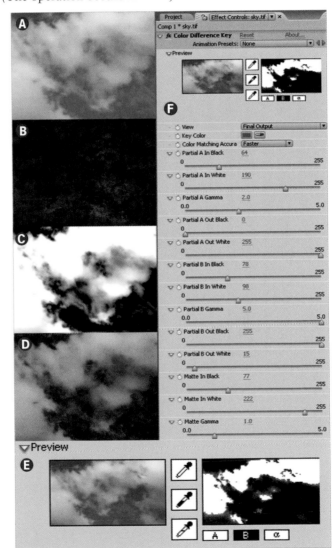

Figure 3.16 *(A) Sky plate (B) New background image (C) Alpha channel created by Color Difference Key (D) Final composite (E) Close-up of matte preview window with A and B buttons and white and black point eyedroppers (F) Color Difference Key settings. The clouds have been color graded toward red. A sample After Effects project is saved as* `color_difference_key.aep` *in the Tutorials folder on the DVD.*

Color Range and Extract

The Color Range effect keys out a specific range of colors in L*a*b* (Lab), YUV, or RGB color space. The range of colors keyed out is centered on a single color chosen by the user through the Key Color eyedropper (see Figure 3.17). The range is then adjusted with a Min and Max slider for each channel (L, a, b or Y, U, V or R, G, B) or by sampling pixels with Plus or Minus eyedroppers. Color Range is useful for removing unevenly lit greenscreen or separating foreground elements that differ in color. For example, in Figure 3.17, a long-exposure night shot features spinning green lights beside the orange and yellow lights of a tent. The green is isolated from the rest of the frame by applying a Color Range and Invert effect.

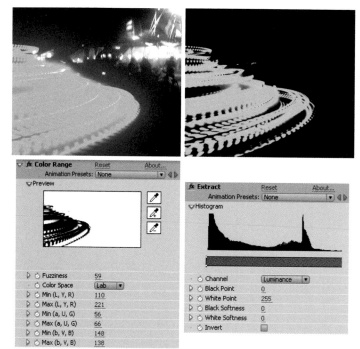

The Extract effect functions in a similar manner to the Color Range effect but keys out a particular value range of a single channel. The range is determined by changing the Channel menu to Luminance, Red, Green, or Blue and determining the White Point (white threshold) and Black Point (black threshold) values for that channel (see Figure 3.17). Extract is the most useful when keying out a background that has a luminance significantly different from the foreground.

Difference Matte

The Difference Matte effect compares a source layer with a difference layer and keys out pixels in the source layer that don't match corresponding pixels in the difference layer. Generally, the source layer contains an object against a background and the difference layer contains the same background without the object. The Difference Matte effect doesn't require a background with a particular color, although the technique would work with chroma key footage. The Difference Layer menu selects its namesake. The Tolerance slider determines the range of pixels that are assigned an alpha value of 1.0. The higher the Tolerance value is, the more accurate the match between source and difference layer pixels must be for pixels to remain opaque. The Matching Softness slider tapers the transition between opaque and transparent pixels. The Blur Before Difference slider applies a blur before creating the matte, which can help reduce noisy artifacts. As an example, in Figure 3.18, a seashell is pulled from an ocean backdrop with the Difference Matte effect. The seashell/ocean layer serves as a source layer and the empty ocean plate serves as the difference layer. Because the effect is prone to create rough edges and trap remnants of shadows, a Simple Choker effect is added. The pulled shell is then composited over a new background.

Figure 3.17 *(Top Left) Long-exposure night photo (Top Right) Photo after application of Color Range effect. (Bottom Left) Color Range settings. A sample After Effects project is saved as* `color_range.aep` *in the Tutorials folder on the DVD. (Bottom Right) Default Extract effect settings.*

Figure 3.18 *(Top Left) Source layer with seashell over an ocean backdrop (Top Center) Difference layer with the ocean by itself (Bottom Left) Result of Difference Matte (Bottom Center) Final composite (Right) Difference Matte and Simple Choker settings. A sample After Effects file is saved as* `difference_matte.aep` *in the Tutorials folder on the DVD.*

Keylight and Inner/Outer Key

Keylight, developed by The Foundry, is the most advanced keyer that's bundled with After Effects. In fact, Adobe documentation suggests employing Keylight before utilizing any other keyer. As such, Keylight is demonstrated with the After Effects tutorials included in this chapter.

Inner/Outer Key, due to its limited functionality and relatively poor success rate, should be skipped. Although the keyer provides the means to establish several mattes to control the alpha matte creation, it's just as easy to create your own holdout or garbage masks while using a more robust keyer. For masking approaches, see Chapter 7, "Masking, Rotoscoping, and Motion Tracking."

Spill Suppressor

The Spill Suppressor effect removes trace amounts of key color left on the foreground element after a plate has been keyed. You can choose the color with the Color To Suppress color swatch. You can control the intensity with the Suppression slider. If the foreground has been properly lit, spill suppression is generally not necessary. However, the effect comes in handy for footage shot in nonideal situations (see Figure 3.19).

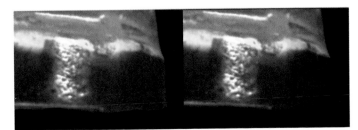

Figure 3.19 *(Left) Close-up of element with green spill along edge (Right) Same element after application of Spill Suppressor*

Alpha in Nuke

Nuke automatically reads the alpha channel of any file imported through a Read node. However, Nuke will not interpret the alpha as premultiplied unless the Premultiplied check box is selected in the Read node's properties panel.

Nuke offers the following additional support for alpha:

- When rendering through a Write node, you can choose to render an alpha channel by changing the node's Channels menu to Rgba (assuming the selected image format supports alpha).
- To render a premultiplied image, select the Premultiplied check box in the Write node's properties panel. If you render a premultiplied image, then re-import the image through a new Read node, the new Read node's Premultiplied check box should be selected to maintain edge quality.
- You can view the alpha channel in a viewer at any time by clicking the Viewer pane and pressing the A key. To return to an RGB view, press A again.
- It's possible to invert the alpha channel by adding an Invert node (Color → Invert) and changing the node's Channels menu to Alpha.

The Merge Node

Images and image sequences are combined in Nuke through the Merge node. Whereas After Effects applies different blending modes to create the combinations, Nuke applies different merge operations through the Merge node. The node's input A is equivalent to layer A, or the top layer. The node's input B is equivalent to layer B, or the bottom layer. The merge operation is set by the node's Operation menu.

Commonly-used merge operations are described in the section "Fundamental Math Operations" earlier in this chapter. For additional documentation on the remaining operations, see the "Merge Operations" section of the Nuke user manual. To quickly examine the math behind each operation, let the mouse hover over the Operation menu; a list of operations and their formulas are displayed in a yellow tooltip box.

There are several ways to apply a Merge node:

- Select the node that will serve as input A. Press the M key, which is the default hotkey for the Merge node. The input A of a new Merge node is connected automatically to the selected node. Manually connect input B.
- In the Node Graph, RMB+click and choose Merge → Merge. This menu option creates a new Merge node and sets the Operation to Over, which is the same as the Normal blending mode in After Effects.
- In the Node Graph, RMB+click and choose Merge → Merges → *merge operation*. Nine of the most commonly used merge operations are included in this menu.

Although only two input pipes appear on a Merge node by default, the node is not limited to two inputs. If you connect additional nodes to a Merge node, additional input pipes are created; input A is relabeled A1 and the new pipes are labeled A2, A3, and so on. In this situation, the input with the highest A number, such as A2, becomes the "top" input. For example, in Figure 3.20, a CG spaceship and a smoke trail render are merged with a sky plate. Because the spaceship is connected to input A2, it occludes both the smoke trail (input A1) and the sky (input B). Unfortunately, all inputs share the same merge operation. While the use of single merge operation on all the inputs of a Merge node might work fine, it limits the flexibility of the composite. A separate solution requires the connection of two or more Merge nodes. In the case of Figure 3.20, the first Merge node is set to Screen and combines the smoke with the sky. The second Merge node is set to Over and combines the spaceship with the smoke/sky output.

By default, the contribution of input A is 100%. However, you can reduce this by lowering the Merge node's Mix slider below 1.0. If more than two inputs are connected to a Merge node, the Mix slider controls the contribution of all the A inputs. (For additional information on Merge node parameters, see Chapter 7, "Masking, Rotoscoping, and Motion Tracking.")

Of the 30 different merge operations available through the Operation menu, only Matte requires unpremultiplied inputs (that is, values that have not been premultiplied). All other operations expect premultiplied inputs. You can apply premultiplication to a node output at any time by adding a Premult node (RMB+click and choose Merge → Premult). To remove the premultiplication from a node, add an Unpremult node (Merge → Unpremult). The various Nuke tutorials in this book use Merge and Premult nodes regularly.

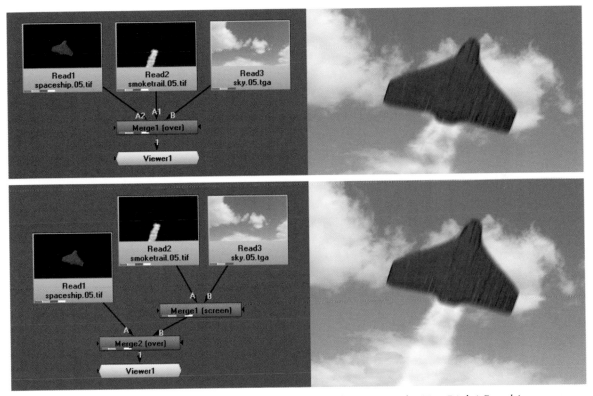

Figure 3.20 *(Top Left) Three Read nodes connected to a single Merge node (Top Right) Resulting composite. A sample Nuke script is included as* `multi_input.nk` *in the Tutorials folder. (Bottom Left) Three Read nodes connected to two Merge nodes with different Operation settings (Bottom Right) Resulting composite. A sample Nuke script is included as* `multi_merge.nk` *in the Tutorials folder on the DVD.*

Additional Blending Nodes

Several other nodes are able to undertake input blending. These are available through the Merge menu:

Blend averages the values of two inputs. By default, the contribution of each node is 50%. However, you can bias one over the other by adjusting the 1 and 2 sliders. For example, raising the 1 slider above the value of 1.0 biases the input 1; input 2 becomes dimmer and more transparent.

Dissolve averages the values of two inputs. The balance between the inputs is controlled by the Which slider. If Which is set to 0.5, the output is a 50% mix of both inputs. If Which is set to 0, only input 0 is visible. If Which is set to 1.0, only input 1 is visible.

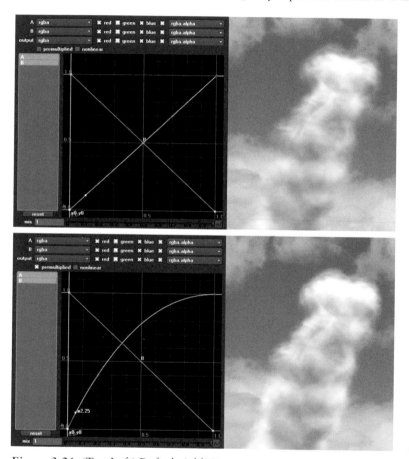

Time Dissolve averages inputs in the same manner as Dissolve. However, instead of providing a Which parameter, Time Dissolve provides an interactive curve and curve editor that changes the dissolve over time. When the curve has a 1.0 value, input B is biased. When the curve has a value of 0.5, input A and input B are mixed. Note that the horizontal axis of the editor runs from 0 to 1.0 and represents the full frame range. The specific start and end frames are set by the In and Out cells. You can move a curve point by LMB+dragging a point in the editor. You can insert a new point by selecting the curve so that it turns yellow and Ctrl+Alt+clicking on the curve.

AddMix supplies a curve editor and creates a color correction curve for the alpha of input A and the alpha of input B. The A curve is multiplied against the A alpha and the B curve is multiplied against the B alpha before the two alpha channels are added together. The ability to alter the curves allows you to fine tune matte edges and alpha opacity. By default, both curves run from 0 to 1.0, although the B alpha curve is inverted so that is has an opposite slope. You can edit the curves in the same manner as you would with the Time Dissolve curve editor (see the previous paragraph). As an example, in Figure 3.21 a CG smoke trail is blended with a sky plate. The Read1 node, which carries the smoke, is connected to the input A of the AddMix1 node. The Read2 node, which carries the sky plate, is connected to the input B. Because the smoke render was premultiplied by the 3D program, the Read1 node's Premultiplied check box is selected. In addition, the AddMix1 node's Premultiplied check box is selected; this forces the AddMix1 node to unpremultiply input A before multiplying color correction curve A. By adjusting the shape

Figure 3.21 (Top Left) Default AddMix settings (Top Right) Result of default settings (Bottom Left) Color correction curve A is adjusted to form an arc. (Bottom Right) Result of adjusted curve. The edge of the smoke becomes brighter and more opaque. A sample Nuke script is included as addmix.nk *in the Tutorials folder on the DVD.*

of color correction curve A in the curve editor, variations in the alpha matte edge quality can be achieved.

KeyMix reveals input A within the mask area established by the node's Mask input. For more information on masking, see Chapter 7, "Masking, Rotoscoping, and Motion Tracking."

CopyRectangle isolates a rectangular section of input A. The node is designed to limit an effect to a particular region of an input, then merge the result with the original, unaffected input. For example, in Figure 3.22, the output of a Read node is connected to a Blur node. The Blur node output is connected to the input A of a CopyRectangle node. The output of the Read node is also connected to the input B of the Copy-Rectangle node. The result is a blur confined to a rectangular region. The CopyRectangle node provides an interactive rectangular region box. To move the box, LMB+drag the box center in the viewer. To resize the box, LMB+drag one of the four box edges.

Figure 3.22 (Left) The CopyRectangle node isolates the effect of a Blur node (Right) The node network. A sample Nuke script is included as copyrectangle.nk *in the Tutorials folder on the DVD.*

MergeExpression allows you to write your own blending mode math with expressions. For an introduction to expressions in Nuke, see Chapter 12, "Advanced Techniques." For examples of common blending mode formulas, see the "Fundamental Math Operations" section earlier in this chapter.

ZMerge creates a blend based on a depth channel. For a demonstration, see Chapter 9, "Integrating Render Passes."

Nuke Keyers

Nuke includes six nodes designed for keying. Each has its own advantages and disadvantages.

The Difference Node

The Difference node outputs an alpha matte after identifying the difference in RGB pixel values between two inputs. Pixels that are identical are assigned 0 alpha values. Pixels that are different are assigned alpha values that range from 0 to 1.0 based on the degree of difference. The RGB output of the Difference node is taken from the B input of the node. For example, in Figure 3.23, a green-blue gradient is connected to the input B of a Difference node. The word *test*, with red, green, blue, and white letters over the same gradient, is connected to the input A of the Difference node. The output of the node is connected to a Premult node and, in turn, to a viewer. The result is the gradient cut out in the shape of the word *test*. Each letter does

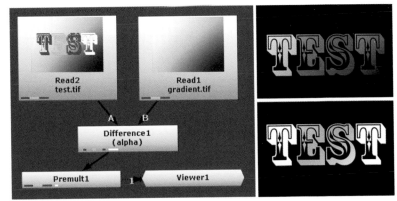

Figure 3.23 (Left) Difference keyer network (Top Right) RGB result (Bottom Right) Alpha result. A sample Nuke script is included as difference.nk *in the Tutorials folder on the DVD.*

not contain 1.0 alpha values, however. The *E* and *S* have alpha values of 0.48 and 0.58 respectively; this is due to green and blue colors of the letters possessing values relatively close to those of the green-blue gradient.

IBKGizmo and IBKColour

The IBKGizmo and IBKColour nodes are two components of an image-based keyer. Whereas color-based keyers base their matte extraction on a baseline color selected by the user (such as blue or green), image-based keying compares pixel values.

The IBKColour node Gaussian-blurs chroma key footage and extracts a hicon (high-contrast) matte. Contrast is determined by comparing the key color, set by the Screen Type menu in the IBKColour properties panel, and the remaining scene colors. Ideally, the RGB output of the node contains only the key color. The output of the IBKColour node is designed to feed into the C (color) input of an IBKGizmo node. The original chroma key footage must be connected to the FG input of the IBKGizmo node. The IBKGizmo node generates a difference matte from the original chroma key footage and IBKGizmo's blurred output. The output of IBKGizmo may then be combined with the new background plate with a Merge node.

For example, in Figure 3.24, a fish is composited over a fish tank. The fish footage is connected to the input of an IBKColour node and the FG input of an IBKGizmo node. The IBKGizmo node's Screen Type menu is set to match the IBKColour node's Screen Type menu; in this case, IBKColour is set to Green and IBKGizmo is set to C-green. Since the default setting for IBKColour did not create a completely clean matte, the Darks/g cell is set to –0.1.

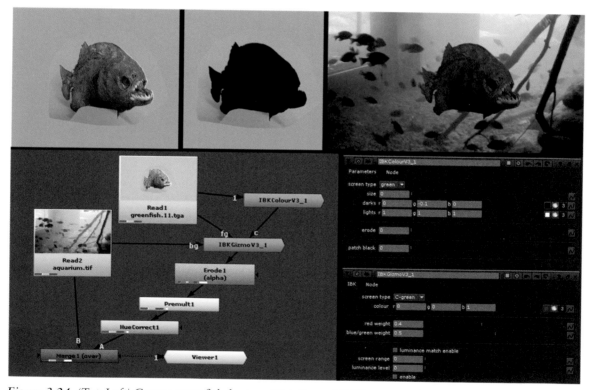

Figure 3.24 *(Top Left) Greenscreen fish footage (Top Center) RGB output of IBKColour node (Top Right) Final composite (Bottom Left) Node network (Bottom Right) IBKColour and IBKGizmo settings. A sample Nuke script is included as* `ibk.nk` *in the Tutorials folder on the DVD.*

The Darks and Lights RGB cells are designed to adjust the upper and lower color thresholds for the matting process. A Darks/g value of −0.1 removes holes appearing in the center of the matte. However, to refine the matte edge, which is not aligned tightly enough to the fish body, the output of the IBKGizmo node is connected to an Erode (Blur) node. The Erode (Blur) node erodes the matte. To create a correct composite, however, the output of the Erode (Blur) node is connected to a Premult node, which is in turn fed into a HueCorrect node. Without a Premult node, the Erode node would create a fine line around the edge. The HueCorrect node simply color-adjusts the fish to match the tank lighting. The output of HueCorrect finally runs into a Merge node, which combines the fish and the fish tank plate.

The Keyer Node

As demonstrated in the Chapter 1 Nuke tutorial, the Keyer node offers a simple way to generate an alpha matte. As determined by its Operation menu, the Keyer can base its output on luminance, greenscreen color, bluescreen color, saturation, minimum value, maximum value, or values within specific RGB channels. Targeted values are controlled by a Range graph (see Figure 3.25). You can LMB+drag the yellow handles to fine-tune the matte. The lower-left handle determines the threshold for transparent pixels (the graph scale is normalized from 0 to 1.0). As you drag the handle to the right, pixels with values lower than the handle value are assigned 100% transparency (an alpha value of 0). For instance, if Operation is set to Saturation Key and the handle value is 0.3, then any pixel with a saturation value less than 0.3 (or 30%) becomes transparent. The upper-right handle of the Range graph sets the threshold for opaque pixels. Any pixel with a value higher than the handle is assigned an alpha value of 1.0. The angle of the curve between the lower-left and upper-right handles determines the degree of falloff from transparent to opaque pixels. A steep slope produces a more severe transition. When the upper-right handle is moved aside, it reveals a third handle in the same position. The third handle sets the upper value limit for pixels that are assigned an alpha value of 1.0. If the second handle is set to 0.5 and the third handle is set to 0.75, then pixels with values between 0.5 and 0.75 receive alpha values of 1.0.

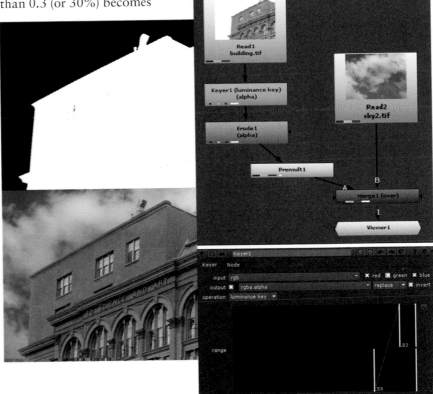

***Figure 3.25** (Top Left) Matte produced by the Keyer node (Bottom Left) Resulting composite over a new sky plate (Top Right) Keyer node network (Bottom Right) Keyer effect's properties panel with Range graph. A sample Nuke script is included as* `keyer.nk` *in the Tutorials folder on the DVD.*

As a working example, in Figure 3.25 a sky is keyed from a plate with a building. Since the Keyer node did not produce a clean edge on the matte, its output is sent through an Erode (Blur) node. In order to successfully use the resulting matte with a Merge node, the Erode (Blur) node's output is sent through a Premult node. Because the sky is significantly brighter than the building, the Keyer node removes the building until the node's Invert check box is selected.

HueKeyer

The HueKeyer node bases its alpha matte on a color range interactively selected through its built-in curve editor. Two curves are provided: Amount and Sat_thrsh (Saturation Threshold). Hues from the input are presented left to right. If an Amount curve point is raised to 1.0, then the corresponding hue is keyed out. That is, the hue receives an alpha value of 0 while the remainder of the image receives a value of 1.0. (You can reverse this behavior by deselecting the Invert check box.) If an Amount curve point is positioned between 0.1 and 1.0, the corresponding hue receives semitransparent alpha values. The Sat_thrsh curve establishes the sensitivity of the key operation. The higher a Sat_thrsh curve point is raised above its default 0.1 value, the greater the saturation a pixel must carry of a particular hue to receive low alpha values. For example, in Figure 3.26, a crayfish is removed from its surroundings with a HueKeyer node. The Amount and Sat_thrsh curves are shaped to target the orange red of the creature. The Invert check box is deselected. Since the HueKeyer is unable to remove the white foam and sections of the black pot that contain red, green, and blue values equally, the HueKeyer output is connected to a Blur and Grade mode, both of which are set to operate on the alpha channel only.

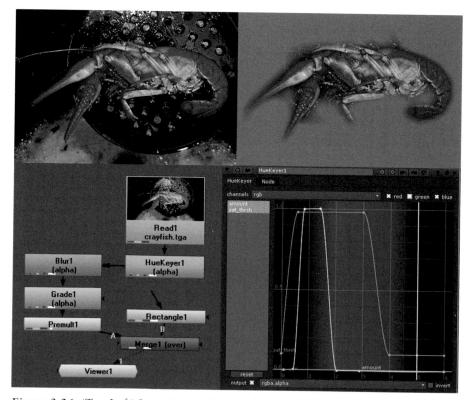

Figure 3.26 *(Top Left) Input image (Top Right) Crayfish separated with a HueKeyer node (Bottom Left) Node network (Bottom Right) HueKeyer curve editor with the Amount curve in yellow and the Sat_thrsh curve in pink. A sample Nuke script is saved as* huekeyer.nk *in the Tutorials folder on the DVD.*

Primatte

Primatte is an advanced keyer written by Imagica that uses a color-based matte extraction process. Primatte is investigated in "Nuke Tutorial 3: Removing Greenscreen" at the end of this chapter.

AE and Nuke Tutorials

With the Chapter 2 tutorials, you had the opportunity to remove a greenscreen from a statue. There are several areas in which the greenscreen removal can be improved. Since Tutorial 2 featured an inanimate object, the chroma key challenges are fairly mild. Hence, additional After Effects and Nuke tutorials are included in this chapter that use video footage of a model.

AE Tutorial 2 Revisited: Refining Color and Edge Quality

Although the greenscreen removal undertaken in Chapter 2 was fairly straightforward, the color balance of the statue and edge quality of the alpha matte can be improved.

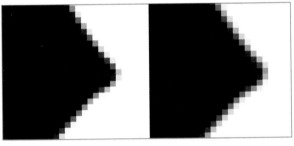

1. Reopen the completed After Effects project file for "AE Tutorial 2: Working with DPX and Cineon Files." A finished version of Tutorial 2 is saved as `ae2.aep` in the Chapter 2 Tutorials folder on the DVD. At this stage, the edge of the statue remains sharper than the edges of surrounding buildings. To soften it slightly, select the `greenscreen.cin` layer and choose Effect → Matte → Matte Choker. In the Effect Controls panel, set Choke 1 to 25 and Gray Level Softness 1 to 40%. To view a before image and an after image, click the small Fx button beside the *Matte Choker* name in the Effect Controls panel. The Matte Choker erodes the edge slightly and creates a greater taper between transparent and opaque pixels (see Figure 3.27).

   Figure 3.27 (Left) Edge of alpha matte (Right) Edge of alpha matte after the application of Matte Choker

2. At this stage, the statue remains heavily saturated. To fit the statue into the environment better, select the `greenscreen.cin` layer and choose Effect → Color Correction → Curves. In the Effect Controls panel, shape the Curves effect's RGB curve to match Figure 3.28. You can LMB+click the curve to insert a new curve point and then LMB+drag the point to a new position. This reduces the brightness in a non-linear fashion. (For more information on color correction effects, see Chapter 4.)

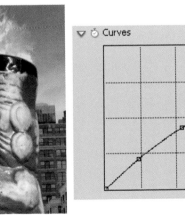

Figure 3.28 (Left To Right) Inappropriately bright and saturated statue; Adjusted Curves effect; Result of Curves effect; Result of Hue/Saturation effect

3. Although the statue's brightness better matches the background, the colors remain too saturated for the environment. To remedy this, select the greenscreen.cin layer and choose Effect → Color Correction → Hue/Saturation. In the Effect Controls panel, set the Master Saturation slider to −40. Save the file under a new name. The tutorial will be revisited in Chapter 10, where shadows and text will be added. A finished revision is saved as ae2_step2.aep in the Tutorials folder on the DVD.

Nuke Tutorial 2 Revisited: Refining Color and Edge Quality

Although the greenscreen removal undertaken in Chapter 2 was fairly straightforward, the color balance of the statue and edge quality of the alpha matte can be improved.

1. Reopen the completed Nuke project file for "Nuke Tutorial 2: Working with DPX and Cineon Files." A finished version of Tutorial 2 is saved as nuke2.aep in the Chapter 2 Tutorials folder on the DVD. At this point, the two Log2Lin nodes used to convert the DPX and Cineon files are left at their default settings. You can adjust the Black (black point), White (white point), and Gamma sliders to fine-tune the color quality of the log-to-linear conversions. For example, to improve the opacity and brightness of the fire element, set the Log2Lin2 node's Gamma parameter to 1.0. To reduce the brightness and improve the contrast of the statue, set the Log2Lin1 node's White to 700 and Gamma to 0.5. (For more information on black and white points, see Chapter 2.)

2. Despite the adjustment of the Log2Lin nodes, the statue's color, saturation, and brightness do not match the background plate. To solve this, select the Keyer1 node in the Node Graph, RMB+click, and choose Color → HueCorrect. The HueCorrect node allows you to alter saturation and luminance precisely throughout the full range of hues. Open the HueCorrect1 properties panel, and select the word *r_sup* in the left column. The r_sup (red suppression) control affects red, green, and blue channels but provides a suppression curve for only the red channel. (For more information on the HueCorrect node, see Chapter 4.) LMB+drag the curve points to form a curve shape similar to the one in Figure 3.29. The heavy red cast disappears. The statue remains too bright, however. Select the word *lum* in the left column. This displays the luminance curve. Select the entire lum curve by LMB+dragging a selection box around the all the curve points. LMB+drag the selected points downward so that the curve sits at approximately 0.7 (see Figure 3.29).

3. At this stage, the statue's edge remains very sharp. Select the HueCorrect1 node, RMB+click, and choose Filter → Erode (Blur). An Erode (Blur) node is inserted between the HueCorrect1 and Premult1 nodes. Open the Erode1 node's properties panel, set the Channels menu to Alpha, and adjust the Size and Blur sliders until the statue edge is slightly softened (see Figure 3.30). To see the effect of the node, use the Alt+MMB camera control to zoom into the statue edge in the viewer. Size controls the amount of edge erosion and Blur adds its namesake to the result. If the statue is supposedly eight stories tall and several hundred yards from the camera, its edge would not be perfectly sharp. Compare the statue's edge to the edges of neighboring buildings. A Size value of 1.6 and a Blur value of 0.65 work well. Save the file under a new name. The tutorial will be revisited in Chapter 10, where shadows and text will be added. A finished revision is saved as nuke2_step2.nk in the Tutorials folder on the DVD.

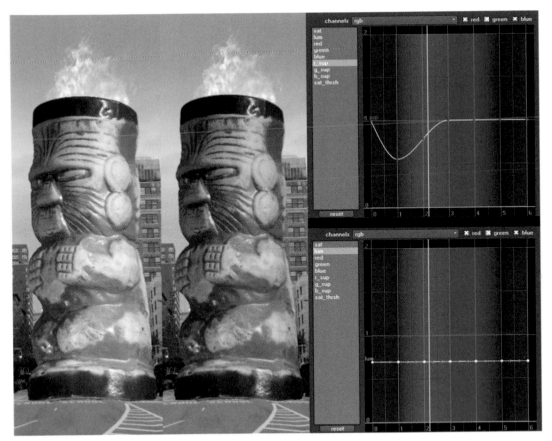

Figure 3.29 *(Left) Statue before color correction (Center) Statue after application of the HueCorrect node (Top Right) Corrected r_sup curve (Bottom Right) Corrected lum curve*

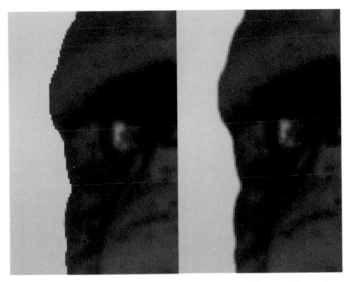

Figure 3.30 *(Left) Close-up of alpha matte edge (Right) Edge after the application of an Erode (Blur) node*

AE Tutorial 3: Removing Greenscreen

Keying out the greenscreen of a live-action shoot always has its challenges. Nevertheless, the Keylight effect offers a robust solution for the chroma key process.

1. Create a new project. Choose Composition → New Composition. In the Composition Settings dialog box, change the Preset menu to HDV/HDTV 720 29.97. Set Duration to 150 frames and Frame Rate to 30. Import the `phonecall.###.tga` sequence from the Footage folder on the DVD (see Figure 3.31).

2. LMB+drag the `phonecall.###.tga` footage from the Project panel to layer outline of the Timeline panel. Review the frames by scrubbing through the timeline. The most challenging aspect of this chroma key removal will be saving the fine hairs on the model's head. In anticipation of this, Comp 1 will be dedicated to creating a custom luma matte.

3. With the layer selected in the layer outline, choose Effect → Color Correction → Hue/Saturation. In the Effect Controls panel, reduce the Saturation slider to –100. Select the layer again and choose Effect → Color Correction → Curves. Shape the curve to match Figure 3.32. With the custom curve, you can impart greater contrast to the image, yet maintain some of the fine detail along the hair's edge. You can insert new points into the curve by LMB+clicking on the curve line. To move a point, LMB+drag it. (For more information on color correction effects, see Chapter 4.)

Figure 3.31 The greenscreen plate

Figure 3.32 (Left) Custom curve for Curves effect (Center) Detail of high-contrast result (Right) Detail of inverted result

4. With the layer selected in the layer outline, choose Effect → Channel → Invert. The RGB is inverted so that the hair becomes white and the background becomes black (see Figure 3.32).

5. Create a new composition. LMB+drag Comp 1 from the Project panel to the layer outline of the Comp 2 tab in the Timeline panel. Toggle off the Video layer switch beside the Comp 1 layer so that it is not visible in the viewer of the Composition panel. LMB+drag a new copy of the phonecall.###.tga footage from the Project panel to the Comp 2 layer outline and place it below Comp 1. With the phonecall.###.tga layer selected within Comp 2, choose Effect → Channel → Set Matte. In the Effect Controls panel, change the Take Matte From Layer menu to Comp 1. Change the Use For Matte menu to Luminance. In this situation, the Set Matte effect converts the luminance information from Comp 1's RGB channels into alpha information for the phonecall.###.tga layer.

Figure 3.33 *(Left) Detail of hair shown over white to illustrate high degree of green spill (Center) Result of Spill Suppressor (Right) Result of Brightness & Contrast and Channel Blur shown over light red background*

6. Since the hair contains a great deal of green, select the phonecall.###.tga layer and choose Effect → Keying → Spill Suppressor. Change the effect's Color To Suppress to the greenscreen color (see Figure 3.33). As a final touch for the layer, choose Effect → Color Correction → Brightness & Contrast and Effect → Blur & Sharpen → Channel Blur. Change the Brightness & Contrast effect's Brightness slider to 10 and the Contrast slider to 10. Change the Channel Blur effect's Alpha Blurriness to 4. This softens the matte edges and adjusts the edge highlights.

7. LMB+drag a new copy of the phonecall.###.tga footage from the Project panel to the Comp 2 layer outline; place it above the previous footage layer so that it's numbered 2 in the layer outline (see Figure 3.34). With the new layer selected, choose Effect → Keying → Keylight. In the Effect Controls tab, use the Screen Colour eyedropper to select the greenscreen color. The green is removed. Since the model's hair was carefully matted on its own layer in steps 5 and 6, her hair will look normal despite heavy erosion by Keylight. In order to see the composite more clearly, create a new Solid and place it at the bottom of the Comp 2 layer outline. To do so, choose Layer → New Solid, select light red as a new color in the Solid Settings dialog box, click OK, and drag the new Solid layer from the top of the layer outline to the bottom of the layer outline.

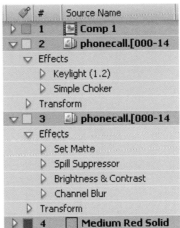

Figure 3.34 *The layer outline showing all the effects used for Comp 2*

8. In this situation, Keylight works fairly well with the remaining options set to default values. However, to fine-tune the keyer, change Keylight's View menu to Status. Status places the viewer in a special mode that indicates pixel values of the alpha matte (see Figure 3.35). White pixels are opaque. Black pixels are transparent. Gray pixels are semitransparent. Green pixels represent green chroma key spill. To reduce and remove the gray pixels appearing where the greenscreen once rested, set the Clip Black slider (in the Screen Matte section) to 50. Any key color pixel encountered with an alpha value below the slider value is assigned a new alpha value of 0. To remove gray pixels from white, opaque areas, set the Clip White slider to 80. Any foreground pixel encountered with an alpha value above the slider value is assigned a new alpha value of 1.0. To soften the edge of the alpha matte and disguise interlacing artifacts along the model's left arm, set the Screen Pre-Blur property to 5.

9. Return Keylight's View menu to Final Result. With the topmost `phonecall.###.tga` layer selected, choose Effect → Matte → Simple Choker. In the Effect Controls panel, set Choke Matte to 1.4. This erodes away the lines along the edge of the chair and the model's arms. Since the luma matte was employed on a lower layer, the erosion does not affect the detail within the hair.

10. At this point, a dark line remains along the model's left arm (see Figure 3.36). To remove the line, as well as repair the reflective arms of the chair, it will be necessary to divide the footage into multiple sections using masking tools. This will be addressed in the Chapter 7 After Effects follow-up tutorial. In the meantime, save the file under a new name. A sample project is saved as `ae3.aep` in the Tutorials folder on the DVD.

Figure 3.35 *(Top) Result of the Keylight effect with the View menu set to Status (Bottom) Same view after the adjustment of the effect's Clip Black and Clip White sliders*

Figure 3.36 *Detail of the final composite. The extraneous pieces of wall, holes in the chair arms, and dark line on the model's left arm will be removed in the Chapter 7 After Effects follow-up tutorial.*

Nuke Tutorial 3: Removing Greenscreen

Keying out the greenscreen of a live-action shoot always has its challenges. Nevertheless, the Primatte node offers a robust solution for the chroma key process. (If you are using the Nuke PLE and don't have access to the Primatte node, other keyer nodes can produce similar results.)

1. Create a new script. Choose Edit → Project Settings. Change Frame Range to 1, 150 and Fps to 30. With the Full Size Format menu, choose New. In the New Format dialog box, set Full Size W to 1280 and Full Size H to 720. Enter a name, such as **HDTV**, into the name cell and click OK.

2. In the Node Graph, RMB+click and choose Image → Read. Browse for and select the phonecall.###.tga sequence from the Footage folder on the DVD. Connect a viewer to the Read1 node to preview the greenscreen footage.

3. With the Read1 node selected, RMB+click and choose Keyer → Primatte. The Read1 node is automatically connected to the FG input of the Primatte1 node. With no nodes selected, RMB+click and choose Draw → Rectangle. Connect the BG input of the Primatte1 node to the output of the Rectangle1 node. Use Figure 3.37 as a reference. Open the Rectangle1 node's properties panel and change Area X to 1280, Area Y to 720, Area R to 0, and Area T to 0. Switch to the Color tab and change Color RGBA to 1, 0.5, 0.5, 1. The light red rectangle will allow you to check the edge quality of the alpha matte while working with Primatte.

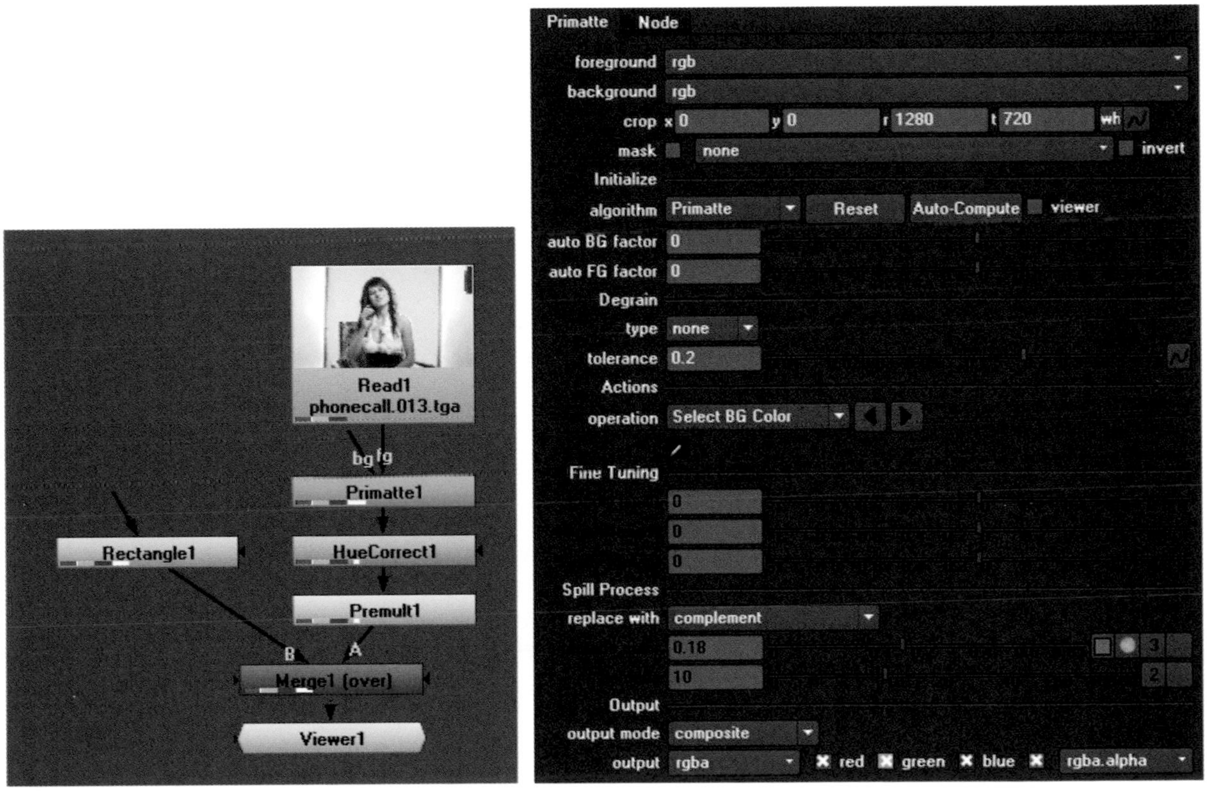

Figure 3.37 *(Left) The final node network (Right) Primatte properties panel with default settings*

Tips & Tricks: Primatte and the PLE

If you are currently using the PLE version of Nuke, the Primatte node is not supported. As such, you can use other keyers in Nuke to remove the greenscreen from the plate. For example, IBKColour and IBKGizmo nodes can produce similar results. For more information on these and other chroma key nodes, see the section "Nuke Keyers" earlier in this chapter.

Figure 3.38 *(Left) Detail of greenscreen plate (Center) Result of Primatte Auto-Compute (Right) Auto-Compute with Auto BG Factor and Auto FG factor set to −0.5*

4. Open the Primatte1 node's properties panel (see Figure 3.37). Click the Auto-Compute button. Auto-Compute undertakes the initial keying steps. It attempts to identify the chroma key color, keys out that color, and nullifies any background and foreground noise. With the phonecall.###.tga footage, Auto-Compute is successful at removing the greenscreen. However, the model's hair is eroded (see Figure 3.38).

5. To improve the result of Auto-Compute, click the Reset button (which removes the key), change Auto BG Factor and Auto FG Factor to −0.5, and click the Auto-Compute button again. This time, the greenscreen is partially removed, but the hair remains intact (see Figure 3.38). Auto BG Factor sets Auto-Compute's aggressiveness toward removing noise found in the background, while Auto FG Factor does the same for foreground noise. The higher the values, the more the noise will be suppressed but the higher the likelihood that fine details of the foreground will be lost.

6. The Auto-Compute routine is optional. If you'd like to select the key color manually, click the Reset button, change the Operation menu to Select BG Color, and select the eyedropper box below the Operation menu. (If the box is selected, it displays an eyedropper icon.) In the viewer, Ctrl+LMB+drag along a section of greenscreen. You can also Ctrl+Shift+LMB+drag to create a selection box. As soon as a color is detected, Primatte keys it out of the image. Note that the manual selection will not employ noise removal. You can employ your own noise removal by changing Type (in the Degrain section) to Small, Medium, or Large and adjusting the Tolerance setting. Higher values reduce the presence of noise and further erode the matte edges.

7. To fine-tune the matte, click the Viewer pane and press the A key. The alpha is revealed (although the alpha from the rectangle is not included). Change the Operation menu to

Clean BG Noise. (Note that the eyedropper should remain visible in the box below the Operation menu.) Ctrl+LMB+drag over the brightest pixels within the greenscreen area. Pixels with the value that you sample are assigned an alpha value of 0. You can repeat the process multiple times. It's not necessary to select every single non-black pixel. Instead, try to balance the removal of the greenscreen with the maintenance of the hair detail.

8. To improve the alpha of the foreground, change the Operation menu to Clean FG Noise. Ctrl+LMB+drag over the darkest pixels within the silhouette of the model in the viewer. Pixels with the value that you sample are assigned an alpha value of 1.0. It's not necessary to drag over every single non-white pixel, but you should strive to make the model and chair white without destroying the detail along their edges (see Figure 3.39). (It will be extremely difficult to make the arms of the chair opaque while keeping the greenscreen transparent. The chair's wood strongly reflects the greenscreen. Thus, rotoscoping will be required to repair these problem areas. Steps to undertake this are discussed in the Chapter 7 Nuke follow-up tutorial.

9. Return to an RGB view in the viewer by pressing the A key again. At this point, there is a great deal of green spill trapped in the hair (see Figure 3.40). To reduce this, change the Operation menu to Spill(-). Ctrl+LMB+drag over strands of hair that are green. The green is removed and the strand color will move toward black. Note that the use of Spill(-) significantly affects the color within the body of hair. If you need to restore the hair detail and thus return some of the spill, change the Operation menu to Spill(+) and Ctrl+LMB+drag over strands of hair that have become too black. Despite the spill operations, you may be left with hair strands that are heavily saturated with green. To remove the green cast, you can change the Primatte basic spill suppression method. By default, Primatte replaces spill color with a complement on the color wheel. However, you can change the Replace With menu (in the Spill Process section) to No Suppression, Solid Color, or Defocused Background. In this case, you can use Solid Color if you change the Replace Color RGB to a brownish-black (see Figure 3.40).

Figure 3.39 *(Top) Initial alpha matte (Bottom) Matte adjusted with the Clean BG Noise and Clean FG Noise functions*

Figure 3.40 *(Left) Green spill trapped in hair (Right) Result of Spill(-) and Solid Color suppression*

10. An alternant approach to removing the green spill is to apply a HueCorrect node, which gives you greater control and generally a better result. To do this, return the spill to its previous condition by either choosing Edit → Undo or using the Spill(+) operation. Select the Primatte1 node, RMB+click, and choose Color → HueCorrect. Open the HueCorrect1 node's properties panel. In the curve editor, click on the word *g_sup* in the left column and LMB+drag the curve point at hue position 3 (green) from a value of 1.0 to a value just above 0 (see Figure 3.41). LMB+drag the curve point at hue position 2 (pale yellow) from a value of 1.0 to a value approximately of 0.75. (Hues run horizontally on a scale of 0 to 6 and values run vertically on a scale of 0 to 2.) This effectively removes the green spill from the hair without damaging the overall hair color. (For more information on the HueCorrect node, see Chapter 4.)

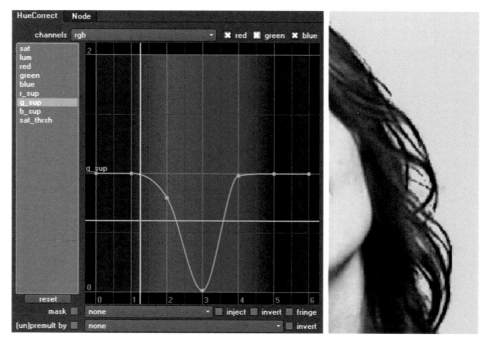

Figure 3.41 (Left) HueCorrect node's curve editor with corrected g_sup curve visible (Right) Result of HueCorrect on hair

11. To see the result of the Primatte1 node through a Merge node, you must premultiply its output. To do so, select the HueCorrect1 node, RMB+click, and choose Merge → Premult. To see the result against a colored background, select the Premult1 node, RMB+click, and choose Merge → Merge. Connect the input B of the Merge1 node to the Rectangle1 node. Attach a viewer to the Merge1 node.

12. If you've managed to refine the matte to maintain the fine details of the hair, odds are that the hair still has a semihard edge or is "lumpy" (see Figure 3.42). To solve this problem, it will be necessary to make a custom luma matte and copy channels between nodes. This will be addressed in the Chapter 4 follow-up Nuke tutorial. In the meantime, save the file under a new name. A sample Nuke script is included as nuke3.nk in the Tutorials folder on the DVD.

Figure 3.42 *Detail of the initial composite. The matte edge will be improved in the Chapter 4 Nuke follow-up tutorial.*

Interview: Johnathan R. Banta, Zoic Studios, Culver City, California

Johnathan R. Banta began creating visual effects when he was 9 years old, shortly after seeing the original *Star Wars*. He started compositing in After Effects in 1996 while at BOSS Film Studios. In 1998, he joined Sassoon Film Design as a lead compositor and digital supervisor. At present, he runs his own visual effects company, Agrapha Productions, and serves as a freelance lead compositor, CG supervisor, and matte painter at various Los Angeles visual effects houses. He's won two VES (Visual Effect Society) awards for his work with IMAX. His credits include over 70 television shows and feature films including *Titantic*, *The Big Lebowski*, *The West Wing*, *Smallville*, and *Revolution*. At the time of this writing, Johnathan was working at Zoic Studios as a lead compositor.

Zoic Studios was founded in 2002 by Chris Jones, Steve Schofield, and Loni Peristere. Zoic is known for its visual effects work for episodic television; however, they also provide services for feature films, commercials, and video games. Zoic's credit list includes the shows *Buffy the Vampire Slayer*, *Angel*, *Battlestar Galactica*, and *CSI* as well as the features *The Day After Tomorrow*, *Spiderman 2*, and *Van Helsing*.

Johnathan R. Banta at his Zoic Studios workstation

Entrance to the Zoic Studios facility in Culver City. The building was originally constructed for an architectural design firm.

(Zoic currently uses After Effects for episodic television work and Shake for feature film effects.)

LL: How often do you work with greenscreen?

JB: It's very common—more so than bluescreen.

LL: Are there any advantages to bluescreen these days?

JB: Bluescreen comes in occasionally. The problem with bluescreen is that it isn't easy to light because it tends to suck in more light. So, DPs (directors of photography) don't like it. Someone at some point convinced everyone that, because YUV [video]...had more luminance information in the green channel, greenscreen was the better way to go. The problem I personally have with greenscreen is that it is closer to human skin tone than was the blue. The logical thought process that the green record is cleaner than the blue record [is flawed]. Most greenscreen [keyers] use the blue record to pull the matte and you get the noise from the blue record anyway.... As long as I have something well lit and in a common color, I'm happy. That being said, not-very-well-lit is the standard.

LL: Was blue or greenscreen an issue with the IMAX projects you worked on?

JB: I [was] working with documentary people who would say, "This is what we have and this is what we want to do with it." It was rarely set up as a visual effects production. Secondly, you have the pressures of [location]—the wind is blowing, the generator blows out... The "fix it in post" saying, although it's a bit of a joke, it's generally part of the production process.

LL: Do you currently work with "dirty" plates; that is, ones with no bluescreen or greenscreen that nevertheless require effects work?

JB: Yes. We matchmove, rotoscope.... Because of the new radical camera approach where the camera is never locked down or it's always on a Steadicam, far [more] often we're off of our screen, so there's always roto involved. Or, the spill is too great or the lighting wasn't there.

LL: Does Zoic ever send rotoscoping work to another studio?

JB: Zoic has a facility in Canada as well. Sometimes roto goes there. For the most part, at least for the team I'm leading on *Fringe*, we make sure everybody has rotoscope ability....

LL: Would there be a disadvantage to sending roto out-of-house?

JB: As long as you have quality control, I don't see a disadvantage to that.

LL: When you remove blue or greenscreen, what tools do you use?

JB: I do anything and everything to get a pull. I'll use any procedural method or layering method that I can come up with as well as "pixel mining." I'm very adept at this personally because of what I've had to do on IMAX. I'll find whatever data I can.... Multiple color operations in different color spaces. I'll use Keylight. I'll use Primatte. I'll use whatever gets me there.

LL: Do you use scripting?

JB: I do lots of scripting. I do a lot of JavaScripting.

Additional Resources: The Full Interview

To read the full interview with Johnathan R. Banta, see the Interviews folder on the DVD.

CHAPTER four

Channel Manipulation

"Understand color and the way computers display images. Try to understand not just what buttons to push, but the underlying and relatively simple math that's happening under the hood."

—ERIK WINQUIST, visual effects supervisor, Weta Digital, Wellington, New Zealand

Channel manipulation gives *a compositor a great deal of control over every step of a composite. While alpha channels are the subject of considerable manipulation, other channels, such as color, luminance, and chrominance, are equally useful. After Effects and Nuke provide a wide array of channel manipulation effects and nodes, including those designed for channel copying and swapping, channel math operations, color space conversions, and color correction. To apply these tools successfully, it helps to understand the underlying math and modes of operations. To assist you in judging the result, histograms are an important device. To practice these concepts, this chapter includes After Effects and Nuke tutorials that integrate CG into degraded live-action footage. In addition, the Chapter 3 Nuke tutorial, which covers greenscreen removal, is revisited.*

Histograms and Tonal Ranges

An image histogram is a graphical representation of tonal distribution. Histograms plot the number of pixels that possess a particular tonal value (that is, color) by drawing a vertical bar. The horizontal scale of a histogram runs from 0 to the total number of tonal steps. Therefore, the left side of a histogram represents shadow areas. The center represents mid-tones. The right represents highlights. For an 8-bit histogram, the horizontal values run left to right from 0 to 255. The vertical scale is generally normalized to run from 0 to 1.0. Histograms may represent a single channel or offer a combined view of all channels, such as RGB.

Reading Histograms

With a histogram, you can quickly determine the quality of an image. For example, in Figure 4.1, an image is biased toward high tonal values, which indicates overexposure. In comparison, a more aesthetic exposure produces a more evenly graduated histogram.

With a low-contrast image, the pixels are concentrated in the center of the histogram. With a high-contrast image, the pixels are concentrated at the low and/or high ends. For example, in Figure 4.2, the same image of a forest is given a shorter exposure. Thus the histogram is biased toward the left. Because the sky in the upper left of the image remains overexposed, however, the last vertical line to the right of the histogram has significant height. The last line indicates pixels with a maximum allowable value. In the case of the example histogram, the value is 255, which implies that clipping is occurring.

Figure 4.1 *(Top) Overexposed digital image and matching histogram (Bottom) Properly exposed image with matching histogram. The bottom image is included as* `forest.tif` *in the Footage folder on the DVD.*

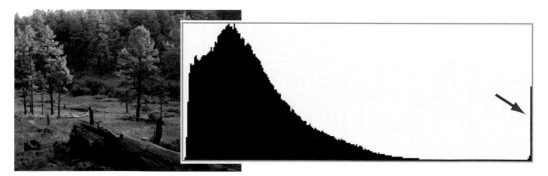

Figure 4.2 *(Left) Underexposed and thus darker image (Right) Matching histogram. Arrow points to the line indicating pixels with a value of 255.*

Histogram Tips

Keep in mind that there is no "ideal" histogram. Histograms react to the subject that is captured. An image taken at dusk naturally produces a histogram biased toward the darker values. An image of an overcast day biases the histogram toward mid-tone values. An image of an intensely sunny day with deep shadows will form a bowl-shaped histogram with concentrations of pixels to the far left and far right. Nevertheless, there a few histogram features to avoid:

Fnd Spikes If the first or last histogram line is significantly taller than neighboring lines, then clipping is occurring and potential detail is lost. For example, a spike at the far left of the histogram indicates that the darkest areas are 0 black with no variation.

Empty Areas If parts of the histogram are empty, then the image is restricted to a small tonal range. Although the image may appear to be fine, it won't be taking advantage of the full bit depth. While this is less likely to occur with a digital camera, compositing effects and nodes can induce such a histogram.

Combing A *combed* histogram is one that has regularly spaced gaps. Combing indicates that some tonal values have no pixels assigned to them. Combing occurs as a result of bit-depth conversions or the strong application of color correction effects and nodes. The only way to remove combing is to use a plug-in that's specifically designed for the task. (Combing and histogram repair plug-ins are discussed in Chapter 2, "Choosing a Color Space.") It's best to take steps to avoid excessive combing because it may lead to posterization (color banding). However, it's possible to reduce the impact of combing by applying noise and blur filters. This process is demonstrated in Chapter 8, "DI, Color Grading, Noise, and Grain."

Tonal Ranges, White Points, and Black Points

Aside from quickly examining the tonal condition of an image, histograms are valuable for the process of color grading, whereby the color of footage is altered or adjusted in anticipation of delivery to a particular media, such as motion picture film or broadcast television. One important aspect of color grading is the establishment of a *white point* and a *black point*. A white point defines the value that is considered white. The term *white* is subjective in that human visual perception considers the brightest point in a brightly lit area to be white and all other colors are referenced to that point. A white point can be neutral, having equal red, green, or blue values, or it can be biased toward a particular channel. If a white point contains an unequal ratio of red, green, and blue, it may be perceived as white by the viewer nonetheless. To make the grading process more difficult, different media demand different black and white points for the successful transfer of color information. Note that white points and black points are often referred to as white references and black references when discussing logarithmic to linear conversions; for more information on such conversions, see Chapter 2. Color grading and the related process of digital intermediates are examined more closely in Chapter 8.

In many cases, the white point of a digital image is at the high end of the scale. With a generic, normalized scale, the value is 1.0. With an 8-bit scale, the value is 255. However, if the subject does not include any naturally bright objects, the white point can easily be a lower value, such as 200. Color correction effects and nodes allow you to force a new white point on an image and thus remap the overall tonal range. If the white point is 255, you can reestablish it as 225. The tonal range is thus changed from 0–255 to 0–225. A black point functions in the same manner, but establishes what is considered *black*. If a black point is 25 and a white point is 225, then the tonal range is 25–225.

Working with Channel Manipulation

A *channel* is a specific attribute of a digital image. Common channels include color and alpha. Whereas many compositing operations are applied to the red, green, and blue channels simultaneously, it often pays to apply an operation to a specific channel, such as the red channel or alpha channel.

Channel Manipulation in AE

After Effects offers 13 channel operation effects and 26 color correction effects as part of the Professional bundle. These are accessible via the Effect → Channel and Effect → Color Correction menus. The most useful effects are discussed in the following sections.

Channel Shifters

With Set Matte, Shift Channels, Set Channels, and Channel Combiner effects, you can move or copy one channel to another within a layer or between layers.

Set Matte

The Set Matte effect allows you to apply the value information of a channel or channels in one layer to the alpha channel of the same or different layer. This is particularly useful when an alpha matte is needed for a layer that currently does not possess one. For example, in Figure 4.3, a carved mask has overexposed highlights along its left forehead and cheek. In order to restore some color detail, two composites are set up. Comp 1 applies Levels and Fast Blur effects to isolate the highlights in the RGB. Comp 2 has the untouched footage as a lower layer and Comp 1 as an upper layer. Since Comp 1 does not have alpha information, a Set Matte effect is applied to it. The Take Matte From Layer menu defines the source used to create the alpha matte. In this example, it's set to Comp 1. The Use Matte For menu determines how the source will be used to generate the alpha matte. Options range from each of the color channels to alpha, luminance, lightness, hue, and saturation. In this example, the menu is set to Luminance, which produces a semitransparent matte. (For an additional example of the Set Matte effect, see "AE Tutorial 3: Removing Greenscreen" in Chapter 3, "Interpreting Mattes and Creating Alpha.")

Figure 4.3 *(Top Left) Unadjusted footage of mask (Top Center) Curves effect applied to isolate highlights (Top Right) Alpha matte generated by Set Matte effect (Bottom Left) Set Matte settings (Bottom Right) Final composite. A sample After Effects project is saved as* set_matte.aep *in the Tutorials folder on the DVD.*

Shift Channels and Set Channels

The Shift Channels effect replaces one channel with a different channel from the same layer. For example, in Figure 4.4, an image is given a surreal color palette by assigning the red, green, and blue channels to lightness, luminance, and green information respectively.

The Set Channels effect takes Shift Channels one step further by allowing you to define a different source for each of the RGBA channels. The sources can be the same layer or a different layer.

Figure 4.4 (Left) Unadjusted image (Right) The result of the Shift Channels effect (Bottom) Shift Channels settings. A sample After Effects project is saved as shift_channels.aep *in the Tutorials folder on the DVD.*

Tips & Tricks: Brightness, Lightness, Luminance, and Luma

Although *brightness*, *lightness*, *luminance*, and *luma* are often used interchangeably, they are not the same quality. In scientific terms, *brightness* refers to the physiological perception of light reflected from an object. As such, brightness is non-quantitative. However, as it's used in the realm of computer graphics, it refers to the relative value of a pixel on a scale from 0 to its bit-depth limit. The term *lightness* also refers to the relative value of the pixel. Lightness is employed by the HSL color space. The HSV color space exchanges lightness for *value*. The HSB color space exchanges lightness for brightness. HSL, HSV, and HSB are related color spaces that attempt to describe perceptual color relationships.

In scientific terms, *luminance* describes the amount of light that is emitted from a particular area defined by a three-dimensional angle. In the realm of video and computer graphics, *luminance* refers to the brightness of a channel as it is biased for human perception and the physical design of display devices. The human visual system is less sensitive to variations in color than it is in variations in the amount of emitted light. Hence, one third of video bandwidth is set aside for the Y luminance channel. In addition, the human visual system does not react equally to red, green, and blue primary colors. Thus luminance values, as they are employed for digital video and computer graphics, are generally reduced to the following formula, where Y represents luminance:

$$Y = 0.3 \text{ red} + 0.59 \text{ green} + 0.11 \text{ blue}$$

This is a rounded-off version of the Rec. 601 specification (also known as CCIR 601), which was established by the International Telecommunication Union. *Luma*, in contrast, is the gamma-corrected sum of the red, green, and blue channels. To differentiate luminance from luma, luma carries the prime symbol ', as in Y'. For example, the Rec. 709 standard is based on the following luma formula:

$$Y' = 0.2126 \text{ red}' + 0.7152 \text{ green}' + 0.0722 \text{ blue}'$$

The word *luma* is often used as shorthand to describe a luminance matte, as in *luma matte*. A luma matte utilizes the brightest information of an image to determine what is opaque and transparent in the alpha channel.

Ultimately, the lightness or brightness of a pixel is equally influenced by all three RGB channels, while the luminance or luma of a pixel is influenced by green and red more heavily than it is by blue.

Channel Combiner

With the Channel Combiner effect, you can convert RGB color space to HLS or YUV color space. This is useful for any operation that needs to operate on a lightness, luminance, or chrominance channel. For example, to convert RGB to YUV, change the From menu to RGB To YUV. To examine the Y channel, change the viewer's Show Channel menu to Red (see Figure 4.5). The U channel is shown by switching to Green. The V channel is shown by switching to Blue. With YUV space, the Y channel encodes luminance, the U channel encodes the blue chroma component, and the V channel encodes the red chroma component. The green chroma component is indirectly carried by the Y channel. (For more information on YUV color space, see Chapter 3.)

In addition, you can premultiply an unpremultiplied layer by changing the From menu to Straight To Premultiplied. Much like the Shift Channels effect, you can also replace one channel with a different channel from the same layer. To do so, change the From menu to a channel you wish to borrow from and change the To menu to the channel you wish to overwrite. The Channel Combiner is demonstrated further in "AE Tutorial 4: Matching CG to Degraded Footage" later in this chapter.

Channel Math Operators

With the Arithmetic and Calculations effects, you can apply standard math operations to the RGB values of a layer.

Arithmetic

With the Arithmetic effect, A is the current pixel value of a channel and B is the value determined by the Red Value, Blue Value, or Green Value slider. The Operator menu sets the math operator to be used with A and B. For example, if Operator is set to Subtract and Red Value is set to 100, the following happens to a pixel with a red channel value of 150:

Figure 4.5 (Top) Y luminance channel (Center) U blue chroma channel (Bottom) V red chroma channel. Note that the V channel contains the most noise.

A - B = C

150 - 100 = 50

Thus, the new red channel pixel value is C, or 50. Note that the effect uses an 8-bit scale. This results in a reduction of red in the image and a relative increase of green and blue. As a second example, in Figure 4.6, the Operator menu is set to Difference, Red Value is set to 88, and Green Value is set to 162. Video footage of a lamp thus takes on psychedelic colors.

In this case, a pixel with a red value of 255 and a green value of 85 undergoes the following math:

```
absolute value of (255 - 88) = 167 (red)

absolute value of (85 - 162) = 77 (green)
```

The Difference operator takes the absolute value of A - B. Hence, the result is never negative. To ensure that none of the operators produce negative or superwhite values, the effect includes a Clip Result Values check box in the Effect Controls panel. If the check box is deselected, values above 255 are "wrapped around." For example, a value of 260 becomes 5.

The Operator menu offers 13 different operators. Add, Min, Max, Multiply, and Screen function like their blending mode counterparts (see Chapter 3 for descriptions). The mathematical equivalents of the remaining operators follow:

And:	If B < A then C = 0 else C = A
Or:	If B < A then C = A + B;
	If B > A then C = B
Xor:	If A = B then C = 0;
	If B < A then C = A + B;
	If B > A then C = B - A
Block Above:	If A > B then C = 0
Block Below:	If A < B then C = 0
Slice:	If A > B then C = 1.0 else C = 0

Calculations

With the Calculations effect, you can apply blending modes to specific channels of different layers. For example, in Figure 4.7 a desert is blended with an abstract background (named `ground.tif`). The chosen blending mode, set by the Blending Mode menu, is Color Dodge. However, the blend only occurs between the red channel of the desert layer and the RGB of the abstract background layer.

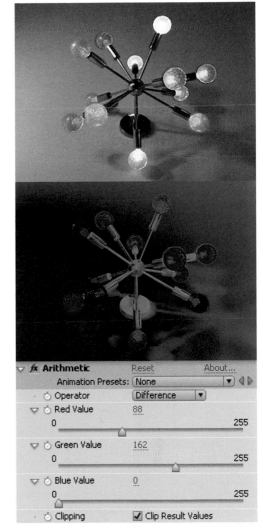

Figure 4.6 *(Top) Unadjusted footage of lamp (Center) Result of the Arithmetic effect (Bottom) Arithmetic settings. A sample After Effects project is saved as* `arithmetic.aep` *in the Footage folder on the DVD.*

Figure 4.7 *(Left) Desert image and abstract background blended with the Calculations effect (Right) Calculations settings. A sample After Effects project is saved as* `calculations.aep` *in the Footage folder on the DVD.*

With blending mode math, the layer to which the Calculations effect is applied is layer A. You can choose layer B by selecting a layer name from the Second Layer menu. The channels used for A are set by the Input Channel menu. The channels used for B are set by the Second Layer Channel menu. The strength of layer B's influence is set by the Second Layer slider.

Channel Color Correctors

The Brightness & Contrast, Curves, Levels, Alpha Levels, Gamma/Pedestal/Gain, Hue/Saturation, Color Balance, and Broadcast Safe effects manipulate the value information of one or more channels. The effects, found in the Effect → Color Correction menu, can have a significant impact on value distribution and thus the shape of an image histogram. In this section, the histogram display of the Levels effect is used to demonstrate these changes.

Brightness & Contrast

The Brightness & Contrast effect shifts, stretches, or compresses tonal ranges. The Brightness slider value is added or subtracted to every pixel of the layer. For example, if Brightness is set to 10, 10 is added. If Brightness is set to –20, 20 is subtracted. Positive Brightness values have the effect of brightening the image while sliding the entire tonal range to the right of the histogram (see Figure 4.8). Negative Brightness values have the effect of darkening the image while sliding the entire tonal range to the left of the histogram. The results are clipped, so negative and superwhite values are not permitted.

Positive Contrast values stretch the tonal range. This has the effect of lowering values below the 0.5 median level and raising values above the 0.5 median level. Resulting values below 0 and above 1.0 are discarded. In addition, the higher the Contrast value, the greater the degree of combing that occurs (see Figure 4.8). As discussed in Chapter 2, combing can create unwanted posterization (color banding). Note that 8-bit, 16-bit, and 32-bit images all suffer from combing if the tonal range is stretched by the Contrast slider. However,

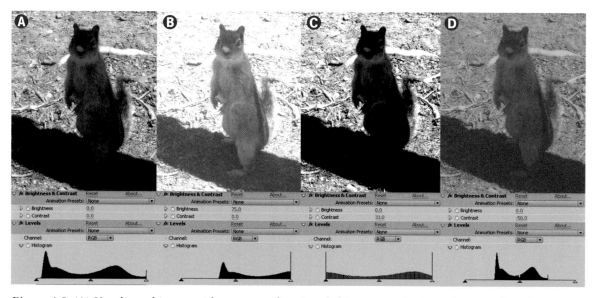

Figure 4.8 (A) Unadjusted image with corresponding Levels histogram. (B) A Brightness value of 75 pushes the tonal values to the right of the histogram. (C) A Contrast value of 33 stretches the tonal range, which leads to the loss of low and high values and a combing of mid-range values. (D) A Contrast value of –50 compresses the tonal range, leaving no low or high values. The image is included as `squirrel.tif` in the Footage folder on the DVD.

posterization is more noticeable with an 8-bit image since there are fewer tonal steps to begin with. When the stretching occurs, a limited number of tonal steps are spread throughout the tonal range, which creates empty gaps in the histogram.

Negative Contrast values compress the tonal range. This has the effect of raising values below the 0.5 median level and lowering values above the 0.5 median level. You can equate the value of the Contrast slider with a percentage that the tonal range is stretched or compressed. For example, if the Contrast slider is set to −50, the tonal range is compressed down to 50%, or half its original size (see Figure 4.8). If the tonal range originally ran from 0 to 255, the new tonal range runs approximately from 64 to 192.

Curves

The Curves effect allows you to remap input values by adjusting a tonal response curve that has 256 possible points. By default, the curve runs from left to right and from 0 to a normalized 1.0. The horizontal scale represents the input tonal values and the vertical scale represents the output tonal values. The functionality is similar to the remapping undertaken by a LUT curve (see Chapter 2). If the curve is not adjusted, an input value of 0 remains 0, an input value of 0.5 remains 0.5, and so on. If you move the start or end points or add new points and reposition them, however, new values are output. (The curve start point sits at the lower left, and the curve end point sits at the upper right.)

For example, you can compress the tonal range toward the high end of the scale by pulling the start point straight up (see Figure 4.9). You can stretch the low end of the tonal range while clipping the high end by moving the end point to the left. You can approximate a gamma function by adding a point to the curve center and pulling it down. You can approximate an inverse gamma function (1 / gamma) by adding a point to the curve center and pulling it up. You can add contrast to the layer by inserting two points and moving the lower point toward 1.0 and the upper point toward 0.

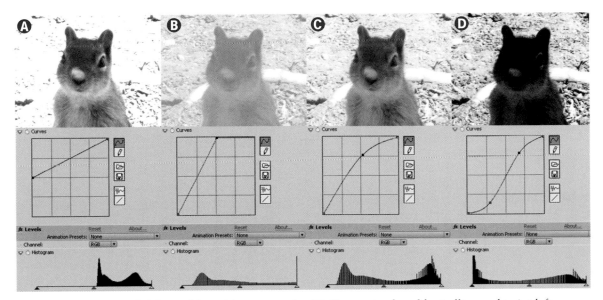

Figure 4.9 *(A) Image brightened by raising start point (B) Contrast reduced by pulling end point left (C) Inverse gamma curve approximated by inserting new point (D) Contrast increased by creating "S" curve with two new points*

To insert a new point on the curve, LMB+click on the curve. To move a point, LMB+ drag the point. To reset the curve to its default state, click the Line button. To smooth the curve and freeze current points, click the Smooth button. The Smooth button, which sits above the Line button, features an icon with a jagged line. To freehand draw the curve shape, select the Pencil button and LMB+drag in the graph area. You can save a curve and reload it into a different instance of the Curves effect by using the File Save and Open buttons. The Curves effect can operate on RGB simultaneously or on an individual channel, such as red or alpha; this is determined by the Channel menu. Note that extreme curve manipulation may lead to excessive posterization or solarization. (Solarization occurs by blending positive and negative versions of an image together.)

Levels and Alpha Levels

As demonstrated, the Levels effect features a histogram. You can adjust the histogram with Input Black, Output Black, Input White, Output White, and Gamma properties (see Figure 4.10). The adjustment is applied to either RGB or individual color and alpha channels, as determined by the Channel menu. Any input values less than the Input Black value are clamped to the Output Black value. If the Input Black value is 0.2, the Output Black value is 0.3, and if a pixel has an input value of 0.1, the pixel receives an output value of 0.3. Ultimately, the Output Black slider establishes the black point of the image (see the section "Tonal Ranges, White Points, and Black Points" earlier in this chapter). Any input values greater than the value of Input White slider are clamped to the Output White value. If the project is set to 8-bit, the maximum clamp value is 255. If the project is set to 16-bit (which is actually 15-bit with one extra step), the maximum clamp value is 32,768. The Output White slider establishes the white point of the image. (Note that the histogram only indicates 256 steps regardless of the project bit depth.) The Gamma slider sets the exponent of the power curve normally used to make the image friendlier for monitor viewing (see Chapter 2 for more information on gamma). If Gamma is set to 1.0, it has no effect on the image. If Gamma is lowered, mid- and high-tones are pulled toward the low end of the tonal range. If Gamma is raised above 1.0, the low and mid-tones are pulled toward the high end of the tonal range. A low Gamma value produces a high-contrast, dark image. A high Gamma value produces a washed-out, bright image.

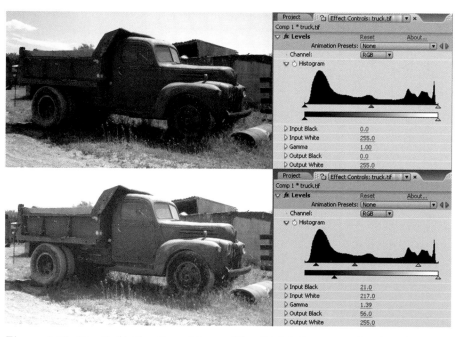

Figure 4.10 *(Top Left) Unadjusted image (Top Right) Corresponding Levels settings (Bottom Left) Image adjusted to bring out detail in shadows (Bottom Right) Corresponding Levels settings. The image is included as* truck.tif *in the Footage folder on the DVD.*

In addition, you can interactively drag the handles below the histogram. The top-left handle controls the Input Black value. The top-right handle controls the Input White value. The top-center handle controls the Gamma value. The two handles below the black and white bar set the Output Black and Output White values. Moving the Input Black and Input White handles toward each other discards low and high values, stretches the mid-tones to fill the tonal range, and leads to combing. Moving the Output Black and Output White handles toward each other compresses the tonal range and leaves the ends of the histogram empty. Note that changing the various sliders or handles does not change the histogram shape, which always represents the tonal range of the input layer *before* the application of the Levels effect. If you wish to see the impact of the Levels effect on the image histogram, you can add a second iteration of the Levels effect and leave its settings with default values.

The Levels (Individual Controls) effect is available if you want to apply separate Input Black, Output Black, Input White, Output White, and Gamma settings for each channel.

The Alpha Levels effect (found in the Effect → Channel menu), allows you to adjust an alpha channel with Input Black Level, Output Black Level, Input White Level, Output White Level, and Gamma sliders. Its functionality is similar to the Levels effect, although it lacks a histogram and has no impact on the RGB channels.

Gamma/Pedestal/Gain

The Gamma/Pedestal/Gain effect offers yet another means to adjust an image's tonal response curve. It splits its controls for the red, green, and blue channels but does not affect alpha. The Red/Green/Blue Pedestal sliders set the minimum threshold for output pixel values. Raising these slider values compresses the tonal range toward the high end. Lowering these slider values stretches the tonal range toward the low end, thus clipping the lowest values. The Red/Green/Blue Gain sliders set the maximum output pixel values. Lowering these slider values compresses the tonal range toward the low end. Raising these slider values stretches the tonal range toward the high end, thus clipping the highest values. The Red/Green/Blue Gamma sliders operate in the same manner as the Gamma slider carried by the Levels effect. The Black Stretch slider, on the other hand, pulls low pixel values toward median values for all channels. High Black Stretch values brighten dark areas. Since you can adjust each of the three color channels separately with the Gamma/Pedestal/Gain effect, you can alter the overall color balance. For example, in Figure 4.11, the colors are shifted to dusklike lighting.

Figure 4.11 (Left) *Image adjusted to emulate the lighting found at dusk (Right) Corresponding Gamma/ Pedestal/Gain settings. A sample After Effects project is included as* `gain.aep` *in the Tutorials folder on the DVD.*

Hue/Saturation

The Hue/Saturation effect operates on the HSL color wheel. It allows you to offset the image colors by interactively adjusting the Master Hue control. For example, if Master Hue is set to 120°, the primary red of a fire hydrant becomes primary green (see Figure 4.12). Setting it to 240° turns the hydrant blue. In terms of the resulting hues, 360° is the same as 0°. However, in order to support smooth keyframe animation, you can make multiple revolutions of the control. The revolutions are tracked as 1×, 2×, 3×, and so on.

Figure 4.12 *(Left) Unadjusted image of hydrant (Center) Master Hue set to 120° (Right) Corresponding Hue/Saturation settings. The sample After Effects project is included as* `hue_saturation.aep` *in the Tutorials folder on the DVD.*

Figure 4.13 *(Top) Master Saturation slider set to 50. (Center) Master Saturation slider set to 100. Note the appearance of noise and compression artifacts. (Bottom) A colorized version using a blue Colorize hue.*

With the Hue/Saturation effect, you can control the image saturation. (As mentioned in Chapter 3, *saturation* is the colorfulness of a color in reference to its lightness.) A high Master Saturation value, such as 75, creates a greater contrast between the RGB channels of a pixel. As a result, the dominant channels, whether they are red, green, or blue, are pushed closer to a value of 1.0 (normalized) or 255 (8-bit). The less-dominant channels are pushed closer to 0. For example, a pixel near the top of the hydrant in the unadjusted hydrant footage (seen at the left of Figure 4.12) has an RGB value of 158, 66, 85. This equates to a ratio of roughly 2.4:1:1.3 where the red channel is 2.4 times as intense as the green channel and the blue channel is 1.3 times as intense as the green channel. If the Saturation slider is set to 50, the pixel's RGB values change to 203, 20, 58 (see the top of Figure 4.13). Thus, the red channel becomes roughly 10 times as intense as the green channel and the blue channel becomes 2.9 times as intense as the green channel.

Master Saturation values less than 0 reduce the contrast between red, green, and blue channels. A Master Saturation value of –100 makes the balance between red, green, and blue channels equal, which in turn creates a grayscale image. A pixel at the top of the hydrant would therefore have a value of 112, 112, 112.

The Hue/Saturation effect offers a Colorize check box. If this is selected, the Master sliders are ignored. Instead, the image is tinted with a hue set by the Colorize Hue control (see the bottom of Figure 4.13). The tinting process increases or decreases channel values in preference of the set hue. For every 25% increase in the Colorize Saturation value, the channels increase or decrease in value by 25%. If Colorize Hue is primary red (0°), green (120°), or blue (240°), only a single channel is increased while the other two are decreased. However, if the hue is a secondary color, two channels are increased while the remaining channel is decreased. For example, a yellow hue (60°) increases the red and green channels while reducing the blue channel. If the hue is a tertiary color, one channel is increased, one channel is left at its input value, and one channel is decreased. For example, an orange hue (30°) increases the red, leaves the green static, and decreases the blue. (For more information on primary, secondary, and tertiary colors, see Chapter 2.)

Color Balance

The Color Balance effect shifts the balance between red, green, and blue channels. Balance sliders are provided for each channel and for three tonal zones (Shadow, Midtone, and Highlight). Negative Shadow slider values stretch the channel's tonal range toward the low end, clipping the lowest pixel values. Positive Shadow slider values shift the channel's tonal range toward the high end. Negative Midtone slider values shift the mid-tones toward the low-end without clipping. Positive Midtone slider values shift the mid-tones toward the high end without clipping. Negative Highlight slider values stretch the channel's tonal range toward the low end without clipping. Positive Highlight slider values shift the channel's tonal range toward the high end, clipping the highest pixel values.

Color Balance (HLS) and Exposure

The Color Balance (HLS) effect operates in a similar fashion to the Hue/Saturation effect. The Hue control offsets the layer colors. The Lightness property sets the brightness and the Saturation property sets its namesake.

The Exposure effect simulates an f-stop change. Although it is designed to adjust 32-bit high-dynamic range images (HDRIs), you can apply the effect to 8- or 16-bit layers. The Exposure slider sets the f-stop value, the Offset slider offsets the Exposure value, and the Gamma slider applies a gamma curve. For additional information, see Chapter 12, "Advanced Techniques."

Broadcast Colors

The Broadcast Colors effect reduces values to a level considered safe for broadcast television. The amplitude of NTSC video is expressed in IRE units, as is the effect's Maximum Signal Amplitude slider. Values between 7.5 and 100 IRE units are considered safe for analog NTSC broadcast as they do not cause color artifacts. The IRE range is equivalent to an 8-bit range of 16 to 235. (See Chapter 2 for information on IRE units and After Effects support of 16–235 color profiles.) Values between 0 and 100 IRE units are considered safe for digital ATSC and DVB HDTV broadcast. You can choose a maximum IRE level by changing the Maximum Signal Amplitude slider. You can choose to reduce the image luminance, reduce the saturation, or key out unsafe areas by changing the How To Make Color Safe menu.

Tips & Tricks: The Levels Effect

You can use the Levels effect to enforce video broadcast safe colors by setting the Output White slider to 235.

Channel Manipulation in Nuke

Nuke offers over two dozen channel operation, color correction, and math nodes. These are accessible via the Channel and Color menus. Before the most useful nodes are examined, however, a closer look at Nuke's channel and node controls is needed.

Channel and Node Controls

The majority of Nuke nodes carry Red, Green, and Blue channel check boxes. These are displayed beside the Channels menu (see Figure 4.14). When a channel check box is deselected, the channel is no longer affected. This is indicated by the Nuke node box itself. If the channel line symbol is short, it's not affected by the node. In other words, the channel is passed through the node without any processing. If the channel line symbol is long, it is affected by the node. An Alpha check box is also included, but only if the Channels menu is set to Rgba or Other Layers → Alpha.

At the same time, the majority of Nuke nodes carry a Mix slider (see Figure 4.15). Mix fulfills its namesake by allowing you to blend the output of the node with the unaffected input. This provides a quick means by which you can reduce the influence of a node without changing its specific sliders or menus.

Figure 4.14 *(Top) Channel check boxes (Bottom) Node box showing channel lines. Long lines for green and blue channels indicate that the channels are affected. Short lines for red and alpha channels indicate that the channels are unaffected. (Although not pictured here, the node box will include channel lines for any existing depth or UV channel.)*

Figure 4.15 *Mix slider*

Channel Shifters

The Copy, ChannelMerge, ShuffleCopy, and Shuffle nodes provide the ability to transfer channels for a single input or between multiple inputs.

Copy

The Copy node allows you to copy one to four channels from one node to another node. The Copy node's input A is designed for connection to the node providing the channel information. The Copy node's input B is designed for connection to the node receiving the channel information. For example, in Figure 4.16, the green channel from an image of the moon is transferred and applied to the blue channel of a fireworks image.

For an additional example of the Copy node in a network, see "Nuke Tutorial 3 Revisited: Creating a Luma Matte" later in this chapter.

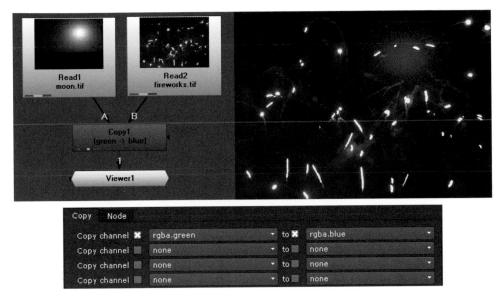

Figure 4.16 (Top Left) Copy node network (Top Right) Final result (Bottom) Copy node settings. A sample Nuke script is included as copy.nk *in the Tutorials folder on the DVD.*

ChannelMerge

The ChannelMerge node is able to merge two channels. It provides a number of standard merging operations, such as plus, minus, multiply, min, and max. As an example, in Figure 4.17, two variations of a CG render are merged together. The first render is in grayscale and is connected to input A of the ChannelMerge node. The second render is in color and is connected to input B of the ChannelMerge node. The ChannelMerge node takes the red channel from A and multiplies it by the green channel of B.

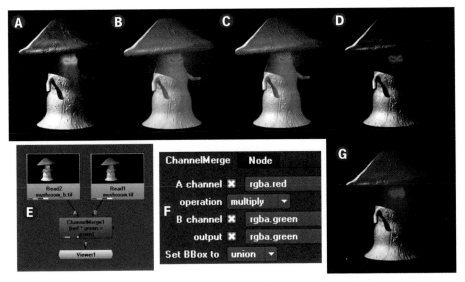

Figure 4.17 (A) Grayscale render (B) Color render (C) Color render's green channel before the application of ChannelMerge (D) Color render's green channel after the application of ChannelMerge (E) Node network (F) ChannelMerge settings (G) Output of ChannelMerge node. A sample Nuke script is included as channelmerge.nk *in the Tutorials folder on the DVD.*

ShuffleCopy and Shuffle

With the ShuffleCopy node, you can rearrange or swap channels between two input nodes and have the result output. Input 1 is fed into the In menu and input 2 is fed into the In2 menu (see the top of Figure 4.18). By default, the node uses the RGBA channels of the inputs; however, you can switch the In and In2 menu to another channel, such as alpha.

You can break the ShuffleCopy properties panel into four sections: InA, In2A, InB, and In2B (see the top of Figure of 4.18). If a channel check box is selected in an In section, then that channel is used for the output, but only for the channel for which it's selected. For example, if the lowest red check box in the InA section is selected, then the red channel is fed into the alpha channel of the output (see the bottom of Figure 4.18).

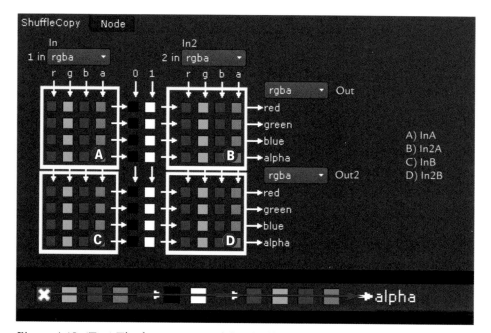

Figure 4.18 *(Top) The four sections of the ShuffleCopy properties panel (Bottom) A red channel check box, in the InA section, is sent to the output's alpha channel.*

By selecting various check boxes in the InA, In2A, InB, and In2B sections, you can quickly rearrange channels. For example, in Figure 4.19, two Read nodes are connected to a ShuffleCopy node. The ShuffleCopy node's check boxes are selected so that the output's red channel is taken from Read2's red channel, the output's green channel is taken from Read1's red channel, and the output's blue channel is taken from Read1's blue channel. Thus the fireworks image loaded into the Read2 node provides only red channel information. In the meantime, the moon image loaded into Read1 has its channels scrambled. This results in red, low-intensity fireworks over a cyan moon.

The ShuffleCopy node's output is ultimately determined by the two output menus, named Out and Out2 (see the top of Figure 4.18). By default, the Out2 menu is set to None. In this case, the InB and In2B sections are nonfunctional. If the Out2 menu is set to specific channels, then the InB and In2B sections become active and add additional processing to the original inputs. If the Out2 channel matches the Out menu, however, Out2 overrides Out. If the Out2 channel is different, then both outputs are able to provide up to eight processed channels. For example, if Out is set to Rgb and Out2 is set to Alpha, the InA and In2A sections create the color while the InB and in2B sections create the alpha information. For example, in Figure 4.20, the output red channel is derived from the green channel of input 2. The output green channel is derived from the green channel of input 1. The output blue channel is derived from the blue channel of input 2. The output alpha channel is derived from the green channel of input 1. Note that the ShuffleCopy node has only one output when connected in a node network. The single output can carry up to eight channels so long as the channels are unique.

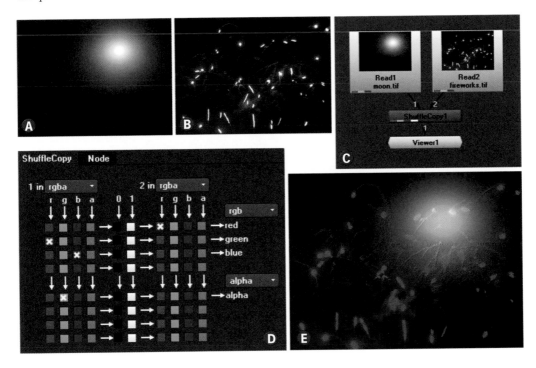

Figure 4.19 (A) Long-exposure shot of moon (B) Footage of fire-works (C) ShuffleCopy node connected to Read nodes (D) Shuf-fleCopy properties panel (E) Resulting composite. A sample Nuke script is saved as `shufflecopy.nk` in the Tutorials folder on the DVD.

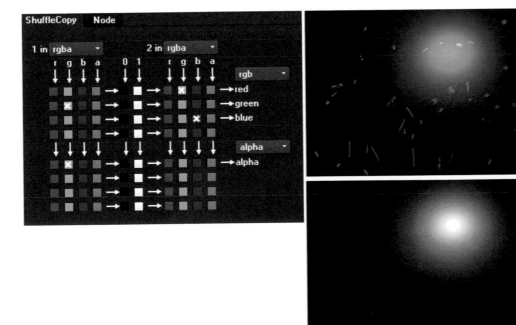

Figure 4.20 (Left) ShuffleCopy settings with Out set to Rgb and Out2 set to Alpha (Top Right) RGB result (Bottom Right) Alpha result. A sample Nuke script is included as `shufflecopy_2.nk` in the Tutorials folder on the DVD.

Aside from Rgb, Rgba, and Alpha, you can set the Out and Out2 menus to Depth, Motion, Forward, Backward, or Mask layers (for example, Other Layers → Depth). Depth is designed for Z-buffer renders and provides a Z channel. Motion is designed for motion vector information and comes with two sets of UV channels: one for forward and one for backward motion blur. The Forward layer carries the forward UV portion of motion vector information. The Backward layer carries the backward UV portion of motion vector information. The Mask layer is designed to read a matte channel that is separate from standard alpha. Depth, Motion, Forward, Backward, and Mask layers and channels are discussed in more detail in Chapter 9, "Integrating Render Passes."

To create a total of eight output channels with the ShuffleCopy node, set one output menu to Rgba and one output menu to Motion. Otherwise, you will need to create a custom layer that carries four channels. To do so, set the Out or Out2 menu to New. In the New Layer dialog box, change the top four Channels menus to channels of your choice.

In addition, ShuffleCopy offers two "constant" channels. These are labeled *0* and *1* in the center of the properties panel. If a 0 check box is selected, it supplies the corresponding output channel a value of 0. If a 1 check box is selected, it supplies the corresponding output channel a maximum value (such as 1.0 on a normalized scale).

The Shuffle node looks identical to the ShuffleCopy node. However, it's designed for only one input. Thus, it's appropriate for rearranging and swapping channels within a single image.

Tips & Tricks: Adding an Alpha Channel

The Shuffle node is useful for adding an alpha channel to a node that does not possess one. To add alpha to a node, connect its output to a Shuffle node, open the Shuffle node's properties panel, and select the *1* constant check box that corresponds to the alpha output. (The check box is the fourth white check box from the top of the *1* column.)

Color Space Converters

The Colorspace, HueShift, and HSVTool nodes are able to convert between color spaces.

The Colorspace Node

The Colorspace node converts an input from one color space to another. Its In set of menus establish the interpretation of the incoming data and its Out menus determine the outgoing conversion. The leftmost column of the menus sets the color space (see Figure 4.21).

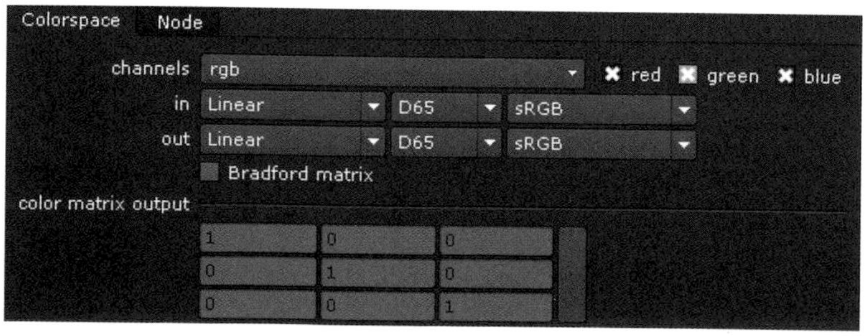

Figure 4.21 *Colorspace properties panel*

If the In menu is set to default Linear, the input data is accepted as is with no filtering. If the In menu is set to a specific space, then the program assumes the data matches that space. For instance, if the menu is set to HSV, the program interprets the red channel as hue, the blue channel as saturation, and the green channel as value.

By default, any image or image sequence imported into Nuke has a LUT applied to it. The LUT is determined by the LUT tab of the Project Settings properties panel. For example, 8- and 16-bit images have a sRGB LUT applied to them. You can override this behavior when preparing to use the Colorspace node by changing the Read node's Colorspace menu to Linear. Also note that the viewer uses a display LUT by default, which may interfere with the proper viewing of the Colorspace output. To avoid this, you can change the Display_ LUT menu to Linear as well.

If the Out menu is set to default Linear, then the node is disabled. However, if the Out menu is set to one of the other 14 color spaces, the channels are reorganized, a log-to-linear conversion occurs, a LUT is applied, or a gamma curve is applied. For example, if L*a*b* is chosen, the RGB channels are converted to an L* luminance channel and a* and b* chroma channels. If Cineon is chosen, an internal linear-to-log conversion occurs. If Rec709 (~1.95) is chosen, the Rec709 LUT is applied utilizing a gamma of 1.95.

Other color spaces, which have not yet been discussed, include YPbPr, CIE-LCH, CIE-XYZ, and CIE-Yxy. YPbPr is an analog variation of Y'CbCr. CIE-LCH is a lightness-saturation-hue-based color space. CIE-XYZ was defined in 1931 and continues to serve as the basis for modern RGB color spaces. X, Y, and Z correspond to tristimulus values that approximate red, green, and blue primary colors. (*Tristimulus values* are the amounts of three primary colors in a 3-component additive color system that are needed to represent a particular color.) CIE-Yxy is formulated from CIE-XYZ color space and is commonly represented by a horseshoe or "shoe sole" chromaticity chart (see the next section for an example). With CIE-Yxy, Y represents luminance, while x and y are coordinates that identify the hue/chroma component. *Hue* is the main property of a color. Specific hues correlate to specific wavelengths of light. Colors with primary hues are given names such as *red*, *green*, and *blue*. *Chroma* is the colorfulness of a color in reference to perceived white (which varies with the environment). *Colorfulness* is the degree to which a color is different from gray at a given luminance. Note that CIE-Yxy is often written as CIE-xyY.

The second column of menus controls the illuminant used. *Illuminants* are standardized profiles that allow images produced under different lighting conditions to be accurately compared. An illuminant profile contains numeric information that represents the spectral quality of a specific light source. Common profiles have been established by the CIE (International Commission on Illumination). When an RGB-based color space is defined, the coordinates of color primaries and a white point (white reference) are established. For example, sRGB color space uses the D65 illuminant to determine the location of the white point. The D65 illuminant replicates midday sun and has a correlated color temperature (CCT) of just over 6500 K. In general, the illuminant menu should match the corresponding color space. For instance, Wide Gamut RGB uses the D50 illuminant (5003 K) and NTSC RGB uses the C illuminant (6774 K).

The third column of menus establishes the color primaries used in the color space conversion. *Color primaries* are numerically-expressed locations within Yxy color space that identify each primary color. For example, sRGB color space assigns its red primary an Yxy location of 0.64 (x), 0.33 (y). In contrast, the SMPTE-C RGB color space assigns its red primary an Yxy location of 0.63 (x), 0.34 (y). (SMPTE-C refers to a color standard set by the Society of Motion Picture and Television Engineers.) Although the visual difference between various color primary settings may be slight, selecting a new primary will alter the numeric values of the output. In general, the color primaries menu should match the corresponding color space. For example, if you are converting to HDTV color space, set the Out menus to Rec709(~1.95), D65, sRGB. For a demonstration of the Colorspace node, see "Nuke Tutorial 4: Matching CGI to Degraded Footage" later in this chapter.

HueShift

The HueShift node converts the input color space to CIE-XYZ. To visualize the CIE-XYZ color space, CIE-Yxy chromaticity charts are used (see Figure 4.22). With the chart, x runs horizontally, y runs vertically, and Y runs on an axis perpendicular to the xy plane and points toward the viewer. While x and y coordinates define the hue/chroma component of a color, Y determines the luminance. The white point of the space is located within the central white spot. Note that the chart is actually a flat, 2D representation of a curved color space.

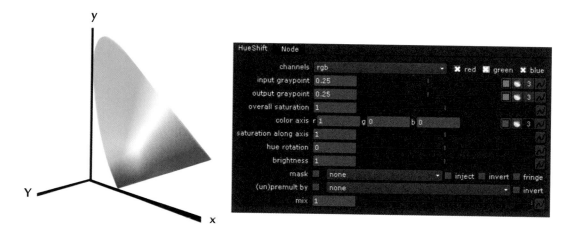

Figure 4.22 *(Left) CIE-Yxy chromaticity diagram (Right) HueShift properties panel*

With the HueShift node, the Hue Rotation slider rotates the color space around the Y axis. The pivot of the rotation is located at the white point. For example, a Hue Rotation value of 180 turns red into cyan. Positive Hue Rotation values rotate the Yxy chart in a clockwise fashion. The Saturation parameter controls standard saturation, while the Saturation Along Axis parameter controls the saturation along either a red, green, or blue axis as determined by the Color Axis cells. Each color axis runs from a corner of the chromaticity diagram toward the white point. You can select an axis between primary colors by clicking the Color Sliders button beside the Color Axis cells and choosing a non-primary color. The Input Graypoint and Output Graypoint parameters offset color values in order to maintain a proper gray mid-tone; the parameters may be left at a default 0.25.

HSVTool

The HSVTool node converts the input color space to HSV color space. As such, it provides a section of parameters for the hue, saturation, and value components. For example, the Hue section includes a Rotation slider that offsets the hue value. The Saturation section includes an Adjustment slider to set the intensity of the saturation. The Brightness section includes an Adjustment slider to determine the brightness. Each section includes Range controls, which you can adjust to limit the effect of a node to a narrow input value range. The HSV Tool node converts the adjusted values back to the input color space in preparation for output.

Channel Color Correctors

Color correction nodes include Saturation, Histogram, Grade, ColorCorrect, and HueCorrect.

The Saturation Node

The Saturation node controls its namesake. A high Saturation property value, such as 2, creates a greater contrast between the RGB channels of a pixel. As a result, the dominant channels, whether they are red, green, or blue, are pushed closer to a value of normalized 1.0. The less-dominant channels are pushed closer to 0. For example, in Figure 4.23, an input gains greater contrast when Saturation is set to 2. As such, the green values are reduced to 0 along the truck body because the body is heavily biased towards red.

Figure 4.23 *(Left) Green channel before application of Saturation node (Right) Green channel after application. The Saturation slider is set to 2 and the Luminance Math menu is set to Maximum. The image is included as* truck.tif *in the Footage folder on the DVD.*

You can choose the style of saturation or desaturation by changing the Luminance Math menu. The CCIR 601 menu option uses a digital video and computer graphics standard that's biased for human perception, which has the formula Y = 0.299 red + 0.587 green + 0.114 blue. The Rec 709 menu option uses a variation of the CCIR standard and is written as the formula Y' = 0.2126 red' + 0.7152 green' + 0.0722 blue'. (For more information, see the Tips & Tricks sidebar about brightness, lightness, luminance, and luma earlier in this chapter.) Of the four menu options, the Maximum menu option applies the maximum amount of contrast between the channels.

The Histogram Node

The Histogram node provides a means to adjust black and white points of an input and its overall tonal range. (See the section "Histograms and Tonal Ranges" earlier in this chapter for more information on points.) There are two sets of sliders: Input Range and Output Range. The leftmost slider handle for Input Range serves as a black value input. Any input values less than the handle value are clamped to the handle value. The rightmost slider handle for Input Range serves as a white value input. Any input values greater than the handle value are clamped to the handle value. Thus, any adjustment of these two sliders will cause a section of the tonal range to be lost. However, the remaining tonal range is stretched to fill the entire histogram. The center slider for Input Range applies a gamma-correction curve; if set to 1.0, the correction is disabled. Movement of the leftmost or rightmost slider will cause the center slider to move automatically. Note that the histogram graphic will superimpose the newly adjusted tonal distribution over the original tonal distribution. The position of the black value input is indicated by a white line that extends the height of the histogram on the histogram's left. The position of the white value input is indicated by a white line that extends the height of the histogram on the histogram's right.

(If the histogram graphic does not update, try clicking the graphic or closing and opening the properties panel.)

The leftmost slider for Output Range determines the image's black point. The rightmost slider for Output Range determines the image's white point. The position of the black point is indicated by a black line that extends the height of the histogram on the histogram's left. The position of the white point is indicated by a black line that extends the height of the histogram on the histogram's right. If either the white point or black point is adjusted, the tonal range is compressed and a section of the histogram will remain empty. For example, in Figure 4.24, an image of a squirrel is adjusted with various Histogram node settings.

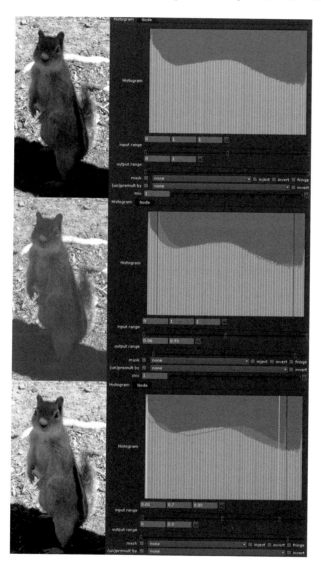

Figure 4.24 *(Top) Unadjusted image with histogram (Center) Washed-out version created by raising the black point and lowering the white point (Bottom) Properly exposed version with an 0.7 gamma, lowered white input value, and lowered white point. A sample Nuke script is included as* histogram.nk *in the Tutorials folder on the DVD.*

The Grade Node
The Grade node provides a more powerful means to adjust the black point, white point, gain, and gamma of an image. The black point, white point, gain, and gamma are predictably controlled by the sliders with the same name (see Figure 4.25). In addition, Lift, Offset, and Multiply sliders are provided for greater fine-tuning.

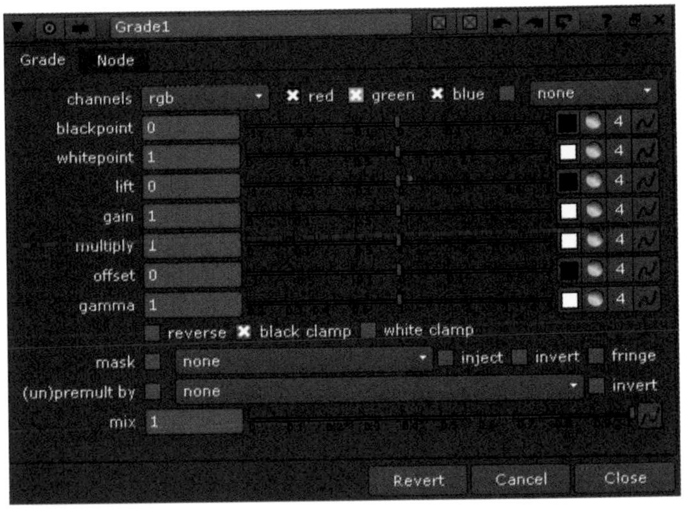

Since the slider scales are unintuitive, here are some approaches to keep in mind when adjusting them:

- Although there is no slider for pedestal, negative Blackpoint slider values are equivalent to positive pedestal values, whereby the values are compressed toward the high end of the tonal range. Positive Blackpoint slider values are equivalent to negative pedestal values. In such a situation, low-end values are clipped and the remaining values are stretched to fit the tonal range.
- Positive Gain slider values create traditional gain, whereby high-end values are clipped and the remaining values are stretched to fit the tonal range.

Figure 4.25 The Grade node properties panel

- If Whitepoint is set above 1.0, the tonal range is compressed toward the low-end of the scale and the upper-end of the range is left empty.
- A positive Lift value produces an almost identical result as a negative Blackpoint value. A negative Lift value produces an almost identical result as a positive Blackpoint value.
- A positive Offset value produces an almost identical result as a negative Blackpoint value. However, negative Offset values produce results similar to a Whitepoint value above 1.0, but the image is darkened.
- High Multiply values increase the brightness of an image and reduce the overall contrast.
- To enter specific numeric color values for a slider, click the 4 button beside the slider.
- To choose a color for a slider interactively, click the Color Sliders button beside the slider name (the button features a small color wheel).

The Grade node will be examined further in Chapter 8, "DI, Color Grading, Noise, and Grain."

ColorCorrect

The ColorCorrect node controls the balance between red, green, and blue channels within an image. Saturation, Contrast, Gamma, Gain, and Offset sliders are provided. These sliders function in the same manner as the ones provided by other color correction nodes and effects, but are targeted toward finite sections of the tonal range (Shadows, Midtones, and Highlights). In addition, a "Master" set of sliders control the entire tonal range. The ColorCorrect node is demonstrated in "Nuke Tutorial 4: Matching CG to Degraded Footage" later in this chapter.

HueCorrect

The HueCorrect node controls the balance between red, green, and blue channels and offers an interactive curve editor with color control and suppression curves. Control curves are supplied for saturation, luminance, red, green, and blue thresholds. Suppression curves are supplied for red, green, and blue channels. The HueCorrect node is demonstrated in the "Nuke Tutorial 2 Revisited: Refining Color and Edge Quality" and "Nuke Tutorial 3: Removing Greenscreen" in Chapter 3.

Math Nodes

Nuke provides basic math nodes, which are found under the Color → Math menu. The Add node adds a value, set by the Value slider, to each pixel value of the input. The Multiply node takes the input values and multiplies them by its own Value slider. The Gamma node applies a gamma curve in the same fashion.

The Expression node, on the other hand, gives you the ability to write your own mathematic formula and have it applied to various channels. Expressions are discussed in Chapter 12, "Advanced Techniques."

The Clamp node, found in the Color menu, clips and throws away sections of tonal range. The minimum value allowed to survive is established by the Minimum slider and the maximum value allowed to survive is established by the Maximum slider. For working examples that use Expression and Clamp nodes, see Chapter 9, "Integrating Render Passes."

The Invert node, found in the Color menu, inverts the input. You can choose specific channels to invert through the Channels menu or through the channel buttons. The basic invert formula is `1 - input`. Thus, a value of 1.0 produces 0, a value of 0 produces 1.0, and a value of 0.5 is unaltered.

AE and Nuke Tutorials

Quality visual effects demand that CG elements possess the same qualities as the live-action footage. Two critical areas of this comparison are the brightest areas and darkest areas of an image; that is, its *whites* and *blacks* are critical. You can identify differences in the whites and blacks by utilizing histograms, luminance information, and various channel effects and nodes.

In addition, you can create custom luma mattes to refine chroma key removal with channel nodes. Although the use of a custom luma matte was demonstrated by AE Tutorial 3 in Chapter 3, Nuke's use of the luma matte is demonstrated in the next section.

Nuke Tutorial 3 Revisited: Creating a Luma Matte

In Chapter 3, Nuke Tutorial 3 left the model with fairly hard edges along her hair. You can solve this by creating a custom luma matte and copying channels.

1. Reopen the completed Nuke project file for "Nuke Tutorial 3: Removing Greenscreen." A finished version of Tutorial 3 is saved as nuke3.nk in the Chapter 3 Tutorials folder on the DVD. In the Node Graph, RMB+click with no nodes selected and choose Color → ColorCorrect. Connect the output of Read1 to the input of ColorCorrect1. In the ColorCorrect1 node's properties panel, set the Master Saturation slider to 0.6 and the Master Gain slider to 1.5. Select the Color-Correct1 node, RMB+click, and choose Color → Invert. Connect a viewer to Invert1. The RGB channels are inverted to create a white hair against a purple background that you can use as a custom luma matte (see Figure 4.26).

Figure 4.26 Result of a ColorCorrect and an Invert node, which can be used as a custom luma matte

2. With no nodes selected, RMB+click, and choose Channel → Copy. Connect the Invert1 node to the input A of the Copy1 node. In the Copy1 node's properties panel, change the topmost Copy Channel menu to Rgba.red and the topmost To menu to Rgba.alpha (see the top of Figure 4.27). With these settings, the red channel from the Invert1 node is copied to the alpha channel of the Copy1 node's output. To see the end result, disconnect the Rectangle1 and Premult1 nodes from the Merge1 node. Connect Copy1 to input A of the Merge1 node. Connect Premult1 to the input B of the Merge1 node. Use Figure 4.27 as a reference. Open the Merge1 node's properties panel. Change the Operation menu to Screen. Switch to the Channels tab. Deselect all the Red, Green, and Blue check boxes so that only the Alpha check box remains selected. When you disable the color channels, the Merge1 node combines the alpha channels of the Premult1 and Copy1 nodes. The color channels are passed through the Merge1 node without any alteration. When you set the Merge1 node's Operation to Screen, the less intense Copy1 alpha val-

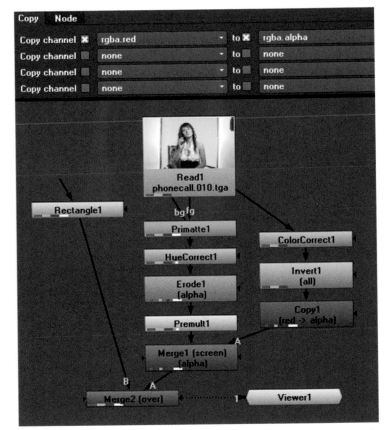

Figure 4.27 *(Top) Copy node's properties panel (Bottom) Revised node network*

ues are added to the more intense Premult1 alpha values while preventing superwhite results. With the Merge1 node selected, RMB+click and choose Merge → Merge. Connect the input B of the Merge2 node to the Rectangle1 node. Connect a viewer to Merge2.

3. Since the fine edge quality of the hair is now supplied by the custom luma matte that is fed into the Copy1 node, you can make the Primatte erosion more aggressive. An easier solution, however, is to add a Blur (Erode) node. Select the HueCorrect1 node, RMB+click, and choose Filter → Blur (Erode). An Erode1 node is inserted between the HueCorrect1 and Premult1 nodes. Open the Erode1 node's properties panel and set Size to 2 and Blur to 0.5. The output of the Erode1 node is aggressively eroded; however, the output of the Merge1 node maintains the fine quality of the hair's edge (see Figure 4.28).

4. The final composite retains the fine details of the hair. However, a bright line remains along the edge of the model's left arm and shoulder. To solve this problem, it will be necessary to divide the footage into multiple sections using rotoscoping tools. This, along with the reflective arms of the chair, will be addressed in the Chapter 7 Nuke tutorial. In the meantime, save the file under a new name. A finished revision is included as nuke3_step2.nk in the Tutorials folder on the DVD.

Figure 4.28 *(Left) Lumpy hair created by Chapter 3 Primatte settings (Center) More aggressive erosion created by Blur (Erode) node (Right) Final composite using the merged alpha of Premult1 and Copy1 nodes*

AE Tutorial 4: Matching CG to Degraded Footage

Matching CG elements can be a challenge, especially when the footage is not in pristine shape.

1. Create a new project. Choose Composition → New Composition. In the Composition Settings dialog box, change the Preset menu to NTSC D1 Square Pixel. Set the duration to 24 frames and Frame Rate to 24. Import the bug.##.tif sequence from the Footage folder on the DVD. In the Interpret Alpha dialog box, select the Premultiplied check box and click OK. In the Project Panel, RMB+click over the bug.##.tif name and choose Interpret Footage → Main. In the Interpret Footage dialog box, change the Assume This Frame Rate cell to 24 and click OK. Import the woman.##.tga sequence from the Footage folder on the DVD. In the Project panel, RMB+click over the woman.## .tga name and choose Interpret Footage → Main. In the Interpret Footage dialog box, change the Assume This Frame Rate cell to 24 and click OK.

2. LMB+drag the woman.##.tga footage from the Project panel to the layer outline of the Timeline panel. LMB+drag the bug.##.tif footage from the Project panel to the layer outline so that is sits on top of the new woman.##.tga layer. Scrub the timeline. The composite places a CG insect on top of the head of an actress (see Figure 4.29). The woman.##.tga footage is taken from a digital copy of a public-domain instructional film. As such, there is heavy degradation in the form of MPEG compression artifacts, film grain, dust, and dirt. The CG, by comparison, is relatively clean. Aside from the lack of noise, the blacks found in the CG are significantly different from the blacks found in the live-action footage. To test this, move your mouse over the various areas and watch the RGB values change in the Info panel (see Figure 4.29). The darkest areas of the CG, such as the shadowed regions of the claws, have RGB values as light as 37, 28, 22. The darkest areas of the live-action footage, such as the region under the chin, have RGB values as dark as 13, 9, 0.

3. To adjust the shadows, you can isolate and adjust the luminance information as well as change the overall color balance. Select the bug.##.tif layer in Comp 1, and choose

Effect → Channel → Channel Combiner. In
the Effect Controls panel, change the From
menu to RGB To YUV. Select the woman.##.
tga layer and choose Effect → Channel →
Channel Combiner. In the Effect Controls
panel, change the From menu to RGB To
YUV. The viewer will display the composite
in YUV space. To examine the Y luminance
channel, change the Composition panel's
Show Channel menu to Red (see Figure 4.30).
Drag your mouse over the dark areas to compare the values in the Info panel. The darkest
areas of the live-action footage have values
around 24, 123, 134. The darkest areas of
the CG have values around 47, 125, 130.
Since the color space is YUV, this disparity between Y values represents a difference
in luminance, or brightness. Note that the
Channel Combiner effect may not display
an accurate result in the viewer if a specific
Working Space is chosen through the Project
Settings dialog box. For example, if Working
Space is set to HDTV (Rec. 709) instead
of None, the output of the composition is
altered by a Rec. 709 LUT before being sent to the monitor.

Figure 4.29 *(Top) The initial composite (Bottom) The Info panel*

4. Select the bug.##.tif layer in Comp 1 and choose Effect → Color Correction → Curves.
In the Effect Controls panel, change the Curves effect's Channel menu to Red. The
displayed curve controls the luminance. Insert points into the curve and adjust it to
match Figure 4.31. This decreases the luminance of the darkest areas of the CG. Drag
your mouse over the viewer and compare the values of the dark areas. The goal is to
get the darkest areas of the CG to have values around 24, 123, 134.

Figure 4.30 *(Left) The Y luminance channel (Right) The Show
Channel menu in the Composition panel*

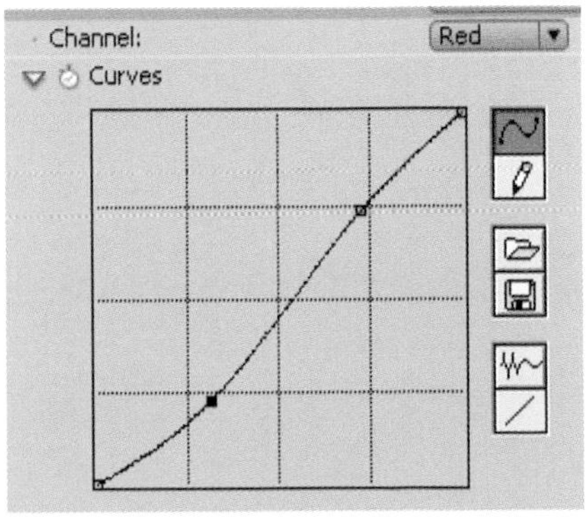

Figure 4.31 *The adjusted Red curve
for the Curves effect. Since the color
space is YUV, the Red curve controls
the Y luminance.*

5. Once you're satisfied with the luminance adjustment, deselect the Fx button in the Effect Controls panel beside the Channel Combiner effect applied to the woman.##.tga layer. Select the bug.##.tga layer and choose Effect → Channel → Channel Combiner. In the Effect Controls panel, change the From menu for the Channel Combiner 2 effect to YUV To RGB. Change the Composition panel's Show Channel menu to RGB. The viewer shows the composite in RGB space once again.

6. Although the luminance values are a better match between the CG and the live-action blacks, the color balance is off. The live-action is heavily biased toward red, whereby the chin shadow produces values around 36, 15, 1. The tail of the insect, in comparison, has RGB values around 25, 20, 15. Select the bug.##.tif layer in the layer outline and choose Effect → Color Correction → Color Balance. In the Effect Controls panel, set Shadow Red Balance to 5, Shadow Green Balance to −5, Shadow Blue Balance to −10, Midtone Red Balance to 5, Midtone Green Balance to −5, and Blue Midtone Balance to −10.

7. At this step, the CG has a higher color saturation than any part of the live-action. To match the washed-out quality of the footage, select the bug.##.tif layer in the layer outline and choose Effect → Color Correction → Hue/Saturation. In the Effect Controls panel, change the Master Saturation slider to −20. This results in more muted colors (see Figure 4.32).

8. At this stage, the colors of the CG match the live-action fairly well. However, the CG does not possess the posterization or pixelization resulting from compression artifacts. You can emulate this with several specialized effects. Select the bug.##.tif layer in the layer outline and choose Effect → Stylize → Posterize. In the Effect Controls panel, change the Posterize effect's Level slider to 10. The effect limits the number of tonal steps in the layer, which causes color banding to occur.

Figure 4.32 Detail of composite shown in RGB after the application of Channel Combiner, Curves, Color Balance, and Hue/Saturation effects

9. With the bug.##.tif layer selected in the layer outline, choose Edit → Duplicate. Select the newly created bug.##.tif layer (labeled *1* in the layer outline). Choose Effect → Stylize → Mosaic. In the Effect Controls panel, change the Mosaic effect's Horizontal Blocks and Vertical Blocks to 200. The effect reduces the number of visible pixels to 200 in each direction but does not shrink the layer (see Figure 4.33). To blend the pixelized version of the CG with the non-pixelized version, change the top bug.##.tif layer's Opacity to 75%.

10. Due to the blending of the two CG layers, the insect becomes darker. To offset this result, select the lowest bug.##.tif layer in the layer outline and choose Effect → Color Correction → Curves. In the Effect Controls panel, insert a new point in the Curves 2 effect's curve and shape the curve to match Figure 4.34. This lightens the insect body. To lighten the shadow, change the Curves 2 effect's Channel menu to Alpha. Insert a new point into the curve and shape it to match Figure 4.34. This

darkens the mid-tone alpha values possessed by the cast shadow but does not unduly impact the higher alpha values of the insect body. Using the Render Queue, render a test movie. The tutorial is complete. A sample After Effects project is saved as `ae4.aep` in the Tutorials folder on the DVD.

Figure 4.33 (Top) Before the application of Posterize and Mosaic effects (Bottom) After the application

Figure 4.34 (Top Left) New RGB curve for the lowest bug layer (Top Right) New Alpha curve for the lowest bug layer (Bottom) Final composite

Nuke Tutorial 4: Matching CG to Degraded Footage

Matching CG elements can be a challenge, especially when the footage is not in pristine shape.

1. Create a new script. Choose Edit → Project Settings. Change Frame Range to 1, 24 and Fps to 24. With the Full Size Format menu, choose New. In the New Format dialog box, change Full Size W to 720 and Full Size H to 540. Enter **D1** into the Name field and click to the OK button.

2. In the Node Graph, RMB+click, choose Image → Read, and browse for the bug.## .tif sequence in the Footage folder on the DVD. Select the Premultiplied check box in the Read1 properties panel. In the Node Graph, RMB+click, choose Image → Read, and browse for the woman.##.tga sequence in the Footage folder on the DVD. Select the Read1 node, RMB+click, and choose Merge → Merge. Read1 is automatically connected to input A of the Merge1 node. Connect input B of Merge1 to Read2. Connect a viewer to the Merge1 node.

3. The composite places a CG insect on top of the head of an actress (see Figure 4.35). The `woman.##.tga` footage is taken from a digital copy of a public-domain instructional film. As such, there is heavy degradation in the form of MPEG compression artifacts, film grain, dust, and dirt. The CG, by comparison, is relatively clean. Aside from the lack of noise, however, the blacks found in the CG are significantly different from the blacks found in the live-action footage. To test this, move your mouse over the various shadow areas and watch the RGB values change at the bottom of the Viewer pane. To switch the readout scale from the default HSVL (HSV/HSL) to 8-bit, change the viewer's Alternative Colorspace menu to 8bit (see Figure 4.35). The dark areas of the CG, such as regions near the claws, have RGB values as high as 52, 43, 34. The dark areas of the live-action, such as the shadow under the chin, have RGB values around 35, 15, 2.

4. To aid in value adjustment, you can isolate the luminance information. Select the Merge1 node, RMB+click, and choose Color → Colorspace. In the Colorspace1 node's properties panel, change the leftmost Out menu from Linear to L*a*b*. Change the Viewer pane's Display_LUT menu to Linear. The viewer will display the composite in L*a*b* space. To examine the L* luminance channel, click the Viewer pane and press the R key (see Figure 4.36). You can also change the Display Style menu at the upper-left corner of the Viewer pane. Drag your mouse over the dark regions to compare the values. The CG has values around 89, 59, 56 in the dark regions while the live-action has values around 46, 40, 54. Since the readout represents L*, a*, and b* channels, the disparity between L* values represents a difference in luminance, or brightness.

5. Select the Read1 node, RMB+click, and choose Color → Grade. This inserts a Grade node between the Read1 node and the Merge1 node. In the Grade1 properties panel, change the Gamma slider to 0.7. The darkest areas of the CG gain values closer to 46, 40, 54.

Figure 4.35 *(Top) The initial composite (Bottom) The Viewer pane's sample color readout and Alternative Colorspace menu*

Figure 4.36 *(Top) The L* luminance channel (Bottom) The Viewer pane's Display Style menu*

6. Select the Colorspace1 node and change the Out menu from L*a*b* back to Linear. Change the Viewer pane's Display_LUT menu back to sRGB. Change the Display Style menu at the upper-left corner of the Viewer pane back to RGB. This effectively turns off the color space conversion. Although the luminance values are a better match between the CG and live-action, the color balance is off. Select the Grade1 node, RMB+click, and choose Color → ColorCorrect. In the ColorCorrect1 properties panel, change the Shadows Gain R cell to 1.4, the Shadows Gain B cell to 0.8, the Midtones Gain R cell to 1.4, and the Midtones Gain B cell to 0.8. To access the RGBA cells, click the *4* button to the right of sliders. The goal is to lower the CG RGB values to approximately 15, 7, 3 in the darkest areas, which is equivalent to the shadow values found around the actress's neck. (That is, you want the red channel to be twice as intense as the green channel and for there to be almost no blue.)

7. At this point, the CG has a higher color saturation than any part of the live-action. To match the slightly washed-out quality of the footage, change the ColorCorrect1's Master Saturation slider to 0.8 (see Figure 4.37).

8. Although the dark areas of the CG are now similar to the dark areas of the live-action, the CG cast shadow remains too light. The cast shadow, in this case, is semitransparent, as is indicated by the gray pixels in the alpha channel. To view the alpha, connect a viewer to the ColorCorrect1 node, select the Viewer pane, and press the A key. To adjust the alpha, select the ColorCorrect1 node, RMB+click,

Figure 4.37 Detail of composite shown in RGB after the application of Grade and ColorCorrect nodes

and choose Color → ColorCorrect. In the ColorCorrect2 node's properties panel, change the Channels menu to Alpha. Change the Master Contrast slider to 1.12. This reduces the opacity and thus darkens the cast shadow (see Figure 4.38). The goal is have the cast shadows retain RGB values around 35, 19, 10, which more closely matches the dark areas of the hair.

9. At this stage, the blacks and overall shadow quality of the CG and live-action footage match fairly well (see Figure 4.38). However, a disparity remains between the posterization and pixelization of the live-action and the pristine quality of the CG. To solve this problem, you can use a Posterize node (Color → Posterize). However, the node tends to produce an output with a high contrast. In this situation, such contrast would interfere with the color balance of the CG and the opacity of its shadow. An alternative solution uses the built-in parameters of the Reformat node. With no nodes selected, RMB+click and choose Transform → Reformat. Disconnect the output of the ColorCorrect2 node from the Merge1 node. Instead, connect the output of ColorCorrect2 to the input of the Reformat1 node. Connect a viewer to Reformat1.

Open the Reformat1 node's properties panel. Change the Type menu to To Box. Select the Force This Shape check box. Change the Width and Height cells to 144, 108. This will scale the input to 1/5 of the project's resolution (720×540). Change Filter to Impulse. The Impulse filter does not employ pixel averaging during the resize process and will thus create a limited-color, pixelized version of the CG. Change the Resize Type menu to Fit.

Figure 4.38 *(Top) Alpha channel (Center) Alpha adjusted with a second ColorCorrect node (Bottom) Detail of resulting cast shadow*

10. With the Reformat1 node selected, RMB+click and choose Transform → Transform. With the Transform1 node selected, RMB+click and choose Merge → Merge. Refer to Figure 4.39 as a reference. Connect the output of ColorCorrect2 to input B of Merge2. Connect the output of Merge2 to input A of Merge1. Connect a viewer to the output of Merge1 to see the result.

11. At this point, the pixelized CG bug is tucked into the bottom left corner of the composite. To fix this, open the Transform1 node's properties panel. Set the Scale slider to 5, the Translate X cell to 289, the Translate Y cell to 216, and the Filter menu to Impulse. The pixelized bug is placed on top of the unpixelized bug.

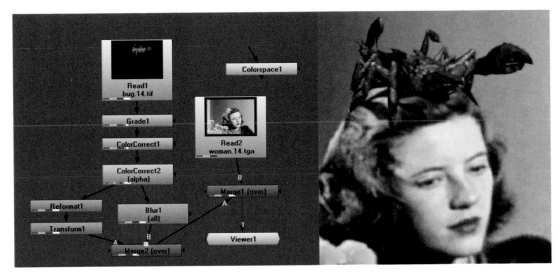

Figure 4.39 *(Left) The final node network (Right) Detail of final composite*

12. To reduce the intensity of the pixelization, reduce the Merge2 node's Mix slider to 0.3. (Mix is equivalent to opacity.) To soften the CG further, RMB+click over an empty area of the Node Graph and choose Filter → Blur. LMB+drag the Blur1 node and drop it on top of the connection line between the ColorCorrect2 and Merge2 nodes. The Blur1 node is inserted into the pipe. Change the Blur1 node's size to 1.5.

13. Render a test movie by disconnecting the Colorspace1 node from the network, selecting the Merge1 node, and choosing Render → Flipbook Selected from the menu bar. The tutorial is complete (see Figure 4.39). A sample Nuke script is included as `nuke4 .nk` in the Tutorials folder on the DVD.

Interview: Andy Davis, Method Studios, Santa Monica, California

Andy Davis attended the Art Center College of Design in Pasadena, California. After working as an illustrator for several years, he was able to apprentice under experienced compositors. He went on to freelance composite for such companies as Imaginary Forces, Asylum, and Big Red Pixel. He joined R!OT in 2006, where he served as a VFX supervisor. In 2009, R!OT merged with its sister company, Method Studios. Over the last 10 years, Andy has worked on commercials, PSAs, and over two dozen feature films including *Gone in Sixty Seconds*, *Pearl Harbor*, *The League of Extraordinary Gentlemen*, and *Live Free or Die Hard*.

Method Studios opened in 1998 and currently has offices in New York and Santa Monica. Method produces visual effects for commercials, music videos, and film. The studio has provided effects for such features as *The Ring* and the *Pirates of the Caribbean* series.

Andy Davis in his Inferno bay. The bay has a half dozen monitors.

The Method Studios facility in Santa Monica, California, a half-mile from the Pacific Ocean

(Method Studios currently uses as a combination of Inferno, Nuke, and Shake for compositing. The Santa Monica studio has over a dozen compositors on staff but expands for large projects.)

LL: Is it still common to work with 35mm footage?

AD: 35mm is still standard. We have quite a lot of Red [HD footage] coming through here nowadays, both for DI and for some commercials, but I think that's going to become more and more the case. The problem is that [HD footage] takes a huge amount of disk space. People make the wrong assumption that just because there's no film processing doesn't mean that it won't need to be converted to DPXs or something [similar]....

LL: What are the main differences between 35mm and high-definition video?

AD: Color depth for one.... The color range is definitely better in film than it is in digital.... The contrast between the lights and the shadows are [more easily] captured on film. I'd say also that most cinematographers are schooled on 35mm. The guys who are the best computer technicians aren't necessarily the best DPs (directors of photography) out there. And everyone seems to understand 35mm. It's pretty much a standard. I'm not really afraid of 35mm going away anytime soon.

LL: What are some advantages of digital video?

AD: What it does is give people the option to shoot [more footage]. With the new cameras [that are being developed], the concept of being able to shoot an IMAX-resolution film on a Steadicam is crazy. Traditional IMAX cameras are gigantic, and all you normally see is boring movies about beavers.... [Digital video camera makers] are really trying to push the envelope. If it wasn't for Red, the Panavisions of the world wouldn't be pushing [the technology]. That said, it isn't perfect. The progressive shutter is a problem for fast movement.... If you're comparing [35mm] to the Red, the Red at least can do 4K, whereas, if you need a hi-res scan of 35mm, the film grain can be a little big.

LL: How important is color grading?

AD: Color is the basis of it all. Color can make or break anything. I really keep an eye out for guys with [a good sense of color]. It's even more critical with film because you have to anticipate what it's going to look like after it goes through the film process…. If the blacks are off a bit, you'll notice it on a 50-foot screen.

LL: How important have DI (digital intermediates) become?

AD: DI is really going to change telecine. The thing that made telecine so handy is that it's fast and interactive. Clients loved being able to walk out with a tape in their hand. DI, however, does give you the ability to be more articulate with mattes…. [DI] just opens up a whole bunch of possibilities.

LL: Do you take any special steps for color grading?

AD: We use 3D LUTs and 2D monitor LUTs. More often than not, when I'm working on film I'll be using monitor LUTs. I'd rather trick the monitor into giving me the right information rather than doing log to lins (logarithmic to linear conversions) and lins to logs all the time.

Additional Resources: The Full Interview

To read the full interview with Andy Davis, see the Interviews folder on the DVD. For more information on 3D LUTs and DI, see Chapter 8.

five

Transformations and Keyframing

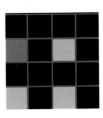

Transformations encompass *translation, rotation, scale, and skew. Each transformation has an unique effect on an output or layer, which necessitates the application for transformation matrices and convolution filters. Keyframing, on the other hand, is necessary for transformations that change over time. After Effects and Nuke provide various means to set keyframes and manipulate the resulting channel curves. Each program offers its own version of a curve editor. So you can practice these concepts, this chapter includes After Effects and Nuke tutorials that let you animate and thereby give life to a static render.*

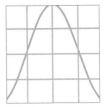

Understanding Transformations

Transformations are an inescapable part of compositing. As such, translation and rotation operations necessitate the remapping of a pixel from an old position to a new position. Scaling operations, on the other hand, require a decrease or increase in the total number of pixels within an image. Transformations involve two important tools: transformation matrices and convolution filters.

Matrix Operations

Transformations are stored within a compositing program as a transformation matrix. A matrix is a rectangular array of numbers arranged into rows and columns. The dimension of matrix is measured by the number of rows, or *m*, and the number of columns, or *n*. Common matrix dimensions are thus expressed as $m \times n$.

A 3×3 transformation matrix, which is common in 2D computer graphics, encodes scale, translation, and skew at specific positions within the matrix. For example, as illustrated in Table 5.1, a common matrix variant encodes the X scale value as *sx*, the Y skew value as *b*, the X skew value as *c*, the Y scale value as *sy*, the X translation as *tx*, and the Y translation as *ty*.

Skew is the amount of shearing present in an image. High skew values cause a rectangular image to become trapezoidal. The right column of the matrix does not change during transformations and is necessary for matrix multiplication. Each position within the matrix is known as an *element*. If a transformation matrix has a skew of 0, 0, a translation of 0, 0, and a scale of 1, 1, it's referred to as an *identity matrix*, as is illustrated in Table 5.2.

In contrast, the position of a pixel within an image is encoded as a vector. (A *pixel* is a point sample which carries an x, y coordinate and a color value; for an image to be stored within a digital system, it must be broken down into a discrete number of pixels.) For example, if a pixel is at 100, 50 in X and Y, the position vector is [100 50 1]. The *1* is a placeholder and is needed for the matrix calculation. If a transformation is applied to a pixel, the position vector is multiplied by the corresponding transformation matrix:

Table 5.1: A 3×3 Transformation Matrix

sx	b	0
c	sy	0
tx	ty	1

Table 5.2: An Identity Matrix

1	0	0
0	1	0
0	0	1

```
                       [sx  b   0]
[x2 y2 1] = [x1 y1 1] [c   sy  0]
                       [tx  ty  1]
```

With this formula, *x1* and *y1* represent the current X and Y positions of the pixel. *x2* and *y2* are the resulting X and Y positions of the pixel. You can also express the formula as follows:

```
x2 = (x1 × sx) + (y1 × c) + (1 × tx)
y2 = (x1 × b) + (y1 × sy) + (1 × ty)
```

If the position of a pixel is 25, 25 and you apply a translation of 100, 100, the following math occurs:

$$[x2\ y2\ 1] = [25\ 25\ 1] \begin{bmatrix} 1 & 0 & 0 \\ 0 & 1 & 0 \\ 100 & 100 & 1 \end{bmatrix}$$

```
x2 = (25 × 1) + (25 × 0) + (1 × 100)

y2 = (25 × 0) + (25 × 1) + (1 × 100)

x2 = 125

y2 = 125
```

The resulting position vector is thus [125 125 1] and the new position of the pixel is 125, 125. Scaling operates in a similar fashion. For example, if a scale of 3, 2 is applied, a point at position 125, 125 undergoes the following math:

$$[x2\ y2\ 1] = [125\ 125\ 1] \begin{bmatrix} 3 & 0 & 0 \\ 0 & 2 & 0 \\ 0 & 0 & 1 \end{bmatrix}$$

```
x2 = (125 × 3) + (125 × 0) + (1 × 0)

y2 = (125 × 0) + (125 × 2) + (1 × 0)

x2 = 375

y2 = 250
```

Hence, the new position vector is [375 250 1]. Because the pixel did not sit at 0, 0, it's moved further away from the origin. (In this situation, pixels must be padded; this is discussed in the section "Interpolation Filters.") In contrast, rotation requires a combination of skewing and scaling. Rotation is thereby stored indirectly in a 3×3 matrix, as is illustrated in Table 5.3.

For example, if an image is rotated 20°, a pixel at position 5, 0 undergoes the following math (the values are rounded off for easier viewing):

Table 5.3: Matrix Representation of Rotation

cosine(angle)	sine(angle)	0
–sine(angle)	cosine(angle)	0
0	0	1

$$[x2\ y2\ 1] = [5\ 0\ 1] \begin{bmatrix} cosine(20) & sine(20) & 0 \\ -sine(20) & cosine(20) & 0 \\ 0 & 0 & 1 \end{bmatrix}$$

```
x2 = (5 x 0.94) – (0 x 0.34) + (1 x 0)

y2 = (5 x 0.34) + (0 x 0.94) + (1 x 0)

x2 = 4.7

y2 = 1.7
```

Thus, the pixel is lifted slightly in the positive Y direction and moved back slightly in the negative X direction. This represents counterclockwise rotation, which is produced by a positive rotation angle in a right-handed coordinate system (where positive X runs right and the positive Y runs up). To generate clockwise rotation, you can the swap the negative and positive sine elements.

Transformation Order and Concatenation

If more than one transformation is applied to a pixel, the transformations are applied one at a time. Hence, *transformation order* is an important aspect of digital imaging. Translating first and rotating second may have a different result then rotating first and translating second. This is particularly true if the anchor point for the layer or output is not centered. (Transformation order, as it applies to Nuke 3D cameras, is discussed in Chapter 12, "Advanced Techniques.")

In certain situations, repeated transformations can be destructive to image quality. For example, these steps might occur in After Effects: 1) a layer is downscaled; 2) the composition the layer belongs to is nested with a second composition; 3) the second composition is upscaled. In this situation, the layer goes through an unnecessary downscale and upscale, which leads to pixel destruction and pixel padding. A similar degradation may occur in Nuke when a node network contains multiple Transform nodes. One way to avoid such problems is to concatenate. *Concatenation*, as it applies to compositing, determines the net transformation that should be applied to a layer or node regardless of the number of individual transformation steps.

Nuke automatically concatenates if multiple Transform nodes are connected in a row. However, if other nodes, such as color or filter nodes, are inserted between the Transform nodes, the concatenation is broken. After Effects, on the other hand, does not offer an automatic method for concatenation. Nevertheless, here are a few tips for avoiding image degradation based on transformations:

- When translating a layer or output, translate by whole-pixel values. Translating by fractional values, such as 10.5, leads to additional pixel averaging.
- In After Effects, avoid nesting whenever possible. If you choose to render out a precomp, choose the highest quality settings and largest resolution you can.
- In Nuke, set the Transform node's Filter menu to the interpolation style that gives you the cleanest results. Interpolation filters are discussed in the following section. Nuke-specific filters are discussed in the section "Choosing an Interpolation Filter in Nuke" later in this chapter.
- In After Effects, toggle on a nested composition's Collapse Transformations layer switch. This forces the program to apply transformations after rendering masks and effects. This allows the transformations of the nested composition and the composition in which the nest occurs to be combined.

Interpolation Filters

Matrix transformations determine the positions of pixels within an image. However, the transformations do not supply pixels with values (that is, colors). This is problematic if an image is enlarged (upscaled). In such a situation, new pixels are inserted between the source pixels (see Figure 5.1). In other words, the source pixels are *padded*. To determine the value of the padded pixels, an interpolation filter must be applied. The simplest form of interpolation filter is named *nearest neighbor*. With this filter, the value of a padded pixel is taken from the closest source pixel. In the case of Figure 5.1, this leads to a magnification of the original pattern. Ultimately, this leads to blockiness on complex images, where *stair-stepping* appears along high-contrast edges. (See Figure 5.5 later in this chapter for an example of stair-stepping.)

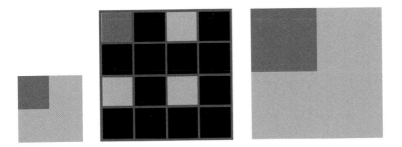

Figure 5.1 *(Left) 4×4 image. (Center) Image scaled by 200 percent, producing an 8×8 pixel resolution. The black pixels are padded. (Right) Final image using a nearest neighbor interpolation.*

A more useful form of image interpolation utilizes a *convolution filter*. A convolution filter multiplies the image by a kernel matrix. A 3×3 kernel can be illustrated as follows:

```
1  1  1

1  1  1

1  1  1
```

If each kernel element is replaced with 1/*divisor* the filter becomes a *mean* or *box filter*, where pixel values are averaged. Pixel-averaging is necessary when the image is shrunk (downscaled). The averaging may also be used as a stylistic method of applying blur. A box filter kernel can be written as follows:

```
1/9  1/9  1/9

1/9  1/9  1/9

1/9  1/9  1/9
```

To determine the effect of a convolution filter, the kernel matrix is "laid" on top of the input matrix. The input matrix is a two-dimensional representation of an input image, where each matrix element holds the value of the corresponding pixel. Since the kernel matrix is smaller than the input matrix, the kernel matrix is "slid" from one pixel to the next until an output value is determined for every pixel. When a single pixel is processed, each kernel matrix element (such as 1/9) is multiplied by the pixel that it overlaps. The resulting products are then added together. For example, in Table 5.4, a 3×3 matrix is laid on top of a portion of an input matrix. The dark gray cell in the center is the targeted pixel for which a new output value is to be generated. Any pixel beyond the edge of the 3×3 matrix is ignored and has an equivalent value of 0. The pixel values are indicated on a normalized range of 0 to 1.0.

Table 5.4: Box Filter Kernel Applied to Input Matrix

0	0	0	0	0
0	1/9 X 1.0	1/9 X 1.0	1/9 X 1.0	0
0	1/9 X 0.75	1/9 X 0.5	1/9 X 0.2	0
0	1/9 X 0.5	1/9 X 0.2	1/9 X 0.1	0
0	0	0	0	0

The math for this example can be written as (1 / 9) × (1.0 + 1.0 + 1.0 + 0.75 + 0.5 + 0.2 + 0.5 + 0.2 + 0.1). The targeted pixel is therefore assigned an output value of roughly 0.58.

Tent Filters

Tent filters undertake averaging but also take into consideration the distance from the targeted pixel to neighboring pixels. For example, a 3×3 tent filter kernel is illustrated here:

1/16   2/16   1/16

2/16   4/16   2/16

1/16   2/16   1/16

With this example, the value of the targeted pixel has the greatest weight (its fraction is the closest to 1.0), while pixels falling at the corners of the matrix have the least weight. Nevertheless, the nine elements within the matrix add up to 1.0, which guarantees that the filtered output retains an overall intensity equal to the source.

When comparing the result of a tent filter to a nearest neighbor filter on a downscaling operation, the differences are subtle but important (see Figure 5.2). With the nearest neighbor filter, every resulting pixel has a value equal to a source pixel. The black diagonal line, due to its position, is completely lost. In contrast, the tent filter averages the values so that several pixels are mixtures of cyan and green, red and green, or black and green. The tent filter thereby allows the black line to survive.

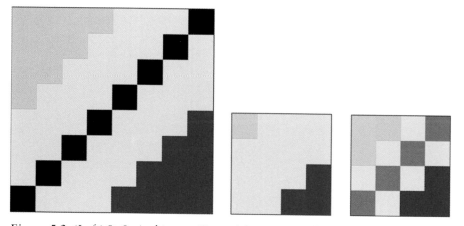

Figure 5.2 *(Left) 8×8 pixel image (Center) Same image downscaled by 50% through a nearest neighbor filter (Right) Same image downscaled by 50% through a tent filter*

Tent filters derive their name from the tent-shaped function curve (see Figure 5.3). With such a graph, the x-axis represents the distance from a source pixel to the targeted pixel. The y-axis represents the weighted contribution of the source pixel. Hence, any pixel that is at a 0.5 pixel distance from the targeted pixel is weighted at 50%. Tent filters can be scaled to produce curve bases with different widths and thereby include a lesser or greater number of source pixels in the calculation. Tent filters are also known as triangle, bilinear, and Bartlett filters.

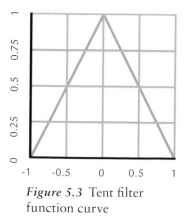

Figure 5.3 Tent filter function curve

Cubic Filters

Cubic filters are a family of filters that employ a bell-shaped function curve (see Figure 5.4). Like tent filters, cubic filters base their weight on distance; however, the weighting is not linear. Cubic filters are well suited for the removal of high-frequency noise and are thus the default scaling method for Photoshop, After Effects, and Nuke. (When image processing is discussed, cubic filters are often referred to as *bicubic* as they must operate in an X and Y direction.)

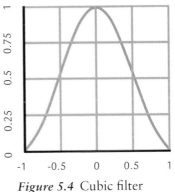

Figure 5.4 Cubic filter function curve

One of the best ways to compare the qualities of various filters is to apply them to high-contrast edges that have gone through a rotation or an upscale. For example, in Figure 5.5, a white square is rotated, revealing the stair-stepping induced by a nearest neighbor filter. In addition, the subtle differences between tent and cubic filters are indicated by different degrees of softening.

Nuke offers additional convolution filters with which to apply transformations. They are discussed in the section "Transformations in Nuke" later in this chapter.

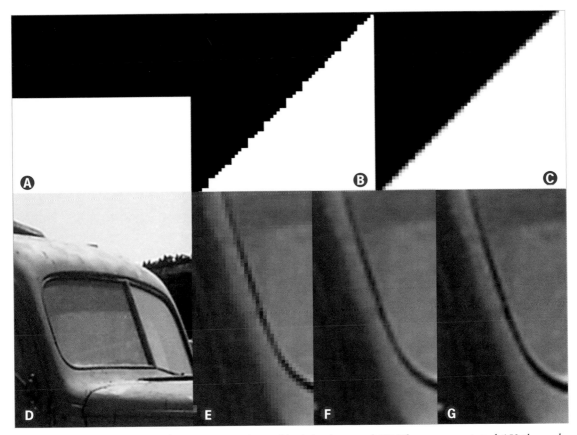

Figure 5.5 *(A) Detail of a white square against a black background (B) The square rotated 45° through a nearest neighbor filter, with stair-stepping along the edge (C) The square rotated through a cubic filter (D) Detail of photo of a truck window (E) Photo upscaled by 500 percent with a nearest neighbor filter (F) Photo upscaled with a tent filter (G) Photo upscaled with a cubic filter. The white square image is included as* `filter.tif` *in the Footage folder on the DVD. The photo is included in the Footage folder as* `truck.tif`*.*

Additional Resources: Convolution Filters Continued

Convolution filters are not limited to transformation operations. They are used as special effect filters in both After Effects and Nuke. For more information, see Chapter 6, "Convolution Filters."

Working with Transformations

After Effects and Nuke support multiple means to translate, scale, and rotate an image. In addition, both programs offer several ways to apply keyframe animation to the transformations. Each program provides editors to refine the resulting curves.

Transformations in AE

After Effects supports 2D and 3D transformations of 2D layers. You can add keyframes through the Timeline panel or the Effect Controls panel. You can edit the resulting curves in the viewer of the Composition panel or the Graph Editor, which supports both speed graph and value graph views.

Moving, Scaling, and Rotating in 2D

Figure 5.6 (Left) Selection tool (Center) Rotation tool (Right) Pan Behind tool

By default, 2D transformations in After Effects occur around an anchor point. The anchor is indicated by a crosshair and is initially placed at the layer's center. You can reposition the anchor point by LMB+dragging with the Pan Behind tool (see Figure 5.6). To reset the layer so that it's centered on the anchor point, Alt+double-click the Pan Behind tool icon.

You can interactively move, scale, or rotate a layer in a viewer within the Composition panel. To move a layer, select the layer with the Selection tool and LMB+drag. You can also move the layer one pixel at a time by using the keyboard arrow keys while the layer is selected. To scale the layer, LMB+drag a point that falls on the layer's corner or edge. To rotate, choose the Rotation tool and LMB+drag.

For a higher degree of precision, you can enter transform values into the layer's Transform section within the layer outline of the Timeline panel (see Figure 5.7). The layer's Anchor Point, Position, and Scale properties are indicated by X, Y values. (The X and Y cells are unlabeled; the left cell is X and the right cell is Y.) Note that the values are based on the composition's current resolution with 0, 0 occurring at the upper-left corner of the layer. The layer's rotation is based on a scale of 0 to 359°. Any rotation below 0 or above 359 is indicated by the *r*× prefix. For example, a rotation of −600 produces -1x -240 and a rotation of 500 produces 1x +140. To update a transform value, click the value cell and enter a new number. You can also interactively scroll through larger or smaller values by placing the mouse pointer over the value so that the scroll icon appears and then LMB+dragging left or right. By default, the Scale X, Y values are linked so that they change in unison. To break the link, deselect the Constrain Proportions link icon. You can enter negative values into the Scale X or Y cells, which serves as a handy way to invert a layer horizontally or vertically.

▽ Transform	Reset	
⚬ Anchor Point	640.0, 360.0	
⚬ Position	640.0, 360.0	
⚬ Scale	🔗 100.0, 100.0%	
⚬ Rotation	0 x +0.0°	
⚬ Opacity	100%	

▽ Transform	Reset	
⚬ Anchor Point	640.0, 360.0, 0.0	
⚬ Position	640.0, 360.0, 0.0	
⚬ Scale	🔗 100.0, 100.0, 100.0	
⚬ Orientation	0.0°, 0.0°, 0.0°	
⚬ X Rotation	0 x +0.0°	
⚬ Y Rotation	0 x +0.0°	
⚬ Z Rotation	0 x +0.0°	
⚬ Opacity	100%	

Figure 5.7 (Top) A 1280×720 layer's Transform section within the layer outline of the Timeline panel (Bottom) Additional properties that appear when the 3D Layer switch is toggled on

Moving, Scaling, and Rotating in 3D

You can convert any 2D layer within After Effects to a 3D layer and thus gain an additional axis for transformation. To do so, toggle on the layer's 3D Layer switch (see Figure 5.8). Anchor Point Z, Position Z, Scale Z, Orientation, X Rotation, Y Rotation, and Z Rotation cells become available in the layer's Transform section (see Figure 5.7). (The Z cells are the furthest to the right.) In addition, an axis handle is added to the anchor point within the viewer of the Composition panel. By default, the x-axis is red and runs left to right, the y-axis is green and runs down to up, and the z-axis is blue and runs toward the camera (that is, toward the user). You can interactively position the layer by LMB+dragging an axis handle.

Orientation is controlled by X,Y,Z cells that use a scale of 0 to 359°. Changing the Orientation values rotates the layer; however, whole rotations below 0° or above 359° are not allowed to exist. If the layer reaches 360°, the value is reset to 0°. In contrast, X Rotation, Y Rotation, and Z Rotation operate with an *r*× prefix and are permitted to reach values below 0° or above 360°. It's not necessary to use both Orientation and X/Y/Z Rotation.

To move a layer away from the camera (as if "zooming out"), increase the Position Z value. To move the layer toward the camera (as if "zooming in"), decrease the Position Z value until it's negative. To offset the layer from its anchor point, increase or decrease the Anchor Point Z value so that it's no longer 0 (see Figure 5.9). If a layer is offset from its pivot, it rotates around the pivot as if it were a moon orbiting a planet. (Changing the Scale Z value has a similar effect, although negative values flip the axis handle by 180° in Y.)

Converting a layer to 3D does not create a new camera. Thus, any changes to the layer's transformations occur from a fixed viewpoint. To create a new camera, you must create a new Camera Layer. This process is detailed in Chapter 11, "Working with 2.5D and 3D."

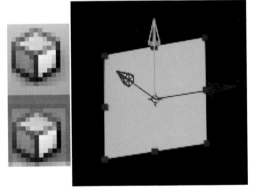

Figure 5.8 (Left) A 3D Layer switch toggled on in the layer outline (Right) A 100×100 layer's 3D transform handle

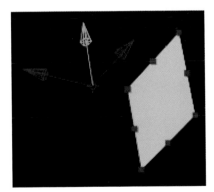

Figure 5.9 Offsetting the pivot of a 3D layer

Keyframing

To set a keyframe in After Effects, you must first toggle on the Stopwatch button beside the property you wish to animate (see Figure 5.10). A property is any layer or effects attribute that carries a channel or channels. Stopwatch buttons are accessible in the layer outline of the Timeline panel or in the Effect Controls panel. As soon as a Stopwatch button is toggled on, a keyframe is laid down for the property for the current frame. By default, keyframes are indicated on the timeline by a diamond-shaped dot (see Figure 5.10). At that point, new keyframes are automatically inserted for the property when there is a change in value.

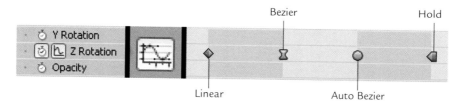

Figure 5.10 (Left) Stopwatch and Include This Property In Graph Editor Set buttons. Both buttons are toggled on. (Center) Graph Editor composition switch (Right) Keyframes displayed on the timeline

If a keyframe already exists for a particular frame, the keyframe is overwritten with a change in property value. You can update values by entering numbers into the property value cells, by adjusting the property sliders, or by interactively manipulating the layer in the viewer of the Composition panel. In addition, you can take the following steps to edit keyframes:

- To delete a keyframe, select it and press the Delete key.
- To select multiple keyframes, LMB+drag a marquee over them.
- To delete all the keyframes for a property, toggle off the Stopwatch button.
- To move a keyframe, LMB+drag it along the timeline.
- To force the creation of a new keyframe when a value hasn't changed, move the current-time indicator (the vertical slider in the Timeline panel) to an appropriate frame, RMB+click over the property name in the layer outline, and choose Add Keyframe.
- To enter specific values for a preexisting keyframe, select the keyframe, RMB+click, and choose Edit Value. Enter new values into the property dialog box and click OK.
- To copy a selected keyframe, press Crtl+C, move the current-time indicator to a new frame, and press Ctrl+V.
- To copy a set of selected keyframes from one property to another, press Crtl+C, highlight the name of the second property by clicking it in the layer outline, and press Ctrl+V. The second property can be part of the same layer or a completely different layer. The keyframes are pasted at the current frame, so it may be necessary to move the current-time indicator before pasting. Note that the paste will work only if the property has compatible channels. For example, you cannot copy keyframes from a Position property, which carries spatial X and Y data, to a Rotate property, which has temporal rotation data.

Using the Graph Editor

Recent releases of After Effects have added to the flexibility of the Graph Editor. To show the editor within the Timeline panel, toggle on the Graph Editor composition switch (see

Figure 5.10). To display curves for a property, toggle on the Include This Property In Graph Editor Set button beside the property name in the layer outline (see Figure 5.10). The Graph Editor utilizes two types of data displays: value and speed. By default, the program chooses the type of display. However, you can change the display at any time by clicking the Choose Graph Type button and selecting Edit Value Graph or Edit Speed Graph from the menu (see Figure 5.11). If you select Edit Value Graph, you can ghost the speed graph within the editor by clicking the Choose Graph Type button and selecting Show Reference Graph. If you select Edit Speed Graph, Show Reference Graph will ghost the value graph.

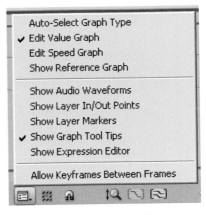

Figure 5.11 (Bottom, Left to Right) Choose Graph Type button and its menu set; Show Transform Box When Multiple Keys Are Selected button; Snap button; Auto-Zoom Graph Height button; Fit Selection To View button; Fit All Graphs To View button

The After Effects value graph is similar to the curve editor used in Nuke or other 3D programs such as 3ds Max or Maya. Time is mapped to the horizontal x-axis and value is mapped to the vertical y-axis. If curves are not immediately visible within the Graph Editor, you can frame them by clicking the Fit All Graphs To View button (see Figure 5.11).

Manipulating Tangent Handles

Many properties, including Scale, Rotate, and Opacity, allow you to manipulate their tangent handles interactively. Tangent handles are referred to as *direction handles* in the After Effects documentation. Tangent handles shape the curve segments as they thread their way through the keyframes. You can change tangent types by selecting keyframes and clicking one of the tangent type buttons at the bottom of the editor (see Figure 5.12).

In addition, you can change the tangent types by RMB+clicking over a keyframe in the Graph Editor or the Timeline panel and choosing Keyframe Interpolation. Within the Keyframe Interpolation dialog box, the Temporal Interpretation menu controls tangent types within the Graph Editor.

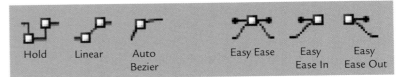

Figure 5.12 Tangent type buttons

By default, keyframes are assigned Linear tangents. That is, the curve runs in a straight line between keyframes. Here is a list of the other tangent types:

Hold creates a stepped curve where values do not change until a new keyframe is encountered. Hold tangents are indicated on the timeline by an icon that has a squared-off side (see Figure 5.10 earlier in this section).

Bezier creates a spline curve that attempts to thread each keyframe smoothly. Bezier tangent handles are broken; that is, you can select and LMB+drag the left and right side of a tangent handle independently. Bezier tangents are indicated on the timeline by an hourglass-shaped icon (see Figure 5.10).

Continuous Bezier also creates spline curves. However, the tangent handles are not broken. Continuous Bezier tangents are indicated on the timeline by an hourglass-shaped icon.

Auto Bezier automatically massages the shape of the curve to maintain smoothness. This occurs when the keyframe value is changed through a property value cell, through a property slider, or through the Edit Value dialog box. If the tangent handle is interactively adjusted through the Graph Editor, the tangent type is instantly converted to a Continuous Bezier. Auto Bezier tangents are indicated on the timeline by a circular icon (see Figure 5.10).

Interpreting the Speed Graph

The speed graph, when compared to the value graph, is less intuitive. Whereas the value graph shows a change in property value over time, the speed graph shows the rate of change for a property value. Hence, the y-axis of the speed graph represents the formula value/second. As a simple comparison, in Figure 5.13, a 100×100 solid is animated moving from the right side of the screen to the left side. On frame 1, the solid has a Position value of 640, 360. At frame 7, the solid has a Position value of 300, 360. If the Graph Editor is set to the value graph view, the Position X curve makes a downward slope, which indicates that the X value is decreasing over time. The Position Y curve, in contrast, is flat, indicating that there is no change to the Y value. If the editor is switched to the speed graph view, the Position X and Y curves become stepped and overlap. Although the solid continues to move in the X direction, the rate of change does not fluctuate. That is, over each of the 7 frames, the solid is moving 1/7 the total distance.

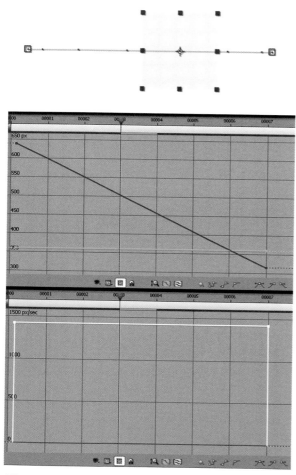

To give the speed graph view curves some shape, you have to change the speed of the solid. Adding an ease in or ease out is a quick way to accomplish this. To add an ease in and ease out, select the curve in the speed graph view and click the Easy Ease button at the bottom of the Graph Editor (see Figure 5.12 earlier in this section). This bows the shape of the Position curve in the speed graph view (see Figure 5.14). This equates to the solid moving slowly at the start and at the end of the animation but rapidly through the middle. The height of the curve for a particular frame indicates the speed of the solid. For example, at frame 1, the solid is moving approximately 925 pixels per second. At frame 4, the solid is moving at approximately 2,105 pixels per second. Again, the y-axis of the speed graph represents value/second or, in this case, pixels moved/second. The slope of the curve, therefore, represents the change in speed. A steep slope indicates a rapid change in speed while a shallow slope indicates an incremental change in speed.

If you switch the Graph Editor to the value graph view, the X curve takes on a more traditional shape. With the application of the Easy Ease button, which creates an ease in and ease out, the slope at the curve's start and end is shallow, indicating an incremental change in value (see Figure 5.14). The center of the curve has a steep slope, indicating a rapid change in value.

To manipulate tangent handles within the speed graph or the value graph view, select a keyframe and LMB+drag the corresponding handle. You can change the length of a handle, and therefore influence the curve shape, by pulling the handle further left or right. If the tangent is set to Bezier and you are using the speed graph view, you can move the left and right side of the tangent handle away from each other vertically. Such a separation

Figure 5.13 (Top) Solid and its motion path in the viewer. (Center) Value graph view. The red curve is Position X. (Bottom) Speed graph view. A sample After Effects project is included as speed_flat.aep in the Tutorials folder on the DVD.

can create a significant change in speed over one frame. In the value graph view, you can rotate the tangent by pulling a tangent handle up or down. However, tangent handles are not available to Linear keyframes in the value graph view. In addition, spatial properties, such as Anchor Point of Position, do not make tangent manipulation available to the value graph view; nevertheless, the tangents are available in the speed graph view or through the overlay of the viewer (see the section "Editing Curves in the Viewer"). Note that Position X, Y, and Z keyframes are linked. Although X, Y, and Z each receive their own curve, their keyframes cannot be given unique frame values or be deleted individually. After Effects CS4 avoids this limitation by allowing you to keyframe each channel separately.

Manipulating Keyframes in the Graph Editor

Whether you choose to work within the speed graph view or the value graph view, there are a number of editing operations you can apply within the Graph Editor:

- To add a keyframe, Ctrl+Alt+click on a curve.
- To delete a selected keyframe, press the Delete key.
- To move a selected keyframe, LMB+drag.
- When multiple keyframe points are selected, a white transform box is supplied if the Show Transform Box When Multiple Keys Are Selected button is toggled on (see Figure 5.11 earlier in this chapter). You can LMB+drag the box left or right and thus move the keyframes as a unit over time. You can LMB+drag the box up or down and thus change the keyframe values. You can scale the keyframes as a unit by LMB+dragging an edge handle.
- You can apply an automatic ease out by selecting a keyframe and clicking the Easy Ease Out button at the bottom of the Graph Editor (see Figure 5.12 earlier in this chapter). To apply ease in, click the Easy Ease In button.

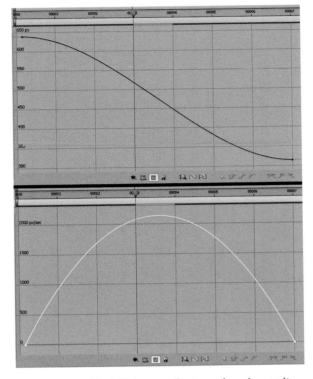

Figure 5.14 (Top) Value graph view after the application of the Easy Ease button (Bottom) The matching speed graph view. A sample After Effects project is included as `speed_ease.aep` in the Tutorials folder on the DVD.

Editing Curves in the Viewer

As a bonus, you can edit keyframes and tangent handles interactively in the viewer of the Composition panel. Within the viewer, keyframes are represented by hollow boxes and the motion path of the layer is indicated by a line running through the keyframes (see Figure 5.13 earlier in this chapter). To select a keyframe, click on its box. To move a selected keyframe, LMB+drag. Any changes applied in the viewer are automatically applied to curves within the Graph Editor.

Tangents found within the viewer have their own set of interpolation properties. By default, the tangents are linear. However, you can change the type by selecting a keyframe, RMB+clicking, choosing Keyframe Interpolation, and changing the Spatial Interpolation to Bezier, Continuous Bezier, or Auto Bezier. The Spatial Interpolation settings do not affect the tangent setting for the curves within the Graph Editor. However, if you move the tangent handles within the viewer, the curves in the Graph Editor automatically update.

Transformations in Nuke

Nuke provides transformation capabilities through specialized nodes. In addition, the program allows keyframe and curve manipulation through its Curve Editor pane.

Moving, Scaling, and Rotating in 2D

In order to move, scale, rotate, or skew the output of a node, you must add a Transform node (Transform → Transform or the default T hotkey). Translate X and Y cells, as well as Rotate, Scale, and Skew sliders, are provided by the Transform node's properties panel (see Figure 5.15). You can also interactively manipulate the resulting transform handle in a viewer. LMB+dragging within the handle circle moves the image. LMB+dragging a point on the circle scales the image in that particular direction. LMB+dragging an arc segment on the circle scales the image in both directions. LMB+dragging the short vertical lines that extend past the top or the bottom of the circle skews the images (turns it into a trapezoidal shape). LMB+dragging the long horizontal line to the right of the circle rotates the image.

Figure 5.15 *(Top) Transform node's properties panel (Bottom) Interactive transform handle in a viewer*

Choosing an Interpolation Filter in Nuke

The Transform node provides several interpolation filters with which to adjust the quality of averaged pixel values. You can select a filter type by changing the Filter menu in the Transform node's properties panel. Brief descriptions follow:

Cubic is the default filter, which offers the best combination of quality and speed. For more information on cubic and similar filters, see the section "Interpolation Filters" earlier in this chapter.

Impulse creates a nearest neighbor style filter whereby the new pixel receives the value of the original pixel or, in the case of scaling, the value of the closest original pixel. The filter takes a minimal amount of computational power but leads to blockiness (see Figure 5.16).

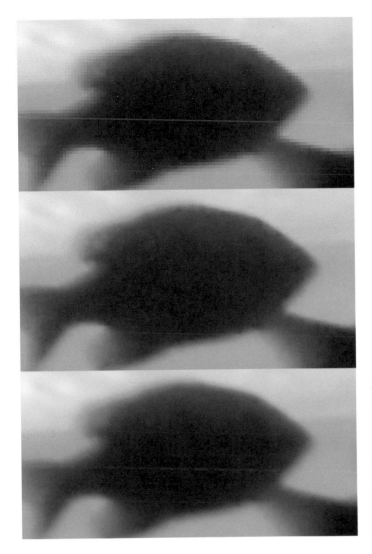

Figure 5.16 *(Top) Image of fish scaled 15 times in X and Y with Impulse filter (Center) Same image with Keys filter (Bottom) Same image with Parzen filter. A sample Nuke script is included as* `filter.nk` *in the Tutorials folder on the DVD.*

Keys uses a bell-shaped function curve but introduces subtle edge sharpening (see Figure 5.16). The Keys function curve is allowed to dip into negative values along the bell base.

Simon is similar to Keys but produces medium-strength sharpening.

Rifman is similar to Keys but produces strong sharpening.

Mitchell is similar to both Cubic and Keys in that it produces smoothing with a very subtle degree of edge sharpening.

Parzen produces the second strongest smoothing among Nuke's convolution filters (see Figure 5.16). Its function curve is a shortened bell curve.

Notch produces the greatest degree of smoothing due to the flattened top of its bell curve.

Additional Resources: 3D Space Transformations

To apply transformations in 3D space within Nuke, you must employ a special setup using 3D geometry, scene, camera, and render nodes. This process is detailed in Chapter 11, "Working with 2.5D and 3D."

Specialty Transform Nodes

Aside from the Transform node, Nuke offers several specialty transformation nodes, all of which are found under the Transform menu:

TransformMasked operates in the same fashion as the Transform node but allows the transformation to occur on a particular channel. For example, you can change the TransformMasked node's Channels menu to Alpha and change the Translate X value to –2, thus subtly shifting the alpha matte to one side.

Position simply translates the image in the X or Y direction. The node automatically streaks the boundary pixels of the image to disguise any gaps that are opened as the image is moved aside.

Mirror flips the image in the horizontal and/or vertical directions.

CameraShake adds its namesake to a node's output (see Figure 5.17). This is useful for re-creating earthquakes, shock waves, handheld camerawork, and the like. The Amplitude slider controls the strength of the shake. The Rotation slider, when raised above 0, inserts rotation along the camera's z-axis. The Scale slider, when above 0, moves the image either closer to or farther from the viewer along the camera's z-axis. The Frequency slider controls the lowest frequency and thus the "graininess" of the underlying noise function. Large Frequency values lead to a small "grain," which causes the shake to be violent and chaotic. Small values lead to large "grains," which cause the shake to be slow and smooth (similar to the float created by a Steadicam). The Octaves cell controls the complexity of the underlying noise. With each whole value increase of the Octaves cell, an additional frequency of noise is layered on the base noise and the more complex and seemingly random the shaking becomes. The CameraShake node automatically adds 2D motion blur to the image; the strength of the blur corresponds to the distance the image is moved for a frame. In addition, the node automatically streaks the boundary pixels of the image to disguise any gaps that are opened as the image is moved aside.

The LensDistortion node creates the subtle spherical distortion of real-world lenses. This is useful for matching live-action footage when motion tracking. The LenDistortion node is detailed in Chapter 10,

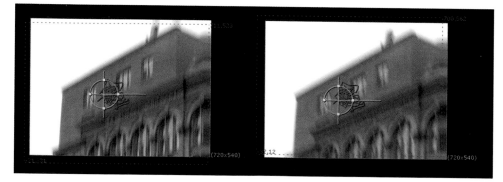

Figure 5.17 *Two frames showing the movement and motion blur introduced by a CameraShake node. The squiggly line in the center is the motion path created by the node for a 30-frame animation. A sample Nuke script is included as* `camerashake.nk` *in the Tutorials folder on the DVD.*

"Warps, Optical Artifacts, Paint, and Text." The SphericalTransform node, on the other hand, is designed for HDRI mapping, which is discussed in Chapter 12, "Advanced Techniques."

Keyframing and the Curve Editor

To set a keyframe, click an Animation button (with a picture of a curve) and choose Set Key from the menu (see Figure 5.18). Animation buttons are provided for any parameter that supports an animation channel. You can also key all the available parameters for a node in one step by RMB+clicking over an empty area of a properties panel and choosing Set Key On All Knobs. (Each keyable parameter is referred to as a knob.) Once a parameter has been keyed, its corresponding numeric cell or check box turns cyan. In addition, cyan tick marks are added to the viewer timeline to indicate the presence of keyframes. (Keyframes are placed at the current frame, so it's important to check the timeline first.) As soon as one keyframe has been set

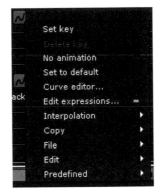

Figure 5.18
Animation button (top left) and menu options

for a parameter, any change in value for that parameter automatically creates a new keyframe. You can delete a keyframe by clicking an Animation button and choosing the Delete key from the menu. You can destroy all the keyframes for a parameter by clicking the corresponding Animation button and choosing No Animation from the menu.

Curve Editor Basics

To edit keyframes and corresponding curves, you can use Nuke's Curve Editor. To launch the editor, click an Animation button for a parameter that carries animation and choose Curve Editor from the menu. The Curve Editor integrates itself into a pane beside the Node Graph. The left column of the editor displays all the parameters for the node that carry keyframes. If a parameter has a single channel, such as Rotate or Skew, only one matching curve is indicated by a : symbol. If a parameter has more than one channel, the matching curves are listed by their names. For example, Translate lists x: and/or y: curves, while Scale lists w: and/or h: curves (see Figure 5.19). To view all the curves of a parameter, click the parameter name. To view specific curves, Shift+click the curve names. You can use the standard camera controls to zoom in or out (Alt+MMB) and scroll (Alt+LMB) within the curve grid. To frame selected curves automatically, press the F key.

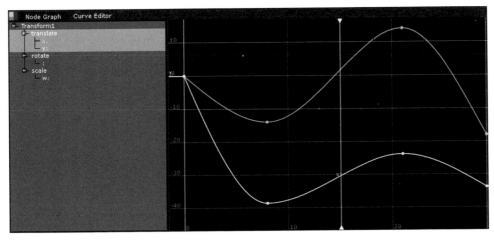

Figure 5.19 The Curve Editor

Here are basic steps to take to select, edit, and delete keyframes and curves:

- To select a keyframe point, click it or LMB+drag a marquee box around it.
- To select multiple keyframe points, Shift+click them or LMB+drag a marquee box around them.
- To move a selected keyframe, LMB+drag. By default, the keyframe is locked to either its current frame or current value, depending on the direction you initially drag the mouse. To move the selected keyframe freely, Crtl+LMB+drag.
- To move a selected keyframe to a specific location, RMB+click and choose Edit → Move. In the Move Animation Keys dialog box, enter specific values in the X and/or Y cells and press OK (see Figure 5.20). You can also enter a specific value for the tangent handle slope. *Slope*, as a term, describes the steepness or incline of a straight line. In Nuke, tangent slopes are measured as a θ (theta) angle. When you select a keyframe, the θ measurement for the right slope is displayed by the right side of the tangent handle (see Figure 5.20). In terms of the Move Animation Keys dialog box, you can enter values into the (Right) Slope or Left Slope cells. If the values of the two slopes are different, the tangent handle is automatically broken; thereafter, you can move each side independently. Slope values are either negative or positive. The range is dependent upon the position of the keyframe on the curve, the type of tangent interpolation, and its proximity to other keyframes. The program automatically clips slope values that are too small or too large. More directly, you can enter a right slope value by clicking the slope readout beside the tangent handle and entering a new value into the cell that appears.

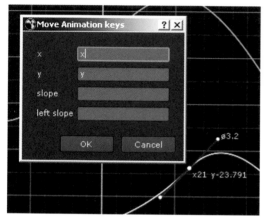

Figure 5.20 *(Top Left) Move Animation Keys dialog box (Bottom Right) Selected tangent handle with X, Y, and θ readout*

- To assign a keyframe to a specific frame, select the keyframe and click the *x* portion of the numeric readout that appears beside it. Enter a value into the cell that opens.
- To assign a keyframe to a specific value, select the keyframe and click the *y* portion of the numeric readout that appears beside it. Enter a value into the cell that opens.
- To delete selected keyframe(s), press the Delete key.
- To insert a new keyframe along a curve's current path, Ctrl+Alt+click the curve at the point where you want a new keyframe.
- To insert a new keyframe at a point that lies off the curve's path, click the curve so that it turns yellow, then Ctrl+Alt+click at a point off the curve. A new keyframe is inserted at that point and the curve is reshaped to flow through the new keyframe.
- To copy a keyframe, select it, RMB+click, and choose Edit → Copy → Copy Selected Keys. Select a different curve through the left column. RMB+click and choose Edit → Paste.
- To impose the shape of one curve onto a second curve, select a curve, RMB+click, and choose Edit → Copy → Copy Curves. Select a different curve through the left column. RMB+click and choose Edit → Paste.
- To reverse a curve, select the curve (or a set of keyframes), RMB+click, and choose Predefined → Reverse. The curve is reversed and its original position is indicated by a dashed line. You can undo the reverse by choosing Predefined → Reverse again.
- To flip a curve vertically, choose Predefined → Negate.
- To smooth a curve automatically, select a set of keyframes, RMB+click, choose Edit → Filter, enter a value into the No. Of Times To Filter cell of the Filter Multiple dialog box, and click OK. The higher the value, the stronger the averaging will be and the flatter the curve will get in that region.
- You can create evenly spaced keyframes along a curve by selecting the curve so that it turns yellow, RMB+clicking, and choosing Edit → Generate Keys from the menu. In

the Generate Keys dialog box, choose Start At and End At frames and an Increment value. If you wish for the new keyframes to have a specific value, enter a number in the curve name cell. For example, if you select the Y curve of a Translate parameter, the curve name cell is *y:* and the cell value is *y*. If you leave *y* in the cell, the new keyframes will be spread along the curve's current path. If you change *y* to a particular value, such as 1, the new keyframes will appear with that value and the old curve path is altered.

Changing Tangent Types

When a keyframe is selected, tangent handles automatically appear. You can LMB+drag any handle to change the curve shape. In addition, Nuke offers seven tangent types that you can select by RMB+clicking and choosing Interpolation → *interpolation type* from the menu. While Linear and Smooth types are identical to those used by other compositing and 3D programs, several types are unique (at least in name):

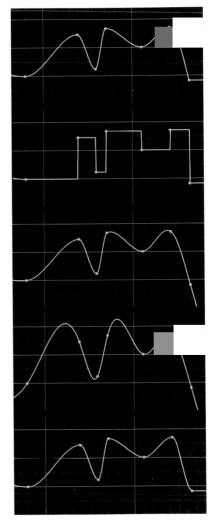

> **Constant** creates a stepped curve. There is no change in value until the next keyframe is encountered (see Figure 5.21).

> **Catmull-Rom** matches the tangent slope to a slope created by drawing a line between the nearest keyframe to the left and right. This generally leads to a subtle improvement in the roundness to curve peaks and valleys (see Figure 5.21).

> **Cubic** aligns the tangent handle to the steepest side of the curve as it passes through the keyframe. This prevents the appearance of sharp peaks within the curve (at least where the cubic tangents are), but it may also lead to the curve shooting significantly past the previous minimum or maximum values (see Figure 5.21).

> **Horizontal** forces the tangent handle to have 0 slope. This may produce results similar to unadjusted Smooth tangents (see Figure 5.21).

> **Break** snaps the tangent in half so that each side can be adjusted independently.

AE and Nuke Tutorials

Although compositing normally involves captured footage of some sort, it's possible to create animation with static images. After Effects and Nuke offer a wide array of keyframing and curve editing tools to achieve this effect.

Figure 5.21 (Top to Bottom) Default Smooth tangents, Constant tangents, Catmull-Rom tangents, Cubic tangents, and Horizontal tangents

AE Tutorial 5: Adding Dynamic Animation to a Static Layer

Editing animation curves within the After Effects Graph Editor gives you a great degree of control. For example, in this tutorial the editor will allow you to give a static ball a believable series of bounces.

1. Create a new project. Choose Composition → New Composition. In the Composition Settings dialog box, set the Preset menu to Film (2K). Set Duration to 36, Start Frame to 1, and Frame Rate to 30. Import the `floor.tga` and `ball.tga` files from the Footage folder on the DVD. Interpret the alpha on the `ball.tga` file as Premultiplied.

2. LMB+drag `ball.tga` from the Project panel into the layer outline of the Timeline panel. Select the Pan Behind tool (Y is the default hot key). LMB+drag the anchor

point for the ball.tga layer so that it rests at the center of the ball (see Figure 5.22). A centered anchor is necessary for any rotational animation. The Anchor Point property, in the ball.tga layer's Transform section, should be approximately 1060, 710 once the anchor point is centered. LMB+drag floor.tga from the Project panel to the bottom of the layer outline. The CG ball is thus composited over the top of a floor photo.

3. Move the timeline to frame 1. Expand the Transform section of the ball.tga layer in the layer outline. Set the Scale to 120%. Set the Rotation to –25. Set the Position to 1160,–80. This places the ball out of frame at the upper right. Toggle on the Stopwatch buttons beside the Position, Scale, and Rotation properties. Keyframes are set on the timeline.

4. Move the timeline to frame 36. You can interactively drag the current-time indicator in the Timeline panel or enter the frame number in the Current Time cell at the top left of the layer outline. Change Position to 875, 1000, Scale to 125%, and Rotation to 50. Because a key has already been set on

Figure 5.22 *Centered anchor point for ball layer*

the properties, new keyframes are automatically laid down with the change in values. As soon as two keyframes exist, a motion path is drawn in the viewer for the ball.

5. Move the timeline to frames 6, 11, 16, 21, 26, and 31, interactively positioning the ball as you go. The ball should bounce three times; that is, the ball should touch the ground at frames 6, 16, 26, and 36 while hitting the peak of a bounce at frames 11, 21, and 31. Each bounce should be shallower than the previous one. You can adjust the position of the keyframes in the viewer by LMB+dragging a keyframe point. Use Figure 5.23 as a reference for the shape of the motion path. To smooth the peak of each bounce, select a keyframe for frame 11, 21, or 31 and LMB+drag the displayed tangent handle. You can lengthen a tangent handle by LMB+dragging it left or right. If it's difficult to see the tangent handle, set the viewer's Magnification Ratio Popup menu to zoom in closer. To make sharp turns with the motion path at the points that the ball touches the ground, shorten the tangent handles for frames 6, 16, and 26.

Figure 5.23 *Ball layer's motion path, as seen in the viewer. The floor layer has been temporarily hidden.*

6. Use the Time Controls panel to play back the timeline. Make sure that the playback occurs at approximately 30 fps. The Info panel will display the playback rate and whether or not it is real time. Adjust the keyframes and motion path of the ball layer until you're satisfied with the overall motion. For additional information on keyframe and curve editing, see the section "Using the Graph Editor" earlier in this chapter.

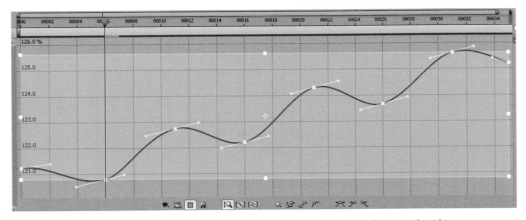

Figure 5.24 The ball layer's Scale curve in the value graph view of the Graph Editor

7. At this stage, the ball is increasing in scale as it bounces toward the foreground. You can refine the scale transition in the Graph Editor. In the layer outline, toggle on the Include This Property In The Graph Editor Set button beside the Scale property. Toggle on the Graph Editor composition switch at the top-right of the layer outline. The Graph Editor opens in the Timeline panel. Click the Choose Graph Type And Options button, at the bottom of the Graph Editor, and choose Edit Value Graph. Click the Fit All Graphs To View button to frame the Scale curve. Since the Scale property's Constrain link remains activated, only one curve is supplied for Scale X and Y. Insert keyframes at frames 6, 11, 16, 21, 26, and 31. To insert a new keyframe, Ctrl+Alt+click the curve. Interactively move the keyframes for frames 6, 16, and 26 to make the scale slightly smaller. This will give the illusion that the ball gets closer to the camera at the peak of each bounce. Use Figure 5.24 as a reference for the shape of the curve. You can add smoothness to the curve by manipulating the tangent handles. To do so, LMB+drag to select all the keyframes, RMB+click over a keyframe, and choose Keyframe Interpolation from the menu. In the Keyframe Interpolation dialog box, set the Temporal Interpolation menu to Bezier and click OK. To move a tangent handle, select a keyframe in the Graph Editor and LMB+drag the left or right tangent handle point.

8. At this stage, the ball feels disconnected due to a lack of shadow (see Figure 5.25). You can create a shadow using the duplicate of the ball layer with Blur and Brightness & Contrast filters. This process, along with the application of artificial motion blur and camera move, will be addressed in the Chapter 6 After Effects follow-up tutorial. In the meantime, save the file for later use. A sample After Effects project is included as ae5.aep in the Tutorials folder on the DVD.

Figure 5.25 The initial composite. A shadow will be added in the Chapter 6 After Effects follow-up tutorial.

Nuke Tutorial 5: Adding Dynamic Animation to a Static Output

Editing animation curves within the Nuke Curve Editor gives you a great degree of control. For example, in this tutorial the editor will allow you to give a static ball a believable series of bounces.

1. Create a new script. Choose Edit → Project Settings. Change Frame Range to 1, 36 and Fps to 30. With the Full Size Format menu, choose 2k_Super_35(Full-ap) 2048×1556. In the Node Graph, RMB+click, choose Image → Read, and browse for the floor.tga file in the Footage folder on the DVD. With no nodes selected, RMB+click, choose Image → Read, and browse for the ball.tga file in the Footage folder on the DVD. In the Read2 node's properties panel, select the Premultiplied check box.

2. With the Read2 node selected, RMB+click and choose Transform → Transform. With no nodes selected, RMB+click and choose Merge → Merge. Connect input A of the Merge1 node to the output of the Transform1 node. Connect input B of the Merge1 node to the output of the Read1 node. Connect the output of the Merge1 node to a viewer. A CG ball is composited over the top of a floor photo. Before you are able to animate, however, it's necessary to center the ball's transform pivot. In the Transform1 node's properties panel, set the Center X cell to 1062 and the Center Y cell to 850 (see Figure 5.26). This centers the transform handle over the ball.

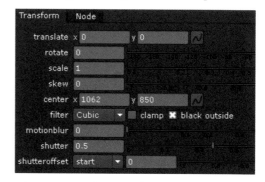

Figure 5.26 The Transform1 node's properties panel after the adjustment of the Center parameter

3. Move the timeline to frame 1. In the Transform1 node's properties panel, set Scale to 1.20. Set Rotation to 50. Set the Translate X and Y cells to 26, 760. This places the ball out of frame. Click the Animation button beside the Translate parameter and choose Set Key. The cell turns cyan and a cyan line appears over frame 1 on the timeline of the viewer. Repeat the Set Key process for the Scale and Rotate parameters.

4. Move the timeline to frame 35. Change the Translate X and Y cells to –196, –196. This moves the ball to the center of the frame. Set the Rotate slider to –25. Set the Scale slider to 1.25. New keyframes are automatically placed on the timeline. As soon as two keyframes exist for the Translate parameter, a motion path is drawn in the viewer.

5. Move the timeline to frames 5, 10, 16, 21, 26, and 31, interactively positioning the ball as you go. The ball should bounce three times; that is, the ball should touch the ground at frames 5, 16, 26, and 35 while hitting the peak of a bounce at frames 10, 21, and 31. Each bounce should be shallower than the previous one. Use Figure 5.27 as reference for the initial shape of the motion path.

6. Check the viewer's Desired Playback Rate cell. It should say 30 by default. Play back the timeline with the viewer Play button. Watch the Desired Playback Rate cell to make sure the playback is approximately 30 fps. If the playback is too slow, then set the viewer's Downrez menu to a value that allows the proper playback speed. (For more information on critical viewer settings, see Chapter 1.) At this point, the bouncing may appear somewhat mechanical or as if the ball is attached to an elastic string.

The duration for which the ball hangs in the air or touches the ground is not ideal. Due to the default Smooth tangent types, there are sharp corners as the ball peaks. In addition, there is an ease in and ease out as the ball nears the ground. To address this, adjust the keyframes and tangent types in the Curve Editor.

7. In the Transform node's properties panel, click the Animation button for an animated parameter and choose Curve Editor from the menu. The Curve Editor opens in a pane beside the Node Graph. Click the *y:* below the word *Translate* in the left column to show the Translate Y curve. Press the F key while the mouse pointer is over the Curve Editor to frame the curve. To improve the arc at each bounce peak, interactively manipulate the tangents for keyframes at 10, 21, and 31. You can move a tangent handle by clicking on a keyframe and LMB+dragging the left or right tangent handle point. The motion path in the viewer will update as the tangent handles are manipulated.

Figure 5.27 The ball's initial motion path (the background is temporarily hidden)

8. To prevent the ease in/out as the ball touches the ground, Shift+select the keyframes at 5, 16, and 26, RMB+click over a keyframe, and choose Interpolation → Break. This breaks each tangent in half. Adjust the left and right side of each tangent handle to remove the ease in and ease out. When you adjust the tangents' handles at the point the ball touches the ground, the tops of each bounce gain additional roundness, which equates to a slightly longer "hang time" for the ball (see Figure 5.28). The only keyframe that doesn't gain additional roundness is the one resting at frame 1. Select the frame 1 tangent handle and adjust it so that the curve no longer makes a linear path from frames 1 to 5.

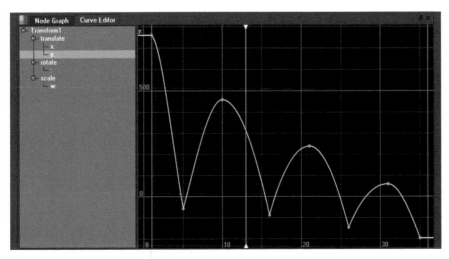

Figure 5.28 The updated Y curve in the curve editor

9. At this point, there may be a slight bend in the ball's motion path as the ball descends from its bounce (see Figure 5.29). This is due to the X curve remaining in its initial state. Select the *x:* below the word *Translate* in the left column of the Curve Editor. Press the F key to frame the X curve. Rotate the tangent handles for frames 5, 16, and 26 until the bend disappears (see Figure 5.29). Play back the timeline. Continue to refine the tangent rotations for all the keyframes of both the X and Y curves.

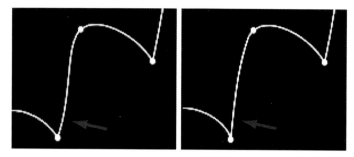

Figure 5.29 *(Left) Bend in motion path due to unadjusted X curve (Right) Result after X curve tangents are rotated*

10. From frame 1 to frame 35, the ball changes from a scale of 1.2 to 1.25. This slight increase will help to create the illusion that the ball is getting closer to the camera. You can exaggerate this scale shift by also changing the ball scale between the peaks and valleys of each bounce. To do so, click the *w:* below the word *Scale* in the left column of the Curve Editor. Press the F key to frame the W curve. (Since the scale occurs equally for the width and height of the ball, only the W curve is provided.) Move the timeline to frame 5. In the Transform1 node's properties panel, click the Scale parameter's Animation button and choose Set Key. This places a new keyframe on the curve without disturbing its current value. Repeat the process for frames 10, 16, 21, 26, and 31. In the Curve Editor, move the keyframes so that the scale is slightly larger at the bounce peaks and slightly smaller at the point where the ball touches the ground. Use Figure 5.30 as reference.

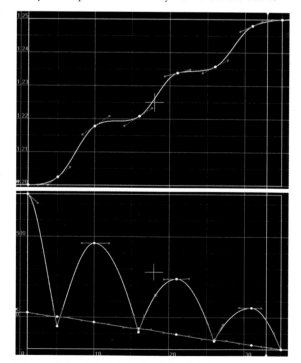

11. At this point, the ball feels disconnected due to a lack of shadow. You can create a shadow using the CG render of the ball with additional Transform, Grade, and Blur nodes. This process, along with the application of artificial motion blur and camera move, will be addressed in the Chapter 6 Nuke follow-up tutorial. In the meantime, save the file for later use. A sample Nuke script is included as nuke5.aep in the Tutorials folder on the DVD.

Figure 5.30 *(Top) The final Scale W curve (Bottom) The final Translate X and Y curves*

Figure 5.31 The initial composite. A shadow will be added in the Chapter 6 Nuke follow-up tutorial.

Interview: Erik Winquist, Weta Digital, Wellington, New Zealand

In 1998, Erik Winquist graduated from the Ringling School of Art and Design with a degree in computer animation. Shortly thereafter, he joined Pacific Data Images as a digital artist. In 2002, he joined Weta Digital as a compositor. After a six-month stint at ILM as a compositor on *Hulk*, Erik returned to Weta to serve as a compositing supervisor on *I, Robot*; *King Kong*; *X Men: the Last Stand*; and *Avatar*. He was also the visual effects supervisor on *The Water Horse* and *Jumper*.

Weta was formed in 1993 by New Zealand filmmakers Peter Jackson, Richard Taylor, and Jamie Selkirk. It later split into two specialized halves: Weta Digital for digital effects and Weta Workshop for physical effects. Weta Digital has been nominated for five visual effects Oscars and has won four.

(Weta Digital keeps a core staff of 40 compositors but expands for large shows.)

LL: What is the main compositing software used at Weta Digital?

Erik Winquist (Image courtesy of Weta Digital)

EW: We've been a Shake house since [*The Lord of the Rings: The Fellowship of the Ring*]. In 2004, during work on *I, Robot*, we started evaluating Nuke, which was used fairly extensively on *King Kong* as an environments tool and has been slowly gaining favor as a compositing package among the compositing department....

LL: What would be the greatest strength of either Shake or Nuke?

EW: With Shake, hands down, it's the user base. It's that package that everyone knows and is easiest to hire artists [for] on short notice.... We also have a large collection of in-house plug-ins that has been written over the years.... Nuke has been a bit more foreign at first glance, but once you get into it, its speed and toolset is just a boon for this increasingly 3D "two-dimensional" work that we do each day. It's definitely a compositing package that has evolved over the years in a production environment. The recent inclusion of Python scripting support has been really great for scripting tools that would otherwise require compiled solutions....

LL: In your experience, do you prefer working with proprietary, in-house compositing software or off-the-shelf, third-party software?

EW: The most flexible solution seems [to be] a third-party application [that] is expandable via software developers' kits (SDKs). That way, you get the benefit of using a tool [that] lots of people will already know but at the same time have the ability to write custom in-house tools to work best with your specific pipeline.

LL: What type of workstations do Weta compositors use?

EW: All of the compositors here are working on dual quad-core Intel boxes running Kubuntu Linux with 8 gigabytes of RAM. We generally don't do fast local storage here, as everything is served from network filers. Most artists have two machines at their desks for better multitasking.

LL: What resolutions do you normally comp at?

EW: That depends on the project really, but the vast majority of shows that have come through Weta have been shot Super35, with a scanning full aperture resolution of 2048×1556 and a 16×9 delivery resolution of 2048×1157. Current HD shows and are being ingested from tape at 1920×1080. We recently completed a special venue project which had a 6:1 delivery ratio with source plates shot on a special tiled rig using three Red One cameras shooting simultaneously.

LL: How is it to work with Red One footage?

EW: There have been a couple shows we've worked on recently [that] used the Red camera for at least a handful of plates, often for pickup shoots. The trouble I've seen early on is that none of the plates were coming in with any consistent color space from show to show, or even shot to shot. For the aforementioned special venue project shot on Red...the images were shot and converted correctly from RAW to linear float EXRs, which were then a breeze to comp with.

The Weta Digital facilities tucked into a quiet corner of Wellington
(Image courtesy of Weta Digital)

LL: Does 35mm footage suffer from any quirks not present with high-definition digital video footage? How about vice versa?

EW: 35mm film still gives your loads more dynamic range than the HD footage that's come across our workstations. Whereas scanned film negative can give you almost four stops above reflected white, the Red footage is only about one stop above. Anything brighter than that is clipped. Where 4:4:4 HD is proving nice is in its lack of film grain and what that can do for extracted keys. Edges and highlights don't suffer from emulsion halation like film.

Additional Resources: The Full Interview

To read the full interview with Erik Winquist, see the Interviews folder on the DVD. For more information on 2.5D techniques, see Chapter 11, "Working with 2.5D and 3D."

Interview: Darren Poe, Digital Domain, Venice, California

Darren Poe began his career as a graphic designer and video postproduction artist. He joined Digital Domain in 1996 as a 3D effects artist. After working on *The Fifth Element* and *Titanic*, he went on to specialize as a compositor. His film roster has since included such features as *Fight Club*, *Daredevil*, *The Day After Tomorrow*, *Charlie and the Chocolate Factory*, *Pirates of the Caribbean: At World's End*, and *Speed Racer*. He currently serves as a digital effects supervisor.

Digital Domain was founded in 1993 by visual effects pioneers Scott Ross, James Cameron, and Stan Winston. The studio has gone on to win seven visual effects and scientific achievement Oscars with its credits exceeding 65 feature films and scores of television commercials.

Darren Poe (Image courtesy of Digital Domain)

LL: Digital Domain developed Nuke in-house. Do you currently use the publicly available commercial version or a custom variation?

DP: Since The Foundry took over the development of Nuke, we're basically using whatever their latest beta is, at least on the show I'm on right now. We have our own in-house custom tools, which are more like plug-ins to Nuke as opposed to variants on the actual build of Nuke itself. (*Nuke* stands for "New Compositor.")

LL: Do you use any other compositing programs?

DP: We do have Shake and will use it in certain circumstance, but 99.9 percent of what we do is Nuke.

LL: Have you used any other packages over the years?

DP: I should go back and say that I'm one of the last people who uses Flame, at least on the feature side. I sometimes forget that I do that. These days, it's primarily used in commercial production. It's a known quantity. Agencies come in knowing what the box can do.

LL: Do you prefer using in-house, proprietary software or off-the-shelf, third-party software?

DP: There are advantages both ways. If you use commercially available software, it broadens the range of people you can bring in to work on a show. One of the things that has changed a lot in the industry is that the model of hiring people has come much closer to the duration and needs of the show. So, you really need to be able to find skilled people who can start immediately—where you don't have that year of ramp-up and training or mentoring....

LL: Is that wide-spread in Los Angeles—hiring a compositor for the duration of a single show or project?

DP: That's pretty much how most places operate. People who have the broadest set of skills with the latest commercial software put them at a great advantage to come in without having to completely learn a new system. But at the same time, with the exception of Nuke, there are a lot of limitations to commercial software that's developed outside of a production context. We build a lot of tools and knowledge over the years based on things that happened on shows and needs that have come up, so that's where the proprietary part of it becomes very important.

LL: As a compositor, what kind of workstation do you use?

DP: We're using Linux. Typically [dual quad-core] machines...usually a dual monitor type of set up.

LL: What resolutions do you normally comp at?

DP: It's completely dependent on the show. We've done a lot of HD (1920×1080) recently (for example, *2012*, which is shot digitally). Right now, we're doing a show that's 4K, so it really runs the gambit.

Inside the modern Digital Domain facility. The arced structure to the right is a large conference room designed by architect Frank Gehry. Miniatures from The Fifth Element *and* Apollo 13 *sit close by. (Image courtesy of Digital Domain)*

LL: Have you worked with Red One footage?

DP: We just did some tests with the Red camera....it's still early [in the testing process]. I don't think any show is really using it—like actually going out and shooting full elements....

LL: So it's still very common to shoot 35mm or VistaVision?

DP: It's still very common, although HD is making huge inroads (*Speed Racer* was shot on HD).

LL: Is it common to work with bluescreen or greenscreen?

DP: Percentage-wise, it's probably less than it has been in the past. As an industry, [we've] moved to a point where rotoscoping and other ways of extraction are seen as possible or even desirable.

LL: What do you use to pull the keys?

DP: Basically, we use Nuke. What's in Nuke is Primatte, Keylight, and Ultimatte...all the main [keyers]....

LL: Do you see more and more "dirty" plates? That is, are visual effects plates now being shot with no blue- or greenscreen at all, preferring to let the compositing team to do whatever they need to do to make the effect work?

DP: Definitely. The cost benefit of properly setting up a shoot with an evenly lit greenscreen can be poor when compared to having the compositing team fix the shot.

LL: Do you rotoscope in house?

DP: We roto in-house.... We basically operate a pool [of rotoscopers] that fluctuates in size depending on the needs of various shows. They [work] across the different shows.

Additional Resources: The Full Interview

To read the full interview with Darren Poe, see the Interviews folder on the DVD. For more information on rotoscoping, see Chapter 7, "Masking, Rotoscoping, and Motion Tracking."

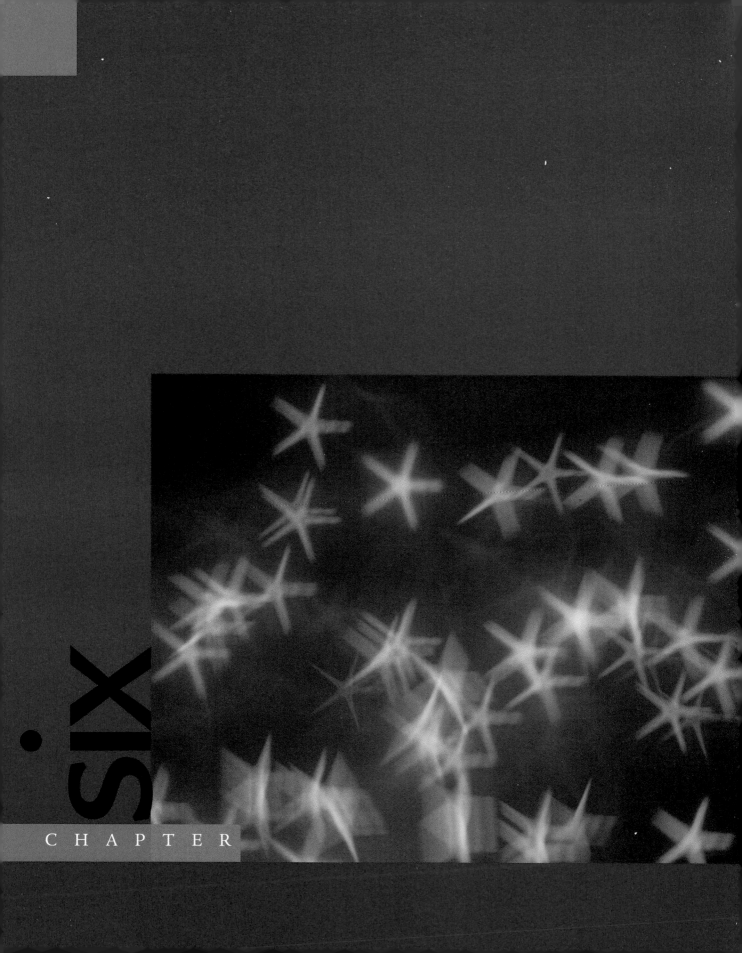

six

Convolution Filters

Filters, in the form of effects *and nodes, are an integral part of compositing. Many common filters, such as blur and sharpen, are based on a convolution kernel. Such kernels, which are detailed in this chapter, are equally capable of creating stylized effects, such as emboss and edge enhance. After Effects and Nuke provide a long list of convolution-style filters. Nuke offers Convolve and Matrix nodes that allow you to design your own custom convolutions. Hence, it's important to understand how kernel values affect the output. A number of sample kernels are included in this chapter. In addition, you will have the chance to update the work started with the Chapter 5 tutorial. In addition, you'll build a custom filter using existing effects and nodes.*

Filter Matrices

As discussed in Chapter 5, using matrices is a necessary step when applying transformations to a layer or node output. Not only is position, rotation, skew, and scale information stored in a transformation matrix, but pixel averaging, which is required to prevent aliasing problems, is undertaken by convolution matrices. You can also apply convolution matrices to create stylistic effects. In fact, such matrices serve as the basis of many popular compositing filters that are discussed in this chapter.

Blurring Kernels

Blurs are one of the most common filters applied in compositing. They may take the form of a box filter, where all the kernel elements are identical and a divisor is employed. They may also take the form of a tent filter, where the weighting of the kernel tapers towards the edges. An example tent filter kernel follows:

```
        1 2 1
1/16   2 4 2
        1 2 1
```

This kernel does not include brackets, although the matrix structure is implied. In addition, the kernel includes a divisor in the form of 1/16. A divisor forces the end sum of the kernel multiplication to be multiplied by its fractional value. The use of a divisor ensures that the resulting image retains the same tonal range as the original. In this case, 16 is derived from the sum of all the matrix elements. You can express the same kernel as follows:

```
1/16 2/16 1/16
2/16 4/16 2/16
1/16 2/16 1/16
```

If a convolution kernel does not indicate a divisor, it's assumed that the divisor is 1.0 / 1.0, or 1.0. If the divisor is a value other than 1.0, averaging occurs across all pixel values found below the kernel. For example, in Table 6.1, a 5×5 input image is represented by an input matrix. Each input matrix cell carries a pixel value. The filter kernel is represented by the dark gray cells. In this position, the kernel determines the output value of the pixel colored light gray, which lies under the kernel's central element. The convolution math for this kernel position can be written in the following manner:

Table 6.1: Blur Kernel Applied to Input Image Matrix

1.0 x 1.0	2 x 1.0	1.0 x 0.5	0	0
2 x 1.0	4 x 1.0	2 x 0.5	0	0
1.0 x 1.0	2 x 1.0	1.0 x 0.5	0	0
1.0	1.0	0.5	0	0
1.0	1.0	0.5	0	0

```
x = ((1.0 × 1.0) + (2 × 1.0) + (1.0 × 0.5) + (2 × 1.0) + (4 × 1.0) +
(2 × 0.5) + (1.0 × 1.0) + (2 × 1.0) + (1.0 × 0.5)) / 16
```

The output value x for the targeted pixel is thus 0.875. The application of this particular filter kernel creates the output image illustrated by Figure 6.1. (For more information on box filters, tent filters, and kernel convolution, see Chapter 5.)

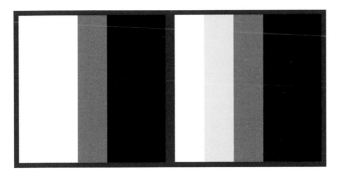

Figure 6.1 (Left) 5×5 pixel image that matches the input matrix illustrated by Table 6.1 (Right) Same image after the convolution of the example blur kernel. A sample Nuke script is included as 5x5blur.nk *in the Tutorials folder on the DVD.*

Tips & Tricks: Kernel Overhang

In order for a convolution kernel to determine the output value of a pixel along the edge of an input matrix, the kernel must "overhang" the input matrix edge. Because part of the kernel is thus covering a region with no pixel values, values must be artificially supplied to the kernel. Compositing programs use several methods to supply the values. The program may automatically supply a fixed value, such as 0. The program may wrap the input matrix and thereby borrow a pixel value from the opposite edge. The program may borrow a value from the nearest valid pixel within the input matrix.

Gaussian Blurs

Blur kernels are not limited to a specific kernel size. For example, Gaussian blurs are often expressed as 5×5 matrices with whole values:

$$1/256 \begin{array}{ccccc} 1 & 4 & 6 & 4 & 1 \\ 4 & 16 & 24 & 16 & 4 \\ 6 & 24 & 36 & 24 & 6 \\ 4 & 16 & 24 & 16 & 4 \\ 1 & 4 & 6 & 4 & 1 \end{array}$$

Gaussian blurs form a bell-shaped function curve and are thus similar to the cubic filters discussed in Chapter 5. The blurs take their name from Johann Carl Friedrich Gauss (1777–1855), a mathematician who developed theories on surface curvature.

Directional Blurs

You can create a directional blur by aligning non-0 elements so that they form a line in a particular direction. For example, the following kernel creates a blur that runs from the bottom left of frame to the right of frame:

```
        0   0    0    0
   1/4  0   0    0.3  1
        0   0.6  0.7  0
        1   0.4  0    0
```

Any pixel that falls under a 0 element is ignored by the pixel averaging process (see Figure 6.2). If the input image has a large resolution, the kernel matrix must have a large dimension for it to have a significant impact. Otherwise, the resulting blur will be subtle.

Figure 6.2 *(Top) Input image (Bottom) Result of a directional blur kernel. Note that the kernel removes the original grain. (Photo © 2009 by Jupiterimages)*

Sharpening Kernels

Sharpening filters employ negative values in their kernels. For example, a generic sharpen kernel can be written in the following manner:

```
    0   -1    0
   -1   11   -1
    0   -1    0
```

As is the case with many sharpening filters, the divisor is 1.0. The negative values, on the other hand, are able to increase contrast within the image by exaggerating the differences between neighboring pixels. For example, in Table 6.2, a 5×5 input image of a soft, diagonal edge is represented by an input matrix. The central element of the matrix kernel is set to 11. The higher the central element, the more extreme the sharpening and the brighter the resulting image.

In Table 6.2, the filter kernel is represented by the dark gray cells. In this position, the kernel determines the output value of the pixel colored light gray. The output value for the targeted pixel is thus 3.6. The application of this particular filter kernel creates the output image illustrated by Figure 6.3.

Table 6.2: Sharpen Kernel Applied to Input Image Matrix

0	0	0	0.4	0.5
0	0	0.4	0.5	0.6
0	0 x 0.4	–1.0 x 0.5	0 x 0.6	1.0
0.4	–1.0 x 0.5	11 x 0.6	–1.0 x 1.0	1.0
0.5	0 x 0.6	–1.0 x 1.0	0 x 1.0	1.0

Because four of the input pixels along the edge of the kernel are multiplied by –1, their values are subtracted from the target pixel value. If the central kernel element does not have a high enough value, either little sharpening occurs or the output image becomes pure black. For example, if the central element is changed from 11 to 2, the output value for the target pixel becomes –1.8 through the following math:

x = 0 − 0.5 + 0 − 0.5 + (2 × 0.6) − 1.0 + 0 − 1.0 + 0

Values below 0 or above 1.0 are either clipped or normalized by the program employing the filter. If they are normalized, the values are remapped to the 0 to 1.0 range.

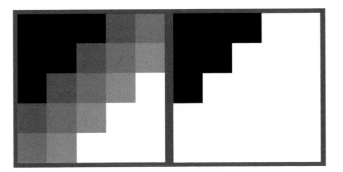

Figure 6.3 *(Left) 5×5 pixel image that matches the input matrix illustrated by Table 6.2 (Right) Same image after the convolution of the example sharpen kernel. A sample Nuke script is included as* 5x5sharpen.nk *in the Tutorials folder on the DVD.*

Tips & Tricks: Kernel Bias

One method for avoiding negative output values when using a convolution filter is to include a bias. A *bias* is a value that is added to the matrix result as a final mathematical step. For example, if the output value is –4.4, a bias of 5 would yield a final output of 0.6.

Unsharpening

Unsharp mask filters apply their own form of sharpening. Although there are different varieties of unsharp masks, they generally work in the following manner:

- An edge detection filter is applied to an input (see the next section).
- The result is inverted, blurred, and darkened.
- The darkened version is subtracted from the unaffected input.

When a strong sharpen filter is compared to the strong unsharp mask filter, differences are detectable. For example, in Figure 6.4, the sharpened image contains numerous fine white lines in the cloth of the jacket. The same lines are more difficult to see in the unsharp mask version. However, the unsharp version creates a greater degree of contrast throughout the image.

For examples of custom unsharp filters, see the AE and Nuke tutorials at the end of this chapter.

Figure 6.4 *(Left) Input image (Center Top) Version with sharpen kernel applied (Center Bottom) Detail of sharpened version (Right Top) Version with unsharp kernel applied (Right Bottom) Detail of unsharp version (Photo © 2009 by Jupiterimages)*

Stylistic Filter Kernels

Several stylistic filters employ negative element values in a limited fashion. These include edge enhance, edge detection, and emboss.

Edge Enhancement

A simple edge enhance kernel can be written like this:

```
0    0    0
0   -8    0
0    8    0
```

With this kernel, any high-contrast edge whose bright side faces the bottom of the frame is highlighted (see Figure 6.5). The remainder of the image is set to black. The variations in line color result from the application of the kernel over pixels with unequal RGB values. To highlight a different set of edges, move the 8 to a different edge element of the matrix.

Edge Detection

Edge detection kernels vary from edge enhance kernels in that they detect edges that run in all directions (see Figure 6.6). Common edge enhance kernels are based upon a Laplace transform, which is an integral transform named after mathematician Pierre-Simon Laplace (1749–1827). Essentially, an integral transform maps an equation from one domain to another in a bid to simplify its complexity.

A Laplacian filter may be expressed as a 3×3 kernel:

```
-1  -1  -1
-1   8  -1
-1  -1  -1
```

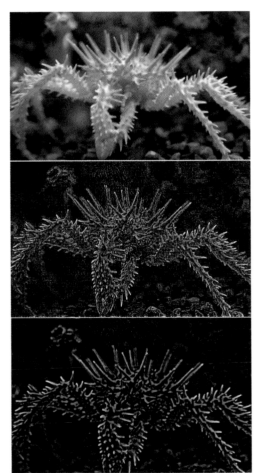

Figure 6.5 *(Top) Input image (Bottom) Result of edge enhance kernel (Photo © 2009 by Jupiterimages)*

Figure 6.6 *(Top) Input image (Center) Edge detection result (Bottom) Edge detection with initial blur (Photo © 2009 by Jupiterimages)*

In the realm of digital image processing and compositing, Laplacian filters often refer to a two-step operation which applies a Gaussian blur kernel first and an edge detection kernel second. Blurring the input matrix first prevents the edge detection kernel from creating fine noise (see Figure 6.6). It's also possible to convolve the Gaussian kernel and the Laplacian filter first, and then convolve the resulting hybrid kernel with the input matrix. The hybrid kernel is referred to as *Laplacian of Gaussian.*

Sobel Filters

Sobel filters only test for high-contrast areas that run in either the X direction or the Y direction. To test for both directions, two kernels are required, as in this example:

```
 1  2  1    −1  0  1
 0  0  0    −2  0  2
−1 −2 −1    −1  0  1
```

Because Sobel filters test horizontally and vertically, they generally do not produce edges as clean as Laplacian filters. Sobel filters, like many edge detection filters, suffer from noise and benefit from an initial blur.

Emboss Filters

Emboss filters lighten pixels in a particular direction while darkening neighboring pixels in the opposite direction. An example of an emboss kernel follows:

```
      −10 −5   1
1/3   −5   10  5
       1   5   1
```

With this kernel, high-contrast edges that favor the lower-right corner of the frame are made brighter (see Figure 6.7). High-contrast edges that favor the upper-left corner of the frame are made darker. When you place a brighter or darker edge along features, you gain the illusion of bumpiness. Since a divisor is used, the original image remains visible within the embossing. Much like Laplacian filters, emboss filters benefit from the initial application of a blur filter.

After Effects and Nuke provide numerous convolution-based filters. In addition, Nuke offers a Convolve and a Matrix node with which you can write your own custom convolutions. These nodes, along with the most useful filters, are discussed later in this chapter.

Figure 6.7 *(Top) Input image (Right) Result of blur kernel and emboss kernel (Photo © 2009 by Jupiterimages)*

Tips & Tricks: Low- and High-Pass Filters

Convolution filters are often referred to as low- or high-pass filters. *Low-pass filters* allow low-frequency signals to survive while they attenuate (reduce the amplitude of) high-frequency signals. *High-pass filters* do the opposite. In the realm of digital imaging, frequency equates to pixel value. Since blur kernels average pixels at the cost of high-frequency detail, they are considered low-pass filters. Since sharpen kernels exaggerate the contrast between pixels while eliminating low-contrast areas, they are considered high-pass filters.

Working with Filters

After Effects and Nuke provide numerous effects and nodes with which to apply convolution filters. The filter types include blurs, sharpens, and stylistic effects.

Filter Effects in AE

Filters are referred to as effects in After Effects. You can find convolution-based effects under the Blur & Sharpen and Stylize menus. In addition, the program provides a layer-based motion blur function.

Layer-Based Motion Blur

After Effects can create motion blur for any layer that transforms over time. The blur length is determined by the distance the layer moves over the duration of one frame. In essence, the blur path lies along a vector that's drawn from each pixel start position to each pixel end position.

To activate motion blur, toggle on the Motion Blur layer switch for a specific layer within the Timeline panel (see Figure 6.8). By default, the blur will not be visible in a viewer. However, if you toggle on the Motion Blur composition switch, the blur appears. Whether or not motion blur is rendered through the Render Queue is determined by the Motion Blur menu of the Render Settings dialog box. By default, the menu is set to On For Checked Layers (checking is the same as toggling on the Motion Blur layer switch). For more information on switches and the Render Queue, see Chapter 1. For an example of layer-based motion blur, see "AE Tutorial 5 Revisited: Creating a Shadow and a Camera Move" at the end of this chapter.

Figure 6.8 (Left) Motion Blur layer switch toggled on for one layer (Right) Motion Blur composition switch toggled on

You can adjust the length of a motion blur trail by changing the composition's Shutter Angle value. To do so, choose Composition → Composition Settings, switch to the Advanced tab of the Composition Settings dialog box, and change the Shutter Angle cell. Lower values shorten the blur trail and higher values lengthen the blur trail. Since the property emulates the spinning shutter disk of a motion picture camera, its measurement runs from 0 to 360°. The Shutter Phase property, which is found in the same tab, controls the time offset of the blur. Positive Shutter Phase values cause the blur to lag behind the moving element. Negative values cause the blur to precede the element. For realistic results, it's best to leave the Shutter Phase set to the equation `Shutter Angle/-2`.

Blurring and Sharpening

After Effects provides several blur and sharpen effect variations. The most useful are discussed in the following sections. The effects are accessible through the Effect → Blur & Sharpen menu.

Gaussian Blur Variations

The Fast Blur effect is an approximation of the Gaussian Blur effect that is optimized for large, low-contrast areas. The Blurriness slider controls the size of the filter kernel and thus the intensity of the blur. You can choose to blur only in the vertical or horizontal direction by changing the Blur Dimensions menu to the direction of your choice. When selected, the Repeat Edge Pixels check box prevents the blur from introducing a black line around the edge of the layer. Instead of allowing the kernel to use 0 as a value when it overhangs the edge of input image matrix, the Repeat Edge Pixels check box forces the kernel to use the nearest valid input pixel value.

In comparison, the Gaussian Blur effect uses a kernel matrix that is similar to the Gaussian filter described in the section "Blurring Kernels" earlier in this chapter. Due to the filter's bell-shaped function curve, the blur is less likely to destroy edge quality. Unfortunately, the effect does not possess a Repeat Edge Pixels check box, which leads to the blackening of the layer edge. Aside from the edge quality, Fast Blur and Gaussian Blur effects appear almost identical when the layer's Quality switch is set to Best. When the layer's Quality switch is set to Draft, however, the Gaussian Blur effect remains superior to the Fast Blur effect, which becomes pixilatcd.

Additionally, the Box Blur and Channel Blur effects base their functionality on the Fast Blur effect. Box Blur adds an Iterations slider that controls the number of sequential blurs that are added and averaged together. If Iterations is set to 1, the result is pixilated but the speed is increased. A value of 3 produces a result similar to Fast Blur. Higher values improve the smoothness of the blur. The Channel Blur effect allows you to set the Blurriness value for the red, green, blue, and alpha channels separately. This may be useful for suppressing noise. For example, you can apply the Channel Blur effect to the blue channel of video footage while leaving the remaining channels unaffected. Thus the noise strength is reduced without drastically affecting the sharpness of the layer.

Directional and Radial Blurs

The Directional Blur effect adds a linear blur as if the camera were moving in a particular direction. With the Direction control, you can choose an angle between 0° and 359°. The length of the blur trail is set by the Blur Length slider.

In contrast, the Radial Blur effect creates its namesake (as if the camera were rotated around an axis running through the lens). The Amount slider controls the blur strength. The center of the blur is determined by the Center X and Y cells. You can interactively choose the center by LMB+dragging the small bull's-eye handle in the viewer of a Composition panel. You can convert the Radial Blur effect to a zoom-style blur by changing the Type menu to Zoom. The blur is thereby streaked from the center to the four edges of the image. The smoothness of the resulting blur is set by the Antialiasing menu, which has a Low and High quality setting.

Control Layer Blurs

The Compound Blur effect bases its blur on a control layer, defined by its Blur Layer menu. High luminance values within the control layer impose a greater degree of blur onto corresponding pixels within the layer to which the effect is applied. For example, in Figure 6.9, a layer with a white star serves as the control layer. The resulting blur is thus contained within the star shape. The maximum size of the kernel and strength of the blur is established by the Maximum Blur slider. By selecting the Invert Blur check box, you can make the blur appear where the control layer has low luminance values.

The Lens Blur effect takes the control layer technique further by offering additional properties. The control layer is selected through the Depth Map Layer menu. (Despite its name, the Depth Map Layer property can use a Z-buffer channel only if it is converted to RGB first.) The Depth Map Channel menu determines what channel information is used for the blur (luminance, R, G, B, or A). Blur Focal Distance determines which pixel values within the control layer are considered to be at the center of the virtual depth of field. The slider operates on an 8-bit scale, running from 0 to 255. If the slider is set to 150, for example, the region is centered at pixels with values of 150. Neighboring pixels with values ranging from roughly 100 to 150 and 150 to 200 are considered "in focus" with the sharpness tapering off toward lower and higher values. As an example of the Lens Blur effect, in Figure 6.10 a boardwalk is given an artificially narrow depth of field. The control layer is a mask that outlines the foreground buildings. In this case, the Blur Focal Distance is set to 98.

Lens Blur provides three properties to control the bokeh shape of the virtual lens: Iris Shape, Iris Rotation, and Iris Blade Curvature. *Bokeh* describes the appearance of a point of light when it is out of focus. (For bokeh examples, see the section "Custom Convolutions" later in this chapter.) You can set the Iris Shape menu to several primitive shapes, including Triangle, Square, and Hexagon. The orientation of the resulting shape is controlled by Iris Rotation. To smooth off the corners of the shape, increase the Iris Blade Curvature value.

The Iris Radius slider sets the size of the filter kernel and the strength of the blur. Since the blurring operation removes noise and grain in the blurred region, Noise Amount and Noise Distribution add noise back to the image. Note that these two properties add noise to the blurred region only. In the same fashion, you can increase the intensity of bright areas within the blurred region by adjusting the Specular Brightness and Specular Threshold sliders. For a pixel to be brightened by Specular Brightness, it must have a value higher than the Specular Threshold value.

Figure 6.9 (Top) A control layer with a white star (Center) Resulting blur created with the Compound Blur effect (Bottom) Same effect with the Invert Blur check box selected. A sample After Effects project is included as compound_blur.aep *in the Tutorials folder on the DVD.*

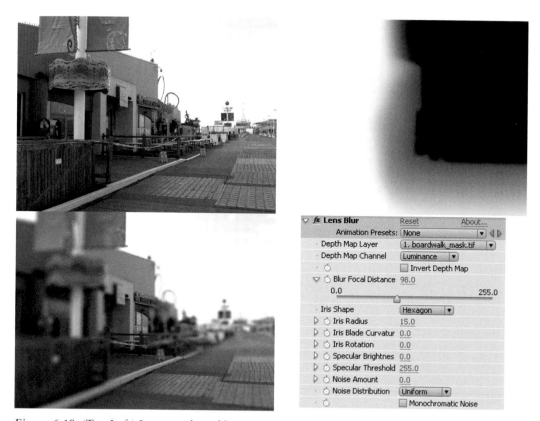

Figure 6.10 *(Top Left) Layer without blur (Top Right) Black-and-white control layer (Bottom Left) Resulting Lens Blur. The foreground and background are blurred, while the mid-ground retains a narrow depth of field. Note that the blur averaging brightens the layer. (Bottom Right) Lens Blur settings. A sample After Effects project is included as* lens_blur.aep *in the Tutorials folder on the DVD.*

Sharpening Effects

The Unsharp Mask effect applies a standard unsharp filter as described in the section "Unsharpening" earlier in this chapter. The Radius slider determines the size of the kernel and the strength of the blur applied to a darkened version of the input. The Threshold slider establishes the contrast threshold. Adjacent pixels, whose contrast value is less than or equal to the Threshold value, are left with their input values intact. Adjacent pixels with a contrast value greater than the Threshold value receive additional contrast through the subtraction of a darker, blurred version of the input.

The Sharpen effect adds its namesake and uses a filter kernel similar to those demonstrated in the section "Sharpening Kernels" earlier in this chapter.

Stylistic Effects

After Effects includes several stylistic filters that utilize convolution techniques. For example, the Smart Blur effect, found in the Blur & Sharpen menu, employs multiple convolution kernels. If the effect's Mode menu is set to Edge Only, the effect becomes an edge detection filter. If Mode is set to Normal, the effect operates as a median filter; this results in a painterly effect where small detail is lost and the color palette is reduced. As such, the effect determines the value range that exists within a group of neighboring pixels, selects the middle value, and assigns that value as the output for the targeted pixel. For example, in Figure 6.11, footage is given a painterly effect. In this case, the Radius slider is set to 50 and the Threshold slider is set to 100. Although a median filter employs a convolution, it also requires an algorithm with the ability to sort values. If Mode is set to Overlay Edge, an Edge Only version is added to the Normal version.

With the Smart Blur effect, the Threshold slider sets the contrast threshold for the filter. If the Threshold value is low, medium-contrast edges are isolated. If the Threshold value is high, a smaller number of high-contrast edges are isolated. The Radius slider, on the other hand, determines the size of the filter kernel. Large values lead to a large kernel, which in turn averages a greater number of pixels. If Mode is set to Edge Only, raising the Threshold reduces the number of isolated edges. If Mode is set to Normal, raising the Threshold reduces the complexity of the image, whereby larger and larger regions are assigned a single value.

Emboss and Find Edges, found in the Stylize menu, create their namesake effects. For more information on these filters, see the section "Stylistic Filter Kernels" earlier in this chapter.

Filter Nodes in Nuke

Nuke groups its filter nodes under a single Filter menu. These include nodes designed for custom convolutions, blurring and sharpening nodes, and stylistic effects nodes. In addition, Nuke provides node-based motion blur.

Figure 6.11 *(Top) Layer with no blur (Bottom) Result of the Smart Blur effect with Mode set to Normal. A sample After Effects project is included as* `smart_blur.ae` *in the Tutorials folder on the DVD.*

Node-Based Motion Blur

The Transform node includes a built-in method for motion blurring the node's output. To activate the blur, raise the Motionblur parameter above 0 (see Figure 6.12). If the node's Translate, Scale, Rotate, or Skew parameter is animated over time, the motion blur appears in the viewer. The quality of the blur is determined by the Motionblur value. The higher the value, the more samples are taken across time and the more accurate the blur trail is. Values between 1 and 3 are generally suitable for creating high-quality results.

By default, the length of the motion blur is dependent on the distance each pixel travels over 1/2 frame. That is, the blur trail extends from the position of the element at the current frame to the position of the element 1/2 frame into the future. The 1/2 is derived from the default setting of the Shutter parameter, which is 0.5.

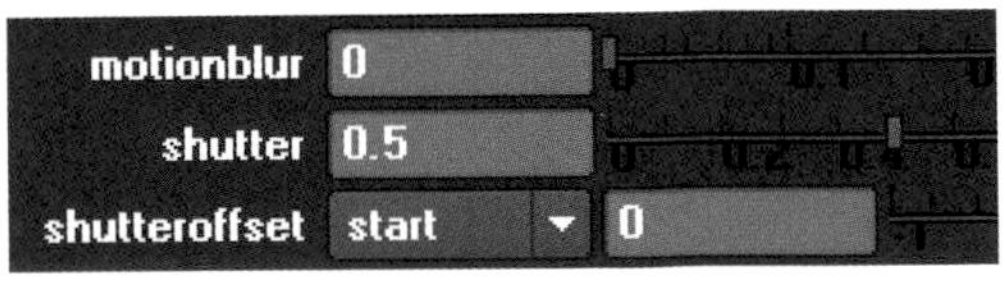

Figure 6.12 *Transform node motion blur parameters*

The motion blur length can be written as the formula `frame to (frame + Shutter)`. To alter this formula, you can change the Shutteroffset parameter. The Shutteroffset menu is set to Start by default but has these additional options:

Centered If Shutter is set to 0.5, the Centered option goes back in time 1/4 frame and forward in time 1/4 frame to create the blur trail. The formula is `(frame - Shutter/2) to (frame + Shutter/2)`.

End The End option uses the formula `(frame - Shutter) to frame`.

Custom The Custom option uses the formula `(frame + offset) to (frame + offset + Shutter)`. The offset is determined by the Shuttercustomoffset cell to the immediate right of the Shutteroffset menu.

For a demonstration of node-based motion blur, see "Nuke Tutorial 5 Revisited: Creating a Shadow and a Camera Move" at the end of the chapter.

Custom Convolutions

Nuke offers the user a way to create a custom convolution kernel. This opens up almost endless possibilities when filters are applied. To create a custom kernel, follow these steps:

1. Select the node to which you want to apply the custom kernel. RMB+click and choose Filter → Matrix. In the Enter Desired Matrix Size dialog box, enter the matrix width and height. Although many standard filters use a matrix with an equal width and height, such as 3×3, you can create one with unequal dimensions, such as 5×4.
2. Connect the Matrix1 node to a viewer. Since the matrix is empty, the image is black. Open the Matrix1 node's properties panel. Enter a value into each matrix element cell. The values can be negative, positive, or 0 (see Figure 6.13).

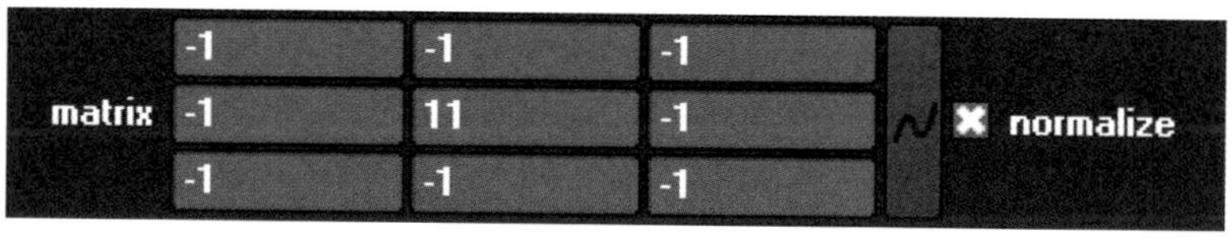

Figure 6.13 A 3×3 matrix provided by the Matrix node. The values entered into the matrix element cells create a sharpening effect.

For sample matrices, see the section "Filter Matrices" at the beginning of this chapter. Several re-creations of common filters have also been included in the Tutorials folder on the DVD:

`sharpen.nk`	Simple sharpen filter kernel
`edge_enhance.nk`	Simple edge enhance kernel
`emboss.nk`	Simple emboss kernel
`laplacian.nk`	Laplacian filter re-created with a Blur and Matrix node
`sobel.nk`	Sobel filter using two Matrix nodes and a Blur node

In addition to the element cells, the Matrix node provides a Normalize check box. If this is selected, the resulting output values are divided by a divisor that is equal to the sum of the matrix elements. When selected, the Normalize check box guarantees that the output intensity is similar to the input intensity. Note that the Normalize check box will function only if the sum of all the matrix elements does not equal 0.

In addition to the Matrix node, Nuke supplies a Convolve node that can interpret a bitmap or other input as a kernel matrix. This is particularly useful when you are creating custom blurs that require a bokeh shape. To create such a blur, follow these steps:

1. Create a new script. In the Node Graph, RMB+click and choose Image → Read. In the Read1 node's properties panel, browse for an image or image sequence. (A sample image, `train.tif`, is included in the Footage folder on the DVD.) With no nodes selected, RMB+click and choose Image → Read. In the Read2 node's properties panel, browse for a bitmap that will serves as the input kernel matrix. (A sample image, `32bokeh.tif`, is included in the Footage folder.)

2. With no nodes selected, RMB+click and choose Filter → Convolve. Connect the output of the Read1 node to the input B of the Convolve1 node. Input B is reserved for the input that is to be affected by the convolution. Connect the output of Read2 to the input A of the Convolve1 node. Connect the output of Convolve1 to a viewer. The image is blurred. A sample script is saved as `convolve.nk` in the Tutorials folder.

The convolution is inherently different from that of a standard Blur node. For example, in Figure 6.14, the two nodes are compared side by side.

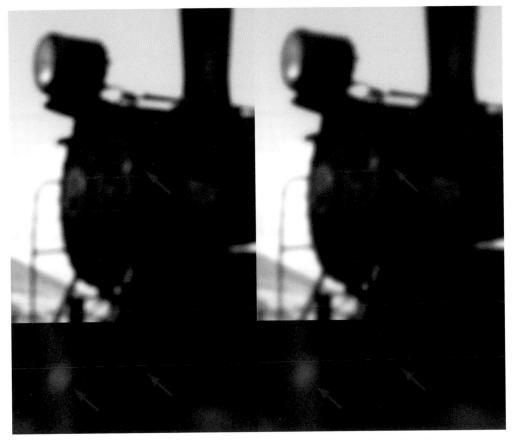

Figure 6.14 (Left) Result of a Convolve node (Right) Result of a Blur node. The arrows point to bokehs created by the nodes. The Convolve node produces sharper bokeh shapes.

Real-world camera lenses create uniquely shaped bokehs when their depth of field is narrow or they are otherwise out of focus (see Figure 6.15). The most common bokeh is roughly circular, which corresponds to the shape of the camera's iris diaphragm, which is composed of overlapping triangular blades. Inexpensive cameras may have fewer blades and thus create bokehs that are more polygonal. It's also possible to create a custom bokeh shape by attaching a lens hood with the desired shape cut into it.

You can create stylized bokeh shapes by creating a bitmap with a particular pattern. The degree to which the input becomes out of focus is related to the size of the bokeh image (see Figure 6.16). That is, the image resolution determines the kernel matrix size. Hence, the 32bokeh.tif image, which is 32×32 pixels, is equivalent to a 32×32 kernel matrix. The larger the matrix is, the greater the degree of pixel averaging and the greater the degree of "out-of-focusness."

Figure 6.15 *(Left) City lights at night from a distance (Center) Brightly colored objects that are close by, but are out of focus (Right) Out-of-focus trees located in the background (Photos © 2009 by Jupiterimages)*

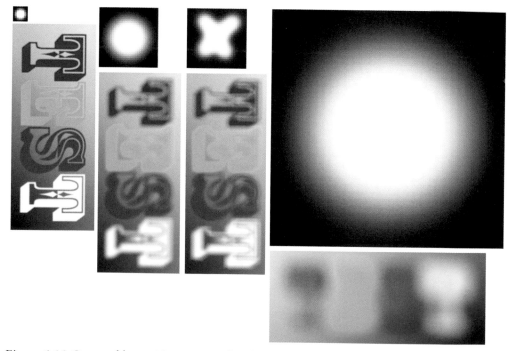

Figure 6.16 *Custom blurs with corresponding bokeh bitmap files. The files are included as* 8bokeh.tif, 32bokeh.tif, 128bokeh.tif, *and* xbokeh.tif *in the Footage folder on the DVD.*

The Convolve node is able to use inputs other than bitmaps. For example, you can connect the output of a Flare node (Draw → Flare) to input A of a Convolve node. If the input resolution is too large, however, the convolution process may be significantly slowed. To make the process efficient, you can pass the input through a Crop node. For example, in Figure 6.17, a Flare node is adjusted to create a multipoint star. The Flare node is connected to a Crop node, which is set to a resolution of 100×100. (For more information on the Crop node, see Chapter 1.) The Flare node, along with similar draw nodes, is detailed in Chapter 10, "Warps, Optical Artifacts, Paint, and Text."

Blurring and Sharpening

Nuke includes a number of nodes that blur and sharpen, all of which are found under the Filter menu.

Blur, Sharpen, and Soften Nodes

The Blur node offers a quick means to apply a standard blur filter (see Figure 6.18). The strength of the blur is set by the Size slider. The higher the Size value is, the larger the kernel matrix and the greater the degree of blurring. The smoothness of the blur is determined by the Quality cell (which is to the right of the Filter menu). Values below 15 downscale the input image; after the kernel is applied, the image is upscaled to its original size using a linear filter. Although the process speeds up the blur, it leads to pixelization. A value of 15, however, produces the most refined result. In addition, you can change the Filter menu to Box, Triangle, Quadratic, and Gaussian. The Box filter, which uses a function curve with no falloff, produces the weakest blur. The Triangle filter uses a tent-style function curve. The Quadratic filter, which uses a bell-shaped curve, produces the most aggressive blur. The Gaussian filter, which uses another variation of a bell-shaped curve, offers a good combination of quality and speed. For more information on blurring matrices, see the section "Filter Matrices" at the beginning of this chapter. For more information on filter function curves, see Chapter 5.

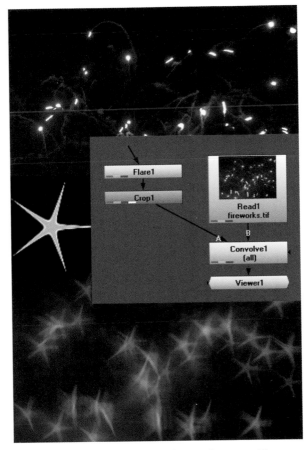

Figure 6.17 (Top) Unaltered fireworks input (Center Left) 100× 100 Flare shape (Center Right) Node network (Bottom) Resulting blur. A sample Nuke script is included as `flare_bokeh.nk` in the Tutorials folder on the DVD.

Figure 6.18 The Blur node properties panel

Despite its name, the Sharpen node applies an unsharp mask to an input (see Figure 6.19). (For more information, see the "Unsharping" section earlier in this chapter.) The Minimum and Maximum sliders set the size of the darkened regions along high-contrast edges. The Amount slider sets the degree to which the darkened regions are subtracted from the original. High Amount values create greater contrast within the image. Size controls the softness of the darkened regions.

The Soften node applies the same process as the Sharpen node. However, the result is added to the original input, creating a brighter, foggy result (see Figure 6.19).

Figure 6.19 *(Left) Result of the Sharpen node (Right) Result of the Soften node. A sample Nuke script is included as* sharpen_soften.nk *in the Tutorials folder on the DVD.*

Defocusing

The Defocus node is designed to create realistic depth-of-field blur that contains specific bokeh patterns. (For more information on bokeh, see the section "Custom Convolutions" earlier in this chapter.) Unlike the Convolve node, however, Defocus bases it bokeh shape on an Aspect Ratio slider. If Aspect Ratio is 1.0, small bright points produce circular spots. If Aspect Ratio is set at a value above 1.0, such as 1.33, 1.85, or 2.35, the circular highlight is stretched horizontally (see Figure 6.20).

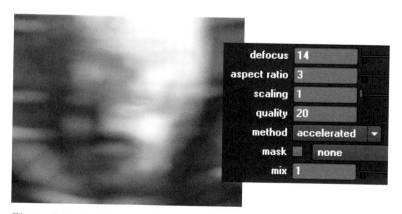

Figure 6.20 *(Left) Input blurred with Defocus with an artificially high Aspect Ratio value of 3. Note the horizontal stretching of the bokeh shapes. (Right) Defocus settings. A sample Nuke script is included as* defocus.nk *in the Tutorials folder on the DVD.*

The Defocus slider sets the degree of blurriness. The Scaling slider serves as a multiplier for the effect of the Defocus and Aspect Ratio parameters. In general, Scaling can be left at 1.0. Quality is true to its namesake with higher values producing better results. The Method menu provides Accelerated and Full Precision methods of interpolation. Accelerated is more efficient but may produce speckled noise in some situations. Full Precision guarantees maximum accuracy.

Specialized Blurs

Nuke includes several specialized nodes that create unique blurs. These include EdgeBlur, DirBlur, Bilateral, and Laplacian.

The EdgeBlur node contains its blur to alpha edges. Size, Filter, and Quality parameters are identical to the Blur node. Edge Mult serves as a multiplier for the blur. Higher Edge Mult values increase the width of the blur; low values sharpen the blur. Tint, if set to a nonwhite value, tints the blurred area in the RGB channels. The ability to tint the edge offers a means to create a light wrap effect. (The Lightwrap node is discussed in Chapter 10.)

The DirBlur node applies a blur in one or more directions, thus emulating camera motion blur. The node offers three styles of blur through the BlurType menu: Zoom, Radial, and Linear (see Figure 6.21). Linear blur creates a blur trail in one direction (even if the input is static). Radial creates a circular blur as if the camera was spun on the axis that runs through its lens. Zoom creates a blur that runs from the center of frame to the four edges.

The center of a Zoom or Radial blur is determined by the BlurCenter parameter, which carries X and Y cells. You can interactively place the center by LMB+dragging the BlurCenter handle in a viewer. If BlurType is set to Linear, the direction of the blur trail is set by the BlurAngle slider. However, you can override BlurAngle by selecting the UseTarget check box. UseTarget activates the Linear Target parameter, which carries X and Y position cells. Linear Target forces the Linear blur trail to follow a vector drawn from the BlurCenter position to the Linear Target position. You can interactively change the Linear Target position by LMB+dragging the Target handle in a viewer. The BlurLength slider sets its namesake. The Samples slider determines how many offset iterations of the input are used to synthesis the blur. High values improve the smoothness of the blur but significantly slow the render. PixelAspect emulates different lens setups, whereby various values affect the shape of the blur trail. Values below 1.0 will warp a Zoom blur as if the virtual lens was wide-angle. Values below 1.0 will also vertically compress a Radial blur. The

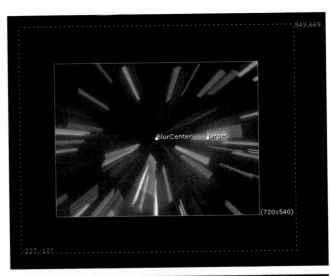

Figure 6.21 (Top) Zoom blur created by DirBlur node. The BlurCenter and Target handles are seen at the center of the viewer. Note that the blur extends the bounding box of the input. (Bottom) DirBlur settings. A sample Nuke script is included as `dirblur.nk` in the Tutorials folder on the DVD.

Quality parameter functions in the manner similar to the Quality parameter of the Blur node; however, a Quality setting of 1.0 creates a refined result, while high values lead to pixelization.

In contrast, the Bilateral node applies a selective blur to the input. Areas of low contrast receive a higher degree of blur, while areas of high contrast receive a lower degree of blur. This approach preserves edge sharpness (see Figure 6.22). The node's Size slider, in combination with the Positional Sigma slider, sets the intensity of the blur. High Positional Sigma values spread the blur into larger regions, obscuring fine detail. The Color Sigma slider determines the ultimate sharpness of high-contrast areas. Low values maintain edge sharpness. Although the Bilateral node produces a unique result, it operates more slowly than other blur nodes.

Figure 6.22 *(Top Left) Detail of unaffected input (Bottom Left) Result of Bilateral node. Note how high-contrast crevices and treetops retain edge sharpness. (Bottom Right) Bilateral settings. A sample Nuke script is included as* `bilateral.nk` *in the Tutorials folder on the DVD.*

The Laplacian node, on the other hand, isolates edge areas by detecting rapid value change across neighboring pixels. Since the filter is prone to noise, however, blur is first applied to the input. The style of blur is controlled by the Filter menu, which is identical to the one provided by the Blur node. Each style affects the resulting thickness of the isolated edges to a different degree. The thickness is also influenced by the Size slider. For more information on Laplacian kernels, see the section "Stylistic Filter Kernels" near the beginning of the chapter.

The Emboss node creates a simple version of its namesake. The emboss kernel is also described in the section "Stylistic Filter Kernels." Additional stylistic Nuke nodes, which are not dependent on convolution techniques, are discussed in Chapter 10.

AE and Nuke Tutorials

In this chapter, you'll have a chance to revisit tutorial 5, in which you'll fabricate a shadow, a camera move, and motion blur. In addition, two new tutorials will show you how to construct a custom unsharp mask using standard effects and nodes.

AE Tutorial 5 Revisited: Creating a Shadow and a Camera Move

In Chapter 5, you gave life to a static render of a ball through keyframe animation. To make the animation more convincing, it's important to add a shadow. An animated camera and motion blur will take the illusion even further.

1. Reopen the completed After Effects project file for "AE Tutorial 5: Adding Dynamic Animation to a Static Layer." A finished version of Tutorial 5 is saved as `ae5.aep` in the Chapter 5 Tutorials folder on the DVD. Play the animation. The ball is missing a shadow and thus a strong connection to the floor. Since the ball is a static frame and no shadow render is provided, you will need to construct your own shadow.

2. Select the `ball.tga` layer in the layer outline of the Timeline panel. Choose Edit → Duplicate. The layer is copied. Choose the lower `ball.tga` layer (numbered 2 in the layer outline). This layer will become the shadow. For the moment, toggle off the Video switch beside the top `ball.tga` layer (numbered 1 in the layer outline). This temporarily hides the top layer. With the lower `ball.tga` layer selected, choose Effect → Color Correction → Curves. In the Effect Controls tab, pull the top-right point of the curve line straight down so that the curve becomes flat (see Figure 6.23). The `ball.tga` layer is changed to 0 black.

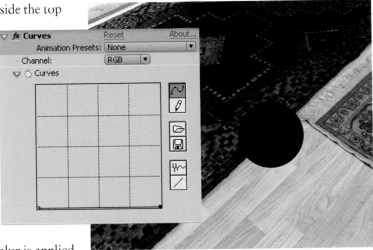

3. With the lower `ball.tga` layer selected, choose Effect → Blur & Sharpen → Fast Blur. Change the Fast Blur effect's Blurriness slider to 100. Note that the amount of resulting blur is dependent on the resolution of the layer to which the blur is applied. Since this project is working at 2K, the Blurriness slider must be set fairly high to see a satisfactory result.

Figure 6.23 (Left) Curves effect with flattened curve (Right) Darkened duplicate of ball layer

4. Move the timeline to frame 6 (where the ball contacts the floor). Toggle on the Video switch beside the top `ball.tga` layer so that the layer is once again visible. The shadow will no longer be apparent because it is directly behind the top layer. To remedy this, select the lower `ball.tga` layer, expand the Transform section, and toggle off the Stopwatch button beside the Position property. The keyframes for Position are removed. Interactively move the lower `ball.tga` layer so that the shadow appears just below and to the right of the ball. Toggle on the Stopwatch button beside the Position property again to reactivate keyframing. A new keyframe is placed at frame 6. Move the timeline to each of the frames where the ball contacts the floor. Interactively move the lower `ball.tga` layer so that the shadow appears just below the ball in each case. At this point, the shadow is inappropriately opaque and heavy. To fix this, change the lower `ball.tga` layer's Opacity to 50% (see Figure 6.24).

Figure 6.24 (Left) Detail of original composite with no shadow (Right) New composite with shadow

5. Move the timeline to each frame where the ball is at the top of a bounce. Interactively move the lower `ball.tga` layer so that the shadow appears away from the ball and to the right. Assuming that the main light source is coming from frame left, the shadow should move toward frame right as the ball bounces up. However, as the bounce height decreases, so should the distance the shadow moves away from the ball. Once all the keyframes have been placed for the lower `ball.tga` layer, select the new keyframes in the Timeline panel, RMB+click over a selected keyframe, and choose Keyframe Interpolation from the menu. In the Keyframe Interpolation dialog box, change Temporal Interpolation and Spatial Interpolation to Continuous Bezier. By changing both Interpolation types, you can interactively move the tangent handles via the Graph Editor and the overlay of the viewer. The layer should form a motion path overlay similar to Figure 6.25.

Figure 6.25 Motion path of ball layer (the vertical curve) and motion path of new shadow layer (the horizontal curve). The background has been temporarily hidden.

6. Play back the timeline. At this point, the shadow opacity is consistent despite the movement of the ball. In a real-world situation, the shadow darkness would fluctuate as more or less ambient light is permitted to strike the shadow area. To emulate this effect, keyframe the Opacity property changing over time. For example, for the frames where the ball contacts the floor, keyframe Opacity at 50%. For the frames where the ball is at the peak of a bounce, keyframe Opacity at a value proportional to the ball's height off the floor. For example, if there are bounce peaks at frames 1, 11, 21, and 31, you can keyframe Opacity at 5%, 10%, 15%, and 20% respectively for those frames. Once the Opacity keyframes have been set, convert the new keyframes to temporal and spatial Continuous Bezier tangents (see step 5). To examine the result, open the Graph Editor (see Chapter 5 for additional details).

7. To add realism to the shadow, you can change the amount of blur applied to it over time. When the shadow is close to the ball, it should be sharper. When the shadow is farther from the ball, it should be softer. You can achieve this by keyframing the Blurriness property of the Fast Blur effect. For example, at frames 1, 11, 21, and 31, set the Blurriness value to 140, 130, 120, and 110 respectively. At frames 6, 16, 26, and 36, key the Blurriness value at 100.

8. At this stage, the ball bounce remains somewhat artificial due to a lack of motion blur. To create motion blur for the ball and shadow, select both `ball.tga` layers and toggle on their Motion Blur layer switches. The blur is not immediately visible but will be added to the final render. To see motion blur in the viewer, toggle on the Motion Blur composition switch at the top of the layer outline of the Timeline panel.

9. Motion blur will also appear if any artificial camera move is created. To create such a move, you will need to nest two composites. Choose Composition → New Composition. In the New Composition dialog box, change Preset to NTSC D1 Square Pixel, Frame Rate to 30, Start Frame to 1, and Duration to 36.

10. LMB+drag Comp 1 from the Project panel and drop it into the Comp 2 tab of the Timeline panel. (For more information on nesting compositions, see Chapter 1.) Since Comp 2 is set to a 720×540 resolution, Comp 1 is oversized by default. Select the Comp 1 layer, expand its Transform section, and change the Scale property to 50%, 50%. This shrinks Comp 1 but makes it large enough to slide around the Comp 2 frame (see Figure 6.26).

11. Select Comp 1 and toggle on the Stopwatch button beside the Position property. Move to different frames and interactively position the Comp 1 layer so that it appears as if the camera is panning or tilting to follow the ball. Because the Stopwatch button is toggled on, keyframes are created each time there is a change in value. Only three of four keyframes are necessary to give the illusion of camera movement. Once you are satisfied with the keyframe placement, select the new keyframes and convert them to temporal and spatial Continuous Bezier tangents (see step 5).

Figure 6.26 Comp 1 scaled and centered within Comp 2, as seen in the viewer of the Composition panel. Note that the orange bounding box of Comp 1 extends past the edge of the viewer frame edge.

12. Play back the timeline. To adjust the smoothness of the artificial camera move, manipulate the motion path overlay within the viewer. With the Comp 1 layer selected, set the viewer's Magnification Ratio Popup menu to 200% or 400% so that the motion path and keyframes are easily seen. Use the Hand tool to scroll the view to various parts of the motion path. To adjust a tangent, LMB+drag a tangent handle. To reposition a keyframe, and thus change the position of the Comp 1 layer for a particular frame, LMB+drag the keyframe box.

13. To add motion blur to the camera move, toggle on the Motion Blur switch for the Comp 1 layer. Render out a test movie using the Render Queue. When you play the rendered movie, you should see motion blur on the ball (see Figure 6.27). In addition, the entire frame will be blurred if the artificial camera makes a sudden move, such as a pan. If you see blur, the tutorial is complete. A sample After Effects project is included as `ae5_step2.aep` in the Tutorials folder on the DVD.

Figure 6.27 Two frames from the rendered composite. Note the subtle camera-style blur added to the left frame by the Motion Blur switch.

Nuke Tutorial 5 Revisited: Creating a Shadow and a Camera Move

In Chapter 5, you gave life to a static render of a ball through keyframe animation. To make the animation more convincing, it's important to add a shadow. An animated camera and motion blur will take the illusion even further.

1. Reopen the completed Nuke project file for "Nuke Tutorial 5: Adding Dynamic Animation to a Static Output." A finished version of Tutorial 5 is saved as nuke5.aep in the Chapter 5 Tutorials folder on the DVD. Play the animation. The ball is missing a shadow and thus a strong connection to the floor. Since the ball is a static frame and no shadow render was provided, you will need to construct your own shadow.

2. In the Node Graph, RMB+click, and choose Color → Clamp. Connect the output of the Read2 node to the input of the Clamp1 node. With the Clamp1 node selected, RMB+click and choose Transform → Transform. Disconnect the input A of the Merge1 node. Instead, connect input A to the output of the new Transform2 node. Refer to Figure 6.28 for node placement. Open the Clamp1 node's properties panel. Change the Channels menu to RGB and the Maximum slider to 0. This series of steps places a black version of the ball, which will become the shadow, on top of the floor.

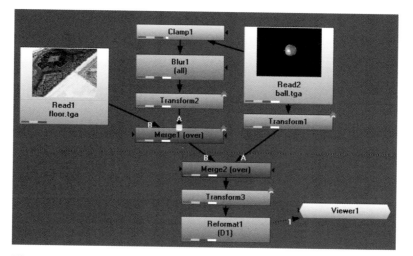

Figure 6.28 The final node network

3. To soften the new shadow, select the Clamp1 node, RMB+click, and choose Filter → Blur. A Blur1 node is inserted between the Clamp1 and Transform2 nodes. Open the Blur1 node's properties panel and set the Size slider to 75. The shadow is softened (see Figure 6.29). To view the result, temporarily connect a viewer to the Merge1 node.

4. With no nodes selected, RMB+click and choose Merge → Merge. Connect the input A of the Merge2 node to the output of Transform1. Refer to Figure 6.28 for node placement. Connect the input B of Merge2 to the output of Merge1. Connect the output of Merge2 to a viewer. The original ball is placed back on top of the shadow and background.

Figure 6.29 Blurred shadow

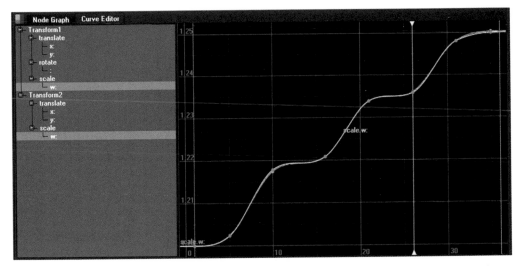

Figure 6.30 *Transform1 and Transform2 nodes overlapping Scale curves in the Curve Editor*

5. Open the Transform1 and Transform2 nodes' properties panels. Move the timeline to frame 5 (where the ball contacts the floor for the first time). Note the scale of the ball in the Transform1 node's properties panel. Set the Transform2 node's Scale value to match. Click the Animation button beside the Transform2 node's Scale slider and choose Set Key from the menu. Continue to every frame where Transfrom1 has a key-frame. Match Transform2's Scale value to Transform1. Any change to Transform2's Scale value will automatically create a new keyframe. To monitor the progress of the Transform2's Scale curve, open the Curve Editor. Match the shape of Transform2's Scale curve to Transform1's Scale curve by changing tangent types and manipulating tangent handles (see Figure 6.30). (For a review of the Curve Editor and tangent set-tings, see Chapter 5.)

6. Return the timeline to frame 5 (where the ball contacts the floor for the first time). Using the viewer transform handle, interactively move the shadow so that it's just below and to the right of the ball. In the Transform2 node's properties panel, click the Animation button beside the Translate parameter and choose Set Key. Move the timeline to each keyframe where the ball contacts the floor and interactively move the shadow to an appropriate location under the ball. New keyframes are automatically added to Transform2's Translate parameter.

7. Play back the timeline. (Make sure the viewer's Desired Playback Rate cell is set to 30 fps.) The shadow follows but stays directly below the ball. If the main light source is arriving from frame left, then a real-world shadow would change position with each bounce of the ball. To add appropriate shadow movement, move the timeline to frame 10 (the peak of the first bounce). Using the viewer transform handle, interactively move the shadow screen right. Move the timeline to each keyframe where the ball is at the peak of a bounce. Interactively move the shadow to an appropriate position. As the bounce height decreases, so should the distance the shadow moves away from the ball. The shadow should form a motion path overlay similar to Figure 6.31. To achieve the appropriately shaped curve, adjust the tangents for the Transform2 node's Translate X and Y curves in the Curve Editor.

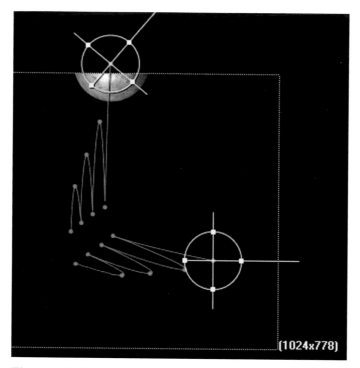

Figure 6.31 *Transform1 node's Translate motion path (vertical curve) and Transform2 node's Translate motion path (horizontal curve), as seen in the viewer. (The background has been temporarily disconnected.)*

8. Play back the timeline. At this point, the shadow is inappropriately opaque and heavy. To fix this, move the timeline to frame 5 (where the ball contacts the floor for the first time). Open the Merge1 node's properties panel. Change the Mix slider to 0.8. The shadow is more believable, yet the opacity is consistent despite the movement of the ball. In a real-world situation, shadow darkness fluctuates as more or less ambient light is permitted to strike the shadow area. To emulate this effect, keyframe the Mix value changing over time. First, move to each keyframe where the ball contacts the floor and force a keyframe for the Mix parameter. To force a keyframe, click the Animation button beside the Mix slider and choose Set Key. Next, move the timeline to the keyframes where the ball is at the peak of its bounce. Set the Mix parameter to a value proportional to the ball's height off the floor. For example, if there are bounce peaks at frames 1, 10, 21, and 31, you can keyframe the Mix value at 0.2, 0.3, 0.4, and 0.5 respectively.

9. To add realism to the shadow, you can change the amount of blur applied to it over time. When the shadow is close to the ball, it should be sharper. When the shadow is farther from the ball, it should be softer. You can achieve this by keyframing the Size parameter of the Blur1 node. For example, at frames 1, 10, 21, and 31, set the Size value to 115, 105, 95, and 85 respectively. At frames 5, 16, 26, and 35, key the Size value at 75.

10. At this stage, the ball bounce remains somewhat artificial due to a lack of motion blur. To create motion blur for the ball, open the Transform1 and Transform2 nodes' properties panels and change the Motionblur slider to 1.0. Motion blur is instantly added and appears in the viewer. Note that the blur significantly slows the speed with which the viewer renders each frame for playback.

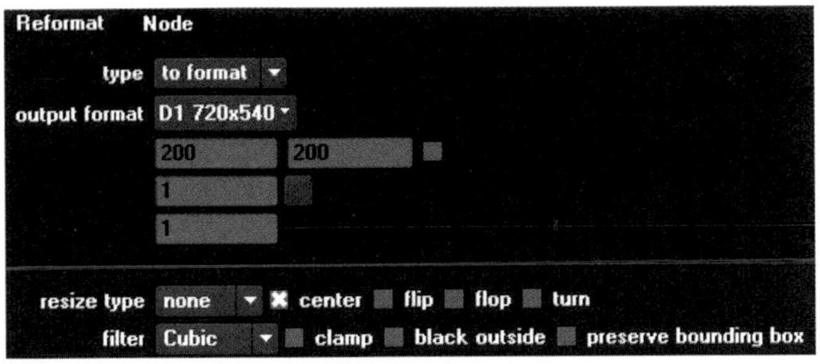

Reformat   Node

type to format ▼

output format D1 720x540 ▼

| 200 | 200 | |

| 1 | |

| 1 |

resize type none   ▼ ✖ center ▢ flip ▢ flop ▢ turn

filter Cubic   ▼ ▢ clamp ▢ black outside ▢ preserve bounding box

Figure 6.32 The *Reformat1 node's properties panel*

11. You can also apply motion blur to any artificial camera move. To create such a move, you will need to reformat the output. Select the Merge2 node, RMB+click, and choose Transform → Transform. Open the Transform3 node's properties panel and change the Scale slider to 0.5. This shrinks the image in anticipation of a smaller output format. With the Transform3 node selected, choose Transform → Reformat. This finishes the node network (see Figure 6.28 earlier in this section for reference). Open the Reformat1 node's properties panel. Change the Output Format menu to New. In the New Format dialog box, change File Size X to 720 and File Size Y to 540. Enter **D1** as the Name and click the OK button. In the Reformat1 node's properties panel, change the Resize Type menu to None (see Figure 6.32). The composited image remains larger than the final output, which will allow you to move the image to create an artificial camera move.

12. Move the timeline to frame 1. Open the Transform3 node's properties panel. Click the Animation button beside the Translate parameter and choose Set Key. Change the timeline to different frames and interactively move Transform3 so that it appears as if the camera is panning or tilting to follow the ball. Only three of four keyframes are necessary to give the illusion of camera movement.

13. To add motion blur to the camera move, change the Motionblur parameter for Transform3 to 1.0. Play back the timeline until all the frames are rendered and the viewer is able to achieve 30 fps. When you stop the playback and scrub through the frames, you should see motion blur on the ball. In addition, the entire frame will be blurred if the artificial camera makes a sudden move, such as a pan. If the timeline is unable to play back the animation in real time, create a flipbook by selecting the Reformat1 node and choosing Render → Flipbook Selected. If you see blur, the tutorial is complete (see Figure 6.33). A sample Nuke script is included as `nuke5_step2.nk` in the Tutorials folder on the DVD.

Figure 6.33 *Several frames from the final animation showing the camera move and motion blur*

AE Tutorial 6: Building an Unsharp Mask from Scratch

Although After Effects includes an Unsharp Mask effect, it's possible to build a custom unsharp mask by combing several other effects.

1. Create a new project. Choose Composition → New Composition. In the Composition Settings dialog box, set Preset to NTSC D1 Square Pixel and Duration to 1. Import flowers.tif from the Footage folder on the DVD. LMB+drag flowers.tif from the Project panel to the layer outline of the Timeline panel. The image features a somewhat washed-out and soft view of a yard (see Figure 6.34).

Figure 6.34 The input image

2. With the flowers.tif layer selected, choose Effect → Stylize → Find Edges. In the Effect Controls panel, select the Invert check box. The Find Edges effect isolates high-contrast edges through a Lapacian kernel. The Invert check box places bright edges over black. Choose Effect → Blur & Sharpen → Fast Blur. Set the Fast Blur effect's Blurriness to 10. Toggle on Repeat Edge Pixels to prevent a black edge. This represents the first step of an unsharp mask, which requires isolated edges to be blurred.

3. Choose Composition → New Composition. In the Composition Settings dialog box, set Preset to NTSC D1 Square Pixel and Duration to 1. LMB+drag Comp 1 from the Project panel to the layer outline of the Comp 2 tab in the Timeline panel. LMB+drag flowers.tif from the Project panel to the layer outline of the Comp 2 tab. The new flowers.tif layer should sit on top of Comp 1.

4. While working within the Comp 2 tab, select the flowers.tif layer and choose Effect → Channel → Compound Arithmetic. The Compound Arithmetic effect was originally designed for older versions of After Effects that did not offer built-in blending modes. Nevertheless, the effect is useful for subtracting one layer from another. In the Effect Controls panel, set the Compound Arithmetic effect's Second Source Layer menu to 2. *Comp 1*. Set Operator to Subtract. Set Blend With Original to 60%. The unsharp mask is finished (see Figure 6.35). To increase the strength of the unsharp mask, lower the Blend With Original value. To increase the size of the soft black border around objects, raise the Size slider of the Fast Blur effect applied to the flowers.tif layer used in Comp 1. The tutorial is complete. A sample After Effects project is included as ae6.aep in the Tutorials folder on the DVD.

Figure 6.35 *The final unsharp filter emulation*

Nuke Tutorial 6: Building an Unsharp Mask from Scratch

Although Nuke's Sharpen node applies an unsharp mask filter, it's possible to build a custom unsharp mask using a Matrix, Blur, Multiply, and Merge node.

1. Create a new script. In the Node Graph, RMB+click and choose Image → Read. Browse for flowers.tif in the Footage folder on the DVD.

2. With the Read1 node selected, RMB+click and choose Filter → Matrix. In the Enter Desired Matrix Size dialog box, enter 3 for Width and Height and click OK. Open the Matrix1 node's properties panel and enter 8 into the central element and −1 into the edge elements (see Figure 6.36). With the Matrix1 node selected, RMB+ click and choose Filter → Blur. In the Blur1 node's properties panel, change the Size slider to 3. With the Blur1 node selected, RMB+click and choose Color → Math → Multiply. Use Figure 6.36 as a reference. In the Multiply1 node's properties panel, set the Value cell to −3. Connect a viewer to Multiply1. The edges of the image are separated through a Laplacian matrix kernel held by the Matrix1 node. The edges are blurred by the Blur1 node and darkened and inverted by the Multiply node. (Multiplying by a negative number is the same as inverting.) This represents the first step of an unsharp mask.

3. With no nodes selected, RMB+click, and choose Merge → Merge. Connect the output of Multiply1 to input B of Merge1. Connect the output of Read1 to input A of Merge1. Open the Merge1 node's properties panel and change the Operation menu to Minus. Connect a viewer to Merge1. A custom unsharp mask is created (see Figure 6.37). To increase the intensity of the unsharpen effect, change the Multiply1 node's Value cell to a larger negative number, such as −10.

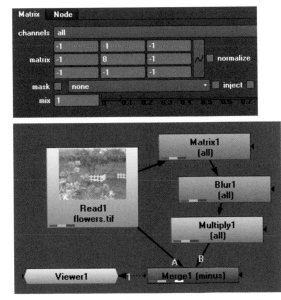

Figure 6.36 (Top) The Matrix1 node properties panel (Bottom) The final node network

To fine-tune the sharpness of the unsharpen effect, adjust the Size slider of the Blur1 node. The tutorial is complete. A sample Nuke script is saved as `nuke6.nk` in the Tutorials folder on the DVD.

Figure 6.37 *(Left) Unaltered input (Right) Result of a custom unsharp mask*

Interview: Alex Lovejoy, The Mill NY, New York City

Alex Lovejoy began his career in 1994 at Triangle TV as a VT (videotape) operator. In 1996, he moved to the Moving Picture Company, where he became a VFX supervisor. While at the Moving Picture Company, Alex oversaw high-end effects on commercials for clients such as Volkswagen, Guinness, Audi, and Levis. In 2006, he joined The Mill NY as a senior flame artist. He currently oversees the studio's 2D artists.

The Mill was launched in 1990. At present, the company has offices in New York, London, and Los Angeles and specializes in postproduction and visual effects for commercials, music videos, and episodic television. Mill Film, a subsidiary specializing in effects for feature film, received an Oscar in 1992 for its work on *Gladiator.*

(The Mill NY operates with a team of 18 compositors split between Flame, Smoke, and Combustion. Additionally, the London and Los Angeles offices employ between 80 and 100 compositors for film and episodic television work.)

Alex Lovejoy (Photo courtesy of The Mill NY)

LL: How have high-definition formats affected the compositing process?

AL: The attention to detail is much greater when compositing in HD. The picture quality is so good (it's not far from feature film resolution) that any discrepancies with matte edges, bluescreen color spill, [and so on] become very noticeable.

LL: At what resolution does The Mill normally composite?

AL: The last few years have seen a dramatic rise in finishing at HD, and this is now the norm. It is more unusual to finish a project at standard-definition nowadays.

LL: Have you worked with 4K footage? If so, what are the advantages?

AL: It is rare to work with 4K images when compositing, especially in the commercial world. The main advantage of working with 4K is the ability to "pan and scan," for example, adding a camera zoom into the final composite. If we are dealing with footage shot at 4K, we would more likely grade at 4K resolution and then convert that to a more manageable format such as 2K or HD to composite with. Digital matte paintings are often completed at very high resolutions. 4K and 8K are common sizes we work with.

LL: Is it still common to work with 35mm? If so, what are the main differences between working with 35mm footage and digital video footage?

AL: Yes, 35mm is still very common. One of the main differences at present is the luminance—film has a lot more information in the black and white areas of an image, giving more range in the grading process. Depth of field and color temperature all have subtle differences too. The shutters in digital cameras work differently—they scan the frame in a progressive motion, just like an image on a television, which scans from top to bottom. This can cause problems when tracking a fast moving camera as the image on a frame can be slightly distorted. Film cameras work with a mechanical shutter, which eradicates this problem. The technology in digital cameras improves all the time and with great speed. It won't be long before film is the VHS of today.

LL: Are there major differences in workflow when creating effects for commercials as opposed to creating effects for feature films? If so, what are they?

AL: The biggest difference is time. A particular effect in a feature may have had a couple of years' worth of research and development behind it. The blockbusters have the budgets and time to achieve the massive visual effects, whereas commercials want the same effect done in three weeks! Film workflow has a much more separated pipeline: one person will animate, one will light, one will texture, one will rotoscope, and so on. A compositor can spend four weeks working on one shot in film. That's a full 60-second spot in the commercials world.

Additional Resources: The Full Interview

To read the full interview with Alex Lovejoy, see the Interviews folder on the DVD.

seven

CHAPTER

Masking, Rotoscoping, and Motion Tracking

"Tracking is something that a Flame artist will do every day, be it making a garbage mask to follow a simple move or tracking a new head onto someone."

—ALEX LOVEJOY, senior Flame artist and 2D supervisor, The Mill NY, New York City

Masking, which is the process *of creating mattes, is an inescapable step for complex compositing. Masking may be as simple as drawing a spline path with a dedicated masking tool. However, the task becomes more complicated when the matte needs to travel and the masking turns into rotoscoping. Motion tracking, on the other hand, requires the software to track features or patterns with a piece of footage and convert that information to animation curves. Once the curves exist, they may be used to apply motion to a different layer or input, remove the jitter from a shaking camera, or change the perspective of an element so that it fits a scene with a moving camera. Although the motion tracking process is semi-automated, special care must be taken when positioning tracking points. To help you practice this technique, as well as various masking and rotoscoping tasks, a new tutorial is added to this chapter. In addition, you'll have to chance to revisit the tutorial from Chapter 3.*

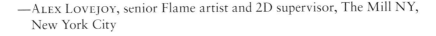

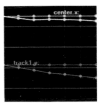

Mattes vs. Masks

Although the terms *matte* and *mask* are often used interchangeably, they refer to two separate parts of the same process. As discussed in Chapter 3, a matte establishes pixel opacity for a digital image and is thus needed to composite multiple images together. Matte values, as expressed by an alpha channel, range from 0 to 1.0 on a normalized scale. Hence, a matte is black and white, with additional shades of gray to establish tapering transparency.

A *mask*, in comparison, is the device that creates the matte. For example, the Pen tool in After Effects creates a closed spline path. Pixels falling inside the path are assigned an alpha value of 1.0, while pixels falling outside the path are assigned an alpha value of 0. The path is a mask; the resulting alpha channel is a matte. In contrast, many Nuke nodes carry a Mask parameter that establishes what input will be used as a matte. Despite the confusion in terminology, *masking* may be considered the process of creating a matte.

Tips & Tricks: Garbage Mattes, Soft Mattes, and Matte Paintings

Garbage mattes, or *garbage masks*, are hastily created mattes used to remove unwanted elements from as image. For example, a garbage matte may be used to remove light equipment from the edge of a greenscreen frame. *Soft mattes* are often created as part of the blue- or greenscreen keying. They are intentionally left with noise in the alpha channel to preserve fine detail, such as hair. A *matte painting*, on the other hand, is a painting of a set, set piece, or location that is impossible or impractical to shoot in real life. Although matte paintings were originally painted on glass plates and combined with footage optically, current matte paintings are created digitally and often involve 2.5D compositing. For more information on 2.5D, see Chapter 11, "Working with 2.5D and 3D."

The History of Rotoscoping

Rotoscoping is the process by which animators trace over live-action footage one frame at a time. The rotoscope process was developed by Max Fleischer, who patented the idea in 1917. Originally, it was a means by which traditional animators were able to add more realism to their work. The process has been used, on a somewhat limited basis, by traditional animators ever since. Rotoscoping found a place in such feature work as *Snow White and the Seven Dwarves*, *Wizards*, and *Heavy Metal*.

In the 1940s, animator U. B. Iwerks adapted the process to create traveling holdout mattes for visual effects work involving optical printing. Optical printing applies multiple exposures to a single piece of film utilizing a specially adapted projector and camera (see Figure 7.1). To prevent double exposure, holdout mattes are exposed on a separate strip of film and are then placed in front of the optical printer projector throw so that the projector light reaches only a limited area of the film held by the optical printer camera.

The process of creating holdout mattes was similar to that used in traditional animation. Reference footage was projected, one frame at a time, onto paper with registration holes. The rotoscoper traced the critical element and then inked or painted each drawing to create a solid black and white image.

Figure 7.1 *The optical printer used for* Star Wars *(1977). Projector A projected source footage. Projector B, which lacked a lens and lamp, held matte footage created through rotoscoping. Camera C exposed new film stock, but only in the region of the frame permitted by Projector B's footage. The white section of the matte footage, once processed, became transparent, while the black section became opaque. (Image courtesy of Industrial Light & Magic)*

Rotoscoping has survived into the digital age and continues to be applied through compositing software and stand-alone programs. Rotoscoping, as used for digital compositing, is often referred to as *roto.*

Rotoscoping Approaches

The most difficult aspect of digital rotoscoping is the creation of accurate mask shapes. Although different programs, tools, and plug-ins exist to make the process easier, you must nevertheless decide where to keyframe the mask. You can key every single frame of the animation, but it is generally more efficient to key specific frames while letting the program interpolate the mask shape for the remaining, unkeyed frames. As such, there are two approaches you can take to plan the keyframe locations: bisecting and key poses.

Bisecting

The process of *bisecting*, as applied to rotoscoping, splits the timeline into halves. For example, you can follow these basic steps:

- Move to frame 1, create a mask path, and set a key for the mask shape.
- Move to the last frame of the sequence. Change the path shape to match the footage and set a new key.
- Move to the frame halfway between frame 1 and the last frame. Change the mask shape and set a new key.
- Continue the process of moving to a frame halfway between previous keyframes.

When you approach the keyframing in such a manner, fewer adjustments of the vertex positions are necessary than if the mask was shaped one frame at a time. That is, instead of keying at frames 1, 2, 3, 4, 5, 6, and so forth, key at frames 1, 60, 30, 15, 45, and so on.

Key Poses

Key poses, as used in the world of traditional animation, are the critical character poses needed to communicate an action or tell a story. If an animator is working pose-to-pose, they will draw the key poses before moving on to in-between drawings, or *inbetweens*. For example, if an animation shows a character lifting a box, the key poses include the character's start position, the character bent down touching the box, and the character's end position with the box lifted into the air.

To simplify the rotoscoping process, you can identify key poses within a piece of footage. Once the poses are identified, shape the mask to fit the key poses and key the mask path. Because key poses usually involve an extreme, less-critical frames are left to interpolation by the program. An *extreme* is a pose that shows the maximum extension of appendages or other character body parts. For example, if an actor is doing jumping jacks, one extreme would show the character in a start position (see Figure 7.2). A second extreme would show the character jumping with his arms stretched out to the side. A third extreme would show the character's hands touching with his arms over his head. Once you have shaped and keyed the mask to fit all the key poses, you can shape and key the mask to fit the most critical inbetween poses.

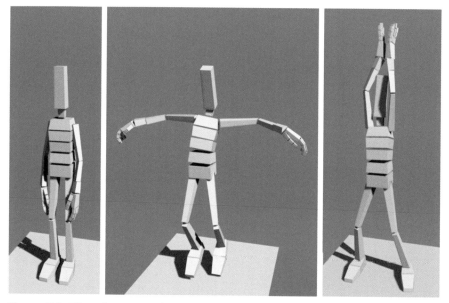

Figure 7.2 Three key poses showing extremes for arms and legs (Rig created by Jason Baskin)

Industry Perspective: The Persistence of Roto

Despite recent developments in compositing technology, rotoscoping has not disappeared. In fact, the roto tools have advanced to the degree that it is sometimes more cost effective to rotoscope than it is to shoot a scene with a proper blue- or greenscreen setup. It's not unusual for a production to shoot "dirty" plates intentionally, where no greenscreen has been supplied. A few of the larger visual effects studios, such as Sony Pictures Imageworks, have established satellite facilities dedicated to the task of roto. Some studios, such as Digital Domain, keep skilled rotoscopers within their 2D department. At numerous other visual effects and commercial production companies, compositors are expected to be skilled in the art of roto. While all major compositing packages contain a set of rotoscope tools, plug-in or stand-alone (SA) roto software is often employed. Silhouette FX and Imagineer Systems Motor are two such SA programs.

Motion Tracking Overview

Motion tracking, which tracks the position of a feature within live-action footage, falls into four main categories:

Transform Tracking If the live-action camera is static, this type of motion tracking is relatively simple. Unique features within the footage, sometimes as small as several pixels, are tracked so that composited elements can inherent the motion identified by the tracking. For example, you might motion track an actor's hand so that you can place a CG prop behind the fingers (see Figure 7.3). A similar but more complex challenge might involve tracking a CG head over the head of an actor in a scene. If the live-action camera is in motion, the tracking becomes more complex. If the camera's motion is significant and occurs along multiple axes, then matchmoving becomes necessary.

Matchmoving With this form of motion tracking, you can replicate the complex movement of a live-action camera so that elements can be composited into the scene with proper position, translation, rotation, scale, and lens distortion. For instance, handheld or Steadicam camera work would generally require matchmoving as the camera is rotating and translating in all three axes and thus shifting the perspective of objects in the scene. (Note that *matchmoving* is often used as a generic term to cover all types of motion tracking.)

Plate Stabilization Through the process of plate stabilization, motion tracking data is used to remove jitter and other 2D camera shakes and motions.

Hand Tracking Hand tracking refers to transform tracking or matchmoving that is beyond the automated capabilities of motion tracking tools. If the hand tracking involves transform tracking, a 3D prop is keyframe animated so that its position lines up with a point appearing in imported footage. If the hand tracking involves matchmoving, a 3D camera is keyframe animated so that a virtual set lines up to the imported footage. (For more information on 3D cameras, as they apply to After Effects and Nuke, see Chapter 11, "Working with 2.5D and 3D.")

Figure 7.3 (Top) Detail of video composite with CG jar tracked to the hand of an actress (Center) Isolated jar layer. The jar's motion path, derived through transform tracking, is visible as the white line. (Bottom) Rotoscoped hand, which is placed back on top of the tracked jar. The yellow path is a mask.

Industry Perspective: Motion Tracking Options

As with rotoscoping, visual effects and commercial production studios take many different approaches to motion tracking. While some compositors stick to the tools built within standard compositing programs, others prefer to use stand-alone programs such as Boujou, PFTrack, 3D Equalizer, Mocha, and SynthEyes. It's not unusual to switch between different programs on a project as each tool tends to have particular strengths when tracking specific footage.

Motion tracking becomes more complex when it's necessary to matchmove a camera. At large studios, such a Weta Digital, this task is turned over to specialized camera departments. Advanced technology is often employed to capture data from the shoot so that a virtual set and virtual camera can be accurately re-created in a 3D program or a compositing program with 3D capabilities. For example, data may be captured with a Light Detection and Ranging (LIDAR) system. Pertinent measurements may also be noted in writing. The notes will include positional information of the camera and set pieces. To replicate the camera accurately, lens information is also critical. (High-dynamic range images and other lighting information may be captured to aid the lighting department.) Occasionally, camera data from a robotic motion control system may be imported directly into the 3D or compositing program.

Despite the impressive array of motion tracking solutions available to compositors, it still may be necessary to hand-track a shot. For example, the ongoing trend to shoot action-oriented feature film work with violent, handheld camera moves ensures that some effects shots are beyond the automated capabilities of the best tracking software.

Applying Masking and Tracking Techniques

Masking and rotoscoping in After Effects and Nuke is carried out through various tools designed to create animatable spline paths. Motion tracking, on the other hand, is created through specific tracking effects and nodes.

Masking and Tracking in AE

The Pen tool supplies the primary means by which to create a mask in After Effects. However, Auto-trace and AutoBezier functions present alternative approaches. Motion tracking is carried out through the Track Motion tool.

Masking with the Pen Tool

In After Effects, all masks are dependent on a path. A *path* is a Bezier spline that indicates the area that the mask occupies. The path includes a number of vertex points, which define the curvature of the Bezier.

To create a path with the Pen tool manually, follow these steps:

1. Select a layer through the layer outline of the Timeline panel. Select the Pen tool (see Figure 7.4). LMB+click in the viewer of the Composition panel. Each click places a vertex point.
2. To close the path, LMB+click on or near the first vertex. The mouse pointer must be close enough

Figure 7.4 Pen tool menu with Add Vertex, Delete Vertex, and Convert Vertex options

to change to a close-path icon (a small pen icon with a circle beside it). Once the path is closed, any area outside the mask is assigned an alpha value of 0 and thus becomes transparent.

3. To end the path without closing it, choose the Selection tool. A nonclosed path will not function as a mask. However, you can close the path at a later time by selecting the path in the viewer and choosing Layer → Mask And Shape Path → Closed.

Manipulating Paths and Masks

By default, the segments between each vertex of a mask path are linear. The vertex points themselves are considered corner points. However, smooth points are also available. A smooth point carries a direction handle and produces curved segments. To draw a smooth point, LMB+drag during the path-drawing process. That is, LMB+click where you want the vertex; without releasing the mouse button, continue to drag the mouse. The direction handle extends itself from the vertex point. The direction handle length, which affects the curvature of surrounding segments, is set once you release the mouse button. (*Direction handles* is Adobe's name for tangent handles.)

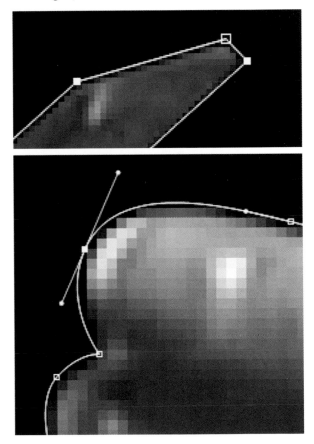

You can convert a corner point to a smooth point by selecting the Convert Vertex tool and LMB+clicking the vertex point in the viewer. Once the point is converted, a direction handle appears. You can move each side of the direction handle separately by LMB+dragging with the Convert Vertex tool or the Selection tool (see Figure 7.5). To return a smooth point to a corner point, LMB+click the point a second time with the Convert Vertex tool. You can delete a vertex point with the Delete Vertex tool. To insert a new vertex point into a preexisting path, choose the Add Vertex tool and LMB+click on the path at the position where you want the new vertex to appear.

Mask Properties

As soon as a mask is drawn, a Masks section is added for the corresponding layer in the layer outline (see Figure 7.6). A subsection is named after the new mask, such as Mask 1. The subsection includes Mask Opacity, Mask Feather, and Mask Expansion. Mask Opacity controls the alpha value of pixels within the mask. For example, a value of 50% assigns an alpha value of 0.5 on a 0 to 1.0 scale. Mask Opacity does not affect the alpha value of pixels that lie outside the mask. Mask Feather, on the other hand, introduces falloff to the alpha values at the edge of the mask. A value of 10, for example, tapers the alpha values from 1.0 to 0 over the distance of 10 pixels. Note that the mask is eroded *inward* when Mask Feather is raised above 0. In contrast, Mask Expansion expands the mask effect (if positive) or shrinks the effect (if negative). Both Mask Feather and Mask Expansion carry X and Y direction cells, which can be adjusted individually.

Figure 7.5 (*Top*) *Detail of mask path drawn with the Pen tool. Default linear segments span the vertex points. Selected vertex points are solid. The large hollow point at the top represents the first vertex drawn. (Bottom) Detail of mask with smooth points and curved segments. The selected vertex point is solid and displays its direction handle.*

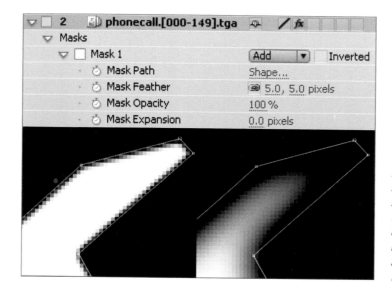

Figure 7.6 (Top) Masks section of a layer as seen in the layer outline (Bottom Left) The alpha channel of a masked layer (Bottom Right) Same mask with Mask Feather set to 5

Transforming and Keyframing a Mask

To select a mask vertex, LMB+click with the Selection tool. To select multiple vertices, select the mask name in the layer outline and then LMB+drag a selection marquee around the vertices you wish to choose. Direction handles are displayed only for selected vertices and the vertices directly to each side of those selected (assuming that they have smooth points).

You can use the keyboard arrow keys to translate selected vertex points one pixel at a time. To translate all the vertices of a mask as a single unit, double-click the mask path in the viewer with the Selection tool. A rectangular path transform handle appears (see Figure 7.7). To translate the path, LMB+drag the handle. To scale the path, LMB+drag one of the handles' corner points. To rotate the path, place the mouse pointer close to a handle corner; when the rotate icon appears, LMB+drag.

You can delete a mask at any time by selecting the mask name in the layer outline and pressing the Delete key. To hide the mask paths in the viewer temporarily, toggle off the Mask And Shape Path Visibility button at the bottom of the Composition panel (see Chapter 1).

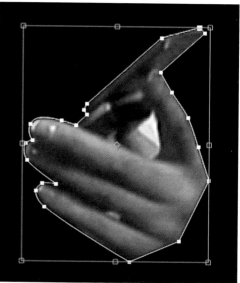

Figure 7.7 A mask transform handle

You can animate the shape of a mask by toggling on the Stopwatch button beside the Mask Path property in the Masks section of the layer. Once the Stopwatch button is toggled on, you can LMB+drag one or more path vertex points in the viewer, which forces the current shape (and all the current point positions) of the path to be keyframed.

You can use the Smart Mask Interpolation tool to refine the way in which the program interpolates mask vertex positions between keyframes. To reveal the tool's controls, choose Window → Smart Mask Interpolation. The Smart Mask Interpolation panel opens at the bottom right of the After Effects workspace (see Figure 7.8).

To apply the tool, follow these steps:

1. Select two or more adjacent keyframes of a mask within the Timeline panel.
2. Set the options within the Smart Mask Interpolation panel.
3. Click the Apply button. The tool places new keyframes between the selected keyframes.

The following suggestions are recommended when setting the tool's options:

- If you do not want a new keyframe at every frame of the timeline, reduce the Keyframe Rate value. For example, if the project frame rate is 30 and Keyframe Rate is set to 10, ten keyframes are added per second with a gap of two keyframes between each one. (Additionally, the tool always adds a keyframe directly after the first keyframe selected and directly before the last keyframe selected.)
- Deselect Use Linear Vertex Paths. This forces the vertex motion paths to remain smooth.
- If the mask shape does not undergo a significant shift in shape between the selected keyframes, set Bending Resistance to a low value. This ensures that relative distance between vertex positions is maintained— that is, the path bends more than it stretches. If the mask shape undergoes a significant change in shape, set Bending Resistance to a high value. A high value allows the vertices to drift apart and the mask shape to stretch.
- If you do not want the tool to add additional vertices, deselect the Add Mask Shape Vertices check box. That said, complex interpolations are generally more successful if vertices are added.
- Leave Matching Method set to Auto. Otherwise, the tool may change each vertex type from linear to smooth or vice versa.

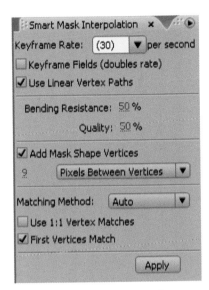

Figure 7.8 The Smart Mask Interpolation panel with default settings

Keep in mind that Smart Mask Interpolation tool is purely optional. Nevertheless, it offers a means to set a series of keyframes automatically. In addition, it can produce a mask interpolation different from the interpolation the program normally creates between pre-existing keyframes.

Choosing a Mask Mode

You can draw multiple masks for any layer. Each new mask is consecutively numbered (Mask 1, Mask 2, and so on). If more than one mask exists for a layer, it's important to choose a mask mode (blending mode) for each mask. You can find the mask modes menu beside the mask name in the layer outline (see Figure 7.6 earlier in this chapter). Here's how each mode functions:

None disables the mask.

Add adds the mask to the mask above it. If there is only one mask for the layer, Add serves as an on switch.

Subtract subtracts the mask from the mask above it (see Figure 7.9).

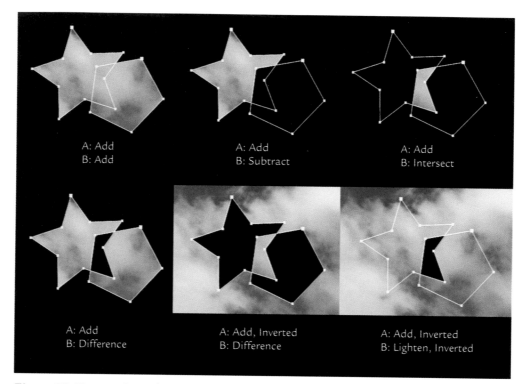

Figure 7.9 Two masks with six mask mode combinations. Mask A is shaped like a star and is the upper mask. Mask B is shaped like a pentagon and is the lower mask. With these examples, the Mask Opacity is 100% for both masks.

Intersect adds the mask to the mask above it but only for the pixels where the masks overlap. The masks are made transparent where they do not overlap (see Figure 7.9).

Lighten adds the mask to the mask above it. However, where masks overlap, the highest Mask Opacity value of the two masks is used.

Darken adds the mask to the mask above it. However, where masks overlap, the lowest Mask Opacity value of the two masks is used.

Difference adds the mask with the mask above it. However, where masks overlap, the lower mask is subtracted from the upper mask (see Figure 7.9).

To invert the result of any mask, select the Inverted check box beside the mask name in the layer outline. The mask blend modes take into account Mask Opacity values for the masks assigned to a layer. For example, if Mask A is set to Add and has a Mask Opacity of 100% and Mask B is set to Subtract with a Mask Opacity of 50%, the area in which the masks overlap receives an opacity of 50%. That is, 50% is subtracted from 100%.

Tips & Tricks: Copying a Mask

You can copy a mask from one layer to another. To do so, select the mask name in the layer outline and press Ctrl+C to copy. Select the second layer in the layer outline and press Ctrl+V to paste.

Masking with Shapes

After Effects offers several ready-made mask shapes. To apply one, select a layer in the layer outline, select a shape tool (see Figure 7.10), and LMB+drag in the viewer. Once the mouse button is released, the size of the shape path is set. Nevertheless, using the Selection tool, you can manipulate any of the resulting vertex points as you would a hand-drawn path. The resulting path is added to the Masks section in the layer outline and receives a standard name, such as Mask 3.

Figure 7.10 *The Shape tool menu*

If a layer is *not* selected when a shape tool is applied, the shape becomes a separate shape layer and does not function as a mask. However, you can convert a shape to a mask path by employing the Auto-trace tool (see the next section).

Masking with Auto-Trace

The Auto-trace tool automatically creates a mask based on the RGB, alpha, or luminance values within a layer. To apply it, follow these steps:

1. Select the layer that you want to trace. Choose Layer → Auto-trace. The Auto-trace dialog box opens (see Figure 7.11). The selected layer becomes the input layer.

2. Change the Channel menu to Red, Green, Blue, Alpha, or Luminance to determine how the tool will generate the mask path or paths. Select the Preview check box to see the result of the tool. One or more mask paths are automatically drawn along high-contrast edges.

3. Adjust the dialog box properties to refine the paths (see the list after this set of steps).

4. Deselect the Apply To New Layer check box. Click the OK button to close the dialog box. The new path (or paths) is added to the input

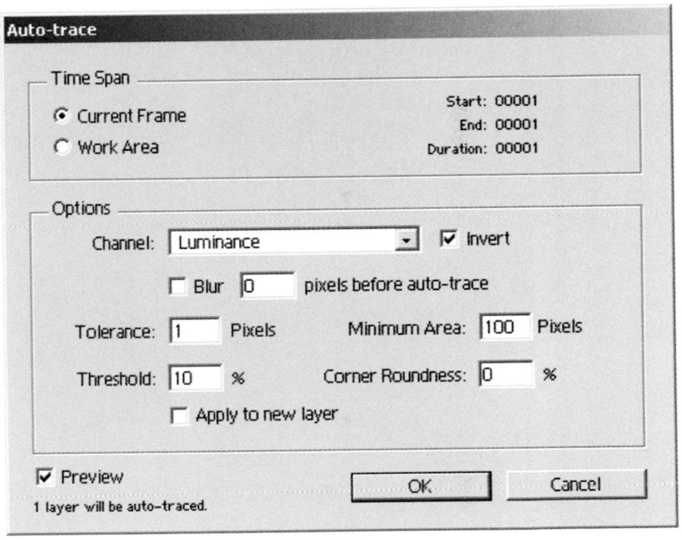

Figure 7.11 *The Auto-trace dialog box*

layer (see Figure 7.12). By default, the mask blend mode menu (beside the mask name in the layer outline) is set to None. To see the resulting matte in the alpha channel, change the menu to Add.

The Auto-trace tool is best suited for fairly simple layers that contain a minimal number of high-contrast edges. Nevertheless, the Auto-trace dialog box contains several properties with which to adjust the results:

Current Frame, if selected, creates paths for the current timeline frame.

Work Area, if selected, creates paths for every frame of the timeline work area. The vertex positions are automatically keyframed over time.

Invert, if selected, inverts the input layer before detecting edges.

Blur, if selected, blurs the input layer before detecting edges. This reduces the amount of noise and minimizes the number of small, isolated paths. The Pixels Before Auto-Trace cell sets the size of the blur kernel and the strength of the blur.

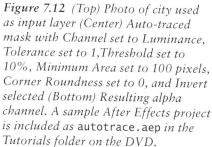

Figure 7.12 *(Top) Photo of city used as input layer (Center) Auto-traced mask with Channel set to Luminance, Tolerance set to 1,Threshold set to 10%, Minimum Area set to 100 pixels, Corner Roundness set to 0, and Invert selected (Bottom) Resulting alpha channel. A sample After Effects project is included as* `autotrace.aep` *in the Tutorials folder on the DVD.*

Threshold sets the sensitivity of the edge detection. Input pixel values above the Threshold value earn an alpha value of 1.0; input pixels below the Threshold value earn an alpha value of 0. Paths are drawn at the borders between resulting sets of pixels with 0 and 1.0 alpha values. The Threshold cell operates as a percentage; nevertheless, this is equivalent to a 0 to 1.0 scale where 50% is the same as 0.5.

Minimum Area specifies the pixel area of the smallest high-contrast feature that will be traced. For example, a value of 25 removes any path that would normally surround a high-contrast dot that is less than 5×5 pixels in size.

Tolerance sets the distance, in pixels, a path may deviate from the detected edges. This is necessary to round the path at vertex positions when using the Corner Roundness property. The higher the Corner Roundness value, the smoother and more simplified the paths become.

Apply To New Layer, if selected, places the paths on a new Auto-trace layer. The Auto-trace layer is solid white; the result is a white shape cut out by the new masks.

Rotoscoping with RotoBezier

You can use any closed path to rotoscope in After Effects. Once the Stopwatch button beside the Mask Path property is toggled on, you can reposition the vertices over time and thus allow the program to automatically place keyframes for the mask shape.

At the same time, you can convert any preexisting path to a RotoBezier path to make the rotoscoping process somewhat easier. To do so, select a mask name in the layer outline and choose Layer → Mask And Shape Path → RotoBezier. RotoBezier paths differ from manually drawn paths in that they do not employ direction handles. Instead, each RotoBezier vertex uses a tension value that affects the curvature of the surrounding segments (see Figure 7.13). You can adjust the tension value by selecting a vertex with the Convert Vertex tool and LMB+dragging left or right in the viewer. LMB+dragging left causes surrounding segments to become more linear. LMB+dragging right causes the segments to gain additional curvature.

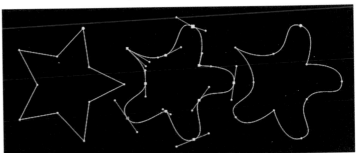

Figure 7.13 *(Left) Mask path with default linear segments (Center) Mask path converted to smooth points with direction handles visible (Right) Mask path converted to RotoBezier*

You can adjust the direction handles of a path with smooth points and thus match any shape that a RotoBezier path may form. However, such adjustments are considerably more time intensive than manipulating the RotoBezier tension weights. Hence, RotoBezier paths tend to be more efficient during the rotoscoping process. Nevertheless, if a required mask needs numerous sharp corners, it may be more practical to stick with a manually drawn path that has default corner points.

Motion Tracking in AE

After Effects comes equipped with a built-in motion tracker, which is called Track Motion or Stabilize Motion, depending on the settings. To apply Track Motion, follow these steps:

1. Select the layer you wish to track in the layer outline. Choose Animation → Track Motion. A Tracker Controls panel opens at the bottom right of the After Effects workspace (see Figure 7.14). In addition, the layer is opened in the Layer panel.

2. A single track point, Track Point 1, is supplied and is placed in the viewer of the Layer panel (see Figure 7.15). The inner box establishes the feature region, which the tracker attempts to follow across multiple frames. For successful tracking, the feature should be an identifiable element, such as the iris of an eye, which is visible throughout the duration of the timeline. The outer box establishes the search region, in which the tracker attempts to locate the feature as it moves across multiple frames. The center + sign is the attach point, which is an X, Y coordinate to which a target layer is attached. The target layer receives the tracking data once the tracking has been completed. You can choose the target layer by clicking the Edit Target button in the Tracker Controls panel and choosing a layer name from the Layer menu of the Motion Target dialog box.

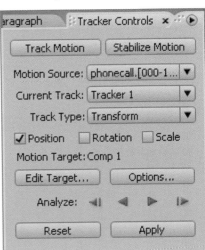

Figure 7.14 *The Tracker Controls panel*

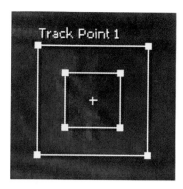

Figure 7.15 Track Point 1 icon, as seen in a viewer of the Layer panel

3. Position Track Point 1 over an identifiable feature. Scrub through the timeline to make sure the feature you choose is visible throughout the duration of the footage. The smaller and more clearly defined the selected feature, the more likely the tracking will be successful. You can adjust the size of the region boxes to change the tracker sensitivity; LMB+drag one of the region box corners to do so.

4. To activate the tracker, return the timeline to frame 1 and press the Analyze Forward play button in the Tracker Controls panel. The tracker advances through the footage, one frame at a time, and creates a motion path for Track Point 1 (see Figure 7.16). The motion path includes keyframe markers, in the form of hollow points, for each frame included in the tracking.

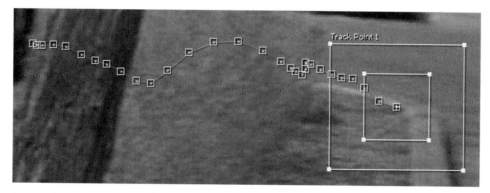

Figure 7.16 A motion path for Track Point 1. Each hollow point is a keyframe marker.

5. Scrub through the timeline. If Track Point 1 successfully follows the feature selected in step 3, you can transfer the data to the target layer. To do this, click the Apply button in the Tracker Controls panel and press OK in the Motion Tracker Apply Options dialog box. Keyframes are laid down for the target layer's Position property. The target layer thus inherits the motion identified by the tracker. Note that the view automatically changes to the viewer of the Composition panel when the Apply button is pressed.

If the motion to be tracked is complicated, you can add a second tracking point and corresponding icon by selecting the Rotation and/or Scale check boxes in the Tracker Controls panel. Track Point 2's icon is attached to the Track Point 1 icon in the viewer. However, you can adjust each icon separately. When you add a second point, the tracker is able to identify motion within footage that undergoes positional, rotational, and scale transformations (see Figure 7.17). If Position, Rotation, and Scale check boxes are selected, the target layer receives keyframes for the corresponding properties.

The Track Motion tool stores the position of the keyframe markers for the tracked layer as keyframes under a Motion Trackers section in the layer outline (see Figure 7.18). Each track point is given its own subsection. Within these subsections, the keyframes are divided between Feature Center, Confidence, and Attach Point properties. Feature Center stores the X and Y position of the Track Point icon. Attach Point stores the X and Y position of its namesake. By default, Feature Center and Attach Point values are identical.

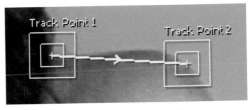

Figure 7.17 Track Points 1 and 2

However, you can reposition the attach point + icon in the viewer before using the Analyze Forward button; this offsets the inherited motion of the target layer and creates unique values for the Attach Point property. If adjusting the attach point + icon proves inaccurate, you can enter new values into the Attach Point Offset property cells *after* the keyframes arc laid down in the Motion Trackers section. For example, entering –100, 0 causes the target layer to move 100 pixels further to the left once the Apply button in the Tracker Controls panel is clicked.

2   🗐 hydrant.[00-29].tga 🖵 /

- ▽ Motion Trackers
  - ▽ Tracker 1
    - ▽ Track Point 1
      - ⏱ 🗠 Feature Center   504.6, 185.7   ◇ ◇ ◇ ◇ ◇ ◇ ◇ ◇
      - Feature Size   ⊜ 22.0, 12.0
      - Search Offset   0.0, 0.0
      - Search Size   ⊜ 40.0, 40.0
      - ⏱ 🗠 Confidence   96.6%   ▣ ▣ ▣ ▣ ▣ ▣ ▣ ▣
      - ⏱ 🗠 Attach Point   504.6, 185.7   ◇ ◇ ◇ ◇ ◇ ◇ ◇ ◇
      - ⏱ Attach Point Offset   0.0, 0.0

Figure 7.18 Motion Trackers section of a tracked layer

The Confidence property represents the motion tracker's estimated accuracy. With each frame, the tracker reports a Confidence value between 0% and 100%. If Track Point 1 suddenly loses its selected feature and goes astray, the Confidence valuc drops. This is an estimated accuracy, however. The value may stay relatively high even if Track Point 1 jumps to a completely inappropriate part of the frame. Nevertheless, you can use the Confidence to drive the action of the tracker. To do so, click the Options button in the Tracker Controls panel. In the Motion Tracker Options dialog box (Figure 7.19), you can choose a Confidence threshold by changing the % cell in the lower-right corner. You can choose an action for the tracker if it drops below the threshold by changing the If Confidence Is Below menu. The Continue Tracking option is the default behavior, which may allow the track points to run astray. The Stop Tracking option stops the tracker when the Confidence level drops too low. This gives the user a chance to adjust the track point positions before applying the Analyze Forward or Analyze Backward buttons again. The Extrapolate Motion option attempts to relocate the selected feature if the Confidence level drops too low. The Adapt Feature option forces the tracker to identify a new pattern within the search rcgion, which mcans that the feature identified for the first frame is no longer used.

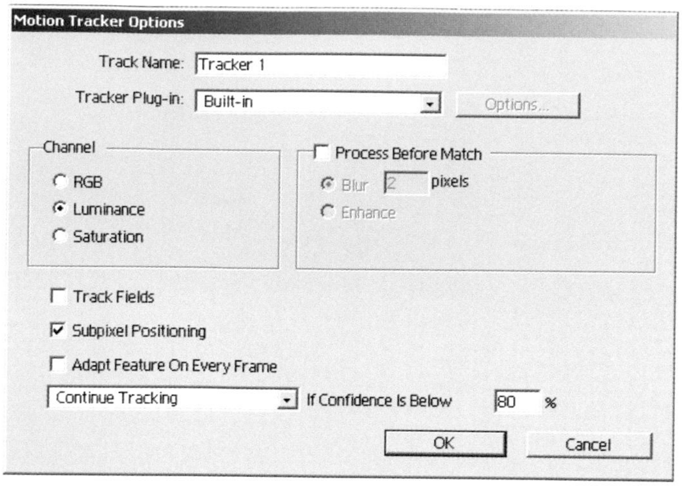

Figure 7.19 Motion Tracker Options dialog box

In addition to the Confidence settings, several other options provide flexibility. Through the Channel section, you can switch the tracker to Luminance, RGB, or Saturation examination. If you select the Process Before Match check box, you can force the tracker to blur or enhance (edge sharpen) the image before tracking. Blurring the image slightly may help remove interference created by film or video grain. Enhancing may aid the tracker when there is significant motion blur. The strength of the blur or enhance is set by the Pixels cell. Subpixel Positioning, when selected, allows track point position values to be stored with decimal values. If Subpixel Positioning is unselected, the positions are stored as whole pixel numbers. With low-resolution material, Subpixel Positioning may help perceived accuracy.

Motion Tracking Problem Solving

Aside from adjusting the properties within the Motion Tracker Options dialog box, you can apply the following techniques if the tracking proves to be inaccurate:

- Move to the frame where a track point has "lost sight" of its chosen feature. Manually position the track point icon so that it is centered over the selected feature once again. Press the Analyze Forward button again. New keyframes are laid over old keyframes.
- If the problem area is only a few frames in duration, manually step through with the Analyze 1 Frame Forward or Analyze 1 Frame Backward button.
- If a track point slips away from its feature, LMB+drag the corresponding keyframe marker to an appropriate position within the viewer. The keyframes in the Timeline panel are automatically updated.
- Adjust the errant track point's search and feature regions. If the feature region is too small, the track point may suddenly lose the feature. If the search region is too large, the track point may be confused by similar patterns that lie nearby.
- Edit the keyframes in the Timeline panel using standard editing tools, such as the Graph Editor or Keyframe Interpolation. You can delete keyframes to remove "kinks" in the track point motion path.
- If you decide to return to the Motion Tracker after working with other tools, change the Motion Source menu in the Tracker Controls panel to the layer that carries the tracking information.

Motion Tracking Variants

By default, the Track Motion tool operates as a transform tracker. However, you can change the functionality by switching the Track Type menu in the Tracker Controls panel to one of the following options:

Parallel Corner Pin tracks skew and rotation. It utilizes four track points (see Figure 7.20). You can adjust the position and size of the first three track points. Track Point 4, however, stays a fixed distance from Track Points 2 and 3 and cannot be manually positioned. Nevertheless, the Parallel Corner Pin tracker is ideal for tracking rectangular features shot with a moving camera. TV screens, billboards, and windows fall into this category. When the tracking data is applied, the target layer is given a specific Corner Pin transform section with keyframes matching each of the four points. In addition, the Position property is keyed.

Perspective Corner Pin tracks skew, rotation, and perspective changes. It utilizes four track points. Unlike with Parallel Corner Pin, however, all four point icons can be adjusted in the viewer. Perspective Corner Pin is ideal for tracking rectangular features that undergo perspective shift. For example, you can place a CG calendar on the back of a live-action door that opens during the shot. When the tracking data is applied,

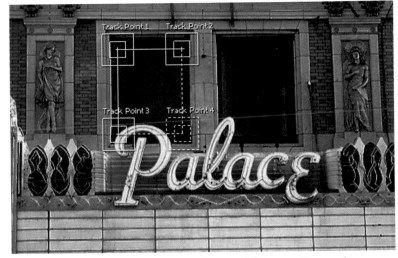

Figure 7.20 *The four track points of a Parallel Corner Pin tracker are placed over a window. Other rectangular features in this image, such as the marquee sections or individual building tiles, are equally suitable subjects. (Photo © 2009 by Jupiterimages)*

the target layer is given a Corner Pin transform section with keyframes matching each of the four points; in addition, the Position property is keyed. Perspective Corner Pin is demonstrated in "AE Tutorial 7: Corner Pin Tracking with a Non-Square Object" at the end of this chapter.

Raw operates as a transform tracker but does apply the tracking data to a target layer. Instead, the keyframes are stored by the layer's Feature Center, Confidence, and Attach Point properties. The Raw option is designed to provide keyframe data to expressions or operations where the copying and pasting of tracking data keyframes may prove useful.

Stabilize tracks position, rotation, and/or scale to compensate for (and thus remove) camera movement within the layer. If the Rotation and/or Scale check boxes are selected, two tracker points are provided. In contrast to Transform mode, the tracking data is applied to the layer that is tracked and there is no target layer. As such, the layer's Anchor Point, Position, Scale, and Rotation properties are keyframed.

Tips & Tricks: Mocha and AE

CS4 includes Mocha for After Effects, a standalone motion tracking and rotoscoping program developed by Imagineer Systems. Mocha utilizes 2.5D planar tracking tools that are well-suited for footage that suffers from motion blur, heavy grain, or objects that move in and out of frame. Motion tracking data is transferred from Mocha to After Effects as Corner Pin transform keyframes. For more information, see the CS4 documentation, or visit www.imagineersystems.com.

Masking and Tracking in Nuke

You can create a mask in Nuke by connecting the output of a node to a second node's Mask input. You can also create a mask with the Bezier node, which is automatically keyframed in anticipation of rotoscoping. The Tracker node, in contrast, can track motion with one, two, three, or four track points.

Using the Mask Input

Numerous Nuke nodes, including filter nodes and merge nodes, carry a Mask input. This is symbolized by an arrow stub appearing on the right side of a node. You can LMB+drag the arrow stub and thereby extend the pipe to another node (see Figure 7.21). Once the Mask input is connected, the Mask check box is selected automatically in the masked node's properties panel. By default, the Mask menu is set to Rgb.alpha, which means that the mask values are derived from the input node's alpha. However, you can change the Mask menu to Rgb.*channel*, Depth.Z, or other specialized channel.

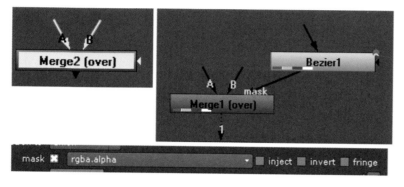

Figure 7.21 *(Top Left) Merge node's Mask input arrow stub, seen on the right side of the node icon (Top Right) Merge node's Mask input pipe connected to the output of a Bezier node (Bottom) Merge node's Mask parameter with Inject, Invert, and Fringe check boxes*

Here are a few example connections that take advantage of the Mask input:

- A Read node, which carries a black-and-white bitmap of text, is connected to the Mask input of a Defocus node. Thus the blur appears only where the bitmap is white (see Figure 7.22). With this example, the Defocus node's Mask parameter is set to Rgb.red. Again, the Mask parameter determines which Mask input channel contributes values to the alpha matte. Rgb.green or Rgb.blue would work equally well in this situation.
- A Ramp node is connected to the Mask input of a Merge node. Thus the Merge node's input A wins out where the ramp is white (see Figure 7.22). The Merge node's input B wins out where the ramp is black. (This assumes that input A and input B possess solid-white alpha channels.) With this example, the Merge node's Mask parameter is set to Rgb.alpha (the Ramp node pattern appears in the RGB and alpha channels).
- A Bezier node is connected to the Mask input of a Merge node, thus determining which portion of the Merge node's input A is used. For a demonstration of this technique, see the next section plus the section "Nuke Tutorial 3 Revisited: Finalizing the Composite" at the end of this chapter.

Tips & Tricks: Invert, Inject, and Fringe

You can invert the values passed to the Mask input by selecting the Invert check box in the masked node's properties panel. You can pass the resulting alpha matte to a downstream node by selecting the Inject check box. Inject allows the alpha matte to be used by the masked node— plus it places the alpha matte values in *mask.a* channel, which can be passed to other nodes through a new pipe connection. The Fringe check box, on the other hand, fringes the mask, whereby the centers of transparent areas are given solid cores. Fringe is useful for placing an effect along the edge of an object.

Figure 7.22 (Top Left) The output of a Read node is connected to the Mask input of a Defocus node. (Top Right) The resulting blur is contained to parts of the Read node's bitmap that are white. A sample Nuke script is included as filter_mask.nk *in the Tutorials folder. (Bottom Left) The output of a Ramp node is connected to the Mask input of a Merge node. (Bottom Right) The resulting merge fades between input A and input B. A sample Nuke script is included as* ramp_mask.nk *in the Tutorials folder on the DVD.*

Drawing Beziers

Perhaps the easiest way to create a mask is to use a Bezier node. To apply a Bezier, you can follow these steps:

1. In the Node Graph, RMB+click and choose Draw → Bezier. Open the new Bezier node's properties panel.

2. In the viewer, Ctrl+Alt+click to place a vertex. Continue to Crtl+Alt+click to place additional vertices. By default, the Bezier path is closed.

3. You can edit the Bezier path at any point as long as the Bezier node's properties panel is open. To move one vertex, LMB+drag the vertex point. To move multiple vertices, LMB+drag a selection marquee around the points and use the central transform handle for manipulation. To move a tangent handle, LMB+drag one of the two handle points. To insert a new vertex, Ctrl+Alt+click on the path. To delete a vertex, select it in the viewer and press the Delete key.

The path tangents are smooth by default (see Figure 7.23). However, you can convert a tangent by RMB+clicking over the corresponding point and choosing Break or Cusp from the menu. Cusp forces linear segments to surround the vertex and is therefore appropriate for making sharp corners on the path. Break splits the tangent handle so that the two ends can be moved independently. You can affect the curvature of the corresponding path segment by LMB+dragging the tangent handle to make it shorter or longer.

By default, the pixels within the closed path receive an alpha value of 1.0, while the pixels outside the path receive an alpha value of 0. However, you can reduce the Bezier node's Opacity slider and thus lower the alpha value within the path. To feather the edge of the resulting alpha matte, do one of the following:

- Adjust the Extra Blur slider of the Bezier node. Positive values feather the edge outward. Negative numbers feather the edge inward. To soften the resulting edge even further, lower the Falloff parameter below 1.0.

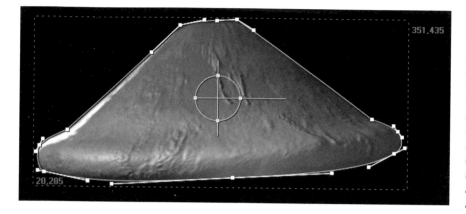

Figure 7.23 A Bezier path with selected vertices. Cusp vertices are identifiable by their lack of tangent handles. Break tangents possess left and right tangent handles that can be rotated individually. Smooth vertices feature tangent handles that are fixed in a straight line. The transform handle is the central circle.

- Ctrl+LMB+drag a vertex in the viewer. By holding down the Ctrl key, you can create a duplicate vertex point. When you release the mouse key, the edge is feathered from the original vertex position to the position of the duplicate vertex. To delete the duplicated vertex and remove the feather, RMB+click over the duplicate vertex and choose Unblur.
- In the viewer, RMB+click over a vertex and choose Blur. A duplicate vertex is created and is slightly offset from the original vertex.

Tips & Tricks: Bounding Boxes

A Bezier path includes its own bounding box, as is indicated by a dotted line in the viewer. A *bounding box* is an enclosed rectangular area that defines which pixels are considered valid by Nuke. (Pixels outside the bounding box are ignored.) The X, Y coordinates of the bottom-left and top-right box corners are indicated in the viewer. If a node output is smaller or larger than the project resolution, or is otherwise uncentered, a bounding box is drawn in the viewer. While Bezier nodes receive a bounding box that fits tightly to the path shape, Read nodes receive a bounding box that is the same size as the imported image. In either situation, you can adjust the bounding box size by connecting an output to an AdjustBBox node (in the Transform menu). Reducing a bounding box size may be useful for removing empty space within an imported CG render. If a bounding box edge intersects non-0 alpha values, however, the RGB edge pixels are streaked to the project resolution frame edge. To remove the streaked pixels, connect a Black-Outside node (in the Transform menu) to the AdjustBBox node's output.

Combining Beziers

A Bezier node can only support a single path. However, you can combine the results of two or more Bezier nodes with one of the following techniques:
- Connect the output of the one Bezier node to the input of another Bezier node. The paths are added together and the output alpha channel is identical to the RGB (see Figure 7.24).
- Connect each Bezier output to a Merge node with default settings. The result is the same as connecting the Beziers directly to each other. You can continue to connect additional Bezier nodes through the A2, A3, and A4 inputs.
- To use Merge nodes with nondefault Operation menu settings, connect the Bezier nodes in pairs (see Figure 7.24). For example, to subtract the Bezier connected to the Merge node's input B from the Bezier connected to Merge node's input A, set the Operation menu to Minus.

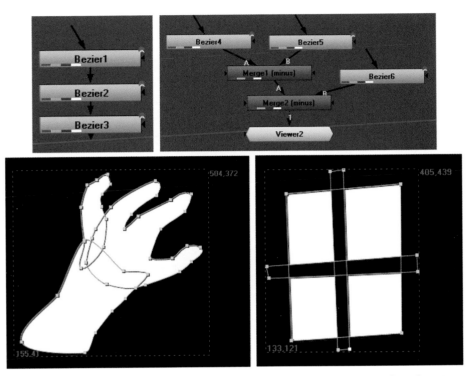

Figure 7.24 *(Top Left) Three Bezier nodes connected in a series (Top Right) Three Bezier nodes connected in pairs to two Merge nodes (Bottom Left) Result of Bezier nodes connected in a series (Bottom Right) Result of Bezier nodes connected to Merge nodes with the Operation menus set to Minus. A sample Nuke script is included as* three_beziers.nk *in the Tutorials folder on the DVD.*

Rotoscoping with Beziers

The Bezier node is designed for animation. When the Bezier is drawn, the shape of its path is automatically keyed for the current frame of the timeline. The keyframe is indicated by the cyan shading of the Shape parameter of the Bezier node's properties panel (see Figure 7.25). The Shape parameter is represented by two cells. The leftmost cell indicates the shape number. The second cell indicates the total number of shapes. If you move the timeline to a different frame and adjust the path, the shape is automatically keyframed, the shape is assigned a new number, and the total number of shapes increases by 1. Once multiple shapes exist, Nuke morphs between shapes. The morph is based on a spline interpolation between vertex points. You can force the interpolation to be linear, however, by selecting the Linear Interpolate check box.

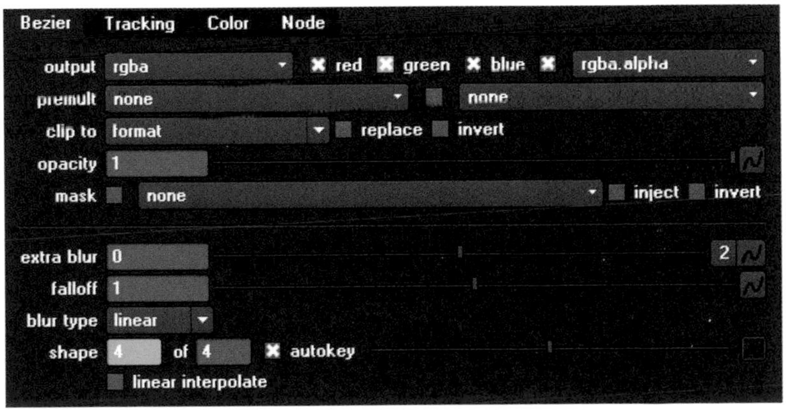

Figure 7.25 *The properties panel of a Bezier node. The Bezier has four shapes that have been keyed.*

You can alter the nature of the shape morph by changing the Shape bias slider, which is found to the right of the Shape cells. If you LMB+click and drag the slider, the interpolation updates the path in the viewer. If you move the slider toward 1.0, the interpolation is biased toward the keyframed shape with the higher frame number. If you move the slider toward –1, the interpolation is biased toward the keyframed shape with the lower frame number. Note that the slider returns to 0 when the mouse button is released and the resulting shape is automatically keyframed. You can revise a keyframe at any time by moving the timeline to the keyed frame and either moving vertex points in the viewer or adjusting the Shape bias slider.

Tips & Tricks: Transforming a Mask

In addition to animating a Bezier path shape changing over time, you can animate the path, as a whole, by translating, rotating, scaling, or skewing through the Tracking tab of the Bezier node's properties panel.

Tracking with the Tracker Node

Nuke provides a Tracker node (in the Transform menu). The node offers five main modes, each of which can be set by changing the Transform menu in the Transform tab of its properties panel. The modes follow:

None is the mandatory mode when calculating the motion track. It operates in the same manner as the Match-Move mode but does not apply the transforms to the connected input. (See the next section for more information.)

Match-Move serves as a transform tracker and is designed to match the movement detected through the motion tracking process.

Stabilize removes 2D camera movement by neutralizing the motion detected through the tracking process. Selected features are pinned to points within the frame without concern for where the edge of the frame may wind up.

Remove Jitter removes 2D camera movement but only concerns itself with high-contrast movement. The mode does not attempt to pin selected features to specific points within the frame. In the other words, Remove Jitter neutralizes small-frequency noise, such as camera shake, without disturbing large-frequency noise, such as a slow camera pan or slow handheld drift.

Add Jitter allows you to transfer the camera motion from a piece of footage to an otherwise static node.

Calculating the Motion Track

By default, the Transform menu of the Tracker node is set to None. It is therefore ready to calculate the motion track with one to four track anchors (tracking points). By default, one track anchor, Tracker 1, is activated. Each track anchor is represented in the viewer by a double-box icon and is named Track*n* (see Figure 7.26). The inner box establishes the pattern area, which the tracker attempts to follow across multiple frames. For successful tracking, the pattern should be an identifiable element, such as the iris of an eye, that is visible throughout the duration of the timeline. The outer box establishes the search area in which the tracker attempts to locate the pattern as it moves across multiple frames.

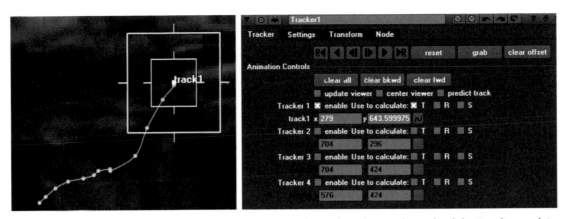

Figure 7.26 (Left) Tracker 1 anchor with a motion path (Right) The Tracker tab of the Tracker node's properties panel

To activate additional track anchors, select the Tracker 2, Tracker 3, and/or Tracker 4 Enable check boxes in the Tracker tab of the Tracker node's properties panel (see Figure 7.26). Each track anchor has the ability to track translation, rotation, and scale. You can activate this ability by selecting the T, R, or S check box beside each track anchor name in the Tracker tab. You can position a track anchor by LMB+dragging its center point in the viewer. You can adjust the size of the inner or outer box by LMB+dragging one of its boundaries (edges).

Once the anchors are positioned, you can calculate the motion tracks by using the track play buttons in the Tracker tab. The buttons offer a means to track forward, backward, one frame at a time, or through a defined frame range. You can apply the track play buttons multiple times and thus overwrite preexisting tracking data. Once tracking data exists, each anchor is given a motion path in the viewer (see Figure 7.26). Points along the paths represent the location of an anchor for any given frame. You can interactively move a point for the current frame by LMB+dragging the matching anchor.

Once motion tracks exist, you can utilize the tracking data. If you are transform tracking (which Nuke calls match-moving) or adding jitter, you can disconnect the Tracker node from the tracked source and reconnect it to the output of the node to which you want to apply the tracking data. You can also duplicate the Tracker node and connect the duplicated node to the output of the node to which you want to apply the tracking data. If you are stabilizing the footage or removing jitter, the Tracker node can stay in its current position within the node network. In any of these situations, the Transform menu must be set to the appropriate mode. The workflows for each of these scenarios are detailed in the following sections.

Match-Move and Add Jitter Workflow

To use the Tracker node in the Match-Move mode, you can follow these basic steps:

1. Select the node that you wish to track. For instance, select a Read node that carries video footage. RMB+click and choose Transform → Tracker.
2. In the Settings tab, set the Warp Type menu to an appropriate transformation set. If the footage you are tracking has a static camera or a camera that has no significant pan or tilt, set the menu to Translate. If the camera does go through a sizable pan or

tilt, set the menu to Translate/Rotate. If the camera zooms, set the menu to Translate/ Rotate/Scale. If the feature or pattern you plan to track goes through any type of rotation or moves closer to or farther from the camera, set the menu to Translate/Rotate/ Scale (even if the camera is static).

3. In the Tracker tab, select the Tracker 1 T, R, and S check boxes to match the Warp Type menu. For instance, if Warp Type is set to Translate/Rotate, then select the T and R check boxes (see Figure 7.26). It may be possible to undertake the tracking with one track anchor. However, this is dependent on the complexity of the footage. You can start with one track anchor and, if the tracking fails or is inaccurate, add additional track anchors by selecting their Enable check box and matching T, R, and/or S check boxes.

4. Position the anchor or anchors using the suggestions in the previous section. Calculate the tracks by using the track play controls in the Tracker tab, which include a means to play forward to the end, play backward to the beginning, or step one frame at a time in either direction. To refine the results, readjust the anchor positions and anchor regions and use the track play buttons multiple times.

5. Once you're satisfied with the tracking results and have motion paths that run the complete duration of the timeline, select the Tracker node and choose Edit → Duplicate. Connect the duplicated Tracker node to the output of the node to which you wish to apply the motion. For instance, connect the Tracker node to a Read node that carries a CG render of a prop or a static piece of digital art. Open the duplicated Tracker node's properties panel. Switch to the Transform tab and change the Transform menu to Match-Move. (If the menu is left set to None, the tracking data is not used.) For example, in Figure 7.27, a starburst graphic is transform-tracked to the shoulder of a model. Because the camera zooms in and is shaky, three track anchors are used. A duplicate of the Tracker node (Tracker2) feeds the tracking data to the Read2 node, which carries the graphic. To offset the graphic so that it rests on a desirable portion of the shoulder, a Transform node is added between the Read2 node and the Tracker2 node. The graphic and the original video footage are combined with a Merge node.

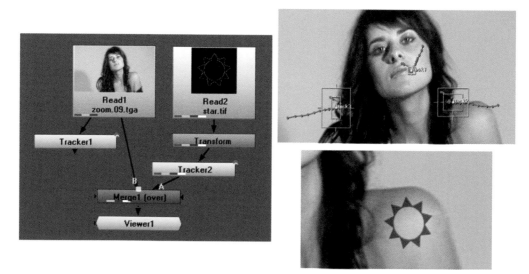

Figure 7.27 (Left) Transform tracking network. A starburst graphic is transform tracked to the shoulder of a model. (Top Right) The three track anchors used by the Tracker1 node. The Tracker2 node is a duplicate of the Tracker1 node and has its Transform menu set to Match-Move. (Bottom) A detail of the starburst merged with the footage after the tracking data is applied. A sample Nuke script is included as transform_track.nk *in the Tutorials folder on the DVD.*

It's not unusual for the Track To The First Frame or Track To The Last Frame buttons to suddenly stop midway through the footage. This is due to an anchor "losing sight" of a selected pattern. This may be caused by a sudden camera movement, heavy motion blur, or a significant change in perspective, deformation, or lighting. Heavy film or video grain can also interfere with the process. When this occurs, there are several approaches you can try:

- With the timeline on the frame where the tracker has stopped, reposition the anchor that has gone astray. Press the track play buttons again.

- Move ahead on the timeline by several frames. Position all the anchors so that they are centered over their selected patterns. Press the track play buttons again. If the tracking is successful, there will be gaps in the corresponding curves where no keyframes are placed. You can edit the gaps in the Curve Editor.

- If the problem area is only a few frames in duration, manually step through with the Track To The Previous Frame or Track To The Next Frame buttons. If an anchor slips away from its pattern, manually reposition it in the viewer.

- Adjust the errant anchor's search and pattern boxes. If the pattern box is too small, the anchor may suddenly lose the pattern. If the search box is too large, the anchor may be confused by similar patterns that lie nearby.

- Raise the Max_Error parameter value (found in the Settings tab of the Tracker node). This allows for a greater deviation in detection to exist. Although this may prevent the tracker from stopping, it may cause an anchor to jump to a neighboring pattern.

The Add Jitter mode uses the same workflow as the Match-Move mode. However, Match-Move is designed to add motion to an otherwise static element, which in turn is composited on top of the tracked footage. Add Jitter, in contrast, is suited for adding artificial camera movement to an otherwise static frame. For example, you can use a Tracker node to motion track the subtle camera shake of video footage, then use a duplicate of the Tracker node with the Transform menu set to Add Jitter to impart the same camera shake to a matte painting held by a Read node.

Stabilize and Remove Jitter Workflow

To use the Tracker node in the Stabilize mode, you can follow these basic steps:

1. Select the node that you wish to stabilize. RMB+click and choose Transform → Tracker. Open the Tracker node's properties panel. In the Settings tab, set the Warp Type menu to an appropriate transformation set. If the footage you are stabilizing has only a minor motion, such as a slight pan or down-to-up tilt, set the menu to Translate. If the camera has chaotic or aggressive motion, set the menu to Translate/ Rotate. If the camera tilts side to side (as with a "Dutch" angle), set the menu to Translate/Rotate. If the camera zooms, set the menu to Translate/Rotate/Scale.

2. In the Tracker tab, select the Tracker 1 T, R, and S check boxes to match the Warp Type menu. For instance, if Warp Type is set to Translate/Rotate, then select the T and R check boxes. It may be possible to undertake the tracking with one track anchor. However, this is dependent on the complexity of the footage. You can start with one track anchor and, if the tracking fails or is inaccurate, add additional track anchors by selecting their Enable check box and matching T, R, and/or S check boxes.

3. Position the anchor or anchors using the section "Tracking with the Tracker Node" as a guide. Calculate the tracks by using the track play buttons in the Tracker tab. To refine the results, readjust the anchor positions and anchor regions and use the track play buttons multiple times. For problem-solving suggestions, see the previous section.

4. Once you're satisfied with the tracking results and have motion paths that run the complete duration of the timeline, change the Transform menu to Stabilize. The footage is automatically repositioned so that the selected patterns are fixed to points within the

frame. For example, in Figure 7.28, an extremely shaky piece of footage is stabilized so that the model appears perfectly still.

The Remove Jitter mode uses the same workflow as the Stabilize mode. However, Remove Jitter makes no attempt to fix selected features to specific points within the frame. Instead, Remove Jitter neutralizes low-frequency noise without disturbing larger camera movements. To see the difference between the two modes, you can change the Transform menu from Remove Jitter to Stabilize or vice versa.

Applying Data to the CornerPin and Stabilize Nodes

Nuke provides two additional nodes for applying motion tracking data: CornerPin2D and Stabilize2D. Both nodes require that you transfer data from a Tracker node through the process of linking.

Figure 7.28 (Left) Tracker1 node used to stabilize footage held by Read1 node (Right) Four track anchors used by Tracker1 node. A sample Nuke script is included as `stabilize.nk` *in the Tutorials folder on the DVD.*

CornerPin2D (Transform → CornerPin) is designed for corner pin tracking, whereby four anchors are used to define the corners of a rectangular feature that moves through a scene. In turn, the track data is used to translate, rotate, scale, and skew the output of a target node so that it fits over the rectangular feature. For example, corner pin tracking is necessary when replacing a TV screen with a video news broadcast that was shot at a different location. A CornerPin2D node is connected to the output of the target node. The output of the CornerPin2D node is then merged with the node that is tracked. The tracking data is transferred from the Tracking node through linking. To create a link, you can follow these steps:

1. Move the mouse pointer over the Animation button beside the Track1 X and Y cells in the Tracker tab of the Tracker node. Ctrl+LMB+drag from the Track1 Animation button to the To1 Animation button in the CornerPin2D tab of the CornerPin2D node. As you Ctrl+LMB+drag, the mouse icon changes and a small + sign appears. Once the mouse pointer reaches the To1 Animation button, release the mouse button. A link is created, the To1 cells turn gray blue (see Figure 7.29), and a green connection is drawn between the two nodes in the Node Graph.

2. Repeat the process of linking Track2 and To2, Track3 and To3, and Track4 and To4.

For additional details on the process, see the section "Nuke Tutorial 7: Corner Pin Tracking with a Non-Square Object" later in this chapter.

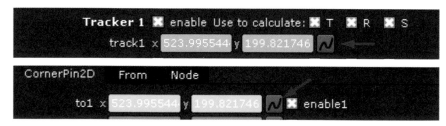

Figure 7.29 (Top) Track1 X and Y cells (Bottom) To1 X and Y cells after the link is established. Animation buttons are indicated by arrows.

Stablize2D (Transform → Stabilize) stabilizes an input through the use of two track points. The Track1 and Track2 parameters must be linked to the equivalent track points of a Tracker node. Since the result is likely to place the input outside the frame edge, Offset X and Y parameters are provided.

Editing Track Curves in the Curve Editor

Once motion tracks are calculated, they are stored within the Tracker node. You can edit a motion track as a set of curves by clicking the Animation button beside the track name (such as Track1) in the Tracker tab and choosing Curve Editor from the menu. If the T, R, and S check boxes were selected before the calculation, the Curve Editor will display Track*n* X, Track*n* Y, Center*n* X, Center*n* Y, Translate X, Translate Y, Rotate, and Scale W curves (see Figure 7.30). If the Transform menu of the Tracker node is set to Stabilize, Match-Move, Remove Jitter, or Add Jitter, updates to the curves will instantly alter the appearance of the tracked footage or element in the viewer.

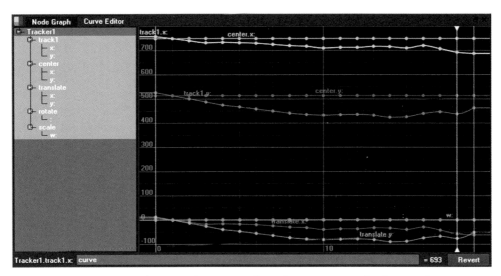

Figure 7.30 Motion track curves for one track anchor, as seen in the Curve Editor

The type of tracking you are attempting determines which curves should be edited. Here are a few guidelines:

- If you are transform tracking, edit the Center X and Center Y curves to offset the tracked element. Offsetting may be necessary when the track anchors are not positioned at the location where you wish to place the tracked element. Adjusting the Center X and Y curves may prevent the need for an additional Transform node, as is the case in the example given for Figure 7.27 earlier in this chapter.
- If you are stabilizing a plate and there are minor flaws in the stabilization, it's best to refine the track anchor motion paths in the viewer interactively, but only after the Tracker node's Transform menu is temporarily set to None. Although you can alter the Track*n* X and Track*n* Y curves in the curve editor, it's difficult to anticipate the altered curves' impact on the stabilization.
- If you are corner pin tracking, whereby the Tracker node is linked to a CornerPin node, edit the Track*n* X and Track*n* Y curves. There will be four sets of Track*n* curves to edit (one for each anchor). Adjusting these curves allows you to fine-tune the perspective shift of the tracked rectangular element.

AE and Nuke Tutorials

Masking is a necessary step for most compositing jobs. Even if rotoscoping is not required, a garbage matte is often needed to remove unwanted elements from footage. As such, you'll have a chance to clean up the greenscreen removal started in the Chapter 3 tutorial. In addition, you'll have the opportunity to corner pin motion track video footage.

AE Tutorial 3 Revisited: Finalizing the Composite

In the Chapter 3 tutorial, you removed the greenscreen from a piece of video footage. However, additional masks must be drawn to remove the unwanted walls and to restore the missing arms of the chair.

1. Reopen the completed After Effects project file for "AE Tutorial 3: Removing Greenscreen." A finished version of Tutorial 3 is saved as ae3.aep in the Chapter 3 Tutorials folder on the DVD. Scrub through the animation. At this stage, the walls remain on the left and right side. In addition, the chair arms are transparent due to the reflection of the greenscreen. Finally, the edges are not as clean as they could be.

2. Open Comp 2 so that it's visible in the Timeline panel. Select the lower phonecall.### .tga layer (numbered 3 in the layer outline). Using the Pen tool, draw a mask around the model's hair (see Figure 7.31). Expand the Mask 1 section of the layer in the layer outline and toggle on the Stopwatch button beside the Mask Shape property. Move through the timeline and adjust the shape of the path so that the hair remains within the mask but the cell phone and the model's hand are never included. This step limits the effect of the luma matte and removes a dark line at the edge of the chair and the model's arm.

3. Select the upper phonecall.###.tga layer (numbered 2 in the layer outline). Using the Pen tool, draw a U-shaped mask around the walls (see Figure 7.31). Expand the Mask 1 section and select the Inverted check box beside the Mask 1 property. The walls are removed.

4. Import room.tif from the Footage folder on the DVD. LMB+drag room.tif from the Project panel to the layer outline of the Comp 2 tab in the Timeline panel so that's the lowest layer. Toggle off the Video layer switch beside the red Solid layer to hide it. The model appears over the background photo.

Figure 7.31 *(Left) Mask applied to the lower* phonecall.###.tga *layer as seen at frame 64. (Right) Mask applied to upper* phonecall.###.tga *layer*

5. The holes left in the arms of the chair are the last problem to solve. The holes exist because the wood reflected the greenscreen so strongly that the wood detail was obliterated. In this situation, it's necessary to add a small matte painting. Import the touchup.tga file from the Footage folder on the DVD. LMB+drag touchup.tga from the Project panel to the layer outline of the Comp 2 tab in the Timeline panel so that it's the highest layer. Since touchup.tga is a full frame of the video, the chair arms must be isolated.

6. With the touchup.tga layer selected, use the Pen tool to draw several paths around the two chair arms (see Figure 7.32). Since the model moves through the footage, you will need to animate the paths changing shape over time.

7. Using the Render Queue, render a test movie. If necessary, adjust the mask shapes and various filters to improve the composite. Once you're satisfied with the result, the tutorial is complete (see Figure 7.33). A finished revision is saved as ae3_final.aep in the Tutorials folder on the DVD.

Figure 7.32 *(Top) Detail of matte painting used to restore the chair arms (Bottom) Two mask paths drawn on the* touchup.tga *layer isolate the painted arms.*

Figure 7.33 (Top) Original greenscreen plate (Bottom) Final composite

Tips & Tricks: Adding a Shadow

To create a more believable integration with Tutorial 3, consider creating a soft, artificial shadow of the model and the chair against the lower-left part of the background. For approaches to creating a shadow using available footage, see "AE Tutorial 5 Revisited: Creating a Shadow and a Camera Move" in Chapter 6.

Nuke Tutorial 3 Revisited: Finalizing the Composite

In the Chapter 4 follow-up tutorial, you improved the greenscreen removal around the model's hair by creating a luma mask. However, additional masks must be drawn to remove the unwanted walls and to restore the missing arms of the chair.

1. Reopen the completed Nuke project file for "Nuke Tutorial 3 Revisited: Creating a Luma Matte." A matching version of Tutorial 3 is saved as nuke3_step2.nk in the Chapter 4 Tutorials folder on the DVD. Scrub through the animation. At this stage, the walls remain on the left and right side. In addition, the chair is missing parts of its arms due to the reflection of the greenscreen. Finally, the matte edges are not as clean as they could be.

2. With no nodes selected, RMB+click and choose Draw → Bezier. Rename the Bezier1 node HairMask through the node's Name cell. Connect the output of HairMask to the Mask input of the Merge1 node. Move the timeline to frame 1. With the HairMask node's properties panel open, Ctrl+Alt+click in the viewer to draw a path around the model's hair (see Figure 7.34). Animate the path over time by advancing to additional frames and moving the path vertices. The goal is to remove everything beyond the edge of the model's hair. Note that her hand is intentionally left out of the mask area.

3. With no nodes selected, RMB+click and choose Draw → Bezier. Rename the new Bezier node BodyMask through the node's Name cell. Connect the output of BodyMask to the Mask input of the Merge2 node. Use Figure 7.35 as reference for the node network. The BodyMask node allows you to remove the unwanted walls with a second garbage matte. With the BodyMask node's properties panel open, Ctrl+Alt+click to draw a path around the walls in a U shape (see Figure 7.34). Select the Invert check box. The walls are removed.

Figure 7.34 *(Left) Mask path drawn for the HairMask node, as seen for frame 64 (Right) Mask path drawn for BodyMask node*

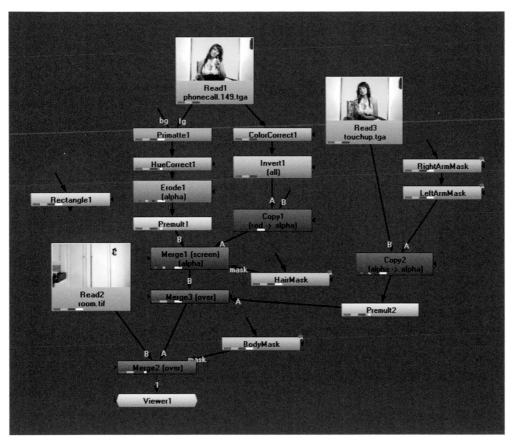

Figure 7.35 *The final node network*

4. Disconnect the Rectangle1 node. With no nodes selected, RMB+click and choose Image → Read. Open the Read2 node's properties panel and browse for the `room.tif` file in the Footage folder on the DVD. Connect input B of the Merge2 node to the output of the Read2 node. A photo of a room is placed behind the model. Since the room is white, a dark halo close to the model's hair is revealed (see Figure 7.36). This is generated by the luma matte created by the ColorCorrect1, Invert1, and Copy1 nodes. The luma matte is a soft matte that maintains the detail of the hair but leaves a noisy alpha channel. To remove this noise, open the ColorCorrect1 node's properties panel and change the Gamma slider to 0.8 and the Gain slider to 2.2 (see Figure 7.36).

5. The holes left in the arms of the chair are the last problem to solve. The holes exist because the wood reflected the greenscreen so strongly that the wood detail was obliterated. In this situation, it's necessary to add a small matte painting. With no nodes selected,

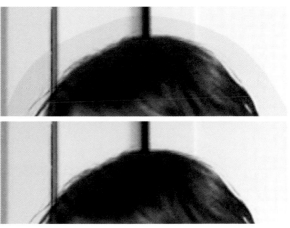

Figure 7.36 *(Top) Dark halo around the model's hair created by a soft matte (Right) Result of fine-tuning applied to the ColorCorrect1 node*

RMB+click and choose Image → Read. Open the Read3 node's properties panel and browse for the touchup.tga file in the Footage folder on the DVD. Connect a viewer to the Read3 node. The image is taken from the first frame of the sequence. However, the arms of the chair have been restored through Photoshop painting (see Figure 7.37). Since touchup.tga is a full frame of the video, the chair arms must be isolated.

Figure 7.37 *(Top) Detail of matte painting used to restore the chair arms (Bottom) Result of masks used to isolate arms from background*

6. With no nodes selected, RMB+click and choose Draw → Bezier. Rename the new Bezier node RightArmMask through the node's Name cell. With no nodes selected, RMB+click and choose Draw → Bezier. Rename the new Bezier node LeftArmMask through the node's Name cell. Connect the output of RightArmMask to the input of LeftArmMask. With no nodes selected, RMB+click and choose Channel → Copy. Connect the output of LeftArmMask to input A of the Copy2 node. Connect the output of the Read3 node to input B of the Copy2 node. With the Copy2 node selected, RMB+click and choose Merge → Premult. Connect a viewer to the Premult2 node. This series of connections allows you to draw a mask for the right arm, draw a mask for the left arm, merge them together, and use the resulting matte to separate the arms from the matte painting image. To draw the first mask, open the RightArmMask node's properties panel and Ctrl+Alt+click to draw a path around the right chair arm. Since the model moves through the shot and covers this arm, the path must be animated over time. To draw the second mask, open the LeftArmMask node's properties panel and Ctrl+Alt+click to draw a path around the left chair arm. The last few frames of this path will require animation as the model swings out her hand. Once both masks are drawn, the result is an isolated pair of chair arms (see Figure 7.37).

7. With no nodes selected, RMB+click and choose Merge → Merge. LMB+drag the Merge3 node and drop it on top of the connection line between Merge1 and Merge2. This inserts the Merge3 node after Merge1 and before Merge2. Connect input A of Merge3 to the output of Premult2. This places the isolated arms over the remainder of the composite, thus filling in the holes.

8. Test the composite by selecting the Merge2 node and choosing Render → Flipbook Selected. If necessary, make adjustments to the mask, color correction, or greenscreen removal nodes. Once you're satisfied with the result, the tutorial is complete (see Figure 7.38). A finished revision is saved as nuke3_final.nk in the Tutorials folder on the DVD.

Figure 7.38 *(Top) Original greenscreen plate (Bottom) Final composite*

Tips & Tricks: Improving the Composite

There are several areas of the revisited Tutorial 3 composite that you can improve. For example, to tie the model to the background in a more convincing manner, create a soft, artificial shadow of the model and the chair against the lower-left part of the background. For approaches to creating a shadow using available footage, see the section "Nuke Tutorial 5 Revisited: Creating a Shadow and a Camera Move" in Chapter 6. In addition, you can selectively apply a Lightwrap node to create the illusion that ambient light is wrapping around the chair and the model's hair and arms. For more information on the Lightwrap node, see Chapter 10, "Warps, Optical Artifacts, Paint, and Text." Last, additional rotoscoping of the model's left arm would help remove the subtle vertical stairstepping left as an artifact of the video interlacing.

AE Tutorial 7: Corner Pin Tracking with a Non-Square Object

Corner pin tracking is easiest to apply when a rectangular object exists within a piece of footage. However, you can apply the technique to odd shaped objects.

1. Create a new project. Choose Composition → New Composition. In the Composition Settings dialog box, set Preset to HDV/HDTV 720, Duration to 30, and Frame Rate to 30. Import the hydrant##.tga footage from the Chapter 4 Footage folder on the DVD. Import sign.tif from the Chapter 7 Footage folder.

2. LMB+drag the hydrant.##.tga footage from the Project panel to the layer outline of the Timeline panel. LMB+drag sign.tif from the Project panel to the layer outline so that it sits above the hydrant.##.tga layer. The goal of this tutorial is to track the sign to the side of the fire hydrant so it looks like it was in the scene from the start.

3. Select the hydrant##.tga layer and choose Animation → Track Motion. The Tracker Controls panel opens at the lower-right side of the program. Change the Track Type menu to Perspective Corner Pin. Four track points appear in the viewer of the Layer panel.

4. Although corner pin tracking usually entails the positioning of four track points over the corners of a square or rectangular object, such as a TV screen, billboard, window, and so on, it's possible to apply corner pin tracking to whatever has four distinct features arranged in a rectangle manner. For instance, the fire hydrant has a series of bolts on the base and top lip that you can use for this purpose. As such, move Track Point 3 over the left base bolt (see Figure 7.39). Move Track Point 4 over the right base bolt. Move Track Point 2 over the top-right lip bolt. Move Track Point 1 over the top-left lip bolt. Scale each of the track point icons so they fit loosely over their respective bolts. If the icons fit too tightly, the tracker may lose sight of the bolts.

Figure 7.39 (Left) The four track points of the Perspective Corner Pin tracker placed over the fire hydrant footage, as seen at frame 1 (Right) Resulting motion path for Track Point 1 and 4, as seen at frame 30

5. Press the Analyze Forward button in the Tracker Controls panel. The tracker moves through the footage one frame at a time. If it's successful, a motion path is laid for each track point (see Figure 7.39). If the tracker fails, adjust the track point positions and region sizes using the trouble-shooting suggestions in the section "Motion Tracking Problem Solving" earlier in this chapter.

6. Once you're satisfied that the tracking and motion paths exist for the entire duration of the timeline, click the Apply button in the Tracker Controls panel. The animation curves are automatically transferred to the sign.tif layer. (Since the sign.tif layer sits above the hydrant.##.tga layer, it's automatically assigned as the target layer.) Note that the view automatically changes to the viewer of the Composition panel when the Apply button is pressed. Henceforth, the sign appears properly scaled and skewed over the side of the hydrant (see Figure 7.40). Play back the timeline.

7. At this stage, the sign is stretched over the top lip of the hydrant. To avoid this, you can offset the top tracking points. In the layer outline, expand the new Corner Pin section of the sign.tif layer. Toggle on the Include This Property In The Graph Editor Set button for the Upper Left and Upper Right properties. Toggle on the Graph Editor composition switch. Convert the Graph Editor to the value graph view by changing the Choose Graph Type And Options menu to Edit Value Graph. Click the Fit All Graphs To View button to

Figure 7.40 *With the tracking data applied, the sign is scaled and skewed to fit the side of the hydrant.*

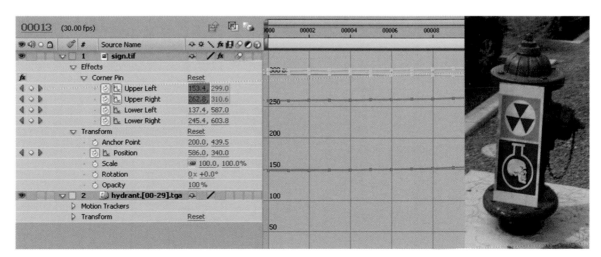

Figure 7.41 *(Left) The layer outline and Graph Editor with Upper Left and Upper Right curves of the sign layer revealed. The Y curves are colored green. (Right) The resulting sign with a lowered top edge*

frame all the curves. (The button features two lines surrounded by brackets.) The Upper Left Y and Upper Right Y curves are colored green. Draw a selection marquee around all the keyframes for the two Y curves. (Although the X curve keyframes become highlighted, they are not affected.) LMB+click one of the selected Y curve keyframes and drag the curves straight up. The top of the sign will move in the viewer of the Composition panel as you do this. Release the mouse button once the top of the sign is just below the top of the hydrant lip (see Figure 7.41).

8. Toggle off the Graph Editor composition switch to return to the timeline view. Play back the footage. The sign remains sharper than the background footage. To add motion blur, toggle on the `sign.tif` layer's Motion Blur layer switch. To see the blur in the viewer, toggle on the Motion Blur composition switch. The blur will also appear when the composition is rendered through the Render Queue.

The tutorial is complete. A sample After Effects project is included as `ae7.aep` in the Tutorials folder on the DVD.

Nuke Tutorial 7: Corner Pin Tracking with a Non-Square Object

Corner pin tracking is easiest to apply when a rectangular object exists within a piece of footage. However, you can apply the technique or odd shaped objects.

1. Create a new script. Choose Edit → Project Settings. Change Frame Range to 1, 30 and Fps to 30. With the Full Size Format menu, choose New. In the New Format dialog box, change Full Size W to 1280 and Full Size H to 720. Enter a name, such as **HDTV**, into the Name field and click the OK button.

2. In the Node Graph, RMB+click and choose Image → Read. Open the Read1 node's properties panel and browse for `hyrdant.##.tga` in the Chapter 4 Footage folder. With no nodes selected, choose Image → Read. Open the Read2 node's properties panel and browse for `sign.tif` in the Chapter 7 Footage folder. The goal of this tutorial will be to track the sign to the side of the fire hydrant so it looks like it was in the scene from the start.

3. With the Read1 node selected, RMB+click and choose Transform → Tracker. Open the Tracker1 node's properties panel. While the Tracker tab is open, select the Enable check box beside Tracker 2, Tracker 3, and Tracker 4. Select the T, R, and S check boxes for all four trackers. Switch to the Settings tab and change the Warp Type menu to Translate/Rotate/Scale.

4. Change the timeline to frame 1. Switch back to the Transform tab. (If the Transform tab is not visible, the track anchor icons are hidden in the viewer.) Although corner pin tracking usually entails the positioning of four anchors over the corners of a square or rectangular object, such as a TV screen, billboard, window, and so on, it's possible to apply corner pin tracking to whatever has four distinct patterns arranged in a rectangular manner. For instance, the fire hydrant has a series of bolts on the base and top lip that you can use for this purpose. As such, place the Track1 anchor over the left base bolt (see Figure 7.42). Place the Track2 anchor over the right base bolt. Place the Track3 anchor over top-right lip bolt. Place the Track4 anchor over the top-left lip bolt. Scale each of the anchors so they fit loosely over their respective patterns. If the anchor regions are too tight, the tracker may lose track of the pattern.

5. Click the Track To The Last Frame button. The program steps through the footage one frame at a time. If the program stops short of frame 30, the tracker has lost one of the patterns. To avoid this, follow the problem-solving suggestions set forth in the section "Match-Move and Add Jitter Workflow" earlier in this chapter.

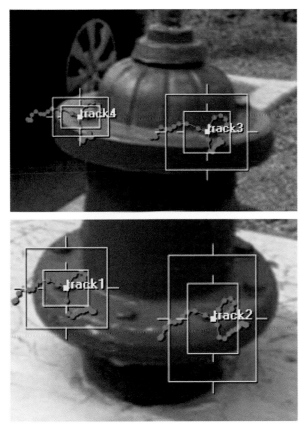

Figure 7.42 *Four track anchors of the Tracker1 node*
positioned over the fire hydrant footage

6. Once you're satisfied with the motion track calculation, choose the Read2 node, RMB+ click, and choose Transform → CornerPin. With no nodes selected, RMB+click and choose Merge → Merge. Connect Read1 to input B of Merge1. Connect CornerPin2D1 to input A of Merge1. Connect a viewer to Merge1. The sign graphic appears at the left of the frame. To apply the motion tracking information to the sign, you must link the Tracker1 node to the CornerPin2D1 node.

7. Open the properties panels for the new CornerPin2D1 node and the Tracker1 node. The CornerPin2D1 node is designed to take tracking data from another node and cannot create tracking data on its own. Thus, you must create links to retrieve information from the Tracker1 node. To do so, Ctrl+LMB+drag the mouse from the Animation button beside Track1 in the Tracker tab of the Tracker1 node to the Animation button beside the To1 cells in the CornerPin2D tab of the CornerPin2D1 node. This creates a link between the two Animation buttons. (For more information on linking, see Chapter 12, "Advanced Techniques.") The link is indicated by the To1 cells turning a gray blue and a green arrow line appearing between the Tracker1 node and the CornerPin2D1 node (see Figure 7.43). In addition, a small green dot appears at the lower-right side of the CornerPin2D1 node with a small letter *E*, indicating that a link expression exists. Repeat the process of linking Track2 and To2, Track3 and To3, and Track4 and To4. As you create the links, the sign image is stretched and distorted until each of its corners touch corresponding track anchors. Note that the Transform menu of the Tracker1 node remains set to None.

8. Play back the timeline using the viewer controls. Since the sign corners meet the anchors, the top of the sign is stretched over the lip of the hydrant. You can off-set the effect of this stretching by switching to the From tab of the CornerPin2D1 node and entering new values into the From1, From2, From3, and/or From4 X and Y cells (see Figure 7.44). For example, to lower the top of the sign, change From3 Y and From4 Y to 950. You can also adjust the horizontal stretch of the sign by changing From2 X to 415 and From3 X to 390. This makes the sign more rectangular and less trapezoidal.

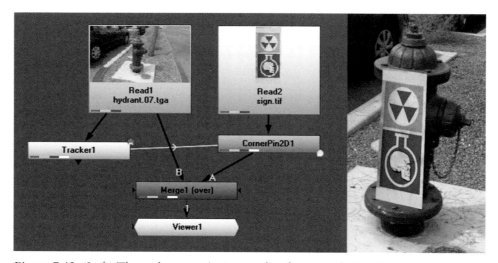

Figure 7.43 *(Left) The node network. A green line between the Tracker1 node and the CornerPin2D1 node indicates a link. (Right) With the tracking data applied, the sign is scaled and skewed to fit the side of the hydrant.*

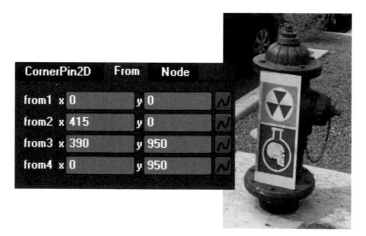

Figure 7.44 *(Left) The From tab in the properties panel of the CornerPin2D1 node (Right) The result of the offset*

9. At this stage, the sign is much sharper than the background. You can activate motion blur for the CornerPin2D1 node by setting the Motion Blur slider, found in the CornerPin2D tab, to 1.0. Motion blur has a tendency to exaggerate minor imperfections in the tracking, however, especially when the motion is relatively subtle. For a less drastic result, change the Filter menu to Notch, which is an inherently soft interpolation method.

10. If imperfections remain in the tracking, you can continue to adjust anchor positions and use the track play buttons of the Tracker1 node to update the tracking information. Because the CornerPin2D1 node is linked, it will automatically update. You can also edit the tracking curves generated by the Tracker1 node. To do so, click the Track1 Animation button in the Tracker tab and choose Curve Editor. Keep in mind that the CornerPin2D1 node is using the Track1, Track2, Track3, and Track4 X and Y curves to determine the positions of the sign corners. It is *not* using Translate X, Translate Y, Rotate, or Scale W curves.

The tutorial is complete. A sample Nuke script is saved as nuke7.nk in the Tutorials folder on the DVD.

Interview: Entae Kim, Freestyle Collective, New York City

Born in Seoul, South Korea, Entae Kim attended Binghamton State University of New York. He switched majors from biology to graphic design and transferred to the Parsons School of Design. After graduation, he worked at several design firms as a web designer. He returned to the School of Visual Arts in New York to study 3D animation. In 2005, he began freelancing as a 3D generalist. Shortly thereafter, Entae joined the Freestyle Collective as head of the CG FX department. Since then, he's worked on numerous television commercials and network packages for clients such as the Cartoon Network, HBO, Nickelodeon, and Comedy Central.

Freestyle Collective is a collaborative design and production studio. Freestyle's services include creative advertising for commercial, broadcast, and corporate clients. Recent projects include identification spots for TCM, VH1, and MTV. The studio also sets aside resources for experimental animation, logo design, and print work.

Entae Kim at his workstation (Photo courtesy of Freestyle Collective)

(Left) The Freestyle Collective office in the heart of Manhattan (Right) Freestyle Collective artists hard at work (Photos courtesy of Freestyle Collective)

(Freestyle Collective keeps five After Effects compositors on staff. The studio's sister company, New Shoes, runs additional Flame bays.)

LL: At what resolutions do you usually composite?

EK: We do a great deal of HD - 1080 (1920×1080). I'll say that 8 out of 10 [projects] are HD.

LL: So SD projects are fairly rare?

EK: It's always a good idea to work with HD since you can always down-convert [to SD].

LL: How have hi-def formats affected the compositing process?

EK: It's definitely been slow on the machine side—reading all these high-resolution files through a server. Also, adding effects and detail [means that] you have to double-check to make sure it works on the [HD] screen. When it was SD, you could get away with mistakes....

LL: Are there any special steps you take in preparation for color grading?

EK: Everyone here uses the same monitor—the same brand. They're calibrated once every week. You can actually correct them to look like NTSC color. Even with that, we bring the work into QC (quality control) monitors and check the vectorscope.

LL: What tools do you use to key blue- or greenscreen?

EK: After Effects has a great one—Keylight. But, almost always, you have to do some kind of roto. You always roto....

LL: Would you say the rotoscoping remains a common technique?

EK: All the postproduction houses have a team of rotoscopers.

LL: What tools do you use for tracking?

EK: Boujou. We sometimes use the After Effects tracking [tools].

LL: Do you use 2.5D or multiplane techniques?

EK: All the time. People want to get more dynamic camera motions. We actually have a matte painter, [so we] use 2.5D matte paintings with camera projections.

LL: Are there any limitations for using camera projections on cards or geometry?

EK: It only works for certain camera angles. It won't work [with] crazy moves through the scene, because the image is projected from the 3D camera onto the models you've set up.

LL: Do you prefer projecting on cards or geometry?

EK: It's better to use geometry, but it [doesn't have to] be super-detailed.

LL: Do you have 3D animators create the geometry?

EK: Yes, animators, modelers…. Normally, what we would do is set up the scene in 3D, render a couple of frames, give the [frames] to the matte painter—the matte painter will break down his layers in Photoshop, then give it to [the compositors], who project it from a 3D camera [in the composite]. It's 3D, then 2D, then it comes back into 3D.

LL: When you were in school, what style of compositing were you taught?

EK: Layers…. Now it's all 3D.

Additional Resources: The Full Interview

To read the full interview with Entae Kim, see the Interviews folder on the DVD. For an example composite created by Entae, see Chapter 1.

eight

DI, Color Grading,
Noise, and Grain

"If you're comparing 35mm to the state-of-the art digital video, digital video cameras can at least capture 4K. If you need a hi-res scan of 35mm, the film grain gets a little big."

—ANDY DAVIS, VFX supervisor, Method Studios, Santa Monica, California

The digital intermediate (DI) *represents one of the most significant changes to filmmaking to occur in recent years. Hence, it's important for compositors to understand the DI process, even if they are not directly involved with the editing, conforming, calibration, or color grading process. Nevertheless, color grading approaches used by DI colorists may be applied by compositors to projects that do not have the luxury of DI. Whereas DI is ultimately an optional step for a production, noise and grain are a permanent part of the production equation. That is, all film and video footage contains some form of noise or grain. Hence, the artifacts must be removed from footage or added to imported CG, digital artwork, or motion graphic elements so that the end composite is coherent and consistent. With the tutorials in this chapter, you'll have the chance to practice color grading techniques as well as disguise unwanted posterization with noise.*

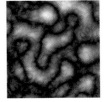

Digital Intermediates

A digital intermediate (DI) is digital copy of a captured image. The copy is created for the purpose of digital manipulation. Once the manipulation is complete, the manipulated copy is output to the original capture format. Hence, the copy serves as an "intermediate."

DI for Film

In the realm of motion pictures, DI has come to indicate a common practice whereby the following workflow is used:

1. Motion picture footage is digitized.
2. The footage is edited offline (see the next section).
3. An edit decision list (EDL) is created for the edit. The EDL is used to conform the footage for the color grading process.
4. LUTs are generated and applied for proper viewing.
5. Titles, motion graphics, and visual effects shots may be added, but only after the editor has determined their placement and length (in which case, the EDL and conform are brought up-to-date).
6. The resulting footage is color graded. Color grading is carried out by specialized artists known as *colorists*.
7. The color graded result is rendered at full resolution and *filmed out* (captured onto film through a film recorder).

Digitizing Film

Motion picture footage is digitized with dedicated pieces of hardware. Although the hardware varies by manufacturer, it shares basic similarities:

- The film is moved through the device, one frame at a time. Each frame is illuminated. The illumination is provided by a laser, LEDs, or more traditional metal halide bulbs. The light is separated into RGB components by a prism or dichroic (color-splitting) mirrors.
- The RGB light is captured by charge-coupled device (CCD) chips, complementary metal oxide semiconductor (CMOS) chips, or a set of photodiodes. The RGB information is encoded into the image format of choice.

Common film formats that are scanned include 16mm, Super 16mm (single-sprocket 16mm with expanded image area), full-aperture 35mm (35mm lacking an optical soundtrack but possessing an expanded image area), and VistaVision (a 35mm variant where the image is rotated 90° for better resolution). Common scanning resolutions include standard SD, standard HD (1920×1080), and 2K full aperture (2048×1556). The digitized frames are generally stored as 10-bit log Cineon or DPX files (see Chapter 2, "Choosing a Color Space"). Other format variations, such as 16-bit linear TIFF or 16-bit log DPX, are not unusual. Some scanner manufacturers provide software that can automatically detect dust, scratches, and similar defects and remove them from the scanned image.

Conforming the Footage

Conforming, as it applies to DI, is the organization and assembly of sequences and shots in preparation for color grading. The conforming process is driven by an EDL, which is updated as the editing of the footage progresses. The actual editing does not occur as part of the color grading session. Instead, editing is created *offline*. For offline editing, a low-resolution copy of the original footage is used. The lower resolution is necessary for speed and efficiency. Because the editing is applied to a copy, the original digitized footage remains unscathed. When the editing is complete, the EDL is exported as a specialized file that includes pertinent information for each cut shot (film reel, starting frame number, and so on).

Conforming may be carried out by specialized software, such as Autodesk Backdraft Conform. This assumes that the conformed footage is accessible by compatible color-grading software, such as Autodesk Lustre. It's also possible to conform and color grade with a single piece of software. For example, Assimilate Scratch and Da Vinci Resolve are designed to carry out both tasks. (While some DI systems are purely software based, others require matching hardware.)

Applying 3D LUTs

An equally important step in the DI process is the application of LUTs. As discussed in Chapter 2, color calibration is an important consideration to a compositor. A compositor should feel confident that their work will look the same on a workstation as it does in the final output, whether it is film or video. In addition to the careful selection of working color spaces, it's important to apply monitor calibration. When a monitor is calibrated, a LUT is stored by a color profile. The LUTs discussed thus far are one-dimensional arrays of values designed to remap one set of values to a second set. If a LUT is designed to remap a single color channel, it is considered a *1D LUT*. If a LUT is designed to remap three channels, such as RGB, then a 1D LUT is applied three times. Because monitor and projector calibration is critical for DI and color grading, however, 1D LUTs become insufficient. Thus, 3D LUTs are employed.

A *3D LUT* is a three-dimensional look-up table that defines input and output colors as triplets (three values corresponding to three channels, such as RGB). 3D LUTs can be represented by an XYZ color cube (see the top of Figure 8.1). Two of the corners of the cube correspond to black and white. Three of the corners correspond to primary red, green, and blue. Three of the corners correspond to secondary colors yellow, cyan, and magenta. Any given color has an X, Y, Z location within the cube. When two different color spaces are compared, they do not share the same space within the visible spectrum. Hence, the deformation supplied by a 3D LUT fits one color space within a second color space. As such, the alteration of a single color channel affects the remaining color channels. The influence of one color component on the remaining components is known as *color cross-talk*. Color cross-talk is a natural artifact of motion picture film, which relies on cyan, magenta, and yellow dyes; when film stock is developed, it's impossible to affect a single dye without affecting the other two. In comparison, a 1D LUT can only affect one channel at time (see the bottom of Figure 8.1). For example, remapping the red channel does not affect the green and blue channels. For efficiency, the 3D LUT deformation is carried out by a deformation lattice. The lattice has a specific resolution, such as 17×17×17. Color points that do not fall on a lattice point must be interpolated. Software that employs 3D LUTs may apply its own unique interpolation method.

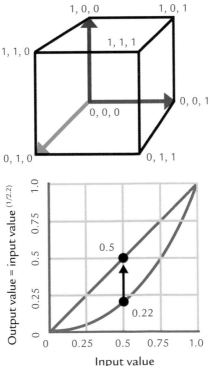

Figure 8.1 (Top) *XYZ color cube used by a 3D LUT* (Bottom) *Single channel remapped with a 1D LUT*

Based on their architecture, 3D LUTs offer the following advantages over 1D LUTs:

- The saturation of an input can be altered.
- Cross-talk is intrinsically present. Thus, the color space of motion picture film can be more accurately represented.
- Color space conversions between devices with different gamuts are easily supported.
- Soft clipping is feasible. Whereas a standard clip leaves a hard transition between non-clipped and clipped values, *soft clipping* inserts a more gradual transition. Soft clipping is useful when converting to or from a low-bit-depth color space.
- Posterization is less likely to occur with the color space conversion.

At the same time, 1D LUTs retain some advantages:

- They're easy to generate with a wide range of calibration software.
- Interpolation of color points is not required, so accuracy may be greater in some situations.

1D LUTs and 3D LUTs are both stored as text files that feature columns of numeric values. 1D and 3D LUTs can be carried by ICC profiles. Due to their complexity, 3D LUTs are usually generated by specialized software. For example, Arricube Creator, part of Arri's family of DI tools, is able to create 3D LUTs and package them as color profiles for a wide range of devices. In addition, Nuke can generate 3D LUTs internally, as is discussed in the section "3D LUTs in Nuke" later in this chapter.

Bringing Effects Work into DI

If a project is slated for DI, a decision must be made whether or not an effects shot (using titles, motion graphics, or visual effects) should be pre-graded (color graded in advance). For example, if an animation/compositing team is given a live-action plate to which effects must be added, three approaches are possible:

- The animation/compositing team matches the effects work to the ungraded plate.
- The plate is pre-graded at the visual effects studio and is handed off to the animation/compositing team.
- The sequence that will host the effects shot is color-graded by a colorist at an outside color grading facility. The plate to be used for the effects shot is color-graded to match the sequence and then is delivered to the visual effects studio.

With pre-grading, the plate may be neutralized, whereby the median pixel value is established as 0.5, 0.5, 0.5. Neutralization prevents bias toward red, green, or blue, which creates a *color cast*. In addition, neutralization allows the colorist to provide the animation/compositing team with color grading values so that they can roughly preview the final color look on their own workstations. Alternately, the colorist may apply a quick color grade to the plate to match the final look of the surrounding scene. Pre-grading is particularly useful on effects-heavy feature film work, where hundreds of effects shots would otherwise slow the final color grading process. However, pre-grading may lead to an accentuation of undesirable artifacts as the plate is repeatedly color graded. In comparison, if the effects work is matched to the ungraded plate, the color may be significantly different from what the director, art director, or visual effects supervisor may have imagined. In such a case, the effects approval process may prove difficult. In addition, matching CG to an ungraded plate may be more challenging if the footage is underexposed, has a heavy color cast, or is otherwise washed out.

Once an effects shot is completed, it is imported into the DI system and conformed to the EDL (the editor receives a copy so that it can be included in the offline edit). A final color grading is applied to match the surrounding scene. If the effects shot utilized a pre-graded plate, the final grading is less intensive.

DI Color Grading

Color grading generally occurs in several steps, brief descriptions of which follow:

Primary Grading Each shot is graded to remove strong color cast or to adjust the exposure to match surrounding shots. The grading is applied to the entire frame.

Secondary Grading Grading is applied to specific areas of a shot. For example, the contrast within unimportant areas of the composition may be reduced, thus shifting the focus to the main characters. Specific pools of light may be given a different color cast for aesthetic balance. Areas with an unintended mistake, such as an unwanted shadow, may be darkened so that the mistake is less noticeable.

Specific areas within a shot are isolated by creating a mask, through the process of keying, or via the importation of a matte rendered in another program, such as After Effects. Masking may take the form of primitive mask shapes or spline-based masking tools. Keyers are able to key out specific colors or luminance levels and thus produce hicon (high-contrast) or luma mattes. Built-in rotoscoping and tracking tools are also available (although they are generally less refined to those found in compositing packages). Masked areas within a frame on a color grading system are commonly known as *power windows*.

The actual grading is carried out by a set of standard tools, which provide a means to adjust brightness, contrast, gamma, gain, pedestal (lift), hue, saturation, and exposure per channel. Each of these functions in a manner similar to the various sliders supplied by the effects and nodes found in After Effects and Nuke. (For more information on color manipulation, see Chapter 4, "Channel Manipulation.") In addition, tools are used to affect the color balance and tint. Color balance adjusts the strength and proportion of individual color channels. Tint increases or decreases the strength of a particular color.

If a project is destined for multiple media outlets, multiple color grading sessions may be applied. For example, separate color grades may be created for a traditional theatrical release and an HDTV broadcast.

Ultimately, the goal of color grading can be summarized as follows:

- To make the color balance of all shots within a scene or sequence consistent and cohesive
- To correct or accentuate colors recorded by cinematographers, who may have a limited amount of time on set to fulfill their vision
- To produce color schemes that match the intention of the director, production designer, and art director
- To have the color-graded result appear consistent in a variety of outlets, including movie theater screens and home living rooms

Industry Perspective: Color Pipelines

Just as there is no industry standard for color calibration, there is no universally accepted color pipeline. A *color pipeline* is a methodology and a matching physical infrastructure that is capable of ensuring that all the artists, management, and clients involved with a film or video project see the same output. A functional color pipeline is difficult to achieve when the display devices vary greatly and are employed in large numbers. For example, a studio may equip 60 animators with standard 8-bit LCDs, 30 lighters and compositors with 30-bit (10 bits per channel) LED LCDs, and an editorial staff with 8-bit CRT video broadcast monitors. In addition, dailies may be reviewed with a 15-bit DLP digital cinema projector, an Inferno bay with 8-bit HD CRTs, or a 35mm projector. Even worse, clients may be located in a different city, state, or country, requiring that some shots be reviewed through the Web. To complicate matters further, a project may require a stereoscopic workflow, which necessitates stereo rendering and special viewing equipment (such as polarized-lens projectors).

The emergence of DI, however, is creating a greater impetus for reliable color pipelines. In fact, makers of DI software have begun to address this by creating toolsets that construct portions of the pipeline outside the immediate task of conforming and color grading. For example, Cine-tal cineSpace, a family of DI tools, supplies equalEyes, which matches monitors on a facility-wide basis.

DI for Video and Animation

DI is not limited to motion picture film. Digital video or computer animation footage is equally suitable for the DI process and can benefit from DI color grading tools. The main advantage of video and animation in this situation is that scanning is not necessary. Thus, the basic workflow follows:

1. Video or animation is transferred to the DI system.
2. The footage is conformed to an EDL.
3. LUTs are generated and applied for proper viewing.
4. In the case of video, titles, motion graphics, and/or visual effects shots are integrated. In the case of animation, titles and/or motion graphics are integrated. In both situations, the editor determines the placement and duration and updates the EDL.
5. The resulting footage is color graded.
6. The color-graded result is recorded to video or film.

Although tape-based video must be captured, tapeless systems that utilize hard disks or flash memory are becoming common. In fact, various DI software systems, including Autodesk Lustre and Digital Vision, have recently added direct support for propriety Raw formats generated by digital video camera systems such as RED One and Arri.

Television commercials, music videos, and other short-form video projects have enjoyed the benefits of the DI process for over two decades. For example, Autodesk Flame (developed by Discreet Logic) has been in use since the mid-1990s and has provided efficient digital footage manipulation throughout its history. Going back further in time, the Quantel Harry allowed the manipulation of stored digital video as early as 1985.

Telecine machines, which are able to convert motion picture film to video in real time, have been in use since the early 1950s. Real-time color-grading capacity was added to the telecine process in the early 1980s. In contrast, high-quality motion picture film scanners were not available until Kodak introduced the Cineon DI system in 1993. Film scanners share much of their technology, including dichroic mirrors and color-sensitive CCDs, with telecine machines. In fact, there is such a high degree of overlap between the two systems that the word *telecine* is used as a generic term for all film transfers.

Fully animated CG features have also tapped into the power of the DI process. For example, with *The Incredibles* (2004) and *Surf's Up* (2007), no shot was filmed out until the entire project was sent through the DI process. DI offers the ability to fine-tune colors across sequences in a short amount of time. Without DI, matching the color quality of every shot in a sequence tends to be time-consuming because multiple artists may work on individual shots for weeks or months.

Industry Perspective: The Future of Film

For the last decade, industry professionals have contemplated the disappearance of motion picture film. The rapid developments in digital cinematography, the DI process, and digital theatrical projection have certainly diminished the role of film in filmmaking. For a compositor, however, this shift in technology does not affect the ultimate goal of compositing, which is to create work that is believable and aesthetically pleasing.

Color Grading without DI

As a compositor, you may not be directly involved with the DI process. In fact, you may work on a project that does not employ DI or color-grading sessions by a dedicated colorist. As such, you may find it necessary to apply your own color adjustments. In this situation, the techniques developed by colorists are equally applicable.

Color Grading in AE

As discussed in the section "DI Color Grading" earlier in this chapter, color grading generally occurs in two steps: primary and secondary. Primary grading applies adjustments to the entire frame of a shot. Secondary grading applies adjustments to limited areas within the frame. To isolate areas with After Effects, you can use the Pen tool to draw masks or create hicon or luma mattes through the combination of various effects. For more information on masking, see Chapter 7, "Masking, Rotoscoping, and Motion Tracking." For an example of luma matte creation, see Chapter 3, "Interpreting Alpha and Creating Mattes."

For grading adjustments, standard color correction effects supply sliders for the most common grading tasks. A list of tasks and corresponding effects follows:

Brightness: Brightness & Contrast, Curves, Levels

Gamma: Gamma/Pedestal/Gain, Levels, Exposure

Contrast: Brightness & Contrast, Curves, Levels

Gain: Gamma/Pedestal/Gain

Pedestal: Gamma/Pedestal/Gain, Exposure (Offset property)

Hue: Hue/Saturation

Saturation: Hue/Saturation

Exposure: Exposure

Color Balance: Color Balance, Curves, Levels (Individual Controls)

Tint: Hue/Saturation, Tint

For details on each of the listed effects, see Chapter 4, "Channel Manipulation." The section "AE Tutorial 8: Color Grading Poorly Exposed Footage" at the end of this chapter steps through the grading process.

Tips & Tricks: Color Finesse

Recent versions of After Effects include a demo of the Color Finesse 2 effect by Synthetic Aperture. The effect includes its own interface with a full set of color grading tools. The tools include standard sliders that affect the layer's hue, saturation, brightness, contrast, gain, gamma, and pedestal. By default, the sliders operate on all channels equally. However, additional slider sets are available for individual channels and color spaces. For example, you can work in HSL, RGB, CMY (CMYK without the K), and Y'CbCr. In addition, the effect includes several waveform monitor and vectorscope readouts. A *waveform monitor* is an oscilloscope that is used to measure voltage of a video signal and, in turn, the brightness of a video image. A *vectorscope* is another specialized oscilloscope that measures the hue and saturation components of a video signal. Although electronic oscilloscopes were originally designed for analog video and television broadcast, the software facsimiles are equally useful for determining the color quality of a digital image. For more information on Color Finesse 2, visit www.synthetic-ap.com.

Color Grading in Nuke

As discussed in the section "DI Color Grading" earlier in this chapter, color grading generally occurs in two steps: primary and secondary. Primary grading applies adjustments to the entire frame of a shot. Secondary grading applies adjustments to limited areas within the frame. To isolate areas with Nuke, you can use the Bezier node to draw masks or create hicon or luma mattes through the combination of various nodes. For more information on masking, see Chapter 7, "Masking, Rotoscoping, and Motion Tracking." For an example of luma matte creation, see Chapter 4, "Channel Manipulation." As for grading adjustments, standard Color nodes supply sliders for the most common grading tasks. A list of tasks and corresponding effects follows:

Brightness: HSVTool, HueShift, Grade

Gamma: ColorCorrect, Grade

Contrast: ColorCorrect

Gain: ColorCorrect, Grade

Lift (Pedestal): ColorCorrect, Grade

Hue: HSVTool, HueCorrect, HueShift

Saturation: HSVTool, HueCorrect, ColorCorrect, Saturation

Color Balance: HueCorrect

Although the word *Brightness* can only be found in the HSVTool's or HueShift's properties panel, the adjustment of Gain, Offset, or Whitepoint sliders of other nodes will have a similar effect. As for color balance, you are not limited to the HueCorrect node. Any node can affect a single channel and thereby change the balance of all three color channels. For example, if you deselect the Red and Green check boxes of a Grade node, the Grade node affects only the Blue channel. If the Grade node is then adjusted, the overall color balance changes.

As for tinting an image, there is no direct correlation to the After Effects Tint effect or Colorize option of the Hue/Saturation effect. However, to create a similar look, you can merge the output of a Constant node (Image → Constant) with a Read node. If the Merge node's Operation menu is set to Multiply, the tinting is thorough (see Figure 8.2).

It's also possible to tint an image by assigning the Whitepoint or Blackpoint parameters a non-monochromatic value. For a demonstration of this technique, see the section "Nuke Tutorial 8: Color Grading Poorly Exposed Footage" at the end of this chapter. For details on each of the nodes listed in this section, see Chapter 4, "Channel Manipulation."

3D LUTs in Nuke

As discussed in Chapter 2, Nuke provides a set of 1D LUTs (which may be viewed through the Project Settings properties panel). The LUTs are designed to convert the color space of a file to Nuke's internal color space. The goal is to display the file image correctly on the system monitor via Nuke's viewer. In addition to 1D LUTs, Nuke supports the importation and creation of 3D LUTs. You can find the nodes in the Color and Color → 3D LUT menus.

Reading 3D LUTs

The TrueLight node loads 3D LUTs created by FilmLight TrueLight. TrueLight is a color management system comprising hardware and software modules. The TrueLight node is designed to display film-based images on a linear RGB monitor properly.

The Vectorfield node loads a custom 3D LUT. The 3D LUT can take the form of a TrueLight LUT (.cub or .cube), Assimilate Scratch and Autodesk Lustre LUTs (.3dl), or native Nuke vector field (.vf) text file.

Figure 8.2 (Top) Input image (Center) Node network with a red-colored Constant node (Bottom) Tinted result. A sample Nuke script is included as tint.nk *in the Tutorials folder on the DVD.*

Tips & Tricks: Expanded LUT Support

Nuke v5.2 expands its LUT integration by supporting additional 1D and 3D LUT formats. 1D LUTs are used to interpret imported files and to preview outputs through the viewer. Newly supported 1D LUTs include those designed for the logarithmic encoding of specific HD video cameras. Newly-supported 3D LUTs, which are read and written by GenerateLUT and Vectorfield nodes, include cineSpace (.csp) and Houdini binary (.blut).

Generating 3D LUTs

When CMSTestPattern and GenerateLUT are used together, they create a custom 3D LUT. CMSTestPattern is a special test pattern that features colored stripes of known values. The output of the CMSTestPattern node must be connected to some type of color correction node (or nodes). In turn, the output of the color correction node is connected to a GenerateLUT node (see Figure 8.3) Whatever adjustments are made to the color correction node are stored as a 3D LUT when the Generate And Write LUT File button is pressed in the GenerateLUT node's properties panel. You can chose to save the 3D LUT as a TrueLight LUT (.cub or .cube), Assimilate Scratch or Autodesk Lustre LUTs (.3dl), native Nuke vector field (.vf), or color management system format (.cms). The 3D LUT may then be used by another program or by Nuke's Vectorfield node. The size of the 3D LUT is set by the CMSTestPattern node's RGB 3D LUT Cube Size cell. Although the cell defaults to 32, a common size used for 3D LUTs is 17. (17 implies that the color cube is 17×17×17.)

If you rename a Vectorfield node VIEWER_INPUT, the listed 3D LUT will be applied to the viewer when the Input Process (IP) button is toggled on. The IP button rests to the right of the Display_LUT menu at the top right of the Viewer pane (see Figure 8.4).

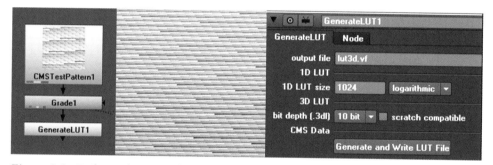

Figure 8.3 *(Left) Node network designed to create a custom 3D LUT. In this case, the color correction is supplied by a Grade node. (Center) Test pattern created by the CMSTestPattern node (Right) The GenerateLUT properties panel*

Figure 8.4 *(Top Left) IP button to the right of the Display_LUT menu in the Viewer pane (Bottom Left) Vectorfield node renamed as VIEWER_INPUT (Right) Vectorfield properties panel*

Tips & Tricks: Viewer Process Support

Nuke v5.2 supplements the v5.1 Display_LUT menu with a Viewer Process support that allows you to define a custom list of gizmos (groups of Nuke nodes). The gizmos can operate as a LUT or apply any combination of filter nodes to the viewer output. For more information, see the Nuke 5.2v1 release notes at www.thefoundry.co.uk. For more information on gizmos, see Chapter 12, "Advanced Techniques."

Viewing Log Files with the IP Button

By creating a custom 3D LUT, loading it into a Vectorfield node, and activating it with the IP button, you can quickly view log images as if they have been converted to a linear color space. To do so, follow these steps:

1. Choose Color → 3D LUT → CMSTestPattern and Color → Colorspace. Connect the output of the CMSTestPattern node to the input of the Colorspace node (see Figure 8.5). In the Colorspace node's properties panel, set the In menu to Cineon. Set the Out menu to sRGB.

2. Choose Color → 3D LUT → GenerateLUT. Connect the output of the Colorspace node to a GenerateLUT node. In the GenerateLUT node's properties panel, enter an output file name and click the Generate And Write LUT File button.

3. Choose Color → 3D LUT → Vectorfield. Rename the Vectorfield node **VIEWER_INPUT**. In the Vectorfield's node's properties panel, load the recently written 3D LUT file. A sample LUT file is included as 3dlut.vf in the Footage folder on the DVD.

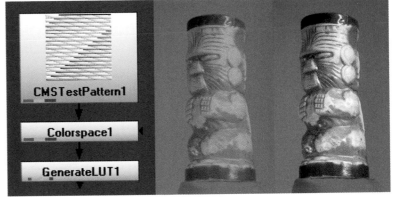

Figure 8.5 (Left) The final node network (Center) Input Cineon file appearing washed out in viewer (Right) Same Cineon after IP button is selected and VIEWER_INPUT Vectorfield node is activated. A sample Nuke script is included as generatelut.nk in the Tutorials folder on the DVD.

4. Using a Read node, import a Cineon or DPX file. Open the Read node's properties panel. Select the Raw Data check box. This prevents the Read node from applying a log-to-linear conversion. Change the Display_LUT menu (in the Viewer pane) to Linear. The file appears washed out in the viewer. Toggle on the IP button (so that the letters turn red). The viewer temporarily shows a log-to-linear color space conversion without affecting the imported log file or altering the node network.

Note that the Display_LUT menu applies a 1D LUT *after* the application of the 3D LUT that is activated by the IP button. To see an accurate color space conversion, set Display_LUT to Linear, which essentially disables the 1D LUT application. (For more information about project 1D LUTs, see Chapter 2, "Choosing a Color Space.")

Noise and Grain

Noise, in the realm of image processing, is a random fluctuation in image brightness. With a CCD or CMOS chip, noise takes the form of *shot noise*, which is visible as 1-pixel deviations in the image (see Figure 8.6). Shot noise is a result of statistical variations in the measurement of photons striking the sensor. In common terms, this arises from an irregular number of photons striking the sensor at any given moment. Shot noise is most visible when the exposure index (ISO speed) is high, which is often necessary when you're shooting in a low-light situation. This is due to a relatively small number of photons striking the sensor. With few photons, variations in the photon count are more noticeable. Hence, you may not see shot noise when you're photographing a brightly lit subject. Shot noise can also occur within an electronic circuit where there are statistical variations in the measurement of electron energy.

Figure 8.6 (Left) Night shot with low light level (Right) Detail of shot noise visible in the lower-right sky (Photo © 2009 by Jupiterimages)

When 1-pixel noise is intentionally applied to an image, it's known as *dither* and the application is referred to as *dithering*. Dithering is often necessary to disguise *quantization errors*, which are unwanted patterns created by the inaccurate conversion of analog signals to digital signals. For example, the conversion of analog video to digital images may create posterization due to mathematical rounding errors. Dithering is also useful for improving the quality of low-bit-depth display systems, although improvements in hardware have made this no longer necessary.

A third type of noise occurs as a result of image compression. For example, digital video must be compressed. Most compression schemes are *lossy*; that is, the compression operates on the assumption that data can be lost without sacrificing basic perceptual quality. Compression allows for significantly smaller files sizes. However, the compression leads to artifacts such as posterization and irregular pixelization. Although the artifacts may be very subtle, adjustments to the image contrast or gamma soon make them visible (see Figure 8.7). Similar pixelization may also result from the improper de-interlacing of video footage, where blockiness appears along high-contrast edges.

Figure 8.7 (Left) Detail of video greenscreen footage. White box indicates area of interest. (Center) Enlargement of greenscreen with an increase in contrast (Right) Same enlargement in grayscale

Grain, on the other hand, is a form of noise inherent in motion picture film and film-based photography. The grain occurs as a result of the irregular silver-halide crystals embedded in the film emulsion (see Figure 8.8).

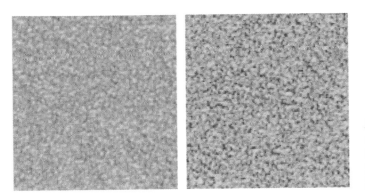

Figure 8.8 (Left) Enlargement of 35mm film grain (Right) Same grain desaturated. Note the similarity to Perlin noise in Figure 8.9

In contrast, CG and similar digital graphics do not carry electronic noise or grain (unless there is improper anti-aliasing). As such, it becomes necessary to add noise to the graphics or remove noise from live-action footage. If this step is not taken, the integration of the graphics with the live action will not be as successful. At the same time, noise and grain are useful when you want to make one format emulate another. For example, if you apply grain to video, you can emulate motion picture footage.

3D, digital imaging and compositing programs can generate noise. This is often a handy way to create an organic, seemingly random pattern. Once the noise is generated, it can be used as matte or other input to help create a specific compositing effect.

When a compositor generates noise, it is usually based upon a Perlin noise function. Perlin noise was developed in the mid-1980s by Ken Perlin as a way to generate random patterns from random numbers. Perlin noise offers the advantage of scalability; the noise can be course, highly detailed, or contain multiple layers of coarseness and detail mixed together (see Figure 8.9).

Perlin noise is a form of fractal noise. A *fractal* is a geometric shape that exhibits *self-similarity*, where each part of the shape is a reduced-sized copy of the entire shape. Fractal patterns occur naturally and can be seen within fern fronds, snowflakes, mountain ranges, and various other plant, crystal, and geographic occurrences.

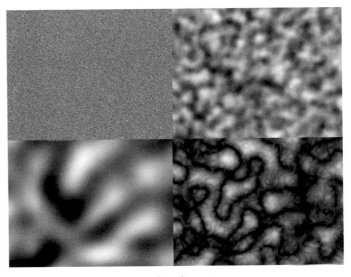

Figure 8.9 Four variations of Perlin noise

Working with Noise and Grain

After Effects and Nuke provide several effects and nodes with which to create or remove noise and grain.

Noise and Grain in AE

After Effects noise and grain effects are found under the Noise & Grain menu. Five of the most useful ones are detailed in the following three sections.

Fractal Noise, Noise, and Add Grain

The Fractal Noise effect creates a Perlin-style noise pattern. You can choose one of 17 variations of the noise by changing the Fractal Type menu. By default, the layer to which the effect is applied is completely obscured. However, you can override this by switching the Blending Mode menu to one of the many After Effects blending techniques. By default, Fractal Noise is not animated, but you can keyframe any of its properties. For example, the Evolution control sets the point in space from which a noise "slice" is taken. If Evolution changes over time, it appears as if the camera moves through a solid noise pattern along the z-axis. The Complexity slider, on the other hand, determines the detail within the pattern. Low values create a simple, blurry noise pattern. High values add different frequencies of noise together, producing complex results.

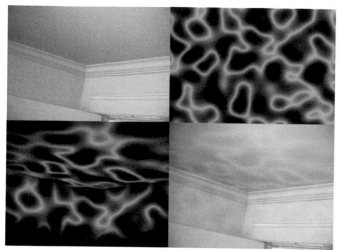

The Fractal Noise effect provides a means to generate a soft, irregular, organic pattern. For example, you can adjust the Fractal Noise effect so that it mimics the specular caustic effect created when bright light hits the top of a body of water (see Figure 8.10). The result is then positioned, masked, and blended with a background plate.

Figure 8.10 (Top Left) Background plate (Top Right) Animated pattern generated with Fractal Noise (Bottom Left) Two iterations of the pattern positioned in 3D space and masked (Bottom Right) Iterations combined with the plate with the Screen blending mode. A sample project is saved as `fractal_spec.ae` *in the Tutorials folder on the DVD.*

In contrast, the Noise effect creates randomly colored, 1-pixel noise and adds the noise to the original layer (see Figure 8.11). By default, the Clip Result Values check box guarantees that no pixel value exceeds a normalized 0 to 1.0 range. The noise pattern automatically shifts for each frame; the animation is similar to television static.

Figure 8.11 (Left) Noise effect with Amount Of Noise set to 20% (Right) Add Grain effect with Intensity set to 3. A lower setting will make the noise much more subtle.

The Add Grain effect differentiates itself from the Noise effect by creating an irregular noise pattern (see Figure 8.11). That is, the noise is not fixed to a 1-pixel size. Additionally, the effect provides property sliders to control the intensity, size, softness, and various color traits, such as saturation. The grain pattern automatically shifts for each frame, but the rate of change can be adjusted through the Animation Speed slider. A value of 0 removes the animation. Due to its irregularity, Add Grain is superior to Noise when replicating the grain pattern found in motion picture footage and the compression artifacts found within digital video. You can emulate specific motion picture films stocks, in fact, by changing the Preset menu, which lists 13 stock types. However, when replicating the shot noise found in digital video, Noise proves superior. For more information on compression grain and shot noise, see the section "Noise and Grain" earlier in this chapter.

Removing Grain

Although its task is fairly mundane, the Remove Grain filter employs sophisticated signal processing techniques. Since its operation is unusual, you can use the following steps as a guide:

1. Apply the Remove Grain effect to a layer containing grain. The effect will remove a portion of the grain immediately. Note that the result appears only in the white preview window in the viewer. You can interactively LMB+drag the preview window box to a new position within the viewer. To see the result of the effect over the entire layer, change the Viewing Mode menu to Final Output. To change the size of the preview window, adjust the Width and Height slider in the Preview Region section.

2. To reduce the aggressiveness of the removal process and any excessive blurring, lower the Noise Reduction value (in the Noise Reduction Settings section). To increase the accuracy of the suppression, raise the value of the Passes slider. If there is no change in the resulting image, return the Passes slider to a low value. High values are better suited for large, irregular grain.

Figure 8.12 *(Left) Remove Grain settings (Right) White preview window within the viewer. A sample project is saved as* `remove_grain.ae` *in the Footage folder on the DVD.*

3. To refine the result further, adjust the sliders within the Fine Tuning section. For example, if the grain is heavily saturated, raise the Chroma Suppression slider. The Texture slider, on the other hand, allows low-contrast noise to survive. To reintroduce a subtle noise to an otherwise noise-free image, increase the Texture value. Noise Size Bias targets grains based on their size. Negative values aggressively remove fine grains, while positive values aggressively remove large grains. The Clean Solid Areas slider serves as a contrast threshold; the higher the Clean Solid Areas value, the greater the number of median-value pixels averaged together (high-contrast edges are not affected).

4. To help identify the best property settings, you can change Viewing Mode to Noise Samples. A number of small windows are drawn in the viewer and indicate the sample areas. The program chooses sample areas that contain a minimal amount of value variation between the pixels. Such areas are used as a base reading for the noise-suppression function. In addition, you can change Viewing Mode to Blending Matte. The viewer displays a matte generated by the edge detection of high-contrast areas. The matte is used to blend the unaffected layer with the degrained version. The blending occurs, however, only if the Amount slider (in the Blend With Original section) is above 0.

5. If the grain is present across multiple frames, select the Enable check box in the Temporal Filtering section. Test the effect by playing back the timeline. If unwanted streaking occurs for moving objects, reduce the Motion Sensitivity value.

6. If the grain removal is too aggressive, high-contrast edges may become excessively soft. To remedy this, raise the Amount slider, in the Unsharp Mask section, above 0. This adds greater contrast to edges, creating a sharpening effect.

Matching Grain

The Match Grain effect is able to identify the grain within a source layer and apply it to a target layer that carries the effect. You can use the following steps to apply Match Grain:

1. Create a new composition. LMB+drag the source footage (the footage that contains the grain) into the layer outline of the Timeline panel. LMB+drag the target footage (the footage that will receive the grain) into the layer outline so that it sits on top.

2. Select the target footage layer and choose Effect → Noise & Grain → Match Grain. A white selection box appears in the viewer (see Figure 8.13). The box indicates the area from which the grain is sampled. The sample is used to construct a new grain pattern that is applied to the entire target image. In the Effect Controls panel, change the Noise Source Layer menu to the source footage layer name. Grain appears within the selection box.

3. To sample the grain from a different area of the source image, LMB+drag the center handle of the selection box to a different portion of the frame. To see the result on the entire frame, change the Viewing Mode menu to Final Output.

To adjust the size, intensity, softness, and other basic traits of the grain, change the properties within the Tweaking and Color sections. To change the style of blending, adjust the properties within the Application section. If the source layer is in motion and the grain pattern changes over time, the target layer will gain animated grain.

Tips & Tricks: Dust & Scratches

The Dust & Scratches effect, which removes small, high-contrast details such as dust particles, operates as a median filter. The Radius and Threshold sliders operate in a fashion similar to the Smart Blur effect, which was detailed in Chapter 6, "Convolution Filters."

Figure 8.13 *(Top Left) Match Grain properties (Top Center) The selection box, as seen in the viewer (Top Right) Source layer. Note that the video shot noise and compression artifacts, which will serve as a grain source, are not immediately visible. (Bottom Left) Grain-free target layer (Bottom Right) Result of Match Grain effect. A sample project is included as* match_grain.ae *in the Footage folder on the DVD.*

Noise and Grain in Nuke

Nuke includes several nodes that are able to replicate fractal nose, shot noise, and film grain. In addition, the program offers two nodes with which to remove film grain. The nodes are found in the Draw and Filter menus.

The Noise Node

The Noise node creates two styles of Perlin noise: Fractional Brownian Motion (FBM) and Turbulence. You can switch between the two styles by changing the Type menu. FBM noise takes advantage of mathematical models used to describe Brownian Motion, which is the seemingly random motion of particles within a fluid dynamic system. By default, FBM noise is soft and cloudlike. In contrast, Turbulence noise produces hard-edged, spherical blobs. Regardless, both noise styles rely on the same set of parameters. The X/Y Size slider sets the frequency, or scale, of the noise pattern. Larger values "zoom" into the noise pattern detail. The Z slider allows you to choose different "slices" of the pattern. That is, if you slowly change the Z value, the virtual camera will move through the pattern as if it was traveling along the z-axis. If you want the noise to change its pattern over time, you must animate the Z parameter. The Octaves cell sets the number of Perlin noise function iterations. In essence, Octaves controls the number of noise patterns that are at different scales and are layered together. For example, if Octaves is set to 2, two noise patterns, each at a different scale, are combined through the equivalent of a Max merge. The Lunacarity slider determines the difference in scale for each noise pattern layered together. (*Lunacarity*, as a term, refers to the size and distribution of holes or gaps within a fractal.) The higher the Lunacarity value, the greater the difference in scale between each layered pattern. Hence, larger Lunacarity values produce a greater degree of fine detail.

Perlin-style noise is useful for creating soft, organic, animated mattes. For example, in Figure 8.14, the fluctuating illumination on a wall is created by combining a properly exposed and an underexposed version of the same wall plate. The combination of the two versions is controlled by a Noise node, which is connected to the Mask input of a Merge node. Since the Noise creates a soft, blobby pattern in grayscale, the end effect is similar to the flickering light of a flame.

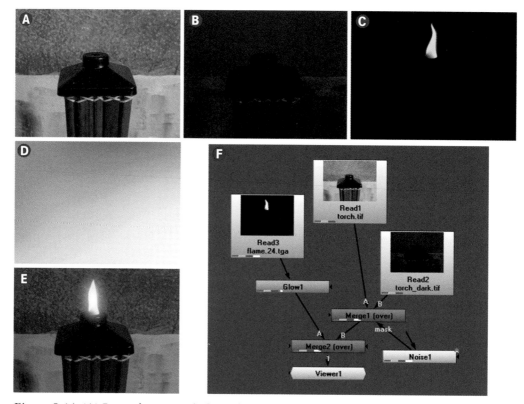

Figure 8.14 (A) Properly-exposed plate of a torch and wall (B) Underexposed version of plate (C) Flame element (D) Soft fractal pattern created by Noise node (E) Final composite (F) Node network. To see the flickering effect of the Noise node, open and play back the noise_flicker.nk script from the Tutorials folder on the DVD.

Adding Dither and Grain

The Dither node creates a 1-pixel random pattern and is suitable for emulating shot noise. To function, it requires an input connection. The Amount slider controls the degree to which the noise pattern is mixed with the input. By default, the noise is colored. You can create a monochromatic variation by selecting the Monodither check box. The noise pattern automatically changes over time and is similar to TV static.

The Grain node reproduces grain found in specific film stocks. You can select a stock by changing the Presets menu to one of six Kodak types (see Figure 8.15). You can create a custom grain by changing any of the parameter sliders. You can set the grain size and irregularity for red, green, and blue grains. To reduce the grain's strength, lower the Red, Green, and Blue Intensity sliders. To increase the contrast within the grain pattern, increase the Black slider value. Note that the Grain node is designed for 2K motion picture scans; thus, default settings may create overly large grain sizes on smaller resolution inputs.

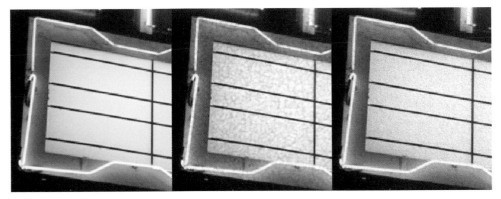

Figure 8.15 Detail of image with no grain (Center) Result of Grain node with Kodak 5248 preset (Right) Result of Grain node with Kodak 5217 preset. A sample script is included as grain.nk *in the Footage folder on the DVD.*

Using Scanned Grain

The ScannedGrain node (in the Draw menu) allows you to replicate the noise found within an actual piece of footage. To prepare a suitable piece of footage, follow these steps:

1. Shoot a gray card (see Figure 8.16). Scan or transfer the footage. Only 2 or 3 seconds are necessary.
2. Import the footage into Nuke through a Read node. Connect the output of the Read node to a Blur node. Raise the Blur node's Size parameter value until the noise is no longer visible. Create a Merge node. Connect the output of the Read node to input A of the Merge node. Connect the output of the Blur node to input B of the Merge node. Set the Merge node's Operation parameter to Minus. This network subtracts the gray of the gray card, leaving only the grain over black (see Figure 8.16).
3. Connect the output of the Merge node to the input of an Add node (Color → Math → Add). Change the Add node's Value cell to 0.5. When you add 0.5, the

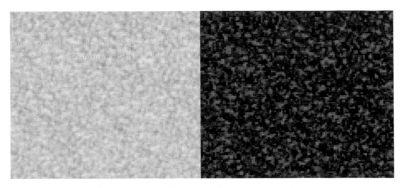

Figure 8.16 (Left) Extreme close-up of grain appearing against a gray card (Right) Grain isolated in Nuke

grain becomes brighter and the black gaps turn gray. This offset is required by the ScannedGrain node.

4. Write the result to disk with a Write node.

To apply the ScannedGrain node, follow these steps:

1. Import grain-free footage through a Read node. Connect the output of the Read node to the input of a ScannedGrain node. Connect the viewer to the output of the ScannedGrain node.

2. Open the ScannedGrain node's properties panel. Browse for the grain footage through the Grain cell (see Figure 8.17). The grain is added to the grain-free footage. Initially, the grain is very subtle. To increase its intensity, you can adjust the Amount parameter. The Amount parameter is split into red, green, and blue channels. In addition, you can interactively adjust the intensity of each Amount channel through the built-in curve editor. If the output becomes too bright, adjust the Offset slider.

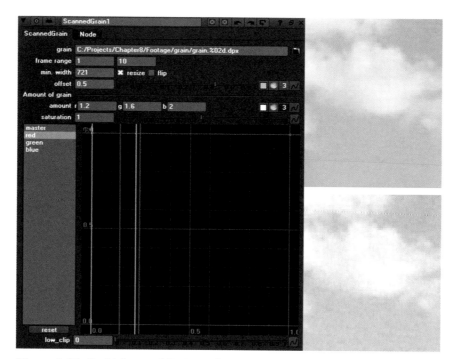

Figure 8.17 *(Left) ScannedGrain node's properties panel (Top Right) Detail of grain-free footage (Bottom Right) Same footage after the application of the ScannedGrain node. (The contrast has been exaggerated for print.) A sample script is included as* scannedgrain.nk *in the Footage folder on the DVD.*

Degraining

In Nuke, there are two specialized nodes that can remove grain: DegrainSimple and DegrainBlue. Both are found under the Filter menu.

The DegrainSimple node is suitable for removing or reducing light grain (see Figure 8.18). The aggressiveness of the grain removal is controlled by Red Blur, Green Blur, and Blue Blur sliders.

The DegrainBlue node targets noise within the blue channel without affecting the red or green channel. In general, the blue channel of scanned motion picture film and digital video is the grainiest. A single slider, Size, controls the aggressiveness of the removal.

Keep in mind that aggressive grain removal may destroy desirable detail within the frame. While the removal is most successful on areas with consistent color, like skies or painted walls, it is the most damaging in areas when there are numerous objects or intricate textures. Therefore, it often pays to control the effect of degraining by limiting it to a masked area. In addition, Nuke's degraining nodes are unable to address irregular artifacts created by compression.

Figure 8.18 (Left) Detail of a grainy image (Right) Result after the application of a DegrainSimple node. Note the preservation of high-contrast edges. A sample script is included as `degriansimple.nk` in the Footage folder on the DVD.

AE and Nuke Tutorials

With these tutorials, you'll have the opportunity to color grade an otherwise unusable plate. In addition, you'll disguise posterization with blur and noise.

AE Tutorial 8: Color Grading Poorly Exposed Footage

Although footage delivered to a compositor usually carries proper exposure, occasions may arise when the footage is poorly shot, is faded, or is otherwise damaged. Hence, it's useful to know how to color grade in less than ideal situations.

1. Create a new project. Choose Composition → New Composition. In the Composition Settings dialog box, change the Preset menu to NTSC D1 Square Pixel, Duration to 30, and Frame Rate to 30. Import the `road.##.tga` footage from the Footage folder on the DVD. LMB+drag the `road.##.tga` footage from the Project panel into the layer outline of the Timeline panel. Scrub the timeline. The footage features a highway as shot through the windshield of a car (see Figure 8.19). The footage is extremely washed out. In addition, the colors have shifted toward red (not unusual for old motion picture film). Choose File → Project Settings. In the Project Settings dialog box, set Depth to 16 Bits Per Channel. A 16-bit space will allow for color manipulation and is necessary for such poorly balanced footage. (Generally, you should pick a specific color space through the Working Space menu to match your intended output; however, for this exercise, Working Space may be set to None.)

2. With the `road.##.tga` layer selected, choose Effect → Color Correction → Brightness & Contrast. Set Brightness to 25 and Contrast to 80. This restores contrast to the footage (see Figure 8.20). However, the sky becomes overexposed when the road and countryside is properly adjusted. In addition, the heavy red cast becomes more apparent.

Figure 8.19 The imported footage

Figure 8.20 *Result of the Brightness & Contrast effect*

3. LMB+drag a new copy of the road.##.tga footage from the Project panel to the layer outline so that it sits on top. With the new layer selected, use the Pen tool to separate the sky (see Figure 8.21). Expand the new layer's Mask 1 section in the layer outline and set Mask Feather to 100, 100. With the new layer selected, choose Effect → Color Correction → Brightness & Contrast. Set Brightness to 10 and Contrast to 40. By separating the sky, you are able to color grade it without unduly affecting the road or countryside. Since the camera is moving, animate the mask to match the horizon line throughout the duration. (For more information on the Pen tool and masking, see Chapter 7, "Masking, Rotoscoping, and Motion Tracking.")

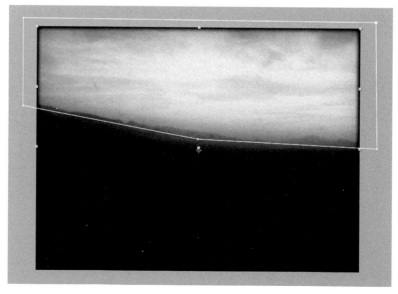

Figure 8.21 *A mask separates the sky.*

4. At this point, the footage remains extremely red. To adjust the color balance of both layers, however, you will need to nest the composites. Choose Composition → New Composition. Set Comp 2 to match Comp 1. Open the Comp 2 tab in the Timeline panel. From the Project panel, LMB+drag Comp 1 into the layer outline of the Comp 2 tab. With the new Comp 1 layer selected in Comp 2, choose Effect → Color Correction → Color Balance. Adjust the Color Balance effect's sliders to remove the red and bring the colors back to a normal range. For example, the following settings produce the result illustrated by Figure 8.22:

Shadow Red Balance: –20

Shadow Green Balance: 10

Midtone Red Balance: –30

Midtone Green Balance: –10

Hilight Red Balance: –10

Hilight Green Balance: 15

Hilight Blue Balance: 20

Figure 8.22 The final composite

5. At this stage, the footage appears fairly desaturated. To add saturation, choose Effect → Color Correction → Hue/Saturation and set the Master Saturation slider to 20. The tutorial is complete. A sample After Effects project is included as ae8.aep in the Tutorials folder on the DVD.

Nuke Tutorial 8: Color Grading Poorly Exposed Footage

Although footage delivered to a compositor usually carries proper exposure, occasions may arise when the footage is poorly shot, is faded, or is otherwise damaged. Hence, it's useful to know how to color grade in less than ideal situations.

1. Create a new script. Choose Edit → Project Settings. In the properties panel, set Frame Range to 1, 30 and Fps to 30. Change the Full Size Format menu to New. In the New Format dialog box, set File Size W to 720 and File Size H to 540. Enter **D1** as the Name and click OK. In the Node Graph, RMB+click and choose Image → Read. Through the Read1 node's properties panel, browse for the road.##.tga footage from the Footage folder on the DVD. Connect a viewer to the Read1 node. Scrub the timeline. The footage features a highway as shot through the windshield of a car (see Figure 8.23). The footage is extremely washed out. In addition, the colors have shifted toward red (not unusual for old motion picture film).

Figure 8.23 The imported footage

2. Since the footage has no alpha channel, select the Read1 node, RMB+click, and choose Channel → Shuffle. In the Shuffle1 node's properties panel, select the white 1 check box that corresponds with the alpha channel (see Figure 8.24). An alpha channel will be necessary for proper masking.

3. With the Shuffle1 node selected, RMB+click and choose Color → Grade. Connect a viewer to the Grade1 node. In the Grade1 node's properties panel, change the Blackpoint slider to 0.08 and the Whitepoint slider to 0.3. This restores the contrast to the footage. However, the sky becomes overexposed (see Figure 8.25). In addition, the heavy red cast becomes more apparent.

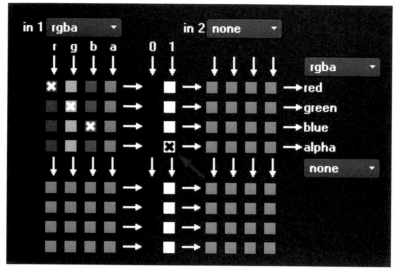

Figure 8.24 *The Shuffle1 node's properties panel. The red arrow points to the selected alpha check box.*

Figure 8.25 *Result of Grade node*

4. With no nodes selected, RMB+click and choose Merge → Merge. Connect input A of the Merge1 node to the output of the Shuffle1 node. See Figure 8.26 as a reference.

With no nodes selected, RMB+click and choose Draw → Bezier. Connect the Mask input of Merge1 to the output of the Bezier1 node. Connect a viewer to the Merge1 node. With the Bezier1 node's properties panel open, Crtl+Alt+click to draw a mask around the sky in the viewer (see Figure 8.26). Change the Extra Blur slider to 25 and the Falloff slider to 0. Animate the mask to match the moving camera. (See Chapter 7 for more information on masking.) By separating the sky, you are free to grade it without affecting the road or countryside. With the Merge1 node selected, RMB+click and choose Color → Grade. In the Grade2 properties panel, click the 4 button beside the Blackpoint parameter. The slider is replaced by four cells. Click the Color Sliders button beside the cells. In the Color Sliders dialog box, choose a brownish color. Note how the sky shifts its color as you interactively change the color sliders or color wheel. By assigning a non-monochromatic Blackpoint value, you are able to tint the sky. In this case, the sky becomes blue when the Blackpoint RGB values are 0.2, 0.1, 0. (The mask should sit at edge of the mountain range; if the mask is too low, the Grade2 node will darken the mountain peaks.) To brighten the sky, set the Grade2 node's Multiply parameter to 1.8.

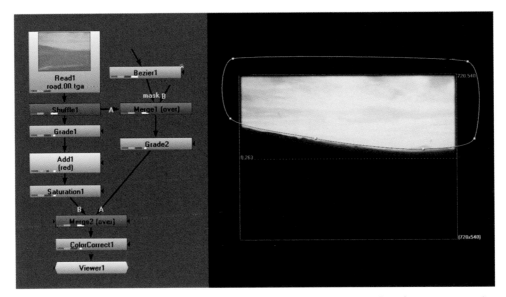

Figure 8.26 (Left) The final node network (Right) The sky separated with a Bezier mask and tinted with the Grade2 node

5. With no nodes selected, RMB+click and choose Merge → Merge. Connect input B of the Merge2 node to the output of the Grade1 node. Connect input A of Merge2 to the output of Grade2. This places the separated sky on top of the remainder of the image. At this stage, the road and countryside remain extremely red. Select the Grade1 node, RMB+click, and choose Color → Math → Add. In the Add1 properties panel, change the Channels menu to Rgb. Deselect the Green and Blue check boxes so that the node impacts only the red channel. Enter −0.1 into the Value cell; −0.1 is thus subtracted from every pixel and the color balance is improved. However, the road and countryside become desaturated. With the Add1 node selected, RMB+click and choose Color → Saturation. In the Saturation1 node's properties panel, change the Saturation slider to 2.

6. As a final adjustment, select the Merge2 node, RMB+click, and choose Color → Color Correction. In the ColorCorrection1 node's properties panel, set Saturation to 0.9, Contrast to 1.2, and Gain to 1.1. This adjusts the brightness and contrast of the composited footage. The tutorial is complete (see Figure 8.27). A sample Nuke script is included a nuke8.nk in the Tutorials folder on the DVD.

Figure 8.27 The final color-graded result

AE Tutorial 9: Disguising Posterization with Blur and Grain

Posterization often results from the compression inherent with digital video footage. In addition, posterization can occur when filters are applied to low bit-depth footage. In either case, it's possible to reduce the severity of the color banding by applying a blur.

1. Create a new project. Choose Composition → New Composition. In the Composition Settings dialog box, change the Preset menu to HDV/HDTV 720 29.97 and set Duration to 30 and Fps to 30. Choose File → Project Settings. In the Project Settings dialog box, set Depth to 16 Bits Per Channel. A 16-bit space will allow for a more accurate blur, which is required by step 4. (Generally, you should pick a specific color space through the Working Space menu to match your intended output; however, for this exercise, Working Space may be set to None.)

2. Import the banding.##.tga footage from the Footage folder on the DVD. LMB+drag the footage from the Project panel to the layer outline in the Timeline panel. The footage features two palm trees against a cloudy sky. Scrub the timeline and examine the footage quality. Over the entire frame, there is a moderate amount of blocky noise created by the video compression. In addition, the sky shows signs of posterization, where the blue creates several bands.

3. If the banding is difficult to see on your monitor, you can temporarily exaggerate it by changing the Adjust Exposure cell in the Composition panel. Although Adjust Exposure is measured in stops, you can enter non-whole values, such as 1.9 (see Figure 8.28). As the exposure is raised, the banding becomes apparent in the

upper-right portion of the sky. When you are finished examining the banding, click the Reset Exposure button.

4. To disguise the color banding, you can add a blur. With the banding.##.tga layer selected, choose Effect → Fast Blur. In the Effect Controls panel, change the Blurriness to 12 and select the Repeat Edge Pixels check box.

5. To prevent the clouds and trees from taking on the heavy blur, draw a mask around the blue of the sky using the Pen tool (see Figure 8.29). Once the mask is complete, expand the Mask 1 section in the layer outline and change Mask Feather to 50, 50. This will soften the edge of the mask and disguise its position. (See Chapter 7 for more information on the Pen tool and masking.) LMB+drag a new copy of the banding.##.tga footage from the Project panel to the layer outline so that it is at the lowest level. This fills in the remaining frame with an unblurred copy of the footage.

6. At this stage, the sky is fairly featureless and doesn't match the clouds or trees, which retain subtle noise. To add noise back to the sky, select the highest banding.##.tga layer and choose Effect → Noise & Grain → Add Grain. LMB+drag the white preview window to a point that overlaps the masked sky. In the Effect Controls panel, change the Add Grain effect's Intensity to 0.04, Size to 3, and Softness to 0.5. Play back the timeline. The sky now has subtle, animated noise. The tutorial is complete. To compare the result to the original footage, toggle on and off the Video layer switch for the top banding.##.tga layer. Additionally, you can raise the value of the Adjust Exposure cell for the viewer. Although the posterization has not been removed completely, it has been significantly reduced. An example After Effects project is saved as ae9.aep in the Tutorials folder on the DVD.

Figure 8.28 (Top) Reset Exposure button and Adjust Exposure cell (Center) Unadjusted footage (Bottom) Detail of banding revealed with adjusted exposure. The band transitions are indicated by the gray lines.

Nuke Tutorial 9: Disguising Posterization with Blur and Grain

Posterization often results from the compression inherent with digital video footage. In addition, posterization can occur when filters are applied to low bit-depth footage. In either case, it's possible to reduce the severity of the color banding by applying a blur.

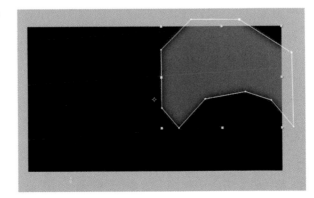

Figure 8.29 Blurred sky separated with a feathered mask

1. Create a new script. Choose Edit → Project Settings. In the properties panel, set Frame Range to 1, 30 and Fps to 30. Change the Full Size Format menu to New. In the new

Format dialog box, set File Size W to 1280 and File Size H to 720. Enter **HDTV 720** as the Name and click OK. In the Node Graph, RMB+click and choose Image → Read. Through the Read1 node's properties panel, browse for the banding.##.tga footage from the Footage folder on the DVD. Connect a viewer to the Read1 node. Scrub the timeline and examine the footage quality. Over the entire frame, there is a moderate amount of blocky noise created by the digital video compression scheme. In addition, the sky shows signs of posterization, where the blue creates several bands.

2. If the banding is difficult to see on your monitor, you can temporarily exaggerate it by adjusting the Gain controls in the Viewer pane (see Figure 8.30). Adjusting the Gain slider will cause the pixel values to be multiplied by the Gain slider value. You can also alter the Gain values by pressing the F-stop arrows. Each time an arrow is pressed, the Gain value is increased or decreased by a stop. Thus the Gain value follows the classic f-stop progression (1, 1.4, 2, 2.8, and so on), where each stop is twice as intense as the prior stop. As the Gain value is raised, the banding becomes apparent in the upper-right portion of the sky. When you are finished examining the banding, return the Gain value to 1.0.

Figure 8.30 (Top) Gain controls. The f-stop is indicated by the red f/n value. The Gain value appears to the right of the F-stop arrows. (Center) Footage with banding area indicated by box. (Bottom) Detail of banding revealed with adjusted Gain value. The band transitions are indicated by the gray lines.

3. Since the footage has no alpha channel, select the Read1 node, RMB+click, and choose Channel → Shuffle. In the Shuffle1 node's properties panel, select the white 1 check box that corresponds with the alpha channel (this is the fourth white box from the top of the 1 column). An alpha channel will be necessary for proper masking.

4. To disguise the color banding, you can add a blur. With the Shuffle1 node selected, RMB+click and choose Filter → Blur. In the Blur1 node's properties panel, set the Size slider to 12. A heavy blur is added to the footage, which hides the banding in the sky. However, the trees and clouds are equally blurred.

5. To restore sharpness to the foreground, you can mask the blurred sky and merge it with an unblurred copy of the footage. With no nodes selected, choose Draw → Bezier. With the Bezier1 node's properties panel open, Crtl+Alt+click in the viewer to draw a mask. In the Bezier1 node's properties panel, set Extra Blur to 40. With node nodes selected, RMB+click and choose Merge → Merge. Connect the output of the Blur1 node to input A of the Merge1 node (see Figure 8.31). Connect the Mask input of the Merge1 node to the output of the Bezier1 node. Connect a viewer to the Merge1 node. The blurred sky is cut out by the mask (see Figure 8.31). Connect the output of the Shuffle1 node to input B of the Merge1 node. The masked, blurred portion of the sky is placed on top of an unaffected version of the footage.

Figure 8.31 *(Left) Final node network (Right) Blurred sky separated with a blurred mask*

6. Although the color banding is significantly reduced, the sky has lost its inherent noise. To add noise, choose the Blur1 node, RMB+click, and choose Draw → Grain. A Grain1 node is inserted between the Blur1 and Merge1 nodes. Open the Grain1 node's properties panel. Reduce the Size Red, Green, and Blue sliders to values between 5 and 10. Reduce the Intensity Red, Green, and Blue sliders to values between 0.05 and 0.1. Play back the timeline. By default, the grain changes its pattern over time. If the grain remains too heavy, slowly reduce the Intensity values. The tutorial is complete. An example Nuke script is saved as nuke9.nk in the Tutorials folder on the DVD.

Interview: Shawn Jones, NT Picture & Sound, Hollywood

Shawn Jones began his career as a director of photography in the early 1990s. He transitioned to audio engineering when he was hired by Sony Electronics to help develop the Sony Dynamic Digital Sound (SDDS) format. In 1996, he joined NT. In 2007, he received an Academy Award in the scientific and technical category for the Environmental Film Initiative, an industry-wide effort to eliminate silver from 35mm film release prints. At present, Shawn serves as chief technology officer for NT and is the studio's resident colorist.

NT Picture & Sound is a division of NT, a studio with 30 years experience in the fine art of optical soundtrack mastering, film scanning and recording, and sound transfer. The NT Picture & Sound facility in Hollywood offers color grading, conforming, and DI services. NT has contributed to such recent feature films as *Watchmen*, *Star Trek*, *Inglourious Basterds*, *District 9*, and *Angels & Demons*.

Shawn Jones at a Da Vinci Resolve color grading station

LL: What is the practical goal of color grading?

SJ: In general, you're simply trying to eliminate the bumps that occurred [during] the production…. You're trying to do the same thing with photo-chemical developing—you're just trying to smooth out what you were given for that particular day [of the shoot]. My direction is to [color balance] the faces…. As long as nothing jumps out at you, that's the starting point. From there, you're [working on] the director's intent—darker, lighter, warmer, colder…and then playing with power windows (masked areas of a frame)….

LL: How critical is color grading to a project?

The NT sign at the studio's Hollywood facility

SJ: A general audience will not notice the subtle things that you've done, but they'll notice anything gross that you've missed. So, you're really just trying to smooth out the deficiencies in the original material…. No matter what show I've [worked on], the director of photography has always botched something for whatever reason—it's not usually their fault—they had a bad day, the sun went down, somebody put the wrong gel on the light….

LL: What color grading system is used at NT?

SJ: Da Vinci Resolve…. We also have [Assimilate] Scratch and Color from Apple.

LL: What image format do you use for color grading?

SJ: 10-bit DPX. It's all log. Sometimes, on some of the effects work, it will be 16-bit linear [TIFFs]….

LL: So, you'll play back 10-bit log files in real time?

SJ: Yes, with a film LUT or a video LUT.

LL: How do you manage your color calibration?

SJ: We use cineSpace as our color engine at the moment with some modifications that we've done…. Every day that we're [color grading], the projector's calibrated—it's a continual process. If it drifts a little, you're screwed.

LL: How often do you update your LUTs?

SJ: The [output quality of a film developing lab] yo-yos every day, but on a whole it's pretty consistent….What varies is the bulb in the projector, the DLP chip as it heats up—from day to day, that changes…so our LUTs get updated based more on what happens in the room and the environment than on what happens on the film.

LL: Do you use multiple LUTs for different displays?

SJ: Every device has its own LUT. [We use cineSpace] to do the profiling and LUT creation.

LL: What's the main advantage of a 3D LUT over a 1D LUT?

SJ: If you're trying to emulate film, it's the only way you can do it…. The only reason you really need a 3D LUT is the [color] cross-talk….

LL: Any other advantages of a 3D LUT?

SJ: A 3D LUT allows you to translate between differing devices with different gamuts. You can soft-clip the variance a little bit better. A blue that's clipping in a video [color] space that doesn't clip in the film [color] space, [can be soft-clipped]…at least you can roll into it (that is, you can gradually transition to the clipped values)….

LL: What resolutions do you work at?

SJ: It's gone from SD to 4K. It really depends on the job. We've done a few 6K elements.

Additional Resources: The Full Interview

To read the full interview with Shawn Jones, see the Interviews folder on the DVD.

Integrating Render Passes

—MICHAEL COLEMAN, After Effects product manager, Adobe, Seattle, Washington

Compositing CG elements *has its own unique challenges. Of these, the fact that CG is often divided into multiple layers leads to a different compositing workflow than may be present with live-action footage. The process becomes even more complicated when each layer is broken into specific render passes. Common render passes include beauty, diffuse, specular, and shadow. More complex passes, such as depth, motion vector, surface normal, and RGB lights, are not unusual. Although render passes increase the compositor's ability to fine-tune, they also require more complex layer stacks and node networks. With the tutorials in this chapter, you'll have the chance to practice compositing CG that is broken into numerous render passes. At the same time, you'll have the opportunity to relight a CG shot with a single RGB light pass.*

Dividing a CG Render

When a shot is animated in a 3D program on a professional production, it is rarely rendered out as is. Instead, the shot is divided into layers and/or render passes. Dividing a shot into layers allows key elements—including characters, backgrounds, shadows, effects, and props—to be rendered separately. By dividing the shot into layers, you gain efficiency. Not only do the separate layers render faster than the complete shot, but revising the shot becomes easier because a specific layer can be re-rendered without affecting other layers. With this method, the background can be held with a single frame if the shot has a static camera. Since background models, whether they are an outdoor environment or an indoor set, are often the most complex part of a CG scene, they are therefore the most time-consuming to render.

Render passes take the division further by breaking down each layer into specific shading components, light contributions, shadowing effects, or compositing encoders. Color, diffuse, ambient, and reflectivity are common shading components (see Figure 9.1). The contributions of CG lights may be rendered separately or given unique colors in anticipation of additional processing. Shadows may be isolated from the rest of the scene. Compositing encoders, designed for specialized compositing tasks, include depth, ambient occlusion, reflection occlusion, surface normal, UV information, and motion vector renders.

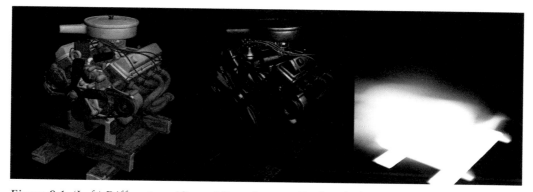

Figure 9.1 *(Left) Diffuse pass (Center) Specular pass (Right) Shadow pass (Engine model by Ian Wilmoth)*

Render passes give the compositor a great deal of control over the look of the shot. For instance, the intensity of the specular highlight can be increased, reduced, or animated in the composite. In addition, the compositor can insert their own motion blur, depth of field, or atmospheric effects. If light contributions are rendered as passes, the compositor can interactively relight the scene. With proper pass preparation, it's even possible to retexture moving CG elements in the composite.

Combining Layers

When a CG shot is rendered as layers, the main difficulty lies in the combination of alpha mattes. For example, if a character is holding a prop yet the character and prop are rendered separately, the renders will not fit together in the composite (see the top left of Figure 9.2). A similar situation arises when two characters are rendered separately but interact closely (hug, shake hands, wrestle, and so on). Fortunately, this can be remedied by applying a form of holdout matte known as an *occlusion matte* or *black hole matte*. An occlusion matte is produced by a type of material or material override that renders the assigned object as black and renders the object's alpha channel with 0 (transparent) values. This effectively cuts a hole into any object that sits behind the one assigned to the occlusion matte. As long as the rendered layers are properly premultiplied, they will fit together perfectly (see the bottom right of Figure 9.2). Popular 3D programs and rendering systems all provide some means to create an occlusion matte. For example, Autodesk Maya provides the Use Background material for this purpose. In addition, Maya materials contain a Matte Opacity Mode attribute that can be set to Black Hole. The mental ray renderer provides the Transmat shader, which produces similar results. Autodesk 3ds Max supplies the Matte/Shadow material. A shader used to create an occlusion matte is often referred to as a *matte shader*.

Common Render Passes

Many render passes, including beauty, diffuse, specular, shadow, reflection, and depth, may be considered universal because they are commonly used. Other passes, such as ambient occlusion, reflection occlusion, custom holdout mattes, motion vector, UV texture, and various light passes, are common but not mandatory for every project. Note that you will have a chance to combine and composite the majority of these passes in the tutorials at the end of this chapter.

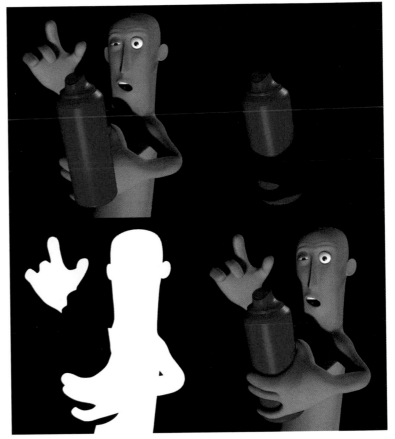

Figure 9.2 *(Top Left) Render of spray paint can composited on top of character render (Top Right) Render of spray paint can with occlusion matte material assigned to character (Bottom Left) Alpha channel of render where character is assigned to normal material and occlusion matte material is assigned to the spray paint can (Bottom Right) Composite using occlusion matte passes. A sample After Effects project is included as* bloke_matte.ae *in the Tutorials folder on the DVD. (Character rig by Jason Baskin. Spray paint model by Ecleposs.)*

Industry Perspective: CG Layers and Passes

While it is common to render CG as different layers, each layer is not consistently divided into render passes. Some studios trust that their animators and lighters are skilled enough to supply beauty renders suitable for compositing as is. Other facilities prefer renders to be delivered as specific, predefined render passes. Even if render passes are expected, the number and type of passes vary per show or project. For example, one project may require only a basic set of passes, such as diffuse, specular, reflection, shadow, and depth. Another project may be more complex and thus require diffuse, ambient, specular, ambient occlusion, depth, RGB light, motion vector, reflection, reflection occlusion, and shadow passes. When render passes are required, there are two methods with which they may be handed off to compositing: OpenEXR and separate frame sequences. The OpenEXR format is able to hold an arbitrary number of custom passes in a single file. Due to compatibility issues with proprietary software, it remains relatively unusual to use OpenEXRs in this manner. The more common method requires that each pass be rendered out as its own image sequence. For example, the diffuse pass may be rendered as 11a_diffuse.###.tga, while the shadow pass may be rendered as 11a_shadow.###.tga.

Beauty, Diffuse, and Specular Passes

A *beauty pass* utilizes all the available shading components, lighting contributions, shadowing effects, and render effects (see Figure 9.3). A beauty pass is created by 3D program by default when no render passes are established.

Diffuse, as a term, describes that which is not concentrated but is widely spread. A diffuse surface is one that reflects light rays in a random pattern, thereby preventing a specular highlight from appearing. Real-world diffuse surfaces include paper, cardboard, and dull cloth. A diffuse render pass, on the other hand, has two variations. The first variation contains the surface colors without reference to lighting (see the top right image of Figure 9.3). This variation, also known as a *texture pass*, must rely on some form of *shading pass* to give the render a sense of depth and roundness. (*Shading* refers to the variation of lightness to darkness across a surface.) For example, the shading pass may use the lighting and shadowing established for the beauty pass but assigns gray Lambert materials to the surfaces (see the bottom left image of Figure 9.3). In addition, ambient occlusion and similar skylight passes may be used as shading passes; however, due to their diffuse nature, they cannot contribute any strong sense of directional lighting.

The second variation of a diffuse pass includes surface color and shading but omits the specular information and self-shadowing (see the top-left image of Figure 9.4). When this variation is combined with a specular pass and a self-shadowing pass, it approximates the beauty pass. A self-shadowing pass is similar to a shadow pass but includes only shadows cast by an object onto itself.

Specular highlights, as created by 3D programs, are artificial constructs. Real-world specular highlights are reflections of intense light sources. 3D surfaces emulate these reflections by increasing the surface brightness where the angle between a reflection vector and view vector is small. A specular pass, also known as a *highlight pass*, is one that contains the specular "hot spots" over a black background in RGB (see the top-right image of Figure 9.4). Depending on the program and method used to create the pass, it may or may not contain matching alpha channel information.

Figure 9.3 *(Top Left) Beauty pass (Top Right) Diffuse pass, which lacks shading, specularity, and self-shadowing (Bottom Left) Shading pass (Bottom Right) Diffuse pass multiplied by shading pass. A sample After Effects project is included as* `girl_diffuse.ae` *in the Tutorials folder on the DVD.*

Figure 9.4 *(Top Left) Diffuse pass with surface color and shading component, but no specularity or self-shadowing (Top Right) Specular pass (Bottom Left) The alpha channel of a self-shadowing pass (Bottom Right) Diffuse pass after the merge of the self-shadowing pass and screen blend of the specular pass. A sample After Effects project is included as* `girl_diffuse_2.ae` *in the Tutorials folder on the DVD.*

Shadow and Depth Passes

A *shadow pass* "traps" cast shadows in the alpha channel. Since the shadow shape is defined as an alpha matte, the RGB channels are left as black. Shadow passes may include cast shadows and/or self-shadowing. (For a cast shadow example, see Figure 9.1 earlier in this chapter.)

A *depth pass*, also known as a Z-depth or Z-buffer pass, encodes the distance from the camera to objects within the scene. The encoding takes the form of a grayscale where objects close to the camera have values closer to 1.0 (see Figure 9.5). Depth passes may take the form of a special fifth channel in a Maya IFF or OpenEXR file. Depth passes may also be rendered in parallel to the RGB render. For example, Maya can render the beauty RGB pass as a Targa file and automatically generate a Z-buffer pass as a separate Targa file with a *_depth* suffix. In either a case, the channel can be viewed only with a program that can properly interpret it (which Photoshop cannot do, but compositing programs can). On the other hand, a specialized material override, such as a depth luminance shader, can render the depth information to standard RGB channels. Depth passes are useful for applying effects that increase or diminish with distance. For example, a depth pass can create an artificial fog that "thickens" with distance (see Figure 9.5).

Holdout Matte and ID Passes

Holdout matte passes may be used to control specific areas of a CG set, character, or prop. For example, a holdout matte may be generated for the glass of a vehicle (see Figure 9.6). The holdout matte render is then used to isolate the glass within a beauty render. Thus, the glass can be adjusted in the composite separately. Such mattes can be created by assigning material overrides in the 3D program. They can also be generated by rendering an *ID pass*, whereby a custom attribute, material color, or depth value is assigned to a surface, a set of polygon faces, or a group of objects. Because the elements carry unique values, they can be isolated in the composite. If an ID pass assigns saturated, non-shaded material colors to various elements, it's known as an *RGB* or *RGB ID pass*. If an ID pass bases its value on material assignments, it's known as a *material ID pass*. If an ID pass is based on custom attributes assigned to specific surfaces, it's known as an *object ID pass*. For examples of ID pass renders, see the section "Using Holdout Matte and RGB ID Passes" later in this chapter.

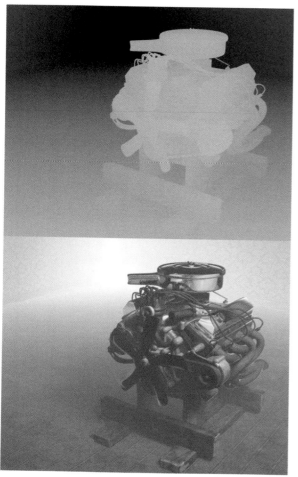

Figure 9.5 *(Top) Depth pass (Bottom) Depth pass used to create artificial fog in the composite that thickens with distance. A sample After Effects project is included as* `engine_fog.ae` *in the Tutorials folder on the DVD.*

Figure 9.6 *(Top) Beauty pass render of truck paint and glass (Center) Holdout matte pass (Bottom) Windows separated in composite using holdout matte. A sample After Effects project is included as* `truck_holdout.ae` *in the Tutorials folder on the DVD.*

Reflection and Refraction Passes

A *reflection pass* isolates any reflection or separates reflective surfaces. A *refraction pass* isolates any refractive surfaces. With both passes, the remainder of the frame is left black in the RGB and transparent in the alpha channel. The passes are useful for creating degraded or blurred reflections and refractions, which would otherwise be expensive to render in the 3D program. Because reflection and refraction passes can be difficult to set up in a 3D program, it is sometimes necessary to create a matching holdout pass. The holdout pass provides occlusion matte information to the passes so that they can fit into the composite without incorrectly covering nearby surfaces. For example, in Figure 9.7, a lamp's reflection and refraction are rendered separately. However, for the glass base to "fit" on top of the beauty render, its upper bend must be cut off with the aid of a holdout pass.

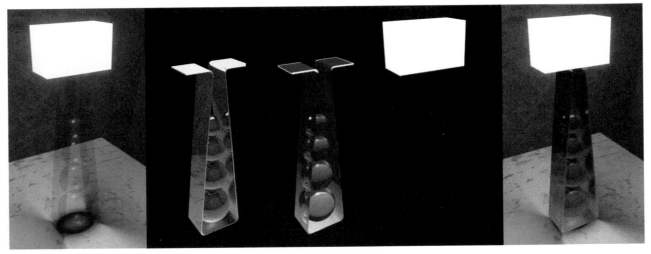

Figure 9.7 (Left to Right) Beauty pass without reflections or refractions; Reflection pass; Refraction pass; Holdout matte pass; final composite. A sample After Effects project is included as `lamp_reflect.ae` *in the Tutorials folder on the DVD. (Lamp by ModelUp Models)*

Refraction is the change in direction of a light wave due to a change of speed. When light passes between air, water, glass, and other semitransparent materials, the resulting refraction causes a distorted view. For example, a straw resting in a glass of water appears unnaturally bent below the water line.

Light Passes

Light passes take several forms. The simplest style of light pass renders a separate beauty pass for each light (see Figure 9.8). The separate beauty passes are then combined in the composite and the individual light contributions are adjusted. The beauty passes can also be color-corrected or tinted for a stylized result.

A second variation of a light pass involves the relighting of the set between beauty renders. For example, one beauty pass is rendered with an initial light setup. The lights are repositioned or adjusted and then a second beauty pass is rendered. This approach is useful when a single lighting setup is not satisfactory for all the objects within in scene.

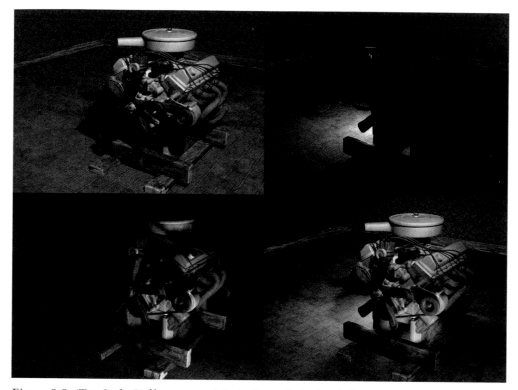

Figure 9.8 (Top Left) Diffuse pass, with shadows, lit by key light (Top Right) Diffuse pass lit by fill light (Bottom Left) Diffuse pass lit by second fill light (Bottom Right) Three passes combined with masking and color correction. A sample After Effects project is included as engine_lights.ae *in the Tutorials folder on the DVD.*

A more complex light pass is known as an *RGB light pass*, where each CG light is assigned to a red, green, or blue primary color. When the RGB light pass render is brought into the composite, each light's illumination is separated by isolating the matching red, green, or blue channel. The light's illumination is then used to create an alpha matte. When the alpha matte is applied to a matching beauty render that uses noncolored lights, the light's contribution to the beauty pass is separated out (see Figure 9.9). The separated light contributions are then recombined. Since each light becomes a separate layer or node, it can be adjusted. Thus it's possible to "turn off" lights, rebalance the intensities of all the lights, and even tint each light a different color.

If a 3D scene contains more than three lights, setting up RGB light passes becomes more complicated. For example, nine lights would require three separate RGB light passes with three lights in each pass. Nevertheless, RGB light passes are easily handled by After Effects and Nuke. Example workflows are included in the tutorials at the end of this chapter.

Ambient Occlusion and Reflection Occlusion Passes

Ambient occlusion describes the blocking of indirect light. Creases, crevices, and areas around adjacent surfaces of real-world objects are often darker due to the indirect light being absorbed or reflected away from the viewer. You can multiply a beauty or diffuse pass by an ambient occlusion pass to replicate this phenomenon (see Figure 9.10). An ambient occlusion pass occurs in RGB and is identifiable by an overriding white material with a soft, nondirectional shadow.

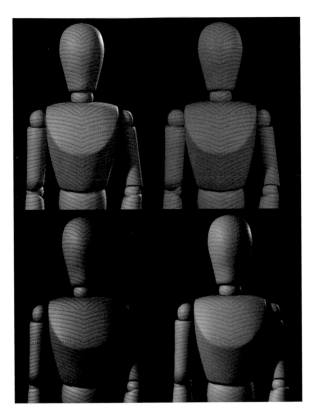

Figure 9.9 *(Top Left) Beauty pass of CG mannequin using three-point lighting (Top Right) RGB light pass with red key, green fill, and blue rim light (Bottom Left) Key light illumination of beauty render isolated in composite (Bottom Right) Lights recombined in composite. The overall light balance and light color has been changed without the need to re-render the CG. A sample After Effects project is included as* man_rgb.ae *in the Tutorials folder on the DVD.*

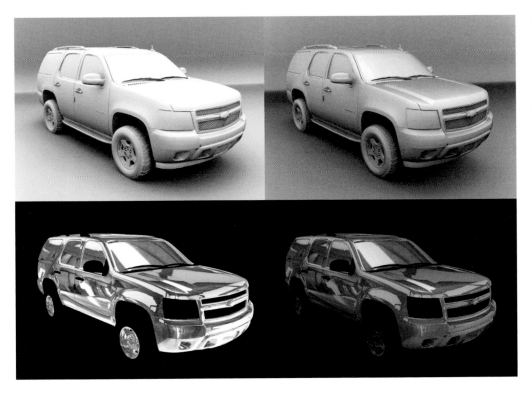

Figure 9.10 *(Top Left) Ambient occlusion pass (Top Right) Reflection occlusion pass (Bottom Left) Reflection pass for paint, window glass, and rims (Bottom Right) Reflection pass matted by reflection occlusion pass and merged with beauty pass. The strength of the reflection is reduced in areas of the reflection occlusion pass that are dark. Thus the red paint of the beauty pass is allowed to show through the reflection. A sample After Effects project is included as* truck_ro.ae *in the Tutorials folder on the DVD. (Truck model by Digimation)*

A reflection occlusion pass is closely related to an ambient occlusion pass. Whereas an ambient occlusion pass can be used to reduce diffuse intensity in areas with a high degree of surface convolution or where multiple surfaces are close together, a reflection occlusion pass can be used to reduce the reflection intensity in those same areas. Visually, both passes appear similar. However, reflection occlusion passes tend to contain less contrast and maintain fine detail around undulations in the surface. For example, in Figure 9.10 the reflection occlusion pass maintains more detail around the hood and headlights. In a composite, you can use a reflection occlusion pass as a matte with which to reduce the opacity of the reflection pass.

Rim Passes

A *rim pass* is designed to emulate light wrap in the composite. A rim pass takes the form of an RGB render where the objects are lit only along their edges (see Figure 9.11). The result can be created with custom shading networks within the 3D program, allowing the rim to survive regardless of the camera position or object motion.

Figure 9.11 *(Left) Rim pass (Center) Separate rim pass on fan blade (Right) Beauty pass after the screen blend of the rim passes. A sample After Effects project is included as* engine_rims.ae *in the Tutorials folder on the DVD.*

Motion Vector and UV Texture Passes

A *motion vector pass* encodes motion as special U and V channels. The U channel represents the horizontal screen distance an object moves over one frame. The V channel represents the vertical screen distance an object moves over one frame. The U and V channels can represent either forward motion or backward motion. Forward motion vectors encode the motion from the current frame to the next frame. That is, if the current frame is n and the camera shutter is set to 0, the motion vector runs from frame n to $n + 1$. Backward motion vectors encode the motion from the prior frame to the current frame. That is, the motion vector runs from frame $n - 1$ to n. A limited number of file formats, such as OpenEXR and Maya IFF, are able to store UV channels. In some situations, the file may carry both forward and backward vectors as UVUV.

In addition, it's possible to render the U and V motion vector information as red and green channels using custom shaders. For example, in Figure 9.12, a primitive shape is animated spinning. If a surface point moves in a strictly horizontal direction in screen space during one frame, pixels are laid down in the red channel. If a surface point moves in a strictly vertical direction in screen space during one frame, pixels are laid down in the green channel. If a surface point moves in both directions, it receives corresponding pixels in the red and green channels. The red and green pixels produce yellow where they overlap. With the example in Figure 9.12, the blue channel is reserved for blur magnitude, which is an optional output of various 3D motion vector shaders. The blur is then applied in the composite by an effect or node that is able to reinterpret the colors as motion vectors.

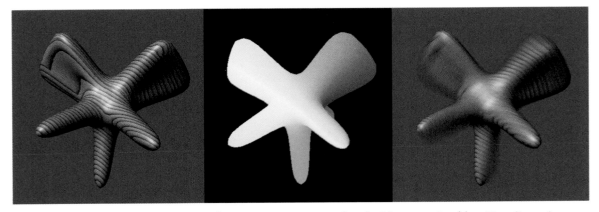

Figure 9.12 (Top Left) Beauty pass of spinning primitive rendered without motion blur (Top Center) Motion vector pass (Top Right) Resulting motion blur created in the composite. A sample Nuke script is included as motion_blur.nk *in the Tutorials folder on the DVD.*

This form of blur is referred to as 2D motion blur since the blurring only happens in screen space in two directions. 3D motion vectors, on the other hand, are useful for blurring objects along three-dimensional vectors and are discussed in Chapter 11, "Working with 2.5D and 3D."

UV channels, as used for motion vectors, differ from those used for UV texture passes. *UV texture passes* render UV texture space so that it's visible in RGB. *UV texture space* is a coordinate space that relates the pixels of a texture to points on a surface. The proper preparation of UV texture points, which are often referred to as *UVs*, is a necessary step in 3D modeling. Nuke is able to read UV texture passes and use them to retexture a 3D render in the composite. This process is documented in Chapter 12, "Advanced Techniques."

Surface Normal Passes

Surface normal passes capture the normal directions of surface points. The XYZ vector of a normal is translated to RGB values. The X axis corresponds to the red channel, the Y axis corresponds to the green channel, and the Z axis corresponds to the blue channel. You can use the surface normal information to apply effects to areas of a surface that point in a particular direction as compared to the camera. For example, you can use a surface normal pass to relight or color-correct a surface in the composite (see Figure 9.13).

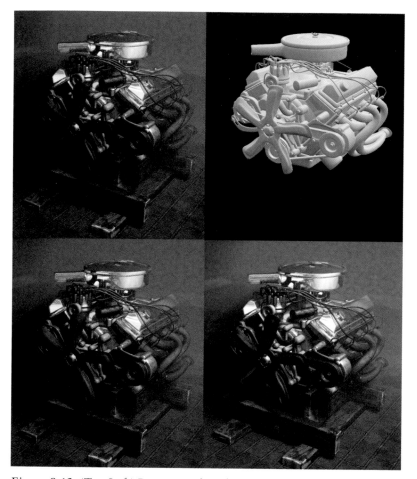

Figure 9.13 *(Top Left) Beauty render of engine and room (Top Right) Surface normal pass of engine (Bottom Left) Surface normal pass used to tint surface areas facing camera orange (Bottom Right) Surface normal pass used to tint surface area aligned to Y axis green. Sample Nuke scripts are included as* surface_normal_orange.nk *and* surface_normal_green.nk *in the Tutorials folder on the DVD.*

Ambient, Translucence, and Subsurface Scatter Passes

The ambient component of a shader simulates diffuse reflections arriving from all surfaces in a scene. In essence, the ambient component is the color of a surface when it receives no direct light. Most shaders have their ambient attribute set to 0 black by default. A non-black value, however, can give the sense that a surface has an inner glow or translucence. If the ambient component is rendered by itself, it can be adjusted in the composite (see Figure 9.14). The translucence component, on the other hand, simulates the diffuse penetration of light into and through a solid surface. In the real world, you can see this effect by holding a flashlight to your hand at night. Translucence occurs naturally with flesh, hair, fur, wax, paper, and leaves. If the translucence component is rendered as its own pass, it can be color-graded to give the illusion that the source light is a different color. In comparison, subsurface scattering techniques attempt to reproduce translucence with more physically accurate shading models and rendering techniques. Nevertheless, you can integrate a sub-surface scatter pass into a composite using techniques similar to those applied to translucence passes.

Figure 9.14 *(Top Left) Ambient pass (Top Right) Translucence pass (Bottom Left) Diffuse pass (Bottom Center) Ambient pass combined with diffuse pass with screen blending mode (Bottom Right) Translucence pass combined with diffuse and ambient passes through screen blending mode. A sample After Effects project is included as* `ambient_translucence.ae` *in the Tutorials folder.*

Text and Effects

It's not unusual for titles and similar text to be generated by a 3D program (as opposed to a 2D program such as Adobe Illustrator). Hence the text is rendered separately. In fact, several 3D programs may be used to generate character animation, prop animation, text, and visual effects. For example, Autodesk Softimage may be used to create character animation while Maxon Cinema 4D is used for the text and Side Effects Houdini is used to generate particle simulations.

Visual effects passes will vary greatly. They may be delivered to the compositor in a finished form, requiring little adjustment. On the other hand, they may be delivered in a raw, untextured, unlit form that necessitates a great deal of manipulation. For example, a 3D fog effect may be ready for compositing as a single beauty pass, while a water drop simulation may require multiple render passes, including reflection, refraction, rim, and surface normal.

Working with Render Passes

After Effects and Nuke provide simple methods by which you can combine common render passes. However, specialized passes, such as depth and motion vector, require more complex layer organization or node networks.

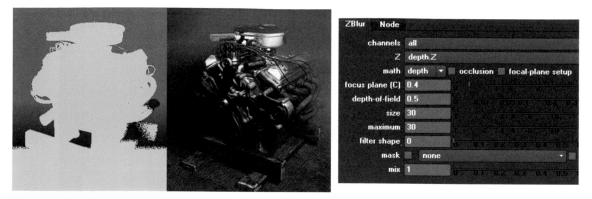

Figure 9.19 *(Left) ZBlur output with Focal-Plane Setup check box selected. Green represents area in focus. (Center) Resulting blur on background (Right) ZBlur properties panel. A sample Nuke script is included as* zblur.nk *in the Tutorials folder on the DVD.*

The ZMerge node creates a merge by evaluating the Z channels and alpha channels of the inputs. For example, in Figure 9.20, two parts of a lamp are merged together. The ZMerge Z Channel menu is set to Depth.Z, while the Alpha channel check box is unselected. The lamp's central stack of spheres and remaining base fit together because they carry unique Z channel values. Wherever surfaces are close together, however, the ZMerge node is prone to create intersections. To avoid this, you can adjust the values of a Z channel with a Grade node. In the Figure 9.20 example, a Grade node is added to Read2, which carries a render of the isolated lamps spheres. You can reverse the interpretation of the Z channel, whereby low values are assumed to be in the distance, by selecting the Smaller Z check box. Note that the ZMerge node tends to creates aliased edges.

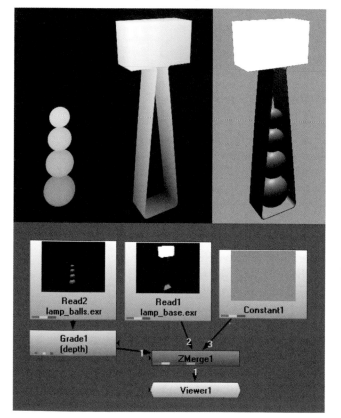

Figure 9.20 *(Top Left) Depth render of lamp center spheres (Top Center) Depth render of lamp base and shade (Top Right) Corresponding RGB channels combined with ZMerge (Bottom) Node network. A sample Nuke script is included as* zmerge.nk *in the Tutorials folder on the DVD.*

Creating Blur with Motion Vectors

You can employ the UV channels of a motion vector pass by using the VectorBlur node (in the Filter menu). Here are a few tips to keep in mind:

- VectorBlur requires that its input contain RGB and UV channels. If the UV motion vector information is carried by the red and green channels of an RGB file, it will be necessary to transfer the channel information via a Copy or ShuffleCopy node.

- For best results, the motion vector pass should be rendered as a floating-point image sequence (such as OpenEXR). Select the Raw Data check box of the Read node that carries the pass.

- Ideally, the motion vector pass should be unpremultiplied. If necessary, you can connect the output of the Read node to an Unpremult node.
- Nuke expects the motion vector values to represent pixel displacement values in the negative (left/down) and positive (right/up) directions. Since many 3D motion vector renders output normalized motion vector values that run between 0 and 1.0, it may be necessary to adjust the values through the VectorBlur's Add, Multiply, and Offset parameters or by adding an Expression node to the network.
- The VectorBlur node offers two forms of motion vector interpretation, which are set by the Method menu. The Backward interpretation is a fast algorithm suited for animation with simple translations. The Forward interpretation plots every pixel's motion path and thus can handle complex translations and rotations.
- If the edge of the resulting motion blur is pixilated or otherwise harsh, add a Blur node to the UV channels before feeding them into the VectorBlur node.

As an example, in Figure 9.21, a motion vector pass and beauty pass of a primitive torus are imported through two Read nodes. The motion vector pass encodes the UV directional information in the red and green channels. The magnitude of the displacement is encoded in the blue channel. The motion vector pass is connected to an Unpremult, Blur, and Expression node before reaching a ShuffleCopy node. The Expression node adjusts the UV values in anticipation of their use with a VectorBlur node. The red channel is fed the expression formula (r − 0.5) × (b × 500). In this case, r stands for the red channel and b stands for the blue channel. To create a suitably long blur trail, the normalized red channel values must be significantly increased so that they run along a negative and positive scale. The green channel has a similar expression formula: (g − 0.5) × (b × 500). (For more information on expressions, see Chapter 12.) The ShuffleCopy node combines the beauty pass RBG channels with the motion vector pass UV channels. The VectorBlur node takes the combined channels and applies the blur. The VectorBlur's UV Channels menu is set to Forward, while the Offset cell is set to −0.5. The Offset cell determines the start of the virtual shutter. By increasing or decreasing the Offset value, you can push the motion blur forward or backward in time. The Multiply cell, which controls the strength of the blur, is left at a default 1.0. If the Expression node was not present, it would be necessary to increase the Multiply node to a large value, such as 25.

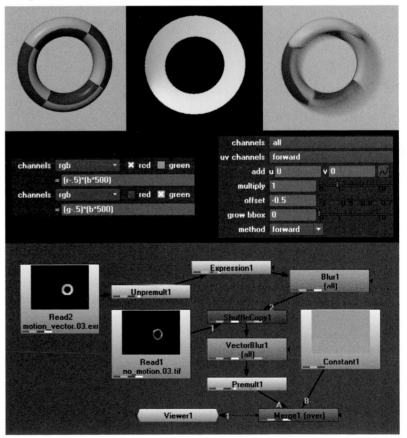

Figure 9.21 (Top Left) Beauty render of moving torus (Top Center) Matching motion vector pass showing red and green channels (Top Right) resulting motion blur (Center Left) Expression node formulas (Center Right) VectorBlur node settings (Bottom) Node network. A sample script is included as `motion_vector.nk` *in the Tutorials folder on the DVD.*

As an alternative approach, you can use the MotionBlur2D node to pull motion vector information from a Transform node. For example, in Figure 9.22, a line of text is scaled and thus gains blur. In this case, a Text node is connected to a Transform node, the Scale parameter of which is animated changing over 30 frames. The output of the Transform node is connected to both inputs of a MotionBlur2D node. One input, which is not labeled, passes the RGB values to the node. The second input, labeled 2D Transf, derives UV channel information from the Transform node. Note that the node icon has violet and cyan channel lines to indicate the presence of UV channels. The output of the MotionBlur2D node is connected to a VectorBlur node, which results in a blur suitable for a change in scale. In this case, the VectorBlur node's UV Channels menu is set to Motion, which is the default motion vector output of the MotionBlur2D node.

Figure 9.22 (Left) Node network (Top Right) Text without blur (Bottom Right) Text with application of MotionBlur2D and VectorBlur. A sample Nuke script is included as `motionblur2d.nk` *in the Tutorials folder on the DVD.*

AE and Nuke Tutorials

In this chapter, you'll have the opportunity to combine render passes from a CG engine as well as extract lighting information from an RGB light pass of a brass horn.

AE Tutorial 10: Combining CG Render Passes

Render passes give the compositor a great deal of flexibility when compositing a shot. The trickiest part of this process, however, is determining the correct layer order and appropriate blending modes.

1. Create a new project. Choose Composition → New Composition. In the Composition Settings dialog box, change the Preset menu to HDV/HDTV 720 29.97, set Duration to 1, and click OK. Choose File → Project Settings. In the Project Settings dialog box, change the Working Space menu to a color space suitable for your monitor. Since this tutorial involves balancing the contributions of multiple render passes, it's important that the color space settings for the project are appropriate. Although sRGB IEC6 1996-2.1 will work for projects that remain on a PC, the Working Space menu lists all the color profiles available on your system, including those designed for film and video. (See Chapter 2 for more information on color space settings.)

2. Import the files listed below from the Footage folder on the DVD. If the filename has an asterisk beside it, select the Premultiplied radio button when the Interpret Footage dialog box pops up. If a filename doesn't have an asterisk beside it, you can select the Ignore radio button.

```
engine_ao.tga*
engine_background.tga
engine_depth.tga
engine_diffuse.tga*
engine_fan_rim.tga
engine_fog.tga
engine_self_shadow.tga*
engine_ref_holdout.tga*
engine_reflect.tga*
engine_rim.tga
engine_shadow.tga*
engine_spec.tga
```

Figure 9.23 Shadow blended over background with Normal mode

3. LMB+drag engine_background.tga from the Project panel to the layer outline of the Timeline panel. LMB+drag engine_shadow.tga on top of engine_background.tga. A cast shadow is placed on top of the empty background. Because the shadow pass features a shadow in the alpha channel, the shadow shape is automatically cut out (see Figure 9.23). To reduce the strength of the shadow, you can reduce the engine_shadow.tga layer's Opacity slider.

4. LMB+drag engine_diffuse.tga to the top of the layer outline. LMB+drag engine_self_shadow.tga to the top of the layer outline. Change the engine_self_shadow.tga layer's Opacity to 95%. The self-shadow pass works in the same manner as the cast shadow pass but includes shadows only on the engine. LMB+drag engine_ao.tga to the top of the layer outline. Change the engine_ao.tga layer's blending mode to Multiply. This multiplies the values within the ambient occlusion render by the diffuse render. Areas of the ambient occlusion pass that are white have no affect on the diffuse render. Areas of the ambient occlusion layer that are gray or black darken the diffuse render (see Figure 9.24). To change the blending mode of a layer, you can select the layer name in the layer outline, RMB+click, and choose Blending Mode → *blending mode*. You can also click the Toggle Switches/ Modes button at the bottom of the Timeline panel to reveal the Mode menus beside each layer.

Figure 9.24 Diffuse and self-shadow passes are blended with Normal mode, while the Ambient occlusion pass is blended with Multiply mode.

5. LMB+drag engine_reflect.tga to the top of the layer outline. The chrome air cleaner and value covers occlude parts of the diffuse render inappropriately. To solve this, LMB+drag engine_ref_holdout.tga to the top of the layer outline. Use Figure 9.25 as a reference. Toggle off the Video layer switch beside the engine_ref_holdput.tga layer to hide

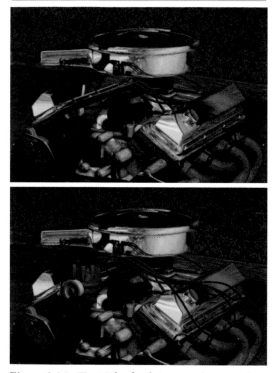

👁	🔊	○	🔒	🏷	#	Source Name	Mode	T
👁				▷ ☐	1	engine_fog.tga	Screen ▼	
👁				▷ ☐	2	engine_spec.tga	Screen ▼	
👁				▷ ☐	3	engine_fan_rim.tg	Screen ▼	
👁				▷ ☐	4	engine_rim.tga	Screen ▼	
				▷ ☐	5	engine_ref_holdou	Normal ▼	
👁				▷ ☐	6	engine_reflect.tga	Normal ▼	
👁				▷ ☐	7	engine_ao.tga	Multiply ▼	
👁				▷ ☐	8	engine_self_shado	Normal ▼	
👁				▷ ☐	9	engine_diffuse.tga	Normal ▼	
👁				▷ ☐	10	engine_shadow.tg	Normal ▼	
👁				▷ ☐	11	engine_backgroun	Normal ▼	

Figure 9.25 *(Top) The final Comp 1 layer outline with Mode menus displayed (Center) Detail of reflection pass without holdout matte. Note that the chrome inappropriately covers the distributor cap and spark plug wires. (Bottom) Detail of reflection pass with holdout matte applied*

it. Select the `engine_reflect.tga` layer and choose Effect → Channel → Set Matte. In the Effect Controls panel, change the Take Matte From Layer Menu to *1.engine_ref_holdout .tga*. Select the Invert Matte check box. The reflection layer is properly integrated into the composite (see Figure 9.25). The Set Matte effect borrows the alpha information from the `engine_ref_holdout.tga` layer, inverts it, and applies the matte information to the `engine_reflect.tga` layer. Set the `engine_ reflect.tga` layer's Opacity to 90% to dull the reflection. With the `engine_reflect.tga` layer selected, choose Effect → Blur & Sharpen → Gaussian Blur. Set the Gaussian Blur effect's Blurriness to 0.5 to reduce the fine noise trapped in the reflection render.

6. LMB+drag `engine_rim.tga` to the top of the layer outline. Change the `engine_rim.tga` layer's blending mode to Screen. This places a white rim along the engine edges. Reduce the `engine_rim.tga` layer's opacity to 15% to make the rim less severe. LMB+drag `engine_fan_rim.tga` to the top of the layer outline. Change the `engine_fan_rim.tga` layer's blending mode to Screen and reduce its opacity to 15%. LMB+ drag `engine_spec.tga` to the top of the layer outline. Change the `engine_spec.tga` layer's blending mode to Screen and reduce its opacity to 35%.

7. LMB+drag `engine_fog.tga` to the top of the layer outline. Change the `engine_fog tga` layer's blending mode to Screen. This places a beam of spotlight fog over the engine. Unfortunately, the edge of the fog cone is sharp in the upper-left corner. To soften this, select the `engine_fog.tga` layer and draw a mask with the Pen tool to establish new fog cone edges (see Figure 9.26). In the `engine_fog.tga` layer's Mask 1 section, change the Mask Feather cells to 200, 200. To reduce the fog intensity, set the `engine_fog.tga` layer's opacity to 15%. To prevent the fog from washing out the details of the engine, select the `engine_fog.tga` layer and choose Effect → Color Correction → Curves. In the Effect Controls panel, adjust the Curves effect's curve to add additional contrast to the fog. The goal is to keep the engine shadows fairly dark. To soften the fog, select the `engine_fog.tga` layer and choose Effect → Blur & Sharpen → Fast Blur. In the Effect Controls panel, set the Fast Blur effect's Blurriness slider to 5.

8. Choose Composition → New Composition. In the Composition Settings dialog box, change the Preset menu to HDV/HDTV 720 29.97 and set Duration to 1. LMB+drag `engine_depth.tga` to the Comp 2 tab of the Timeline panel. With the new layer selected, choose Effect → Brightness & Contrast. Set the Contrast slider to 50. This adjusts the RGB depth pass so that it will be useful as a matte for creating artificial depth of field.

9. Choose Composition → New Composition. In the Composition Settings dialog box, change the Preset menu to HDV/HDTV 720 29.97 and set Duration to 1. LMB+drag two copies of Comp 1 from the Project panel to the Comp 3 tab of the Timeline panel. LMB+drag Comp 2 to the top of the Comp 3 layer outline (see Figure 9.27).

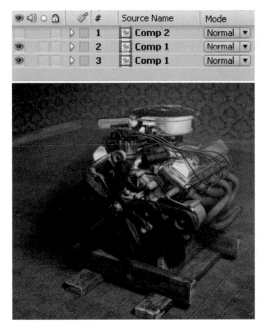

Figure 9.26 *(Top) Rim, specular, and fog passes are blended with the Screen mode. (Bottom) Mask drawn to soften the edge of the fog pass layer*

Figure 9.27 *(Top) The final Comp 3 layer outline (Bottom) Background blurred with Set Matte and Gaussian Blur effects*

Toggle off the Video layer switch beside Comp 2. With the middle Comp 1 layer selected (marked 2 in the layer outline), choose Effect → Channel → Set Matte. In the Effect Controls panel, set Take Matte From Layer to *1. Comp 2*. Set the Use Matte For menu to Luminance and select the Invert Matte check box. This uses the luminance information from the Comp 2 layer to supply an alpha matte to the middle Comp 1 layer. With the middle Comp 1 layer selected, choose Effect → Blur & Sharpen → Gaussian Blur. Set the Gaussian Blur effect's blurriness to 5. Because the layer was matted with the Set Matte effect, the layer opacity decreases from the background to the foreground. Therefore, the result of the Gaussian blur appears over the background only when the middle Comp 1 layer is blended with the bottom Comp 1 layer. (To see the blur by itself, temporarily toggle off the Video layer switch beside the bottom Comp 1 layer.)

10. At this stage, the engine remains somewhat washed out. To restore contrast to the composite, select the middle Comp 1 layer and choose Effect → Color Correction → Curves. In the Effect Controls panel, adjust the Curves effect's curve to darken the background (see Figure 9.28). Select the lower

Figure 9.28 *The final composite*

Comp 1 layer and choose Effect → Color Correction → Brightness & Contrast. In the Effect Controls panel, set the Contrast slider to 10 to darken the engine's shadows. The tutorial is complete. A sample After Effects project is included as ae10.aep in the Tutorials folder on the DVD.

Nuke Tutorial 10: Combining CG Render Passes

Render passes give the compositor a great deal of flexibility when compositing a shot. The trickiest part of this process, however, is determining the correct node order and appropriate Merge node Operation menu settings.

1. Create a new script. Choose Edit → Project Settings. In the Project Setting properties panel, change the frame range to 1, 1. Change Full Size Format to New. In the New Format dialog box, change the File Size W cell to 1280 and the H cell to 720. Enter **HDTV** into the Name cell and click OK. Note that the Display_LUT menu of the viewer panel is set to sRGB by default. Since the contributions of multiple render passes must be balanced in this tutorial, it's important that the color space you're working in is appropriate for your monitor. If the tutorial were destined for film or video, for example, a different Display_LUT setting would be necessary. (See Chapter 2 for more information on color space settings.)

2. Import the files listed below from the Footage folder on the DVD via Read nodes. If the filename has an asterisk beside it, select the Premultiplied check box in the corresponding Read node's properties panel.

   ```
   engine_ao.tga*
   engine_background.tga
   engine_depth.tga
   engine_diffuse.tga*
   engine_fan_rim.tga
   engine_fog.tga
   engine_self_shadow.tga*
   engine_ref_holdout.tga*
   engine_reflect.tga*
   engine_rim.tga
   engine_shadow.tga*
   engine_spec.tga
   ```

3. Due to the number of render passes, you will need eight Merge nodes. Create these by RMB+clicking over an empty area of the Node Graph and choosing Merge → Merge. Rename the Merge nodes as follows:

   CombineRims
   AddSelfShadow
   AddRims
   AddSpec
   AddAO
   AddReflect
   AddFog
   AddFGToBG

4. Connect the engine_fan_rim.tga Read node to input A of CombineRims. Use Figure 9.29 as reference for the final node network. Connect the engine_rim.tga Read node to input B of CombineRims. This merges the two rim light passes.

5. Connect the engine_self_shadow.tga Read node to input A of AddSelfShadow. Connect the engine_diffuse.tga Read node to input B of AddSelfShadow. This places the

self-shadow over the engine. Connect CombineRims to input A of AddRims. Connect AddSelfShadow to input B of AddRims. Set the AddRims node's Operation menu to Screen. This places the rim light over the engine. Set the Mix slider of the AddRims node to 0.2 to reduce the rim intensity.

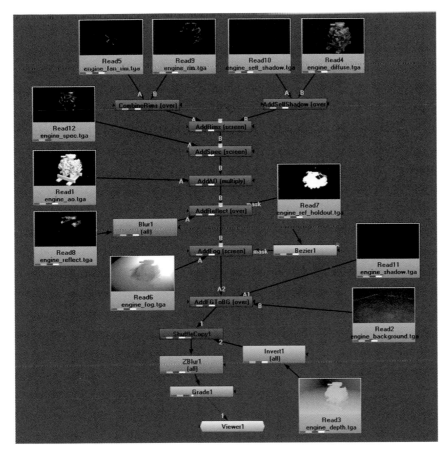

Figure 9.29 *The final node network*

6. Connect the engine_spec.tga Read node to input A of AddSpec. Connect AddRims to input B of AddSpec. This adds specular highlights to the otherwise diffuse engine. Set the AddSpec node's Operation menu to Screen. Set the Mix slider of the AddSpec node to 0.2 to reduce the specular intensity. Connect the engine_ao.tga Read node to input A of AddAO. Connect AddSpec to input B of AddAO. Set the AddAO node's Operation menu to Multiply. This darkens the surface convolutions of the engine by multiplying the color values by an ambient occlusion pass (see Figure 9.30).

7. Select the engine_reflect.tga Read node, RMB+click, and choose Filter → Blur. Set the Blur1 node's Size slider to 1.25. The blur softens fine noise found within the

Figure 9.30 *Diffuse, self-shadow, rim, specular, and ambient occlusion passes merged*

reflection render. Connect the Blur1 node to input A of AddReflect. Connect AddAO to input B of AddReflect. Connect the engine_ref_holdout.tga Read node to the Mask input of AddReflect. In the AddReflect node's properties panel, select the Invert check box. The engine_ref_holdout.tga features an alpha matte that defines what does and what does not occlude the chrome valve covers and air cleaner. If the engine_ref_holdout.tga file is removed, the chrome components will block the spark plug wires, manifold, and distributor inappropriately. Set the AddReflect node's Mix slider to 0.8 to dull the reflection slightly (see Figure 9.31).

8. Connect the engine_fog.tga Read node to input A of AddFog. Connect AddReflect to input B of AddFog. Open the AddFog node's properties panel. Change the Operation menu to Screen and set the Mix slider to 0.025. This places light-driven atmospheric fog into the scene. Unfortunately, the edge of the fog cone is sharp. To soften the edge, you can draw a mask. To do so, RMB+click with no nodes selected and choose Draw → Bezier. With the Bezier1 node's properties panel open, Ctrl+Alt+click and draw a mask shape in the viewer to define a new fog edge (see Figure 9.32). To add sharp corners to the mask, RMB+click over each mask vertex and choose Cusp from the menu. Connect the Bezier1 node to the Mask input of the AddFog node. Set the Bezier1 node's Extra Blur slider to 200 and its Falloff slider to 1.0. The edge of the fog becomes soft.

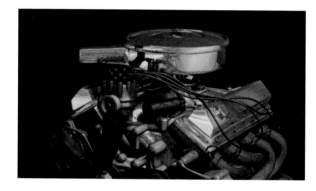

Figure 9.31 Detail of merged reflection pass

Figure 9.32 Bezier mask drawn to soften edge of fog pass

9. Connect the `engine_shadow.tga` Read node to input A of AddFGToBG. Connect the `engine_background.tga` Read node to input B of AddFGToBG. Connect AddFog to input A2 of AddFGToBG. (As soon a third connection is made to a Merge node's input, input A is relabeled A1.) The engine and cast shadow is placed over the background (see Figure 9.33).

10. Select the `engine_depth.tga` Read node, RMB+click, and choose Color → Invert. The `engine_depth.tga` file features a Z-buffer depth pass rendered in RGB. However, to be useful as a means to create artificial depth of field and atmosphere, it must be inverted so that the brightness areas are in the distance. With no nodes selected, RMB+click and choose Channel → ShuffleCopy. Connect AddFGToBG to input 1 of ShuffleCopy1. Connect Invert1 to input 2 of ShuffleCopy1. Open

Figure 9.33 Engine and shadow pass are merged over the background.

the ShuffleCopy1 node's properties panel. Change the In2 menu to Rgba and the Out2 menu to Depth (see Figure 9.34). (For more information on the ShuffleCopy node, see Chapter 4, "Channel Manipulation.") Select the check box in the In2 red column that lines up horizontally with Out2's Z channel. The ShuffleCopy1 node thereby applies the red channel values of the Invert1 node to its Z channel output. At the same time, the RGB values of AddFGToBG are passed through.

11. Select the ShuffleCopy1 node, RMB+click, and choose Filter → ZBlur. Open the ZBlur1 node's properties panel. Set the Z menu to Depth.Z, the Math menu to Direct, Focus Plane to 0.6, Depth-Of-Field to 0.25, Size to 15, and Maximum to 15. A blur is applied to the background without affecting the foreground. To see the focal range more clearly, temporarily select the Focal-Plane Set-Up check box. Green represents the region that remains in focus. Normally, red signifies the area behind the focal region; however, because the depth information is inverted with the Invert node, the blue foreground color is swapped with the red background color.

12. As a final step, select the ZBlur1 node, RMB+click, and choose Color → Grade. In the Grade1 node's properties panel, set Blackpoint to 0.002 and Gain to 0.8. This returns some of the contrast lost when the fog was added to the composite (see Figure 9.35). The tutorial is complete. A sample Nuke script is included as `nuke10.nk` in Tutorials folder on the DVD.

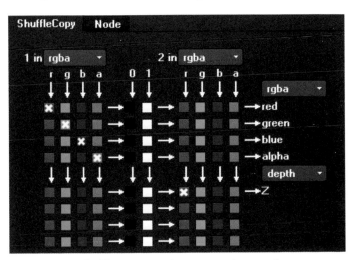

Figure 9.34 ShuffleCopy1 node's properties panel

Figure 9.35 *The final composite*

AE Tutorial 11: Employing RGB Light Passes

With an RGB light pass, each light is colored a primary color. This gives you the ability to re-light a shot in the composite.

1. Create a new project. Choose Composition → New Composition. In the Composition Settings dialog box, change the Width cell to 1280 and the Height cell to 960, set Frame Rate to 24, and set Duration to 24. Enter **Red Key** into the Composition Name cell and click OK. Repeat the process to create three more compositions. Name the second composition Green Fill, the third composition Blue Rim, and the fourth composition Combination.

2. Import the horn_beauty.##.tga footage from the Footage folder on the DVD. The render features a CG horn lit by a key light, a fill light, and a rim light. Import the horn_rgb.##.tga footage from the Footage folder on the DVD. The footage features the same CG render; however, each of the three lights is tinted a primary color. The key is red, the fill is green, and the rim is blue. Note that the horn_rgb.##.tga render carries shadows while the horn_beauty.##.tga render does not.

3. LMB+drag the horn_beauty.##.tga footage from the Project panel to the layer outline of the Red Key tab of the Timeline panel. LMB+drag the horn_rgb.##.tga footage to the top of the layer outline of the Red Key tab. Toggle off the Video layer switch for the horn_rgb.##.tga layer to hide it. Select the horn_beauty.##.tga layer and choose Effect → Channel → Set Matte. In the Effect Controls panel, set the Set Matte effect's Take Matte From Layer to *1. Horn_rgb.[1-24].tga*. Set Use Matte For to Red Channel. The Set Matte effect converts the light contribution of the CG key, which is colored red, to an alpha matte (see Figure 9.36). The horn_beauty.##.tga layer thereby gains new alpha channel values and thus only reveals the key light illumination.

4. Apply step 3 to the Green Fill and Blue Rim compositions. For the Green Fill composition, set the Set Matte effect's Use Matte For menu to Green Channel. For the Blue Rim composition, set the Set Matte effect's Use Matte For menu to Blue Channel.

5. Open the Combination composition in the Timeline panel. LMB+drag Red Key, Green Fill, and Blue Rim from the Project panel to the Combination layer outline. The three isolated lights are recombined. You can adjust each light's contribution to the composite by adjusting the corresponding layer's Opacity slider. For example, to reduce, or even turn off, the contribution of the rim light, reduce the Blue Rim layer's Opacity slider. Because the horn_rgb.##.tga render contains shadow information for the key and rim light, adjusting the corresponding Opacity sliders causes the shadows to fade in and fade out appropriately.

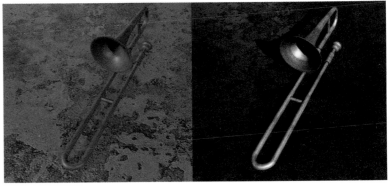

6. Since each light is isolated as a layer in the Combination composition, you are free to change the color of one or more lights. For example, to change the rim light to green, apply a Hue/Saturation effect (in the Effect → Color Correction menu) to the Blue Rim layer (see Figure 9.37). Set the Master Hue control to 80 and the Master Saturation slider to 80. You can also fine-tune each light's brightness by adjusting the Hue/Saturation effect's Master Lightness slider.

Figure 9.36 (Top) The Red Key layer outline with the Set Matte effect revealed (Bottom Left) RGB light pass render of horn. The key light has a red color. (Bottom Right) Key light illumination isolated by Set Matte effect

7. Experiment with the intensity balance of all three lights by adjusting the layers' Opacity sliders. If you've added Hue/Saturation effects, experiment with different color settings. Once you're satisfied with the colors and balance, the tutorial is complete. A sample After Effects script is included as ae11.aep in the Tutorials folder on the DVD.

Figure 9.37 Three variations of the horn created by adjusting the Opacity sliders and Hue/Saturation effects of the layers belonging to the Combination composition

Nuke Tutorial 11: Employing RGB Light Passes

With an RGB light pass, each light is colored a primary color. This gives you the ability to re-light a shot in the composite.

1. Create a new script. Choose Edit → Project Settings. In the Project Setting properties panel, change Frame Range to 1, 24. Change Full Size Format to New. In the New Format dialog box, change the File Size W cell to 1280 and the H cell to 960. Enter **1280×980** into the Name cell and click OK. In the Node Graph, RMB+click and choose Image → Read. In the Read1 node's properties panel, browse for the `horn_beauty.##.tga` footage in the Footage folder on the DVD. Connect a viewer to the Read1 node. The render features a CG horn lit by a key light, a fill light, and a rim light.

2. With no nodes selected, RMB+click and choose Image → Read. In the Read2 node's properties panel, browse for the `horn_rgb.##.tga` footage in the Footage folder on the DVD. The footage features the same CG render; however, each of the three lights is tinted a primary color. The key is red, the fill is green, and the rim is blue. Note that the `horn_rgb.##.tga` render carries shadows while the `horn_beauty.##.tga` render does not.

3. With no nodes selected, create three Copy nodes (Channel → Copy) and three Premult nodes (Merge → Premult). Using Figure 9.38 as reference, create these connections:

   - Connect Read1 to input B of the Copy1, Copy2, and Copy3 nodes.
   - Connect Read2 to input A of the Copy1, Copy2, and Copy3 nodes.
   - Connect Copy1 to Premult1.
   - Connect Copy2 to Premult2.
   - Connect Copy3 to Premult3.

   Open the properties panel for Copy1. Change the Copy Channel menu to Rgb.red. Open the properties panel for Copy2. Change the Copy Channel menu to Rgb.green. Open the properties panel for Copy3. Change the Copy Channel menu to Rgb.blue.

   This series of steps converts each CG light's illumination into an alpha matte. Because each light is colored a primary color, it can be isolated by a Copy node. For example, the red key light has a strong presence in the red channel of the `horn_rgb.##.tga` render. The Copy1 node therefore converts the red channel to an alpha channel. The RGB colors of the `horn_beauty.##.tga` render are passed through by the Copy nodes unharmed.

4. Create three Merge nodes (Merge → Merge). Create these connections and adjustments:

   - Connect Premult1 to input A of Merge1.
   - Connect Merge1 to input B of Merge2.
   - Connect Premult2 to input A of Merge2.
   - Connect Merge2 to input B of Merge3.
   - Connect Premult3 to input A of Merge3.

   By connecting the Merge nodes in this fashion, you can balance each light's contribution in the composite by adjusting the Merge nodes' Mix sliders. For example, in reduce, or even turn off, the contribution of the rim light, reduce the Merge3 Mix slider (see Figure 9.39). Because the `horn_rgb.##.tga` render contains shadow information for the key and rim light, adjusting the corresponding Mix sliders causes the shadows to fade in and fade out appropriately.

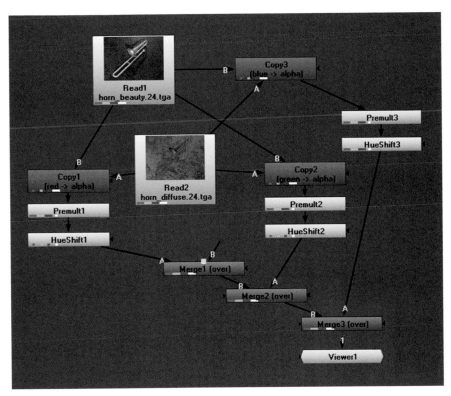

Figure 9.38 *The final node network (HueShift nodes are optional.)*

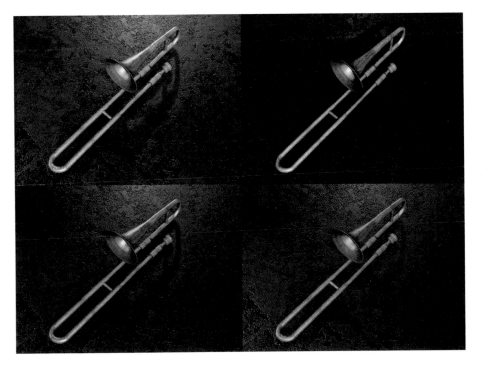

Figure 9.39 *(Top Left) Initial composite with all three Merge nodes' Mix sliders set to 1.0. (Top Right) The rim light and fill light are disabled by setting the Merge2 and Merge3 nodes' Mix sliders to 0. Note the appearance of the key shadow. (Bottom Left) The rim light is tinted green with a HueShift node. (Bottom Right) All three lights are tinted by HueShift nodes.*

5. Since each light is isolated by the node network, you are free to change the color of one or more lights. For example, to change the rim light to green, insert a HueShift node between the Premult3 node and the Merge3 node. Set the HueShift node's Hue Rotation slider to −80. If you want to adjust the colors of all three lights, insert a HueShift node after each Premult node. You can also fine-tune each light's brightness by adjusting the HueShift nodes' Brightness sliders.

6. Experiment with the intensity balance of all three lights by adjusting the Merge nodes' Mix sliders. If you've added HueShift nodes, experiment with different color settings. Once you're satisfied with the colors and balance, the tutorial is complete. A sample Nuke script is included as `nuke11.nk` in the Tutorials folder on the DVD.

Interview: Dan Rice, Blur Studio, Venice, California

Dan Rice's first major in college was biotechnology. Recognizing the creative potential in computer graphics, he switched studies and enrolled at the Art Institute of Pittsburgh. His

first job at Interactive Media allowed him to combine graphic design with 3D artwork. In 2002, Dan joined Blur and has since worked his way to the positions of art director and CG supervisor. He specializes in look development and oversees game cinematics, commercials, and short films that involve a "more cartoony" style. His involvement with "Gopher Broke" helped lead the short to an Oscar nomination in 2004.

Blur Studio was founded in 1995 by Tim Miller and David Stinnett. It provides visual effects and animation for feature films, ride films, commercials, game cinematics, and broadcast design. The studio has also produced highly respected animated shorts, including "In the Rough" and "Gentlemen's Duel."

Dan Rice at his workstation. All the animators share a single open workspace.

(Blur currently uses After Effects and Fusion for compositing. The studio keeps two dozen compositors on staff, although many compositors model, texture, and light.)

LL: Which game cinematics have you worked on?

DR: The cartoonier ones. For example, *Fable...Sonic the Hedgehog....*

LL: Are there differences between compositing something that's cartoony as opposed to something that's supposed to look real?

DR: I come from a graphic design background, so I'm really schooled in color design and color theory.... From the art direction standpoint, I think we go through a heftier look-development phase.... We're coming up with art direction, color scripts, moods for the piece—we're establishing all that stuff ourselves as artists.... What I like to do at the beginning of my projects is to have a look-development time, and so I'll explore the look-development in terms of rendering and lighting. I'll talk to the concept artists and try to work out an aesthetic—even before we get into CG…. A good analogy would be the [Pixar] art books—our CG supervisors here are more involved in the [concept art] stage, as opposed to other studios where it's preproduction [where] all the preproduction art is created by 2D artists and then it's handed off to the CG team….

LL: How important is color theory to an animator?

DR: If you want to be a lighter or compositor, having an eye that is color sensitive is extremely important. That's what we look for. It's all about the color aesthetic.

LL: As a supervisor, when you composite a shot to develop the look of a sequence, how do you treat the rendering passes?

DR: My work process here is to break out my passes to give me the most control in my compositing package…. So, I'll use a diffuse color pass, an ambient skylight pass that has no shadows, an ambient occlusion pass, and then each and every single [3D] light as a separate pass—and [finally] a reflection pass, and Z-depth…. I combine those together [in the comp] to

The Blur facility in Venice, California

define the look. [The problem is], I don't want to give all that control [back to the lighter]…. What we'll [do instead] is collapse all that back down in 3D to match the look [gained in the comp]…. [We used] to give the lighters a lot of passes and they could make it work. Now, we're getting away from that. We're going toward the direction where the senior people here—the supervisors—can establish the look [by using all the passes], but then simplify the look for the [lighter] so that they can focus on lighting…. [The passes require a great deal of] rendering, management of assets….

Additional Resources: The Full Interview

To read the full interview with Dan Rice, see the Interviews folder on the DVD.

ten

TIKI DAZE

Warps, Optical Artifacts, Paint, and Text

"If your text goes from hard black to white, you'll get video signal distortions. I would definitely make sure that the video signal can ease across the colors."

—JERRY VAN DER BEEK, co-founder, designer, and compositor, Little Fluffy Clouds, Marin, California

Aside from the common tasks *of transforming, merging, and keyframing, it's often expeditious to employ warps and morphs. In addition, various filters and nodes re-create unique qualities in a composite that would otherwise be time-consuming or complicated to capture on film or video. These include ones that reproduce real-world optical artifacts, including lens flares, glints, atmospheric glows, and spherical distortions. When you're faced with footage that must be touched up or repaired, built-in paint programs support a quick resolution to the problem. Although it's relatively straightforward, there are advantages and disadvantages to generating text within the compositing program. In this chapter, you'll have the chance to finish the Chapter 2 tutorial by adding shadows, glows, and text.*

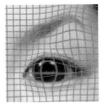

Warping and Morphing

Warping perturbs pixels within a layer or input. It differs from a transformation in that the pixels are not affected to the same degree. Warping is often localized, thus ignoring the remainder of the image (see Figure 10.1). In contrast, *morphing* warps a source layer/input to match a target layer/input. Morphs happen over time, thereby allowing the transition to be gradual. In addition, the output pixel colors are gradually shifted from the source values to the target values.

Warping may be employed when an image or a portion of an image needs to take on a new shape. This may range from the localized warping of a character's hand to fit a CG prop to an intense warping of an exterior in anticipation of its use as a reflection in artificial water. Morphing, on the other hand, may be employed when one element needs to take on the appearance of a second element. The most common type of morph involves a human face transforming into that of an animal or a monster. However, morphing may be employed more subtly. For example, a stunt double shot in front of greenscreen may be morphed to match the position and orientation of an actor shot on location.

On a more technical level, morphing generally requires some type of 2D source control mesh and 2D target control mesh. The source mesh defines specific features of the image. The target mesh defines which source pixels will be repositioned over time and how far they travel. The meshes are defined by horizontal and vertical splines. Control vertices lie at the spline intersections. Each vertex influences the source pixels close by it. The influence of a vertex overlaps the influence of nearby vertices but degrades and disappears over distance. Keyframing is applied to each vertex or the overall mesh shape. The color transition from the source to the target is instigated by a change in opacity or a similar blending technique. In comparison, warping is generated by a wide array of approaches that produce horizontal and vertical pixel perturbation. These range from spline deformations to displacement maps to predefined warps based upon mathematical formulas.

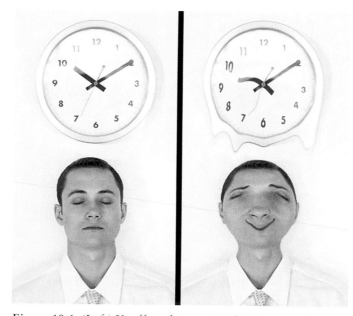

Figure 10.1 *(Left) Unaffected image (Right) Image with warp applied. Some pixels remain unaffected while other areas are severely distorted. (Photo © 2009 by Jupiterimages)*

Adding Text

Aside from aesthetic choices that involve font, color, placement, and typographical concerns (tracking, kerning, and so on), the successful use of text requires that it's readable on the target output. For example, if a line of text is designed for SDTV but features letters with fine features, the interlacing process may produce fuzzy results (see Figure 10.2). Resizing the font or choosing a font type with stronger features can solve this.

Even though HDTV solves many of the resolution issues present with SDTV, broadcast safety remains a concern for text elements. For example, while the NTSC SDTV broadcast-safe color range is 7.5 to 100 IRE, which equates to 16 to 235 on an 8-bit scale, ATSC or DVB HDTV broadcast has a safe range of 0 to 100 IRE, or a 0 to 235 scale. With both broadcast

Figure 10.2 (Top) Close-up of 20-point font in 720×480 interlaced composite (Bottom) Close-up of 24-point font with thicker features in same composite

standards, values above 235 may create display errors that include buzzing (random noise), color bleeding, line flickering, line crawling (pixel drift between lines), and audio distortion. To keep within the broadcast-safe range, you can do the following:

- In After Effects, apply the Levels effect with Output White set to 235.
- In Nuke, apply a Histogram node and set the Out cell of Output Range to 0.92.

Even if the text possesses broadcast-safe values, it may induce errors through high edge contrast. For example, if black text is placed over a white background, the sudden transition from 235 white pixels to 0 black pixels may cause display errors. Fortunately, when TrueType fonts are applied through the text tools of After Effects and Nuke, anti-aliasing does occur and the transition at the text edge is never perfectly sharp. The same holds true for text imported from other programs, such as Adobe Illustrator. Nevertheless, the anti-aliased transition may be as small as 1 or 2 pixels. To soften the transition between background and text, you can employ one of the following techniques:

- Blur the text slightly. For example, adding a Gaussian blur with its strength set below 1.0 slightly softens the text (see Figure 10.3).

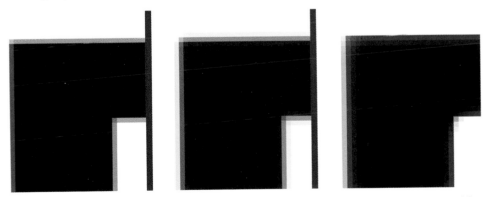

Figure 10.3 (Left) The letter D, enlarged by 1600% in a 720p HDTV composition. Note the 1-pixel transition from white to black. (Center) Same letter after the application of a Gaussian blur with an 0.4 strength. The transition stretches to 3 pixels. (Right) Same letter after the application of a glow effect. The transition stretches to 5 pixels. Sample After Effects projects are included as `text_blur.aep` *and* `text_glow.aep` *in the Tutorials folder on the DVD.*

- Add a glow effect to the text. The glow will brighten and blur the edge slightly (see Figure 10.3).
- Add an "invisible noise" to the composited text. The noise should be adjusted so that it is too faint to see with the naked eye but strong enough to affect the values slightly. For example, if black text is placed over a white background, the noise will ensure that there is more variation in a horizontal scanline of pixels (see Figure 10.4).

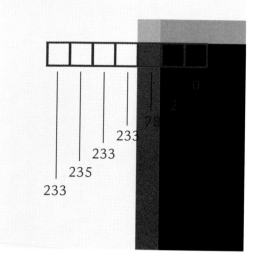

Figure 10.4 *The letter* D, *enlarged by 1600% in a 720p HDTV composition. The application of a subtle "invisible noise" adds variation to the pixel values. Since the text is made broadcast safe, no value is over 235. A sample After Effects project is included as* text_noise.aep *in the Tutorials folder on the DVD.*

Tips & Tricks: Broadcast Variations

The broadcast safe range of PAL, SECAM, and their digital successor, DVB, runs from 0 to 700 mV (millivolts) whether the broadcast is SDTV, EDTV, or HDTV. The 0 to 700 mV range is equivalent to 0 to 100 IRE. The broadcast safe range of ATSC, which is replacing the NTSC standard, is also 0 to 100 IRE.

The standardization of digital broadcasting has not eliminated interlacing. For example, 1080 HDTV exists as progressive-frame and interlaced versions.

Adding Optical Artifacts

Since compositors often work with live-action film and video footage, it's necessary to re-create some of the optical artifacts that are unintentionally captured. These artifacts include lens flares, lens debris, atmospheric glows, glints, light wrap, and spherical lens distortion.

A *lens flare* is an identifiable pattern created by the scattering of light through an optical system. The scattered light reflects off the individual glass elements common to compound lenses and creates overexposure in limited areas. The source of the scattered light is usually intense and must be pointed toward the lens. For example, the sun, bright artificial lighting, and strong specular reflections produce lens flares. In cinematography and videography, lens flares are generally not desired. However, since flares are common, they are often added to visual effects work to create a sense of photographic realism. Although artificial lens flares generally consist of a string of roughly circular shapes, real-life lens flares vary with the camera, lens, and lighting situation. For example, flares produced by anamorphic lenses used in the motion picture industry take the form of thin horizontal lines (see Figure 10.5).

Figure 10.5 *(Top Left) Common flare with polygonal string (Top Right) Flare with halo arc (Bottom Left) Vertical flare (Bottom Right) Anamorphic lens flare (Photos © 2009 by Jupiterimages)*

Lens debris, such as dirt, dust, water drops, or water vapor, often forms patterns similar to lens flares. Because the debris is situated outside the focal plane of the lens, it appears as out-of-focus circles or simple polygonal shapes (see Figure 10.6). The brightness and apparent transparency of the debris change with the position of the lens and the relative lighting of the location.

Atmospheric glow occurs when a bright light source scatters through haze, fog, smog, or smoke (see Figure 10.6). (Air saturated with light-scattering particles is referred to as a *participating media*.) The glow may be intense and focused or extremely diffuse, whereby it spreads over a large area. When the sun forms focused shafts of light, they're known as *god rays*. Compositing programs usually offer a filter that can re-create atmospheric glow. Generally, the filters blur and lighten a source layer and then blend the result back on top of the source. This results in the brighter areas of the image "bleeding" over the edges of the darker areas.

Figure 10.6 *(Top Left) Lens debris. (Top Right) A spotlight creates an intense atmospheric glow in a well-defined cone. (Bottom Left) City lights create a diffuse glows over a large area. (Bottom Right) Strongly lit background haze creeps around the edge of trees, creating a variation of light wrap. In addition, shafts of light break through the leaves, forming god rays. (Photos © 2009 by Jupiterimages)*

Figure 10.7 *Glints on water. Each glint forms an eight-pointed starburst, as seen in the inset. (Photo © 2009 by Jupiterimages)*

Light wrap is the result of bounced light "wrapping" around the edges of an object. In essence, atmospheric glow produces its own light wrap effect (see Figure 10.6). Thus, if a specific light wrap tool is not available in a compositing program, a glow filter can be used to create a similar result. In any case, when CG elements are integrated into a live-action plate, the light wrap is generally not present. Hence, ways to add light wrap in the composite are desirable.

Glints are related to lens flares in that they are an artifact of light scatter through an optical system. However, glints are not limited to a single large artifact but occur at points within a shot that are intense (see Figure 10.7). In addition, glints may occur only momentarily. In fact, the term *glint* is synonymous with *sparkle*.

Spherical lens distortion, on the other hand, occurs with low-quality or otherwise wide-angle lenses. In fact, "fisheye" lenses take advantage of the distortion to display a wide field of view (see Figure 10.8). When matching elements to live-action footage, it is sometime necessary to match the spherical distortion. Conversely, it may be advantageous to identify the distortion and remove it.

After Effects and Nuke offer effects and nodes that re-create lens flares, atmospheric haze, glows, glints, light wrap, and spherical distortion. These effects and layers are demonstrated throughout the remainder of this chapter.

Painting in the Composite

The presence of paint tools in a compositing program expands the tasks a compositor is able to carry out. For example, a compositor can undertake

Figure 10.8 Spherical lens distortion, as seen on background buildings (Photo © 2009 by Jupiterimages)

frame repair, paint-based rotoscoping, wire removal, render patching, or clean plate creation. Frame repair includes scratch, dirt, and dust removal. Paint-based rotoscoping allows the compositor to use paint tools to create mattes instead of using various spline path mask tools. Hand-painted masks may be easier to create when the masking job is complex and the motion changes radically with each frame. Wire removal includes a wide range of visual effects work that requires the removal of lighting, camera, or effects rigs that are captured in a live-action shoot. Render patching is similar to frame repair but instead addresses 3D render glitches. Such glitches may include aliasing noise, light flickers, or errant hairs in a hair simulation. Clean plate creation involves the manufacture of a clean plate using footage partially obscured by actors, props, or set pieces.

Industry Perspective: Clean Plates and Paint Fixes

A *clean plate* is footage containing an empty set or location. For example, a shot is filmed with actors; the actors step off camera and then the camera operator captures the clean plate without moving or altering the camera. Clean plates are often needed in visual effects work when an actor must go through some type of transformation. The clean plate guarantees that the actor can be removed from the background, even if only for a few frames. Clean plates are also a requirement for location motion capture work. For example, if an actor is filmed on location in a motion capture suit, the compositor must remove them from the frame so that the CG double can be added. As such, time limitations, handheld cameras, and other on-set problems can prevent a clean plate for being captured. At that point, it's left to the paint artist or compositor to assemble a clean plate from pieces of the footage.

Large studios often maintain a paint or "paint fix" department. The tasks assigned by each studio vary, but they generally include those discussed in this section. If a studio lacks such a department, the problematic shot is assigned to a compositor. Note that paint fix departments are usually separate from texture painting or matte painting departments.

Warps, Optical Artifacts, Paint, and Text in AE

After Effects includes a large array of special effects. Since coverage of every effect is beyond the scope of this book, only a few of the most useful ones are discussed here. Among these, warping effects, simulation effects, and text are discussed.

Warping and Distorting Layers

After Effects includes a Distort menu with effects designed to perturb pixels. These range from the simple Warp to the more advanced Mesh Warp.

Bezier and Mesh Warps

The Bezier Warp effect applies a set of vertices and Bezier handles to the four corners of a layer (see Figure 10.9). You can interactively LMB+drag the vertices or tangent handles in the viewer. Each vertex and set of tangent handles has a corresponding property, so you can animate the vertices and handles moving over time. With this method, you can simulate a flapping flag or distorted piece of cloth.

Figure 10.9 *Bezier Warp effect applied to rectangular layer. A sample After Effects project is included as* `bezier_warp.aep` *in the Tutorials folder on the DVD.*

In contrast, the Mesh Warp effect lays a mesh over the layer. You can change the effect's Rows and/or Columns properties to change the mesh density. You can select and LMB+drag any vertex that lies at the intersection of a column and row line. The layer is instantly distorted in that region (see Figure 10.10). Note that the Mesh Warp effect must be selected through the Effect Controls panel or the layer outline of the Timeline panel for the mesh to be visible in the viewer. Each mesh vertex carries a vertical and horizontal tangent handle (see Figure 10.11). To move a handle, LMB+drag a handle end point. To animate the mesh deforming over time, toggle on the Stopwatch button beside the Distortion Mesh property and proceed to change the mesh shape at different frames.

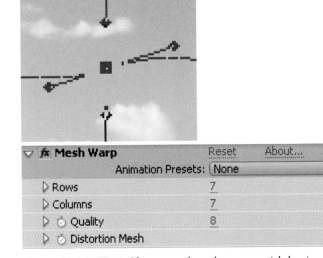

Figure 10.10 (Top) Unaffected layer (Center) The mesh of the Mesh Warp effect with some vertices repositioned (Bottom) Resulting warp. The road has been given a bend and the distant mountains have been shortened. A sample After Effects project is included as `mesh_warp.aep` in the Tutorials folder on the DVD.

Figure 10.11 (Top) Close-up of mesh vertex with horizontal tangent handle repositioned (Bottom) The Mesh Warp effect's properties

Displacement Effects

The Effect → Distort menu includes a number of effects that produce their namesake distortion. These include Twirl, Bulge, Ripple, and Spherize. The Warp effect, on the other hand, produces a number of Photoshop-style distortions that include arcs and waves; you can select the distortion type through the Warp Style menu. For an example of the Warp

effect, see the section "AE Tutorial 2 Revisited: Adding Shadows, Glow, and Text" at the end of this chapter. In comparison, the Wave Warp effect creates a horizontal and vertical wave distortion that may be suitable for re-creating a reflection on rippling water (see Figure 10.12).

The Turbulent Displace effect, on the other hand, bases its distortion on a Perlin-style fractal noise. The Complexity slider determines the number of octaves and thus the amount of detail. High Complexity values lead to coarse and fine detail mixed together. The Size slider determines the scale of the base noise. Higher Size values "zoom" into the fractal pattern. You can change the quality of the distortion by changing the Antialiasing For Best Quality menu from Low to High. By default, the four edges of the affected layer are pinned. That is, they are not distorted. You can override this behavior and allow the image edges to pull away from the frame edges by changing the Pinning menu from Pin All to None or one of the other options. The Evolution control selects different 2D noise slices along the z-axis. If you animate the Evolution property, you can create the distorted refraction of objects under water. For example, in Figure 10.13, the center of a child's pool is distorted over time.

Figure 10.12 (Top) Sky layer (Bottom) Sky layer with Wave Warp effect applied. A sample After Effects project is included as `wave_warp.aep` *in the Tutorials folder on the DVD.*

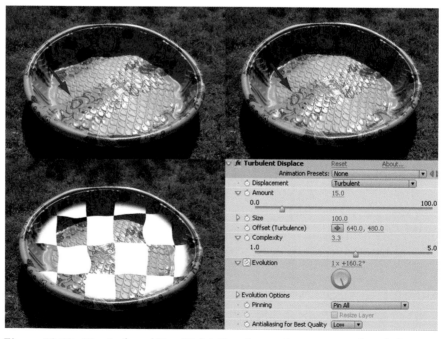

Figure 10.13 (Top Left and Top Right) Two frames from animated Turbulent Displace effect, which distorts the center of the pool. Note the difference near the arrows. (Bottom) Same effect applied to an otherwise square checkerboard to show the degree of distortion. (Bottom Right) The Turbulent Displace effect's properties. A sample After Effects project is included as `turbulent_displace.aep` *in the Tutorials folder on the DVD.*

Re-creating Optical Effects

After Effects includes the Lens Flare, Optics Compensation, and Glow effects to re-create specific optical artifacts.

Lens Flare and Optics Compensation

The Lens Flare effect (in the Generate menu) creates a flare with a starburst at its origin and a string of polygonal shapes extending from that point (see Figure 10.14). The location of the origin is determined by the Flare Center property. You can interactively position the flare center by LMB+dragging the bull's-eye handle in the viewer. To affect the way in which the string of polygonal shapes is sized, change the Lens Type menu to one of three preset lens types. The flare is automatically blended with the layer to which the effect is applied. To fade out the flare, raise the Blend With Original slider above 0%.

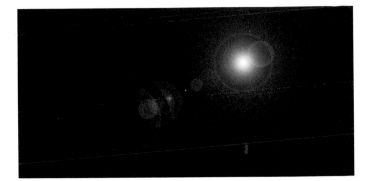

Figure 10.14 *After Effects Lens Flare effect. A sample After Effects project is included as* `lens_flare.aep` *in the Tutorials folder on the DVD.*

The Optics Compensation effect (in the Distort menu) re-creates the spherical distortion created by real-world lenses. The higher the value of the Field Of View (FOV) slider, the greater the distortion and the more the outer edges of the layer move toward the center. For example, in Figure 10.15, a grid is distorted with the Optics Compensation effect in order to match the distortion found in a background plate. You can choose a new central point for the distortion by changing the View Center X and Y values.

You can invert the result and have the center move toward the outer edges by selecting the Reverse Lens Distortion check box. You can use this feature to remove or reduce the optical distortion present in a plate (see Figure 10.15). Note that the effect leaves a gap along the frame edges when the Field Of View value is high and the Reverse Lens Distortion check box is unselected.

Figure 10.15 *(Top) The Optics Compensation effect is applied to a grid, thus warping it to match the spherical distortion of a background plate. (Bottom) The Optics Compensation effect is applied to the plate with the Reverse Lens Distortion check box selected. The spherical distortion of the plate is removed, as is indicated by its alignment to the square grid. Sample After Effects projects are included as* `optics_match.aep` *and* `optics_remove.aep` *in the Tutorials folder on the DVD.*

The Glow Effect

The Glow effect (in the Stylize menu) creates atmospheric glow (see Figure 10.16). The Glow Threshold slider determines where the glow is applied. The higher the Glow Threshold value, the brighter the pixels must be to receive the glow effect. Glow Intensity serves as multiplier for the glow effect. The higher the Glow Intensity value, the brighter the glow areas become. By default, the glow is added to the input layer. This may lead to clipping as values reach the bit-depth limit. You can choose a different blending mode, such as Screen, by changing the Glow Operation menu. In addition, the Glow effect uses the colors of the input layer to create the glow colors. However, you can force your own colors on the glow by changing the Glow Color menu to A & B Colors. You can then choose the colors through the Color A and Color B cells. The A & B Midpoint slider controls the mixture of the two. Lower values use less of Color A and more of Color B. When you switch to A & B Colors, the colors loop. That is, the glow area is ringed by the two colors. You can choose different methods of forming the rings by changing the Color Looping menu. For example, Triangle B > A > B alternates between B and A. To create additional rings, increase the Color Loops menu.

As mentioned earlier in this chapter, glow filters can be used to emulate a light wrap effect. For example, in Figure 10.17, a CG ball is given light wrap through a Glow effect and four nested compositions. The compositions undertake the following steps:

- Comp 1 places a darkened copy of a CG ball over a sky plate.
- Comp 2 adds a Glow effect to nested Comp 1.
- Comp 3 screen blends nested Comp 2 over an unadjusted copy of the CG ball. Thus the blurry glow creeps over the edge of the ball. Adding a Hue/Saturation effect to nested Comp 2 reduces the saturation of the glow.
- Comp 4 places the nested Comp 3 over a new copy of the sky plate. In order to prevent the glow from appearing over the sky, the alpha channel for nested Comp 3 is adjusted with a Curves effect.

Figure 10.16 *(Top) Unaffected layer (Center) Layer after application of the Glow effect. (Bottom) Glow effect settings. A sample After Effects project is included as* glow.aep *in the Tutorials folder on the DVD.*

Figure 10.17 *(Top Left) Comp 1 places a darkened CG ball over a sky. (Top Right) Comp 2 adds a Glow effect to Comp 1. (Bottom Left) Comp 3 places Comp 2 over the unadjusted ball. The blurry glow along the ball's edge replicates light wrap. (Bottom Right) Comp 4 combines Comp 3 with the sky. A sample After Effects project is included as* `glow_lightwrap.aep` *in the Tutorials folder on the DVD.*

Generating Text

There are several methods by which you can create text in After Effects. These include the use of text tools as well as Basic Text, Timecode, and Path Text effects.

Text Tools

You can select the Horizontal Type tool, LMB+drag a text box in the viewer, and type the text directly into the text box. This method creates a new text layer in the layer outline of the Timeline panel. The font type, size, and other typographical properties are found in the Character panel (found along the right side of the program by default). Text justification (align left, align right, center, and so on) and text indentation options are set by the Paragraph panel (see Figure 10.18). You can create an empty text layer at any time by choosing Layer → Text. If you would like to create text vertically, choose the Vertical Type tool, which is accessible through the Horizontal Type tool button menu. If at any time you want to retype a portion of the text or alter its properties, use the Horizontal or Vertical Type tool to LMB+drag and highlight the text in the text box. You can also alter text properties for each layer by selecting a text layer in the layer outline.

Figure 10.18 *(Top) Horizontal Type tool menu (Center) Character panel (Bottom) Paragraph panel*

After Effects treats the text outline (the stroke) and text fill separately (see Figure 10.19). To change the thickness of the stroke, adjust the Stroke Width cell (the icon with three horizontal lines in the Character panel). A Stroke Width value of 0 turns off the stroke and leaves only fill. You can also disable the stroke by clicking the Stroke Color cell (the hollow box in the Character panel) so that it sits on top of the Fill Color cell and then clicking the small No Stroke Color button (a white box with a red diagonal line). You can disable the fill by clicking the Fill Color cell so that it sits on top of the Stroke color cell and clicking the same "No" button. To change either color, double-click a color cell to open the Text Color dialog box.

Figure 10.19 (Top Left) Stroke Width cell. (Bottom Left) Stroke Color cell set to red and Fill Color cell set to yellow. The small white box with the red diagonal line is the "No" button. (Right) Text box in viewer.

Basic Text and Timecode Effects

If the quality of the text is not overly important, choose Effect → Text → Basic Text. A Basic Text dialog box opens. You can enter the required text and choose a font, font size, and font orientation. In the Effect Controls panel, you can change the Basic Text effect's color and tracking (space between letters). Unlike the Text tool, Basic text does not create a new layer but adds the text to the layer to which the effect is applied. Due to its relatively limited number of controls, Basic Text is suitable for labeling tests and works in progress.

Along those lines, the Timecode effect automatically adds its namesake to a layer. You can switch between Frame Numbers, Feet + Frames (for 16mm or 35mm), or SMPTE HH:MM:SS:FF (hours:minutes:seconds:frames) by changing the Display Format menu. You can also change the Time Units cell to the project's frames per second.

Path Text

The Path Text effect creates text along a Bezier spline, a circle, or a line that can be animated to transform or deform over time. To apply the effect, follow these steps:

1. Select the layer to which you want to add text. Choose Effect → Text → Path Text. In the Path Text dialog box, select a font and style. Type the text in the text field and click OK.
2. The text is added but obscures the original layer. To composite the text on top of the layer with proper transparency, select the Composite On Original check box in the Advanced section of the Effect Controls panel.
3. By default, the text is added to a Bezier spline (see Figure 10.20). You can LMB+drag the tangent base point to reposition the ends of the spline. You can LMB+drag the tangent handle point to change the shape of the spline. Note that the handles are visible only if the Path Text effect is selected in the layer outline of the Timeline panel or the Effect Controls panel.

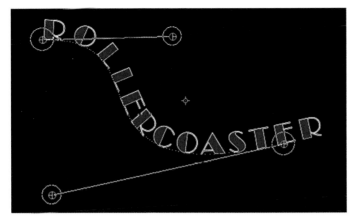

Figure 10.20 Path Text effect with Shape Type set to Bezier

4. To change the spline to a circle or straight line, change the Shape Type menu in the Path Options section. The central circle handle positions the circle while the outer handle scales and rotates the circle. The two handles of the line position the ends and ultimately determine the line length and orientation.

5. To change the text color, adjust the properties in the Fill And Stroke section. Typographical options are found in the Character section. Justification is found in the Paragraph section.

Painting in AE

Several tools and effects allow you to paint interactively within the viewer of a Layer panel. The stroke information is saved as a vector path. You can animate the path's properties over time. This makes the paint tools and effects ideal for touching up footage. For example, you may use the Clone Stamp tool to remove a film scratch, a smudge on a lens, a special effect wire rig, unwanted lighting equipment, or an undesirable sign.

Painting with the Paint Tool

To use the Paint tool, follow these steps:

1. Double-click a layer name in the layer outline of the Timeline panel. This opens the layer in the Layer panel with its own viewer. The Layer panel will sit beside the Composition panel. Note that the Layer panel carries its own timeline slider.

2. Click the Paint tool icon at the top left of the program (see Figure 10.21). Select a brush size in the Brush Tips panel. Choose a brush color and opacity through the Paint panel. If the Brush Tips or Paint panel is not visible, activate it by selecting its name in the Window menu.

3. LMB+drag in the Layer panel viewer to draw a paint stroke. When you release the mouse button, the stroke ends. The stroke is stored in the Paint section of the layer outline. Each stroke receives its own subsection with its own set of properties. For example, the first stroke you paint with the Paint tool is named Brush 1. By default, the stroke exists for the remainder of the timeline (starting with the frame it was drawn on) and receives its own timeline bar, which you can lengthen or shorten (see Figure 10.22).

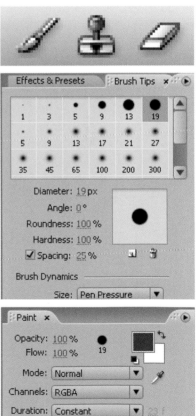

Figure 10.21 (Top) The Paint, Clone Stamp, and Eraser tools (Center) The Brush Tips panel (Bottom) The Paint panel

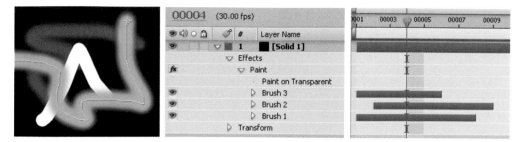

Figure 10.22 *(Left) Three brush strokes in the viewer of the Layer panel. The green stroke is selected, revealing its path. (Center) The same strokes revealed in the layer outline. (Right) The strokes' timeline bars. In this case, each bar is set for a different duration.*

Once a stroke is drawn, you can select it with the Selection tool and LMB+drag it in the viewer of the Layer panel to reposition it. You can hide a stroke by toggling off the Video switch beside its name in the layer outline. Each stroke carries its own blending mode, which is set by the Blend Mode menu (also found beside its name in the layer outline).

When you paint a stroke with the Paint tool, you can force the stroke to exist only for one frame by changing the Duration menu in the Paint panel to Single Frame. You can also choose a specific frame length by changing the Duration menu to Custom and entering a number into the nearby F cell. The stroke is laid down from the current frame to the F cell frame number. If Duration is set to Write On, the stroke will automatically draw itself over time as if handwriting.

You can animate stroke properties over time. The properties are carried by the Stroke Options and Transform subsections in the layer outline. Aside from common properties such as Position, Rotation, Scale, Color, Diameter, Channels, and Opacity, you can adjust and keyframe the following:

Start and End If Start is above 0% or if End is less than 100%, only a portion of the stroke is displayed. For example, if Start is set to 50%, the stroke is displayed from the halfway point along its length to the end point.

Hardness, Roundness, and Angle Hardness determines the sharpness of the stroke edge. The lower the value, the more feathered the edge becomes. Roundness determines the consistency of the stroke width. If the Roundness value is low, the stroke takes on the look of calligraphy, where the stroke thickness differs vertically and horizontally. In this case, the Angle property determines in which direction the thin section of the stroke runs. If the angle of a stroke section matches the Angle value, that section becomes thin. The angle of a stroke is measured from the bottom of a frame. Therefore, a perfectly horizontal stroke has a 0° angle.

Spacing and Flow In reality, a stroke is a number of overlapping shapes lined up along the vector path. The Brush Tip panel determines the shape. Hence, a brush tip may be hard-edged and circular or feathered and ellipsoid. You can control the coarseness of the overlapping by adjusting the Spacing property. The higher the Spacing value, the more spread out the shapes become. The Flow property, on the other hand, controls the opacity of individual shapes. If the Flow value is lowered, the shapes become more transparent. However, the areas where the shapes overlap remain more opaque. In contrast, the Opacity property affects the transparency equally for all areas of the stroke.

The Paint effect (Effect → Paint → Paint) operates in the same manner as the Paint tool. In fact, as soon as a stroke is painted with the Paint tool, the program automatically adds the Paint effect to the layer. It's the Paint effect that holds all the stroke properties.

Tips & Tricks: Painting on an Empty Layer

If you prefer to paint a stroke on an empty layer, create a Solid layer, change the layer's color to pure black or white, open the Solid layer in the Layer panel, and paint the stroke. To ensure that the stroke carries proper transparency, toggle on the Paint On Transparent property in the Effect Controls panel or layer outline. When you switch back to the Composition panel, the stroke will sit on top of lower layers with appropriate transparency.

Painting with the Eraser and Clone Stamp Tools

The Eraser tool creates a black stroke with 0 alpha. If the erase stroke is painted over a layer with an image, the image has a hole cut into it. At the same time, the tool cuts a hole into any paint strokes the eraser stroke overlaps.

The Clone Stamp tool is able to sample areas of the layer on which the clone stroke is painted. To sample an area, Alt+click within the viewer of the Layer panel. If the layer contains footage with multiple frames, the clone stroke contents will update with the changing image. This is useful for capturing subtle changes in film grain when repairing dust, dirt, scratches, or compression artifacts in film or video footage. For example, in Figure 10.23, the Clone Stamp tool is used to remove a dirt spot from the windshield of a car. A single stroke is painted over the dirt. Because the camera and car are moving chaotically, the stroke's Position is animated over time. In addition, the Clone Position property is animated so that the clone source is always to the immediate right of the clone stroke. For example, if the stroke, named Clone 1, is at 142, 148, the Clone Position property is set to 152, 148 (10 pixels to the right). Aside from the Clone Position property, clone strokes provide a Clone Time Shift property. If set above or below 0, Clone Time Shift samples frames in front of or behind the current frame.

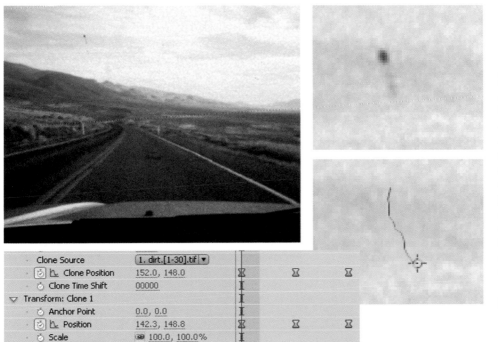

Figure 10.23 (Top Left) Footage with dirt on windshield (Top Right) Detail of dirt (Bottom Left) Clone Stamp stroke in layer outline with animated Position and Clone Position properties (Bottom Right) Detail of Clone Stamp stroke. The dirt spot is covered. A sample After Effects project is included as paint_dirt .aep *in the Tutorials folder on the DVD.*

Painting with Vector Paint

The Vector Paint effect allows you to paint strokes but has a slightly different functionality than the Paint tool or Paint effect. To apply the Vector Paint effect, follow these steps:

1. Select the layer to which you want to add a stroke. Choose Effect → Paint → Vector Paint. Select the Vector Paint effect in the Effect Controls panel. Set the brush Radius, Opacity, Feather, and Color.

2. When the effect is applied, a paint toolbox is added to the top left of the Composition panel (see Figure 10.24). Click the toolbox paintbrush icon and LMB+drag in the viewer to create a stroke. By default, the stroke appears only at the current frame. To have the stroke appear from the current frame until the end of the timeline, change the Playback Mode menu, in the Effect Controls panel, to Hold Strokes.

If you paint multiple strokes with the Vector Paint effect on a single layer, all the strokes are stored in a single Vector Paint section in the layer outline. In other words, you cannot affect the strokes individually. However, the Vector Paint effect does offer a Wiggle Control with which you can make the strokes take on irregular, undulating thickness over time.

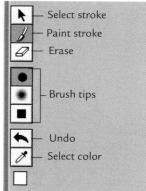

Figure 10.24 *The Vector Paint toolbox*

To add the wiggle, toggle the Enable Wiggling switch on. Five additional options appear below Enable Wiggling that control the speed and variation of the wiggle.

Painting with Liquify

With the Liquify effect, you can interactively push pixels in the viewer as if the image was a liquid medium. A hidden control mesh controls the distortion. The Liquify effect differs from the Mesh Warp and Bezier Warp effects in that the control mesh is denser and tangent handle manipulation is not required. To apply the Liquify effect, follow these steps:

1. Select the layer you wish to distort. Choose Effect → Distort → Liquify. In the Warp Tool Options section of the Effect Controls panel, select a brush size.

2. LMB+drag in the viewer. Pixels are instantly dragged along with the brush. You can release the mouse button and reclick and drag as many times as you like. If you LMB+click without moving the mouse, the warp is applied to the pixels below the brush; however, the warp is amplified with each click. The deformations are discretely stored by the effect and will continue to appear for the duration of the timeline.

The Liquify effect has several different modes of operation; you can switch among them by using the mode icons in the Effect Controls panel (see Figure 10.25). By default, the Warp mode is activated. Warp simply drags pixels behind the brush center. The Turbulence mode scrambles pixels under the brush but does so in a smooth fashion. Twirl Clockwise and Twirl Counterclockwise modes rotate the pixels below the brush as a unit. Pucker moves pixels toward the brush center while Bloat moves pixels away from it. The Shift Pixels mode lines up pixels in a line perpendicular to the brush motion. The Reflection mode flips pixels in the direction the brush is moving. The Clone mode copies distortions from sampled areas (to sample an area, Alt+click in the viewer). The Reconstruction mode repairs previous distortions by returning the control mesh to its prior state.

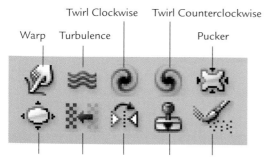

Figure 10.25 *The Liquify effect's mode icons*

When a brush stroke is applied in the viewer, the control mesh vertices are perturbed (see Figure 10.26). Pixels close to a mesh vertex are thus pulled along to the vertex's new position. You can examine the perturbed sections of the mesh by selecting the View Mesh check box (in the View Options section). You can deform the mesh over time by toggling on the Stopwatch button beside the Distortion Mesh property.

Figure 10.26 (Left) Unaffected layer (Center) The Liquify effect's distortion (Right) Distortion mesh displayed with View Mesh check box selected (Photo © by 2009 Jupiterimages)

Industry Perspective: Using Warps and Morphs

Although many of the example warps and morphs in this chapter are fairly extreme, those used in production are often just the opposite—they are fairly subtle. For example, an actor's hand may be morphed to fit a CG prop or a prop shot against greenscreen. A live-action car may be warped to match up to a CG car wreck. Many times, the required warp or morph will last only a few frames.

Warps, Optical Artifacts, Paint, and Text in Nuke

Nuke provides several nodes designed to create warps, morphs, optical effects, paint strokes, and text.

Warping Inputs

With the GridWarp and SplineWarp nodes (in the Transform menu), you can warp or morph an input.

Warping with GridWarp

The GridWarp node warps an image based on the relative positions of points in a source and destination grid (which are essentially meshes). You have the option of warping a single input or blending two inputs to create a morph. To warp a single input, follow these steps:

1. Choose a source node whose output you wish to warp. With the source node selected, RMB+click and choose Transform → GridWarp. By default, the Src (Source) input to the GridWarp node is connected to the source node. Connect a viewer to the source node (see Figure 10.27).

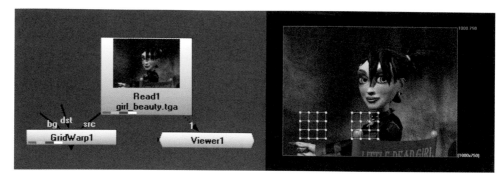

Figure 10.27 (Left) Initial GridWarp node setup (Right) Initial state of GridWarp source and destination grid

2. Open the GridWarp node's properties panel. Two grids appear in the viewer (see Figure 10.27). The pink grid establishes the source grid, which defines the area that is to be warped. The purple grid establishes the destination grid, which defines how the warping will occur. To snap the grids to the resolution of the source node, click the Image Size buttons in the Source Grid and Destination Grid sections of the GridWarp node's properties panel.

3. Select the Hide check box in the Destination Grid section. LMB+drag the grid points of the pink source grid to encompass the feature you want to warp. For example, if you want to warp a character's mouth, shape the grid so that it surrounds the mouth and follows major contours of the lips, nearby cheeks, chin, and so on (see Figure 10.28). When you select a grid point, a tangent handle becomes available. You can move a tangent handle by LMB+dragging a handle point. Shortening a handle will cause the tangent to form a sharper corner. If the grid resolution is insufficient, you can add more subdivisions by clicking the Add button in the Source Grid section and LMB+clicking on a grid curve. A new point is inserted and a new grid curve is drawn in the direction that is perpendicular to the curve you click on. By default, any curve added to the source grid is added to the destination grid.

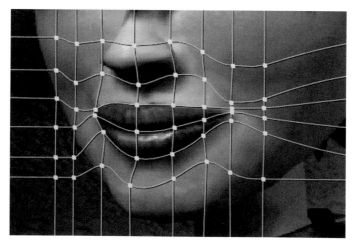

Figure 10.28 Detail of source grid after it's fit to image size and has additional curves inserted. The grid is shaped to surround the mouth.

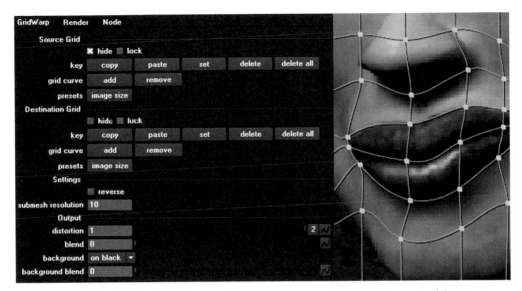

Figure 10.29 (Left) The GridWarp node's properties panel (Right) Close-up of destination grid adjusted to create warp. A sample Nuke script is included as `gridwarp.nk` *in the Tutorials folder on the DVD.*

4. Once you're satisfied with the shape of the source grid, select the Hide check box in the Source Grid section and deselect the Hide check box in the Destination Grid section (see Figure 10.29). Click the Copy button in the Source Grid section. Click the Paste button in the Destination Grid section. This copies all the point transformations from the source grid to the destination grid.

5. Shape the purple destination grid to create the warp. For example, if you want to make the character's mouth sneer, pull the destination grid points upward in that area (see Figure 10.29). If you would like to see the warp update as you adjust the destination grid, connect a viewer to the GridWarp node. As long as the GridWarp node's properties panel is open, you can display and manipulate the source and destination grids. Note that the length of any given vertex handle controls the influence of the matching vertex. Short tangent handles reduce the distance a vertex is able to influence surrounding pixels. Adjust the Distortion slider to increase or decrease the strength of the warp. To increase the accuracy of the distortion, raise the Submesh Resolution value.

You can animate the source or destination grid deformations over time. To set a key for the source grid, move to the appropriate frame on the timeline and click the Set button in the Source Grid section of the GridWarp node's properties panel. To set a key for the destination grid, click the Set button in the Destination Grid section. Once a keyframe has been set, any updates to the grid points will automatically produce additional keyframes. If the GridWarp node's input is film or video footage, it may be useful to animate the source grid changing shape to follow a particular target. For example, if you plan to warp a person's eye, then animate the source grid following the person's eyes. If you want the warp to scale over time, animate the destination grid. For example, if you want to have the eyes suddenly become smaller, animate the destination grid points drawing closer together.

To adjust the way in which the pixels are averaged or padded to create the warp, you can choose a different convolution filter through the Filter menu of the Render tab. You can add an additional layer of anti-aliasing by changing the Antialiasing menu from None to Low, Medium, or High.

Morphing with GridWarp

As mentioned, you can use the GridWarp node to morph together two inputs. This requires a slightly different set of steps:

1. Connect the Src (Source) input of a GridWarp node to the output of a node you wish to morph. Connect the Dst (Destination) input of the GridWarp node to the output of a node that will serve as a destination. (In other words, the source image will become the destination image through the morph.) For the GridWarp node to work smoothly, it's best for the source and destination inputs to be the same resolution. Connect a viewer to the source node (see Figure 10.30).

2. Open the GridWarp node's properties panel. Two grids appear in the viewer. The pink grid establishes the source grid, which defines the area that is to be warped. The purple grid establishes the destination grid, which defines how the warping will occur. Click the Image Size button in the Source Grid and Destination Grid sections to snap the grids to the project resolution. Select the Hide check box in the Destination Grid section. Shape the source grid by adjusting vertex and tangent handle positions to follow key features of the source input (see Figure 10.30). If the source input is footage that changes over time, animate the grid following the key features. To animate the grid, click the Set button in the Source Grid section and proceed to adjust the grid at different frames. If necessary, increase the grid's resolution by inserting curves with the Add button in the Source Grid section.

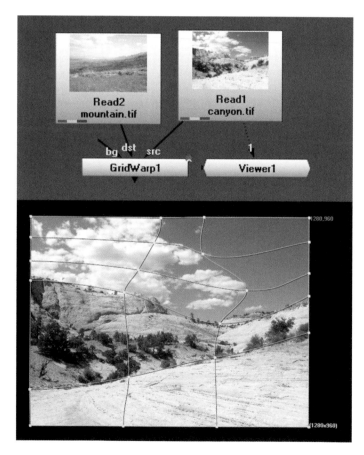

Figure 10.30 (Top) *Initial node setup for creating a morph with GridWarp (Bottom) Source grid shaped to fit landscape features*

3. Once you're satisfied with the shape of the source grid, select the Hide check box in the Source Grid section and deselect the Hide check box in the Destination Grid section. Connect the viewer to the destination node. Shape the purple destination grid to conform to the features that are a relative match to the source. For example, if the source and destination both feature a face, match the vertex positions around the eyes, nose, mouth, chin, ears, and so on. In the example illustrated by Figure 10.30, the horizon lines and cloud edges are matched between the two landscapes (see Figure 10.31). If the destination input is footage that changes over time, animate the destination grid following the selected features. To animate the grid, click the Set button in the Destination Grid section and adjust the grid at different frames. Once you are satisfied with the destination grid's shape, connect the viewer to the GridWarp node.

4. To animate the morph over time, keyframe the Distortion and Blend sliders running from 0 to 1.0 or vice versa. If Distortion and Blend are set to 1.0, the destination input is output with no deformation. If Distortion and Blend are set to 0.5, the morph occurs at half strength. That is, any given source pixel is moved half the distance between its original position and the end position determined by the destination grid. In addition, the output pixel color is a 50% mixture of the source and target. If Distortion and Blend are set to 0, the source input is output with no deformation.

Warping with SplineWarp

The SplineWarp node allows you to apply a warp through the manipulation of Bezier splines. To use the SplineWarp node with a single input, follow these steps:

1. Choose a source node whose output you wish to warp. With the source node selected, RMB+click and choose Transform → SplineWarp. By default, the Src (Source) input to the SplineWarp node is connected to the source node.

2. Open the SplineWarp node's properties panel (see Figure 10.32). Select the First Bezier Masks Deformation check box. In the viewer, Ctrl+Alt+click to draw a mask to isolate the area you wish to warp. Any area outside the mask will be unaffected by the SplineWarp node. To close the mask, RMB over a spline vertex and choose Open\/Close Curve.

Figure 10.31 *(Top) Destination grid (Bottom) Four frames of morph after the animation of the Distortion and Blend sliders. A sample Nuke script is included as* `gridwarp_morph.nk` *in the Tutorials folder on the DVD.*

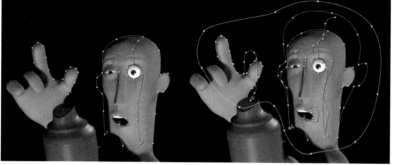

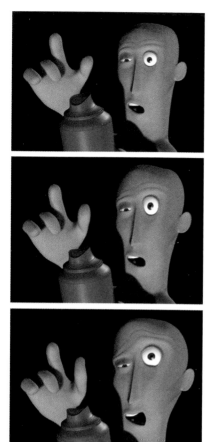

Figure 10.32 *(Top) SplineWarp node's properties panel (Bottom Left) Four pink source splines defining a thumb, finger, and features of face (Bottom Right) Green mask spline and purple destination splines*

3. Change the Show menu to Src (Source). Ctrl+Alt+ click to draw one or more splines in the viewer to define the specific feature or features that will be warped. As an option, you can close a spline by RMB+clicking over a spline vertex and choosing Open\/Close Curve. To move the selected vertex or vertex handle, LMB+drag. To view the mask spline and the source splines simultaneously, select the Show Both Curves check box. The source splines are rendered pink.

Figure 10.33 *Results of Distortion slider set to 0.2, 0.6, and 1.0. A sample Nuke script is included as* splinewarp.nk *in the Tutorials folder on the DVD.*

4. If the source input features footage that changes over time, animate the source splines so that they consistently match or follow the chosen feature. By default, the Autotkey check box is selected in the SplineWarp node's properties panel. Therefore, any change you make to a spline shape throughout the timeline is automatically keyed.

5. Change the Show menu to Dst. The mask spline is shown in green while the destination splines are shown in purple. Move the vertices of the destination splines to create the warp. To see the final deformation, change the Show menu to Blend. The warp updates as you move each vertex. To set the strength of the deformation, adjust the Distortion slider (see Figure 10.33). To dissolve between the undeformed and deformed version, adjust the Blend slider. You can animate the destination splines to alter the effect of the warp over time.

Morphing with SplineWarp

To use the SplineWarp node with two inputs to create a morph, follow these steps:

1. Connect the Src (Source) input of a SplineWarp node to the output of a node you wish to morph. Connect the Dst (Destination) input of the SplineWarp node to the output of a node that will serve as a destination. (In other words, the source image will become the destination image through the morph.) If the source and destination nodes are not the same resolution, you will need to feed them through Reformat nodes first. Connect a viewer to the SplineWarp node.

2. Open the SplineWarp node's properties panel. Select the First Bezier Masks Deformation check box. In the viewer, Ctrl+Alt+click to draw a mask to isolate the area you wish to warp. Any area outside the mask will be unaffected by the SplineWarp node. To close the mask, RMB over a spline vertex and choose Open\/Close Curve.

3. Change the Show menu to Src (Source). Ctrl+Alt+click to draw a splines in the viewer to define the specific feature that will be morphed (see Figure 10.34). Change the Show menu to Dst (Destination). The destination input is shown. The destination splines are rendered purple. Move the vertices of the destination splines to outline specific features. For example, if the source splines outline the head of a character provided by the source input, outline the head of the corresponding character that's provided by the destination input.

4. If the source and/or target inputs feature footage that changes over time, animate the source and/or target splines so that they consistently match or follow the chosen feature. By default, the Autotkey check box is selected in the SplineWarp node's properties panel. Therefore, any change you make to a spline shape throughout the timeline is automatically keyed. You are also free to animate the mask spline.

5. To see the end effect of the morph, change the Show menu to Blend. Set the Distortion and Blend sliders to 1.0. To see the morph at half strength, set the Distortion and Blend sliders to 0.5. To animate the morph over time, animate the Distortion and Blend sliders changing from 0 to 1.0 or vice versa.

Figure 10.34 (Top) Source image with six source splines. (Center) Adjusted destination splines. The destination splines and mask spline are animated to match the changing target footage. (Bottom) Resulting morph with Distortion and Blend set to 0.5. A sample Nuke script is included as `splinewarp_morph.nk` *in the Tutorials folder on the DVD.*

Re-creating Optical Artifacts

Nuke includes seven nodes that re-create specific optical artifacts: LensDistortion, Glow, Flare, Glint, Sparkles, GodRays, and LightWrap.

Lens Distortion

With a LensDistortion node (in the Transform menu), you can create a spherical distortion. The Field Of View slider sets the degree of distortion. High values press the upper and lower edges of the input toward the center of frame. The Reverse check box, if selected, pushes the upper and lower edges of the input away from the center of frame. In both cases, there is no distortion applied to vertical elements of the input. That is, vertical elements are not given curvature. At the same time, there is no built-in means to reposition the center of the distortion. Since distortion always occurs from the exact center of frame, it's difficult to match the node's effect to plates that have been cropped or transformed so that the original framing no longer exists. That said, it is possible to use a Transform node to prescale and preposition the input before feeding it to the LensDistortion node.

Lens Flares, Glints, and Sparkles

The Flare, Glint, and Sparkles nodes are found in the Draw menu. The Flare node replicates a lens flare, but without the string of polygonal shapes extending to the frame edge (see Figure 10.35). By default, the flare is circular. You can give it a polygonal or starlike shape by increasing the Edge Flattening parameter. You can position the flare by interactively LMB+dragging the Position handle (a small dot with the word *Position*) in the viewer. The node provides parameters to adjust the brightness, size, rotation, number of rays, ray softness, and chroma shift. In addition, you can select different colors for the inner and outer rings.

As mentioned, glints and sparkles refer to temporary flashes of light. The Sparkles node differs from the Glint node, however, by placing a single star-shaped highlight over the input (see Figure 10.35). You can choose one of three styles through the Sparkle Type menu. If the menu is set to Rays, the highlight features thin, long rays. If the menu is set to Sparkles, the highlight is similar to a spark in that the rays are broken into short, irregular segments. If the menu is set to Fireworks, the rays are broken into segments; however, each segment is thicker near its end. The properties for the Sparkles node are straightforward and control the size, number of rays, color, and so on.

The Glint node reproduces the temporary nature of its optical namesake by placing a star-shaped highlight over the most intense pixels of an input (see Figure 10.36). The No. Of Rays, Length, and Odd Ray Length sliders control the density of the star rays, the size of each star ray, and the ray irregularity. The node places individual glints over pixels whose values exceed the Tolerance slider. For example, if Tolerance is set to 0.5, a glint is placed over every pixel with an RGB value above 0.5. By default, the Glint node interprets the input

Figure 10.35 A Flare and a Sparkles node are merged to create a more complex lens flare. A sample Nuke script is included as flare.nk *in the Tutorials folder on the DVD.*

as is. However, you can influence the Glint output by changing the Gamma, From Color, and To Color sliders. Gamma discretely applies a gamma curve to the input before applying the glint effect. Higher Gamma values increase the brightness of individual glints. The From Color slider tints the input through multiplication before applying the glint effect. If the

From Color is set to a non-white color, the glint rays take on the same color. The To Color slider, on the other hand, tints the input through multiplication *after* applying the glint effect. The To Color slider also affects the color of the rays, but the saturation is more intense and the rays become more opaque. The overall quality of the glint render is determined by the Steps parameter: the higher the Steps value, the smoother the result.

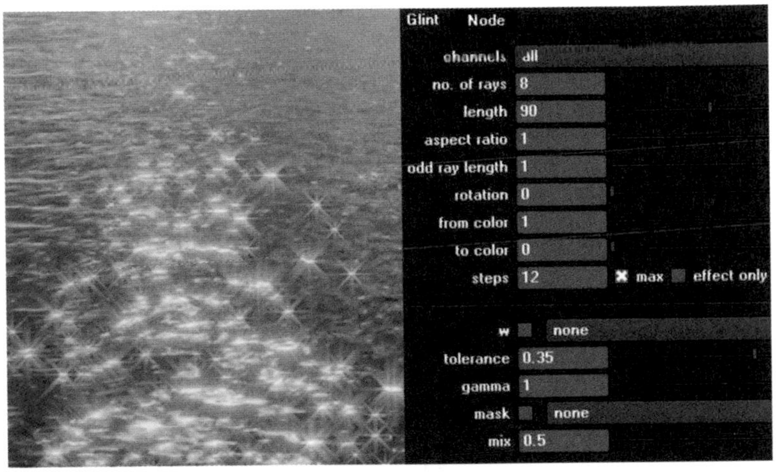

By default, The Glint node applies glints to the entire input. However, you can control its output by masking it. You can connect a mask node, such as a Bezier, to the node's Mask input. You can also use matte information, contained within the input, by choosing a channel from the W channel menu and selecting the W check box. If you prefer to merge the effect outside of the Glint node, select the Effect Only check box.

Figure 10.36 (Left) The Glint effect creates numerous star-shaped flares. (Center) Glint node settings. A sample Nuke script is included as `glint.nk` *in the Tutorials folder.*

God Rays and Glow

The GodRays node (in the Filter menu) shares many of the same attributes as the Glint node. However, GodRays creates its namesake light streaks by averaging together multiple, offset copies of the input (see Figure 10.37). The Center property determines the origin of the rays and may be interactively positioned in the viewer. The Steps property determines the smoothness of the averaging and must be set high to avoid pixelization. The GodRays node offers an additional means to create the illusion of motion blur for an input. As such, the Translate, Rotation, and Scale properties are included so that the "motion blur" streak can be adjusted.

The Glow node (in the Filter menu) creates atmospheric glow (see Figure 10.37). This is achieved by color adjusting and blurring a portion of the input based on a value threshold and adding the result to the unaffected input. The Tolerance slider sets the threshold below which no glow

Figure 10.37 (Top) Light streaks created by the GodRays node (Bottom) The same input with the Glow node applied. A sample script is included as `godrays_glow.nk` *in the Tutorials folder.*

occurs. For example, if Tolerance is set to 0.5, pixels with a value below 0.5 are clipped and are not used as a source of the glow. The Filter and Quality parameters are identical to the Blur node. You can adjust the saturation and brightness of the resulting glow through the sliders of the same name. The Tint cell allows the glow to be tinted a specific color. The Glow node carries a Width property, which functions in the same manner as the W property of the Glint node (see the previous section).

LightWrap

The LightWrap node accepts two inputs. Input A is designed for the element that requires the light wrap. Input B is designed for the background plate. The node cuts a thin sliver from the background, blurs it, and places it on top of the A input. The sliver is cut along any detected edges of input A's alpha matte. The thickness and opacity of the light wrap sliver is determined by the node's Intensity slider (see Figure 10.38). The higher the Intensity value, the thicker and more opaque the resulting sliver. The softness of the sliver's edge is controlled by the Diffuse slider. You can increase the background blur, as it appears in the sliver, by raising the BGBlur slider. In contrast, the FGBlur slider blurs the alpha matte of the light wrap sliver. High FGBlur values cause the light wrap effect to penetrate further into the object. In addition to blurring, you can color-balance the background input by adjusting the Saturation slider or adjusting the long list of standard color correction parameters provided by the node's CCorrect tab.

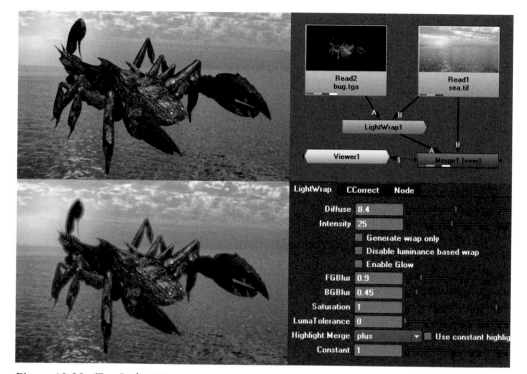

Figure 10.38 (Top Left) CG creature merged over ocean plate (Top Right) Node network (Bottom Left) LightWrap node applied to CG render. Note the softening of the edge, particularly around the tail. (Bottom Right) Matching LightWrap settings. A sample Nuke script is included as `ligthwrap.nk` in the Tutorials folder on the DVD.

You can choose different blending modes for the light wrap sliver by changing the Highlight Merge menu. You can forgo blending the background input by selecting the Use Constant Highlight check box. In this case, the color of the light wrap is taken from the Constant color parameter. You can force the node to output only the light wrap by selecting the Generate Wrap Only check box.

Painting in Nuke

With the Paint node (in the Draw menu), you can touch up and repair an input. To apply the node, follow these steps:

1. Select the node that you wish to paint, RMB+click, and choose Draw → Paint. Open the Paint1 node's properties panel. The various provided paint modes are listed at the top left (see Figure 10.39). Select the Freehand Paint brush. Set the Brush Size, Brush Hardness, and Opacity parameters in the Selection section. To select a specific brush color, change the Source menu to Color. You can enter values into the Color R, G, and B cells, use the Color Sliders button, or sample the viewer by activating the eyedropper button.

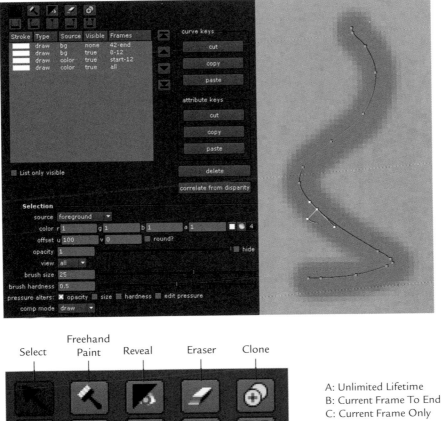

Figure 10.39 (Top Left) The Paint node's properties panel. Four strokes are listed in the stroke window. (Top Right) Close-up of painted stroke in viewer showing path and one selected vertex with tangent handle (Bottom) Paint modes and "lifetime" buttons

2. To paint a stroke, LMB+drag in the viewer. When you release the mouse button, the stroke is ended. A path in the viewer represents the stroke. In addition, the path is listed in the large stroke window in the properties panel. You can select a stroke by highlighting the stroke name in the stroke window or by using the Select tool in the viewer. Once a stroke is selected, you can move it by selecting all the path vertices and using the transform handle. You can also select individual path vertices and reposition them or manipulate their tangent handles. You can delete selected vertices by pressing the Delete key. You can delete the entire path by clicking the Delete button in the properties panel.

3. To erase a painted stroke, select the Eraser brush and LMB+drag in the viewer. The erased stroke cuts a hole into paint strokes but doesn't affect the original input.

4. To clone the input, select the Clone brush. The mouse pointer becomes two circles (see Figure 10.40). The circle with the crosshair defines the clone source. The empty circle defines the paintbrush. By default, the clone source circle is a fixed distance from the paintbrush circle. You can change this by positioning the brush circle over the area you wish to sample and Ctrl+clicking. When you click Ctrl, the clone source circle is repositioned under the brush circle. As you Ctrl+drag, the brush circle is once again distanced from the clone source circle. When you release the mouse button, the distance becomes fixed. Once you've sampled an area, you can LMB+drag to paint a stroke.

Figure 10.40 *The Clone brush in the viewer. The crosshair circle establishes the clone source.*

By default, each stroke lasts the entire timeline. However, you can change this behavior by selecting one of the "lifetime" buttons *before* painting the stroke (see Figure 10.39 earlier in this section). You have the option to change each stroke's blending method by selecting a stroke and changing the Comp Mode menu to Luma, Chroma, or Alpha. Each stroke shape is automatically animated. If you move the timeline to a different frame, transform vertices, or adjust tangent handles, the stroke is automatically keyframed and the keys are indicated by cyan highlights on the timeline. Unfortunately, you can't edit the keys in the Curve Editor. However, you can remove a keyframe by moving to the appropriate frame number and clicking the Cut button in the Curve Keys section of the properties panel.

When you paint with the Freehand Paint brush, the brush lays down a color defined by the Source parameter. However, by changing the Source menu from Color to Foreground, Background1, Background2, or Background3, you can select pixel values from other inputs. Thus, you can "paint through" a virtual stack of images. This is often useful when cleaning up a plate by sampling a cleaner version. You can even paint "across time" by offsetting the source through its Read node. For example, in Figure 10.41, a heavy scratch appears across the face of an actor in a vintage film. The footage is loaded into the Read1 node, which is connected to the unlabeled Fg input of the Paint1 node. The same footage is loaded into the Read2 node, which is connected to the Bg input. However, the Read2 node's Frame cell is set to frame−2. The Frame cell accepts expressions to offset the footage. Thus Read2 displays its footage two frames earlier than the Read1 node. When the Freehand Paint brush is used with Source set to Background1, the brush samples pixels from Read2. Since the scratch only lasts a few frames, sampling the footage two frames earlier produces a scratch-free section of the man's face. To limit the effect of the paint stoke, the brush is given a duration of frames 12 to 14 through the Frame Range button of the Paint1 node. Note that the duration is based on the Nuke timeline and not the actual frame numbering of the footage. In this example, two additional strokes are painted above the man's head and on his cheek with the Clone brush and the Source menu set to Foreground.

Generating Text

With the Text node (in the Draw menu), typesetting becomes an easy process. The node supports the majority of TrueType (.ttf) and PostScript fonts found on the operating system. Size, Kerning (space between characters based on character pairs), Leading (space between lines of text), and Justify sliders are included in the Font section. You can type or paste text into the Message cell. The Message cell also supports Nuke scripting commands in brackets. Three sample commands follow:

> [frame] Prints the current frame number.
>
> [value root.name] Prints the current script name with path.
>
> [memory usage] Prints the current number of Kilobytes used.

For additional scripting examples, see Chapter 12, "Advanced Techniques."

AE and Nuke Tutorials

In this chapter, you'll have the chance to finish the Chapter 2 tutorial with the tiki statue by adding shadows and optical artifacts. In addition, you'll have the opportunity to repair footage using paint tools.

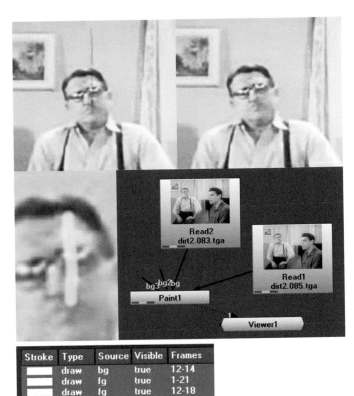

Stroke	Type	Source	Visible	Frames
	draw	bg	true	12-14
	draw	fg	true	1-21
	draw	fg	true	12-18

Figure 10.41 (Top Left) Scratched footage (Top Right) Footage after fix with Paint node (Center Left) Freehand Paint brush stroke shown over face (Center Right) Node network (Bottom) Strokes shown in Paint node properties panel. A sample Nuke script is included as paint_scratch.nk *in the Tutorials folder on the DVD.*

AE Tutorial 2 Revisited: Adding Shadows, Glow, and Text

In the Chapter 2 and 3 tutorials, you composited a tiki statue over a city background plate. There are several areas in which you can improve the composite. In particular, the addition of shadows will help tie all the elements together in a more believable fashion.

1. Reopen the completed After Effects project file for "AE Tutorial 2 Revisited: Refining Color and Edge Quality." The revisited version of Tutorial 2 is saved as ae2_step2.aep in the Chapter 3 Tutorials folder on the DVD. At this stage, the statue matches the background fairly well. However, the statue does not cast a shadow on the ground or nearby buildings.

2. Select the bg_plate.tif layer in the Comp 1 layer outline and choose Edit → Duplicate. The duplicate layer is placed above the original. With the new layer selected, choose Effect → Color Correction → Curves. In the Effect Controls panel, shape the curve to match Figure 10.42. With the Pen tool, draw a mask that will emulate a shadow cast on the ground and nearby buildings. Use Figure 10.42 as a reference. In the new layer's Mask 1 section of the layer outline, change Mask Feather to 150, 150.

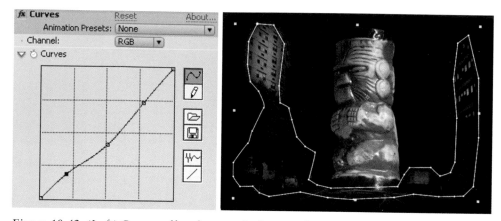

Figure 10.42 *(Left) Curves effect for cast shadow (Right) Masked shadow area*

3. To create a darker core shadow near the statue's base, make a second duplicate of the lowest `bg_plate.tif` layer. Place this duplicate just below the `effect.##.dpx` layer. With the new layer selected, choose Effect → Color Correction → Curves. In the Effect Controls panel, shape the curve to match Figure 10.43. With the Pen tool, draw a mask that will emulate a shadowed area at the base of the statue. Use Figure 10.43 as a reference. In the new layer's Mask 1 section of the layer outline, change Mask Feather to 35, 35.

4. At this point, the lower half of the statue is too bright for the shadowed street. Select the `greenscreen.cin` layer and choose Edit → Duplicate. Place the new layer at the highest level of the layer outline. When a layer is duplicated, all the effects assigned to the layer are copied. Hence, the newest layer is given a Curves and Hue/Saturation effect. In the Effect Controls panel, adjust the new layer's Curves effect to match Figure 10.44. Reduce the Hue/Saturation effect's Master Saturation value to −60. With the Pen tool, draw a mask that isolates the lower half of the statue. Use Figure 10.44 as a reference. Set the new layer's Mask Feather to 100, 100.

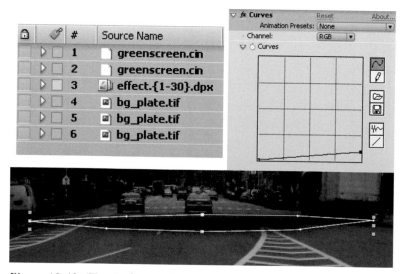

Figure 10.43 *(Top Left) Final Comp 1 layer outline (Top Right) Curves effect for core shadow (Bottom) Masked shadow core area*

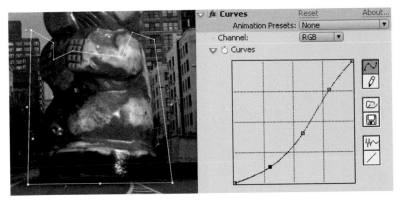

Figure 10.44 (Left) Masked bottom of statue (Right) Matching Curves effect

5. The base of the statue remains disconnected to the ground due to its different perspective. You can fix this with the Liquify effect. Choose New → New Composition. Match the settings of Comp 1. Name the new composition **Add Glow And Paint.** LMB+ drag Comp 1 from the Project panel to the layer outline of the new composition's tab in the Timeline panel. With the new layer selected, choose Effect → Distort → Liquify. In the Effect Controls panel, expand the Warp Tools Options section and set Brush Size to 6 and Brush Pressure to 100. Select the Warp mode icon (a hand pushing a line). In the viewer, use the brush to straighten the bottom of the statue so it better matches the plate perspective (see Figure 10.45).

6. The base of the statue retains two bright areas that don't match the lighting of the scene. One is a thin tan line that runs around the base edge and the other is a specular highlight. To remove these, you can use the Paint tool. Double-click the Comp 1 layer to open it in the Layer panel. Select the Paint tool at the top left of the program. In the Paint panel, set the Duration menu to Constant. In the viewer of the Layer panel, Alt+click to sample the dark brown of the statue base. Using the Brush Tip panel, set the brush diameter to 9. Paint a stroke to cover up the specular highlight. Open the Brush 1 section of the Comp 1 layer, expand the Stroke Options subsection, and set Opacity to 85%. This allows the specular highlight to show through subtly so that the base isn't too monochromatic. Alt+click to pick a

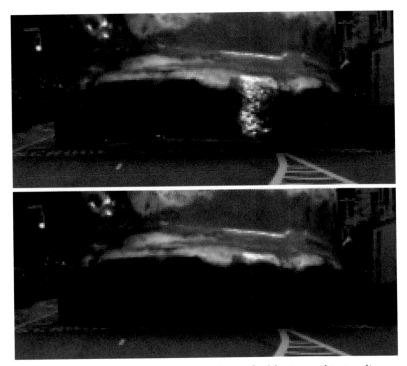

Figure 10.45 (Top) Base of statue with crooked bottom, thin tan line, and specular highlight (Bottom) Result of Liquify and Paint effects

darker color from the scene. You can sample the black tire of the nearby truck. Using the Brush Tip panel, set the brush diameter to 4. Paint a thin stroke along the base of the statue to cover the thin tan line. Switch to the Composition panel to see the end result (see Figure 10.45).

7. LMB+drag a second copy of Comp 1 from the Project panel to the Comp 2 tab of the Timeline panel. With the new layer selected, choose Effect → Color Correction → Brightness & Contrast. Set the Brightness slider to 50. This brightens up an otherwise fairly dull image. Choose Effect → Blur & Sharpen → Gaussian Blur. Set the Bluriness slider to 15. This throws the layer severely out of focus. Change the layer's Opacity setting to 50%. Change the layer's blending mode to Screen. By brightening, blurring, and lowering the opacity of the top layer, you've created a simple glow effect. The glow brightens the scene and makes it less dim and dingy. To limit the glow to the sky, which would be the part of the frame most likely to produce a glow effect, draw a mask with the Pen tool. Use Figure 10.46 as a reference. Set Mask Feather to 250, 250.

Figure 10.46 *Masked layer with stylistic glow*

8. Choose New → New Composition. Match the settings of Comp 1. Name the new composition **Camera Move**. LMB+drag the Add Glow And Paint composition from the Project panel to the layer outline of the Camera Move tab. Move the timeline to frame 1. Toggle on the Stopwatch button beside the Scale property. A keyframe is placed on the timeline. Move the timeline to frame 30. Set Scale to 103%, 103%. This creates a slow "zoom" into the scene. With the Add Glow And Paint layer selected, choose Effect → Distort → Optics Compensation. Move the timeline to frame 1. In the Effect Controls panel, toggle on the Stopwatch button beside the Field Of View (FOV) property. A keyframe is added to the timeline with a value of 0. Move the timeline to frame 30. Set Field Of View (FOV) to 35. Select the Reverse Lens Distortion check box. This adds an inverted spherical distortion to the layer. Because Field Of View (FOV) is animated over time, it creates the illusion of parallax. Although more accurate parallax can be created using a 3D camera and cards,

the Optics Composition effect is sufficient for a short shot. (For more information on 2.5D techniques, see Chapter 11, "Working with 2.5D and 3D.") Note that the Optics Composition effect does soften the image when the Field Of View (FOV) value is high. Thus the effect should be used with caution.

Tips & Tricks: Understanding Parallax

Parallax is the perceived displacement of an object between two lines of sight. Since humans possess binocular vision, parallax is an inherent part of human visual perception. The existence of parallax helps the human mind perceive depth and distance. Nearby objects possess a large parallax, as measured by the angle between each line of sight for each eye, and therefore appear "close."

9. Choose New → New Composition. Match the settings of Comp 1. Name the new composition **Add Text**. LMB+drag the Camera Move composition from the Project panel to the layer outline of the Add Text tab. Use the Horizontal Type tool to draw a text box in the viewer. Type **Tiki Daze** or another phrase of choice. In the Character panel, choose a font that fits the mood of the scene. Set the font size to 90 px (or similarly large size). The T icon just below the Font Style menu indicates the Font Size cell. In the Paragraph menu, select the Center Text button. Change the text fill color to a light tan through the Fill Color cell in the Character panel. Change the stroke color (the color of the font edges) to an orange brown through the Stroke Color cell in the Character panel. If the Fill Color cell covers the Stroke Color cell, click the Stroke Color cell to bring it to the top. Position the text roughly to match Figure 10.47.

Figure 10.47 Initial text placement

10. With the new text layer selected, choose Effect → Distort → Warp, Effect → Blur & Sharpen → Gaussian Blur, Effect → Stylize → Glow, and Effect → Color Correction → Levels. These effects will be used to add character to the otherwise plain text. In the Effect Controls panel, set the Warp effect's Bend slider to –20. This bends the text downward. However, the effect also stretches the text horizontally. Select the text box in the viewer and LMB+drag to rescale the text so that it once again fits the frame. Move the timeline to frame 1. Toggle on the Stopwatch button beside the Blurriness property of the Gaussian Blur effect. Set Blurriness to 12. Move the timeline to frame 6. Set Blurriness to 0.4. Move the timeline back to 1. Set the Glow effect's Glow Radius property to 20. Move the timeline to frame 6. Set Glow Radius to 60. Move the timeline to frame 10. Set Glow Radius to 20. Move the timeline back to 1. Set the text layer's Opacity property (in the Transform section of the layer outline) to 0%. Move the timeline to frame 6. Set the text layer's Opacity property to 100%. This series of steps causes the font to fade in with a glow that fades in and out.

11. Set the Levels effect's Output White property to 235. This guarantees that the text will not produce colors with values over 235, which is equivalent to 100 IRE for NTSC or ATSC broadcast TV. To make sure that the rest of the composite is broadcast safe, copy the Levels effect from the text layer to the Camera Move layer. Render a test movie through the Render Queue. The tutorial is complete (see Figure 10.48). A sample After Effects project is include as `ae2_final.aep` in the Tutorials folder on the DVD.

Figure 10.48 *The final composite*

Nuke Tutorial 2 Revisited: Adding Shadows, Glow, and Text

In the Chapter 2 and 3 tutorials, you composited a tiki statue over a city background plate. There are several areas in which you can improve the composite. In particular, the addition of shadows will help tie all the elements together in a more believable fashion.

1. Reopen the completed Nuke project file for "Nuke Tutorial 2 Revisited: Refining Color and Edge Quality." The revisited version of Tutorial 2 is saved as `nuke2_step2.aep` in the Chapter 3 Tutorials folder on the DVD. At this stage, the statue matches the background fairly well. However, the statue does not cast a shadow on the ground or nearby buildings.

2. Select the Merge2 node in the Node Graph, RMB+click, and choose Channel → Shuffle. This node is necessary to give the final output an opaque alpha channel. At present, the alpha channel contains an opaque statue and a transparent background plate. Open Shuffle1 node's properties panel. Select the 1 check box for outgoing alpha.

3. With the Shuffle1 node selected, RMB+click and choose Color → HueCorrect. With no nodes selected, RMB+click and choose Merge → Merge. Connect the HueCorrect2 node to input A of the Merge3 node. Connect the output of Shuffle1 to input B of

Merge3 (see Figure 10.49). Connect a viewer to Merge3. Open the HueCorrect2 node's properties panel. Highlight the word *lum* in the left column. Select all the luminance curve points and drag them down to a value of approximately 0.5. This darkens the entire plate. To isolate the darkness and have it emulate a shadow, create a mask. To do so, RMB+click with no nodes selected and choose Draw → Bezier. Rename the Bezier1 node **Shadow**. Connect the Shadow node to the Mask input of Merge3. Open the Shadow node's properties panel. Set the Extra Blur slider to 125. Ctrl+Alt+click in the viewer to draw the mask. Use Figure 10.49 as a reference.

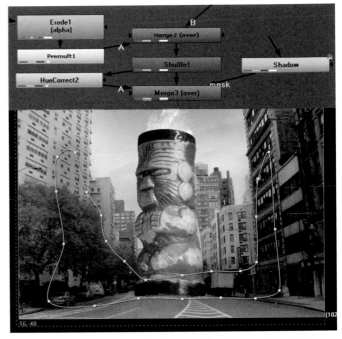

Figure 10.49 *(Top) Detail of network with new Shuffle1, HueCorrect2, Merge3, and Shadow (Bezier) nodes (Bottom) Mask drawn to create cast shadow*

4. To create a darker, core shadow near the statue's base, you can repeat the basic process of step 3. With the HueCorrect2 node selected, RMB+click and choose Color → HueCorrect. With no nodes selected, RMB+click and choose Merge → Merge. Connect the HueCorrect3 node to input A of the Merge4 node (see Figure 10.50). Connect the output of Merge3 to input B of Merge4. Connect a viewer to Merge4. Open the HueCorrect3 node's properties panel. Highlight the word *lum* in the left column. Select all the luminance curve points, and drag them down to a value of 0.2. This darkens the entire plate. To isolate the darkness and have it emulate a core shadow, create a mask. To do so, RMB+click with no nodes selected and choose Draw → Bezier. Rename the new Bezier node **CoreShadow**. Connect the CoreShadow node to the Mask input of Merge4. Open the Core-Shadow node's properties panel. Set the Extra Blur slider to 50 and the Falloff slider to 2. Ctrl+Alt+click in the viewer to draw the mask. Use Figure 10.50 as a reference.

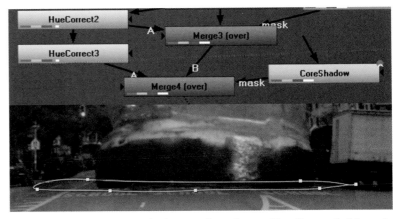

Figure 10.50 *(Top) Detail of network with new HueCorrect3, Merge4, and CoreShadow (Bezier) nodes (Bottom) Mask drawn to create core shadow*

5. At this point, the lower half of the statue is too bright for the shadowed street. Select the HueCorrect1 node. Choose Edit → Duplicate. Connect the output of Keyer1 to the input of the new HueCorrect4 node. With no nodes selected, RMB+click and choose Merge → Merge. Connect the output of HueCorrect4 to input A of Merge5. Disconnect the output of HueCorrect1 from the Erode1 node and connect it to input B of Merge5 instead. Use Figure 10.51 as a reference. Connect the output of Merge5 to Erode1.

With no nodes selected, RMB+click and choose Draw → Bezier. Rename the new Bezier node **LowerStatue**. Connect the LowerStatue node to the Mask input of Merge5. Open the LowerStatue node's properties panel. Set Extra Blur to 100. Ctrl+Alt+click in the viewer to draw a mask to isolate the lower portion of the statue. Open the HueCorrect4 node's properties panel. Highlight the word *lum* in the left column. Select all the luminance curve points and drag them down to a value of 0.25.

6. At this stage, the composite is fairly dull. To give the face of the statue and the fire more interesting contrast and brightness, isolate them and apply a Glow node. To do so, select the Merge4 node, RMB+click and choose Filter → Glow. With no nodes selected, RMB+click and choose Merge → Merge. Connect the output of Glow1 to input A of Merge6 (see Figure 10.52). Connect the output of Merge4 to input B of Merge6. Open the Glow1 node's properties panel. Set the Brightness slider to 0.6, the Saturation slider to 1.5, and the Size slider to 5. With no nodes selected, RMB+click and choose Draw → Bezier. Rename the new Bezier node **Sky**. Connect the Sky node to the Mask input of Glow1. Open the Sky node's properties panel. Set Extra Blur to 200. Ctrl+Alt+click in the viewer to draw a mask around the sky and head of the statue. Use Figure 10.52 as reference.

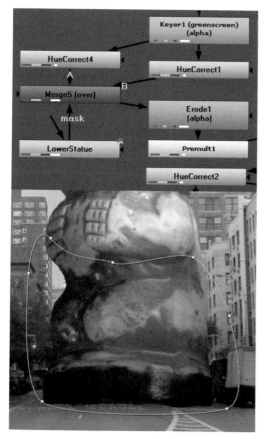

Figure 10.51 (Top) Detail of network with new HueCorrect4, Merge5, and LowerStatue (Bezier) nodes to create darker statue base (Bottom) Mask drawn to isolate base

Figure 10.52 (Top) Detail of network with new nodes to create glowing head and sky (Bottom) Mask drawn to isolate head and sky

7. Due to the way in which the statue was shot against a greenscreen, the base is not flat and does not match the perspective of the scene. In addition, the specular highlight along the base is too intense for the present lighting. To solve this, select the Merge6 node, RMB+click, and choose Draw → Paint. Paint several strokes to disguise the specular highlight and to straighten the base (see Figure 10.53). See the section "Painting in Nuke" earlier in this chapter for more information on using the Paint node.

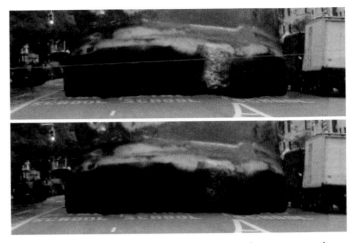

Figure 10.53 (Top) Crooked statue base and strong specular highlight (Bottom) Same area after the application of the Paint node

8. Select the Paint1 node, RMB+click and choose Transform → Transform. Move the timeline to frame 1. Open the Transform1 node's properties panel. Click the Animation button beside the Scale parameter and choose Set Key. Move the timeline to frame 30. Change the Scale slider to 1.03. This creates a subtle, artificial zoom. Select the Transform1 node, RMB+click, and choose Transform → LensDistortion. Open the PerspDistort1 node's properties panel. Move the timeline to frame 1. Set the Field Of View slider to 0. Click the Animation button beside the Field Of View parameter and choose Set Key. Move the timeline to frame 30. Set Field of View to 20. Select the Reverse check box. The LensDistortion node creates an inverted spherical distortion during the artificial zoom. Because Field Of View is animated over time, it creates the illusion of parallax. Although more accurate parallax shift can be created using a 3D camera and cards, the effect is sufficient for a short shot. (For more information on 2.5D techniques, see Chapter 11, "Working with 2.5D and 3D.") Note that the LensDistortion effect may soften the image when the Field Of View value is high. Thus the effect should be used with caution.

9. With no nodes selected, RMB+click and choose Draw → Text. Open the Text1 node's properties panel. Select a font of your choice. Type **TIKI DAZE** into the Message box. Set the Size slider to 600. With the Text1 node selected, RMB+click and choose Filter → Glow. Open the Glow2 node's properties panel. Set the Brightness slider to 1.45. With the Glow2 node selected, RMB+click and choose Merge → Merge. Connect the PerspDistort1 node to input B of Merge7 (see Figure 10.54). Connect a viewer to Merge7.

Figure 10.54 (Left) End of node network (Right) The final composite

10. Reopen the Text1 node's properties panel. Interactively position the text in the viewer to match Figure 10.54. Open the Merge7 properties panel. Move the timeline to frame1. Set the Mix slider to 0. Click the Animation button beside the Mix parameter and choose Set Key. Move the timeline to frame 6. Set the Mix slider to 1.0. This fades in the text. Reopen the Glow2 node's properties panel. Move the timeline to frame 1. Set the Size slider to 50. Click the Animation button beside the Size parameter and choose Set Key. Move the timeline to frame 6. Set the Size slider to 100. Move the timeline to Frame 10. Set the Size slider to 75. This increases, then decreases, the spread and intensity of the glow as the text fades in.

11. With the Merge7 node selected, choose Render → Flipbook Selected to create a test render. If you're satisfied with the settings, the tutorial is complete (see Figure 10.54). A sample Nuke script is included as nuke2_final.nk in the Tutorials folder on the DVD.

Interview: Aron Baxter, Guava / Nice Shoes, New York City

Aron Baxter graduated with a degree in graphic design from Ravensbourne College of Design and Communication in London. He joined the Moving Picture Company, where he learned compositing on Quantel Henry, HAL, and Harry systems. In 2003, he joined Nice Shoes as a senior VFX artist. He later moved to Guava to serve as a VFX supervisor. Shortly

Aron Baxter by his Flame station at the Guava facility

after the interview for this book, Aron returned to Nice Shoes as creative director. His credits include commercials for Nike, Castrol, Fiat, BBC, and Volvo. His feature credits include *The Borrowers* and *GoldenEye*.

Nice Shoes serves as New York's largest provider of postproduction services for the advertising industry, offering high-end visual effects work as well as color-grading services. Founded in 1996, Nice Shoes has a client roster that includes such companies as IBM, Maybelline, VH1, Kodak, GMC, and Calvin Klein. In 2001 and 2002, Nice Shoes formed two sister companies: Freestyle Collective and Guava. Guava served as a boutique house specializing in visual effects design and supervision for effects-driven commercials. At the time of this writing, the artists working at Guava have rejoined Nice Shoes and Guava no longer operates as an independent company.

(Nice Shoes uses Flame, Inferno, Nuke, and After Effects.)

LL: Outside the compositor, what programs do you use to generate text?

AB: Photoshop, Illustrator, Fontographer....

LL: You practice calligraphy. Are you able to use that skill?

AB: With all this technology, I very much want to keep my feet on the ground, so whenever there's any sort of text involved, I [try to] hand-draw, then scan [the text]. The interesting aspect of that type of work lies in the imperfections, or the differences, or the nuances, or the subtleties from character to character rather than just using a straight font, where all the *T*s are exactly the same.... We can still turn a hand-drawn font into a usable file format, [whether] it's a 2D spline or 3D geometry (such as an OBJ file).

LL: Are there any advantages to premade fonts?

AB: There are so many fonts out there.... [However,] whenever you download a free font or buy a particular font, you do see the repetitive nature. Whenever we do handwriting, every time we write a letter, it's different....

LL: When you serve as the VFX supervisor on a commercial spot, do you have a chance to sit down and composite?

AB: How would I describe myself? A visual effects artist or a visual effects supervisor? When [I supervise] a project, I'll sometimes comp in After Effects or Nuke or Flame. [Supervisors should] know what's going on in the [compositing] packages so that they have an understanding and can oversee the team that's working on [the project].

LL: You've worked as a compositor for over 15 years. That's a long time....

AB: When I started compositing, there weren't many people doing [it]. And now, [the industry] is flooded with compositors. But it's the people who do the imaginative work, who are doing their very best, that are lauded. There are people in this industry who are visible who can serve as inspirations or role models.

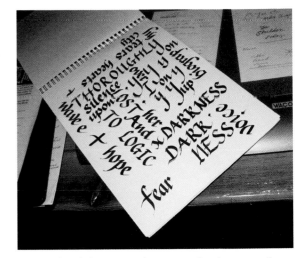

A sample of the original typography Aron employs on his projects

Additional Resources: The Full Interview

To read the full interview with Aron Baxter, see the Interviews folder on the DVD.

eleven

Working with 2.5D and 3D

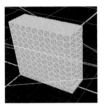

2D compositing is limited by *its lack of depth.*

That is, the virtual camera can move in the X or Y direction but not along the z-axis. You can add the third dimension, however, by creating a 3D camera. In that case, 2D layers and outputs may be arranged in 3D space. This combination of 2D and 3D is often referred to as 2½D or 2.5D. Both After Effects and Nuke support 2.5D workflows by making 3D cameras, lights, and materials available. Nuke goes so far as to add a complete set of shaders and geometry manipulation tools. With this chapter, you'll have the chance to set up a 2.5D environment complete with cameras, lights, materials, and texture projections.

2D vs. 2.5D vs. 3D

By default, compositing programs operate in a 2D world. Layers and outputs of nodes are limited to two dimensions: X and Y. The ability of one layer or output to occlude another is based upon the transparency information of its alpha channel.

Compositing programs offer the ability to add the third dimension, Z, by creating or adding a 3D camera. The layers or outputs remain 2D, but they are viewable in 3D space. When a 2D image is applied to a plane and arranged in 3D space, it's commonly referred to as a *card*. Cards display all the perspective traits of 2D objects in 3D space (diminishing size with distance, parallel edges moving toward a vanishing point, and so on). Thus, once a card is in use, the compositing has entered 2.5D space. 2.5D, or 2½D, is a name applied to a composite that is not strictly 2D or 3D but contains traits of both. 2.5D may encompass the following variations:

- 2D layers stacked and offset (*multiplaning*)
- 2D cards arranged in 3D camera space
- 2D images projected on 3D geometry in 3D space
- Combinations of all of the above

The ultimate goal of a 2.5D scene is to create the illusion of three-dimensional depth without the cost. The earliest form of 2.5D may be found in the multiplaning techniques developed by the pioneering animators at Fleischer Studios. With multiplaning, individual animation cels are arranged on separated panes of glass. (*Cel* is short for celluloid, which is a transparent sheet on which animators ink and paint their drawings.) The panes are positioned in depth below or in front of the camera. The cels are then animated moving at slightly different speeds. For example, a foreground cel is moved quickly from left to right, while the mid-ground cel is moved more slowly from left to right; the background painting of a distant landscape or sky is left static. The variation in speed creates the illusion of parallax shift. (See Chapter 10, "Warps, Optical Artifacts, Paint, and Text," for more information on parallax.) In addition, the assignment of cels to different glass panes allows the foreground cel to be out of focus. The combination of parallax approximation and real-world depth of field imparts a sense of three-dimensional depth to otherwise flat drawings.

Multiplaning in the Composite

You can replicate the multiplaning technique in a compositing program. For example, in Figure 11.1, a foreground layer, two mid-ground layers, and a background layer are arranged in After Effects. The foreground layer is blurred slightly and animated moving left to right. The mid-ground layers are animated moving more slowly in the same direction. The background layer is left static. In this example, the four layers were derived from a single digital photograph. Each layer was prepped in Photoshop and masked inside After Effects.

Using 2D Cards and 3D Projections

Although often successful, multiplaning is limited by the inability to move the camera off axis. That is, the camera must always point straight down the z-axis. Panning, tilting, or aggressively moving the camera about in 3D space will ruin the illusion of depth. However, if each layer of the multiplane is converted to a card and arranged in 3D space, the limitations are reduced. Using 2D cards in a 3D space is a common technique for visual effects work and is often employed to give depth to matte paintings and other static 2D backgrounds.

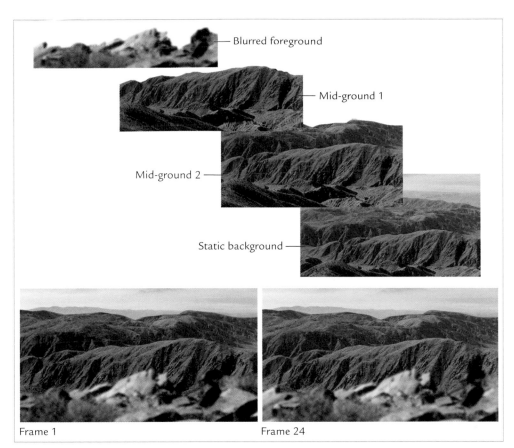

Figure 11.1 (Top) Four layers used to create multiplaning (Bottom Left) Resulting composite at frame 1 (Bottom Right) Resulting composite at frame 24. Note the shift in parallax. The foreground rocks are at a different position relative to the background. A sample After Effects project is included as `multiplane .aep` in the Tutorials folder on the DVD.

For example, in Figure 11.2, cards are arranged to create a hallway. With this example, a single photo of a real hall is cut apart to create texture maps for each card. The gaps are only temporary; the final arrangement allows the cards to touch or slightly intersect. (See the After Effects tutorial at the end of this chapter for a demonstration of this technique.)

The use of cards in 3D space allows for greater movement of the camera. However, restrictions remain because excessive transforms in the X, Y, or Z direction will ruin the illusion. One way to reduce the limitations of cards is to project 2D images onto simple 3D geometry (see Figure 11.3). (See the Nuke tutorial at the end of this chapter for a demonstration of this technique.) The geometry may be imported from a 3D program, such as Maya, or may be constructed from 3D primitives provided by the compositing program (an ability of

Figure 11.2 Seven cards arranged to create a hallway

Flame, Inferno, and Nuke, for example). If physical measurements or laser scan information is collected from a live-action shoot, a location or set can be replicated as 3D geometry in exacting detail. In addition, such detailed information often includes the relative positions of the real-world camera and the real-world lights used to illuminate the scene. If the only reference available to the modeler is the captured film or video footage, the geometry may only be a rough approximation.

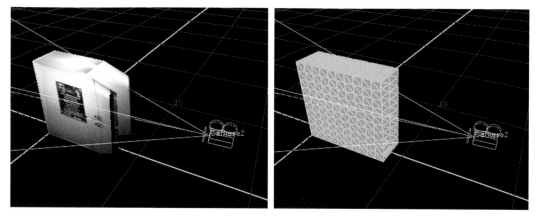

Figure 11.3 *(Left) Image projected onto geometry through camera (Right) Wireframe of imported geometry*

Ultimately, projections suffer the same limitations as the other 2.5D techniques. If the camera is moved too aggressively, the limited resolution of the projected image or the geometry itself may be revealed.

Once again, it's important to remember that the goal of a 2.5D scene is to create the illusion of three-dimensional depth without the necessity of rendering all the elements in 3D. Hence, in many situations, 2.5D techniques are perfectly acceptable when you're faced with scheduling and budgeting limitations. When successfully employed, 2.5D is indistinguishable from 3D to the average viewer.

Industry Perspective: 3D vs. 3-D

As a term, *3D* has developed multiple connotations. It is often used to describe computer animation created by programs such as Maya, 3ds Max, and Softimage. At the same time, such animation is often referred to as *CG* (computer graphics) or *CGI* (computer-generated imagery). This book, for example, refers to all renders created by 3D programs as CG. In the realm of compositing, *3D* refers to a 3D camera that is able to view 2D layers or 3D geometry within a three-dimensional space with an x-, y-, and z-axis. To confuse matters somewhat, *3D* is used to describe stereoscopic projects. Those working closely with stereoscopic technology, however, generally prefer the term *stereoscopic 3-D*, or *stereo 3-D* (note the hyphen). *Stereoscopy* is any technique that creates the illusion of depth through the capture of two slightly different views that replicate human binocular vision. Stereoscopic 3-D, as it applies to compositing, is discussed in detail in Chapter 12, "Advanced Techniques."

Compositing 2.5D and 3D

After Effects and Nuke support 3D cameras, lights, and materials, allowing for the set up of 2.5D scenes.

2.5D and 3D in AE

After Effects supplies several means by which to convert a 2D layer into a 3D layer, thus making it a card. In addition, the program provides 3D cameras and 3D lights that let you work with a full 3D environment.

3D Layers and Cameras

As described in Chapter 5, "Transformations and Keyframing," you can convert any After Effects layer into a 3D layer. You can do so by toggling on the 3D Layer switch for a layer in the layer outline or choosing Layer → 3D Layer. Once the layer is converted to 3D, you are free to transform, scale, or rotate the layer in the X, Y, or Z direction. However, the virtual camera used to view the 3D layer remains fixed. You can create a 3D camera, however, by following these steps:

1. Create a composition with at least one layer. Select the layer and choose Layer → 3D Layer. The 3D transform handle appears in the viewer. A 3D camera is functional only if a 3D layer exists.

2. Choose Layer → New → Camera. The Camera Settings dialog box opens (see Figure 11.4). Choose a lens size from the Preset menu. The lenses are measured in millimeters and are roughly equivalent to real-world lenses. Click the OK button.

3. A new 3D camera is created and is named Camera 1. The camera receives its own layer in the layer outline. However, the camera is not immediately visible in the viewer. The Composition panel, by default, shows a single view through a single viewer. You can switch to other views by changing the Select View Layout menu from 1 View to 4 Views (see Figure 11.5). The 4 Views option displays four views that cor-

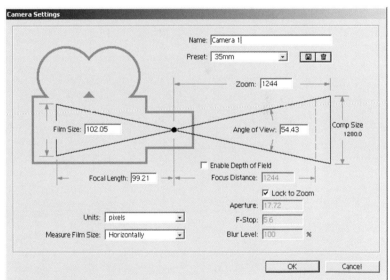

Figure 11.4 The Camera Settings dialog box

respond to top (XZ), front (XY), and right (XZ) cameras, plus the active perspective camera. Note that you can change a view by selecting the corresponding viewer frame (so that its corners turn yellow) and changing the 3D View Popup menu to the camera of your choice (see Figure 11.5). In addition, you can change the Magnification Ratio Popup menu for the selected view without affecting the other views.

4. You can translate the 3D camera by interactively LMB+dragging the camera body icon or camera point-of-interest icon in a viewer (see Figure 11.6). (The camera layer

must be selected in the layer outline for the camera icons to be fully visible.) You can rotate the selected camera by interactively using the Rotate tool (see Figure 11.5). You can also adjust and keyframe the camera's Point Of Interest, Position, Orientation, and Rotation properties through the camera layer's Transform section in the layer outline.

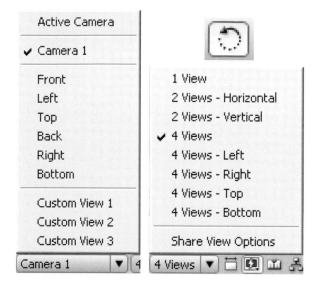

Figure 11.5 *(Left) 3D View Popup menu (Top Right) Rotate tool (Bottom Right) Select View Layout menu*

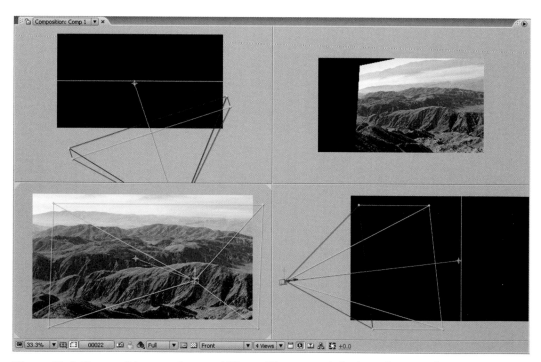

Figure 11.6 *Composition panel set to 4 Views. The camera's body and point-of-interest icons are visible. Note that the yellow corners of the front view indicate that a particular viewer is selected.*

If you need to reframe a view, select the Orbit Camera, Track XY Camera, or Track Z Camera tool and LMB+drag in the corresponding viewer (see Figure 11.7). Orbit Camera rotates the 3D camera around the camera's point of interest. (You can only use the Orbit Camera tool in a perspective view.) Track XY Camera scrolls the view left/right or up/down. Track Z Camera zooms in or out.

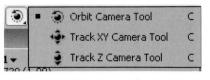

Figure 11.7 Camera tools menu

Tips & Tricks: Orientation vs. Rotation

In After Effects, the Orientation and Rotation properties are easily confused. Both properties rotate a 3D layer or 3D camera and have X, Y, and Z channels. However, an Orientation channel resets itself to 0° when it surpasses 359°. When a Rotation channel surpasses 359°, it counts the number of revolutions with the *n*× prefix. Hence, you can keyframe, and keep track of, multiple revolutions with the Rotation property. When you interactively rotate a 3D layer or 3D camera in a viewer, however, the Orientation values are altered and the Rotation values remain unaffected.

Importing Maya Camera Data

After Effects is able to import camera data from a Maya scene file. However, special steps must be taken to ensure the successful importation. The steps include:

1. In Maya, create a non-default perspective camera. Animate the camera. Delete any static animation channels. Bake the animation channels by using the Bake Simulation tool. Baking the channels places a keyframe at every frame of the timeline.

2. In Maya, set the render resolution to a size you wish to work with in After Effects. It's best to work with a square-pixel resolution, such as 1280×720. Export the camera into its own Maya ASCII (.ma) scene file. A sample scene file is included as camera.ma in the Footage folder on the DVD.

3. In After Effects, import the Maya ASCII file through File → Import. The camera data is brought in as its own camera layer in a new composition. The Position and XYZ Rotation properties of the layer are automatically keyframed to maintain the animation. The Zoom property is set to match the focal length of the Maya camera.

4. To look through the imported camera, set the 3D View Popup menu to the new camera name. If need be, add a 3D layer to the composition. To see the camera icon in motion, change the Select View Layout menu to 4 View and play the timeline.

If the camera is at 0, 0, 0 in Maya world space, it will appear at the top-left edge of the After Effects viewer when the view is set to Front or Top. Hence, it may be necessary to correct the imported camera animation by editing the keyframes in the Graph Editor or parenting the camera layer to a layer with offset animation.

After Effects also supports the importation of Maya locators (null objects that carry transformations). For more information, see the "Baking and Importing Maya Data" page in the After Effects help files.

3D Depth of Field

3D cameras in After Effects carry built-in depth of field. To activate this feature, toggle on the Depth Of Field property in the layer outline. The Focus Distance property, which is measured in pixels, sets the center of the focal region. The Focal Distance plane is represented as a subdivision in the camera icon's frustum, which is the pyramidal shape representing the camera's field of view (see Figure 11.8). The Aperture property establishes the camera's virtual iris size and f-stop. Higher Aperture values widen the iris and reduce the f-stop, thus leading to a narrower depth of field. The Blur Level property sets the degree of blurriness for regions outside the focal region. To reduce the strength of the blur, reduce the Blur Level value. The F-Stop property is accessible through the Layer → Camera Settings dialog box. If you manually change the F-Stop value, the Aperture value automatically updates.

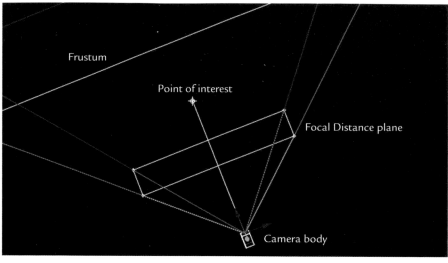

Figure 11.8 Close-up of camera

Arranging 3D Layers

A single composite can carry multiple 3D layers and cameras. Here are a few guidelines to keep in mind:

- If you create a new layer by LMB+dragging footage from the Project panel to the layer outline, the new layer will remain a 2D layer. In fact, it will appear in every view as if fixed to the camera of that view. Once you convert it to a 3D layer, however, it will appear in the 3D space as a card.
- To move a 3D layer, select the layer in the layer outline and interactively LMB+drag the corresponding card in a viewer. You can also adjust the layer's Transform properties, which include Position, Scale, Orientation, and Rotation.
- 3D layers support alpha channels. Shadows cast by the 3D layers accurately integrate the transparency.
- A quick way to open the Camera Setting dialog box is to double-click the camera layer name. By default, camera distance units are in pixels. However, you can change the Units menu to Inches or Millimeters if you are matching a real-world camera.
- You can activate motion blur for a 3D layer by toggling on the Motion Blur layer switch in the layer outline. By default, the blur will appear when the composite is rendered through the Render Queue. However, if you toggle on the Motion Blur composition switch (at the top of the Timeline panel), the blur will become visible in the viewer. The quality of the motion blur is set by the Samples Per Frame property, which is located in the Advanced tab of the Composition Settings dialog box. Higher values increase the quality but slow the viewer update. In contrast, the quality of motion

blur applied to non-3D compositions is determined by the Adaptive Sample Limit property (the number of samples varies by frame with the Adaptive Sample Limit setting the maximum number of samples).

- When you render through the Render Queue, the topmost camera layer in the layer outline is rendered. Camera layers at lower levels are ignored.

3D Materials and Lights

As soon as a layer is converted into a 3D layer, it receives a Material Options section in the layer outline. These options are designed for 3D lights. To create a light, follow these steps:

1. Select a layer and choose Layer → 3D Layer. The 3D transform handle appears in the viewer. A light is functional only if a 3D layer exists.
2. Choose Layer → New → Light. In the Light Settings dialog box, choose a light type and intensity and click the OK button. A new light is added to the composition and receives its own layer in the layer outline. A light illuminates the 3D layer. Areas outside the light throw are rendered black.
3. You can manipulate the light by interactively LMB+dragging the light body icon or light point-of-interest icon in a viewer. (The light layer must be selected in the layer outline for the light icons to be fully visible.) You can rotate the selected light by interactively using the Rotate tool. You can also adjust and keyframe the light's Point Of Interest, Position, Orientation, and Rotation properties through the Transform section of the layer outline.

You can readjust the light's basic properties by selecting the light layer and choosing Layer → Light Settings. There are four light types you can choose from:

Parallel creates parallel rays of light that replicate an infinitely far source. The icon is composed of a spherical origin and a line extending to the point of interest (see Figure 11.9). You must "aim" the light by rotating the origin or positioning the point of interest. The position of the entire light icon does not affect the light quality. Direct lights are appropriate for emulating the sun or moon.

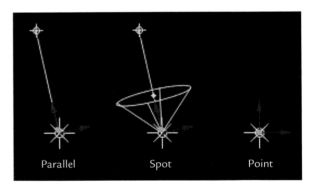

Spot creates a classic spot light with a light origin and cone. The origin is represented by a small sphere (see Figure 11.9). By default, the edge of the cone produces a hard, circular falloff. You can adjust the cone through the light's Cone Angle and Cone Feather properties.

Figure 11.9 Three light types that produce icons in the viewer

Point creates an omni-directional light emanating from the center of its spherical icon (see Figure 11.9). Point lights are equivalent to incandescent light bulbs. Point lights have a Position property but no point of interest.

Ambient creates a light that reaches all points of the 3D environment equally. Hence, an ambient light does not produce an icon for the viewer and does not include a Transform section within its layer. Only two properties are available with this light type: Intensity and Color.

You can access the following properties through the Light Options section of the layer outline:

Intensity determines the brightness of the light.

Color tints the light.

Cone Angle and **Cone Feather** control the diameter and softness of light's cone if Light Type is set to Spot.

Casts Shadows allows cards to cast shadows onto other cards if toggled on (see Figure 11.10).

Shadow Darkness sets the opacity of the cast shadows.

Shadow Diffusion sets the edge softness of the cast shadows. High values slow the composite significantly.

Once a light exists, the properties within the Material Options section of the 3D layer take effect. A list of the Material Options properties follows:

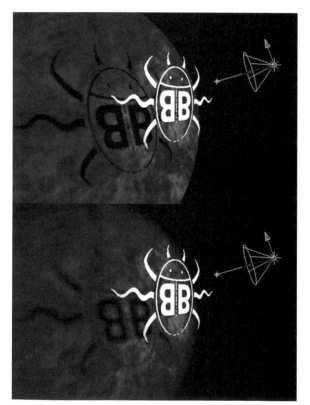

Figure 11.10 (Top) A spot light casts a shadow onto a 3D layer with a red abstract image. A second 3D layer, with the bug logo, carries transparency through an alpha channel. The light's Cone Feather and Shadow Diffusion are set to 0. (Bottom) Same setup with Cone Feather set to 35% and Shadow Diffusion set to 15. A sample After Effects project is included as shadow.aep *in the Tutorials folder on the DVD.*

Casts Shadows determines whether the 3D layer casts shadows onto other 3D layers. If Casts Shadows is set to Only, the layer is hidden while the shadow is rendered.

Light Transmission, when raised above 0%, emulates light scatter or translucence whereby light penetrates and passes through the 3D layer (see Figure 11.11).

Accepts Shadows determines whether the 3D layer will render shadows cast by other 3D layers.

Accepts Lights determines whether the 3D layer will react to 3D lights. If toggled off, the footage assigned to the layer is rendered with all its original intensity. Accepts Lights has no effect on whether the 3D layer receives shadows, however.

Diffuse represents the diffuse shading component—the lower the value, the less light is reflected toward the camera and the darker the 3D layer. (For more information on shading components, see Chapter 9, "Integrating Render Passes.")

Specular controls the specular intensity. The higher the value, the more intense the specular highlight (see Figure 11.12).

Shininess sets the size of the specular highlight. Higher values decrease the size of the highlight.

Metal controls the contribution of the layer color to the specular highlight color. If Metal is set to 100%, the specular color is derived from the layer color. If Metal is set to 0%, the specular color is derived from the light color. Other values mix the layer and light colors.

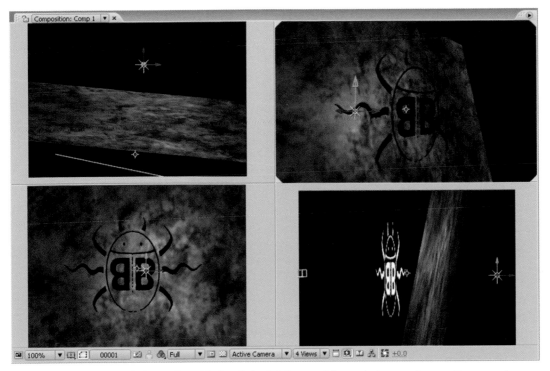

Figure 11.11 *A point light is placed behind the 3D layer with a red abstract image. Because the layer's Light Transmission property is set to 100%, the light penetrates the surface and reaches the camera. The 3D layer with the bug logo has a Light Transmission value of 0% and thus remains unlit from the front. A sample After Effects project is included as* transmission.aep *in the Tutorials folder on the DVD.*

Figure 11.12 *(Left) 3D layer lit by a point light. Diffuse, Specular, Shininess, and Metal properties are set to 100%. (Right) Same setup with Diffuse set to 70%, Specular set to 40%, Shininess set to 5%, and Metal set to 50%. A sample After Effects project is included as* specular.aep *in the Tutorials folder on the DVD.*

2.5D and 3D in Nuke

Nuke supplies a comprehensive 3D environment for working with cards, 3D cameras, 3D lights, and imported geometry. At its simplest, the 3D environment requires the following nodes to operate:

Camera creates a 3D camera and defines the 3D projection used by the renderer.

Card is a primitive plane that carries the 2D input.

Scene groups together 3D lights and geometry, such as planes created by Card nodes. This node is fed into the ScanlineRender node.

ScanlineRender provides a default renderer for use with the 3D environment. The 3D environment must be rendered out as a 2D image before it can be used as part of a non-3D node network.

Setting Up a 3D Environment

To set up a 3D environment, follow these steps:

1. In the Node Graph, RMB+click and choose Image → Read. Choose a file or image sequence through the Read node's properties panel. With the Read1 node selected, choose 3D → Geometry → Card. With the Card1 node selected, choose 3D → Scene.
2. With no nodes selected, chose 3D → Camera. With no nodes selected, choose 3D → ScanlineRender. Connect the Obj/Scn input of the ScanlineRender1 node to the Scene1 node. Use Figure 11.13 as a reference. Connect the Cam input of the Scanline-Render1 node to the Camera1 node. Connect a viewer to the ScanlineRender1 node.

Once you set up a 3D environment, you can view it with a standard viewer. To do so, change the View Selection menu, at the upper right of the Viewer pane, to 3D (see Figure 11.14). Because the camera and card are created at 0, 0, 0 in 3D world space, the card is not immediately visible. Change the Zoom menu, directly to the left of the View Selection menu, to Fit.

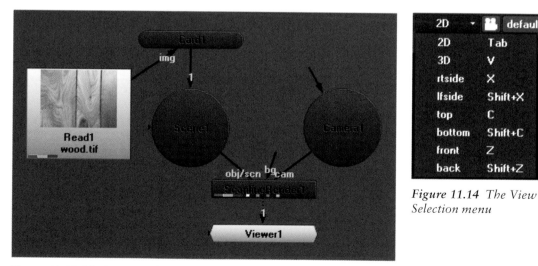

Figure 11.14 The View Selection menu

Figure 11.13 Node network of a 3D environment. A sample Nuke script is included as `simple_3D.nk` *in the Tutorials folder on the DVD.*

You can select specific orthographic views by changing the View Selection menu to Top, Bottom, Front, Back, Lfside, or Rtside. If you set the View Selection to 3D, you can orbit around the origin by Alt+RMB+dragging. You can scroll by Alt+LMB+dragging in any of the views. You can zoom by Alt+MMB+dragging in any of the views. To return the viewer to the point of view of the camera, change the View Selection menu back to 2D. (If the camera intersects the card, translate the camera backward.)

The 3D camera is represented by a standard icon that includes the camera body and frustum (pyramidal shape that represents the field of view). You can interactively move the camera in the viewer by selecting the Camera node or by clicking the camera icon (see Figure 11.15). Once the camera is selected, you can LMB+drag an axis handle that appears at the base of the lens. To rotate the camera, Ctrl+LMB+drag. (You must keep the properties panel open to manipulate the camera interactively.) In addition, the Camera node's properties panel contains a full set of transform parameters, which you can change by hand and animate via corresponding Animation buttons. You can change the camera's lens by entering a new Focal Length value in the Projection tab.

You can transform a Card node in the same manner as a Camera node. Once the Card node is selected, a transform handle appears at its center.

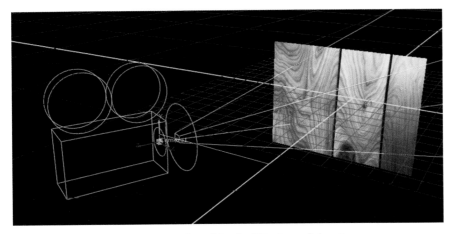

Figure 11.15 A camera icon and card in the 3D view of the viewer

Tips & Tricks: Camera Projections

By default, the Camera node functions as a virtual motion picture or video camera. Hence, objects are rendered with depth and perspective. However, you can alter this functionality by changing the Projection menu in the Perspective tab of the Camera node's properties panel. If you switch the menu to Orthographic, the scene is rendered with parallel projection and objects are flattened. If you switch the menu to Spherical, the entire 3D environment, in 360°, is rendered to a spherical environment map; such maps are useful for image-based lighting techniques and are discussed in Chapter 12, "Advanced Techniques." If you switch the menu to UV, each piece of geometry has its full UV texture space rendered. No part of the texture space is cropped or otherwise lost. For example, if a Sphere node has a Read node connected to its Img input, the UV mode of the camera will display the flattened UV texture space of the sphere with the Read node image laid out. Since lighting information is retained, this provides a convenient way to "cook" or "bake" a texture map.

Geometry Types, Group Nodes, and Constraints

A Card node is only one of four primitive geometry types available through the 3D → Geometry menu. Each type carries an Img input, which you can use to texture the geometry. However, each type treats the texture mapping in a different way:

Cube applies the Img input to each of its six sides.

Cylinder stretches the Img input as if it were a piece of paper rolled into a tube. By default, the cylinder has no caps. You can force a top or bottom cap by selecting the Close Top or Close Bottom check box in the node's properties panel. With caps, the top or bottom row of pixels is stretched to the center of the cap.

Sphere stretches the Img input across its surfaces, pinching the top and bottom edge of the image into points at the two poles.

If you create more than one piece of geometry, you must connect each piece to a Scene node, which in turn must be connected to a ScanlineRender node. The connections to a Scene node are numbered 1, 2, 3, and so on. If a piece of geometry is not connected to a Scene node, it remains visible in the 3D view of the viewer but will not appear in the 2D view of the viewer. Again, the 2D view, set by the View Selection menu, represents the view of the camera and the ultimate output of the ScanlineRender node.

You can interactively scale, rotate, or translate the geometry of a Cube, Card, Cylinder, or Sphere node. You can group multiple pieces of geometry together by connecting their outputs to a MergeGeo node (in the 3D → Modify menu). To transform the resulting group, connect the output of the MergeGeo node to a TransformGeo node (in the 3D → Modify menu). See Figure 11.16 for an example. When the TransformGeo node is selected, a single transform handle appears in the viewer. The TransformGeo node's properties panel contains all the standard transform parameters, which you can adjust and animate.

The TransformGeo node includes two inputs with which you can constrain the group: Look and Axis. You can connect the Look input to a geometry or light node. This forces the TransformGeo node always to point its local z-axis toward the connected object. You can also connect the Look input to a Camera or second TransformGeo node that is not part of the same node network. On the other hand, you can connect the Axis input to an Axis node. An Axis node (in the 3D menu) carries a transformation without any geometry. When an Axis node is connected to the Axis input, it serves as a parent node and the TransformGeo node inherits the transformations. If the Axis node is located a significant distance from the TransformGeo node, the geometry connected to the TransformGeo node will suddenly "jump" to the Axis location. The Axis node is represented in the viewer as a six-pointed null object (see Figure 11.17).

Tips & Tricks: The Card3D Node

The Card3D node, in the Transform menu, converts an input to a 3D card, but does not require a 3D camera or 3D environment. The node offers a Rotate property, allowing the input to appear oriented in 3D space. The Lens-In Focal property functions as a zoom, creating the illusion that the card is closer to or farther away from the 2D camera. To interactively position the card in the viewer, LMB+drag the transform handle. To rotate the card, Ctrl+LMB+drag.

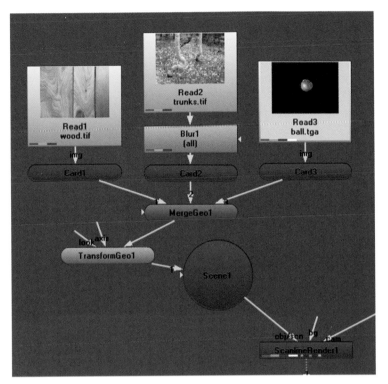

Figure 11.16 *Multiple cards grouped by a MergeGeo node. The group is made transformable by a TransformGeo node. A sample Nuke script is included as* mergegeo.nk *in the Tutorials folder of the DVD.*

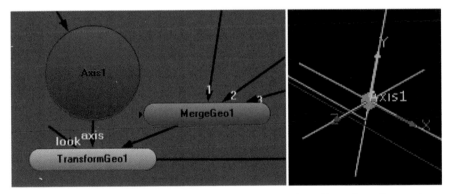

Figure 11.17 *(Left) An Axis node serves as a parent for a TransformGeo node. (Right) An Axis icon in the viewer.*

Reading and Writing Geometry

The ReadGeo node is able to import polygonal OBJ and FBX files. UV information survives the importation. To apply the node, follow these steps:

1. With no nodes selected, RMB+click and choose 3D → Geometry → ReadGeo. Open the ReadGeo node's properties panel. Browse for an OBJ or FBX file through the File parameter. A sample OBJ file is included as geometry.obj in the Footage folder of the

DVD. A sample FBX file is included as geometry.fbx. If there is more than one geometry node in an FBX file, set the Node Name menu to the node of choice. Connect the output of the ReadGeo node to the Scene node currently employed by the 3D environment. The imported geometry appears in the viewer.

2. If you are opening an FBX file and wish to import the node's animation, set the Take Menu to Take 001 or the take of your choice. If takes were not set up in the 3D program, Take 001 will hold the primary animation.

Tips & Tricks: OBJ and FBX Formats

OBJ, developed by Wavefront Technologies, is a widely accepted geometry file format that stores vertex positions, UV texture coordinates, and normal information. FBX is a 3D data interchange file format designed to transfer scenes between Autodesk's line of 3D programs, including Maya, 3ds Max, and Softimage. The format is able to carry all major geometry types, character rigs, cameras, lights, materials, textures, and animation channels. In addition, the FBX format supports *takes*, whereby a single channel can carry parallel sets of curves. That is, each set of curves creates a different animation cycle or different variation of the animation.

3. To texture the geometry, connect a Read node to the Img input of the ReadGeo node. Load a texture file into the Read node. A sample texture file, which matches geometry.obj, is included as texture.tga in the Footage folder on the DVD. If you switch to the 2D view of the viewer (which is the camera's point of view), geometry that carries UV information will display its texture by default (see Figure 11.18). At this stage, however, the surface will not possess any sense of shading. To add shading, you must connect a shader node and add at least one 3D light (see the sections "Creating 3D Lights" and "Adding Shaders" later in this chapter). If you switch to the 3D view of the viewer, the geometry is also textured by default. To display a wireframe version, change the ReadGeo node's Display menu to Wireframe.

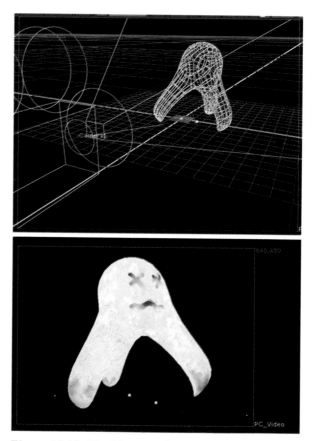

Figure 11.18 (Top) Imported OBJ geometry, as seen in wireframe in the 3D view of the viewer (Bottom) Textured geometry, as shown in the 2D view of the viewer. A shader and light node must be added to give a sense of shading.

The WriteGeo node exports geometry as an OBJ file when its Execute button is clicked. If the WriteGeo node's input is connected to a geometry node, the exported OBJ carries no transformation information. If you connect the WriteGeo node's input to a TransformGeo node, the exported OBJ inherits the transformation information as it stands for frame 1. If you connect the WriteGeo node's input to a Scene node, the exported OBJ includes *all* the geometry connected to the Scene node. Before you can use the Execute button, however, you must select a filename through the File parameter. Include the .obj extension for the exportation to work. Once you click the Execute button, the Frames To Execute dialog box opens. Despite this, the node can accept a frame range of only 1, 1.

Creating 3D Lights

You can light geometry within Nuke's 3D environment with the 3D → Lights menu. Once a light node is created, its output must be connected to a Scene node for its impact to be captured by the camera. The available light types follow:

Light creates a point light icon by default, but it is able to emulate three styles of lights through its own Light Type menu. These include point, directional, and spot. Each style of light functions in a manner similar to the Point, Direct, and Spot nodes. The Light node supports the ability to import lights through an FBX file, which is described in the section "Importing and Exporting Data" later in this chapter.

Point creates an omni-directional light emanating from the center of its spherical icon (see Figure 11.19). Point lights are equivalent to incandescent light bulbs.

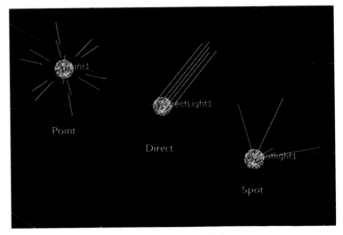

Direct creates parallel rays of light that replicate an infinitely distant source. The icon is a small sphere with lines extending in one direction (see Figure 11.19). The lines indicate the direction of the light rays; hence, you must "aim" the light by rotating it. The light's position does not affect the light quality. Direct lights are appropriate for emulating the sun or moon.

Figure 11.19 Point, direct, and spot lights

Spot creates a classic spot light with a light origin and cone. The origin is represented by a small sphere, while the cone is represented by four lines extending outward (see Figure 11.19). The edge of the cone produces a hard, circular falloff. You can adjust the cone through the node's properties panel. The Cone slider controls the cone spread; valid ranges are 0 to 180°. The Cone Penumbra Angle slider sets the size of the cone's edge falloff. Negative values fade the cone from the edge inward. Positive values fade the cone from the cone edge outward. In contrast, the Cone Falloff slider determines how quickly the light intensity diminishes from the cone center to the cone edge. The higher the value, the more focused the light.

Environment uses a spherically mapped input to determine its intensity. The Environment node is designed for image-based lighting and is therefore discussed in more detail in Chapter 12, "Advanced Techniques."

All the light nodes share a set of parameters, which are described here:

Color allows the light to be tinted.

Intensity controls the strength of the light.

Falloff Type determines the light decay. By default, the light intensity does not diminish with distance. To create real-world decay, where the intensity is reduced proportionally with the square of the distance (intensity/distance^2), set the menu to Quadratic. If you set the menu to Linear, the intensity diminishes at a constant rate and thus travels farther than it would with Quadratic. If you set the menu to Cubic, the decay is aggressive as the intensity is reduced proportionally with the cube of the distance (intensity/distance^3).

Shared 3D Parameters

Camera, geometry, and light mode's share a set of parameters:

Display allows you to change the node icon's appearance in the 3D view of the viewer. Menu options include Off (hidden), Wireframe, Solid (shaded), and Textured.

Pivot sets the XYZ position of the pivot point of the node (as measured from the node's default pivot location, which may be the volumetric center of geometry or the world origin). Scaling, rotations, and translation occur from the pivot. For example, if the pivot is set outside a geometry node, the geometry will rotate as if orbiting a planet.

Transform Order sets the order that the node will apply scale, rotate, and translation transformations. For example, SRT, which is the default setting, applies scaling before rotation or translation. The transform order can affect the transformation result if the object's pivot point is not volumetrically centered.

Rotation Order determines the order in which each axis rotation is applied to a node. Although the ZXY default is fine for most situations, the ability to change rotation order is useful for specialized setups.

Uniform Scale scales the object equally in all three directions. Uniform Scale serves as a multiplier to Scale XYZ. For example, if Scale XYZ is 0.5, 1, 0.2 and Uniform Scale is 2, the net result is a scale of 1, 2, 0.4.

Adding Shaders

Any light you add to the scene will illuminate the surface of the geometry. However, the geometry will appear flat unless you connect a shader. The 3D → Shader menu includes five basic shaders, any of which you can connect between the Img input of a geometry node and the output of the node providing the texture information:

Diffuse adds the diffuse component to a surface. The term *diffuse* describes the degree to which light rays are reflected in all directions. Therefore, the brightness of the surface is dependent of the positions of lights within the environment. The node only provides a White slider, which establishes the surface color.

Specular adds the specular component to the surface. A *specular highlight* is the consistent reflection of light in one direction. In the real world, a specular highlight results from an intense, confined reflection. In the realm of computer graphics, specular highlights are artificially constructed "hot spots." You can control the size of Nuke's specular highlight by adjusting the Min Shininess and Max Shininess sliders.

Emission adds the emissive or ambient color component to the surface. *Ambient color* is the net sum of all ambient light received by the surface in a scene. High Emission slider values wash out the surface. The Emission shader ignores all light nodes.

BasicMaterial and **Phong** combine the Diffuse, Specular, and Emission nodes. Phong has a slight advantage over BasicMaterial in that it calculates specular highlights more accurately. However, in many situations, the shading appears identical.

Tips & Tricks: The FillMat Node

Nuke 5.2 adds a FillMat node to the 3D → Shader menu. FillMat assigns a constant color to chosen RGBA channels and therefore can create a holdout matte or black hole matte, which cuts holes into the opaque alpha of geometry assigned to other shaders.

Each of the five shaders carries various inputs. The mapD input is designed for diffuse or color maps. The map may come in the form of a bitmap loaded into a Read node, a Draw menu node, or any other node that outputs useful color values (see Figure 11.20). The mapS input is designed for specular maps. The mapE input is designed for emissive (ambient color) maps. The mapSh input is designed for shininess maps. If a shader node has a Map input, the input represents the key component. For example, the Diffuse shader Map input represents the diffuse component, while the Emission shader Map input represents the emissive component.

If you wish to merge two shaders together, use the MergeMat node (in the 3D → Shader menu). For example, connect a Specular node to input A of a MergeMat node (see Figure 11.21). Connect a Diffuse node to input B of the MergeMat node. Connect the output of the MergeMat node to the Img input of the geometry node. The MergeMat node's Operation menu determines the style of merge. When combining a Diffuse and Specular node, set the Operation menu to Plus.

You can also chain an unlimited number of shader nodes together by connecting the output of one to the unlabeled input of the next (see Figure 11.21). Since the outputs are added together, however, this may lead to an overexposed surface unless the shader properties are adjusted.

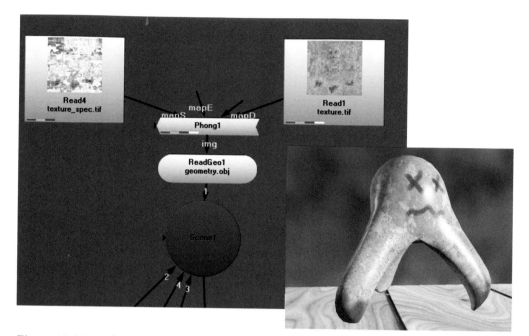

Figure 11.20 *(Left) A specular map is connected to the mapS input of a Phong node. A diffuse (color) map is connected to the mapD input. (Bottom Right) The resulting camera render. A sample Nuke script is included as* `shaded.nk` *in the Tutorials folder on the DVD.*

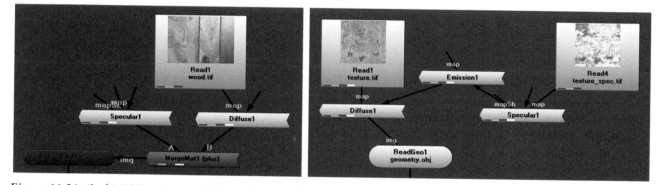

Figure 11.21 *(Left) A MergeMat node is used to combine Specular and Diffuse shader nodes. A sample Nuke script is included as* `mergemat.nk` *in the Tutorials folder. (Right) Diffuse, Emission, and Specular shaders are chained through their unlabeled inputs. A sample Nuke script is included as* `shader_chain.nk` *in the Tutorials folder on the DVD.*

Tips & Tricks: The ApplyMaterial Node

To assign a single shader to a MergeGeo node, use the ApplyMaterial node (in the 3D → Shader menu). Connect the unlabeled input of ApplyMaterial to the output of the MergeGeo node. Connect the Mat input of ApplyMaterial to a shader node. Connect the output of ApplyMaterial to the appropriate Scene node.

Additional Geo Nodes

The 3D → Modify menu includes a number of nodes designed to manipulate geometry. UVProject, Normals, and DisplaceGeo are described in the following sections.

UVProject and Project3D

The UVProject node projects an image onto a piece of geometry while overriding the geometry's inherent UV values. To apply the node, follow these steps:

1. With no nodes selected, RMB+click and choose 3D → Modify → UVProject. LMB+drag the UVProject node and drop it on top of the connection line between a geometry or MergeGeo node and its corresponding Scene node (see Figure 11.22).

2. Connect an Axis node to the Axis/Cam input of the UVProject node. As soon as the connection is made, the projection functions and is visible in the viewer (see Figure 11.22). (This assumes that the geometry node's Display and Render menus are set to Textured).

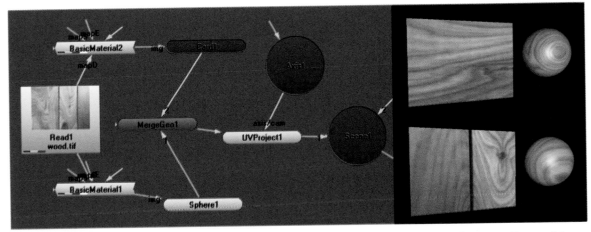

Figure 11.22 *(Left) Card and Sphere nodes are combined with a MergeGeo node. The MergeGeo node's UV texture space is provided by a UVProject node with an Axis node supplying the projection coverage information. (Top Right) Resulting render with Projection set to Planar. (Bottom Right) Resulting render with Projection set to Cylinder. A sample Nuke script is included as* uvproject.nk *in the Tutorials folder on the DVD.*

You can also attach a new Camera node to the Axis/Cam input. You can create a new Camera or Axis node for the sole purpose of working with the UVProject node. If you connect an Axis node, the projection coverage is based upon the node's Translate, Rotate, and Scale parameter values. If you connect a Camera node, the projection coverage is based upon the node's Translate, Rotate, Scale, Horiz Aperture, Vert Aperture, and Focal Length parameter values. As you change the various parameters, the projection updates in the viewer. If the Scale value is too small, the edge pixels of the texture are streaked to fill the empty area of the surface.

The UVProject node carries four projection types, which you can access through the Projection menu. If you set the menu to Planar, the projection rays are shot out in parallel. Planar is suitable for any flat surface. If you set the menu to Spherical, the input image is wrapped around a virtual sphere and projected inward. Spherical is suitable for geometry representing planets, balls, and the like. If you set the menu to Cylinder, the projection is similar to Spherical; however, it is less distorted than the Spherical projection because it does not pinch to the input image edges along the top and bottom. The default menu setting, Perspective, projects from the view of the node. Thus the Perspective setting is the most appropriate if a Camera node is connected. Note that the Focal Length, Horiz Aperture, and Vert Aperture parameters of the Camera node affects the projection only if the UVProject node's Projection menu is set to Perspective.

Tips & Tricks: UV Coordinates, UV Channels, and Normals

UV texture space is a coordinate space that relates the pixels of a texture to points on a surface. U and V each represent a particular direction along a two-dimensional surface. Even if a piece of geometry is not two-dimensional, it must be "unwrapped" and fit within two-dimensional UV coordinate space in order to be textured. UV coordinates differ from UV channels in that the UV coordinates are carried by the vertices of a surface while UV channels are encoded in a bitmap render. For example, UV channels are used to encode motion blur vectors in Nuke.

Normals (short for *surface normals*) are vectors that point directly away from a surface (and at a right angle to the surface). Normals are stored at each vertex position of each polygon face. However, in order for a surface to be shaded smoothly, normals are derived along the interior of each polygon face.

The Project3D node (in the 3D → Shader menu) can produce results similar to the UVProject node. However, its application is slightly different:

1. With no nodes selected, RMB+click and choose 3D → Shader → Project3D. LMB+ drag the Project3D node and drop it on top of the connection line between a shader node and a geometry node. For a texture map to be projected, a Read node with the texture map must be connected to the appropriate map input of the shader node.
2. Connect a Camera node to the Cam input of the Project3D node. As soon as the connection is made, the projection functions and is visible in the viewer (so long as the geometry's Display and Render menus are set to Textured). The orientation of the camera frustum determines the projection coverage. If the connected Camera node is positioned in such a way that the frustum coverage is incomplete, the uncovered part of the surface will render black.

Normals

With the Normals node, you can manipulate the normals of primitive or imported polygon geometry. To utilize the node, place it between the geometry node and the corresponding Scene node. For the results of the node to be seen, the Img input of the geometry node must be connected to a shader node. The Invert check box, beside the Action menu, flips the normals by 180°. The Action menu supports the following options:

Set orients all normals along a vector established by the Normal XYZ cells. If the Normal XYZ values are 0, 0, 0, the normals are "set to face," which facets the resulting render. If the Normal XYZ values are non-default values, the normals are oriented in the same direction. For example, if the camera is looking down the –z-axis, which is the default, you can set the Normal XYZ cells to 0, 0, 1 and thus have all the normals point toward the camera (this creates a flat-shaded "toon" result).

Build determines how smoothly the surface is rendered across adjacent polygons (see Figure 11.23). If the Angle Threshold slider is set to 0, no smoothing occurs and the surface appears faceted. If Angle Threshold is set above 0, only adjacent polygons that possess an angle less than the Angle Threshold value are smoothed. The angle is measured between the normals that exist at shared vertices of the corner of two adjacent faces. A slider value of 180 smooths all the polygons.

Lookat points all the surface normals toward the node that is connected to the Normals node's Lookat input. For Lookat to function in an expected fashion, Normal XYZ must be set to 0, 0, 0.

Delete removes a particular surface attribute. The attribute is established by the Attr Name cell, which uses code. N stands for normal, *uv* stands for UV points, and so on. For a complete list of attributes, hover the mouse pointer over the cell.

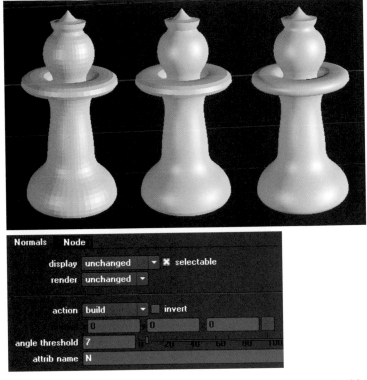

Figure 11.23 *(Top Left) Geometry with Action menu set to Build and Angle Threshold set to 0 (Top Center) Angle Threshold set to 7. Note the faceting that remains around the central collar. (Top Right) Angle Threshold set to 180 (Bottom) Properties panel of the Normals node. A sample Nuke script is included as* `normals.nk` *in the Tutorials folder on the DVD.*

DisplaceGeo

The DisplaceGeo node displaces the surface of a geometry node by pulling values from an input. The input may be any node that outputs color values. For example, you can connect the DisplaceGeo node's Displace input to a Checkerboard node or a Read1 node that carries a texture map. (The DisplaceGeo node is placed between the geometry node and the corresponding Scene node.) The strength of the displacement is controlled by the Scale slider. To soften the displacement, increase the Filter Size value. By default, the displacement is based on luminance, but you can change the Source menu to a particular channel. If you wish to offset the resulting displacement in space, adjust the Offset XYZ values.

Adjusting the Scanline Renderer

Initially, the ScanlineRender node produces poor results in the 2D view of the viewer. You can improve the render quality through the node's various parameters. The following are found in the ScanlineRender tab of the node's properties panel:

Filter applies the standard set of convolution filters to the render to avoid anti-aliasing issues.

Antialiasing, when set to Low, Medium, or High, reduces or prevents stairstepping and similar aliasing artifacts at surface edges and surface intersections.

Z-Blend Mode controls how intersecting surfaces are blended together along the intersection line. If the menu is set to None, a hard edge remains. If the menu is set to Linear or Smooth, a smoother transition results. The distance the blend travels along each surface is set by the Z-Blend Range slider (see Figure 11.24).

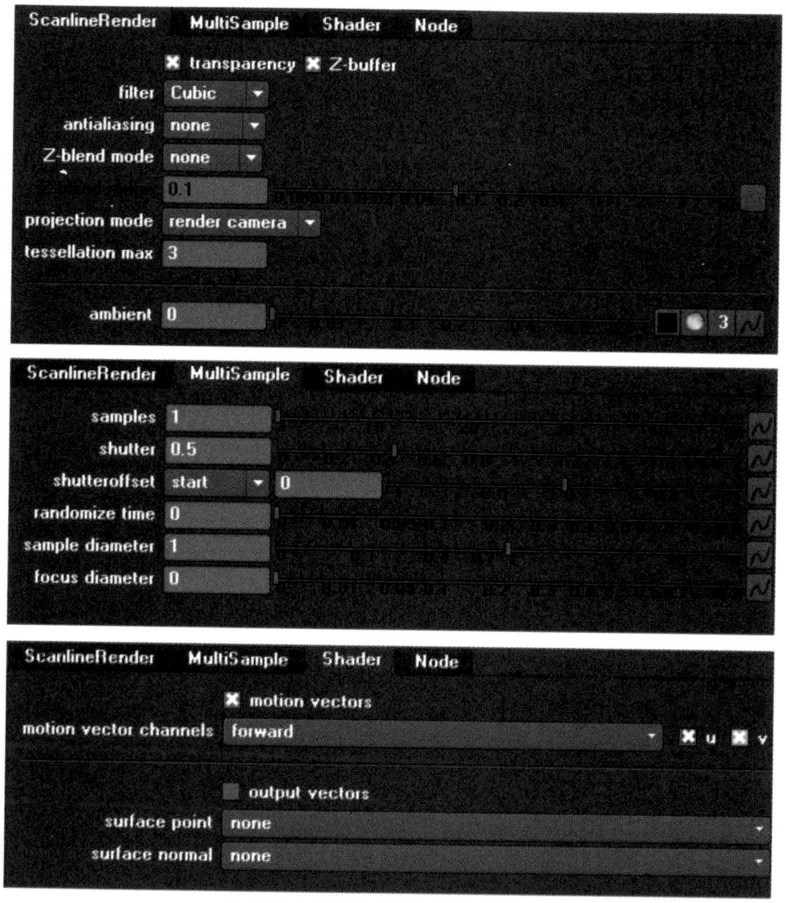

Figure 11.24 (Top) The ScanlineRender tab of the ScanlineRender node (Center) The MultiSample tab (Bottom) The Shader tab

Additional parameters are available through the MultiSample tab:

Samples sets the number of subpixel samples taken per pixel. The higher the Samples value, the more accurate the result will be and the higher the quality of the anti-aliasing. If Samples is set to a high value, you can leave the Antialiasing menu, in the ScanlineRender tab, set to None.

Shutter and **Shutter Offset** determine motion blur length. See the "Tips & Tricks" note at the end of this section for information on the handling of motion blur.

Randomize Time adds jitter to the subpixel sampling. This prevents identifiable patterns from appearing over time. Unless you are troubleshooting aliasing artifacts, however, you can leave this set to 0.

Sample Diameter sets the filter kernel size for the anti-aliasing process. Values over 1 may improve the quality.

Any improvement to the render quality will significantly slow the update within the viewer. However, for acceptable results to be rendered through a Write node, high-quality settings are necessary.

Tips & Tricks: Scanline Motion Blur

The ScanlineRender node produces motion blur only if its Samples parameter is set above 1. To create high-quality blur, you must set Samples to a high value, such as 36. However, you have the option to use a VectorBlur node instead. The ScanlineRender node encodes the motion blur vectors as UV channels. This is set by the Motion Vectors check box and Motion Vectors Channel menu (in the Shader tab). You can connect a VectorBlur node (in the Filter menu) between the ScanlineRender node and a viewer. If the VectorBlur node's UV Channels menu is set to Forward, the motion blur appears.

Importing and Exporting Data

You can import cameras, lights, and transforms from an FBX file through Nuke's Camera, Light, and Axis nodes. In addition, Nuke offers the Chan (.chan) file format for quickly importing and exporting animation data.

Importing an Animated Camera

The Camera node can import an animated camera. For example, you can import a Maya camera with the following steps:

1. Open a Camera node's properties panel. Select the Read From File check box. This ghosts the transform parameters.
2. Switch to the File tab. Browse for an FBX file through the File parameter. A sample FBX file is included as camera.fbx in the Footage folder on the DVD. A warning dialog box pops up. Click Yes. Any prior settings are destroyed for the Camera node with which you are working.
3. The imported camera icon appears in the 3D view of the viewer. If the FBX file contains more than one camera, you can switch between them by changing the Node Name menu to another listed camera (see Figure 11.25). Note that the FBX format attaches a *Producer* suffix to default camera nodes, such as Producer Top. With the sample camera.fbx file, the custom camera is named Panavision.
4. At this point, the camera's animation will not appear. To import the keyframes, change the Take Name menu to Take 001. If you did not set up takes in the 3D program, Take 001 will hold the primary animation. To see the camera in motion, switch the View Selection menu to 3D and play the timeline.
5. If you would like to transform the imported camera, return to the Camera tab and deselect the Read From File check box. The keyframes are converted to Nuke curves and are editable through the Curve Editor. In addition, the transform properties become available through the Camera tab.

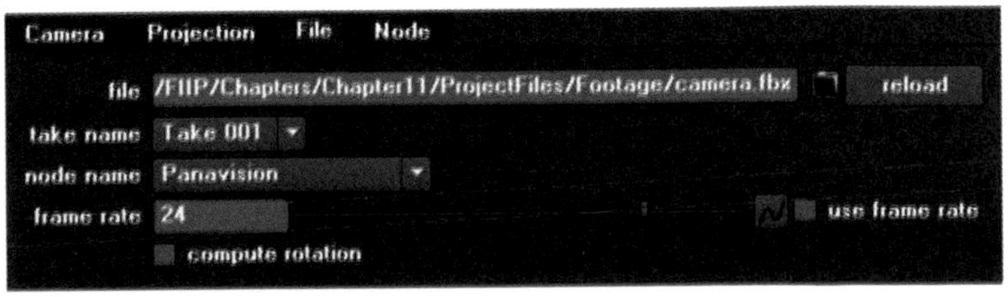

Figure 11.25 The File tab of a Camera node's properties panel. A sample Nuke script is included as fbx_camera.nk in the Tutorials folder on the DVD.

Aside from the transformations, Nuke is able to import the camera's focal length and the project's frames per second. You can force a different frame rate on the FBX file by changing the Frame Rate slider in the File tab.

Tips & Tricks: Solving Importation Problems

If the importation of a camera, light, or transform fails or has no apparent effect on your 3D environment, there are several steps you can take to remedy the problem. First, make sure the node you are using to import is connected, through its output, to a Scene node. The Scene node, in turn, should be connected to a ScanlineRender node. Second, if the FBX file you are importing does not contain useful animation, it may nevertheless help to set a single keyframe on each node while working in the 3D program. For example, while in Maya, set a key for frame 1 for each camera or light. When you set a single key, no motion appears, but the FBX file is forced to carry a take (Take 001). When you select Take 001 through the Take Name menu of the File tab, the imported transform information is more likely to transfer successfully. You can edit or delete the keys once you deselect the Read From File check box.

Importing Lights

The Light node can import a light from an FBX file. You can follow these steps:

1. Open a Light node's properties panel. Select the Read From File check box. This ghosts the transform parameters.
2. Switch to the File tab. Browse for an FBX file through the File parameter. A sample FBX file is included as lights.fbx in the Footage folder on the DVD. A warning dialog box pops up. Click Yes. Any prior settings are destroyed for the Light node you are working with.
3. The imported light icon appears in the 3D view of the viewer. Nuke will match the light type to the type contained with the FBX file. Nuke supports spot, directional, and point light types but is unable to read ambient lights. If the FBX file contains more than one light, you can switch between them by changing the Node Name menu to another listed light.
4. At this point, any animation on the imported light will not appear. To import the keyframes, change the Take Name menu to Take 001 (if you did not set up takes) or the take number of your choice.
5. If you would like to transform the imported light, return to the Light tab and deselect the Read From File check box. The keyframes are converted to Nuke curves and are editable through the Curve Editor. In addition, the transform properties become available through the Light tab.

Aside from the transformations, Nuke is able to import the light's intensity value and the project's frames per second. As you are importing the light, you can change the Frame Rate and Intensity Scale values through the File tab.

Importing Transformations

The Axis node can extract transformation information from a targeted node in an FBX file. Follow these steps:

1. Open an Axis node's properties panel. Select the Read From File check box. This ghosts the transform parameters.

2. Switch to the File tab. Browse for an FBX file through the File parameter. A sample FBX file is included as transform.fbx in the Footage folder on the DVD. A warning dialog box pops up. Click Yes. Any prior settings are destroyed for the Axis node with which you are working.

3. The Axis icon jumps to the same coordinates in space as the imported node. If the FBX file contains more than one node, you can switch between them by changing the Node Name menu to another listed node.

4. At this point, any animation will not appear. To import the keyframes, change the Take Name menu to Take 001 (if you did not set up takes) or the take number of your choice.

5. If you would like to transform the imported axis, return to the Axis tab and deselect the Read From File check box. The keyframes are converted to Nuke curves and are editable through the Curve Editor. In addition, the transform properties become available through the Axis tab.

Importing and Exporting Chan Files

Camera, Light, and Axis nodes support the Chan file format (.chan), which carries animated transform information. To import a Chan file, click the Import Chan File button and browse for the file. The imported transformation data is applied to the node and the animation curves are updated. To export a Chan file, click the Export Chan File button. Each Chan file is a text list that includes each frame in the animation sequence with transformation values for each animated channel. The ability to import and export the files allows you to transfer animation quickly from one node to another within the same script or different scripts.

The MotionBlur3D Node

The MotionBlur3D node, in the Filter menu, creates motion blur for cameras and objects moving within a 3D environment. It offers the advantage of a high-quality linear blur at relatively little cost. For the node to function, the outputs of the ScanlineRender node and the Camera node are connected to the MotionBlur3D node (see Figure 11.26). In turn, the output of the MoitonBlur3D node is connected to the input of the VectorBlur node. If the VectorBlur's UV Channels menu is set to Motion, the motion blur appears in the 2D view of the viewer.

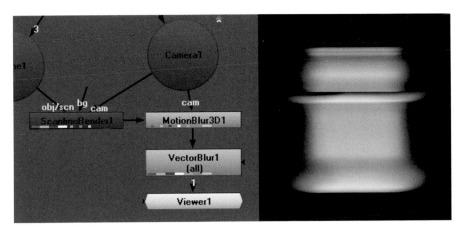

Figure 11.26 (Left) MotionBlur3D node in network (Right) Resulting heavy blur on a chess piece caused by a dollying camera. A sample Nuke script is included as motionblur3d.nk in the Tutorials folder on the DVD.

AE and Nuke Tutorials

In these tutorials, you'll have the opportunity to turn a 2D photo of a hallway into a 3D model within the composite.

AE Tutorial 11: Replicating a Hallway with 3D Layers

By arranging 3D cards in 3D space, you can replicate a hallway.

1. Create a new project. Choose Composition → New Composition. In the Composition Settings dialog box, change the Preset menu to HDV/HDTV 720 29.97 and set Duration to 30. Import the following files:

   ```
   hall_wall_fg_l.tga
   hall_wall_fg_r.tga
   hall_wall_l.tga
   hall_wall_r.tga
   hall_ceiling.tga
   hall_floor.tga
   hall_door.tga
   ```

   The files are derived from a single photo of a hallway. By splitting the photo into seven images, you can place them on separate 3D layers in After Effects.

2. Choose Layer → New → Camera. In the Camera Settings dialog box, set Preset to 35mm. 35mm is equivalent to the lens used on the real-world camera that took the original photo. Click OK. Change the Select View Layout menu, in the Composition panel, to 4 Views.

3. LMB+drag the imported images into the layer outline of the Timeline panel. As long as they sit below the Camera 1 layer, the order does not matter. Convert the new layers to 3D by toggling on each layer's 3D Layer switch. Interactively arrange the resulting 3D layers, one at a time, in the viewer. The goal is to create the shape of the hallway. Use Figure 11.27 as a reference. You can scale a 3D layer by LMB+dragging any of the edge points. You can rotate any 3D layer by using the Rotate tool. For greater precision, enter values into the Position, Scale, and Rotate cells in each layer's Transform section. To make the transformations easier to see, place a Solid layer at the lowest level of the layer outline (Layer → New → Solid). You can also create a second camera to serve as a "working" camera to view the 3D layers from different angles. Interactively position Camera 1, however, so that its view looks down the hall without seeing past its edges. Camera 1 will serve as the render camera at the completion of the tutorial.

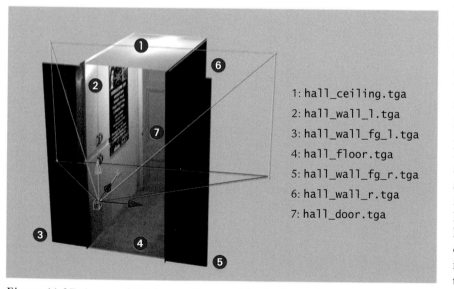

1: hall_ceiling.tga

2: hall_wall_l.tga

3: hall_wall_fg_l.tga

4: hall_floor.tga

5: hall_wall_fg_r.tga

6: hall_wall_r.tga

7: hall_door.tga

Figure 11.27 Arranged 3D layers. Camera 1 looks down the hallway.

4. To light the geometry, create two point lights. To do so, choose Layer → New → Light. In the Light Settings dialog box, change the Light Type menu to Point and click OK. Position Light 1 near the ceiling and the door (see Figure 11.28). Position Light 2 near the floor and foreground walls. Set the Intensity value of Light 2 to 150%. You can access the Light Options section for each light in the layer outline. Adjust the Material Options values for each 3D layer so that the lighting feels consistent. For example, set the hall_door.tga layer's Diffuse property to 50% and Specular property to 0%. This prevents a hot spot from forming on the door and making it inappropriately bright compared to the rest of the hallway.

5. To test the depth of the scene, animate Camera 1 moving slowing across the hall. Play back the timeline to gauge the amount of parallax shift that's created. Create a new 3D layer and animate it moving through the hallway. For example, in Figure 11.29, an image with the word *AE* is converted to a 3D layer. Create a test render through the Render Queue. To render with motion blur, toggle on the Motion Blur layer switch for each of the 3D layers in the layer outline. If you'd like to see the blur in the viewer, toggle on the Motion Blur composition switch. The tutorial is complete. A sample After Effects project is included as ae11.aep in the Tutorials folder on the DVD.

Figure 11.28 *Positioned point lights, indicated by their star-shaped icons*

Figure 11.29 *Three frames of animation showing parallax shift. The most significant shift occurs along the left wall.*

Nuke Tutorial 11: Replicating a Hallway with Imported Geometry

Nuke allows you to import geometry and project textures within the 3D environment.

1. Create a new script. Choose Edit → Project Settings. In the Project Settings properties panel, change Frame Range to 1, 24. Change the Full Size Format value to 1K_Super_35 (Full App). In the Node Graph, RMB+click and choose Image → Read. Browse for hallway.tga in the Footage folder in the DVD. Connect a viewer to the Read1 node. hallway.tga features a hall and door. The goal of this tutorial will be to create a sense of 3D by projecting the image onto imported geometry.

2. With no nodes selected, RMB+click and choose 3D → Geometry → ReadGeo. With the ReadGeo1 node selected, RMB+click and choose 3D → Scene. With no nodes selected, chose 3D → Camera. With no nodes selected, choose 3D → ScanlineRender. Connect the Obj/Scn input of the ScanlineRender1 node to the Scene1 node. Connect the Cam input of the ScanlineRender1 node to the Camera1 node. Connect the Read-Geo1 node to the Scene node. Connect a viewer to the ScanlineRender1 node. Use Figure 11.30 as a reference.

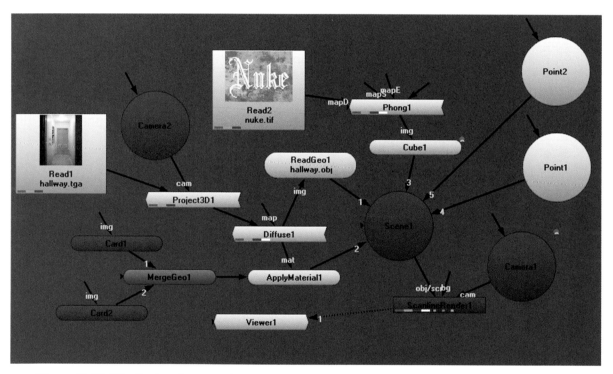

Figure 11.30 The final node network

3. Open the ReadGeo1 node's properties panel. Browse for hallway.fbx in the Footage folder on the DVD. At this stage, nothing is visible in the viewer. Change the View Selection menu, at the top right of the Viewer pane, to 3D. The imported geometry is visible, but it is so large that it extends past the edge of the frame. The geometry is a simplified model of the hallway. However, because it was accurately modeled on inch units in Maya, it becomes extremely large when imported into a 3D environment that utilizes generic units. In the ReadGeo1 node's properties panel, change the Uniform

Scale slider to 0.032. A uniform scale of 0.032 makes the geometry approximately 8 units tall, which is equivalent to 8 feet, or 96 inches. Use the camera keys (Alt+LMB, Alt+MMB, and Alt+RMB) in the viewer to frame the camera icon and imported geometry. The Camera1 icon remains inside the geometry. Select the Camera1 icon and translate it to 0, 4, 12 (see Figure 11.31).

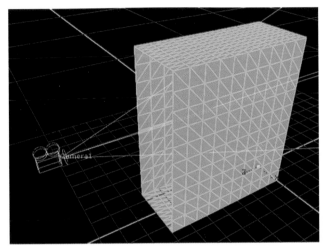

Figure 11.31 *Resized, imported geometry and repositioned Camera1 icon as seen in the 3D view of the viewer*

4. With no nodes selected, RMB+click and choose 3D → Shader → Project3D. Connect the output of Read1 to the unlabeled input of Project3D1. With no nodes selected, RMB+click and choose 3D → Shader → Diffuse. Connect the output of Project3D1 to the input of Diffuse1. Connect the Img input of ReadGeo1 to Diffuse1. Select the Camera1 node and choose Edit → Duplicate. Connect the output of the new Camera2 node to the Cam input of Project3D1. Use Figure 11.30 earlier in this section as a reference. This projects the hallway image onto the hallway geometry from the point of view of Camera2.

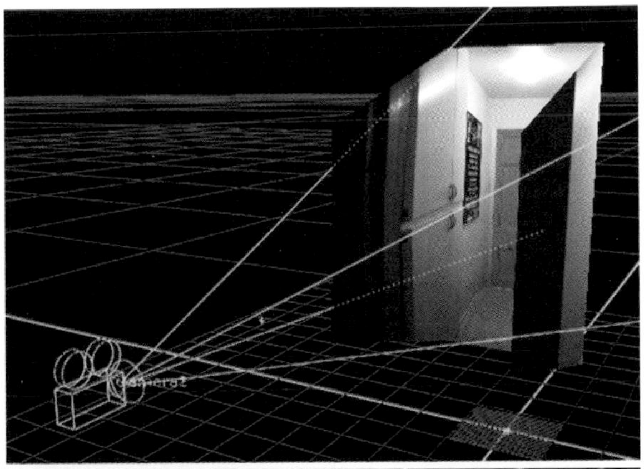

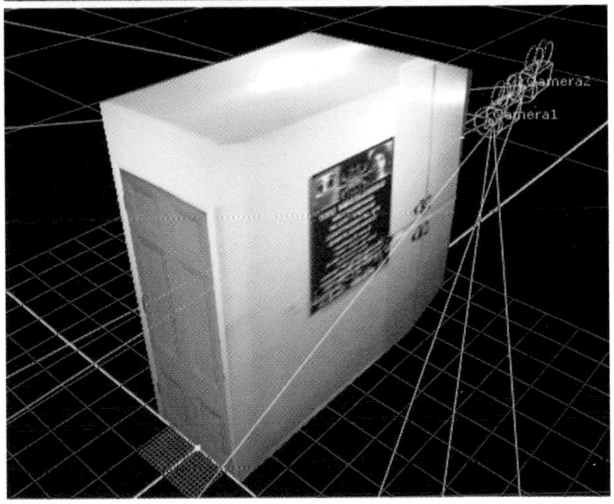

5. Initially, the projection is too small (see Figure 11.32). Select the Camera2 icon and interactively translate and rotate it until the projection covers the entire geometry. The goal is to align the edges of the geometry with the perspective lines of the image. For example, the ceiling-to-wall intersections of the image should line up with the side-to-top edge of the geometry.

Figure 11.32 *(Top) The initial projection. The Camera1 and Camera2 icons overlap. (Bottom) Camera2's Focal Length, Translate, and Rotate parameters are adjusted, creating better projection coverage. Note how the door is aligned with the back plane of the geometry and the ceiling is aligned with the top plane.*

A translation of 0.4, 4.2, 16 and a rotation of –1.5, 3, 0 work well. One important consideration is the focal length of the projecting camera. Ideally, the focal length of Camera2 should match the focal length of the real-world camera used to capture the image. However, since hallway.tga was doctored in Photoshop, an exact match is not possible. Nevertheless, if Camera2's Focal Length property is set the 45, the match becomes more accurate. An additional trick for aligning the projection is to examine the hallway geometry from other angles in the 3D view. In such a way, you can check to see if the image walls are aligned with the geometry planes (see Figure 11.32). For example, the door should appear on the back plane of the geometry without overlapping the side planes. In addition, the floor and ceiling shouldn't creep onto the back or side planes.

6. You can fine-tune the projection by adjusting Camera2's Window Scale parameter (in the Projection tab). The parameter allows you to scale the projection without manipulating the camera's transforms. In addition, you can stretch the projection in the X or Y direction. With this setup, a Window Scale value of 1.1, 1.35 provides a more exact match. You can also adjust the Translate, Rotate, and Scale properties of the ReadGeo1 node if necessary. Since the geometry is too short in the Z direction, which causes the cabinets to be cut off, set the ReadGeo node's Scale Z value to 1.25.

7. Return to the 2D view. The projection is working at this stage. However, the geometry doesn't cover the left and right foreground walls. To create walls, add two cards. With no nodes selected, RMB+click and choose 3D → Geometry → Card two times. With no nodes selected, RMB+click and choose 3D → Modify → MergeGeo. Connect the output of Card1 and Card2 to MergeGeo1. Use Figure 11.30 earlier in this section as a reference. With MergeGeo1 selected, RMB+click and choose 3D → Shader → Apply-Material. Connect the output of ApplyMaterial1 to Scene1. Connect the Mat input of ApplyMaterial1 to the output of Diffuse1. These connections allow the Camera2 projection to texture both cards. Open the Card1 and Card2 nodes' properties panels. Change the Uniform Scale setting for each one to 10. Translate Card1 in the viewer so that it forms the left foreground wall (see Figure 11.33). Translate Card2 in the viewer so that it forms the right foreground wall.

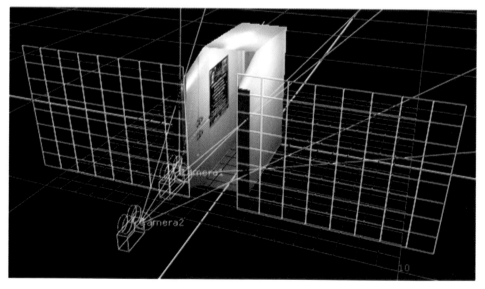

Figure 11.33 Card1 and Card2 are scaled and translated to form foreground walls.

8. Create two point lights (3D → Lights → Point). Connect both Point nodes to Scene1. Position Point1 in the viewer so that it sits near the ceiling of the hall. Position Point2

near the floor between Card1 and Card2 (see Figure 11.34). Set the Intensity slider for Point2 to 0.1. Although the hallway geometry does not require lighting (the Project3D1 node brings in the projected texture at 100% intensity), any additional geometry must be lit to be seen.

9. To test the depth of the 3D environment, animate Camera1 moving slowly across the hall. Play back the timeline to gauge the amount of parallax shift that's created.

Create a new piece of geometry and animate it moving through the hallway. For example, in Figure 11.35, a Cube node is added. The cube is textured with a Phong shader and a Read node with a texture bitmap. Animate the geometry moving toward the camera to increase the sense of depth in the scene. Test the animation by rendering with Render → Flipbook Selected. To increase the render quality and activate motion blur, increase the Samples slider in the MultiSample tab of the ScanlineRender node's properties panel. The tutorial is complete. A sample Nuke script is included as `nuke11.nk` in the Tutorials folder on the DVD.

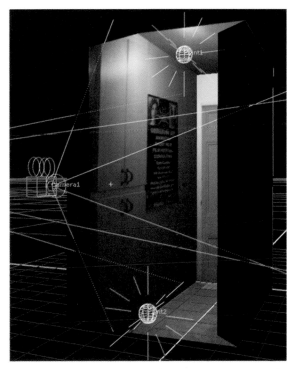

Figure 11.34 Two point lights are positioned inside the hallway.

Figure 11.35 Three frames of animation showing parallax shift. The most significant shift occurs along the left wall.

Interview: David Schnee, Tippett Studio, Berkeley, California

In 2002, David Schnee graduated from the Academy of Art University in San Francisco. While at school, he specialized in compositing and visual effects, working in Combustion, After Effects, and Flint. Four months after graduation, he was hired by Tippett to work on *Starship Troopers 2*. Thrown into a production environment, he quickly learned to use Shake. His feature credits now include *Constantine*, *Cloverfield*, *The Spiderwick Chronicles*, *Drag Me to Hell*, and *X-Men Origins: Wolverine*.

David Schnee at a workstation. Note that the compositing program, in this case Shake, is spread over two monitors.

Phil Tippett founded Tippett Studio in 1984. The venture literally started in Phil's garage, where he created stop-motion animation. It has since grown to a world-class facility with five buildings and over 200 employees in Berkeley, California. Over the past two decades, Tippett has created visual effects for over 60 feature films and has earned multiple Emmys, CLIOs, and Academy Awards. Feature credits include *Robocop*, *Ghost Busters*, *Jurassic Park*, and *Hellboy*.

(Tippett uses Shake and, secondarily, After Effects. At present, the studio keeps 25 compositors on staff, but the total expands and contracts depending on the projects on hand. Compositors are separated into their own compositing department.)

LL: What has been the biggest change to compositing in the last 10 years?

DS: [T]he biggest change includes a couple of things —one is [the] blurry line between 2D and 3D in the composite. [The second is] the ever-increasing…responsibility of the compositing artist. This includes becoming more responsible earlier in the pipeline [by] performing re-times (color grades) on plates, working with every breakout (render) pass imaginable, [and the need] to re-light and fix [problems created by] departments up stream…. [For] artists working with higher-end software such as Nuke, [this includes] using projection mapping techniques [with imported] geometry. [I]n some cases, [this entails] lighting environments with HDRI images or building a new camera move from the existing plate with projections…. [The] ability to…build an entire environment…in the composite is most definitely a big change for us. At Tippett, we perform these same techniques, but it's handled in our matte painting department. It's only a matter of time before we will be performing these same tasks in our [compositing] department.

LL: What is the most exciting change that you see on the horizon?

DS: 3-D. If the stereoscopic thing takes off (we'll find out in the next year or so), we'll need to think and composite in…new ways, accounting for each eye and manipulating layers of each eye to get the most from the 3-D and convergence points. We'll also need better asset management due to the doubling of the amount of rendering and layers to account for both left and right eye.

LL: Is there any leap in technology that you would like to see happen?

DS: I would love to be able to work more in "real time." [T]oo much time is spent waiting on GUI updates, filtering, and processing math operations. I'm not sure what the answer is, but it would be great to work in an environment where you can build and test operations and see the results much faster.... [W]orking at 2K in real time could happen, but as projects demand more detail and better quality, working at 4K will [become] the norm, and doubling up on just about everything in the pipeline will eat away at that real-time workflow we might get [if we just worked with] 2K.

(Top) One of several rooms dedicated to animators at Tippett Studio (Bottom Left) A sound stage used to shoot miniatures and other live-action elements (Bottom Right) The main lobby, which includes numerous models from feature film work, including The Empire Strikes Back *and* Starship Troopers

Additional Resources: The Full Interview

To read the full interview with David Schnee, see the Interviews folder on the DVD. For more information on stereoscopic techniques, see Chapter 12, "Advanced Techniques."

Interview: Aaron Vasquez, Click 3X, New York City

Aaron Vasquez graduated from the School of Visual Arts in New York City, where he specialized in CG modeling and texturing. He began his career with SMA Realtime, where he was able to train himself on an Inferno station. He made the transition to visual effects work when he later moved to Sideshow Creative. In 2005, he joined Click 3X as a Flame artist. In the past four years, he's provided effects for a variety of brands, including Pantene, Sharp, Time Warner, and Samsung.

Aaron Vasquez at his Flame station

Click 3X was founded in 1993, making it an early adopter of digital technology. The studio offers branding, image design, motion graphics, and visual effects services for commercials, music videos, and feature film as well as the Web and mobile media. The studio's recent client roster includes MTV, Burger King, and E*Trade.

(Click 3X uses Flame, Smoke, After Effects, Shake, and Nuke. The studio has five compositors in-house.)

LL: Do you visit the set when there is a live-action shoot?

AV: Yes. I'll go sometimes and serve as visual effects supervisor. A lot of times I'll take my laptop with me—get a video tap straight into my laptop and I'll do on-set comps for the clients, who are usually nervous about what's going to happen.... It's a great tool to ease their fears....

LL: What do you use on location to create the composites?

AV: I'll use After Effects to do the comps on the fly.

LL: Since you're on set, what data is important to bring back with you?

AV: If it's motion control, any of the motion control data—the ASCII files (text data files) that they provide...any measurements—that's always important.... [W]hat I'm finding now too is that the CG guys will ask me to [take] 360° panoramas for them so that they can re-create the lighting with HDRIs. I'll bring a lighting ball (a white ball used to capture the on-set light quality) with me...and a mirror ball.... We have a Nikon D80 we use for the photos.

LL: How common is it to work with 2.5D?

AV: It's very common. Almost every other job is multiplaning these days. A lot of the work I've been doing lately is taking [the 2.5D] to the next level—instead of just multiplaning on cards, I'll project [images] onto CG geometry in Flame.... One of my strengths originally was as a [CG] modeler, so I'll model objects in Lightwave…and bring it in as an OBJ or Max 3DS files. I usually take care of the texturing in Flame. It's instantaneous. [Flame] has built-in geometry also.…

Additional Resources: The Full Interview

To read the full interview with Aaron Vasquez, see the Interviews folder on the DVD. For an example composite created by Aaron, see Chapter 1.

twelve

Advanced Techniques

"Stereoscopic technology certainly holds interesting possibilities once we get over the 'we must put the sword in the viewer's face' phenomenon."

—RICHARD SHACKLETON, Nuke product manager, The Foundry, London

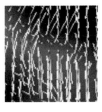

After Effects and Nuke contain *toolsets*

that may be considered "advanced." This does not mean that they are necessarily difficult to apply. However, they do tend to be unintuitive— or they are at least based on unusual algorithms or workflows. The tools include those that process HDRI, prepare multiple views for stereoscopic 3D, time-warp footage, retexture CG in the composite, simulate physical effects, and provide various scripting languages for customization or automation. There are no tutorials in this chapter. However, at the end, the reader is encouraged to use all the techniques discussed in this book to combine provided footage and image files creatively.

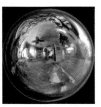

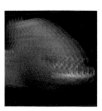

High Dynamic Range Images

High Dynamic Range Imaging (HDRI) techniques store extremely large dynamic ranges. A *dynamic range* is the ratio of minimum to maximum luminous intensity values that are present at a particular location. For example, a brightly-lit window in an otherwise dark room may produce a dynamic range of 50,000:1, where the luminous intensity of the light traveling through the window is 50,000 times more intense than the light reflected from an unlit corner. Such a large dynamic range cannot be accurately represented with a low bit-depth. Even if you use a suitably large bit-depth, such as 16-bit with 65,536 tonal steps, the intensity values must be rounded off and stored as integers; this leads to inaccuracy. Hence, high dynamic range (HDR) image formats employ 16- or 32-bit floating-point architecture. The floating-point architecture supports a virtually unlimited number of tonal steps, plus it maintains the ability to store fractional values. (For more information on floating-points, see Chapter 2, "Choosing a Color Space.")

HDRI is commonly employed in professional photography. A common approach to taking HDR photographs follows these steps:

1. A camera is fixed to a tripod. Multiple exposures are taken so that every area of the subject is properly exposed (see Figure 12.1). Each exposure is stored as a standard 8-, 10-, 12-, or 16-bit low dynamic range (LDR) image.

2. The multiple exposures are brought into an HDR program, such as HDRShop or Photomatix, where they are combined into a single HDR image. The image is exported as a 16- or 32-bit OpenEXR, .hdr, or a floating-point TIFF. Note that HDR refers to high dynamic range images in general, while .hdr refers specifically to the Radiance file format. HDR image formats are discussed in the section "HDR Formats and Projections" later in this chapter.

3. If the HDR image is destined for print, a limited tonal range is isolated by applying an exposure control, or the entire tonal range is compressed through tone mapping (which is described later in this chapter).

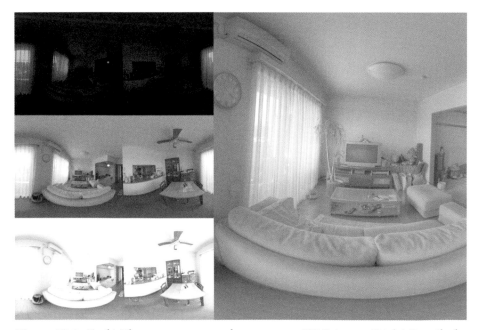

Figure 12.1 (Left) Three exposures used to create an HDR image (Right) Detail of tone-mapped result (HDR image by Creative Market)

HDRI in Visual Effects

HDR photography is often employed in the visual effects industry to capture the lighting on location or on set. The resulting HDR images are used by animators to light CG within a 3D program. Similar lighting approaches are occasionally applied by compositors in a compositing program. There are several approaches to these techniques:

- A single HDR image captures an entire location or set. The image is loaded into an image-based lighting tool. The image is projected from the surface of a projection sphere toward a CG element at its center. A renderer utilizing radiosity, global illumination, or final gather is employed. The pixel values of the projected HDR image are thereby interpreted as bounced, ambient, or indirect light. In addition, the HDR information is used as a reflection source. (Although this process usually happens in a 3D program, some compositing packages are able to light 3D geometry with an HDR image; for a demonstration in Nuke, see the section "Environment Light and SphericalTransform" later in this chapter.)

- HDR images of real-world light sources are mapped to planar projections or area lights, which are placed an appropriate distance from the CG camera and CG elements. A renderer utilizing radiosity, global illumination, or final gather converts pixel values into light intensity values. Such virtual lights are known as *HDR lights*.

- HDR images of the set are projected onto a polygonal reproduction of the set. The point of view of the hero element (such as a CG character or prop) is captured and a new environmental HDR map is created. The new map is then used to light the hero element through an image-based lighting system. If the hero element moves through the shot, the environmental HDR map changes over time to reflect the changing point of view. Animated maps using this technique are referred to as *animated HDRs*. (For a simple demonstration of this process in Nuke, see the section "Creating Animated HDRs" later in this chapter.)

- An HDR image is loaded into a compositing program. A light icon is interactively positioned in a viewer. Wherever the light icon rests, a higher exposure level within the HDR is retrieved. Thus, the compositor is able to light within the composite interactively while using the real-world intensity values contained within the HDR image.

Nuke supports the ability to light geometry with an HDR image through the Environment node. In addition, Nuke can convert between different styles of HDR projections with the SphericalTransform node. These nodes are described in the section "HDRI Support in Nuke" later in this chapter. Both After Effects and Nuke can read and manipulate various HDR file formats, which are described in the next section.

HDR Formats and Projections

Here's a quick review of commonly used HDR formats. Additional information can be found in Chapter 2:

> **OpenEXR (.exr)** was created by Industrial Light & Magic. It is widely used in the visual effects industry. OpenEXR has a 16-bit half float and a 32-bit full float variation, both of which can support HDR photography.

> **Radiance (.hdr, .rgbe, .xyze)** was developed by Greg Ward and was the first widely used HDR format.

> **Floating-Point TIFF** is a 16-bit half float or 32-bit full float variation of the common TIFF format. This format is the least efficient of the three and produces significantly larger file sizes.

When HDRI is employed for professional photography, the images are left in a recognizable form. That is, they remain rectangular with an appropriate width and height. When HDRI is used to light a scene within a 3D program or compositing program, however, the images must be remapped to fit a particular style of projection. Different projection styles are required by different image-based lighting tools, projections, and nodes. There are several different projection types:

Light probe projections capture the reflection of an environment in a highly reflective chrome ball or sphere (see Figure 12.2). Through an HDR or paint program, the reflection of the camera or photographer is removed. This style has 180×180° and 360×360° variations. The 180×180° image is taken from a single point of view, while the 360×360° image is assembled from two views offset by 90°. Light probe images appear similar to those simply named *mirrored ball*. However, the light probe algorithm retains more information along the edge of the sphere when compared to the mirrored ball versions. Light probe HDRs are also referred to as *angular*.

Lat long projections are rectangular and often feature a complete panoramic view of a location (see Figure 12.2). This style of HDR is also referred to as *spherical*, *latitude/longitude*, and *equirectangular*.

Cubic cross projections feature an unfolded cube, which encompasses a complete 360° view of a location (see Figure 12.2). This style has vertical and horizontal variations.

Figure 12.2 *(Left) Light probe HDR (Center) Lat long HDR (Right) Vertical cubic cross HDR (HDR image by Creative Market)*

Exposure Adjustment and Tone Mapping

The main disadvantage of HDR images is the inability to display their entire tonal range on a low-bit-depth monitor or television. There are two solutions to this predicament: choose a narrow tonal range through an exposure control or apply tone mapping. HDR-compatible programs provide exposure controls for the purpose of previewing or exporting at a lower bit depth. For example, Photoshop includes an Exposure slider through the 32-Bit Preview Options dialog box. After Effects provides the Exposure effect for the same purpose. Nuke's Grade node can be used to the same end.

Choosing a tonal range through an exposure control ignores or discards the remaining tonal range. In comparison, the process of *tone mapping* remaps the entire tonal range to a lower-bit-depth space, such as 8-bit. Hence, tone mapping creates an image where everything is equally exposed, leading to a low-contrast, washed-out look (see Figure 12.1 earlier in the chapter). The stylistic quality of tone mapping is prized by many photographers. However, tone mapping is generally not used in the realm of compositing unless such a stylistic look is desirable. Nevertheless, After Effects supports tone mapping through its HDR Compander effect. After Effects's and Nuke's support of HDR is discussed in detail later in this chapter.

Stereoscopic 3-D

Stereoscopy is any technique that creates the illusion of depth through the capture of two slightly different views that replicate human binocular vision. Because left and right human eyes are separated by a distinct distance, each eye perceives a unique view. Objects at different distances from the viewer appear to have different horizontal positions in each view. For example, objects close to the viewer will have significantly different horizontal positions in each view, while objects far from the viewer will have almost identical horizontal positions. The difference between each view is known as *binocular* or *horizontal disparity*. The horizontal disparity is measurable as an angle between two lines of sight, where the angle is defined as *parallax*. The human mind uses the horizontal disparity as a depth cue. When this cue is combined with monocular cues such as size estimation, the world is successfully perceived as three-dimensional. The process of yielding a depth cue from horizontal disparity is known as *stereopsis*.

The earliest form of stereoscopy took the form of stereoscopic photographs developed in the mid-1800s. Stereoscopic photos feature slightly divergent views that are printed side by side. When the photos are viewed through a stereoscope (a handheld or table-mounted viewer with two prismatic lenses), the illusion of depth is achieved (see Figure 12.3).

The stereoscopic process was applied to motion pictures in the late 1890s. The peak of commercial stereoscopic filmmaking occurred in the early 1950s with dozens of feature films released. By this point, the term *3-D* referred to stereoscopic filmmaking (although earlier cartoons used the phrase to advertise multiplaning). While pre-2000 3-D films generally relied on anaglyph methods to create the depth illusion, post-2000 films usually employ polarization. In both cases, the audience member must wear a pair of glasses with unique lenses.

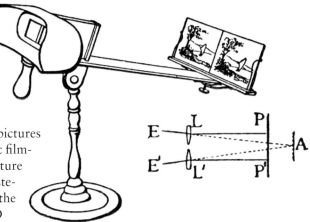

Figure 12.3 *Stereoscope with mounted stereoscopic photograph (Image © 2009 by Jupiterimages)*

Anaglyphic 3-D

Anaglyphs carry left and right eye views; however, each view is printed with a chromatically opposite color. The views are overlapped into a single image (see Figure 12.4). Each lens of the viewer's glasses matches one of the two colors. For example, the left view is printed in red and the right view is printed in cyan. The left lens of the viewer's glasses is therefore tinted cyan, allowing only the red left view to been seen by the left eye. The right lens of the viewer's glasses is tinted red, allowing only the cyan right view to been seen by the right eye.

Because cyan is used, blue and green portions of RGB color space are included. That said, it's possible to create anaglyphs with black-and-white images. Nevertheless, early color motion picture anaglyphs relied on red-green or red-blue color combinations (see Figure 12.4).

Polarized 3-D

Polarization relies on an unseen quality of light energy. Light consists of oscillating electrical fields, which are commonly represented by a waveform with a specific wavelength. When the light oscillation is oriented in a particular direction, it is said to be *polarized*. *Linear polarization* traps the waveform within a plane. *Circular polarization* causes the waveform to corkscrew. When light is reflected from a non-metallic surface, it's naturally polarized; that is, the light energy is emitted by the surface in a specific direction. Sky light, which is sunlight scattered through Earth's atmosphere, is naturally polarized. Polarized filters take advantage of this phenomenon and are able to block light with specific polarization. For example, polarized sunglasses block light that is horizontally polarized (roughly parallel to the ground), thus reducing the intensity of specular reflections (which forms glare). Professional photographic polarizers can be rotated to target different polarizations. Stereoscopic 3-D systems apply polarized filters to the projected left and right views as well as to each lens of the viewer's glasses. The polarization allows each view to be alternately hidden from sight.

Figure 12.4 *(Top and Center) Red-cyan anaglyphs (Bottom) Red-blue anaglyph glasses (Anaglyphs available via Wikimedia Commons. Bottom image © 2009 by Jupiterimages.)*

3D Projection and Display

When a stereoscopic project is presented, there are several different projection and display methods to choose from:

Dual Projectors One projector is tasked with the left view, while a second projector is tasked with the right view. Early stereoscopic motion pictures, which relied on this method, employed anaglyph color filters. Current IMAX systems use a polarized projector lenses.

Passive Polarization A single projector alternatively projects left and right views. The views are retrieved from interlaced video footage (where each view is assigned to an upper or lower field) and filtered through a linear or circular polarization filter. As the left view is projected, the polarization of the viewer's right lens blocks the left view from the right eye. As the right view is projected, the polarization of the viewer's left lens blocks the right view from the left eye. The term *passive* is used because the viewer's glasses are not synchronized with the projection, as is possible with an active shutter system (see the next description). The frame rate of a passive polarization system may be quite high. For example, the RealD system projects at 144 fps, where each view of a single frame is shown three times (24 fps × 2 views × 3).

Active Shutter A single projector or display is used in combination with *shutter glasses*, which contain polarizing filters and liquid crystals that can switch between opacity and transparency with the application of voltage. The voltage application is cued by an infrared emitter driven by the projector or display. Active shutter systems have the advantage of working with consumer digital projectors, televisions, and PC monitors. Active shutter systems can use either interlaced frames or *checkerboard wobulation*, whereby the two views are broken into subframes and intertwined in a fine checkerboard pattern.

Recording 3-D

There are several methods used to capture footage for a stereoscopic project. A common approach utilizes two cameras. The cameras are either positioned in parallel (side by side) or are converged so that their lines of sight meet at a particular point on set. To make the stereoscopic effect successful, the lenses must be the same distance apart as human eyes— roughly 2.5 inches. The distance between eyes is known as *interocular distance*. The distance between lenses is referred to as *interaxial separation*. The correct distance may be achieved with beamsplitters, mirrors, or lenses positioned at the end of optical fiber cables (see Figure 12.5). If such a setup is not possible on set, the footage for each view is transformed in the composite to emulate an appropriate distance.

When stereoscopic footage is prepared, a convergence point must be selected. A *convergence point* is a depth location where the horizontal disparity between the left and right eye views is zero (that is, the disparity is 0° parallax). When the footage is projected, objects in front of this point appear to float in front of the screen (possessing negative parallax). Objects behind the point appear to rest behind the screen (possessing positive parallax). If the footage is

Figure 12.5 A 1930s Leitz stereoscopic beamsplitter fed left and right views to a single piece of film (Image © 2009 by Jupiterimages)

shot with converged cameras, the convergence point may be selected by the cinematographer while on the set. More often, however, it is more efficient to select a convergence point while the compositor is working in the composite.

After Effects and Nuke provide stereoscopic effects and nodes specifically designed for reading and preparing stereoscopic 3-D footage. These are discussed later in this chapter.

Time Warping and Optical Flow

Time warping is a generic term for the retiming of footage. If the motion within a piece of film of video footage is too slow or too fast, the frame rate can be altered. Before the advent of digital filmmaking, this was achieved by *skip printing* or *stretch printing* motion picture film; with these techniques, film frames from the camera negative were skipped or repeated as positive film stock was exposed. Skipping or repeating frames is a basic time warping technique that continues to be applied by compositing programs. However, compositing programs have the advantage of *frame blending*, whereby sets of neighboring frames are averaged so that new, in-between frames are generated.

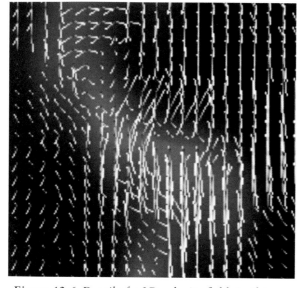

Figure 12.6 Detail of a 2D velocity field. In this example, the source footage is curling white smoke over a dark background.

There are multiple approaches to frame blending. Simple frame blending merely overlaps neighboring frames with partial opacity. Advanced frame blending utilizes optical flow. *Optical flow* is a pattern created by the relative motion of objects as seen by an observer. In compositing, optical flow is represented by a *2D velocity field* that places pixel motion vectors over the view plane (see Figure 12.6). Optical flow, as it's used for time warping, employs *motion estimation* techniques whereby pixels are tracked across multiple frames. By accurately determining the path a pixel takes, it is easier to synthesize a new frame. If a pixel starts at position A and ends at position B, it can be assumed that a point between A and B is suitable for a new, in-between position. (When discussing optical flow, pixels are point samples with a specific color value that can be located across multiple frames.) However, if the footage is high resolution, tracking every image pixel may prove impractical. Thus, optimization techniques allow the images to be simplified into coarser blocks or identified homogeneous shapes.

Optical flow techniques have inherent limitations. For example, footage that contains inconsistent brightness, excessive grain or noise, or multiple objects moving in multiple directions is problematic.

Industry Perspective: Retiming Footage

As time warping software has steadily improved over the last several years, the frequency with which retiming occurs has increased. This is particularly true for compositors working in the visual effects or commercial production arena. That said, if a piece of footage must be significantly retimed, it is usually preferable to shoot the footage at a higher or lower frame rate to begin with. This is especially critical for slow-motion effects. For example, if shattering glass, exploding concrete, or a water splash must be captured, a slow-motion film of a video shoot is superior to time warping footage shot at a normal frame rate.

Working with Advanced Techniques

After Effects and Nuke support a wide range of advanced techniques that include HDRI, time warping, stereoscopic preparation, and scripting. In addition, After Effects provides the ability to create dynamic, physically based simulations while Nuke allows you to remap UV texture space of pre-rendered CG.

Advanced Techniques in AE

After Effects offers several effects with which you can interpret HDR images, change the duration of a piece of footage, create stereoscopic images, automate functions with a script, and create particle simulations.

HDRI Support in AE

After Effects supports a 32-bit floating-point color space. As discussed in Chapter 2, you can set the Depth menu of the Project Settings dialog box to 32 Bits Per Channel (Float). In addition, the program can import OpenEXR, floating-point TIFF, and Radiance files (which include files with .hdr, .rgbe, and .xyze filename extensions). The program can write out the same floating-point formats. When an HDR image is written, the full 32-bit floating-point color space is encoded, even if the dynamic range is not fully visible through the viewer.

Because the tonal range of an HDR image file is far greater than the tonal range of an 8-bit or 10-bit monitor, it may be necessary to compress the range or select a specific exposure. The HDR Compander, the HDR Highlight Compression, and the Exposure effects are designed for these tasks.

HDR Compander

The HDR Compander effect (in the Effect → Utility menu) is specifically designed to compress a 32-bit tonal range down to 8-bit or 16-bit color space, where lower-bit-depth effects can be applied; once those effects are applied, a second iteration of the HDR Compander effect can expand the tonal range back to 32 bits.

As an example, in Figure 12.7, a floating-point TIFF of a shelf is imported

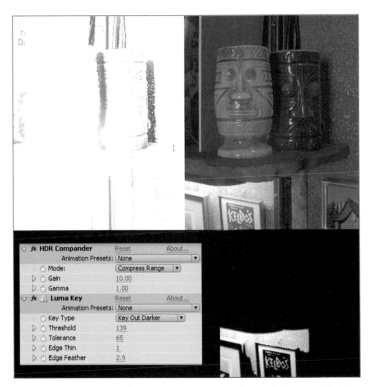

Figure 12.7 *(Top Left) An HDR image is brought into a 32-bit project. Due to the limited tonal range of the 8-bit monitor, it appears overexposed. (Top Right) The same image after the application of the HDR Compander effect with its Gain slider set to 10. (Bottom Left) The HDR Compander effect is placed before a Luma Key effect in order to compress the 32-bit space to a 16-bit tonal range. Normally, the Luma Key cannot operate in 32-bit space, as is indicated by the yellow warning triangle. (Bottom Right) The result of the Luma Key, which is able to operate with the addition of the HDR Compander effect. A sample After Effects project is included as* compander.aep *in the Tutorials folder on the DVD.*

into a project with its Depth menu set to 32 Bits Per Channel (Float). A sample pixel within its brightness area has a value of 3460, 1992, 0 on an 8-bit scale of 0 to 255. The same pixel has a value of 444, 662, 255, 918, 0 when examined using a 16-bit scale of 0 to 32,768. The same pixel has a value of 13.57, 7.81, 0 when examined using a 0 to 1.0 scale. In this situation, the brightest pixel is 13.57 times brighter than the 255, 32,768, or 1.0 limit. (You can change the scale the Info panel uses to display pixel values by changing the Info panel menu to 8-bpc, 10-bpc, 16-bpc, or Decimal.) Hence, the TIFF possesses values far beyond range that an 8-bit monitor can display. In addition, the TIFF possesses values beyond the range in which an 8- or 16-bit effect can operate.

When the HDR Compander effect is applied to the TIFF layer, the effect's Mode menu is set to Compress Range and the Gain slider is set to 10. When the Info panel menu is set to Decimal (0.0-1.0), the same pixel values become 1.36, 0.78, 0. The Gain slider operates with the following formula: input pixel value / Gain. The formula holds true whether the Info panel menu is set to 8-bpc, 10-bpc, or 16-bpc. The Gain slider operates in a linear fashion. That is, all areas of the tonal range are compressed equally. You can bias a particular area of the tonal range, however, by adjusting the effect's Gamma slider, which applies a gamma curve to the result. For example, Gamma values above 1.0 will favor the low end of the tonal range while values below 1.0 will favor the high end of the tonal range.

If a second iteration of the HDR Compander is added with the Mode menu set to Expand Range and the Gain slider set to match the first HDR Compander iteration, the original tonal range is restored. Note that the second HDR Compander effect is optional and is useful only if you plan to render out 32-bit floating-point image sequences.

Tips & Tricks: Effects and Bit Depths

Many of the effects in After Effects do not support all bit depths. If an effect is unable to operate properly in a project's current bit depth, a yellow, triangular warning icon appears beside the effect's name in the Effect Controls panel. If you would like to see what bit depths an effect supports, search through the After Effects help files for the effect name. The page for the effect will include a bit-depth information line.

The Exposure Effect

Although you can apply the Exposure effect to 8- or 16-bit images, as discussed in Chapter 4, its Exposure slider is designed for 32-bit footage. For example, in Figure 12.8, a light probe .hdr of a brightly colored room appears underexposed when first imported. If Exposure is set to 3, the room becomes easier to see, but the reflected windows remain overexposed. If Exposure is set to −2, the windows are properly exposed, but the rest of the room becomes darker. The Exposure effect multiplies each pixel value by a constant and is not concerned with the overall tonal range. The unit of measure of the Exposure slider is an f-stop; each whole f-stop value has twice the intensity of the f-stop below it. By default, the effect is applied equally to all channels. However, you can set the Channels menu to Individual Channels and thus produce separate red, green, and blue controls. Note that the effect operates in linear (non-gamma-adjusted) color space and not the inherent color space of the imported footage. However, you can override this trait by selecting the Bypass Linear Light Conversion check box.

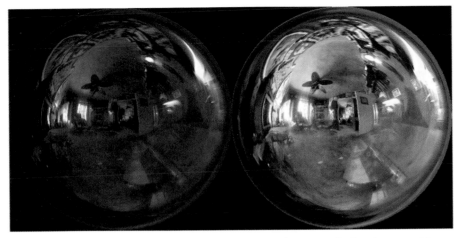

Figure 12.8 (Left) A light probe image appears underexposed when imported into a 32-bit project. (Right) The same light probe gains better balance when an Exposure effect is applied with its Exposure slider set to 3. A sample After Effects project is included as exposure.aep *in the Tutorials folder in the DVD.*

HDR Highlight Compression

To combat highlights within HDR images that become overexposed, After Effects provides the HDR Highlight Compression effect (in the Effect → Utility menu). For example, if the Exposure effect is applied to the floating-point TIFF of the shelf with an Exposure slider set to –5.5, the wall below the shelf light remains overexposed with RGB values over 1,000 on an 8-bit scale (see Figure 12.9). If the HDR Highlight Compression effect is applied, the overexposed area is tone mapped so that the values no longer exceed the 8-bit monitor color space. The HDR Highlight Compression effect has a single slider, Amount, which controls the strength of the tone mapping.

Figure 12.9 (Top) Overexposed area of HDR image (Bottom) Result of HDR Highlight Compression effect. A sample After Effects project is included as highlight.aep *in the Tutorials folder in the DVD.*

Stereoscopic Workflow in AE

The 3D Glasses effect (in the Effect → Perspective menu) creates stereoscopic images. To use the effect, follow these steps:

1. Create a new composition. Import the left eye view and right eye view footage. LMB+drag the footage into the outline layer. Toggle off the Video switches for each new layer.
2. Create a new Solid (Layer → New → Solid). With the Solid layer selected, choose Effect → Perspective → 3D Glasses. In the Effect Controls panel, change the 3D Glasses effect's Left View menu and Right View menu to the appropriate view layer names.
3. Change the 3D View menu to the anaglyph style of choice. For example, switching the menu to Balanced Colored Red Blue tints the left view cyan and the right view red (see Figure 12.10).

Figure 12.10 *(Top Left) Left view (Bottom Left) Right view (Top Right) 3D Glasses effect properties (Bottom Right) Resulting red-cyan anaglyph. A sample After Effects project is included as* stereoscopic.aep *in the Tutorials folder on the DVD.*

The 3D View menu has additional settings, which are tailored toward specific outputs:

Stereo Pair sets the left and right view side by side. You can use this mode to create a cross-eyed stereo view. *Cross-eyed stereo* does not use glasses but requires the viewer to cross their eyes slightly until a third stereo image appears in the center. However, for a cross-eyed view to be successful, the left and right images must be swapped; you can perform the swap with the 3D Glasses effect by toggling on the Swap Left-Right property.

Interlace Upper L Lower R places the left view into the upper field and the right view into the lower field of an interlaced output. This mode is necessary when preparing stereoscopic footage for a polarized or active shutter system. If toggled on, the Swap Left-Right property switches the fields.

Red Green LR and **Red Blue LR** create red-green and red-blue color combinations based on the luminance values of the left and right view layers.

Balanced Colored Red Blue creates a red-blue color combination based on the RGB values of the left and right view layers. This allows the resulting anaglyph to retain the layers' original colors. However, this setting may produce *ghosting*, which occurs when the intensity of one stereo color exceeds that of the paired color. For example, the red view may bleed into the cyan view. You can adjust the Balance slider to reduce ghosting artifacts; in essence, the slider controls the amount of saturation present for the paired stereo colors.

Balanced Red Green LR and **Balanced Red Blue LR** produce results similar to Red Green LR and Red Blue LR. However, the settings balance the colors to help avoid ghosting artifacts.

You can adjust the horizontal disparity and the location of the convergence point by raising or lowering the Convergence Offset value. Positive values slide the right view to the right and the left view to the left. This causes the convergence point to occur closer to the camera and forces a greater number of objects to appear behind the screen. Negative Convergence Offset values have the opposite effect. You can identify a convergence point in an anaglyph by locating the object that does not have overlapping colors. For example, in Figure 12.10, the convergence point rests at the central foreground tree.

Time Warping

After Effects includes several approaches to time warping imported footage. These include time stretching, blending, and remapping.

Time Stretch and Frame Blending

The simplest way to time-warp a piece of footage is to apply the Time Stretch tool (Layer → Time → Time Stretch). In the Time Stretch dialog box, the Stretch Factor value determines the final length of the footage. For example, entering 50% makes the footage half its prior length, while 200% makes the footage twice its prior length. The Time Stretch tool does not blend the frames, however. If the footage is lengthened, each frame is duplicated. If the footage is shortened, frames are removed. This may lead to judder in any motion found in the footage.

To avoid judder, you can apply one of two frame-blending tools, both of which are found under Layer → Frame Blending. Frame Mix applies an efficient algorithm that is suitable for previews and footage that contains fairly simple motion. Pixel Motion applies a more advanced algorithm that is more appropriate for footage that has been significantly stretched (whereby the motion has been slowed down). Once frame blending has been applied, you can switch between Frame Mix and Pixel Motion styles by toggling the Frame Blending layer switch (see Figure 2.11). The backslash, which is considered draft quality, activates Frame Mix, while the forward slash, considered high quality, activates Pixel Motion. Frame blending, with either tool, averages the pixels between two original frames, thus creating new in-between frames. Frame-blended frames, in general, are softer than the original frames. (To see frame blending in the viewer, you must toggle on the Frame Blending composition switch.)

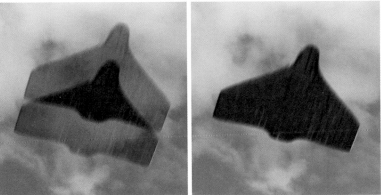

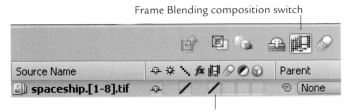

Frame Blending composition switch

Frame Blending layer switch

Figure 12.11 (Top Left) Detail of time-stretched footage with Frame Mix blending. Significantly lengthening the duration of the footage (in this case, 200%) creates overlapping images of the ship. (Top Right) Same time-stretched footage with Pixel Motion blending. (Bottom) Frame Blending switches in the layer outline. A sample After Effects project is included as `frame_blending.aep` *in the Tutorials folder on the DVD.*

Tips & Tricks: Converting Frame Rates

By default, dropping footage with a lower frame rate into a composition with a higher frame rate forces After Effects to repeat frames. For example, if 24 fps footage is dropped into a 30 fps composition, the program repeats 6 frames per second. To avoid the judder resulting from a 24 fps to 30 fps conversion, apply Pixel Motion frame blending. As an option, you can return the footage to its original length (that is, number of frames) by applying the Time Stretch tool to the layer with the Stretch Factor cell set to 80%. If you are converting 25 fps footage to a 30 fps composition, set the Stretch Factor cell to 83%.

On the other hand, if you drop footage with a higher frame rate into a composition with a lower frame rate, the footage is shortened and frames are discarded. For example, if 48 fps footage is dropped into a 24 fps composition, the timeline bar for the footage becomes half its normal length. If the footage has 48 frames, the timeline bar becomes 24 frames long. This ensures that any moving objects maintain a correct speed. Nevertheless, the lengths of motion blur trails for the moving objects are no longer accurate because frames are lost. To return the footage to its original length, apply the Time Stretch tool to the layer with the Stretch Factor cell set to 200%. Set the cell to 125% for a 30 fps to 24 fps conversion. Set the cell to 120% for a 30 fps to 25 fps conversion. Apply Pixel Motion frame blending.

Time Remapping and Timewarp

A limitation of the Time Stretch tool is its linear nature. If you wish to change the duration of a piece of footage in a nonlinear fashion, use the Time Remapping tool. To use the tool, follow these steps:

1. Select the layer you wish to remap. Choose Layer → Time → Enable Time Remapping. A Time Remap property is added to the layer in the layer outline (see Figure 12.12).

Figure 12.12 Time Remap property in the layer outline

2. Toggle on the Include This Property In The Graph Editor Set button beside the Time Remap property name. Open the Graph Editor by toggling on the Graph Editor composition switch at the top right of the layer outline.

3. By default, the Time Remap curve runs from 0 to 1.0 over the current duration of the footage. Manipulate the Time Remap curve shape to change the speed of the motion contained within the footage. For example, to give the motion a slow start, a fast middle, and a slow end, create an S-shaped curve in the value graph view (see Figure 12.13). You can use any of the standard Graph Editor tools and options to change the curve shape. (See Chapter 5 for more information on the Graph Editor.)

4. If you wish to shorten or lengthen the footage, select the top-right curve point and LMB+drag it to a new frame number. If you lengthen the footage, you will also need to extend the footage bar in the timeline view of the Timeline panel.

5. To frame-blend the result, activate Frame Mix or Pixel Motion (see the prior section). If the Time Remap curve is significantly altered, it will be necessary to use Pixel Motion to produce acceptable results. To remove a Time Remap property from a layer, toggle off the Stopwatch button beside the Time Remap name.

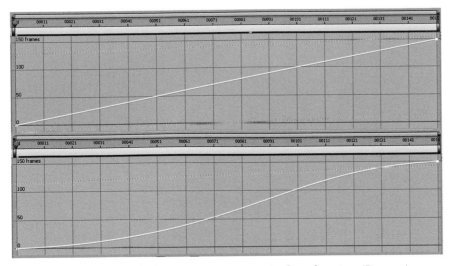

Figure 12.13 (Top) *Default Time Remap curve in the value view (Bottom) Curve reshaped to create a slow start and end for the motion contained within the footage. A sample After Effects project is included as* time_remap.aep *in the Tutorials folder on the DVD.*

Industry Perspective: Non-Linear Time-Warping

Since the release of *The Matrix* in 1999, the non-linear time warping of footage has become popular in feature films, television commercials, and video games. Non-linear time-warping is identifiable by a sudden change in speed during a continuous shot. For example, the motion may suddenly change from a normal speed to slow motion. You can achieve such an effect by using the Time Remapping tool in After Effects.

The Timewarp effect (Effect → Time → Timewarp) operates in a manner similar to the Time Stretch tool. However, if the Speed property is set to a value below 100%, the footage is lengthened. If the Speed property is set to a value above 100%, the footage is shortened. In either case, the footage bar in the Timeline panel remains the same length. If the footage is shortened, the last frame of the footage is held until the end of the footage bar. If the footage is lengthened, any frame beyond the end of the footage bar is ignored. You can activate Frame Mix or Pixel Motion frame blending through the Method menu. Timewarp differentiates itself by providing a Tuning section if the Method menu is set to Pixel Motion. The Tuning section includes the following important properties:

Vector Detail determines how many motion vectors are drawn between corresponding pixels of concurrent original frames. The vectors are necessary for determining pixel position for blended frames. A value of 100 creates one motion vector per image pixel. Higher values produce more accurate results but significantly slow the render.

Filtering selects the convolution filter used to average pixels. If this property is set to Normal, the filtering is fairly fast but will make the blended frames soft. If it's set to Extreme, the blended frames will regain their sharpness but the render time is impacted greatly.

In addition, the effect provides motion blur for blended frames if the Enable Motion Blur check box is selected (see Figure 12.14). You can adjust the blur length by setting the Shutter Control menu to Manual and changing the Shutter Angle value. The length of the motion blur trail, which is driven by the virtual exposure time, is based on the following formula: exposure time = 1 / ((360 / Shutter Angle) × frames per second). The larger the shutter angle, the longer the motion blur trail becomes.

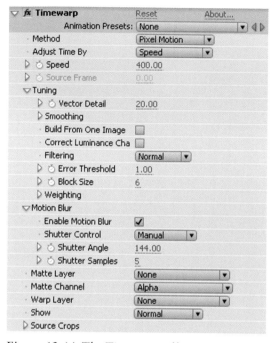

Figure 12.14 The Timewarp effect properties

Other Time Effects

Several additional time tools and effects are included in the Layer → Time and the Effect → Time menus. Descriptions of the most useful effects follow:

Time-Reverse Layer This tool reverses the frame order of a layer. What runs forward is made to run backward.

Freeze Frame This tool adds a Time Remap property and sets a keyframe at the current frame. The keyframe's interpolation is set to Hold, which repeats the frame for the duration of the timeline. However, you can alter the curve in the value view of the Graph Editor to make the Freeze Frame effect occur at a certain point in the timeline. For example, in Figure 12.15, frames 1 to 4 progress normally, while frame 5 is "frozen" for the remainder of timeline. In this situation, a keyframe must be inserted into the curve at frame 1, and both keyframe tangent types must be changed from Hold to Linear.

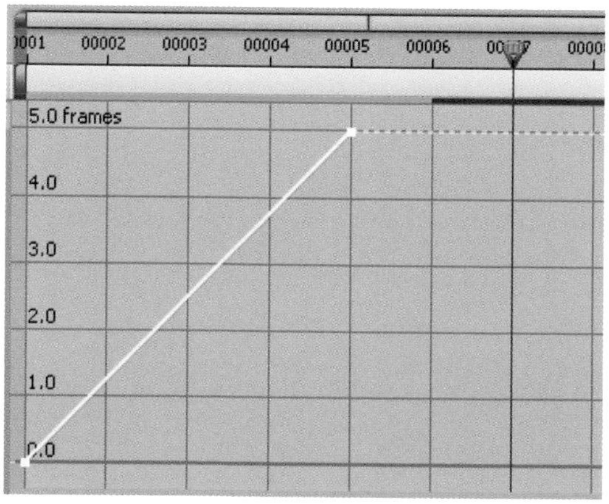

Figure 12.15 The Time Remap curve is altered in the value view of the Graph Editor so that frame 5 freezes for the remainder of the timeline. A sample project is included as `freeze_frame.aep` *in the Tutorials folder on the DVD.*

Echo The Echo effect purposely overlaps frames for a stylized result. The Echo Time (Seconds) property sets the time distance between frames used for the overlap. The Number Of Echoes slider sets the number of frames that are blended together. For example, if the project is set to 30 fps, Echo Time is set to 0.066, Number Of Echoes is set to 2, and the timeline is currently on frame 1, then frame 1 is blended with frames 3 and 5. The value 0.033 is equivalent to 1 frame when operating at 30 fps (1 / 30). By default, the effect adds the frames together, which often leads to overexposure. To defeat this, you can adjust the Starting Intensity slider or choose a different blending mode through the Echo Operator menu.

Posterize Time The Posterize Time effect locks a layer to a specific frame rate regardless of the composition settings. This allows you to create a step frame effect where each frame is clearly seen as it is repeated. The Frame Rate property sets the locked frames per second.

Time Difference The Time Difference effect determines the color difference between two layers over time. Each output pixel value is based on the following formula: ((source pixel value − target pixel value) × Contrast property percentage) + 128. The source layer is the layer to which the effect is assigned. The target layer is determined by the effect's Target menu. If the source and target pixel are identical, the output pixel value is 128. The Time Difference effect is useful for generating a moving matte. For example, in Figure 12.16, an empty greenscreen plate serves as the target layer, while footage of a model serves as the source layer. The background is removed from the output.

Figure 12.16 (Top Left) Empty background plate (Top Right) Plate with model (Bottom Left) Result of Time Difference effect with Absolute Difference toggled on and Alpha Channel menu set to Original (Bottom Right) Result seen in alpha channel with Absolute Difference toggled on and Alpha Channel menu set to Lightness Of Result. A sample project is included as `time_difference.aep` *in the Tutorials folder on the DVD.*

If the Absolute Difference property is toggled on, the formula switches to the following: (absolute value of (source pixel value − target pixel value)) × (Contrast property percentage × 2). By default, the alpha for the output is copied from the source layer.

However, you can alter this behavior by switching the Alpha Channel menu to options that include, among others, the target layer, a blended result of both layers, and a grayscale copy of the output (Lightness Of Result).

Simulation Effects

After Effects includes a number of effects designed for simulation, whereby a phenomenon is re-created as the timeline progresses. The simulations either replicate basic laws of physics or re-create the proper look of a phenomenon in the real world. The simulations include generic particles, raindrops, soap bubbles, snow, and foam. Since the list of effects and their properties is quite long, only the Particle Playground effect is covered in this section. Additional documentation on non-third-party effects, such as Card Dance, Caustics, and Shatter, are included in the Adobe help files.

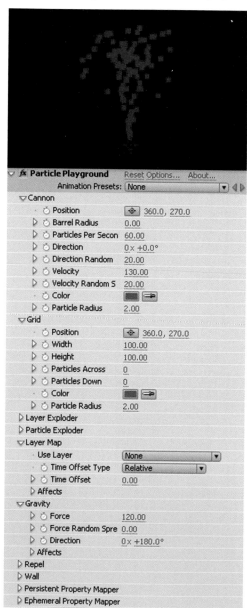

Particle Playground

The Particle Playground is one of the most complex effects in the program. The generated particles are able to react to virtual gravity and interact with virtual barriers. To apply the effect, you can follow these steps:

1. Create a new Solid layer. With the layer selected in the layer outline of the Timeline panel, choose Effect → Simulation → Particle Playground.

2. By default, dot particles are generated from a "cannon." That is, they are shot upward from an emitter. The emitter is represented in the viewer by a red circle (see Figure 12.17). You can reposition the emitter interactively by LMB+dragging it. To see the particle simulation, play back the timeline from frame 1.

3. By default, the particles possess a slow initial velocity. Within a short time, they begin to fall toward the bottom of the frame through a virtual gravity. To adjust the strength of the gravity, change the Force property (in the Gravity section). You can alter the direction of the gravity, and thus emulate wind, by changing the Direction property. To alter the number of particles, initial velocity, initial direction, and randomness of movement, adjust the properties in the Cannon section (see Figure 12.17). To widen the throat of the virtual cannon,

Figure 12.17 (Top) Default particle emission with the emitter at the base of the particles (Bottom) Default Particle Playground properties

raise the Barrel Radius property. To change the size of the particles, adjust the Particle Radius property. Since the particles are dots, they will remain square.

4. If you wish to generate particles from a grid instead of the cannon, set Particles Per Second in the Cannon section to 0 and raise the values for the Particles Down and Particles Across properties in the Grid section. With the grid emitter, particles are born at each grid line intersection. The size of the grid is set by the Width and Height properties, although the grid resolution is determined by Particles Down and Particles Across. If Particles Down and Particles Across are both set to 2, the grid has a resolution of 2×2, even if it's 100×100 pixels wide.

The red, square particles are rarely useful as is. You can take two approaches to making them more worthy of a composite—apply additional effects or use the Layer Map property. Two examples follow.

Creating a Light Trail

To create a light trail with the Particle Playground effect (where a moving light streaks over a long exposure), choose the grid style of particle generation. Set the Particles Across and Particles Down properties to 1.0. So long as the Force Random Spread property (in the Gravity section) is set to 0, the particles will flow in a perfectly straight line. To prevent the particles from drifting, set the Force property to 0. To create the illusion that the light is streaking, animate the Position property (in the Grid section) moving over time. You can then blur and color adjust the result before blending it over another layer (see Figure 12.18).

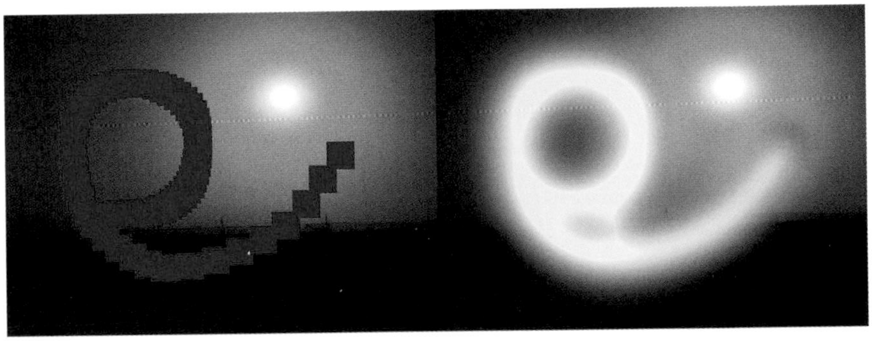

Figure 12.18 (Left) Grid-style particles formed into a path by animating the grid's Position property over time (Right) Same particles after the application of Fast Blur and Glow effects. A sample After Effects project is included as light_trail.aep in the Tutorials folder on the DVD.

Using the Layer Map

To use the Particle Playground's Layer Map property, prepare a bitmap sequence that is suitable for mapping onto a particle. For instance, create a low-resolution sequence featuring a bird, bat, or insect flapping its wings (see Figure 12.19). Import the bitmap sequence into a project. LMB+drag the sequence from the Project panel to the layer outline of the composition that carries the Particle Playground effect. Toggle off the Video switch beside the sequence layer to hide it. Change the Particle Playground's Use Layer menu (in the Layer Map section) to the sequence layer name. The sequence is automatically mapped onto the particles. If the bitmaps include alpha, the transparency is applied to the particles. To loop a short sequence, increase the Loop value (found in the Interpret Footage dialog box). To offset each particle so that all the particles aren't lock-stepped in their animation, incrementally raise the Random Time Max value (which is based on seconds). For example, in Figure 12.19, the bitmap sequence has only eight frames, so Random Time Max is set to 0.1. To randomize the motions of the particles, adjust the Direction Random Spread, Velocity Random Spread, and Force Random Spread properties. To add motion blur to the particles, toggle on the Motion Blur layer switch; to see the blur in the viewer, toggle on the Motion Blur composition switch.

Figure 12.19 (Left) 25×25 pixel bitmap sequence representing a bug flapping its wings. Red represents alpha. (Right) Result when sequence is used by Layer Map property of a Particle Playground effect. A sample After Effects project is included as `layer_map.aep` *in the Tutorials folder on the DVD.*

Additional Resources: Particle Playground

For additional information on the Particle Playground effect and its ability to explode particles or have particles interact with virtual barriers, see the "Particle Playground Effect" page in the After Effects help files.

Industry Perspective: Simulations in the Composite

The ability to generate simulations within a compositing program can be useful for quick fixes. For example, a particle simulation tool may be employed to create a puff of dust when a foot or object hits the ground. However, at medium to large animation studios, visual effects houses, and commercial production facilities, it's more common for the compositor to receive rendered effects from a CG animation team. If the project is large enough, such as an animated feature film, an entire department will be dedicated to creating effects work, including simulations that replicate water, dirt, mud, smoke, fire, explosions, and so on. Perhaps the one area where built-in simulation tools prove the most useful is for motion graphics, where abstracted patterns are often incorporated with animated logos and text.

Scripting in AE

Two scripting methods are supported by After Effects: ExtendScript and expressions. ExtendScript is a programming language that allows you to write external scripts to control the program. Expressions provide a means to link and automate various properties.

An Introduction to ExtendScript

After Effects supports scripting through the Adobe ExtendScript language. ExtendScript is an extended variation of JavaScript. ExtendScript is suitable for performing complex calculations beyond the capacity of standard effects, automating repetitive tasks, undertaking "search and replace" functions, communicating with outside programs, and creating custom GUI dialog boxes.

Each time After Effects launches, it searches the Scripts folder (for example, `C:\ Program Files\Adobe\Adobe After Effects CS3\Support Files\Scripts`). Encountered scripts are accessible through the File → Scripts menu. You can also manually browse for a script file by choosing File → Scripts → Run Script File.

ExtendScript files carry the `.jsx` filename extension and are text based. You can edit a script in a text editor or through the built-in After Effects JavaScript editor, which you can launch by choosing File → Scripts → Open Script Editor. The Script Editor offers the advantage of automatic debugging and color-coded syntax.

Each ExtendScript script must begin with an opening curly bracket { and end with a closing curly bracket }. Lines that are not part of conditional statements or comments end with a semicolon. Comment lines, which are added for notation, begin with a double slash //. An ExtendScript script may be several pages long or as short as this example:

```
{
    //This script creates a dialog box
    alert("Compositing Rules!");
}
```

ExtendScript is an object-oriented programming language and therefore includes a wide array of objects. *Objects*, many of which are unique to After Effects, are collections of properties that perform specific tasks. Optionally, objects carry methods, which allow the object to operate in a different manner based on the specific method. The syntax follows *object.method(value)*. Here are a few example objects, which are demonstrated by the `demo.jsx` script in the Tutorials folder on the DVD:

`alert("`*message*`");` writes a message in pop-up dialog box.

`app.newProject();` creates a new project after prompting you to save the old project.

`app.project.save();` saves the current project so long as it has been saved previously.

`scriptFile.open();`, `scriptFile.read();`, and `scriptFile.close();` open, read, and close a separate JSX script file, respectively.

Although many objects in ExtendScript are "ready-made," it's possible to create new objects within a script. The creation of an object is tasked to a *constructor function*, which defines the properties of the object. For example, in the `demo.jsx` script, `var my_palette = new Window("palette","Script Demo");` creates a new object based on the constructor function named `Window`. The resulting `my_palette` object creates the dialog box GUI.

ExtendScript supports the use of variables through the `var` function. There are three common variables types:

`var test = 100;`	integer
`var test = 12.23;`	float
`var test = "Finished";`	string

Once a variable is declared, it's not necessary to use `var` when updating the variable value. ExtendScript supports common math operators. These include + (add), – (subtract), * (multiply), and / (divide).

Additional Resources: ExtendScript Guide

For an in-depth look at ExtendScript, see the "Adobe After Effects CS3 Professional Scripting Guide" that's available at the Adobe website (`www.adobe.com`).

An Introduction to Adobe Expressions

Expressions, which are programmatic commands, link two or more properties together. A destination property is thereby "driven" by one or more source properties, whereby the destination receives the source values.

After Effects expressions rely on two naming conventions:

```
section.property[channel]

effect("name")("property")
```

section refers to the section in the layer outline where the property resides. For example, Transform is a section while Opacity is a property. When a property has more than one component that can be animated, it earns a *channel*. For example, X, Y, Z and Red, Green, Blue are channels. Channels are represented by a position number starting with 0. Hence, X, Y, Z channels are given the positions 0, 1, 2. When an effect property is used, it's signified by the effect prefix. The effect name, such as Fast Blur, is contained in the first set of quotes.

To create an expression, follow these steps:

1. Select the property name in the layer outline and choose Animation → Add Expression. An expandable Expression field is added to the timeline to the right of the property name (see Figure 12.20). The name of the property and its channel is added to the Expression field.

1 2 3 4   5

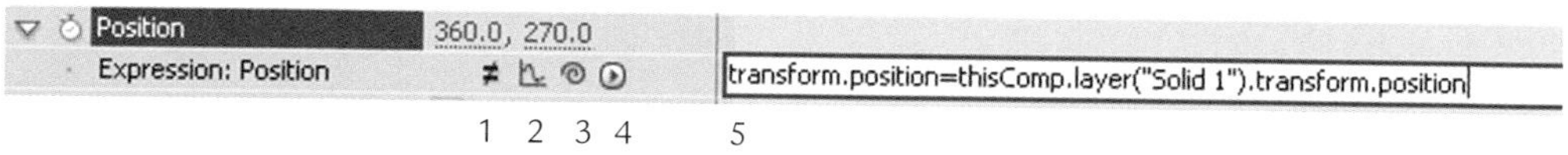

Figure 12.20 Expression added to Position property. The added expression features include: 1) Enable Expression switch, 2) Show Post-Expression Graph switch, 3) Expression Pick Whip tool, 4) Expression Language Menu button, and 5) Expression field (click to edit).

2. To finish the expression, click the Expression field to activate it for editing. Type the remainder of the expression. If the expression is successful, the Enable Expression button is automatically toggled on and the property values turn red. If the expression fails due to mistyping, syntax error, or mismatched channels, the Enable Expression button remains toggled off and a yellow warning triangle appears beside it. In addition, a pop-up warning box identifies the error.

You can also pull property and channel names into the field by using the Expression Pick Whip tool. To use this tool, LMB+click and hold the Expression Pick Whip button. Without letting go of the button, drag the mouse to another property or channel (on any layer). A line is extended from the button to the mouse. Valid properties and channels turn cyan. Release the mouse over a property or channel. The property name and channel(s) are added to the Expression field. To prevent the Expression Pick Whip tool from overwriting the current property, add an = sign before using it. For example, if you create a new expression and the expression reads `transform.position`, update the expression to read `transform.position=` before using the Expression Pick Whip tool.

A simple expression equates one property to another. For example, you can enter the following:

```
transform.position=thisComp.layer("Solid1").transfrom.position
```

With this expression, the Solid1 layer provides Position property values that drive the position of the layer with the expression. You can make expressions more complex by adding math operators. Basic operators include + (add), − (subtract), × (multiply), / (divide), and ×–1 (invert). To double a value of a source property, include ×2 in the expression. To reduce the value by 25%, include /4 in the expression. An expression can contain more than one source property and/or channel. For example, you can enter the following expression:

```
transform.opacity=
transform.position[1]-effect("Brightness & Contrast")("Brightness")
```

With this expression, the Opacity value is the result of the layer's Position Y value minus the Brightness value of a Brightness & Contrast effect.

To delete an expression, select the property name in the later outline and select Animation → Remove Expression. You can temporarily turn off an expression by toggling off the Enable Expression switch (see Figure 12.20 earlier in this section). To insert expression functions into the Expression field, click the Expression Language Menu button and choose a function from the menu. Functions are code words that launch specific routines or retrieve specific values.

Additional Resources: AE Expression Examples

For additional After Effects expression examples, choose File → Browse Template Projects. Template files are saved with the `.aet` filename extension. The `expression_sampler.aet` file contains several dozen unique expressions.

Advanced Techniques in Nuke

With Nuke, you can light a scene with an HDR image, prepare anaglyph stereoscopic footage, apply optical flow, automate functions with scripts and expressions, and retexture CG renders.

HDRI Support in Nuke

Nuke operates in 32-bit floating-point linear color space at all times. Lower bit-depth footage is converted to 32-bit as it's imported. The composite is viewed at a lower bit depth through the viewer, which applies a LUT determined by the project settings.

Nuke reads and writes `.hdr`, OpenEXR, and floating-point TIFF formats. To examine or utilize different exposure ranges within an HDR image, you can apply a Grade node and adjust the Whitepoint slider.

In addition, Nuke supplies the SoftClip node (in the Color menu), which compresses an HDR image's tonal range to a normalized range of 0 to 1.0. The node's Conversion menu determines whether the image's brightness or saturation is preserved. The Softclip Min and Softclip Max sliders determine the value range within the HDR that's compressed.

Environment Light and SphericalTransform

The Environment light allows you to create reflections and specular highlights in a 3D environment with an HDR bitmap. Assuming you have a 3D scene set up with geometry (see Chapter 11 for more detail), you can follow these steps:

1. Import an HDR bitmap through a Read node. A sample OpenEXR file is included as `room.exr` in the Footage folder of the DVD. With the Read node selected, RMB+click and choose Transform → SphericalTransform. With the SphericalTransform node selected, RMB+click and choose 3D → Lights → Environment. Connect the Environment1 node to the appropriate Scene node (see Figure 12.21).

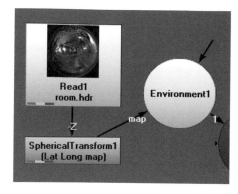

Figure 12.21 SphericalTransform and Environment nodes in a node network. A sample Nuke script is included as `hdr_lighting.nk` *in the Tutorials folder on the DVD.*

2. Open the SphericalTransform node's properties panel. This node is designed to convert an environment bitmap, such as an HDR file, from one projection style to another. Change the Output Type menu to Lat Long Map. Lat long maps are designed to fit spherical projections (in fact, they are often referred to as spherical maps). Change the Input Type menu to the appropriate projection style. For a review of projection types, see the section "HDR Formats and Projections" earlier in this chapter. In the case of `room.exr`, the menu should be changed to Angular Map 360.

3. For the Environment light to have an effect on geometry, the geometry must be connected to a shader that possesses specular quality. The strength of the light's influence is therefore controllable through the shader's Specular, Min Shininess, and Max Shininess parameters.

You can adjust the overall brightness of the Environment light through the Environment node's Intensity slider. If Intensity is high and there are no other lights in the scene, the Environment light creates a strong reflection on the surface (see Figure 12.22). If other lights are present, the Environment light's influence is diminished; however, the light colors will be visible in the areas where there is a strong specular highlight. The Environment light's influence is also affected by the shader's Diffuse parameter. If Diffuse is set to 0, the surface will appear mirror-like. If the resulting reflection appears too sharp, you can blur it by raising the Environment node's Blur Size value. If the Diffuse value is high and other lights are present in the scene, the Environment's light contribution is reduced (see Figure 12.22).

The position and scale of the Environment light icon does not affect the end result. However, the rotation does. You can change the Rotate XYZ values of the Environment node or the RX, RY, and RZ values of the SphericalTransform node to offset the resulting reflection along a particular axis.

Figure 12.22 (Left) Reflection on 3D chess piece created by Environment light node when no other lights are present (Right) More subtle reflection created when a Direct light node is added to the scene

Creating Animated HDRs

As mentioned earlier in this chapter, an animated HDR is a rendered sequence from the point of view of a CG character or prop that is used for lighting information. The creation of an animated HDR generally occurs in two steps: (1) a CG re-creation of an set is modeled and textured with HDR photos captured at the real location, and (2) the point of view of the character or prop is captured through an animated camera and is rendered as a spherically mapped floating-point image sequence. You can spherically map the view of a camera in Nuke by setting the Camera node's Projection menu (in the Projection tab of the properties panel) to Spherical.

As an example of this process, in Figure 12.23, the 3D hallway created in Chapter 11 is reutilized. The point of view of the animated cube is converted to a spherically mapped image sequence. This requires that the Camera1 node follows the cube's motion path exactly. To do this, the Cube1 node's animation is exported as a Chan file. The Chan file is then imported into the Camera1 node. Since the translation is desired but the rotation is not, the resulting rotation keyframes are deleted. An extra card is placed at the hall opening to prevent a black hole from appearing; the card is textured with a copy of the door photo. To prevent the cube from appearing in the render, it's temporarily disconnected from the Scene1 node. The Camera1 node's Projection menu is set to Spherical and an OpenEXR image sequence is rendered. (Although the 3D hallway is textured with low-dynamic-range bitmaps and is lit with standard Nuke lights, the process is essentially identical to one using a set textured with HDR bitmaps and lit with HDR lights.) A sample Nuke file for this step is included as `animated_hdr_a.nk` in the Tutorials folder on the DVD.

The resulting OpenEXR sequence can be used for lighting information if it's loaded into a Read file and the Read file is connected to an Environment light node. However, the Environment light is only able to use the image sequence for the specular lighting component. This is suitable for creating a reflection pass or roughly emulating the diffuse lighting quality. For example, in Figure 12.24, the OpenEXR is brought into an adapted script. The 3D hallway and light are removed. The cube remains. The Phong1 node, however, is connected to the Read2 node through the MapS (specular) connection. The Phong1 node's Diffuse property is set to 0, Specular is set to 4, Min Shininess is set to 2, and Max Shininess is set to 2. To prevent flickering and distinct reflective patterns from appearing across the cube, the Read1 node,

Figure 12.23 *(Top) First frame of animated HDR sequence created by rendering a Camera node with its Projection property set to Spherical (Bottom) Last frame of sequence*

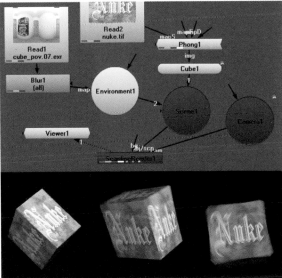

Figure 12.24 *(Top) Node network created to light the cube with a spherically mapped, animated HDR (Bottom) Three frames from the resulting render of the cube. Variations in light quality are due to the change in the cube's rotation relative to its point of view as captured by the OpenEXR sequence.*

which carries the OpenEXR sequence, is connected to a Blur node with its Size property set to 15. Although the Environment light does not move during the animation, the view of the cube updates with each frame of the OpenEXR. The lighting therefore changes based on the cube's rotation relative to its point of view as captured by the OpenEXR sequence. For example, any side of the cube pointing downward is rendered darker as the view in that direction sees the carpet, which is less intensely lit than the walls. A sample Nuke file for this step is included as `animated_hdr_b.nk` in the Tutorials folder on the DVD.

Stereoscopic Workflow in Nuke

Nuke can create anaglyphs and interlaced stereoscopic outputs appropriate for polarized and active shutter systems. You can combine views, split views, and separate various parameters for individual views. In addition, the program takes advantage of the OpenEXR format and is able to store multiple views within a single file.

Setting Up a Stereoscopic Script

To set up a stereoscopic script, follow these steps:

1. Choose Edit → Project Settings. In the properties panel, switch to the Views tab. Click the Set Up Views For Stereo button. A left and right view are listed in the Views field. You can switch between the views by clicking the Left or Right button that's added to the Viewer pane (see Figure 12.25). You can color-code any future connection lines by selecting the Use Colors In UI check box in the properties panel. By default, left view outputs are color-coded red and right view outputs are color-coded green.

2. Create two Read nodes. Load the left view into one Read node and the right view into the second Read node. With no nodes selected, RMB+click and choose View → Join Views. Connect the left-view Read node to the Left input of the JoinView1 node. Connect the right-view Read node to the Right input of the JoinView1 node. Connect a viewer to the JoinView1 node. You can look at the left and right view in the viewer by clicking the Left and Right buttons.

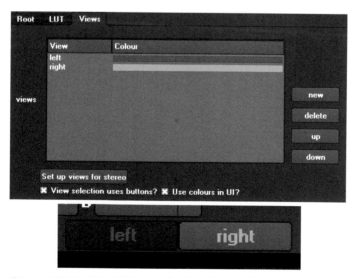

Figure 12.25 *(Top) Views tab of the Project Setting properties panel set up for a stereoscopic script (Bottom) Left and Right buttons added to the Viewer pane*

Preparing for Stereoscopic Output

To convert two views to a single anaglyph image, connect an Anaglyph node (in the Views →
Stereo menu) to a JoinViews node. The Anaglyph node converts each view into a monochromatic image. The left view is filtered to remove blue and green. The right view is filtered
to remove red. The output of the node contains a red left view superimposed over a cyan
right view (see Figure 12.26). The output is thus ready for viewing with red-cyan anaglyph
glasses. You can write out the combined view with a standard Write node.

Figure 12.26 (Left) Two views combined with a JoinViews node and converted with an
Anaglyph node (Right) Resulting Anaglyph. A sample Nuke script is included as `anaglyph.nk`
in the Tutorials folder on the DVD.

The saturation of the anaglyph is controlled by the Amtcolour slider. If Amtcolour is
set to 0, the anaglyph becomes black and white. High Amtcolour sliders maximize the colors
contained within the original images but may lead to ghosting. You can invert the colors,
thus making the right view red, by selecting the Anaglyphs node's (Right=Red) check box.
You can adjust the horizontal disparity and the location of the convergence point by raising or lowering the Horizontal Offset value. Positive values slide the left view to the left and
the right view to the right. This causes the convergence point to occur closer to the camera,
which places a greater number of objects behind the screen. Negative Horizontal Offset
values cause the convergence point to occur farther from the camera, which places a greater
number of objects in front of the screen.

You can also change the convergence point by using the ReConverge node (Views →
Stereo → ReConverge). However, the ReConverge node requires that the left and right views
are carried as two separate channels in an OpenEXR file. In addition, the node requires a
disparity field channel. A *disparity field* maps pixels in one view to the location of corresponding pixels in the second view. A specialized plug-in, such as The Foundry's Ocula, is
required in this case. Disparity fields are also necessary to transfer Paint node strokes from
one view to another. The Ocula plug-in also provides support for interlaced and checkerboard stereoscopic output, which is otherwise missing from Nuke.

Writing and Reading OpenEXR Files with Multiple Views

You can write left and right views into a single OpenEXR file. If stereo views have been set
up through the Project Settings properties panel, a Write node automatically lists the left
and right views through its Views menu (see Figure 12.27). Once the OpenEXR is written,
it can be reimported through a Read node. If an OpenEXR contains multiple views, a small

V symbol appears at the top left of the Read node icon. You can connect a viewer to the Read node and switch between left and right views by clicking the Left and Right buttons in the Viewer pane.

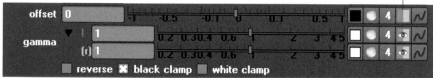

Figure 12.27 (Left) View menu in a Write node's properties panel (Right) V symbol at top left of Read node signifying multiple views

Additionally, you can force the left and right views to be written as separate files by adding the %V variable to the File cell of the Write node. For example, entering **filename.%V.exr** will add the view name to each render.

If you connect a node to a Read node that carries a multi-view OpenEXR, the connected node affects both views equally. However, if stereo views have been set up through the Project Settings properties panel, each node parameter receives a View menu button (to the immediate left of each Animation button). If you LMB+click a View menu button and choose Split Off Left or Split Off Right from the menu, the parameter is broken into left and right view components (see Figure 12.28). To access each component, click the small arrow to the immediate right of the parameter name.

If an OpenEXR contains both views, you can extract a single view by connecting a OneView node (in the Views menu). The OneView node carries a single parameter, View, with which you select Left or Right. The OneView node allows you to manipulate one view without disturbing the other.

If you need to flop the views so that the left becomes right and the right becomes left, connect a ShuffleViews node (in the Views menu). Once the ShuffleViews node is connected to an output with two views, click the Add button in the node's properties panel. A Get column and From column appear. The Get column determines what view is being affected. The From column determines what source is used for the selected view. To swap the left and right views, click the Add button twice and click the buttons to match Figure 12.29.

View menu buttons

offset	0	-1	-0.5	-0.1	0.1	0.5	1
gamma	1	0.2	0.3 0.4 0.6	2	3 4 5
(r)	1	0.2	0.3 0.4 0.6	2	3 4 5

reverse ✗ black clamp white clamp

Figure 12.28 Gamma parameter of Grade node split into left and right view components

ShuffleViews	Node
	get	from	
views to use	left	right	right	delete
	right	left	right	delete
	add			

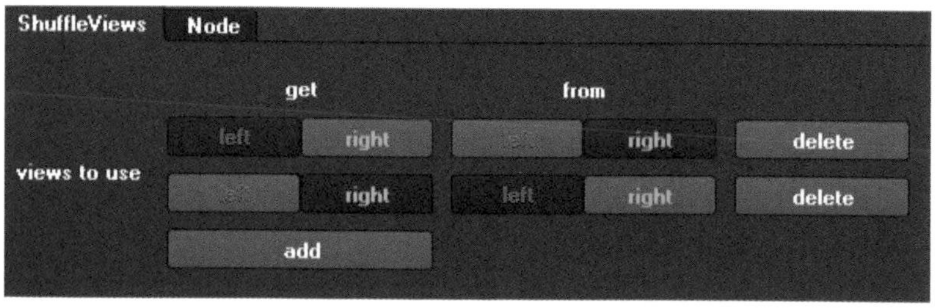

Figure 12.29 ShuffleViews node set to flop left and right views

Finally, you can use a multi-view OpenEXR in the following ways:

- You can connect an Anaglyph node directly to a Read node that carries an OpenEXR with two views.
- To examine two views simultaneously in the viewer, connect a SideBySide node (in the Views → Stereo menu). The SideBySide node will create a cross-eyed stereo view if the left and right views are first swapped with a ShuffleViews node (that is, the left view should be on the right and the right view should be on the left).
- To blend two views into a single view, connect a MixViews node (in the Views → Stereo menu). The blend is controlled by the Mix slider.

Time Warping Nodes

Nuke includes several nodes with which you can stretch, shorten, and blend footage.

Retime and OFlow

The simplest way to time-warp a piece of footage is to connect a Retime node (Time → Retime). In the Retime node's properties panel, Speed determines the final length of the footage. For example, entering 2 makes the footage half its prior length, while entering 0.5 makes the footage twice its prior length. In other words, 2 speeds the motion up while 0.5 slows the motion down. If the footage is stretched, the frames are duplicated without blending. If the footage is shortened, the frames are overlapped with partial opacity.

To avoid the motion artifacts created by the Retime node, you can connect an OFlow node instead (Time → OFlow). OFlow employs an optical flow algorithm to produce superior blending. The node includes the following parameters:

Method sets the style of blending. If Method is set to Motion, optical flow motion vectors are plotted for each pixel. If Method is set to Blend, the frames are simply overlapped, which produces results similar to the Retime node. If Method is set to Frame, frames are simply discarded or duplicated.

Timing offers two approaches to retiming. If Timing is set to Speed, you can enter a value in the Speed cell. Values above 1.0 speed up the motion (shorten the duration). Values below 1.0 slow down the motion (lengthen the duration). If Timing is set to Source Frame, you can remap one frame range to another. For example, you can move the timeline to frame 10, change the Frame parameter to 20, and key the Frame parameter using its Animation button. This step tells the OFlow node to remap old frames 1 to 20 to new frames 1 to 10. For the Source Frame mode to work, however, at least two keyframes must be set. Hence, in this case it's necessary to move to frame 1 and key the Frame parameter with a value of 1.0. By using the Source Frame option, you can create a non-linear time warp and cause the motion to switch from a normal speed to a sped-up or slowed-down speed at any point during the timeline.

Filtering provides two quality levels. The Normal level is suitable for mild retiming, while the Extreme level may be necessary for severely stretched footage.

Warp Mode determines which algorithm variation is used. The Occlusions mode is designed for footage with overlapping foreground and background objects. The Normal mode is the default and works for most footage. The Simple mode is the fastest, but it may produce inferior edge quality.

Correct Luminance, if selected, attempts to correct for variations in luminance between frames. Fluctuating luminance can result from moving specular highlights or similar changes in lighting. Whatever the origins, the fluctuations can interfere with the local motion estimation applied by the optical flow techniques.

Vector Detail sets the number of motion vectors created for the footage. A value of 1.0 creates one motion vector per image pixel, but it will slow the node significantly.

Show Vectors, if selected while Speed is less than 1.0 and Method is set to Motion, displays the motion vector paths in the viewer (see Figure 12.30).

Figure 12.30 *A detail of the motion vectors displayed by the OFlow node's Show Vectors parameter. A sample Nuke script is included as* oflow.nk *in the Tutorials folder on the DVD.*

Additional quality parameters, including Smoothness, Block Size, Weight Red, Weight Green, and Weight Blue, work well with their default setting and should be adjusted only when problem solving. For additional information on these parameters, see the Nuke user guide.

Tips & Tricks: Frame Rates in Nuke

The frame rate set by the Project Settings' Fps parameter does not affect the frames of imported footage. That is, frames are not permanently discarded or duplicated to match the frame rate. For example, if a 20-frame sequence is imported through a Read node, all 20 frames can be viewed on the timeline whether the Fps parameter is set to 24, 25, or 30. If the footage is played with the time controls, the speed of the playback is controlled by the Desired Playback Rate cell. During the playback, frames are held or skipped to achieve the correct playback rate. However, the playback is non-destructive and all the imported frames remain when the playback is stopped. Nevertheless, you can change the total number of frames carried by an output by connecting an OFlow node. For example, you can convert an output lasting 24 frames to an output lasting 30 frames by setting the OFlow node's Speed cell to 0.8.

Other Time Nodes

Additional time-based nodes are included under the Time menu. A few are described in the following list:

FrameBlend and TimeEcho The FrameBlend node overlaps frames. You can select the number of adjacent frames to blend through the Number Of Frames cell. You can also select the Use Range check box and enter values into the Frame Range cells. If you select the Use Range check box, the result will not change over the duration of the timeline but will stay fixed. The FrameBlend node is useful for adding motion blur to objects that otherwise do not possess blur (see Figure 12.31). In addition, it provides a means to reduce or remove noise or grain from a plate shot with a static camera. The TimeEcho node produces results similar to FrameBlend, but it offers only three parameters. You can select the number of adjacent frames to blend through the Frames To Look At cell. The blending mode, set by the TimeEcho Method menu, includes Plus, Average, or Max options. If TimeEcho is set to Average or Plus, you can give greater blending weight to frames close to the current timeline frame by raising the Frames To Fade Out value.

FrameHold The FrameHold node repeats one frame of its input through the duration of the timeline. The Frame is determined by the First Frame parameter. However, if the Increment parameter value is raised above 0, First Frame is deactivated. Instead, every *n*th frame, as determined by Increment, is output. For example, if Increment is set to 5, Nuke holds frame 1 for frames 1 to 4, then holds frame 5 for frames 5 to 9, and so on.

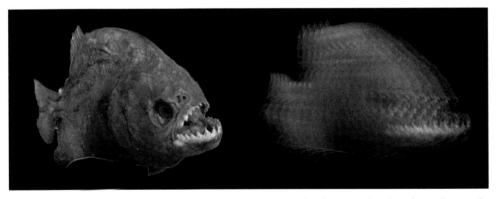

Figure 12.31 *(Left) Footage with no blur (Right) Result of FrameBlend node with Number Of Frames set to 5. A sample Nuke script is included as* `frameblend.nk` *in the Tutorials folder on the DVD.*

UV Retexturing

The STMap node replaces input pixel values with values retrieved from a source input. The retrieval from the source input is controlled by the distortion channels of a distortion map. The distortion channels are labeled U and V where U determines the horizontal location of values within the source and V determines the vertical location of values within the source. Due to this functionality, it's possible to retexture a CG object in the composite (see Figure 12.32). In this situation, the distortion channels are derived from a UV shader render of the CG object. A UV shader converts UV texture coordinate values carried by the geometry into red and green colors.

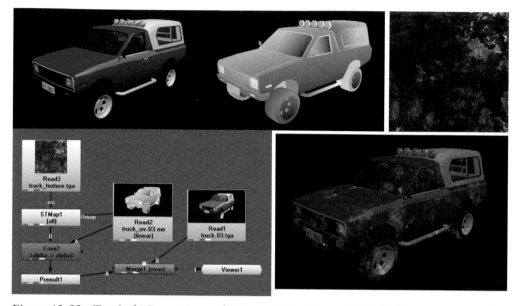

Figure 12.32 *(Top Left) Beauty pass of CG truck (Top Center) UV shader pass (Top Right) Dirt bitmap used for the source input (Bottom Left) STMap node in node network (Bottom Right) Resulting dirtied truck. A sample Nuke script is included as* `stmap.nk` *in the Tutorials folder on the DVD. (Truck model by Pieter Steyn.)*

To use the STMap node in this fashion, it's necessary to create a high-quality UV shader render pass. Ideally, the pass should be rendered as a 32-bit float format, such as OpenEXR. Lower bit depths are prone to create noise when the texture is remapped. In addition, the UV render pass should be interpreted as Linear through the Colorspace menu of the Read node that imports it.

The STMap node, which is found in the Transform menu, has two inputs. The Src (source) input connects to the node that provides the new pixel colors. The Stmap input connects to the node carrying the distortion channels. For example, in Figure 12.32, a texture map featuring dirt is loaded into a Read node and connected to the Src input. A UV pass is loaded into a second Read node and is connected to the Stmap input. To establish which channels are used as distortion channels, the STMap node's UV Channels menu is set to Rgb. With this setting, the U is derived from the red channel and the V is derived from the green channel, as is indicated by Red and Green check boxes.

The STMap node does not process the alpha channel properly. Thus, it's necessary to retrieve the alpha by connecting a Copy node and a Premult node. In the Figure 12.32 example, the result is merged with the beauty render of the truck. When the STMap node is used, the truck can be dirtied without the need to re-render the CG sequence. In addition, the dirt map can be altered, updated, or replaced within the composite with little effort. The STMap node is able to remap a render even when the CG objects are in motion.

Gizmos, Scripts, Links, and Expressions

Nuke projects are called *script files* or *scripts*. Nuke also supports Python and TCL scripting. A *scripting language* is any programming language that allows a user to manipulate a program without affecting the program's core functions. As part of the scripting support, Nuke utilizes expressions and groups of nodes known as gizmos.

Gizmos and Group Nodes

In Nuke, a *gizmo* is a group of nodes. Gizmos are useful for passing node networks from one artist to another or reapplying a proven node network to multiple shots on a single project. For example, the reformatting, color grading, and greenscreen removal sections of a node network may be turned into separate gizmos. A gizmo is stored as a text file with the .gizmo filename extension.

To create and save a gizmo, follow these steps:

1. Shift+select the nodes that you wish to include in a gizmo. In the Node Graph, RMB+click and choose Other → Group. A new Group node is created. The contents of the Group node are displayed in a new tab, which is named Group*n* Node Graph (see Figure 12.33). In addition, Input and Output nodes are connected. The number of Input and Output nodes corresponds to the number of inputs and outputs that the originally selected nodes possessed.

2. Switch back to the Node Graph tab. Note that the new Group node is placed in the work area but is not connected to any other node. Nevertheless, the number of input and output pipes matches the input and output nodes in the Group*n* Node Graph tab. The numbered pipe labels also correspond. For example, with the example in Figure 12.33, a node connection to the Group node's 2 input is actually a connection to the Scene1 node through the Input2 node.

3. Open the Group node's properties panel. Rename the node through the Name cell. To save the Group node as a gizmo, click the Export As Gizmo button.

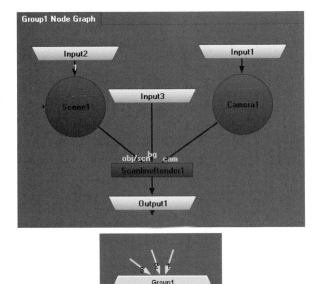

Figure 12.33 (Top) Group node network, as seen in the Group*n* Node Graph tab (Bottom) The same Group node, as seen in the Node Graph tab

A Group node has the same functionality as the originally selected nodes and can be connected to a preexisting node network. You can adjust the parameters of the original nodes without affecting the Group node or the duplicated nodes that belong to the group. If you want to adjust the Group node, switch back to the Group*n* Node Graph tab and open the properties panel for any contained nodes. To simplify the adjustment process, you can borrow knobs from the contained nodes and add them to the Group node (*knobs* are parameter sliders, check boxes, or cells). To do so, follow these steps:

1. Open the Group node's properties panel. RMB+click over the dark-gray area of the panel and choose Manage User Knobs. A Manage User Knobs dialog box opens (although the dialog box is labeled *Nuke5.1*).

2. In the dialog box, click the Pick button (see Figure 12.34). In the Pick Knobs To Add dialog box, the nodes belonging to the Group node are listed. Expand the node or choice, highlight the knob name, and click OK. The knob, whether it is a slider,

check box, or cell, is added to the Group node's properties panel under a new User tab. Repeat the process if you wish to add multiple knobs. To save the updated Group node as a gizmo, switch back to the Node tab of the properties panel and click the Export As Gizmo button.

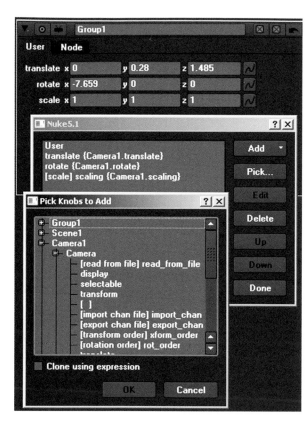

Figure 12.34 *(Top Box) Group1 node properties panel with Translate, Rotate, and Scale knobs borrowed from the Camera1 node (Center Box) Manage User Knobs dialog box with list of added knobs (Bottom Box) Pick Knobs To Add dialog box with list of nodes belonging to Group1 along with the nodes' available knobs*

You can edit the added knob by clicking the Edit button in the Manage User Knobs dialog box. You have the option to change the knob's name, which is the channel name used for scripts and expressions. In addition, you can enter a new label, which is the word that appears to the left of the knob in the properties panel. You can also enter a ToolTip, which is the text that appears in a yellow box when you let your mouse pointer hover over the knob parameter in the properties panel. In fact, you are not limited to editing Group nodes, but can add or edit knobs for any node that appears in the Node Graph.

To open a preexisting gizmo, choose File → Import Script. The imported Gizmo node is named gizmo*n*. Gizmo files are saved in a text format that contains a list of included nodes, custom parameter settings, custom knob information, and the node's XY position within the Node Graph.

Tips & Tricks: Exporting Ungrouped Nodes

You can export a set of ungrouped nodes by Shift+selecting the nodes in the Node Graph, RMB+clicking, and choosing File → Export Nodes As Script. The nodes are saved in their own script with a .nk extension. You can bring the selected nodes back into Nuke by choosing File → Import Script.

Python Scripting

Nuke supports the use of Python, which is a popular object-oriented programming language. To begin Python scripting, LMB+click a content menu button (see Figure 12.35) and choose Script Editor from the menu. By default, the editor opens as a pane on the left side. The lower, light-gray area of the editor is the Input window, while the darker, upper area is the Output window. To enter a script command, click the Input window so that it's highlighted and type or paste in the command. For example, you can type **print** "Hello there". To execute the script command, press Crtl+Enter. The result of the command is displayed in the Output window. A message following the phrase # Result will list whether the command was successfully or unsuccessfully carried out. If it was unsuccessful, a specific error is included.

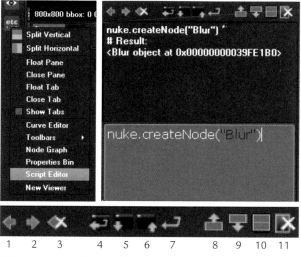

The Script Editor includes a number of menu buttons along the top of the Output window (see Figure 12.35). You can source, load, save, or execute by using the center buttons. Loading a script places it into the Input window but does not execute it. Sourcing a script executes the script immediately. Choosing the Save A Script button saves the script currently displayed in the Input window to a Python text file with a .py filename extension. To clear the contents of the Input window, click the Clear History button on the left. To clear the contents of the Output window, click the Clear Output Window button on the right.

Since Python is object oriented, it includes a wide array of objects. *Objects*, many of which are unique to Nuke, are collections or properties that perform specific tasks. Optionally, objects carry *methods*, which allow the object to operate in a different manner based on the specific method. The syntax follows object.method(value). Here are a few sample objects and methods (note that Python is sensitive to capitalization):

Figure 12.35 (Top Left) Script Editor option in a content button menu (Top Right) Script Editor with Output window at top and Input window at bottom (Bottom) Script Editor buttons, which include (1) Previous Script, (2) Next Script, (3) Clear History, (4) Source A Script, (5) Load A Script, (6) Save A Script, (7) Run The Current Script, (8) Show Input Only, (9) Show Output Only, (10) Show Both Input And Output, and (11) Clear Output Window

> nuke.undo() and nuke.redo() execute an undo or a redo.
>
> nuke.getColor() launches the Get Color dialog box.
>
> nuke.createNode("*name*") creates a node and places it in the Node Graph. *name* is the proper name of a node, such as Blur or Merge.
>
> nuke.message("*text*") pops up a dialog box with a message included between the quotes.
>
> nuke.plugins() lists currently loaded plug-ins with their paths.

To alter a node's parameter with Python, it's necessary to assign a variable to the node name. For example, entering gr=nuke.nodes.Grade() creates a Grade node and assigns it to a variable named gr. To alter one the of the Grade node's parameters, you can then enter gr["*name*"].setValue (*value*), where **name** lists the specific parameter. For example, you can enter gr["gamma"].setValue (1.5).

Final Inspiration

As a final example of digital compositing, two composites created for Mercedes by Jerry van der Beek at Little Fluffy Clouds are included here. Aside from the CG car, which was rendered in Maya, all the elements were generated in After Effects with a combination of standard effects and a single additional plug-in (Trapcode Particular). These composites demonstrate that amazing visuals can be created within the compositing program by a single compositor.

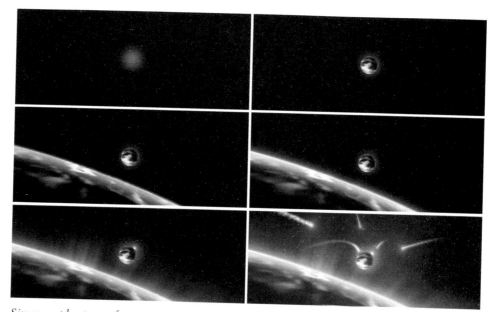

Six example steps of a composite featuring a planet approached by shooting stars (Images courtesy of Little Fluffy Clouds)

Six example steps of a composite featuring abstract light flares dancing around a car (Images courtesy of Little Fluffy Clouds)

AE and Nuke Tutorial Challenge

Formal tutorials have not been included with this chapter. Instead, I'd like to encourage you to create your own unique projects using the source files included on this book's DVD along with the techniques discussed in this book's 12 chapters. There are almost endless possibilities with digital compositing, and no two compositors will produce the same results if set free with the same footage. In fact, if you come up with a unique composite using the resources from this book that you'd like to share, I'll post it on my website (www.BeezleBugBit.com). Just drop me at line at comp@beezlebugbit.com. Have fun and good luck!

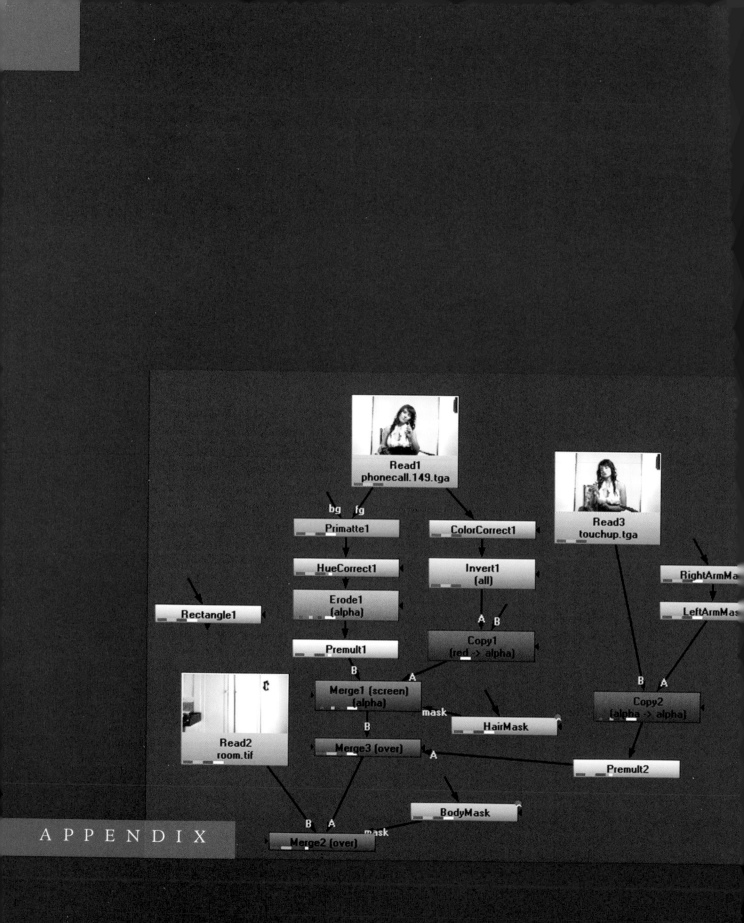

About the Companion DVD

What You'll Find on the DVD

If you need help installing the items provided on the DVD, refer to the installation instructions in the section "Using the DVD."

Support Files

The DVD includes more than 1 gigabyte of After Effects project files, Nuke scripts, video footage, CG renders, texture bitmaps, and digital stills. The files are organized by chapter. Within each chapter you will find Tutorials and Footage folders:

- Tutorials folders contain After Effects project files and Nuke scripts.
- Footage folders contain video footage, CG renders, texture bitmaps, and digital stills.

For the After Effects projects and Nuke scripts, it is assumed that the source files are located on a C: drive. For best results, copy the DVD contents onto your own C: drive. If space is not available, you can reload the necessary files once you are in the program. Methods for reloading the files are discussed in Chapter 1.

System Requirements

This book was written with Adobe After Effects CS3 and The Foundry Nuke 5.1v1. Newer versions of the software packages are available. However, CS3 and 5.1v1 were chosen to ensure backward compatibility and stability. Since the differences between these versions and the latest releases are minor, it will not affect your learning experience.

If you do not own After Effects and Nuke, free trials are available through the software developers. Adobe offers a 30-day, fully functional trial of After Effects at www.adobe.com, while The Foundry offers a Personal Learning Edition (PLE) of Nuke at www.thefoundry.co.uk. (Note that the PLE version of Nuke places a dotted watermark on any render and does not support the Primatte keyer, which is discussed in this book.)

Using the DVD

To install the items from the DVD to your hard drive, follow these steps:

1. Insert the DVD into your computer's DVD-ROM drive. The license agreement appears.

   Windows users: The interface won't launch if Autorun is disabled. In such a case, click Start → Run (for Windows Vista, Start → All Programs → Accessories → Run). In the dialog box that appears, type **D:\Start.exe**. (Replace **D** with the proper letter if your DVD drive uses a different letter. If you don't know the letter, see how your DVD drive is listed under My Computer.) Click OK.

2. Read through the license agreement, and then click the Accept button if you want to use the DVD.

   The DVD interface appears. The interface allows you to access the content with just one or two clicks.

   Alternately, you can access the files at the root directory of your hard drive.

   Mac users: The DVD icon will appear on your desktop; double-click the icon to open the DVD and then navigate to the files you want.

Troubleshooting

Wiley has attempted to provide programs that work on most computers with the minimum system requirements. Alas, your computer may differ, and some programs may not work properly for some reason.

The two likeliest problems are that you don't have enough memory (RAM) for the programs you want to use or you have other programs running that are affecting the installation or running of a program. If you get an error message such as "Not enough memory" or "Setup cannot continue," try one or more of the following suggestions, and then try using the software again:

Turn off any antivirus software running on your computer. Installation programs sometimes mimic virus activity and may make your computer incorrectly believe that it's being infected by a virus.

Close all running programs. The more programs you have running, the less memory is available to other programs. Installation programs typically update files and programs, so if you keep other programs running, installation may not work properly.

Have your local computer store add more RAM to your computer. This is, admittedly, a drastic and somewhat expensive step. However, adding more memory can really help the speed of your computer and allow more programs to run at the same time.

Customer Care

If you have trouble with the book's companion DVD, please call the Wiley Product Technical Support phone number at (800) 762-2974. Outside the United States, call +1(317) 572-3994. You can also contact Wiley Product Technical Support at http://sybex.custhelp.com. John Wiley & Sons will provide technical support only for installation and other general quality control items. For technical support on the applications themselves, consult the program's vendor or author.

To place additional orders or to request information about other Wiley products, please call (877) 762-2974.

Index

Wiley Publishing, Inc.
End-User License Agreement